GUN TRADER'S GUIDE TO HANDGUNS

A Comprehensive, Fully Illustrated Reference for Modern Handguns with Current Market Values

Edited by Robert A. Sadowski

Skyhorse Publishing

Skyhorse Publishing books may be purchased in bulk at special discounts for sales promotion, corporate gifts, fund-raising, or educational purposes. Special editions can also be created to specifications. For details, contact the Special Sales Department, Skyhorse Publishing, 307 West 36th Street, 11th Floor, New York, NY 10018 or info@skyhorsepublishing.com.

Skyhorse® and Skyhorse Publishing® are registered trademarks of Skyhorse Publishing, Inc.®, a Delaware corporation.

Visit our website at www.skyhorsepublishing.com.

10 9 8 7 6 5 4 3 2 1

Library of Congress Cataloging-in-Publication Data is available on file.

Cover design by Tom Lau
Cover photos courtesy of Glock, Kimber, Luger, Magnum Research, Ruger, Sig Sauer, Taurus, and Uberti

Print ISBN: 978-1-5107-1969-9
Ebook ISBN: 978-1-5107-1970-5

Printed in China

Contents

Introduction

This is the first edition of the *Gun Trader's Guide to Handguns*, or *GTG Handguns* for short. In the same tradition of other *Gun Trader's Guide* books, *GTG Handguns* gives handgun collectors a complete reference for identifying and determining the value of modern cartridge handguns produced from the late nineteenth century through the early twenty-first century.

SPECS AND PHOTOS

Included in this volume are specifications and illustrations or photographs for thousands of handguns. The format is simple and easy to use. All handguns are listed in alphabetical order by manufacturer or importer name, and the models are also in alpha-numeric order so the reader can locate a specific model fast. The index also makes it easy to find a specific model from a manufacturer. In some cases, where gun manufacturers have both revolver and pistol models, those models are also divided into revolver and pistol sections under that manufacturer. Each entry includes:

- Manufacturer
- Model Name
- Model Number
- Model Specifications
- Distinguishing Features
- Variations of Different Models
- Grades
- Dates of Manufacture
- Date of Discontinuation (if applicable)
- Current Value (by condition)
- Photos or Illustrations

Inside the full-color section is detailed information on several rare and common handguns. Also included in *GTG Handguns* is a chapter on firearm grading, using an example of a Second Generation Colt Single Action Army (SAA) revolver.

We have included specific chapters on highly collectable handguns like M1911 and M1911A1 pistols, Walther P.38s, Lugers, Ruger Blackhawks, Colt Pythons, Smith & Wesson Model 29s, and more. *GTG Handguns* also features a chapter on handgun provenance, which looks in detail at one of Elmer Keith's personal revolvers, Old No. 5, also known as the "last word" in SAA revolvers. Keith was a single-action aficionado, and Old No. 5 maybe be the most famous Colt SAA ever customized. We also look into a Colt Model 1902 purportedly owned by Bonnie Parker of Bonnie and Clyde infamy. Bob Rayburn provided his expertise and collecting knowledge of the Colt Woodsman pistol, one of the most collectable American-made rimfire pistols ever designed. An appendix offers tips on buying and selling through online auctions, what to expect at gun shows, the AFT definition of curios and relics, and handgun collector organizations.

ACCURATE HANDGUN VALUES

We have made every effort to ensure the information on all handguns is current and up to date. Not every handgun ever manufactured can be listed in any reference book of this size, but we have made every effort to include the makes and models that are most popular with owners and collectors and manufactured from the turn of the twentieth century to present. (Note: *GTG Handguns* does not include antique or recently manufactured blackpowder firearms.) Values shown are based on national averages obtained by conferring with knowledgeable gun dealers, traders, collectors, and auctioneers around the country, and the values listed accurately reflect the nationwide average at the time of publication.

Keep in mind that the stated values are averages based on a wide spectrum of variables. No price given in any such reference book should be considered the "one and only" value for a particular handgun. Value is ultimately determined by the buyer and seller.

In the case of rare items, such as an M1911A1 manufactured by Singer Manufacturing Co. during World War II, wherein only five hundred pistols were manufactured and very little trading of those in existence takes place, active gun collectors were consulted to obtain current market values. Also note that in researching data, some manufacturers' records were unavailable and sometimes completely unobtainable; some early firearms manufacturers' production records have been destroyed in fires, lost, or even simply not accurately maintained. These circumstances resulted in some minor deviations in the presentation format of certain model listings. For example, production dates may not be listed when manufacturing records are unclear or unavailable. As an alternative, then, approximate dates of manufacture may be listed to reflect the availability of guns from a manufacturer or distributor. These figures may represent disposition dates indicating when that particular model was shipped to a distributor or importer.

To ensure *GTG Handguns* has the most accurate information available, we encourage and solicit users to contact the research staff at Skyhorse Publishing.

ACKNOWLEDGMENTS

The editor and publisher wish to express special thanks to the many collectors, dealers, manufacturers, shooting editors, and firearm manufacturers' historians and research personnel who provided us with specifications and updates. We are especially grateful for their assistance and cooperation in compiling information for *GTG Handguns* and for reproducing photographs, illustrations, and descriptions of their collectible firearms.

Special thanks to Mike Bishop of Bishop's Fine Guns (bishopsfineguns.com) in Fitzgerald, Georgia, for many of the detailed color photographs; Bob Rayburn (colt22.com or coltwoodsman.com), for his encyclopedic knowledge of Colt Woodsman models and use of his images and data; James D. Julia auctioneers (jamesdjulia.com) for use of images and descriptions; Rock Island Auctions (rockislandauction.com), for images and descriptions; and Case Antiques (caseantiques.com) for images and descriptions. Thanks also to Roy Jinks, historian and gatekeeper of Smith & Wesson history, for his insight, knowledge, and use of images. Special thanks to Sharps Bros. and Spikes Tactical (spikestactical.com), and IBX Tactical (ibxtactical.com).

Finally, *GTG Handguns* would like to thank all those who collect, hunt, work, compete, plink, shoot, or defend their home with a handgun. We welcome your comments. Please send comments or suggestions to:

Robert A. Sadowski, Editor
Gun Trader's Guide to Handguns
Skyhorse Publishing, Inc.
307 West 36th Street, 11th Floor
New York, NY 10018
info@skyhorsepublishing.com

How to Use *GTG Handguns*

The number one question asked by most owners, collectors, hunters, competition shooters, or those who have inherited a handgun is: What is it worth? To know what a handgun is worth, one must start by knowing what it is. The first questions one should ask are: Who is the manufacturer? Is it a pistol, revolver, or derringer? Model? Caliber? Barrel length? Finish? Are there any distinguishing markings, other than model number or name? Another question that could mean the difference between a junker, shooter, and a valuable firearm is: Who owned it? Some famous people who have owned handguns, for good or bad, give the handgun provenance. A WWII-era Colt 1911A1 owned by a famous general will fetch much more than a Colt 1911A1 brought home by a regular GI. Know what it is to know what it is worth.

The price of handguns can fluctuate, with the value of some models, such as Colt Single Action Army revolvers, Lugers, and certain Smith & Wesson double-action revolvers, steadily increasing in value as time passes. Like they say, "They don't make them like they used to anymore." Other handguns typically keep their value depending on the brand, but prices are subject to the current popularity of certain models.

This is where *GTG Handguns* can be an invaluable resource to identifying models, model specifications, and dates a model was produced or imported in the United States. Included are numerous photographs and illustrations to help in identifying a model. The images in *GTG Handguns* are carefully chosen to provide a representative image of a model, while the text helps to narrow down the model to a specific variant. As they say, a photo is worth a thousand words. Both images and

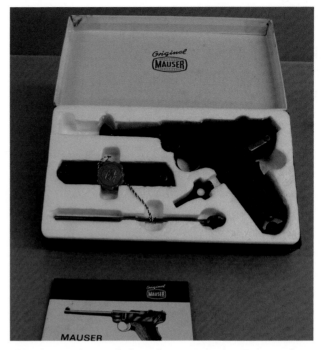

This Luger is graded "NiB" (New in Box) and at first might seem extremely valuable, but it is from neither WWI nor WWII, nor was it even manufactured during those eras. This example was imported by Interarms. It is a Swiss-style Mauser Eagle Luger that was manufactured by Mauser in the 1970s and worth about $1,400. A Luger in less than pristine condition but manufactured in the early twentieth century for commercial or military sale may be more valuable. *Image courtesy Bishop's Fine Guns*

illustrations are extremely helpful when trying to identify a specific model handgun, because to the untrained eye one Ruger Blackhawk looks like all Ruger Blackhawks. Not to the experienced eye, however; see the chapter on Ruger Blackhawks (see page 49) to learn more about original "three-screw" models.

POPULARITY

Some handguns are always going to be popular and in demand. I would hazard to guess that Luger semi-automatic pistols and Colt

SAA revolvers are two of the most coveted and collected handguns. When collecting, trading, buying, and selling any of these handguns, be careful. There are some people willing to sell you a fake and take advantage of your naive nature. Listen to your gut, and if you want more information, ask for a second opinion by contacting an auction house or a dealer with an excellent

Since 1949, the Ruger .22 LR semi-automatic pistol, first as the Standard and then the MK I, has been extremely popular with shooters. The MK IV is the current evolution of the pistol. In the some 67-plus years the pistols have been produced, there have been many variants, with some more valuable than others. The most valuable model is the Standard Model in its original "salt cod" box, that variant built between 1949 and 1952. The "salt cod" box was a wooden box used to ship the Standard Model contained in a red, two-piece cardboard box. Values can range from $3,760 to $3,800 in 100 percent condition.
Image courtesy of Rock Island Auctions

reputation. Some unscrupulous people have artificially aged, changed markings, changed barrel lengths, and done other despicable things to forge a common handgun into one that looks rare and valuable. Be aware and cautious when dollar amounts are high.

The media—TV, movies, books, magazines, video games—can all influence the popularity and, hence, the value of a handgun. The S&W Model 29 .44 Magnum may not have the following it has if it were not for the *Dirty Harry* movie franchise. Personally, I like Colt Pythons, and ever since the TV series *The Walking Dead* has aired, I have seen the price of Colt Pythons increase.

NOT SO NEW
Those who have to have the latest and greatest handgun may at times trade in or want to sell a near-new gun as the novelty of newness wears off. This is a good opportunity to own a slightly used gun at a fraction of the new cost. Yes, slightly used, but near new and not even close to the manufacturer's suggested retail price. The frugal Yankee in me likes slightly used guns a lot.

WHAT'S IT WORTH?
Many times, instead of a buyer or seller searching for a specific handgun, one unexpectedly lands in their lap. A relative or a neighbor may have passed away and the surviving spouse wants to get rid of the guns in the house. Or a friend or acquaintance may need to weed out their collection and make room in their safe for other guns. Such opportunities are unexpected and quick decisions need to be made. The task is to determine the value. Do not assume that the newly acquired firearm is worth a bucket-load of money, but then again don't instantly think you should surrender the firearm to the local police station for a minor reward in a so-called

"buy-back" program. In 2012, a woman in Connecticut dropped off a firearm at a gun buy-back program organized by local police. The firearm was a rare a StG 44 or Sturmgewehr 44 rifle developed in Nazi Germany during World War II and issued to SS troops. The value of the rifle ranged from $30,000 to $40,000. Any collector or museum would have been humbled to have such a specimen in their collection. Fortunately, the police politely declined the rifle, told the woman she had a valuable piece of history, and returned it to her.

Other things to consider: If a handgun is with its original box, it will be worth more. Also, remember that aftermarket grips and nonprofessional customizations may enhance the look or usability of a handgun, but since the handgun will not be in original factory condition, it will usually be worth less. Handguns modified by well-known gunsmiths, however, are a different situation. Some 1911 pistols customized by Armand Swenson, Pachmayr Gun Works, and Jim Hoag will bring top dollar. For example, some Pachmayr 1911 pistols are very rare and exceptionally well built. Many of these custom guns were used extensively in competition and are well worn.

ABBREVIATIONS USED IN THIS BOOK

ACP	=	Automatic Colt Pistol	LR	=	Long Rifle	SA	=	single action
adj.	=	adjustable	M&P	=	Military & Police	Spl.	=	Special
Auto.	=	automatic	Mag.	=	Magnum	Syn.	=	synthetic
Avail.	=	available	mfg	=	manufactured	TH	=	target hammer
bbl.	=	barrel	mm	=	millimeter	TT	=	target trigger
c.	=	circa	NiB	=	new in box	Vent.	=	ventilated
DA	=	double action	NM	=	National Match	VR	=	vent rib
disc.	=	discontinued	oz.	=	ounce	w/	=	with
FN	=	Fabrique Nationale	reintro.	=	reintroduced	w/o	=	without
in.	=	inch	Rem.	=	Remington	Wby.	=	Weatherby
L.H.	=	left-hand	rnd.	=	round	Win.	=	Winchester
lbs.	=	pounds	S&W	=	Smith & Wesson	WMR	=	Winchester Magnum Rimfire
LC	=	Long Colt	S/N	=	serial number	WRF	=	Winchester Rimfire

Second Generation Colt Single Action Army

According to R. L. Wilson in his book *Colt: An American Legend*, the very first production Single Action Army, serial No. 1, was thought lost, before being found in a barn in Nashua, New Hampshire, in the early 1900s. The value of that first Colt revolver would be set according to who had the deepest pockets and the greatest desire to own the first Colt Single Action Army (SAA) revolver ever built. I would hazard to guess it would be in the millions of dollars range.

Reality check: Don't get your hopes up for such a find. Yes, there are gems waiting to be discovered in old barns, behind plastered walls, and in safe deposit boxes and attics. Or those finds of a lifetime could be lost in the back of a gun safe for thirty-some years.

THE RESEARCH BEGINS

Let's say you are the executor to your Aunt Phyllis's estate. You are cleaning out her attic of nearly a lifetime's accumulation of things when you come across an old tin cookie box. You open it and find an oily rag wrapped around something heavy. Carefully removing the dirty cloth like a burial shroud, you find a revolver. It looks like a revolver used by cowboys in the Old West. You have seen them countless times in TV westerns and movies, but before your mind starts racing and thinking this was the gun of Billy the Kid or Pat Garrett, take a breath and let's walk through the steps to identify and determine the value of this revolver to see whether we have a valuable piece of treasure with historic significance or a not-so-valuable piece that Aunt Phyllis kept hidden in the attic for reasons only she understood.

The first step in identifying Aunt Phyllis's revolver is to determine if the handgun is loaded. Once it is rendered safe, the first question you should ask yourself about this mysterious revolver in your hand is, is it a real honest-to-goodness Colt Model P? Also, think logically. If the revolver was used and owned by a famous outlaw or lawman in the late 1800s, then the gun should look well used. Most likely it would also be documented in biographies and other sources. If it looks too new for its age, then be suspect. Either this is a real Colt, or it has been refinished, or it is a replica made in Europe. Refinishing an older firearm typically strips the value from the gun, though it does make it look more appealing. Again, if it looks too new or too clean, then something could be amiss.

Carefully review the markings on the revolver. Take pictures of the markings with your cellphone or camera so you can refer back to them. When writing the markings down, you may inadvertently capitalize or use different punctuation, so it is best to take a photo. On our example revolver, we find markings on the left side of the barrel.

With this general information, we have determined the revolver is a Colt SAA chambered in .38 Special. Using a measuring tape, we also determine the barrel is 5½ inches in length. The finish is blued on the barrel, cylinder, grip frame, trigger guard,

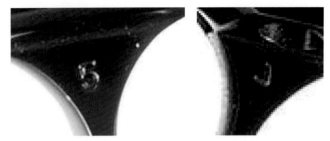

Inspector marks appear on the front side of trigger guard.

The serial number is located on the frame near the front edge of the trigger guard. Second Generation Single Action Army revolvers can primarily be identified by the "SA" suffix on the serial number.

Note the markings on the revolver's barrel.

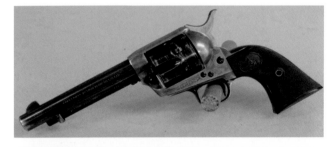

On the left side of the frame we find Colt's two-date/two-line patent markings.

This looks like a Colt Single Action Army manufactured in the twentieth century, since it still retains much of its finish.

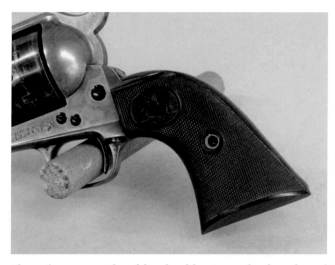

The grips are made of hard rubber, are checkered, and include the Rampant Colt logo, all indicating an early Second Generation model.

and trigger. The frame and the loading gate are case-hardened. The sides of the hammer are polished. The grips or stocks are hard rubber checkered with the Rampant Colt logo on the left and right panels.

The next step is to look up the serial number, which indicates the revolver is indeed a Second Generation Colt SAA, one manufactured in 1957. Serial number ranges for the Colt SAA model are included in this edition of *GTG Handguns*. The Colt website (colt.com) also has a database of Colt serial numbers. Just type in the serial number and what information Colt has on the firearm will show up in the search. Colt also provides archive letter services to authenticate its firearms. There is a fee to obtain this letter. For First Generation Single Action Army revolvers, the fee is $150, while the fee for all other Colt models is $100. Such letters can be a good investment, since they verify a firearm as being built and shipped from the Colt factory. It will also indicate the finish, type of grips, and engraving with which the firearm was shipped from the factory. Remember that modifications done to a firearm not performed at the factory can lessen the value of the firearm.

First Generation (1873–1940)

Year Mfg.	Serial Number Range	Year Mfg.	Serial Number Range	Year Mfg.	Serial Number Range
1873	1–200	1896	163001–168000	1920	338001–341000
1874	201–15000	1897	168001–175000	1921	341001–343000
1875	15001–22000	1898	175001–182000	1922	343001–344500
1876	22001–33000	1899	182001–192000	1923	344501–346400
1877	33001–41000	1900	192001–203000	1924	346401–347300
1878	41001–49000	1901	203001–220000	1925	347301–348200
1879	49001–53000	1902	220001–238000	1926	348201–349800
1880	53001–62000	1903	238001–250000	1927	349801–351300
1881	62001–73000	1904	250001–261000	1928	351301–352400
1882	73001–85000	1905	261001–273000	1929	352401–353800
1883	85001–102000	1906	273001–288000	1930	353801–354100
1884	102001–114000	1907	288001–304000	1931	354101–354500
1885	114001–117000	1908	304001–308000	1932	354501–354800
1886	117001–119000	1909	308001–312000	1933	354801–355000
1887	119001–125000	1910	312001–316000	1934	355001–355200
1888	125001–128000	1911	316001–321000	1935	355201–355300
1889	128001–130000	1912	321001–325000	1936	355301–355400
1890	130001–136000	1913	325001–328000	1937	355401–356100
1891	136001–144000	1914	328001–329500	1938	356101–356600
1892	144001–149000	1915	329501–332000	1939	356601–357000
1893	149001–154000	1916	332001–335000	1940	357001–357859
1894	154001–159000	1917	335001–337000		
1895	159001–163000	1918	337201–338000		

Second Generation (1956–1975)

Year Mfg.	Serial Number Range	Year Mfg.	Serial Number Range	Year Mfg.	Serial Number Range
1956*	0001SA–8800SA	1962	35651SA–37300SA	1969	49001SA–52600SA
1957	8801SA–18500SA	1963	37301SA–38500SA	1970	52601SA–59400SA
1958	18501SA–23400SA	1964	38501SA–40000SA	1971	59401SA–61700SA
1959	23401SA–28500SA	1965	40001SA–41500SA	1972	61701SA–64400SA
1960	28501SA–33600SA	1966	41501SA–43800SA	1973	64401SA–69400SA
1961	33601SA–35650SA	1967	43801SA–46300SA	1975	70501SA–73319SA
		1968	46301SA–49000SA		

*"SA" serial number suffix was added when Second Generation revolver began production.

Third Generation (1976–Present)

Year Mfg.	Serial Number Range	Year Mfg.	Serial Number Range	Year Mfg.	Serial Number Range
1976	80000SA–81999SA	1989	SA94434	2004	S34500A–S37999A
1977	82000SA–90499SA	1990	Not Available	2005	S38000A–S41299A
1978	90500SA–99999SA -SA01001	1991	SA94673–SA96587	2006**	S41300A–S42899A
		1992	SA96588–SA99878	2007**	S42900A and S53000A
1979	SA13000–SA30249	1993	SA99879–SA99999	2008**	S48100A and S57300A
1980	SA30250–SA46899	1994*	S07006A–S10122A	2009**	S48300A and S57300A
1981	SA46900–SA58627	1995	S10123A–S12559A	2010**	S49000A and S64000A
1982	SA58628–SA65255	1996	S12560A–S15885A	2011**	S48000A and S65000A
1983	SA65256–SA66495	1997	S15886A–S21568A	2012	S66200A–S68899A
1984	SA66496–SA70499	1998	S21569A–S26456A	2013	S68900A–S71599A
1985	SA70500	1999	S26457A–S29099A	2014	S71600A–S74299A
1986	Not Available	2000	S29100A–S31499A	2015	S74300A–
1987	SA70813	2001	S31500A–S33399A		
1988	SA71464–SA72269 SA90136–SA94433	2002	S33400A–S33999A		
		2003	S34000A–S34499A		

*Serial number SA suffix dropped and SA changed to "SxxxxxA".
**Serial numbers out of sequence

We find our example is actually an early Second Generation model, which makes it more valuable than a mid- or late-model Second Generation variants and all Third Generation Colt SAA revolvers of the same model type. First Generation SAA revolvers are the most valuable to collectors. If the serial number search had determined this was a First Generation Colt, it would be appropriate to secure a factory letter.

Doing some further data checking in the handgun values section in *GTG Handguns*, we determine the following:

- Colt SAA Second Generation revolvers were made in four calibers: .45 Long Colt, .44 Special, .38 Special, and .357 Magnum, and these calibers presented in this order indicates the value from most valuable to least valuable.
- Barrel lengths available were: 3-inch (Sheriff's model), 4¾-inch, 5½-inch, 7½-inch, and 12-inch (Buntline model). The 3- and 12-inch barrel models are less common. Standard and more common barrel lengths were 4¾-, 5½-, and 7½-inch models. Models with a 4¾-inch barrel typically bring about 10 to 15 percent higher values than other standard barrel lengths.
- Finish choices were all blue, blue and case-hardened, or nickel. Nickel finish typically adds about 20 percent to the value of the revolver.

The rub marks from the cylinder rotating on the bolt indicate the revolver was used. This decreases the total collector value of the revolver and makes this more of a collectable shooter.

- The original box is not with this example, but early Second Generation models came in a black box. Having the original box would increase the value of the revolver by 30 percent. Mid- and late-model Second Generation Colt SAAs had what is referred to as the "stagecoach box." The box top was red and white with an illustration of a stagecoach. The interior of the box was also red and white and die cut to hold the revolver.

The next step is to grade the Colt based on its condition. We can see that this revolver has had some use, and was also somewhat cared for. The muzzle shows signs of being holstered, as the bluing is worn. The cylinder has a ring around it from the cylinder rotating and dragging against the bolt. The back strap has a patina from being handled and not maintained after use, and the grips, too, show use, as the checkering near the backstrap is worn. It is important to note that the wear of the revolver is consistent.

Overall, Aunt Phyllis's revolver would rate about 60 percent to 80 percent, or GOOD condition, using the NRA Firearm Grading Guide in *GTG Handguns*. Going back to the Second Generation Colt SAA section in *GTG Handguns*, we can then look at the GOOD (Gd) column and determine the value of this Colt SAA about $1,500 to $1,900.

The ejector rod housing also shows signs of worn bluing, no doubt from holster wear.

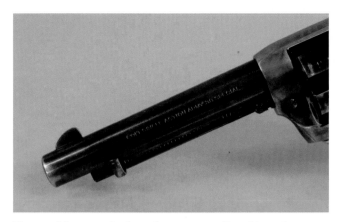

The markings on the barrel are on one line. Note the worn bluing on the muzzle, another indication this revolver was used.

The right stock or grip panel shows use, as the checkering is not sharp and crisp. Worn metal paired with sharply checkered grips can indicate that the original grips were replaced, which would lessen the value of the firearm.

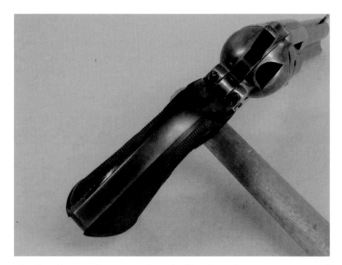

The backstrap has a patina, indicating the gun was used and not cared for or stored properly.

The frothy case color still shows on the frame. The more original the finish on the revolver, the more valuable it will be.

Collecting the Colt Woodsman

By Bob Rayburn

The Colt Woodsman was designed by John Moses Browning in 1912 and went into production in 1915 as the Colt 22 Target Model. It was the first successful magazine-fed .22 LR pistol.

In the very first owner's brochure for the new pistol, the manufacturer confidently declared:

This is the only automatic pistol now made to handle the standard caliber .22 Long Rifle cartridges, and **will prove** *(emphasis added) most popular with shooters, sportsmen, trappers, and others desiring a high-grade pistol adapted for this economical and easily obtained ammunition.*

Those words were prophetic, as the Colt 22 Target Model evolved into the Colt Woodsman and then the various models that evolved from that. In the next sixty-two years, literally hundreds of thousands would be manufactured and sold all over the world.

Advance Notice—A New Colt!

On or about May 1, 1915 we will be prepared to furnish samples of a new Automatic Pistol

The Colt, Caliber .22 Target Model

Announcing the new Colt! This is a copy of the first advertisement for the new Colt .22 LR rimfire pistol, which was originally called the Colt Automatic Target Pistol. This is known as a Pre-Woodsman model.

This chapter describes the major variations in all models of the Colt Woodsman line, from the beginning in 1915 until production ceased in 1977. There are many more variations of interest to advanced collectors, but those details are far too numerous to include in this space.

SERIES AND MODELS

There are three series of Woodsman pistols, corresponding to three basic frame designs. First Series refers to all those built on the first S frame as it existed prior to and during World War II. The second frame design was used from late 1947 until mid-1955, and the third S frame design was used from 1955 to to the end of regular production in 1977.

Each series had a Sport Model with a 4½-inch round barrel, a Target Model with a 6- or 6⅝-inch round barrel, and a Match Target Model with a heavy, flat-sided barrel. The very similar Challenger, Huntsman, and Targetsman were economy models based on the Woodsman design and made only during the post-WWII years.

For the First Series Match Target Model, the barrel was 6⅝ inches in length, while in the post-war versions it was either 4½ or 6 inches. Wherever barrel length is mentioned, it is measured from breech to muzzle, i.e., from where the bullet goes in to where it comes out.

FIRST SERIES (1915–1947)

The First Series Woodsman can be easily recognized by its distinctive profile, which resembles the Luger in its rakish grip angle. The serial number also provides a sure means of identification, since only the First Series lacked an alphabetical suffix.

The Woodsman name was added in 1927, and collectors today generally refer to the earlier guns as Pre-Woodsman. Pistols produced prior to 1931 were manufactured for use with standard velocity ammunition only. Between the introduction of the Woodsman line in 1915 and WWII, three different barrel profiles were used: pencil, medium, and straight taper.

Three different barrel profiles were used on the Woodsman and pre-Woodsman from its introduction in 1915 until WWII:

1. Pencil barrel (1915–1922): Pronounced shoulder that steps down the barrel diameter to .500 inch just forward of the receiver, then tapers slightly to .475-inch at the muzzle.
2. Medium barrel (1922–1934): Smaller step down, then tapers to .525-inch at the muzzle.
3. Straight taper barrel (1934–1947): No step down, tapers from .600-inch at the receiver to .525-inch at the muzzle.

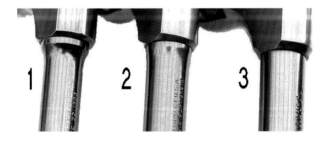

The earliest model in the First Series came in only one version and was known simply as Colt Automatic Target Pistol.

The Woodsman name was added in 1927 and, in 1932, heat-treated mainspring housings that permitted the use of high-velocity ammunition were phased in from serial numbers 81000 to 86000. A grooved pattern enhances identification.

In response to numerous requests from the target shooters of the day for a heavier barrel

PRE-WOODSMAN

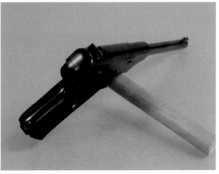

Close-ups of a Colt Automatic Target Pistol, known to collectors as a Pre-Woodsman. Colt added the Woodsman name in 1927. *Image courtesy Bishop's Fine Guns*

Colt Automatic Target Pistol (Pre-Woodsman) with the thin, 6⅝-inch pencil barrel. Serial numbers will be under 31000 (1915–1922). For current values, see page 171. *Image courtesy Bob Rayburn*

and larger grips, Colt responded with a new model in 1938. The Match Target Woodsman, with its slab sided 6⅝-inch barrel, also featured a hand-honed action and an improved

A 1927 ad in the *American Rifleman* magazine, announcing the new name for the Woodsman. *Image courtesy Bob Rayburn*

Mainspring housing differences. Left: This Woodsman takes standard-velocity ammunition only. Right: Standard or high-velocity ammunition can both be used. *Image courtesy Bob Rayburn*

rear sight adjustable for both windage and elevation. The grip frame area is actually the same as the other models, and regular Woodsman stocks will fit perfectly. The larger grip was achieved by fitting the new pistol with oversized, one-piece wraparound stocks commonly called "elephant ear" grips today. To signify the Match Target's intended market, a bull's-eye target pattern was roll-marked onto the left side of the barrel. This led to the nickname of "Bullseye Model" for these First Series Match Target pistols.

Brochure announcing the new Sport Model Woodsman. *Image courtesy Bob Rayburn*

MATCH TARGET WITH "ELEPHANT EAR" GRIPS

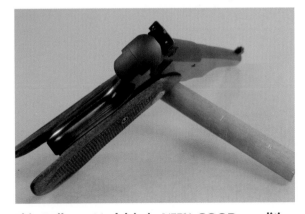

This Bullseye Model is in VERY GOOD condition and comes with the original box, tags, test target, cleaning brush, and manual, all of which add to value of the firearm. For current values, see page **171.** *Image courtesy Bishop's Fine Guns*

The Sport model, with a 4½-inch barrel, was added to the Woodsman line in 1933. Serial Nos. approximately 86000–187423, made 1934–1947. Other than having a shorter barrel and a fixed front sight, the Sport models are the same as the Target models of the same era. Some of the early Sport Models had a lighter, medium-weight barrel, and some of the later pre-WWII Sport Models had an optional elevation-adjustable front sight. For current values, see page 171–172. *Image courtesy Bob Rayburn*

A 1933 advertisement heralding the introduction of the new Colt Match Target Woodsman. *Image courtesy Bob Rayburn*

A First Series Match Target with 6⅝-inch flat-sided barrel and elongated "elephant ear" grips. Serial numbers range MT1 to MT16611. For current values, see page 171. *Image courtesy Bob Rayburn*

SECOND SERIES (1947–1955)

The Second Series Woodsman pistols are the only models that have a push-button magazine release, similar to that of the Colt Government Model pistol and its military versions in the 1911 and 1911A1. All post-WWII-type Woodsmans have an "S" suffix on their serial numbers. Although it is part of the Second Series, the Challenger model, unlike the Woodsman, has a spring catch at the butt and a "C" suffix to the serial number.

No camping trip was complete without the Colt Woodsman, and according to this 1950 ad, it doubled as game-getter and for home-defense.

Left: The Second Series Woodsman, made from 1947–1955, is easily identified by the push-button magazine release. **Center:** With the exception of the 1949–50 Sport model, which had fixed sights, The Second Series Woodsman had the Coltmaster rear sight (bottom) until 1953, and the Accro rear sight (top) from 1953–55. **Right:** A unique feature of the Second Series Woodsman is the provision for a grip adapter on the backstrap. With few exceptions, each came with two grip adapters, a large and a small. The shooter could use either one, or none, for three different grip sizes. *Image courtesy Bob Rayburn*

A Second Series Match Target with 4½-inch barrel. Serial numbers 59468-S to 146137-S, made 1949–1955. For current values, see page 171. *Image courtesy Bob Rayburn*

An example of a Second Series Match Target, with 6-inch barrel. Serial numbers 1-S to 146137-S, made 1947–1955. The Second Series Match Target Model came standard with plastic grips and a left panel thumbrest. Note the thumb magazine release. For current values, see page **171.** *Image courtesy Bob Rayburn*

This is a Second Series Sport Model with 4-inch barrel. Serial numbers 2318-S to 146137-S, made 1948–1955. During this production run, plastic grips and a left-panel thumbrest were standard. For current values, see page **172.** *Image courtesy Bob Rayburn*

SECOND SERIES MATCH TARGET

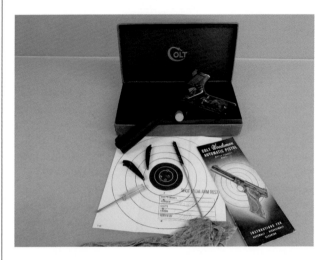

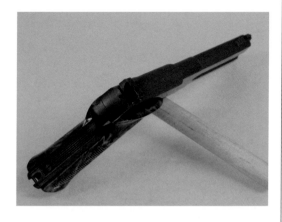

This Second Series Match Target features the original box and accompanying accoutrements. It would rate NiB (NEW IN BOX) and fetch a premium. For current values, see page 171. *Image courtesy Bishop's Fine Guns*

SECOND SERIES SPORT MODEL

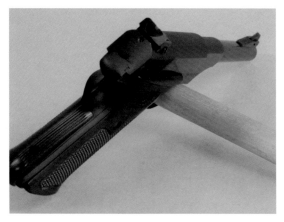 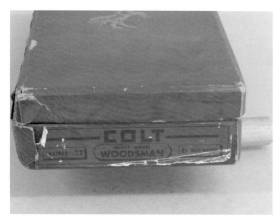

The Second Series Sport Model featured a 4½-inch barrel only. Serial Nos. 1345-S to 146137-S, made 1948–1955. The thumbrest on the left grip panel was added to the Sport Model in 1950, after approximate serial number 71200-S. From mid-1949 to mid-1950, the Sport Model had a fixed rear sight and a different type of front sight. Note the grip adaptor in the backstrap of this Second Series Sport Model. This specimen also includes the original box. For current values, see page 172. *Image courtesy Bishop's Fine Guns*

SECOND SERIES TARGET MODEL

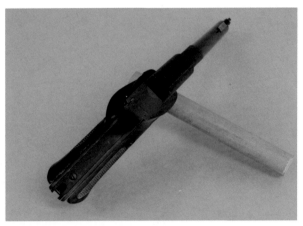

Note the lanyard loop in this Second Series Target model. For current values, see page 172. *Image courtesy Bishop's Fine Guns*

Note the thumb-button magazine release and barrel marking on this Second Series Target model with 6-inch barrel. For current values, see page 172. *Image courtesy Bishop's Fine Guns*

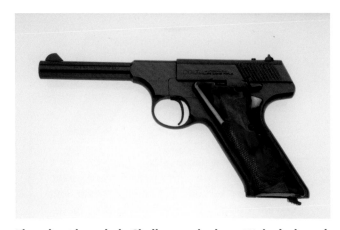

The short-barreled Challenger had a 4½-inch barrel. This model was similar to the Second Series Woodsman, except it came with fixed sights, without an automatic slide stop and with a butt magazine release. Serial Numbers 1-C to 77143-C, made 1950–1955. Plastic grips without a thumbrest were standard. For current values, see page 167. *Image courtesy Bob Rayburn*

An example of a long-barrel Challenger, which featured a 6-inch barrel and plastic grips without a thumbrest. Serial numbers 1-C to 77143-C, made 1950–1955.

THIRD SERIES (1955–1977)

The Third Series replaced the Second Series in mid-1955. The most obvious change was the replacement of the push-button magazine release with a snap catch at the frame butt. The trigger guard was made larger, the grip adapters and lanyard ring were eliminated, and the trigger was reshaped. The magazine safety, which was a feature of the Second series, was carried over to the Third Series for a few months, and then was quietly dropped.

All Third Series Woodsmans have an "S" suffix to the serial number, just as in the Second Series. All Third Series guns have the magazine release on the butt, in the same location as those of the First Series.

In 1955, the Second Series Challenger was replaced in the Third Series by the very similar Huntsman Model. The Targetsman, basically a slightly upgraded Huntsman, was added to the line in 1959. The early Huntsman and Targetsman models continued the Challenger serial numbers with a "–C" suffix.

This is an example of a Huntsman with a 4½-inch barrel. Early versions had black plastic stocks. Later versions, beginning in 1960, had walnut stocks. The Huntsman did not have a thumbrest. Made 1955–977. For current values, see page 167. *Image courtesy Bob Rayburn*

Later Huntsman and Targetsman models, and all Third Series Woodsman models, have a snap catch-type magazine release located in the grip butt. *Image courtesy Bob Rayburn*

This is a Huntsman model with 6-inch barrel. Early versions had black plastic stocks. Beginning in 1960, the pistol had walnut stocks. No Huntsman grips had a thumbrest. Made 1955–1977. For current values, see page 167. *Image courtesy Bob Rayburn*

The Targetsman came only with a 6-inch barrel and had an adjustable rear sight and a pinned front sight. Early versions had black plastic stocks. Later versions, beginning in 1960, had walnut stocks. The Targetsman came standard with left-side thumbrest. Made 1959–1977. For current values, see page 171. *Image courtesy Bob Rayburn*

The Third Series Sport Model came only with a 4½-inch barrel. Standard equipment included a left-panel thumbrest. Early versions had black plastic stocks, while later versions, beginning in 1960, came with walnut stocks. Made 1955–1977. For current values, see page 172. *Image courtesy Bob Rayburn*

The Third Series Target Model featured only a 6-inch barrel. Early versions had black plastic stocks. Later versions, beginning in 1960, had walnut stocks. All Second and Third Series Target models were standard with a left-panel thumbrest. Made 1955–1977. For current values, see page 172. *Image courtesy Bob Rayburn*

The Third Series Match Target was available with either a 4½- or 6-inch barrel. This is a 4½-inch-barreled model. Later versions, beginning in 1960, had walnut stocks. All Second and Third Series Target models were standard with a left-panel thumbrest. Made 1955–1977. For current values, see page 172. *Image courtesy Bob Rayburn*

This is a Third Series Match Target with a 6-inch barrel. It is an early Third Series Woodsman, identified by the black plastic grips and the same rear sight as was used on the late Second Series guns. Beginning in 1960, all Woodsman, Huntsman, and Targetsman models were again equipped with walnut grips. Made 1955–1977. For current values, see page 172. *Image courtesy Bob Rayburn*

THIRD SERIES MATCH TARGET MODEL

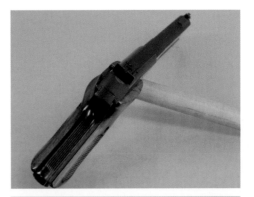

This is an example of a late-production Third Series Match Target with 6-inch barrel. By 1960, all Third Series Woodsman pistols were equipped with walnut grips. For current values, see page 172. *Image courtesy Bishop's Fine Guns*

In total, the Woodsman models were built for sixty-two years with only a brief interruption during WWII. From its introduction in 1915, The Colt .22 Automatic Pistol quickly became a huge success for the company, as proclaimed in the 1937 Colt catalog:

The Colt "Woodsman" Model .22 Automatic Pistol was brought out as a Target Model and instantly gained the recognition of expert shooters because of its accuracy, simplicity, and power. In addition to establishing World Pistol Records this Arm has repeatedly won important pistol matches both here and abroad. Exceptionally popular with Hunters, Trappers, Campers, Tourists and Farmers.

In the Colt .22 Automatic Pistol is found that rare combination of qualities which mark the

THIRD SERIES SPORT MODEL FACTORY ENGRAVED

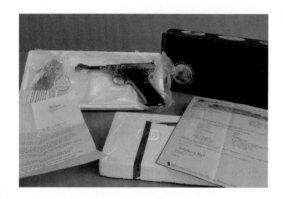

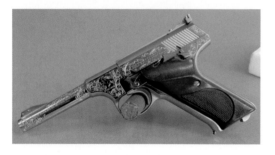

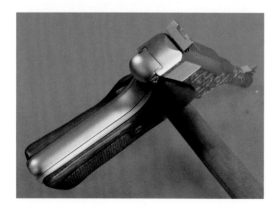

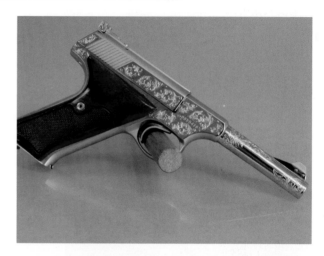

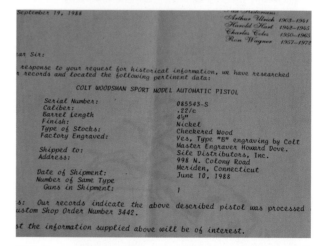

This is a rare example of a factory-engraved Third Series Woodsman Sport Model. It features a nickel finish, checkered wood grips, and Type "B" engraving. Note the factory letter that proves this firearm was engraved at the factory. *Image courtesy Bishop's Fine Guns*

ideal small bore Arm. Chambered for the economical, easy to get .22 Long Rifle Cartridge, it handles the new High Speed ammunition with perfect satisfaction. Here are combined Balance, Range, Accuracy, Convenience, Power and Safety, with every advantage of the single-shot Pistol, plus automatic action for rapid-fire and snap shooting.

Generations of hunters, trappers, marksmen, casual shooters, and collectors have been able to appreciate the quality, reliability, and the aesthetics of the family of guns that grew out of that 1915 Colt Caliber .22 Target Model. By the 1960s and '70s, other manufacturers with more modern and efficient manufacturing methods were producing high-quality but less-costly .22 pistols. High labor costs and other expenses arising from obsolete or obsolescent equipment and manufacturing methods eventually forced Colt to discontinue the Woodsman line.

The series and models detailed above provide a good starting point for the collector. Please note that there are many variations within these, some of which are quite scarce and desirable for the Woodsman collector, such as factory engraved models.

NATIONAL LEAD COMPANY COMBINATION SHOULDER STOCK AND HOLSTER

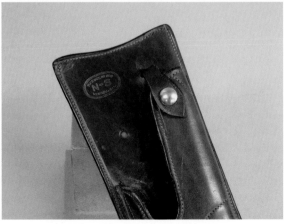

This is another example of the N-S shoulder stock in the original box. Note the EXCELLENT condition. This is valued at about $2,500. *Image courtesy Bishop's Fine Guns*

This pre-Woodsman was manufactured in 1927, the last year before "THE WOODSMAN" was added as the official model name of the pistol. What is unique about this specimen is the N-S patented, National Lead Company combination shoulder stock and holster. The shoulder stock is metal covered in smooth brown leather, with a metal grip-fitting for the pistol. It is marked with "N-S"/patent date/location in a rope circle. These were marketed in the late 1920s and early 1930s specifically for the Woodsman line, but due to the 1934 National Firearms Act, short-barreled rifles and pistols with shoulder stocks were banned, making these variants very hard to find, especially in such a well-preserved state.

Image courtesy Rock Island Auction

COLT WOODSMAN POCKET GUIDE

8th Edition

Series and Models
A Basic Collection
Factory Engraving
Value Factors
Tables of Features
Magazine Compatibility
Tables of Manufacture Dates
Assembly/Disassembly
Exploded Views and Parts Lists
Frequently Asked Questions
Bibliography

© 1985 - 2010 by Robert Rayburn
All rights reserved. No portion may be reproduced
without written permission from the author.

Bob Rayburn has been shooting and collecting Colt Woodsman pistols for more than forty years and has put together quite a collection of First, Second, and Third Series Woodsmans. In fact, he is such an ardent pursuer of these rimfire Colts that he took his collection of handwritten notes and converted it into the *Colt Woodsman Pocket Guide,* now in its eighth edition. This little red book is an invaluable aid to collecting Colt Woodsman pistols, and it can be purchased on Bob's websites, www.colt22.com or www.coltwoodsman.com.

Smith & Wesson Model 29
Make My Day
"The most powerful handgun in the world."—circa 1971

If it hadn't been for Clint Eastwood's *Dirty Harry* series of movies, the Smith & Wesson Model 29, introduced in 1955, may have been dropped from the catalog and strategically reintroduced as consumer demand warranted. Most ardent handgun hunters knew the Model 29 was an excellent hunting revolver chambered in .44 Magnum, but it was the *Dirty Harry* character wielding the massive Model 29 in the early 1970s that propelled the revolver into a pop culture icon.

The Model 29 revolver, in 1971 claimed to be the most powerful handgun in world, has since been ousted from that particular top spot by other handguns and other calibers. Movies, TV shows, and video games, along with the fact that the revolver and caliber combination make a good hunting handgun, has ensured the Model 29 continues to be manufactured to this day.

BEFORE *DIRTY HARRY*
Since its introduction in 1955, many design changes have been made and many model variants offered. When I spoke to Roy Jinks, historian for Smith & Wesson, he said, "The basic difference in the Model 29 series are the four-screw and three-screw models." But the story doesn't start there.

"The Model 29 was the second magnum revolver ever made," said Jinks. "After the introduction of the .357 Magnum, in 1935, there was a push to make a more powerful .44-caliber revolver."

In 1935, Smith & Wesson used its N-frame to produce its first .357 Magnum revolver, known as the Registered Magnum. S&W chose to chamber the powerful .357 Magnum cartridge in a six-shot revolver built from this large, heavy-duty, carbon-steel N-frame. The revolver and caliber combination was an immediate success, and S&W had a hard time filling orders—and this was at the height of the Great Depression, when the revolver cost $60.00. The big N-frame had a pinned barrel, counter-bored cylinder chambers, and checkering across the topstrap of the frame and barrel.

THE IMPACT OF ELMER KEITH
Elmer Keith was a life-long, long-range, big-bore handgun shooting and hunting enthusiast. A noted gun writer and handloader, Keith handloaded the .44 Special cartridge, pushing it to its limits. He shot his hot handloaded cartridges in S&W .44 Hand Ejector 1st Model New Century revolvers to test the effectiveness of the loads. The Hand Ejectors were also known as "Triple Locks," due to a third locking lug on the crane. These were strongly built revolvers and could withstand the increased pressure of Keith's handloaded .44 Special cartridges.

Keith and a few others are primarily responsible for the development of both the .44 Magnum and the .357 Magnum cartridges, but it was Keith who was responsible for convincing Smith & Wesson to build a revolver capable

REGISTERED MAGNUM

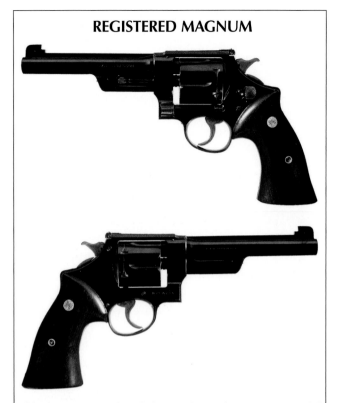

This is an example of the Registered Magnum model introduced by S&W in 1935. It was the first magnum revolver chambered in .357 Magnum. These revolvers were handmade to order by Smith & Wesson and individually registered to the owner. The Registered Magnums had a level of fit and finish beyond the already high standard set by S&W during that time. This revolver is equipped with a raised Patridge blade front sight and an adjustable, rectangular notch rear sight, both set into the signature, full-checkered barrel rib and topstrap. The 6-inch barrel is pinned and the rear cylinder face is counter-bored, with fine case-hardened colors on the serrated trigger and hammer. These grips are not the factory originals. Estimated value: $4,500–$7,100.
Image courtesy Rock Island Auctions

TRIPLE LOCK REVOLVERS

This pair of S&W Hand Ejector First Model (Triple Lock) revolvers in .44 Special that belonged to Elmer Keith. With these revolvers, Keith handloaded the .44 Special cartridge to velocities well above factory ballistics, and that work led to the development of the .44 Magnum cartridge. The revolvers pictured here are virtually identical, with 6½-inch barrels, one with gold bead front sight and the other with Keith's "long-range" modified, thick front sight blade with two gold bars for distance shooting. Both have round topstraps, frames are the five-screw type, and the cranes have a third fastener in the ejector rod housings. Both have standard color case-hardened hammers and smooth triggers. The revolvers are mounted with mirror-image, custom Magna-sized, burl walnut two-piece grips, with "Elmer Keith" and oak leaves carved on one side in deep relief, and the other grip with oak leaves. *Image courtesy James D. Julia, Inc.*

Triple Locks were designed with a third lock-up built into the crane that locks into a detent built into the bottom part of the ejector shroud. The first and second lockups were 1) at the front of the ejector rod, which locked in the detent pin in the ejector rod shroud, and 2) at the rear of the ejector, locking into the rear of the frame behind the cylinder. *Image courtesy James D. Julia, Inc.*

of handling the .44 Magnum cartridge. That revolver would become known as the Model 29.

"Smith & Wesson was working with Remington to develop and produce a more powerful magnum .44 cartridge," explained Jinks.

While Remington was developing the cartridge, S&W was also developing the longer chamber for the .44 Magnum.

The Model 29 was originally produced with a four-screw sideplate. This drawing illustrates the differences between the four-screw and the three-screw sideplates. The fourth screw was eventually replaced with an interlocking tongue. *Collection of Roy G. Jinks*

For $135, tax included, the new Smith & Wesson .44 Magnum revolver was introduced and made available. The original pre-Model 29 was not marked "Model 29" until 1957. *Collection of Roy G. Jinks*

Originally, the new S&W .44 Magnum revolver was simply marked ".44 MAGNUM" on the right side of the barrel. Note the four-screw sideplate. *Collection of Roy G. Jinks*

This catalog illustration of the original S&W .44 Magnum shows the Coke-bottle-style grips with their palm swell and the diamond around the screw hole. *Collection of Roy G. Jinks*

"S&W then made the first .44 Magnum revolver, in December of 1955," Jinks said.

By 1956, the new revolver was cataloged as the Model 29.

"When it came out, it cost $125," Jinks told me, "but S&W quickly raised the price to $140.

"Originally, the Model 29 was only available in 4- and 6½-inch pinned barrels," Jinks said. "The 8 3/8-inch barrel model came out in the late 1950s."

Less common are 5- and 5½-inch barrels. Jinks explained the Model 29 was popular with handgun hunters, but favor with it waned before picking up again with the release of the *Dirty Harry* series of movies in the 1970s.

"In the 1970s, S&W could not make enough of the Model 29 revolver to keep up with demand," Jinks told me.

At that time, the revolvers were selling for four and five times the normal retain price.

IMPROVEMENTS

Over the years, the Model 29 has gone through numerous engineering and cosmetic changes.

"The original .44 Magnums, made between 1956 and late 1957, were still built the old-fashioned way," said Jinks. "They were first soft-fitted, then hard-fitted."

"Soft-fitting" means the originals were hand-fitted with the assembled gun "in the white," or without a cosmetic finish. All the parts were then stamped so that the gun had matching serial numbers throughout. The revolver was then finished as a fully assembled gun in the "hard-fitted" phase, where the revolvers were heat blued. In essence, the guns were assembled twice.

"To increase production and meet demand," explained Jinks, "the soft-fitting step was removed, which meant all the barrels, frames, and cylinders were heat-blued as individual parts. This means slight variances in oven temperatures on indi-

This collectable has gold highlights and is a **Model 29-3 Elmer Keith 1899-1984 Commemorative. It has a wood presentation case with a blue lining. This model was manufactured in 1985 as a limited edition. Only 2,500 were produced. Estimated value is $1,000–$1,500.** *Image courtesy Rock Island Auction*

vidual parts caused the assembled gun to have slight differences in bluing color."

In the late 1970s, the oven bluing method was replaced with a penetrating bluing.

"The brightness of the blue became a little more black," explained Jinks.

With this change, the variances in bluing from the oven process no longer occurred.

The Model 29's original grips were also changed to meet production demands.

"Up until the mid-1960s, the gun had Coke-bottle grips with a palm swell," Jinks explained, "and had a diamond around the screw hole. In the latter part of the 1970s, that grip was dropped to improve production of the grip, and the diamond was eliminated around the screw hole."

S&W's model naming convention of the Model 29 changed as the revolver's design and production changed to include a dash and additional number. For instance, in 1962, the Model 29-1 was being manufactured. This model included changes to the extractor rod to prevent the rod from unscrewing during recoil.

In January 1999, after approximately seven changes, the Model 29 was officially discontinued,

This Smith & Wesson **pre-Model 29 .44 Magnum revolver, with its original black box, was manufactured between 1957 and 1958. It features a 6½-inch barrel, a serrated ramp front sight with orange insert, and a fully adjustable rear notch sight. Other characteristics include a wide, case-hardened checkered hammer and wide, case-hardened serrated trigger. The serial number for these models is stamped on the butt, inside of the yoke cutout, and on the back of the cylinder. Value is estimated at $1,000–$1,500.** *Image courtesy Rock Island Auction*

This variation of the Model 29 is the Model 29-5 Magna Classic, produced in 1990. It is built on the round-butt frame and uses a three-screw sideplate. Only three thousand were produced, and on this one, "1 of 3000" appears on the right side of the barrel on the underlug. For full specifications and values, see page 293. *Image courtesy Rock Island Auction*

The Model 629 Classic was a stainless-steel variant introduced in 1990. It is still in production. It features a round-butt grip frame, full underlug barrel, and Hogue grips. Barrel lengths include 5-, 6½-, and 8³/₈-inch choices with an interchangeable front sight. For full specifications and values, see page 301. *Image courtesy Smith & Wesson*

but it would soon return as the Model 29-8, in 2001. The Model 29-8 employed a new frame design with an internal lock system and reverts back to the four-screw sideplate.

The Model 29 spawned other variations of the model. The Model 629, introduced in 1978, is a stainless-steel version. The Model 29 Silhouette, introduced in 1983, featured a three-screw sideplate

and a 10⅝-inch barrel with an adjustable front sight. In 1991, the Model 29 Classic debuted with a full-lug barrel. The Model 29 Classic DX, introduced in 1992, uses a round-butt N-frame and a three-screw side plate. In 1990, the Model 29 Magna Classic was introduced with all of the features of the Classic DX, but with a 7½-inch barrel. Numerous collectors' editions have also been made over the years.

Model 29 Engineering Changes		
MODEL DESIGNATION	**YEAR**	**ENGINEERING CHANGE**
29	1957	Around serial number S179000, revolvers were stamped with model number
29-1	1962	extractor rod changed to reverse thread; most 29-1 models use a three-screw sideplate
29-2	1962	trigger screw dropped, cylinder stop changed
29-3	1982	pinned barrel and cylinder counter-bore dropped, cylinder length changed
29-4	1988	new yoke retention system, floating hand added
29-5	1990	redesigned bolt block and stop notch in cylinder
29-6	1993	redesigned extractor, frame topstrap drilled and tapped for optics mount, Hogue grips introduced
29-7	1998	frame and internal mechanism redesign, MIM parts introduced
29-8	2001	frame redesign, internal lock mechanism added, four-screw sideplate reintroduced
29-9	2002	Lew Horton (distributor) Heritage series with blued or nickel finishes, 6½-in. barrel, four-screw sideplate, target grips
29-10	2006	square grip frame reintroduced, serrated back strap

The Iconic Luger
Pistole Parabellum 1908

The Luger is perhaps the most iconic pistol ever manufactured. Lugers are prized by collectors, with some variations extremely rare and highly coveted.

Like most semi-automatics in the early twentieth century, the Luger required careful hand-fitting of parts, thus manufacturing was expensive and time-consuming. These pistols generally show great workmanship, as they were originally built at a time when all firearms, and most mechanical items for that matter, were built by hand by machinists and craftsmen.

The Luger was originally produced from 1900 through 1942, and these models are the most sought-after and valuable. What follows in this chapter is a guide to help identify Lugers manufactured during this time period.

Please note that Lugers have continued to be manufactured since 1942.

In the 1970s and '80s Lugers were also produced by Mauser and imported into the US by Interarms.

In the early 1990s, both Stoeger and Aimco began producing Lugers in the US. In 1991, Aimco, Inc., of Houston, Texas, manufactured an all-new remake of the original Luger design that was marketed by Mitchell Arms.

In 1994, Stoeger, Inc., purchased the rights to market a stainless-steel "American Eagle" Luger pistol. Stoeger, it should also be noted, was once a sporting goods retailer in New York City and imported German-produced Lugers, as well as other firearms, in the early twentieth century. The unique stainless-steel variant of the Luger marketed by Stoeger have since been discontinued.

A few pistols have copied the Luger toggle design, notably Erma, which produced .22 LR, .32 ACP, and .380 ACP models that were imported into the US from 1964 through 1968 and are now discontinued. Stoeger also offered a .22 LR

Stoeger contracted the DWM—*Deutsche Waffen-und Munitionsfabriken*—**factory in Germany to produce Lugers and then imported the pistols into the US for the commercial market during the early twentieth century. These are the types of markings one can expect. Note the right side of the barrel extension is stamped "GERMANY" and roll-marked "A.F. STOEGER, INC./ NEW YORK."** *Image courtesy Rock Island Auction*

This is an example of a post-WWI, DWM-manufactured, commercial Luger pistol marked on top of the barrel "ABERCROMBIE & FITCH CO NEW YORK/MADE IN SWITZERLAND." This pistol was originally intended for sale in Switzerland, but was diverted or sold to sporting goods retailer Abercrombie & Fitch Co. in New York, circa 1922. Only one hundred of these Swiss Lugers were imported into the US. *Image courtesy Rock Island Auction*

Luger that was manufactured in the US until it was discontinued in 1985. These pistols have more of a novelty interest with the true Luger collector.

NOTHING ELSE LIKE IT

A description of the Luger pistol is appropriate here, since these pistols are unlike any other contemporary semi-automatic handgun built today.

Lugers feature a toggle mechanism that was invented by Hugo Borchardt, who used the mechanism in the C-93 pistol in 1893. (Borchardt actually based his design on the Maxim machine guns, but that is really getting into the weeds.) George Luger, a designer at the Ludwig Lowe small arms factory in Berlin, Germany, radically redesigned the Borchardt toggle system and patented a new pistol design in 1898.

The firearm is technically defined as a short recoil-operated, toggle-locked, semi-automatic pistol. In operation, the toggle and barrel assembly move rearward after a round is fired. The barrel is then stopped by the frame, but the toggle movement continues and the knee joint bends to extract and eject the case before moving forward to pick up and insert a fresh round from the magazine into the chamber.

The Luger held eight rounds in a detachable magazine. It weighed 30.7 ounces, with the most common barrel length being about 4 inches. The finish was typically a deep blue, with straw-colored controls and sharply checkered wood grips. Specimens with original finish demand high prices, though the finish on wartime-production models suffered, and in some cases the grips were checkered plastic.

In hand, the comfortable grip angle of the Luger makes the pistol a natural pointer, easy for the operator to aim and get on target fast. The Luger is reliable when using high-velocity cartridges that produce enough recoil to operate the mechanism.

These pistols are commonly called "Lugers" and were first available commercially starting in 1900. These first Lugers are what collectors call the "Borchardt Luger Transitional Models," made in 1898 and 1899. Only a few of these Borchardt models are known to exist.

Commercial production ramped up in 1900, with the Luger originally chambered in .30 Luger/7.65x21mm Parabellum and produced by *Deutsche Waffen- und Munitionsfabriken* (DWM). In 1902, the Luger was chambered in a new caliber called 9x19mm Parabellum. Officially, SAAMI—the Sporting Arms and Ammunition Manufacturers' Institute—calls the cartridge "9mm Luger" but it is better known as simply the 9mm, one of the most popular and widely used pistol cartridges ever designed and used by civilians, military, and law enforcement.

The change to a larger caliber was due to the demand by the German military for a sidearm in a larger caliber. At the turn of the twentieth century, revolvers were the most common and wide-spread handgun in use by military forces, and the new semi-automatic pistols of this time were a radical departure. Some were awkward and complex, and all were viewed with a bit a skepticism. Many semi-automatic pistols of this era utilized an internal box magazine housed forward of the trigger guard, such as in the Mauser C96 and the Bergman-Bayard Model 1903 pistols. The Luger was different. The Luger used a magazine housed in the grip of the pistol, and that is how the modern handgun evolved.

The Swiss Military was the first to adopt the Luger, in 1900, in the .30 Luger/7.65x21mm Parabellum caliber. The German Navy also liked the Luger, but wanted a pistol with a more powerful round. Hence the pistol was redesigned by resizing the original bottleneck cartridge case to hold a larger bullet, thus creating the 9x19mm Parabellum, and, in 1904, the Imperial German Navy adopted the Luger chambered in 9mm with a 5.9-inch barrel and a two-position rear sight. The German Army, also enamored with the new pistol, adopted the Luger as the "Pistole 08" or " "P.08" in 1908. with a 3.9-inch barrel is perhaps the most common variant of the Luger encountered. It served with the German Army during WWI and WWII.

Shortly after Germany's adoption, other countries, including Holland, Brazil, Bulgaria, Portugal, and Russia, adopted the Luger as their military sidearm. The US Army even considered the Luger, before it eventually adopted the M1911. Long story short, the Luger holds the distinction as being one of the first successful semi-automatic military sidearms, as well as being the first pistol chambered in 9mm.

TELLING ONE FROM ANOTHER

Since Luger pistols were produced for both commercial and military/police markets, and because there were numerous companies manufacturing the pistols, particularly during World War II, identifying Lugers can be complicated. The best way to go about accurately identifying a Luger is to first check the serial number, manufacturer mark, and production year and proof symbols.

SERIAL NUMBERS

Since there were numerous manufacturers, serial numbers were often repeated on pistols. It should also be noted that serial number sequencing followed a sequential order for commercial models, but for contracts, the serial numbers were started at "1." There may be several Lugers still in existence with serial number "1."

Pistol serial numbers are found in numerous locations on the pistols. Additionally, in some locations the full serial number is used, while in other locations only the last two digits of the full serial number are used.

The location of the serial numbers on pistols varies between military and commercial pistols.

On military Army pistols produced from WWI through WWII, the full serial number is located on the front of the frame, under the barrel, and the left side of the receiver. The breechblock, extractor, front toggle link, inside the grip panels, rear toggle link, sear bar, trigger sideplate, takedown lever,

thumb safety lever, and trigger are all marked with the last two digits of the full serial number.

Commercial, contract pistols, and Navy pistols located the full serial number in a manner similar to the military Army models, with the exception

This is an example of standard military-style serial number placement, with the full serial number "2993" stamped on the underside of the barrel, front of the frame, and the underside of the barrel extension. The other parts are stamped with the last two digits "93." *Image courtesy Rock Island Auction*

This pistol shows military-style serial numbers with number "9473" marked on the barrel extension and receiver, while smaller parts are marked only with the last two digits of the full serial number. Note that "73" is stamped on the locking bolt, trigger sideplate, safety bar, and sear bar. *Image courtesy Rock Island Auction*

of the parts containing the last two digits. Military serialization was not concerned with the aesthetics of the pistols, but on commercial models more care was taken. Thus, the last two digits of the full serial number on commercial models are located on the breechblock, front toggle link, grip safety, inside the grip panels, rear toggle link, sideplate, takedown lever, thumb safety lever, and trigger.

A pistol with matching serial numbers is more valuable than a pistol with non-matching serial numbers. For the serious collector, matching serial numbers are a must, while for the casual collector, one who may shoot the pistols in their collection, a Luger with non-matching serial numbers can make an excellent shooter, since the value of the pistol will not be eroded by use.

MANUFACTURER MARKINGS AND DATES

The manufacturer's roll mark is the next step in identifying a Luger. The top of the front toggle link typically identifies the manufacturer. At times,

This is an example of markings on a mid-production 1906/24 Luger manufactured in Switzerland at the BERN factory for the Swiss Armed Forces. Note that the top of the chamber area is blank and the front toggle link is marked with the small Swiss cross over "WAFFENFABRIK/BERN." About seventeen thousand were manufactured, serial number range 15216-33089. *Image courtesy Rock Island Auction*

This is an example of a Mauser WWII-production Luger. Note the top of the chamber has the full date of "1936," with the "S/42" code marking on the front toggle link. *Image courtesy Rock Island Auction*

importer names and manufacturer names will appear on the side of frame. These marks identify the manufacturer and, in some cases, identify who contracted the manufacturer to produce pistols. Many times, the date of manufacture is located on the chamber area, on top of the barrel.

This is an example of a WWI German Luger manufactured by the DWM factory. Note the top of the chamber is marked the year "1916" and the front toggle link has the DWM logo. *Image courtesy Rock Island Auction*

This is an example of a Simson & Co. Suhl-manufactured pistol. Note the top of the chamber is marked with the year "1925," and "SIMSON & Co./SUHL" is located on the front toggle link. *Image courtesy Rock Island Auction*

These are the markings of a Luger variation manufactured for the Netherlands by the Vickers Ltd. Company in England. Note the blank chamber area and the front toggle link stamped "VICKERS/LTD" in two lines. These Lugers were produced from 1915 to 1917. Approximately ten thousand were made and, so, are very rare today. Many pistols were used in the Far East, and most specimens were in poor condition before being arsenal-refurbished between 1925 and 1933, though this is one instance where that does not detract from the value. *Image courtesy Rock Island Auction*

This is an example of a late-production Mauser pistol. Note the "42" dated chamber area, indicating a manufacturing date of 1942, with the toggle marked "byf," the wartime code for the Mauser factory. *Image courtesy Rock Island Auction*

This is an example of the markings on a Simson & Company-manufactured pistol. Note the "1925" stamp on the chamber, area indicating the date of manufacture, and the "Simson & Co./Suh" markings on the front toggle link. *Image courtesy Rock Island Auction*

This is an example of Erfurt Arsenal markings. Note the "1912" stamp on top of the chamber, indicating date of manufacture, and the crown logo over the "ERFURT" name on the front toggle link. *Image courtesy Rock Island Auction*

This is an example of a pre-WWII, Mauser-manufactured Luger with "42" code markings. Note the chamber area is marked with the full date of "1940," with the "42" code marking for the Mauser factory located on the front toggle link. *Image courtesy Rock Island Auction*

MANUFACTURER AND CONTRACT MARKINGS

This is an example of Krieghoff and Sohn factory markings. Note the chamber area is date-stamped "1936," with the front toggle link marked with the C-1, 1936-pattern Krieghoff and Sohn anchor logo over "KRIEGHOFF/SUHL." *Image courtesy Rock Island Auction*

This is an example of DWM-manufacturer markings for a Swiss military contract. Note the "Cross in Shield" crest on the chamber area and the DWM logo on the front toggle link. Approximately 5,200 pistols were made for non-commercial sales to either military or police. *Image courtesy Rock Island Auction*

This is an example of a DWM Model 1906 American Eagle Luger. Note the large American Eagle crest on the chamber area and the DWM logo on the front toggle link. These are rather rare Lugers, with only about three thousand produced and exported to the United States. *Image courtesy Rock Island Auction*

This is an example of a Garde Nationale Republic of Portugal contract pistol manufactured by Mauser. Only 579 pistols were manufactured, with a serial number range of 1,921–2,500 and with a "v" suffix. Note the chamber area has the intertwined Portuguese "GNR" (Garde Nationale Republicane) logo, while the Mauser banner logo is on the front toggle link. *Image courtesy Rock Island Auction*

This is an example of Bulgarian contract, DWM-manufactured pistol marking. Note the chamber is marked with the DWM scroll monogram, while the Bulgarian crest is located on top of the front toggle link. The crest includes the Bulgarian crown over a shield with a rampant lion inside. *Image courtesy Rock Island Auction*

This is an example of a Persian contract Luger, specifically an artillery Luger manufactured on contract for the government of Persia (now Iran). Note the Persian lion on the chamber area and the use of the Farsi lettering in place of most of the traditional markings. Fewer than a thousand Artillery Lugers were made in this configuration. *Image courtesy Rock Island Auction*

Known as the "Cross in Sunburst" among collectors, this pistol was manufactured by DWM specifically for the Swiss military contract. Note the top of the chamber is marked with the Swiss cross in a sunburst, while the DWM logo is on the front toggle link. *Image courtesy Rock Island Auction*

PROOF MARKS AND UNIT MARKINGS

Proof symbols can be located in numerous locations of the pistol, including on the top or the outer side of the frame. Proof marks used by Luger manufacturers vary widely. Imperial Navy, Imperial Army, Nazi Commercial, Early Nazi Military, Mid Nazi Military, Late Nazi Military, and many others all have unique proof marks, and the list is too extensive to reproduce within these pages.

Unit markings also appear on pistols. These markings indicate which units of the Army, Navy,

This is an example of a pistol marked on the front grip strap. The marking "B.II.2." indicates the pistol was issued to the Second Bavarian Regiment. *Image courtesy Rock Island Auction*

or police received the pistol. For Army pistols, these markings can be found in Roman and Arabic numerals and were stamped on the front grip strap of the pistol. Naval pistols were marked on the backstrap of the grip above the stock lug. Many times, an older pistol was reissued with its original unit markings crossed out with an "X" and new unit markings stamped above or below. Police pistol unit marking appear on the frontstrap of the grip.

Again, unit markings are extensive, having been started in 1909 and running through WWII. A good source to help demystify these marks is Aaron Davis's book *Standard Catalog or Luger,* Jan C. Still's *Imperial Lugers and Their Accessories–The Pistols of Germany and Her Allies in Two World Wars Volume IV, German Small Arms Markings From Authentic Sources* by J. Goertz and D. Bryans, and *World of Lugers Proof Marks Complete Listing of Different Variations of Proof Marks on the Luger* by Sam Costanzo, to name just four.

OTHER WAYS TO KNOW WHAT LUGER YOU HAVE

Luger pistols defy being placed in specific categories, since there are so many variations and small distinctions. Still, and in general, one can divide Lugers into two distinct model types: commercial models manufactured for the civilian markets, and military models made specifically for the various military and police forces.

Military service pistols include the following:

- German Army model, typically with a 3.9-inch barrel
- German Naval model with a 5.9-inch barrel and two-position rear sight
- German Artillery Luger with a 7.9-inch barrel and eight-position tangent rear sight. The Artillery Luger was used with a shoulder stock, as well as a 32-round drum magazine commonly called a "snail magazine," since it resembled a snail.

There are also rare models, like two samples of a Luger chambered in .45 ACP that were part of a group of several pistols from a variety of manufacturers sent as samples to the US Army for testing in 1907. DWM built two test pistols in .45 ACP for the trials. The whereabouts of one of the pistols is known, and in 1989 it was sold for $1,000,000. It came up for sale again in 2010 and fetched only $494,500, so you can see that, even with very rare firearms, the price is set by whatever the buyer will pay.

Following are a few examples of Luger pistol variations produced for commercial and military markets. From a military perspective, the Luger

The "Million Dollar Luger" was one of two pistols chambered in .45 ACP for the US Army trails in 1907. It fetched $1,000,000 in 1989. When it came back on the market in 2010, it sold for $494,500.

was the sidearm for the German military during three distinct eras: the German Empire from 1904 to 1918, the Weimar Republic from 1919 to 1933, and of Nazi Germany from 1933 to 1945. Values shown assume all matching serial numbers.

This is a good example of an early production, German Military 1908 First Issue Contract Luger pistol made by DWM. It has a 4-inch barrel and is chambered in 9mm. A blue finish appears on the frame and barrel, with an original straw finish on the trigger, takedown lever, magazine release, and ejector. Grips are checkered walnut. Note the magazine is not original, but is a replacement magazine that is blue and unmarked and with a black plastic base. This pistol rates EXCELLENT (Ex) or NRA 95 percent. Estimated value is $1,400–$2,250. *Image courtesy Rock Island Auction*

This is an early production and scarce DWM Model 1902 American Eagle model with the fat barrel, often referred to as a "Fat Barrel" American Eagle. Only six hundred to seven hundred of these models were manufactured for commercial sale in the United States. This model features the short, old-style frame with leaf springs but no stock lug, a recessed breechblock, dished toggles with toggle lock, and grip safety. The top of the chamber area is marked with the prominent American Eagle crest, while the front toggle link is marked with the DWM logo. It is chambered in 9mm and has a nickel-plated magazine body with a wooden base, checkered walnut grips, and the pistol has a mostly blue finish with a straw finish on small parts. Condition rates EXCELLENT (Ex) or NRA 90 percent. Estimated value is $4,000–$6,000. *Image courtesy Rock Island Auction*

This is an example of a DWM-manufactured 1914 Artillery Luger. These pistols featured an 8-inch barrel and tangent rear sight. It has a blue finish, checkered walnut grips, and a nickel-plated magazine with a wood base. This pistol rates GOOD (Gd) or NRA 68 percent. Estimated value is $1,300–$1,900. With the original leather holster, shoulder stock, and snail magazine this pistol's value would increase dramatically. *Image courtesy Rock Island Auction*

During WWI, Artillery Lugers were issued with these 32-round magazines, commonly referred to as "snail drum" magazines. This example was manufactured by Bing Brothers of Nuremberg, Germany. Estimated value is $950–$1,400. *Image courtesy Rock Island Auction*

This is a rare DWM Model 1900 American Eagle "Test Luger" purchased by the US Ordnance Department in August 1901, for trials with the US Cavalry. The Ordnance Board authorized an order for 1,000 DWM model 1900 Luger pistols, which were delivered in two lots: approximately eight hundred shipped October 26, 1901, with the remaining two hundred shipping on October 29, 1901. Approximate serial number range is 6,000–7,200. The most distinguishing feature is that there are no German acceptance proof marks and no German export markings. At the completion of the US tests, all these Lugers were sold as surplus. Caliber is 7.65 mm Luger. The chamber area is stamped with the American Eagle, and the pistol features a grip safety, recessed breech bolt, dished toggles with toggle locks on the side, a rust-blue finish with heat-blued grip screws, front sight blade, and connecting pins, as well as the extractor, toggle link, ejector, takedown lever, trigger, magazine release, and thumb safety lever in a straw-colored finish. Walnut checkered grips and a nickel-plated magazine body with a blank wooden base were also included. Condition rates GOOD (Gd) or NRA 60 percent. Estimated value is $4,500–$7,000. *Image courtesy Rock Island Auction*

This is a DWM-made Model 1902 "Fat Barrel" American Eagle Luger pistol that has been upgraded with the addition of a set of non-original "cartridge counter" style walnut grips. This cartridge counter device, also known as the "Powell Indicating Device," consists of two components. The first is a special left grip that has a small slot cut lengthwise down the grip, with a small metal strip inscribed with black numbers (1 through 7) running from the top to the bottom of the strip, to indicate the number of rounds remaining in the magazine. The second was the special cartridge counter magazine that is slotted on the left side of the body and fitted with a special follower that had a small pin/indicator that slides up and down the strip as rounds are fired. Caliber is 9mm Luger and features are a 4-inch barrel, blue finish, and checkered walnut grip. Condition rates as GOOD (Gd) or NRA 60 percent. Estimated value is $5,000–$7,000. *Image courtesy Rock Island Auction*

This late-production, post-WWI DWM Model 1914 Navy Luger, dated 1917, has been refurbished. These Navy Lugers are distinct. There is no grip safety, they are fitted with a stock lug, and they have flat checkered toggles. This specimen has a 6-inch barrel, with the two-position Navy rear sight adjustable from 100 to 200 meters, and it is chambered in 9mm. Condition rates as EXCELLENT (Ex) or NRA 95 percent. Estimated value is $3,000–$4,500. *Image courtesy Rock Island Auction*

This commercial contract Mauser Banner Luger pistol is chambered in the 7.65mm Luger Auto cartridge, something seldom seen in this serial number range. It is in like-new condition. Very few were manufactured prior to the start of WWII. The serial number with its "v" suffix and the "Crown/U" proofs combined with the Mauser Banner indicate that this Luger was manufactured at a time when the Mauser factory was still selling commercial/contract pistols to numerous countries in Europe. Condition rates LIKE NEW/NEW IN BOX (LiB). Estimated value is $6,500–$9,500. *Image courtesy Rock Island Auction*

This variant is commonly called a "Black Widow" Luger. Manufactured by Mauser during WWII, in 1941, this P.08 has the "byf" code on the toggle and "41" on the chamber area. Chambered in 9mm and featuring a 4-inch barrel, the "Black Widow" had a checkered black plastic grip. Condition rates EXCELLENT (Ex) or NRA 95 percent. Estimated value is $1,600–$2,500. *Image courtesy Rock Island Auction*

Dated "1940" on top of the chamber and marked "42" on the toggle, this WWII-era Luger looks to be unissued. This pistol's features include a 3⅞-inch barrel, blue finish, 9mm caliber, and checkered wood grips. Condition rates NEW IN BOX/LIKE NEW IN BOX (NiB). Estimated value is $2,500–$3,750. *Image courtesy Rock Island Auction*

This is an example of a Swiss Model 1929 Bern Luger manufactured by Waffenfabrik Bern and chambered in 7.65mm Luger Auto. It has a 4¾-inch barrel with a matte blue finish and checkered plastic grips. The chamber area is blank. The magazine body wears a nickel finish with a Bakelite base. Note the straight front grip strap, identifying this as a Swiss Luger. Condition rates EXCELLENT (Ex) or NRA 95 percent. Estimated value is $1,800–$2,750. *Image courtesy Rock Island Auction*

Eastern Block Makarovs
Surplus Handguns

Surplus and traded-in military and law enforcement (LE) handguns offer collectability, as in the case of WWII-era Walther P.38 pistols, or, for instance, law enforcement trade-ins like SIGs and Glocks. These used guns cost much less than new models and can be viewed as collectable shooters. The key to understanding surplus guns is knowing that they are released in lots—some small, some large—and once they are gone, there are no more until the next lot is imported.

The conditions of surplus guns range from FAIR to UNISSUED. The value of surplus handguns obviously depends on their condition, availability, and collectability. Take, for instance, the SIG P6, a pistol designed in the mid-1970s to meet the German police requirements of the time and evolved from the models P220 and P225. It was inexpensive to produce, met all the West German police requirements, and was eventually adopted by the West German police. These pistols are coveted by SIG collectors and shooters. In recent years past, West German police trade-ins were imported into the US by CAI (Century Arms International). In 2011, they sold for about $350. There are no more surplus P6 pistols available through surplus firearm sellers today. In 2016, the value of a P6 ranged from $400 to $680. (As an aside, The P6 pistol is so popular that, in 2015, SIG reintroduced its P225, the commercial version of the P6, albeit with modern updates.) This is an example of just one surplus handgun that accrued value, even though it was used and wore import markings.

Two factors that contribute to a surplus handgun's value are import marks and matching serial numbers. Import marks are blatantly and unceremoniously engraved on the slide, receiver, or barrel. The marks do not add value and, in fact, can reduce the value of the gun. All things the same, the gun without import marks will bring a higher price.

Mismatched serial numbers are often found. An example of this is found in P.38 pistols captured by the Soviets during WWII. These pistols were all arsenal-refinished after being disassembled, then reassembled without any effort made to keep like serial numbered parts together. These mismatched serial number pistols offer more shooting value than collectible value.

WHAT'S OUT THERE?

One type of handgun currently on the market and affordable to a budding military pistol collector is the former Soviet Bloc sidearm chambered in 9x18mm Makarov. Generically speaking, these pistols were manufactured in other countries and are called "Polish Makarovs" for models built in Poland, "Czech Makarovs" for those that were built in former Czechoslovakia, and so on. Most countries under the influence of or friendly with the former Soviet Union, like China, had a pistol chambered in 9x18mm Makarov in service since the 1950s.

All of these pistols are chambered in 9x18mm Makarov, but the designs are very different from the original Makarov pistol, or "PM," used by the Soviets. What is similar between them, besides being chambered in 9x18mm Makarov, is that they share a similar blowback operating system and have common features like a double-action/single-action trigger, exposed hammer, fixed sights, external extractor, and the barrel fixed to the frame.

POLAND'S P-64

In Hungary and Poland, two countries that designed their own pistols for the 9x18mm cartridge, pistol designs were influenced by the Walther PP and PPK pistols. Walther pistols were used by German officers during WWII, and numerous examples were captured by the Soviet Army during that war. In fact, the Soviets occupied Zella-Mehlis in Germany, where the Walther factory was located, and the factory's tooling and machines were disassembled and shipped back to the Soviet Union. Walther pistols clearly influenced pistol design and manufacturing in Poland and Hungary. Those made in Czechoslovakia look different than Walthers but they, too, share some design elements and function in a similar way.

In the 1950s, Poland's military held a service pistol design competition for a replacement service pistol, and the winning entry was from the Polish Institute for Artillery Research. Officially designated *9 mm pistolet wz. 1964*, but more commonly called the P-64, this pistol was manufactured at the Łucznik Arms Factory in Radom, Poland. Outwardly it looks like a Walther PPK, but the P-64 has a unique disconnector, one very different from the Walther's. In addition to the outward aesthetics, the similarities between the PPK and P-64 include a loaded chamber indicator at the rear of the slide that can felt and seen; the plastic grip panels form the pistol's backstrap, the barrel fixed to the frame, and a thumb safety decocker. This compact pistol is known for a very heavy DA trigger pull.

The P-64 was officially replaced with the P-83 Wanad, but the P-64 still remains is service with some Polish Military units and police agencies. The Vietnam and Lebanese militaries also issued this pistol. Many P-64 pistols are on the market today and typically include the holster, cleaning rod, and extra magazine. See page 260 for full specifications and values.

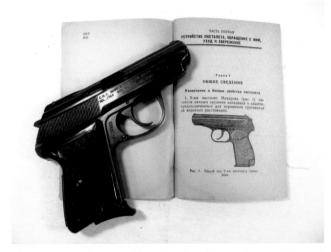

The P-64 was is use with Poland's military from 1951 and is still in use today. This P-64 is shown with an original PM manual. In profile, the P-64 looks very similar to a Walther PPK, but the P-64 has a unique patented disconnector distinctly different from the Walther's.

According to the markings on the left side of the slide, this particular P-64 was manufactured in 1975.

HUNGARY'S PA-63

During WWII, in the late 1940s, the FÉGARMY Arms Factory manufactured a variant of the Walther PP called the "48M." After the war, Hungary came under Soviet influence and was required to adopt a sidearm chambered in 9x18mm; the PA-63 began production in 1963 and was produced through 1990. Similar to the Walther PP in design and function, the PA-63 is

The similarities between the Walther PPK and P-64 include a loaded chamber indicator at the rear of the slide that can be felt and seen, and plastic grip panels that form the pistol's backstrap.

The Hungarian PA-63 has a distinctly different two-tone finish, unusual for a police sidearm. It features a blued steel slide and polished aluminum frame. Note the thumbrest on the plastic grip, something also not typically found on a service weapon.

The magazine holds six rounds and has a finger rest built into the floor plate. Note the butt heel magazine release latch.

The last four digits of the serial number match those of the magazine, receiver, and slide. Matching serial numbers like these can add value to a surplus handgun.

distinct due to a blued steel slide and polished aluminum frame. The two-tone finish actually makes the PA-63 less expensive to manufacture. It is still in use, especially with Hungarian Police.

The PA-63 is not as readily available as, say, the P-64, but, when encountered, they are typically in GOOD to VERY GOOD condition and will most likely come with an extra magazine. See page 196 for specifications and values.

CZECHOSLOVAKIA'S VZ 82
In 1983, the CZ 82, or Vz 82—"Vz" is the Czech abbreviation for "model"—was adopted by the Czech military. What makes this pistol unique is that it features a double-stack 12-round magazine; typical Eastern Bloc Makarovs use a single-stack magazine with either a six-, seven-, or eight-round capacity. Though the CZ 82 holds nearly twice the number of cartridges as similar firearms, it is still compact. Other unique features include an ambidextrous thumb safety—one of the first military pistols to have such an ambidextrous control—and a push-button magazine release located next where a right-hand shooter's thumb would be when gripping the gun, on the grip, rather than the butt of the pistol. The CZ 82 also has a slide release located on the left side of the frame, something not typically found on a blowback pistol.

The CZ 82 was used by the Czech Republic, law enforcement in Israel, and North Korean, Slovakian, and Vietnamese militaries. It is the current sidearm of the Czech Army. CZ-USA imported the model chambered in .380 ACP and 9x18mm for a time in the 1990s. These models will not have the importer's markings. Today, the CZ 82 is less common, with the models chambered in 9x18mm fetching a higher value compared to the .380 ACP models. Many were shipped with an ambidextrous leather holster. See page 187 for specifications and values.

The CZ 82 was issued with an ambidextrous leather holster. Small pockets hold the barrel of the pistol in place so that both left- and right-handed soldiers can use the holster.

The CZ 82 has a large beavertail, so users with larger hands are less likely to experience hammer and slide bite.

Many surplus handguns are resold on the commercial market with a holster, extra magazine, and cleaning rod.

The double-stack magazine of the CZ 82 holds 12 rounds, yet the pistol is still very compact.

POLAND'S P-83

The P-83 Wanad was developed in the late 1970s to replace the shortcomings of the P-64, specifically that firearm's heavy double-action trigger pull, limited magazine capacity, heavy felt recoil, and expensive manufacturing process. The P-83 addressed all these shortcomings, including its problematic manufacturing expenses through the use of modern, cost-effective, welded sheet steel stampings. It was adopted in 1983, hence the model name. The commercial variant differs from the military model by featuring a rounded hammer, different sights, and has import roll marks on the left side of the slide that read "RADOM wz.

P-83 9×18 POLAND Z.M. LUCZNIK." Military models have markings in the same location that read "9mm P-83."

The P-83 still sees limited use with the Polish military. This model is easily found, and many times it will include a holster, extra magazine, and cleaning rod. See page 260 for specifications and values.

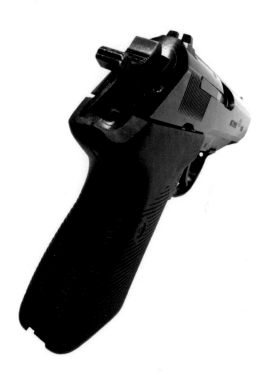

Military models can be identified against by their small sights and spur hammer. Commercial models have different sights and a rounded hammer spur.

This P-83 Wanad pistol was manufactured in 1983. Note the date stamp toward the muzzle.

The magazine has an eight-round capacity, two rounds more than the P-64. The grip is also longer than the P-64's, so the firearm is easier to control.

Ruger Blackhawk
"Old Models" or "Three-Screw" Models

Covered here are the Blackhawk revolvers referred to as "Old Model" or "Three-Screw" Blackhawks, which were manufactured from 1955 through 1973. In 1973, a safety transfer bar was incorporated into the mechanism and the revolver was renamed New Model Blackhawk. These new models are also referred to as "Two-Screw" models. The "screw" is in reference to old Blackhawks having three screws in the frame. New Model Blackhawk models have two screws.

This is an example of a Ruger Blackhawk revolver chambered in .357 Magnum with a barrel length of 4⅝ inches. Finish is blue and grip are hard rubber fitted with the Blackhawk medallions. It was manufactured in 1955, the first year of production.

Blackhawk "Flattop" (1955–1962)		
SERIAL NUMBER RANGE	BARREL LENGTH	TOTAL MANUFACTURING
1–42,690	4⅝	27,200
	6½	14,200
	10	1,300

New Model Blackhawk revolvers have been produced from 1973 to present.

The first Blackhawk revolver, also referred to as a "Flattop," was chambered in .357 Magnum and featured a 4⅝-inch barrel. The topstrap was flat, hence the nickname, and was equipped with an adjustable rear sight. They were blued and sported either checkered rubber grips or smooth walnut grips. Smooth walnut grips became standard around serial No. 30000. These Flattop models were produced from 1955 through 1962. During this production period,

6½-inch and 10-inch barreled variants were offered. Factory ivory and stag grips were also offered and add $2,000 and $600, respectively, to the value. See page 270 for specifications and values.

The Blackhawk .44 Magnum Flattop in the then-new .44 Magnum cartridge was introduced a year after the Blackhawk Flattop chambered in .357 Magnum. To handle the powerful .44 Magnum cartridge, this revolver had a heavier frame and cylinder compared to its .357 Magnum predecessor. In 1959, a Super Blackhawk was introduced with a larger grip frame with a squared-off, Dragoon-style trigger guard. The Super Blackhawk was produced until 1972 and was offered with either a 6½- or 7½-inch barrel. The 6½-inch barrel variant is rare. See page 271 for specifications and values.

In 1962, the Blackhawk went through an engineering change, wherein the shape of the topstrap

The Blackhawk Flattop .44 Magnum had a heavier frame and cylinder than the Blackhawk flattop chambered in .357 Magnum. The Blackhawk Flattop .44 Magnum preceded the Super Blackhawk. Note the fluted cylinder, rounded trigger guard, and smaller grip compared to the Super Blackhawk. *Image courtesy Rock Island Auction*

The Super Blackhawk was available with a brass frame. Note the squared-off, Dragoon-style trigger guard. *Image courtesy James D. Julia*

This is an example of a Blackhawk manufactured between 1962 and 1973. Note the topstrap is beefed up to protect the rear adjustable sight. *Image courtesy Rock Island Auction*

Blackhawk. 44 Magnum "Flattop" (1956–1963)		
SERIAL NUMBER RANGE	BARREL LENGTH	TOTAL MFG.
1–29,860	6½	27,610
	7½	2,700
	10	1,500

Blackhawk (1962-1973)			
CALIBER	BARREL LENGTH(S)	DATES MANUFACTURING	TOTAL MANUFACTURING
.30 Carbine	7½	1967-1973	32,985
.357 Magnum	4⅝, 6½	1962-1973	245,059
.41 Magnum	4⅝, 6½, 7½	1965-1973	39,371
.45 Long Colt	4⅝, 7½	1970-1973	23,0303

was changed from a flat design to one that was beefed up to protect the rear sight. The revolver was also offered in three additional calibers: .30 Carbine, .41 Magnum, and .45 Long Colt. A few revolvers in .357 Magnum, .41 Magnum, and .45 Long Colt were also produced with a brass grip frame. About six hundred brass grip models were manufactured in each caliber, except for the .41 Magnum models, for which only about sixty were produced. These brass frame models fetch a premium.

Walther P.38
The First Modern Combat Pistol

The P.38 was not the first pistol designed by Walther to fire the 9mm cartridge. During WWI, Walther introduced the Model 6 pistol, which had limited success. Developed as a replacement for the Luger P.08, the P.38 was designed for ease of production using stamped steel, alloy steels, and composite grips. The German Military wanted a mass-produced pistol that was dependable, rugged, and suited for combat. The P.38 was the answer. Though it was designed for ease in manufacturing and uses less material than its predecessor, it is a well-designed and reliable pistol. The grips meet to form the P.38's backstrap, meaning the pistol used less metal and was made lightweight. Its design was cutting edge for the time, and many modern pistol designs to this day use features that were first employed on the P.38.

The P.38 was the first combat pistol to include a pivoting locking bolt short-recoil action, double-/single-action trigger mechanism, a safety lever that decocked the hammer, large and well-defined sights, and a loaded chamber indicator. More than one million P.38s were produced by the end of the war in 1945. Walther, Mauser, and Spreewerke all manufactured the pistol during WWII, and the pistols were marked with codes that identified the manufacturer and the year produced. On the left side of slide, an "ac-41" indicated a Walther-manufactured pistol produced in 1941. Walter also used a "480" code on early manufactured guns. Mauser guns wear either "byf" or "svw" codes. All Spreewerke guns are identified by "cyq". For the most part, all P.38 manufacturer code markings were followed by a date.

The Walther contract for military production of P.38s started out with what is referred to as "Zero Series," wherein the numeral "0" preceded the serial number. These models used the Walther banner logo marking on the side instead of the codes. Walther then transitioned and used the "480" code for about seven thousand pistols, then changed to the "ac" code with no date, and then to the "ac" code with a date. The last code used by Walther was "ac 45." The most common or most-produced variants are those coded "ac 44," with about 120,000 manufactured. Approximately one hundred thousand "ac 42"-coded pistols were manufactured. The remainder of Walther-manufactured P.38 models

The more common Walther "ac 44" code on a P.38 that features the standard one-line slide marking and is without a suffix after the serial number. The frame, barrel, and slide are marked with the Walther "eagle/359" *waffenamt* mark, as well as the standard Nazi eagle proofs. It is fitted with ribbed plastic grips. The barrel slide and frame markings have been highlighted in white, and the magazine is marked with a single "eagle/88" stamp. It has 98-percent original finish. Estimated value is $850–$1,300. *Image courtesy Rock Island Auction*

are the early first- and second-issue Zero Series and "480"-code variants. Serial numbers do repeat and do not exceed 10,000. Sequential series were marked with letters: "a" was added to second-series serial numbers, "b" to third-series serial numbers, etc.

Mauser military contract P.38 pistols used the "byf" and "svw" codes and a date. The "byf-43" and "byf-44" variants are the most common, with some 88,000 and 120,000 produced, respectively. These are the least valuable of the Mauser-produced P.38 pistols. Some notable exceptions are pistols with blued and phosphate-finished parts, and collectors refer to these pistols as having a dual-tone finish. All-gray phosphate models also fetch more, as does the "svw-45" variant, which is very rare.

The Spreewerk military contract P.38 pistols used a "cyq" code. These pistols are the least valuable of all to collectors and more valuable to shooters.

POSTWAR P1

Postwar P1 pistols are easily identified by their checkered black plastic grips. The Manurhin P1 (top) was manufactured in France under license from Walther and has a 5-inch barrel. The Walther P1 (center) is dated "7/80" and features a short 3½-inch barrel. The P.38 IV (bottom) has a 4½-inch barrel and was manufactured in 1981 with an "IB" code. Estimated value for each is $900–$1,400. *Image courtesy Rock Island Auction*

G.I. BRING-BACK

A pristine example of a WWII-era Walther P.38 with issue holster. It is a G.I. bring-back without importation marks. *Image courtesy Bishop's Fine Guns*

Large quantities of P.38 pistols were captured by the Soviet Union during the war and, in the late 1990s, showed up on the surplus market.

This post-war P1 is elaborately engraved with a German oak leaf pattern and sports checkered walnut grips. *Image courtesy Bishop's Fine Guns*

Many of these P.38s have mismatched serials numbers, as the Russians inspected and refinished the pistols at the Izhevsk Mechanical Plant. These pistols have less value than G.I. bring-back pistols lacking importation marks.

Postwar pistols differ from war-time specimens, as an aluminum frame replaced the steel frame models built during WWII (among other minor design changes). Walther began to produce the P.38 in 1957, calling it the "P1." In 1972, a design change included a steel hex bolt to reinforce the aluminum frame. The P1 was in service with the Germany *Bundeswehr* from 1957 through about 1992. Commercial variants were available in .22 LR, .30 Luger, and 9mm. The P1 came standard with black checkered grips.

P.38 Manufacturer's Codes		
CODE	MANUFACTURER	DATES OF MANUFACTURE
Walther	Walther	1937–mid-1940
480	Walther	mid-1940–October 1942
ac	Walther	October 1942–end of WWII
byf	Mauser	November 1942–January 1945
SvW	Mauser	January 1945–end of WWII
cyg	Spreewerk	March 1941–end of WWII

AR-15 Pistol
Meet "The Jack"

Today, nearly every AR-15 manufacturer and builder produces an AR-15 pistol and, for the most part, they are as ubiquitous as their parent rifle. The partnership between Spike's Tactical and Sharp Bros., however, has taken the AR-15 pistol to a new level of aesthetics and performance. *Image by Alex Landeen*

One of the first AR-style pistols built for commercial sale was the Olympic Arms model OA-93, introduced in 1993. The Olympic Arms company was a real innovator in the industry and the oldest manufacturer of AR-15 weapons other than Colt. The company ceased operation in 2017.

Now meet "The Jack." The Jack begins with an AR-15 lower receiver with a human skull shape CNC-sculpted on the front of the magazine well. Sharps Bros., which designed the lower, is known for its unique AR designs that both allow for creative expression and enhance performance through the use of oversized trigger guards and flared magazine wells. The lower by itself is distributed through vendor Spike's Tactical, which also builds the lower into a complete AR pistol.

The Jack lower is constructed from 7075-T6 billet aluminum and held to mil-spec or tighter tolerances. It is compatible with all mil-spec

Unique to the Olympic Arms OA-93—the first AR pistol—is the operating system, which incorporates the recoil system into a flattop upper receiver, thus eliminating the need for a buttstock. It is only 17 inches in length and weighs 4.5 pounds. For full specifications and values, see page 258. *Image courtesy Olympic Arms*

standard-issue magazines. Except for a few parts like the Magpul MOE pistol grip, the majority of the parts of the full AR pistol are manufactured by Spike's Tactical. This includes Spike's cold hammer-forged Enhanced Battle

Trigger manufactured from 8620 tool steel. The disconnect is heat-treated 4140 Chromoly with a slick and durable nickel-Teflon finish. It is also relieved of metal to reduce weight and increase the reaction speed for a quick and positive reset. The hammer spring is a Magpul MBUS Pro red hammer spring that offers positive ignition even with harder primers, while maintaining a crisp, ultra-smooth 4.5 to 6.5 pound pull weight. KNS anti-rotation pins are used so nothing loosens up during hard use or frequent maintenance.

The upper receiver is a Spike's Tactical Gen 2 Billet SAR constructed of 7075 aluminum and a Spike's 8.1-inch cold hammer forged barrel with a pistol-length gas system. It has a Melonite coating inside and out and a 1:7 twist. The .750 gas block is tied into a pistol-length gas tube with a coiled roll pin.

The business end sports Spike's Barking Spider 5.56mm muzzle device, which redirects noise, blast, and concussion forward and away from the user. The device also increases the back pressure, which, in return, can increase the reliability. The front end of the Barking Spider incorporates a striking device (i.e., a glass breaker).

The value of this unique AR-15 build is $2,050.

Spike's added its proprietary red-and-black pistol tube cover with the company's trademark spider, for more visual impact and additional comfort when shooting the pistol with the tube touching your cheek.

As much as it is cool-looking, the underside of The Jack skull is a magazine well with a flared edge so that the user can brace it up against a barrier when shooting.

KNS anti-rotation pins are used so that nothing loosens up during hard use or frequent maintenance. Note the ambidextrous magazine release.

US Military M1911 and M1911A1 Pistols

Soon after the US Army test trials in 1910, the Government adopted the Colt semi-automatic pistol in .45 ACP as the M1911. During the trials, the Colt pistol had had some six thousand rounds fired through it over the course of two days, and as the pistol heated up from the extended firing it was dunked into a bucket of water to cool it down. The Colt performed flawlessly. No other pistol in the testing trials could compete against it.

The pistol and caliber combination is today as much a symbol of America's power as it is a powerful and effective combat pistol. With official adoption of the pistol in the year 1911 (hence the model designation), the pistol was officially named "Automatic Pistol, Caliber .45, M1911;" the revised version was named "Automatic Pistol, Caliber .45, M1911A1." Most are simply referred to as 1911s. These early military Colt 1911 and 1911A1 pistols are highly collectable and have numerous variations.

Though Colt was the original manufacturer and still catalogues the 1911 as the Model O, other firearm manufacturers produce a large variety of 1911 pistols. Some are near duplicates of the M1911 and M1911A1. These reproduction pistols are fine shooters and make collecting historic-type 1911 pistols more affordable. Original M1911 pistols were manufactured in the early twentieth century by Colt and three other licensed manufacturers prior to and during World War I, while M1911A1 pistols were manufactured prior to and during World War II by Colt and four other manufacturers.

World War I Production Manufacturers

Colt

Remington-UMC

Springfield Armory*

North American Arms Co. of Quebec

*US Gov't run Arsenal not current commercial firearm manufacturer Springfield-Armory.

The M1911 is a short recoil-operated semi-automatic pistol that feeds from a single-stack, seven-round magazine. Military models featured a 5-inch barrel and were all chambered in .45 ACP (Automatic Colt Pistol).

Two automatic safety devices are utilized in the M1911. The first is a disconnector that prevents the release of the hammer unless the slide and barrel are fully forward and locked in battery. The second is a grip safety that, unless depressed, leaves the trigger locked (i.e., correctly grasping the gun in the firing position disengages the grip safety and allows the gun to fire). A manually operated thumb safety is also built into the design. With the thumb safety engaged, both the slide and the hammer are locked in position.

What follows are variations of the US Military M1911 and M1911A1 pistols. Note that original, mint, LNiB (LIKE NEW IN BOX) condition specimens can be valued double or more compared to specimens graded even 98 percent to 97 percent.

PROOF, Not Talk

You need an automatic pistol for home protection. You know you do. But you're not sure, after reading the different makers' claims, which pistol is the best. Good. Now listen to this:

The Colt was adopted by the U. S. Government because of its "marked superiority to any other known pistol."

The U. S. Ordnance Board made the most exhaustive and rigid tests before it decided on the Colt. It brushed claims aside—its experts decided on *results.*

Marked superiority! A strong statement—from the highest source in the country, too. Be guided by the Government's decision—get a Colt—the automatic pistol that

Fires the First Shot First

the pistol that is automatically safe—those two qualities so essential to a firearm for home protection.

Write for new booklet No. 85 on "How to Shoot."

COLT'S PATENT FIRE ARMS MFG. CO.
Hartford, Conn.

Colt AUTOMATIC **PISTOL**

October 10, 1914

This commercial advertisement from 1914 touted the US Military's success with the M1911 pistol.

Arsenal Overhaul Inspection Stamps

AA	Augusta Arsenal
AN/ANAD	Anniston Army Depot (Anniston, Alabama) observed with a date stamp following it (MM YY) in 1975 and 1977
BA	Benecia Arsenal
MR	Mt Rainer Ordnance Depot
OG	Ogden Arsenal
RA	Raritan Arsenal
RIA	Rock Island Arsenal*
RRA	Red River Arsenal
SA	Springfield Arsenal**
SAA	San Antonio Arsenal

*US government-run arsenal, not current commercial firearm manufacturer Rock Island Arsenal by Armscor.

**US government-run arsenal, not current commercial firearm manufacturer Springfield Armory.

AUTOMATIC PISTOL, CALIBER .45, M1911

The M1911 was produced from 1911 to 1925 and those firearms were marked on the right side of the slide "MODEL OF 1911 U.S. ARMY." Originals featured a blued finish. Arsenal-reworked M1911s have a Parkerized finish. Thousands of M1911 and M1911A1 pistols where refurbished at US arsenals and service depots from the mid-1920s to the mid-1950s and will usually be marked on the frame and/or receiver with the arsenal initials.

DISTINGUISHING CHARACTERISTICS

Original M1911s featured a long trigger and a flat mainspring housing with a built-in lanyard loop.

The sights consisted of a small front blade, and notched rear sight set in a dovetail. Grips were checkered walnut with a double diamond pattern. There was no finger groove on either side of the receiver/frame behind the trigger. The tang of the grip safety was short.

During WWI, it was found that soldiers were firing the M1911 to low impact, so a few design modifications were made to make the firearm easier and more comfortable to shoot accurately. An arched mainspring housing replaced the flat one, which rotated the pistol higher in the shooter's hand, thus effecting higher hits. A shorter trigger was swapped out for the longer one and the wood grips were replaced with checkered brown plastic. Material behind the trigger area on both sides of the receiver was removed to make the pistol more comfortable for the trigger finger of either a left- or right-handed shooter. The tang on the

Inspector Marks

CSR	Charles S Reed, Colt manufacturing serial numbers 717,282-723,000
EB	Ernest Blind, RIA manufacturing
E.E.C	Edmund E. Chapman, Remington UMC manufacturing serial numbers 1-21676
FK	Frank Krack, RIA manufacturing
GHD	Guy H. Drewry, Colt manufacturing serial numbers 845,000 to 2,360,600
GHS Monogram	Gilbert H. Stewart, Colt manufacturing serial numbers 101,500-230,000
JKC	Lt. Col. James K. Christmas, Singer manufacturing
JMG Monogram	J.M. Gilbert, Colt manufacturing serial numbers 230,001-302,000
FJA	Frank J. Atwood, Remington Rand and Ithaca manufacturing
JSB	John S. Begley, Colt manufacturing
RCD	Lt. Col. R. C. Downey, Union Switch and Signal manufacturing
RS	Robert Sears, Colt manufacturing serial numbers 723,000-750,500
WB	Waldemar Broberg, Colt manufacturing serial numbers 750,500-861,000
WGP Monogram	Walter G. Penfield, Colt manufacturing serial numbers 1-101,500
WTG	Walter T Gorton, Colt manufacturing serial numbers 700,000-710,000

Note: Inspection initials are located under the slide stop on the left side of pistol. Pistols rebuilt at an arsenal or service depot were typically marked with the initials of the arsenal as well as the mark by an inspector who stamped his initials or monogram on the gun once it passed final inspection.

THE M1911 CHARACTERISTICS

Blued Finish

No Finger Groove & Long Trigger

Short Grip Safety Tang

Checkered Wood Grip

Flat Mainspring Housing

M1911A1 CHARACTERISTICS

Parkerized Finish

Finger Grooves & Short Trigger

Long Grip Safety Tang

Checkered Plastic Grip

Arched Mainspring Housing

grip safety was also lengthened. The pistol now featured a Parkerized finish. The modified pistol was designated the M1911A1.

Manufacturers placed unique marks on M1911A1 pistols, and these marks can be used to help identify the pistol's manufacturer.

Note that an "X" prefix to the serial number indicates a pistol that has been renumbered by ordnance.

Before WWI ended, a total of 68,533 M1911 pistols had been manufactured. By 1925, that number increased to about 650,000. By WWII, some 1.9 million M1911A1s were purchased for the US government, bringing the total to more than 2.6 million M1911 and M1911A1 pistols produced for WWI and WWII. These numbers do not include models produced for commercial sale during these time periods.

The first M1911 model production is divided up by years and manufacturer, and depending on those factors the value of the pistol varies.

World War II Production Manufacturers

Colt

Ithaca

Remington-Rand

Union Switch & Signal

Singer Sewing Machine Co.

M1911A1 Manufacturer Proof Marks

Colt—A VP proofmark in a triangle at the left front of the triggerguard; a GHD inspector marking or an M1911A1 marking without any spaces between the figures.

Ithaca—A geometric-shape proofmark, such as a triangle, arrowhead or similar on the front left of triggerguard.

Remington-Rand—A serial number preceded by a "NO" instead of a "No".

Singer Sewing Machine Co.—A serial number preceded by an "S" indicates an M1911A1.

Union Switch & Signal—An RCD inspector mark or double spacing between the M and 1911A1.

Model M1911 Military Production				
MANUFACTURING	DATE MFD	VALUE NiB	VALUE Ex	VALUE Gd
Colt	1912	-	$10,000	$6,000
Colt	1913–1915	-	$5,400	$4,300
Colt	1916	-	$5,750	$2,100
Colt	1917–1918[1]	-	$4,300	$3,000
Colt	1919–1925	-	$4,300	$3,000
North American Arms Co.[2]	1918	-	$35,000	$30,000
Remington-UMC[3]	1918–1919	-	$7,000	$3,950
Springfield Armory[4]	1914–1915	-	$6,800	$3,850

[1]Late manufactured pistols have black Army finish.
[2]Very rare, only one hundred pistols made.
[3]Serial number range: 1-21,676
[4]Serial number ranges: 72751-83855, 102597-107596, 113497-120566, 125567-133186

COLT MANUFACTURED 1911

Example of a World War I US Colt Model 1911, this one manufactured in 1918. Fixed sights, with the two-block address/patent markings and Rampant Colt on the left side of the slide, and "MODEL OF 1911. U.S. ARMY" on the right. This is a JMG-inspected frame (see previous table for inspector proof marks), with "UNITED STATES PROPERTY" on the left and the serial number on the right. It is fitted with a long smooth trigger, flat-top rear sight, checkered wide hammer, checkered slide stop and thumb safety, short grip safety, checkered diamond flat grips, a two-tone, pinned base magazine, and a "P/H"-marked barrel. Estimated value is $1,400–$2,250. *Image courtesy Rock Island Arsenal*

No new M1911 or M1911A1 pistols were purchased by the US government after WWII. (Note: A newer variant of the 1911 known as the M45A1 CQBP—Close Quarters Battle Pistol—was purchased in a quantity of twelve thousand, in 2012, by the US Marine Corp.) After WWII, the M1911A1 was used again during the Korean War, the Vietnam War, in Desert Storm, and in all other conflicts up to the present day with Special Forces operators, even though the M1911A1 was officially replaced by the Beretta model 92FS handgun in 1985 (designated by the US military as the M9).

The service life of an M1911A1 is approximately 250,000 rounds. These old work horses are still around and, according to the CMP (Civilian Marksmanship Program), the Secretary of Defense in 2015 has authorized transfer to the CMP surplus M1911 and M1911A1 .45 ACP pistols for sale to the public . . . Currently, the military has some one hundred thousand such pistols that it no longer needs and that are being stored at taxpayer expense. These historically significant firearms can now be transferred to law-abiding owners at a net gain to the government's heavily indebted balance sheet. After more than a century's worth of service, these M1911 and M1911A1 pistols are rendered surplus, and these specimens, because of rework and rebuilds, will not fetch high values but are collectable shooters.

COLT MANUFACTURED 1911A1

An example of a US Model 1911A1, this one manufactured in 1943 by Colt. It has fixed sights, with the two-line, two-block address divided by the Rampant Colt on the left side of the slide. The inspector mark "GHD" (Guy Henry Drewry) is on the left side of the frame, and the property/nomenclature markings are on the right. The pistol is fitted with a flat-top rear sight, short milled trigger, wide checkered hammer, long grip safety, checkered slide stop and thumb safety, arched and checkered mainspring housing, reinforced checkered Coltwood grips, and a "COLT 45 AUTO"-marked barrel. This example would rate EXCELLENT with 97 percent original, dark-green Parkerized finish remaining and having areas of light edge wear, cycling marks, and some light markings. The grips are excellent, with light handling marks. Estimated value is $1,300–$1,900. *Image courtesy Rock Island Arsenal*

US NAVY 1911

Manufactured as part of the final Navy production block of 1913, this Model M1911 pistol bears the "MODEL OF 1911. U.S. NAVY" marking on the right side of the slide. Originally earmarked to receive pistols marked specifically for them, the Navy and the Marine Corps used "ARMY"-marked M1911s and M1911A1s for most of the service life of the pistol. This pistol has fixed sights, with the two-line, two-block Colt patents and address on the left side of the slide ahead of the Rampant Colt. "UNITED STATES PROPERTY" and the "WGP" (Walter G. Penfield) inspector mark are on the left side of the frame. The firearms is fitted with a round-top rear sight, long smooth trigger, wide checkered hammer, short grip safety, checkered slide stop and thumb safety, and flat mainspring housing with a lanyard staple. Checkered hardwood grips have diamond patterns around the screws. It also has a two-tone pinned base magazine and a full blue barrel marked "P H" in-line with the bore. This is a rare model, with only 31,000 produced during the contract period from 1911 to 1914. Low serial number guns get a premium. Note: Since many of these pistols were on ships at sea, many are in FAIR condition; above 70 percent to 80 percent grade are valued higher. This pistol was restored. Estimated value is $3,000–$4,500. *Image courtesy Rock Island Arsenal*

This Remington/UMC-produced M1911 was manufactured in 1918. Note the three-line, two-block patent and address markings flanking the circled "REMINGTON/UMC" logo on the left side and "MODEL OF 1911/U.S. ARMY CALIBER .45" on the right. It wears an "E.E.C."-inspected frame (see table on inspector proof marks), with "E" and "29" on the trigger guard. Checkered grips with diamond patterns around the screws, a "P" barrel, long smooth trigger, wide checkered hammer, short grip safety, and a flat mainspring housing with lanyard staple are also featured. This example has been professionally restored. Estimated value is $1,800–$2,750. *Image courtesy Rock Island Arsenal*

ITHACA GUN CO. PRODUCED 1911A1

This M1911A1 was manufactured by the Ithaca Gun Co., of Ithaca, New York, in 1944, and was shipped to Ogden Arsenal and the Benicia Ordnance Depot in May that same year. The slide and receiver have a gray-green Parkerized finish and the barrel is blued. The receiver feed ramp is bright. The pistol is fitted with checkered brown plastic stocks and is complete with a full-blued magazine. The pistol has a seven-rib mainspring housing, narrow hammer with serrated spur, serrated safety lock and slide stop, and a stamped trigger. The left side of the trigger guard bow is stamped with the distinctive Ithaca factory proof mark. Small Ordnance "Shell and Flame" insignias are stamped in the receiver barrel channel and on the back of the slide above the firing pin hole. The right side of the receiver is stamped with the Ordnance Corps escutcheon behind the grip. "UNITED STATES PROPERTY/No 1451272" is stamped in two lines behind the slide stop hole, and "M 1911 A1 U.S. ARMY" is stamped in one line in front of it. The Ordnance final inspection mark "FJA" is stamped vertically on the left side of the receiver below the slide stop. A "P" proof mark is stamped on the left side of the receiver behind the magazine release. The top of the slide is also stamped with a "P" proof mark, this one between the rear sight and the ejection port. The left side of the slide is roll stamped "ITHACA GUN CO.,/ITHACA, N.Y." in two lines. The blued barrel has the "H.S." (High Standard) marking on the right lug and a "P" proof mark on the left.

The early style Keyes Fibre Co. stocks lack reinforcing rings around the screw holes. There are strengthening ribs, mold marks, and the Keyes star on the inside of the stocks. The full-blued magazine is unmarked. The pistol retains 95 percent of the original gray-green Parkerized finish, with minor edge wear on the high points of the receiver and slide. The slide and receiver have some scattered handling and storage marks. The barrel has about 80 percent of its blue finish. The stocks and stock screws are in excellent condition. The markings on the frame and slide are clear. The magazine retains at least 98 percent of the original blue finish. Estimated value is $1,600–$2,250. *Image courtesy Rock Island Arsenal*

SINGER MFG. CO. PRODUCED 1911A1

A rare example of an authentic M1911A1 manufactured by the Singer Manufacturing Company during WWII. Under the Ordnance Educational Order No. W-ORD-396, the Singer Manufacturing Company produced only five hundred pistols total, with almost all of them issued to the US Army Air Corps. That small number of Singer-manufactured firearms combined with the high attrition rate during WWII makes *any* surviving Singer M1911A1 an extremely rare martial pistol, one highly sought after by collectors.

This specific pistol retains its original WWII blued finish, with the left side of the slide roll-marked with the two-line address of "S. MFG. CO./ELIZABETH, N.J., U.S.A." There are no markings on the slide's right side. The top of the slide is stamped with a "P" proof mark that is oriented toward the left side of the slide, with the left side of the frame having the same corresponding "P" proof above the magazine release button. The slide is correctly *not* numbered to the pistol frame. The right side of the frame is stamped "UNITED STATES PROPERTY/No S800215" in two lines, with "M 1911 A1 U.S. ARMY" towards the front of the frame, the left side stamped with the initials of Col. John K. Clement, "JKC," the Executive officer of the New York Ordnance District. The pistol has the correct wide spur hammer with borderless checkering, checkered thumb safety, slide stop, trigger and main spring housing. It is fitted with an original all-blued barrel that is stamped with only a single "P" proof on the left side of the lug.

This pistol is fitted with a correct set of early WWII, Singer-manufactured, brown plastic, checkered grips with the hollow backs, and with no mold marks or reinforcing ribs on the inside. They have full checkering, with no reinforcing rings around the screw holes. The pistol is complete with one WWII-production, all-blued replacement magazine having no markings on the front lip of the base plate. EXCELLENT condition with more than 90 percent of the original blue finish, having edge and high spot wear overall with only minor blue loss on the front edges of the slide, thinning on the front grip strap and front edge of the trigger guard bow, and with browning on the mainspring housing. There is a patch of pitting present on the forward lower right side of frame. The grips are in excellent condition, with nice sharp distinct checkering on both sides and with no handling marks. Estimated value is $60,000–$90,000. *Image courtesy Rock Island Arsenal*

This is an example of a professionally restored Union Switch & Signal M1911A1 originally manufactured in 1943. Note the left side of the slide is marked with the intertwined "USS" company logo and "U.S. & S. CO./SWISSVALE, PA. U.S.A." Lieutenant Colonel Robert Downie's "RCD" inspector proof is on the left side of the frame. This pistol exhibits M1911A1 features like a thin checkered hammer, stamped trigger, serrated slide catch, checkered thumb safety, arched mainspring housing, Keyes-Fiber grips, and a High Standard barrel. Estimated value is $2,000–$3,000. *Image courtesy Rock Island Arsenal*

TRANSITIONAL MODEL OR "IMPROVED MODEL 1911 PISTOL"

This is a transitional model M1911A1, also referred to as an "Improved Model 1911 Pistol." The transitional M1911s were made in 1924, and while they retained the nomenclature markings of the M1911, they were equipped with the signature features of the M1911A1, which included the dished frame sides, shortened trigger, elongated grip safety, and arched mainspring housing. This example is in 85 percent or better original condition, with its blue finish showing scattered spots of bright corrosion on the slide, including a few tiny patches of pitting, some bright edge wear, and minor handling marks overall. Estimated value is $3,250–$4,500. *Image courtesy Rock Island Arsenal*

This is an example of a M1911 "Black Army," manufactured in 1918. The collector phrase "Black Army" was established due to the dark, brush-blue appearance of late World War I-produced Model 1911s. On the left side of the slide, divided by the Rampant Colt and "MODEL OF 1911. U.S. ARMY" in sans-serif letters on the right. The "eagle/S16"-proofed frame is marked "UNITED STATES PROPERTY" on the right side above the serial number. It is fitted with the long trigger, flat-top rear sight, wide checkered hammer, short grip safety, checkered slide stop and thumb safety, and a flat mainspring housing with lanyard staple. It also has checkered hardwood grips with diamond patterns around the screws and a full-blue barrel marked "S/P" on the lug. This example has about 60 percent original finish, showing streaks of brown patina on the slide, scattered spotting, bright edge wear, and some takedown marks around the slide stop. The grips are also fine, with some dents and flat spots. Estimated value is $1,400–$2,250. *Image courtesy Rock Island Arsenal*

Glock: Thirty Years, Five Generations

Anything, in essence, is collectable, but what makes items truly collectible is their uniqueness, place in history, rarity, and design. It doesn't matter if it's baseball cards, record albums, 1960s muscle cars, or firearms.

Glock pistols may not seem collectible because they are so common. Just take a look at what most law enforcement officers wear on their hips. More than likely it's a Glock pistol. You may even carry a Glock of your own or keep one in the nightstand drawer. Why then, you might ask, would a firearm as common as a Glock be collectible?

GAME CHANGER

The story of Glock is a well-known piece of history and, like smartphones, some of us wonder how we ever got along without these pistols. To say that Glocks were revolutionary is a vast understatement. When introduced, Glock pistols were a game-changer to the firearms industry and the way militaries, law enforcement agencies, and civilians use and think about handguns.

It has been more than thirty years since Glock launched its first pistol in Europe, in 1982, and from then on, its reputation soared. In the US, Glock pistols have been imported since 1986 (Glock, Inc., USA celebrated its thirtieth anniversary as a US factory in 2016), and from nearly the beginning, some people with foresight thought their revolutionary design might just catch on.

It did catch on, so much so that Glocks can be found in more than 65 percent of law enforcement agencies in the US. More than ten million Glock semi-auto pistols have been manufactured since 1983, and the Glock Collectors Association (GCA) has been there every step of the way, chronicling the evolution of Glock pistol designs, cataloging commemoratives, and making note of unique models. What is also so unique about collecting Glock pistols is that some of us have seen the phenomenon first-hand, watching as some gun experts and the media snorted that no one would ever want a "plastic" gun.

THE GLOCK COLLECTORS ASSOCIATION

The GCA was established, in 1995, by Raymond W. Reynolds, Shawn R. McCarver, and Joseph T. Strand, three friends who had the foresight to anticipate the impact Glock pistols would have on the firearm industry.

Monumental changes to the firearms industry don't happen often. You rarely get to witness, say, a Sam Colt introducing a revolver or a John Browning fine-tune a pistol design into the 1911, but these three friends knew there was something to Glock. Reynolds, in fact, was a retired police officer who collected Glocks and eventually joined Glock to tout the pistols' virtues to police chiefs across the nation. Reynolds helped build the brand in the US and, in a way, had a part in creating the destiny of the GCA and the success of Glock itself.

In 1995, the GCA was incorporated as a not-for-profit corporation, with Reynolds as the association's first president. McCarver served as its second president. In 2007, Stanley "Stash" Ruselowski Jr., was appointed the third president of the GCA, with Thomas C. Pietrini as secretary/treasurer. One of the founding members, Joseph T. Strand, remained on the board of directors. All are volunteers to the GCA and serve without compensation.

Like other associations that focus on a specific firearm brand, the GCA's mission is to educate and preserve. It educates the public on the models, variations, and commemoratives built by Glock, as well as provides members with specific information on Glock serial numbers, importation information, and other facts unique to Glock pistols. The group also helps preserve the pistols for generations to come. Raymond Reynolds sold his extensive collection to Glock, Inc., USA, which the company uses as a reference collection.

The GCA is affiliated with the NRA as a recognized gun club and collector's association, and it has a licensing agreement with Glock to use the company's logo in association publications, but there is no affiliation. Gaston Glock, Glock's founder, gave his permission to allow the organization the use of the Glock logo. The association, in turn, made him honorary member #001.

In 1996, Glock issued two paired sets of pistols called the "Defense Set." That issue included five hundred matching 9mm G19 and G26 pistols and 1,500 matching .40 S&W G23 and G27 pistols. Only five hundred full sets of four pistols exist. These pistols are engraved of the right side of the slide "DEFENSE SET/1 of 2" and "DEFENSE SET/2 of 2."

COLLECTING HISTORY

An annual gathering of the GCA is held yearly at the NRA's Annual Meetings, where officers are elected and members can talk all things Glock with each other. Ruselowski travels with his extensive collection of rare and unique Glock models to this event and other gun-collecting shows across the US. The GCA has received several awards since the association started and, under Ruselowski's watch, hopes to receive a Silver Medallion, the NRA's top gun-collecting prize for rare and unique firearms.

Talk with Ruselowski and you'll soon understand the collectability of Glock pistols. Just like Ruger collectors get excited about two-screw and three-screw revolvers, Winchester collec-

tors speak with reverence about pre-'64 models, or those into S&W revolvers discuss models with a pinned barrel, Ruselowski helps decode the Glock serial-numbering system, as well as describe unique transitional models. He has sixty-four Glocks in his collection, which is continually displayed at events attended by the GCA.

The most impressive part of Ruselowski's collection are the models representing the First Run Upon Introduction civilian models, from the G17 (the first model offered by Glock) to Glock's latest model, the G43. These twenty-plus models and more than 170 variations show the evolution of the Glock pistol.

Probably the most noticeable feature of Glocks over the years is the variation in the grip treatment. There are actually five texture treatments that, generally speaking, followed this evolution:

In 1996, Glock produced two thousand "Centennial Georgia Olympic Games" G17 Gen 2 pistols, the right side of the side engraved "Atlanta, Georgia, Security Team USA 1996." These pistols were sold with a walnut display case.

1. Gen1 guns (1986–1988) had a pebbled finish.
2. Gen2 guns (1988–1997) had a checkered "grenade" texture.
3. Gen3 guns (1995–2009) had finger grooves and a checkered texture.
4. Gen4 guns (2010–present) offer a new grip texture and the innovative Modular Backstrap System.
5. Gen5 guns (2017–present) have a flared mag-well, nDLC finish, GLOCK Marksman Barrel, ambidextrous slide stop levers, and a grip that has no finger grooves.

In commemoration of the 9/11 terror attacks, Glock produced a thousand each of the G17, G22, and G21 models, each with a banner that reads "America's Heros." A star-style badge and a firefighter symbol are on either side of the banner, and the date "9-11-01" is under the banner.

Note that a transitional period occurred between Gen3 and Gen4 pistols, and this is where things become very interesting for collectors. The Gen3 pistols started with finger grooves and thumbrests but no front rail. Later models featured accessory rails and a checkered texture on the grip frame.

Cutaway pistols are used by a firearm manufacturer's sales force to show the inner workings of the gun. Ruselowski has a cutaway Glock 17 Gen1—one of eighty made—in "new in box" condition. Then there's the specimen from the first run of OD green Glock 21 Gen3s. He also has a Glock 21 Gen3 with a true Picatinny rail that was submitted for the US military pistol contract pre-2007. His G21SF is unique because of its rail and ambidextrous magazine release. Ruselowski has other unique combinations, including models with serial numbers that match his membership numbers in the GCA, consecutively numbered guns, and serial numbers that match model numbers. Commemorative models in the collection include the America's Heroes set of three pistols (G17, G21, and G22), which commemorate the fallen police and fire personnel lost during 9/11, while others recognize Desert Storm, the Atlanta Olympics, an unusual and specially marked engraved "defense set" of four pistols, and many more.

Glock released one thousand "Desert Storm Commemorative" G17 Gen 2 pistols in 1991. The top of the slide was engraved with all thirty coalition countries, and the side of the slide was engraved with "New World Order" and "Operation Desert Storm, Jan. 16-Feb. 27th, 1991."

JOIN THE CLUB

Those interested in joining the GCA can email, fax, or write Ruselowski for a membership application or go to the club's Facebook Page (facebook.com/glockcollectorsassociation) and download an application. Membership is open to anyone over twenty-one years of age and legally able to own a handgun. Applicants are asked to affirm the NRA safety pledge. Dues are $35 annually, $99 for three years, or $150 for five years.

Upon joining the GCA, members receive the most recent *GCA Journal*, a publication that comes out about once a year and includes articles on unique pistols, history on specific models, and other items of interest. Members can also purchase copies of past journals, as well as the *GCA Master Journal*, which lists the standard production matrix of first-run pistols shipped to the US. This matrix is invaluable to any collector, as it lists Glock models, first-run prefixes, dates shipped, variations, and more interesting information. Members are encouraged to submit articles on their own collections for potential inclusion in the annual journal.

For more information on the GCA, email sjruselowski@gmail.com, fax 203-756-8742, or write to 45 Freight Street, #1-102, Waterbury, Connecticut, 06702.

These are (left) a twentieth anniversary G17 with laser engraving, a facsimile of Gaston Glock's signature, and the number in the series, "34 of 2006," and (right) the twenty-fifth anniversary model with a silver medallion embedded in the left grip.

INSTANT CLASSICS

In the past thirty years, Glock has completely changed the way the military and law enforcement view service handguns. For civilians, the pistols are known to be user-friendly and safe. What Glock did also completely changed the way the world designed and manufactured pistols. In fact, today the basic Glock pistol design—polymer frame and striker-fire system—is copied by most major firearm manufacturers.

Glock pistols leave little to be desired, except for beauty; they are denounced as blocky and ugly and one Glock pistol looks pretty much like all Glock pistols. Indeed, it might seem odd that Glock pistols would be collectible since they are so ubiquitous. But over the short time these pistols have been in use, they have seen four distinct generations. To the casual observer, the differences across the models might not be obvious, while to the astute collector, the differences are well-noted even in transitional models. Here's how to identify the four generations of Glock pistols:

- **Gen1, 1986–1988**—The 9mm G17 was the first pistol and started the brand's extensive line. Gen1 pistols featured a pebble-finished frame and lacks horizontal finger grooves on the front and rear backstraps.
- **Gen2, 1988–1997**—Gen2 pistols have the checkered "grenade" finish and have horizontal grooves on both the front and rear grip straps. Glock also introduced the .40 S&W caliber G22 full-size, G23 compact, and G24 long-slide in this generation, along with the .357 SIG G31 full-size and G32 compact.

With Gen2 models, ported and compensated variants were first offered sporting slots cut into the barrel and a cutout in the top of the slide. The "C" suffix added to model numbers indicates a compensated model.

In 1990, 10mm and .45 ACP calibers were introduced with the G20 and G21, respectively.

The magazines in Gen2 models were modified with an integrated recoil spring assembly. Also, to comply with ATF requirements, a steel plate was embedded into the frame forward of the trigger guard where the pistol's serial number was stamped.

- **Gen3, 1995–2011**—Gen3 pistols are notable for a variation in the frame features. The first Gen3 pistols were transitional and had new finger grooves molded into the front grip strap with thumbrests, but no front accessory rail. Gen3s then transitioned into finger grooves with thumbrests and a checkered finished frame with a front accessory rail. The finger groove transitional models were the G19C, G20, G20C, G21, G21C, G26, G27, G28, G29, G30, G33, G36, and G39.

Other modifications to Gen3 pistols include the introduction of the Short Frame, noted with a the "SF" suffix following the model number. These SF frame pistols shortened the trigger reach and minimized the heel of the pistol to better accommodate shooters with small hands.

At this time, Glock produced a proprietary caliber with Speer called the .45 GAP—Glock Automatic Pistol. Also during this time frame, subcompact models were introduced, including the G26, G27, G29, G30, G33, and G39, as was the single-stack "slimline" G36 in .45 ACP.

A limited number of pistols with frames in Flat Dark Earth and olive drab finishes were offered. Gen3 also saw the introduction of the RTF2 (Rough Textured Frame 2) with an extreme "polymid" traction surface on the grip panels for use in wet environments.

- **Gen4, 2010–present**—In 2010, Glock introduced its Gen4 models, which can be identified with "Gen4" roll-marked after the model number on the left side of the slide. These models feature a recessed thumbrest, finger grooves, and the accessory rail of the previous generation, but now include the RTF4 textured frames whose "polymid" traction is less severe than the previous generation's RTF2 texture. Gen4 models also feature the Short Frame (SF) receiver with four interchangeable backstraps (two with extended beaver tails), a reversible and enlarged magazine catch, dual recoil spring assembly, and a new trigger system. Magazines for Gen4 models were changed to accommodate the new magazine catch, thus rendering earlier generation magazines incompatible with Gen4 models. Nine new models were introduced in the Gen4 era, including the G30S and G41, the G42 (.380 ACP), and G43 (single-stack 9mm), as well as five MOS—Modular Optic System—variants of the G17, G19, G34, G35, and G41, which offer a way to easily mount a number of modern reflex and red-dot optics without costly machining to the slide.

- **Gen5, 2017–present**—The G17 Gen5 and G19 Gen5 pistols were inspired by the GLOCK M pistols used by the FBI and include many features GLOCK users had been asking for. There are over twenty design

changes that differentiate Gen5 pistols from their Gen4 predecessors, including a flared mag-well, a new nDLC finish, the GLOCK Marksman Barrel, ambidextrous slide stop levers, and a grip which has no finger grooves.

Note: Special thanks to the Glock Collectors Association President Stanley J. Ruselowski Jr., for data on Glock pistols and use of his personal collection of First Run Upon Introduction of Civilian Models and cutaways.

Note the differences in the back straps; from left to right Gen1, Gen2, Gen3, and Gen4.

The Gen5 pistols feature over twenty design changes which distinguish them from their Gen4 predecessors. Gen5 models include the G17 and G19 (shown).

Colt Python
Colt's Most Famous Snake

The Colt Python was one of the finest production revolvers ever built and many have called it the "Rolls-Royce of Colt revolvers" and the "best revolver in the world." It is frequently referred to as "the Cadillac of revolvers." In fact, the Python was actually compared to the Cadillac automobile in 1956 advertisements—and that wasn't just Colt's marketing department spinning a tale.

Ask revolver shooters, and more than likely they will agree the Colt Python was and is the best double-action revolver ever produced. This "snake" was used by lawmen, target shooters, and hunters, and today is one of the collector's

Colt produced this specimen in 1966. It has standard markings and features a pinned serrated ramp front and an adjustable rear notch sight, with a wide, borderless checkered hammer and serrated trigger. It is fitted with checkered walnut grips with gold Colt medallions. This Python is graded at 99 percent original blue finish, with only slight handling marks and a faint cylinder drag line. The grips are excellent, with some minor dings on the butt. The checkering is crisp. The gun is mechanically excellent. The value of this Python ranges from $2,750–$4,000. *Image courtesy Rock Island Auctions*

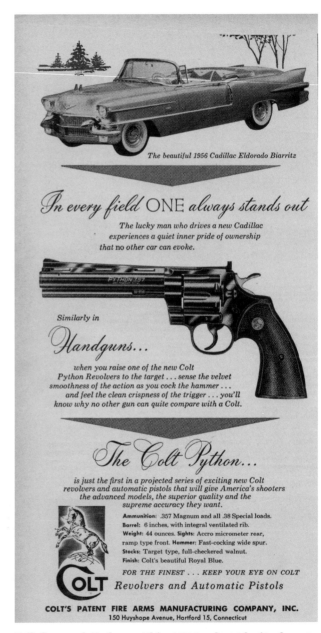

Tail fins and Pythons. This 1956 ad made it clear to shooters that the Python was the revolver you aspired to own.

most sought-after Colt models. Of late, if you are like the Rick Grimes character in *The Walking Dead*, the Python makes an excellent zombie killer.

The Python was not the first Colt revolver to use a snake's name. The Colt Cobra takes that honor, and over the years Colt snakes included the Anaconda, Viper, King Cobra, and Diamondback, but it is the Python that is the most well-known.

When it debuted in 1955, the Python was available with a 6-inch barrel with three vents on its rib, a hollow underlug, fully checkered target grips, and a fully adjustable Colt Accro rear sight. The blue finish was nothing less than brilliant, with a mirror-like quality cataloged as "Colt Royal Blue."

The Python was an immediate success. Hand-fitted with a honed action, it was known for its accuracy, smooth double-action trigger pull, and tight lock-up. Not only was the action exceptionally smooth, the revolver incorporated a full-length lug under the barrel, excellent adjustable sights, and a vent rib. It looked as good as it performed.

A 4-inch barrel model followed and was first cataloged as the Colt New Police Python, though the revolvers were never roll-marked with this name.

The six-shot Python is built on Colt's large I-frame and was chambered in only two calibers, the .357 Magnum in standard models and .38 Special in the Python Target model with an 8-inch barrel. Barrel choices ranged from 2.5, 3 (rare), 4, 6, or 8 inches, with 4- and 6-inch models being the most common. The revolver was equipped with an adjustable rear sight and pinned front blade. Original finish choices included a polished Royal Blue and bright nickel. A plainer blue and satin stainless steel were offered on late-production models. Grips consist of fully checkered walnut on revolvers prior to 1991. After 1991, checkered rubber grip replaced the wood.

Pythons were produced until the late 1990s, when production shifted to the Colt Custom Shop.

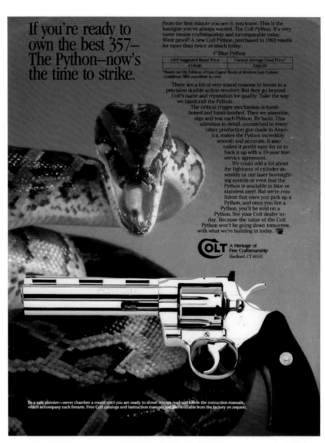

The Python was a high-quality revolver, and this 1980s advertisement even touted its used value.

A matte stainless-steel model was produced from 1983 through 1996. The revolver pictured here features a 6-inch barrel and checkered rubber grips. The value of this Python ranges from $1,700–$2,250. The value of 2.5-inch barrel models increases 100 percent.

To signify the change, the model was renamed to be the Python Elite. It was virtually the same revolver as the previous Python just with "Python Elite" roll-marked on the barrel. The last Python out Colt's doors had a suggested retail price of $1,150, and Colt ceased production altogether in 2006.

This is an example of a Colt Python .38 Special Target model manufactured in 1980, with a total production of only 3,489 produced. This revolver has a pinned, fixed, serrated ramp blade front sight and adjustable rear notch sight, a shrouded ejector rod with checkered knob, serrated trigger, wide borderless checkered hammer, the Rampant Colt logo on left side of frame, and checkered walnut grips with gold Colt medallions. A Colt "woodgrain" box and papers are included. Note the roll mark on the barrel reads "Python Target." Estimated value is $3,000–$4,000. *Image courtesy Rock Island Auctions*

An example of the Colt Python Hunter model with an 8-inch vent rib barrel, blue finish, and rubber grips. This model was manufactured in 1981 and includes a Colt-branded Leupold M8-2x scope, aluminum hard case, cleaning rod, and cleaning tips. The estimated value is $1,500–$2,250. *Image courtesy Rock Island Auctions*

This is a late-production Python manufactured between 1991 and 1997 with standard markings and features. It has checkered grips with silver Colt medallions and the Colt factory blue case. Estimated value $2,000–$3,000. *Image courtesy Rock Island Auctions*

The Python is one of those rare handguns that is not only well made and performs, it has had an impact on pop culture, having been featured in numerous television shows, movies, and video games. It has walked tall and walks among the dead. A nickel-plated, 6-inch Python is currently the weapon of choice of the lead character in the television series *The Walking Dead*, but it has also appeared in the TV series *Starsky & Hutch* (1975–79), the original *Walking Tall* movie with Joe Don Baker (1973), and others, as well as *Call of Duty: Black Ops, Half-Life 2* and other video games.

If you find one, even if it is a beater, it will most likely be expensive. Thanks to *The Walking Dead* television series, the price of Pythons has increased in recent years. While variances of models are fairly extensive, what follows are good guidelines to identifying a Colt Python. See the Colt section, page 181 for current values.

SNAKE EYES

In 1989, Colt manufactured a limited-edition run of cased pairs of Python "Snake Eyes." Five hundred sets were produced. Both Pythons in the sets were equipped with a 2½-inch vent rib barrel and simulated ivory grips. One had a bright stainless finish the other had a blued finish. This pair rates EXCELLENT, with some light handling marks, a very light cylinder drag line, and signs of very light buffing overall. The grips are excellent, with a couple of light handling marks. The boxes are also excellent, with some light handling, edge, and corner wear. A glass-front case with a green fabric interior and Colt-marked poker chips and cards was included. The estimated value is $6,500–$10,000. *Image courtesy Rock Island Auctions*

Smith & Wesson Model 39
First Generation 9mm

The Model 39 was originally developed to compete in the U.S. Army Service Pistol Trials of 1954. The Army eventually dropped the search for a replacement pistol, so Smith & Wesson introduced the Model 39 to the commercial market in 1955.

The Model 39 generates a lot of interest for collectors, since it was the first American-made DA/SA centerfire semi-automatic in 9mm. Part of the Model 39's legacy is that it ushered in the widespread use of semi-automatic pistols with US law enforcement agencies. It also helped usher in the era of the "Wonder Nines," 9mm pistols with DA/SA triggers and high-capacity magazines that became extremely popular starting in the 1980s.

The Model 39 borrowed features found on the Walther P.38. Its barrel was fixed to the frame, and it had a decocking safety lever and the aforementioned DA/SA trigger. It was also chambered in 9x19mm (9mm) and employed a single-stack magazine, but it departed in similarities to the P.38 by using a conventional slide design with a barrel bushing.

Also similar to the P.38, the Model 39 was lightweight—about 27.5 ounces unloaded—due to an aluminum alloy frame, and it was relatively compact in size at just 7.6 inches long. It had all the design elements to be an excellent candidate for a service pistol in law enforcement or military personnel hands. Indeed, when the US Army cancelled its 1954 service pistol trials and the new pistol was brought to the commercial market, law enforcement took note. In 1967, the Illinois State Police became the first LE agency to adopt the Model 39.

An early aluminum alloy frame Model 39 (top) with its long extractor. Note the shorter extractor on the Model 39-2 (bottom). The shorter extractor replaced the longer extractor, which was prone to breakage. The change was made in 1971. *Image courtesy Smith & Wesson*

The Model 39 went through a variety of model generations and became the basis for other models. The Model 52, for instance, is a steel-framed, single-action semi-automatic with a 5-inch barrel, adjustable target sights, and chambered to take .38 Special wadcutter cartridges. It was designed for competition shooting. The Model 59 is also based on the Model 39, except the Model 59 was designed to accommodate a 14-round, double-stack magazine thanks to a wider aluminum frame and a straight grip backstrap. The Model 59 could be considered S&W's first "Wonder Nine". Like the Model 39 it, too, was chambered in 9mm.

"The Model 39 was originally brought out," explained Roy Jinks, Smith & Wesson's historian, "as a candidate for the US military's desire for a 9mm pistol. Two versions were produced, a single-action and a double-action version. Although the single-action models were cataloged, S&W never made more than ten guns."

The single-action Model 39, catalogued as the Model 44, is perhaps the rarest variant of the Model 39 with only ten pistols manufactured. These pistols were built in the 1200 serial number range, when pre-Model 39s were being produced. Depending on condition, an original Model 44 can have a value from $20,000 to $26,000.

Of note to collectors, the first run of Model 39 pistols—about 2,500, according to Jinks—did not have the model number stamped on the receiver. Many of these first-release guns ended up in U.S. and foreign military hands. Some original Model 39 pistols were made with a steel frame in the mid- to late 1950s and were sold in the late 1960s. About 927 of these steel-frame Model 39s were produced. Aluminum alloy frames were produced after the steel frames, but aluminum alloy frames were the first commercially available. Early models did not have the model number markings stamped on the frame. Starting in 1957, the model number was stamped on the left side of the receiver just above the trigger.

"The first guns, pre-Model 39s, had a shorter safety lever," said Jinks, "and the grip was not recessed for the safety, the grip tang was short, and it had a different backstrap. They also did not have a trigger play spring. These pre-Model 39s were not stamped with the model number, nor were they stamped with 'Patent Pending' marks on the slide. Later models have a longer safety lever, as well as the more common characteristics we associate with the Model 39."

Early models are also easily identified by their large pivoting extractor. Prone to failure, a more robust extractor was later used.

Production of pre-Model 39s and Model 39s were mixed. To add confusion to production

dates and serial numbers, the serial numbers of the pre-Model 39s and Model 39s were mixed with those of Model 41 and Model 52 pistols. Military trial pistols were stamped with an "X" prefix to the serial number.

The Model 39 evolved to the Model 39-2, when the long extractor was changed to the short extractor and other improvements were made. The Model 39-2 was only produced with the aluminum alloy frame. For the US market, the Model 39-2 was produced in 9mm, along with a small lot in .30 Luger (7.65mm) for the European market.

A highly modified variant of the Model 39 was officially named the Mk 22 Mod 0 and was the built for Naval Special Warfare operators during the Vietnam War. Operators called it the "hush puppy." The Mk 22 Mod 0 featured a wider grip frame to accommodate a double stack 14-round magazine and was equipped a suppressor and tall sights. Unique to the "hush puppy" was a slide lock that kept the slide from cycling upon firing which greatly decreased the noise produced when the pistol was fired.

The Model 59 is, in essence, a Model 39, except the Model 59 has a wider frame to house a 14-round double-stack magazine. It was produced from 1971 to 1988, before being replaced by the Model 459. *Image courtesy Smith & Wesson*

These pistols manufactured in 1955 are an ultra rare Model 39 (top) with a single-action trigger and a pre-Model 39 (bottom) with DA/SA trigger. It was made in very limited edition in case the US military wanted the 9mm pistol in single-action rather than the double-action. *Image from collection of Roy G. Jinks*

This is an example of a pre-Model 39; note the trigger, small safety lever, short grip tang, and no model markings on the frame above the trigger. *Image from collection of Roy G. Jinks*

Smith & Wesson Model 39 Variations			
MODEL NAME	**MFG DATE**	**SERIAL NUMBER RANGE**	**NOTE**
Model 39 (steel frame)	1966 only	39000, 60000–64000, 81000–82000	no model number
pre-Model 39 (aluminum frame)	1954–1957	1001–2600	no model number
Model 39 (aluminum frame)	1954–1970	"A" prefix serial number began in 1970	model number appeared after approximately serial number 2600
Model 39-2	1971–1982		change from long to short extractor

Handgun Provenance

ELMER KEITH'S OLD NO. 5

Before Elmer Keith (1899–1984) was a gun writer and Executive Editor of *Guns & Ammo* magazine he was cowboy, wrangler, big-game hunter, and firearms enthusiast, though "enthusiast" may be too gentle a term. He was a gun *nut*. Perhaps one of the originals. Hell, he was there (a play on one of Keith's books, *"Hell, I was There!,"* one of his many books on guns and hunting.)

Keith was short of stature, but what he lacked in height he made up for with his no-nonsense opinions on guns and his trademark 10-gallon Stetson. As much as he was vocal and voiced his opinion in print, often to the consternation of his fellow writers like Jack O'Connor, Keith had the stuff. Handguns were a major fancy for him. An avid handloader, Keith loaded cartridges for the .38 Special that would blow apart lesser-quality revolvers. That's why Keith favored S&W revolvers for their strength and quality. He contributed to the development of the first .357 Magnum, along with D. B. Wesson and Phillip Sharpe, in 1934. The same is true of the .44 Magnum (1955) and the .41 Magnum (1964), both of which he helped develop by cajoling extreme velocities out of the .44 Special. Keith loved to push big, heavy bullets beyond the scope of normalcy.

COWBOY, GUN NUT, INNOVATOR

Being a true cowboy in every sense of the word—he was a bronc buster—Keith cut his teeth on old Colt cap-and-ball revolvers and Single Action Army (SAA) revolvers. He especially liked the Colt SAA design, yet thought it could be better. He started tinkering with SAAs and hooked up with Harold Croft, another like-minded revolver enthusiast who, legend has it,

Old No. 5 is the most famous of all customized Colt Single Action Army revolvers. It was a joint project between Harold Croft and Elmer Keith.

showed up at Keith's place in Oregon in the 1920s, with a box full of revolvers for him and Keith to try. The two struck a partnership and began to customize Colt SAA revolvers. The end result was "Old No. 5," perhaps the most famous Colt SAA revolver ever modified.

The Colt SAA was introduced in 1873 and specifically designed for the US government Service Sidearm Trials in 1872. It has been in continual production by Colt ever since, except for a few years during WWII. It is a single-action revolver, meaning the hammer must be cocked to fire the gun. Initially offered in .45 Long Colt, the SAA holds six rounds.

Of any handgun built, it has to be one of the most recognizable. Over the years, the Colt SAA has gone through numerous design modifications, and collectors group the revolvers by generation:

- First Generation, produced 1873 to 1941
- Second Generation, produced 1956 to 1974
- Third Generation, produced 1976 to present day.

Not only are SAAs some of the most collected revolvers, they are highly prized depending on the generation and configuration. The SAA is one of the most copied revolvers, with numerous replicas manufactured in Italy, Germany, and the United States, some with great fanfare. During his movie career, John Wayne used a Great Western Arms SAA made in the United States. Replicas of late, especially those manufactured by companies like Uberti, are fine examples, but they do no match the authenticity of a Colt SAA manufactured in Hartford, Connecticut.

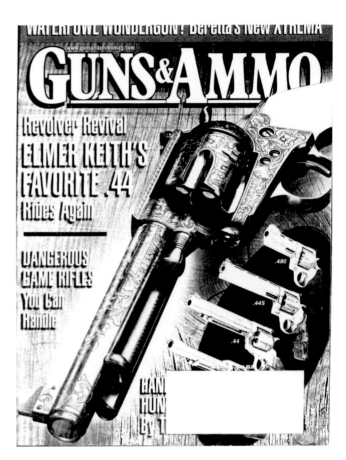

Old No. 5 last appeared on the cover of the May 2003 issue of *Guns & Ammo*, **further proof that Keith was connected to the revolver.**

Harold Croft (left) and Elmer Keith (right) collaborated on the custom Colt SAA revolver design that eventually became known as "Old No. 5."

There were numerous iterations of Keith's custom revolvers, and as the name suggests, "Old No. 5" was the fifth attempt. In Croft's box were revolvers Croft had customized, designs he called "featherweights," which Keith tested and then made final design changes to create what was in his mind the perfect SAA revolver. Keith wrote about the revolver in an April 1929 *American Rifleman* article called "The Last Word," detailing the specifics surrounding the concept and development of the revolver project.

AS THE STORY GOES

No. 5 held a mythical nature for gun enthusiasts, who at one time could not get enough information about the revolver. Numerous individuals had seen Keith with the revolver, and the revolver was in possession of Keith's family for some time.

Determining the provenance of Old No. 5 and its holster was straight forward. The revolver had been written about in the 1929 issue of *American Rifleman*, and that article had accompanying photographs. This revolver is also pictured on page 103 of Keith's book *Six Guns*. On page 169 in the same book, the revolver and Keith-designed Lawrence holster are shown.

When the auction house of James D. Julia, Inc., saw the gun, it described its condition as: *Very fine. Overall retains 96 to 97 percent strong custom blue showing holster wear and sharp edge wear. Grips are sound showing light wear on eagle and retain light ivory patina. Mechanics are crisp, bright shiny bore. Holster is crisp showing only very light wear & retains about all of its original brown finish. This is truly a once in a lifetime opportunity to own handgun history, the iconic "Last Word" from Elmer Keith.*

The details of Old No. 5, described by James D. Julia, Inc., then unfold, illustrating the extent of modifications performed to the original revolver:

The serial number is: M5. Caliber: .44 Special. It has an all blue finish with 5½-inch barrel with a one-line address and dual caliber markings on left side. Bore is six lands and grooves with left hand twist. Muzzle is fitted with a sleeve that is mounted with a Colt double action style adjustable front sight. Top strap has been reworked and redesigned into a flat top style which extends over the hammer slot and has a Colt style, windage adjustable rear sight. The base pin is of custom design that has a ribbed hourglass shaped head and is secured with a swinging latch replacing the screw or spring-loaded crossbolt and is retained by a spring-loaded detent. The hammer is Bisley style that has a widened and extended spur. The trigger is also wider and a little longer than a standard single action trigger. Backstrap is

an altered Bisley part attached to a single action front strap/trigger guard. The hammer spring is a custom design between the originator of this design and Mr. Keith. Mounted with two-piece pre-ban African ivory grips, custom built to fit this frame with a raised, carved Mexican eagle on right side.

A side note on the grips and engraving: According to Keith, they were originally walrus ivory grips but had shrunk, and so Keith had a new pair made from elephant ivory, carved with a Mexican eagle. These were the grips

The muzzle is fitted with a sleeve that is mounted with a Colt double-action style adjustable front sight.

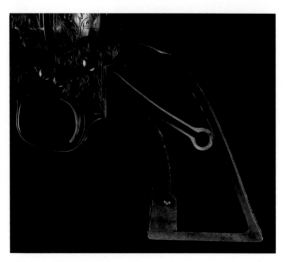

The revolver used a unique flat mainspring that Elmer Keith helped design.

The base pin is a custom design that has a ribbed, hourglass-shaped head. It is secured with a swinging latch, replacing the screw or spring-loaded crossbolt, and is retained by a spring-loaded detent.

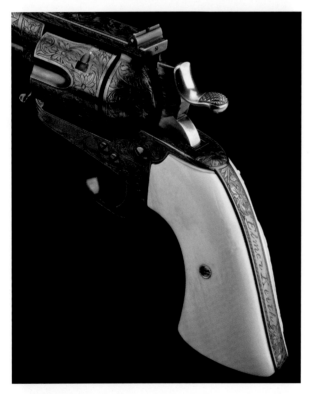

The hammer is a Bisley-style that has a widened and extended spur.

mounted on the revolver at auction. And there was more:

The engraving on this revolver was commissioned by Mr. Croft for Mr. Keith and consists of flowing foliate and floral patterns with about

full coverage on the frame, barrel, cylinder, front strap, and trigger guard. Top strap is engraved with the Masonic symbol of a square and compass. Backstrap is engraved "Elmer Keith" and butt strap is engraved "Durkee, Oregon."

The revolver was actioned March 15–16, 2015, by James D. Julia, Inc., of Fairfield, Maine. The

The revolver is engraved with a flowing foliate and floral pattern, with nearly full coverage on the frame, barrel, cylinder, frontstrap, and trigger guard.

The topstrap is engraved with the Masonic symbol of a marking square and compass.

The buttstrap is engraved "Durkee, Oregon." This is where Keith lived at the time.

Croft had Keith's name engraved on the backstrap.

Keith's signature is engraved on the right side of the frame.

Elephant-ivory grips are carved with a Mexican eagle. These were the second of two sets of ivory grips Old No. 5 wore.

low estimate before the auction was $30,000, while the high estimate was $50,000. The realized final bid was $80,500.

Note: Special thanks to James D. Julia, Inc., (jamesdjulia.com), for use of the Keith estate images and information.

BONNIE PARKER'S COLT MODEL 1902

Most people would not know who Bonnie Parker was were it not for her companion Clyde Barrow.

Together they were Bonnie and Clyde, criminals who, during the Great Depression, robbed banks, small stores, and gas stations. They also murdered and kidnapped people during their crime spree, which landed them on the FBI Public Enemy list between 1931 and 1935. Yet folks in many of the Midwestern states where the couple operated helped the outlaws and hindered law enforcement's effort to capture the pair and their gang of associates.

At the time, the press glamorized the couple, but eventually the events that became known as the Grapevine murders turned the public against Bonnie and Clyde.

KILLERS ON THE ROAD
On Easter morning in 1934, Clyde and a gang member murdered two Texas highway patrolmen at the intersection of Route 114 and Dove Road in

This Colt Model 1902 Sporting was found in Parker's clothing after Parker and Barrow were ambushed by law enforcement and killed. Letters discovered and produced after the couple's death proved it was Parker's pistol.

Grapevine, Texas. It wasn't long before the couple would be permanently stopped by the law. Late the following month, on a rural road in Bienville Parish, Louisiana, lawmen ambushed Bonnie and Clyde.

Reports of the incident vary and have changed over the passage of time, but it is generally understood that law enforcement did not identify themselves before opening fire. Bonnie and Clyde had slowed down to see if they could assist the father of a gang member, when bullets perforated their stolen Ford V8. The officers did clearly remember hearing Bonnie scream at the start of the onslaught. About 130 rounds were fired at the couple by the group of officers. The coroner listed seventeen wounds on Clyde and twenty-six on Bonnie.

Though Bonnie Parker was involved in hundreds of felonies while in the company of Clyde Barrow and their gang members, there is no direct evidence she ever fired at a police officer or civilian. The couple had become folklore legends with tens of thousands attending their funerals, and to this day most refer to them by their first names as if they were pals.

After the ambush, Frank Hamer, the Texas Ranger who was hired to hunt down the criminal pair, inventoried the contents of the felons' vehicle and found a number of fully automatic Browning BAR rifles, Colt 1911 pistols, sawed-off shotguns, and hundreds of rounds of ammunition. Hamer kept the weapons, legal at the time under the terms of the Texas Department of Corrections, which had hired him.

What was not among the arsenal appropriated from the bullet-riddled car was a Colt Model 1902 semi-automatic pistol.

THE HISTORY BEHIND THE HISTORY

The Model 1902 was designed by John Browning for Colt, an improvement over Browning's earlier Model 1900. The Model 1902 was a short recoil operated pistol chambered in .38 ACP. It incorporated a slide stop, but no external manual safety. Both Military and Sporting models were produced. Military models were produced through 1928, Sporting models until 1908.

The Model 1902 featured hard black rubber grips, though custom grips were available from the factory. Most pistols were produced with a highly polished, deep Colt Royal Blue finish, but nickel-plated models were also available. Some early models had a fire-blued finish on the trigger, pins, and grip screws, while the hammers had a case-hardened finish. Early production models had either milled straight line or cross-cut checkered slide serrations on the muzzle end of the slide. These were omitted in later production models.

The hammers on Colt 1902 pistols help identify the production cycle of the pistols. Three hammer types included a high spur hammer and a rounded or "stub" hammer, which appeared on early and mid-production guns. The third hammer, a low-profile spur hammer, appeared on later Model 1902 pistols in both the Military and Sporting variants.

Though the Model 1902 was intended for the military market it was never adopted by the US Government. It was manufactured in sizable numbers: 18,068 Military and 6,927 Sporting models were built.

MORTICIAN'S UNEXPECTED DISCOVERY

A Colt Model 1902, serial number 7362, was found enfolded in Bonnie Parker's skirt at the Conger Funeral Home embalming room in Arcadia, Louisiana. A letter of authentication regarding the gun is dated May 5 and signed by James Lavelle Wade, coroner in charge of the Bonnie and Clyde death investigation and signer of their

This Colt Model 1902 has a rounded hammer, referred to by Colt as the "stub" hammer. Model 1902s had three types of hammer styles.

Note that the cocking serrations are toward the muzzle, which helped the user more easily manipulate the Model 1902's long slide.

The outlaw couple Bonnie and Clyde were mugging at the camera in this photo taken in March 1933. This photograph was found by police after a shootout in Joplin, Missouri.

Six rounds of .38 ACP ammunition were found loaded in the pistol at the time it was discovered by the embalmer.

death certificates, and by Mrs. Alwyn Hightower, an employee of Conger Funeral Home. Affidavit witness signatures include Mrs. Ed Conger, wife of the Conger Funeral Home director.

This letter of authentication is valuable in establishing the provenance of the Model 1902 and connection to Bonnie Parker. Case Antiques, the auction house that auctioned the Colt Model 1902, described how the pistol became connected to Bonnie Parker.

After the shootout the Conger Furniture Store/ Funeral Home received the bodies. [It was common at the time for furniture store to double as funeral homes.] The affidavit states the weapon was enfolded in the skirt of Bonnie Parker and discovered in the embalming room of Congers Funeral Home by the late Mr. Charles Francis Bailey, who was employed at the time by Mr. Ed Conger as an embalmer. The following day, May 24, 1934, Bailey gave the weapon as a souvenir to Mrs. Alwyn Hightower's son, Dr. Robert Hightower, M.D., who was the present consignor. The lot also included six bullets found in the pistol and a photo archive of pictures taken by King Murphy, Mr. Bailey's assistant and amateur photographer. Additionally, a Colt Manufacturing Company letter accompanied

the lot stating the Model 1902 Colt was shipped to Simmons Hardware Company in St. Louis, Missouri on August 22, 1904 with a total shipment of 15 guns of this type. Additional items in the archive includes a 1973 offer letter for the gun and various newspapers referencing the 50th anniversary of the death of Bonnie & Clyde. The dated August 1973 letter from Peter Simon of Jean, Nevada, offers to purchase the gun, the book of actual pictures, and any other memorabilia. Dr. Robert Hightower died October 27, 1973. The letter also has handwritten notes from Dr. Hightower's wife: *Before Dad died he had me write Bob, this fellow wanted to buy the Clyde & Bonnie gun etc. I called him but I never did call and give him a price for I didn't know what to charge. If you ever decided to do so you might call + give him a price if he is still there. The value may go up with time but it could go down for new people don't even remember them. Thought I'd pass this on. It's yours now to do as you wish. I love you Mother.*

The specifications of the Colt Model 1902 Sporting model list by Case Antiques states:

Colt Model 1902 (Sporting) Automatic Pistol: Caliber- 38 rimless, smokeless, 7 shot magazine, 6? barrel, magazine marked PAtD SEPT. 9, 1884, hard rubber grips with molded checkering, the rampant colt design, and the name COLT at the top of the grips. This particular pistol was produced in 1904 with a total production of approximately 7,500. Standard weight 2 pounds, 3 ounces.

The condition according to Case Antiques was as follows:

Colt pistol has aftermarket nickel finish but appears to retain the original factory grips. Minor oxidation to nickel finish. There are no records indicating the pistol has been disassembled or cleaned since acquisition in 1934.

The pistol was auctioned on January 25, 2014, by Case Antiques of Knoxville, Tennessee. The low estimate before the auction was $125,000, while the high estimate was $175,000. The realized price to the winning bidder was $99,450.

Note: Special thanks to Case Antiques (caseantiques.com) for use of the Bonnie Parker Colt and black-and-white photograph images and information.

The nickel finish on the pistol was applied sometime after the pistol was shipped from the factory in 1904. The non-factory nickel finish would reduce the value of this pistol were it not for its infamous provenance.

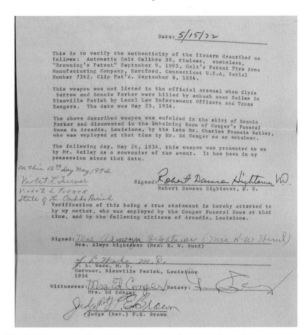

This is the notarized letter attesting to the circumstances of how the Colt pistol was found and who took ownership of the pistol.

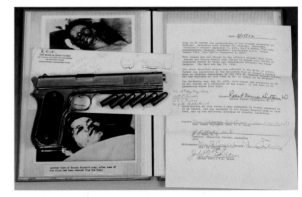

The entire lot auction offered in 2014 included the pistol, ammunition from the pistol, black-and-white photos, and letters authenticating Parker possessed the gun.

Featured Handguns
A Detailed Look at Both Common and Rare Handguns

AMT AUTO MAG II

The Auto Mag II was originally manufactured from 1987 to 2001, and then reintroduced in 2004 by High Standard in Houston, Texas, which also produces High Standard pistols. These two examples were manufactured by AMT.

The Auto Mag II was one of few successful semi-automatic pistols chambered in .22 WMR. These pistols were constructed of stainless steel and used a gas-assisted action. See page 138 for specifications and values. *Images courtesy Bishop's Fine Guns*

BERETTA MODEL 76P STANDARD

This particular Beretta is a .22 LR Model 76P that features a barrel shroud integrated with the frame, and a rail for mounting optics. The Model 76 was produced from 1971 to 1985 and was available with either plastic or wooden grips, with a "P" or "W" suffix on the model number, respectively. See page 145 for specifications and values. *Images courtesy Bishop's Fine Guns*

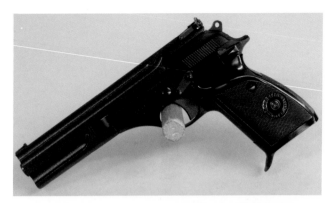
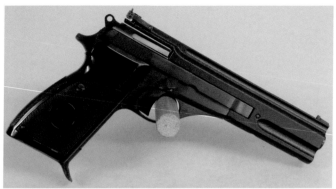

BERETTA MODEL 948

This is a rare Beretta .22 LR Model 948 that is nickel-plated and fully engraved. This example still has the leather presentation case lined in velvet and silk, along with a cleaning rod, brush tip, and extra magazine. Most likely this was manufactured in 1958. See page 148 for specifications and values. *Images courtesy Bishop's Fine Guns*

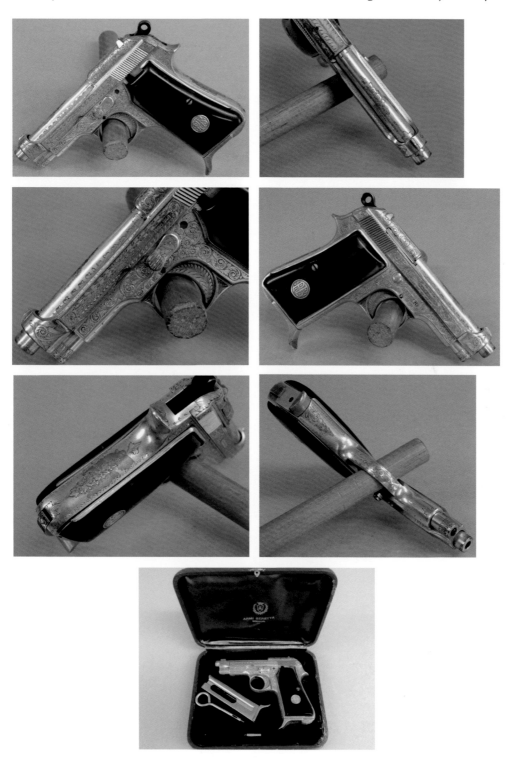

BROWNING FN "BABY" MODEL

The "Baby" subcompact pistol is chambered in .25 ACP/6.35mm and features a 2-inch barrel. Manufactured in Belgium and imported by Browning from 1945 to about 1968, this variation is roll-marked with "Browning Arms Co." on the left side of the slide. Since it still has the original box and looks unused, it will demand a higher price. For full specifications and values, see page 199. *Images courtesy Bishop's Fine Guns*

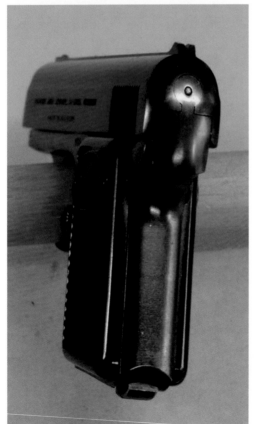

BROWNING HI-POWER STANDARD

Since 1945 and to present day, the Hi-Power has gone through numerous model evolutions. This is a Hi-Power Standard with adjustable rear sight. It was offered in 9mm and .40 S&W (discontinued in 2010). The ambidextrous thumb safety was added in 1989. The pistol parts were manufactured in Belgium and assembled in Portugal. For full specifications and values, see page 156. Note the variant with rear tangent sight adjustable from 50 to 500 meters. These pistols were imported from 1965 to 1978. This is a later model, with a spur hammer, manufactured somewhere between 1972 and 1978. Note that these pistols did not have a polished blue finish like the Hi-Power Tangent Captain pistols that were imported from 1993 to 2000. For full specifications and values, see page 156. *Images courtesy Bishop's Fine Guns*

BROWNING MEDALIST

The Medalist was a .22 LR target pistol manufactured in Belgium by FN and imported by Browning from 1962 to 1975. About 24,000 were manufactured. The pistol was sold in a black case with a red cloth felt interior and was supplied with three barrel weights. For full specifications and values, see page 157. *Images courtesy Bishop's Fine Guns*

BROWNING NOMAD

The Nomad was an entry level .22 LR pistol designed for informal target shooting and plinking. FN in Belgium manufactured the Nomad, and it was imported by Browning from 1961 to 1974. The pistol was available with either a 4½- or 6¾-inch barrel. The frame material was either steel or alloy. Alloy models demand a 10 percent premium over steel-frame models. For full specifications and values, see page 157. *Images courtesy Bishop's Fine Guns*

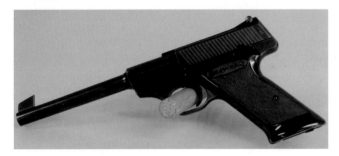

COLT ANACONDA

Colt debuted its first .44 Magnum revolver in 1990 and called it the Anaconda. This larger double-action revolver is built on Colt's "AA" frame and was designed to compete with similar revolvers from Ruger and Smith & Wesson. The Anaconda was only available in stainless steel with what Colt called its Ultimate Stainless finish. First edition revolvers have "Colt Anaconda First Edition" roll-marked on the left side of the barrel. Three barrel lengths were offered: 4, 6, or 8 inches.

A .45 Long Colt model was offered from 1992 through 1999. From 2002 through 2006, when the revolver was discontinued, the Colt Custom Shop produced the Anaconda. For full specifications and values, see page 174. *Images courtesy Bishop's Fine Guns*

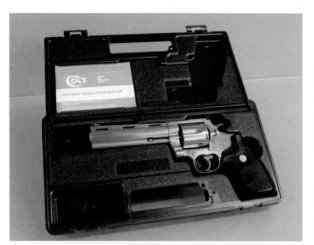

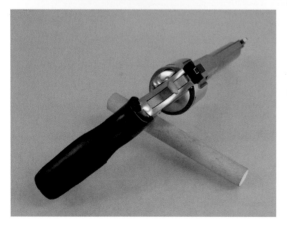

COLT BANKER'S SPECIAL, POSSIBLE "FITZ SPECIAL"

The Banker's Special was a variant of the Colt Detective Special. It was first produced in 1928 in the .38 Colt New Police cartridge, which is the same as the .38 S&W. A few .22 LR models were produced and are more valuable than the .38-caliber model. This specimen is chambered in .22 LR. Production of the model stopped during World War II.

This Banker's Special is interesting since it is highly modified, with the hammer bobbed and the front section of the trigger guard removed, similar to what is known as a "Fitz Special" or "Fitz Colt." John Henry Fitzgerald, an employee of Colt from 1918 to 1944, is credited with coming up with the idea to radically modify Colt revolvers into snubnoses for deep concealed carry. More investigation is needed to verify if this is a true "Fitz Special" but a Colt factory letter indicates the Banker's Special was shipped from the factory to an individual residing in New York City, who was most likely a police officer. The single shipment of the revolver to a possible NYC officer indicates this may be a genuine "Fitz Special." For full specifications and values, see page 175. *Images courtesy Bishop's Fine Guns*

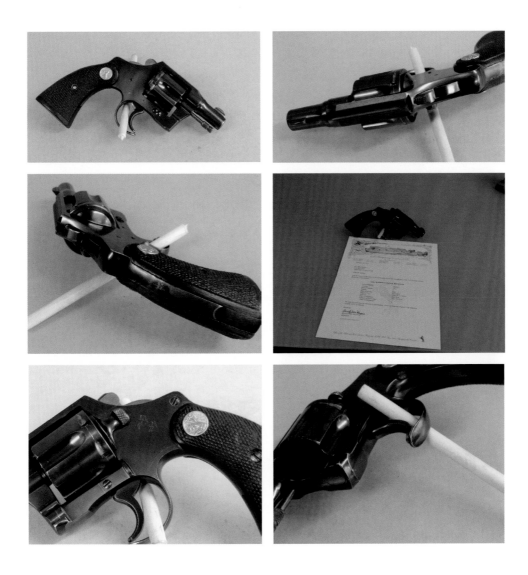

COLT CAMP PERRY MODEL

The Camp Perry Model is a unique handgun, as it is a single-shot built on a revolver frame. Designed from a Colt Officer's Model Target revolver, the Camp Perry is also a target revolver, but one that is a single-shot fitted with flat block in lieu of a round cylinder. The name "CAMP PERRY MODEL" is stamped on the left side of the chamber. The model debuted in 1926, and 2,488 were produced in total when production ceased in 1941. It was only available in .22 LR and originally with a 10-inch barrel. In 1934, an 8-inch barrel model with a modified action producing reduced lock time was offered. These 8-inch barrel models can increase the value from 30 percent to 40 percent. For full specifications and values, see page 173. *Images courtesy Bishop's Fine Guns*

COLT DETECTIVE SPECIAL, SECOND ISSUE

The Detective Special was introduced in 1927. Based off of Colt's "D"-frame Police Positive, the Detective Special featured a 2-inch barrel. It was extremely popular with law enforcement from its inception through the 1970s.

Detective Special models are identified as a First Issue (1927 through 1946), Second Issue (1947 to 1972), Third Issue (1973 through 1986), and a Fourth Issue (1993 to 1995). First Issue models were initially made with a square butt like the Police Positive, but in 1933 a round butt version replaced the square butt. First Issue models also had a half-moon front sight and checkered trigger, hammer, and cylinder latch. Second Issue models had internal changes as well as a round butt, ramp front sight, lengthened ejector rod, and a grooved hammer spur and trigger. Grips were checkered walnut with silver medallions, except from 1948 to 1952 when Coltwood grips or brownish checkered plastic grips were offered. This specimen is a Second Issue. An easy way to determine a Second Issue from a First Issue is to note that a Second Issue has a 1/8-inch deeper frame when measured from the hammer to the bottom of the frame between the trigger guard and the grip. Third Issue models featured a shorter grip frame while Fourth Model revolvers have a heavier barrel with a full ejector rod shroud. For full specifications and values, see page 176.
Images courtesy Bishop's Fine Guns

COLT DIAMONDBACK

Another "snake" in the Colt lineup was the Diamondback, which was introduced in 1966. Built on Colt's "D" frame, just like the Colt Detective Special, Police Positive, and similar revolvers, the Diamondback looks like Colt's iconic Python due to its full lug and vent-rib barrel. But while the Diamondback may look like a small Python, the resemblance stops there since the Diamondback did not have the fit, finish, or tuned action of the Python.

Barrel lengths were 2.5, 4, or 6 inches, and calibers were .22 LR and .38 Special. Note that 2.5-inch barreled models were equipped with service grips, while the other lengths had target grips. The most valuable specimens are the blued, 2.5-inch barrel .22 LR model and the nickel-plated, 6-inch barrel .22 LR. Only about 2,200 of the latter model were produced. The rarest model is a .22 Magnum model. Some of these may or may not have been assembled by Colt. Look for documentation if buying one. For full specifications and values, see page 176. *Images courtesy Bishop's Fine Guns*

COLT SHOOTING MASTER .38

The Shooting Master .38 is a high-grade target revolver built off of Colt's New Service revolver frame. About 2,500 Shooting Master .38 revolvers were manufactured, from 1932 to 1940. These revolvers are identifiable by the 6-inch barrel, flat-top frame, adjustable target front and rear sights, a checkered trigger and backstrap, and checkered walnut grips with silver medallions. Note that the Shooting Master was available with a rounded butt or a square butt after 1933. This particular model is fitted with Ed McGivern front and rear sights. For full specifications and values, see page 179. *Images courtesy Bill Wilson collection*

COLT PEACEKEEPER

Manufactured from 1985 through 1989, the Peacekeeper is very similar to the Colt Trooper MK V, except it had a vent-rib barrel of either 4 or 6 inches. On the left side of the barrel the roll mark reads: "PEACEKEEPER/* .357 MAGNUM CTG.*" on two lines. It was available only in .357 Magnum and had a matte blue finish and rubber finger groove grips. For full specifications and values, see page 180. *Images courtesy Bishop's Fine Guns*

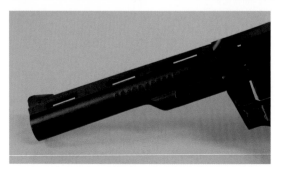

COLT PEACEMAKER 22

The Peacemaker 22 replaced the Frontier Scout model. This is a small-frame, rimfire, Single Action Army revolver with two interchangeable cylinders, one in .22 LR and one in .22 Winchester Magnum Rimfire (WMR). These revolvers were manufactured from 1970 through 1977, with about 190,000 produced. Note that these models can be identified with either a "G" or "L" serial number prefix. This specimen will fetch 10 percent higher, due to the fact it is in the original box and has the original box for the additional cylinder. For full specifications and values, see page 181. *Images courtesy Bishop's Fine Guns*

COLT SAA, SECOND GENERATION BUNTLINE

An easy way to determine the generation of a Colt SAA (Single Action Army) is to look at the serial number. This specimen has a serial number with an "SA" suffix, indicating it is Second Generation SAA. The long, 12-inch barrel also identifies this revolver as a Buntline. Some 3,900 Second Generation Buntlines were produced from 1957 through 1975. Early manufacture Buntlines had checked rubber grips, while later manufacture had smooth walnut. This model was only chambered in .45 Long Colt. For full specifications and values, see page 184. *Images courtesy Bishop's Fine Guns*

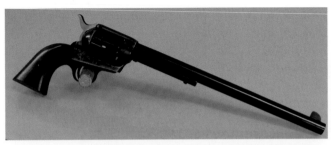

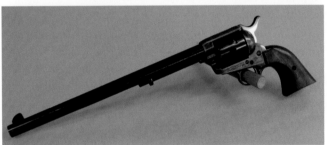

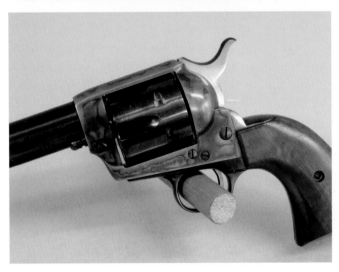

COLT SAA, CLASS C ENGRAVING

Colt's Custom Shop offers a wide variety of SAA options. This SAA revolver wears Class C engraving and an unfluted cylinder. For a true value estimate, a factory letter is needed. *Images courtesy Bishop's Fine Guns*

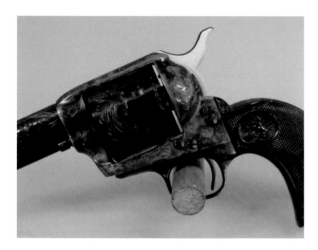

COP DERRINGER

COP, short for Cop Off-duty Police, is a four-barrel derringer with a double-action trigger. It is made of stainless steel and was offered in .22 WMR or .357 Magnum. This specimen is chambered in .357 Magnum and comes with the original holster. It saw limited manufacture in the late 1970s. For full specifications and values, see page 138. *Images courtesy Bishop's Fine Guns*

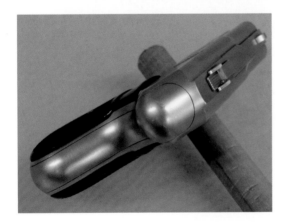

FREEDOM ARMS MODEL 83 (252 VARMINT CLASS)

The five-shot, .22 LR Model 252 Varmint Class was introduced, in 1991, by Freedom Arms of Freedom, Wyoming. Freedom Arms revolvers typically have a matte finish like this specimen possesses. This example also has a fixed front sight and adjustable rear sight. The barrel is marked on the left "FREEDOM ARMS 252 CASULL .22LR / FREEDOM, WYOMING U.S.A." The right side of the frame is marked "FREEDOM ARMS/VARMINT CLASS." An optional .22 WMR cylinder is included. Note the relief holes drilled into the hammer. For full specifications and values, see page 201. *Images courtesy Bishop's Fine Guns*

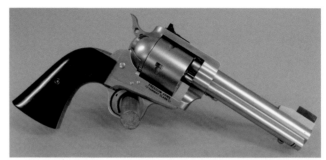

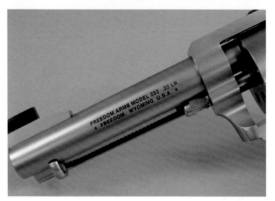

HIGH STANDARD SUPERMATIC TROPHY, 106 SERIES

The 106 Series of pistols debuted in 1965 and was designed with the same grip angle as a Colt Military Model 1911 pistol. They were manufactured in the Hamden, Connecticut, factory, and for that reason are more prized with collectors. Note that the roll mark "MODEL 106/ MILITARY" appears on two lines on the right side of the frame. Supermatic pistols were the deluxe target pistol model, featuring a high-gloss finish on early production models and gold-plated magazine release, safety, and trigger. Also note that pistols in the 106 Series used a magazine with a red plastic bottom. For full specifications and values, see page 227. *Images courtesy Bishop's Fine Guns*

HIGH STANDARD SUPERMATIC CITATION, 103 SERIES

The 103 Series pistols were produced, for the most part, between 1960 and 1963. This example of a Supermatic Citation was manufactured in the Hamden, Connecticut factory. The roll mark "MODEL 103" appears on the right side of the slide above the extractor. On the left side of the frame, the roll mark "SUPERMATIC/CITATION" appears on two lines. Note the two removable barrel weights attached to the underside of the barrel and muzzle brake. These three items add value to the pistol, about $100 and $130, respectively. For full specifications and values, see page 226. *Images courtesy Bishop's Fine Guns*

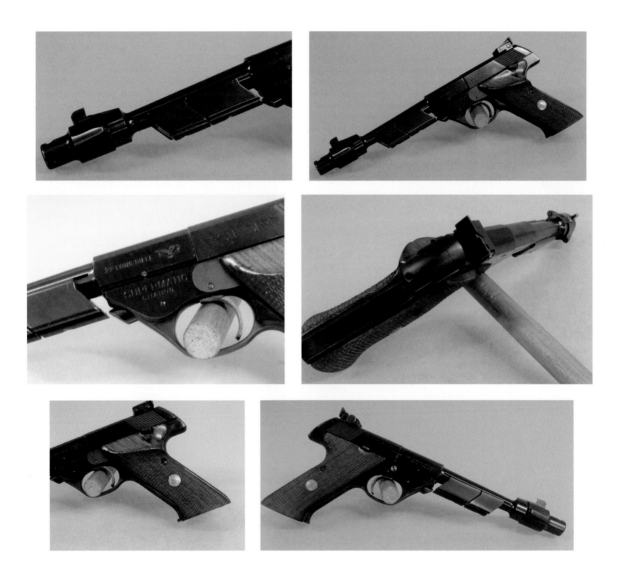

HECKLER & KOCH HK45 TACTICAL

The HK45 Tactical was originally developed for the US military's Joint Combat Pistol program in 2005–06. The program has since been put on hold. The HK45 Tactical was offered for commercial sales staring in 2013. The pistol features Meprolight three-dot tritium night sights, a 10-round steel magazine, a Picatinny mil-std 1913 rail, and a threaded barrel. This polymer-framed pistol is chambered in .45 ACP and utilizes a proprietary internal mechanical recoil reduction system. This example features a DA/SA trigger with safety decocking lever located on the left side of the receiver. A DAO without a safety decocking lever is also available. For full specifications and values, see page 219. *Images courtesy Bishop's Fine Guns*

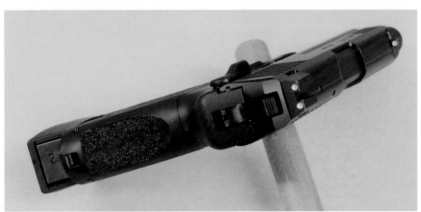

KORTH TARGET MODEL

The Korth revolver is manufactured in Lollar, Germany, and has been imported by a number of companies since 1964. Korth revolvers are renowned for their high quality and very tight tolerances and, thus, are the most expensive revolvers currently produced. They are very expensive new, upwards of $8,000, and used models are rarely encountered. This specimen is a Target Model chambered in .22 LR, featuring stippled walnut grips, a 6-inch vent-rib barrel, and adjustable sights. For full specifications and values, see page 240. *Images courtesy Bishop's Fine Guns*

MAGNUM RESEARCH MARK VII .50 AE DESERT EAGLE

The Desert Eagle series of semi-automatic pistols are known for chambering magnum cartridges typically reserved for large-frame revolvers. This example, chambered in .50 AE (Action Express), is one of the most powerful pistol cartridge currently in production. The Mark VII in .50 AE featured a 6-inch barrel with a ⅞-inch-wide Weaver-style rib. Mark XIX .50 AE models have a full Picatinny top rail. The Mark VII was available only in a matte black finish. It was manufactured for Magnum Research by IMI in Israel from 1991 to 1995. For full specifications and values, see page 251. *Images courtesy Bishop's Fine Guns*

SIG SAUER MODEL 1911 TRADITIONAL COMPACT

SIG began producing 1911-style pistols in 2004, beginning with the GSR (Granite Series Revolution). All SIG 1911s are built in the US with US-produced parts. The example shown is a Model 1911 Traditional Compact. The Traditional series model has a domed slide top. For full specifications and values, see page 280. *Images courtesy Bishop's Fine Guns*

SMITH & WESSON .38/44 OUTDOORSMAN (MODEL OF 1950, PRE-MODEL 23)

The .38/44 Outdoorsman is built on S&W's large, square-butt N-frame and first appeared in 1931. The revolver underwent design transitions after World War II, and those models are known as "Postwar Transitional" models. This example was introduced in 1950 and manufactured until 1957, with a total of 6,039 being produced. The serial number range for this model is S75000 to S261999. The serial number is found stamped on the butt. For full specifications and values, see page 292. *Images courtesy Bishop's Fine Guns*

SMITH & WESSON FOURTH MODEL, THE STRAIGHT LINE TARGET

The Fourth Model, The Straight Line Target, was manufactured from 1925 through 1936 and is a single-shot .22 LR with a unique side-swing barrel for loading and unloading. The pistol was shipped in a fitted metal case lined in green felt and including cleaning and maintenance tools. For full specifications and values, see page 288. *Images courtesy Bishop's Fine Guns*

SMITH & WESSON K-22 MASTERPIECE, PRE-MODEL 17

The K-22 Masterpiece was manufactured from 1946 through 1957 and is similar to the K-22 Outdoorsman and the K-22 Masterpiece ribbed round, 6-inch barrel. Note these revolvers have a "K" serial number prefix. The K-22 Masterpiece transitioned to the Model 17. For full specifications and values, see page 302. *Images courtesy Bishop's Fine Guns*

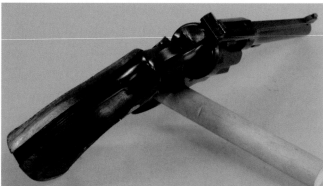

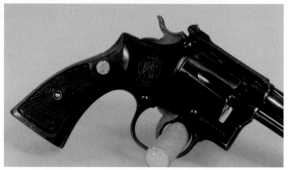

SMITH & WESSON THE HIGHWAY PATROLMAN, PRE-MODEL 28

The Highway Patrolman was built to attract the law enforcement market in the mid-1950s. A budget version of the Model 27, The Highway Patrolman was also chambered in .357 Magnum but had a non-serrated barrel rib, adjustable sights that were non-serrated, and a satin blue finish.

S&W omitted the time-consuming manufacturing and finishing processes of the Model 27, and the Highway Patrolman was the result. It debuted in 1954 and was produced through 1957, then, as the Model 28, was manufactured through 1986. For full specifications and values, see page 293. *Images courtesy Bishop's Fine Guns*

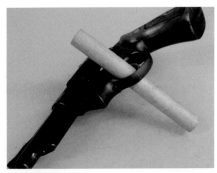

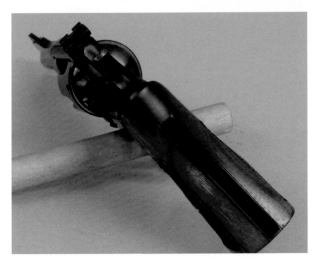

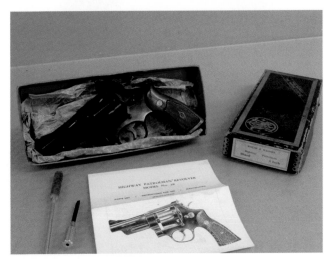

SMITH & WESSON MODEL 34-1

Many anglers, campers, outdoor recreationalists, and plinkers are familiar with the Model 34. Originally it was called The Model of 1953 .22/.32 Kit Gun, which was a small .22 LR revolver with an adjustable sights introduced in 1953. In 1957, the name was changed to Model 34 and the model number stamped on the frame where the crane closes on the frame. This example is a Model 34-1, which began manufacture in 1960 using S&W's J-frame. The Model 34 was discontinued in 1991. For full specifications and values, see page 294. *Images courtesy Bishop's Fine Guns*

SMITH & WESSON MODEL 36, .38 CHIEFS SPECIAL

The Model 36 is one of S&W's iconic snubnose revolvers using the J-frame to create a compact, five-shot, .38 Special revolver. Originally the revolver was known as the Chiefs Special, when it debuted in 1957. As S&W changed to numerically named models, it became the Model 36 in 1957, after serial No. 125000. This specimen is a classic, with blued frame, checkered walnut grips with medallion, and case-colored hammer and trigger. Note that early production models were shipped in a two-piece red box, later in a two-piece blue box. Current models use a one-piece cardboard box. For full specifications and values, see page 294. *Images courtesy Bishop's Fine Guns*

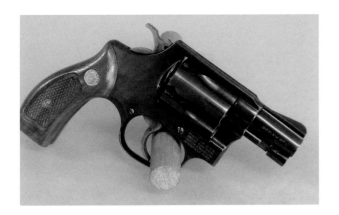

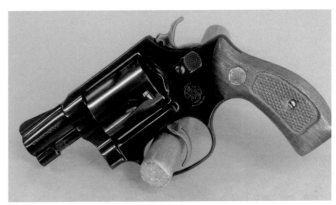

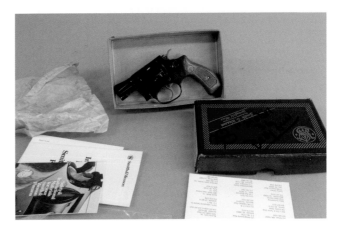

SMITH & WESSON MODEL 41

The Model 41 is a .22 LR match target pistol introduced in 1957. The grip angle of the Model 41 is the same as the grip angle of a Colt Military 1911 pistol. The examples shown here are a 7-inch barreled model, a 5.5-inch heavy barrel, and a 7.375-inch barrel with muzzle brake. All models featured checkered walnut grips with thumbrest. Early manufacture pistols included a cocking indicator (as shown in rear view), and increase value on average 25 percent or more. The cocking indicator was dropped in 1978. For full specifications and values, see page 281. *Images courtesy Bishop's Fine Guns*

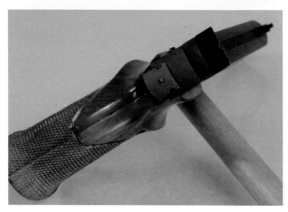

SMITH & WESSON MODEL 52-2

In 1962, S&W introduced the Model 52, a center-fire match target pistol chambered for .38 Special wadcutter ammunition, a round with the bullet seated flush to the case mouth. The grip angle of the Model 52 is similar to the Model 39, and in fact it used the same trigger mechanism, but with a set screw locked-out DA mode. Unique to the Model 52 was a true SA trigger debuting in 1963,

adjustable sights, and screw-down barrel bushing. The specimen is a Model 52-2, which had engineering updates that included a better extractor, adjustable trigger stop, and a counterweight the shooter could attach to the pistol. The Model 52-2 was produced form 1971 through 1993. For full specifications and values, see page 281.
Images courtesy Bishop's Fine Guns

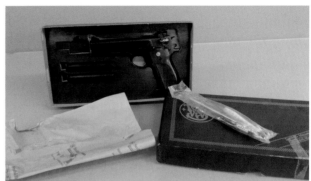

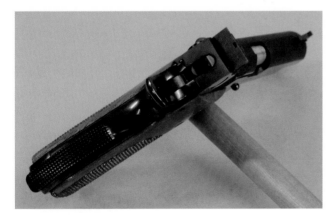

SMITH & WESSON MODEL 63

Small-frame .22 LR revolvers, known generally as "Kit Guns," have been manufactured by S&W over the decades. This is an example of a current-manufacture Model 63, an eight-shot revolver made of stainless steel and debuted in 2008. In 2010, S&W added a fiber optic front sight. A black blade front sight was discontinued in 2009. For full specifications and values, see page 297.

Images courtesy Bishop's Fine Guns

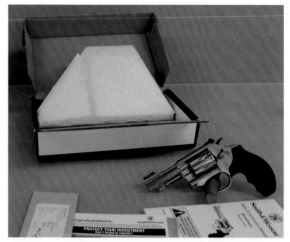

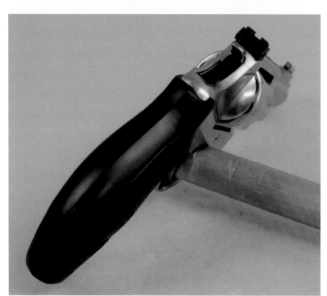

SMITH & WESSON MODEL 296 TI

From 1999 through 2002, S&W offered an L-frame, .44 Special snubnose revolver constructed with an aluminum alloy frame, five-shot titanium cylinder, and 2.5-inch stainless-steel barrel. It weighed 18.9 ounces. Note the roll mark on the right side of the barrel, ".44 S&W SPECIAL CTG./ MAX BULLET 200 GRAINS." These revolvers were shipped in a gray jewel-style box lined with blue velvet. For full specifications and values, see page 298. *Images courtesy Bishop's Fine Guns*

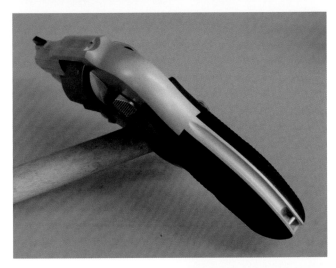

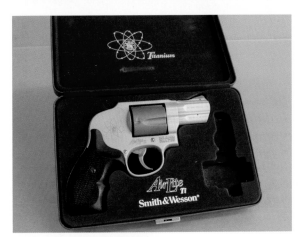

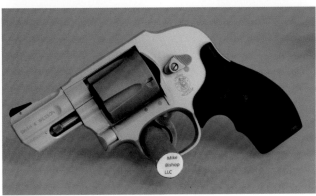

SMITH & WESSON MODEL 325PD AIRLITE SC

The 325PD Airlite Sc is a six-shot .45 ACP revolver that weighs about 21.5 ounces, due to the frame and cylinder material. The frame is made of S&W's proprietary Scandium alloy, and the cylinder is made from titanium. The stainless-steel barrel is covered with an aluminum shroud to further reduce weight. Features include Ahrends smooth wood grips and a fiber optic front sight. This revolver was produced from 2004 through 2007. For full specifications and values, see page 298. *Images courtesy Bishop's Fine Guns*

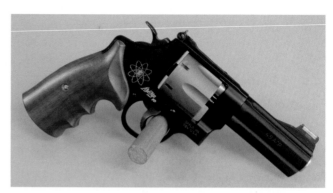

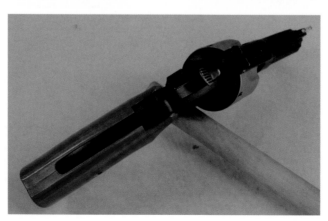

SMITH & WESSON MODEL 351C AIRLITE

The Model 351C Airlite is a Centennial-style variant with an enclosed hammer. Introduced in 2010, this model is a seven-shot .22 WMR. It weighs about 10.6 ounces, since it is manufactured with an aluminum alloy frame and cylinder. The base of the grip features a lanyard pin. For full specifications and values, see page 298. *Images courtesy Bishop's Fine Guns*

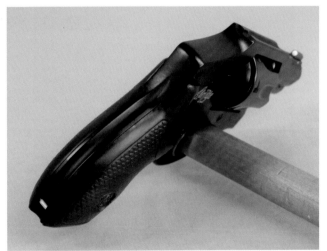

S&W MODEL 386 AIRLITE TI MOUNTAIN LITE

The Model 386 Airlite Ti Mountain Lite is built on S&W's round-butt L-frame, with a scandium frame, seven-shot titanium cylinder, and either a 2.5- or 3.125-inch stainless-steel barrel with an aluminum shroud. This revolver features a Hi-Viz fiber optic front sight and Hogue Bantam rubber grips. Note that "Mountain Lite" is stamped on the left side of the barrel shroud. The 386 Airlite Ti Mountain Lite was manufactured from 2001 to 2007. For full specifications and values, see page 299. *Images courtesy Bishop's Fine Guns*

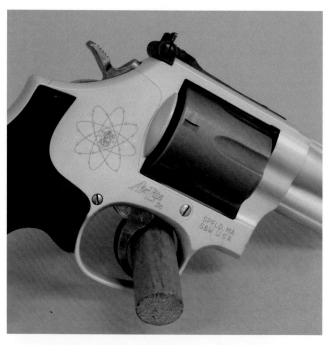

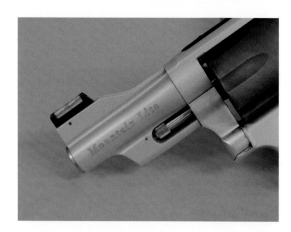

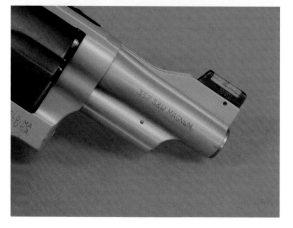

SMITH & WESSON MODEL 500

The Model 500 debuted in 2003 as S&W's new X-frame revolver in the new powerful .500 S&W Magnum cartridge. Both revolver and cartridge are designed for hunting and protection from larger bears and other dangerous game. One unique feature is the integrated and removable muzzle brake/compensator built into the end of the aluminum barrel shroud. The specimen shown here has a 4-inch barrel, which was introduced in 2004. For full specifications and values, see page 299. *Images courtesy Bishop's Fine Guns*

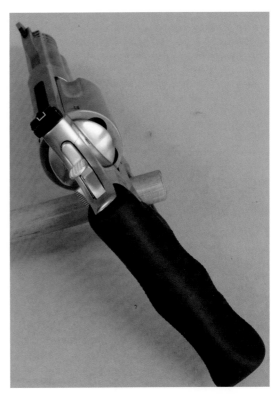

SMITH & WESSON MODEL 547

The Model 547, also known as the M&P 9mm, is based on S&W's K-frame with either a round or square butt. Unique to this revolver is the 9mm chambering, and unlike other revolvers chambered for semi-automatic pistol cartridges, it does not use moon clips to hold the cartridges in the cylinder. Instead, the Model 457 uses a spring-loaded extractor that engages the extractor groove on the 9mm cartridge case. These revolvers were produced from 1980 to 1985. For full specifications and values, see page 299. *Images courtesy Bishop's Fine Guns*

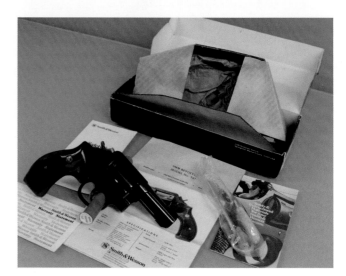

SMITH & WESSON MODEL 625 JM

The Model 625 JM was designed with input from shooting professional Jerry Miculek, hence the "JM" at the end of the model name. This is a six-shot stainless-steel revolver chambered in .45 ACP that has been in production since 1988. A .45 Long Colt model was also offered but since discontinued. Note that early 5-inch barrel models were roll-marked "45 Cal Model of 1989" on the barrel and stamped on the frame "625-2". In 1989, markings started to be laser engraved. For full specifications and values, see page 300.

Images courtesy Bishop's Fine Guns

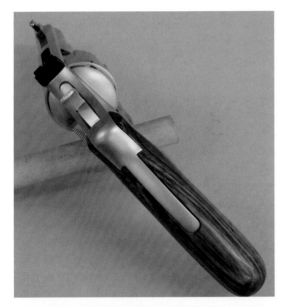

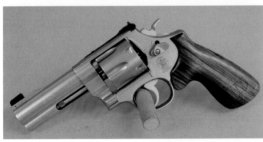

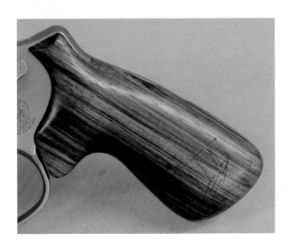

SMITH & WESSON MODEL 625, MODEL OF 1988

The Model 625-2, Model of 1988, is built on S&W's N-frame and features a six-shot cylinder chambered in either .45 ACP or .45 LC. Barrels length available included 3, 4, and 5 inches. Note the roll mark on the right side of the barrel reads "45 CAL MODEL OF 1988." The Model 625 has gone through ten engineering changes since it was introduced in 1989. For full specifications and values, see page 300. *Images courtesy Bishop's Fine Guns*

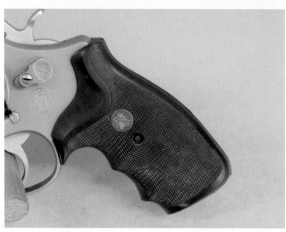

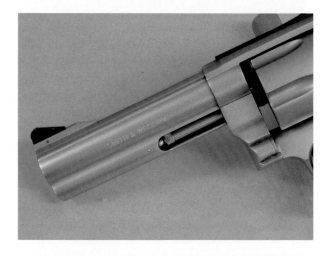

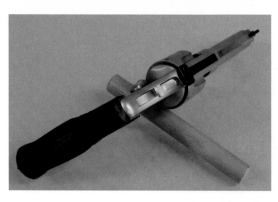

SPRINGFIELD ARMORY MODEL 1911-A1 STANDARD

Springfield Armory produced Model 1911-A1 pistols from 1985 to 1990. The example shown is a 1911-A1 Standard model with a 5.04-inch barrel, Parkerized finish, checkered walnut grips, and three-dot sights. This model has since evolved into the Loaded 1911-A1 series of pistols currently in production. Note that 1985–90 pistols had the Springfield logo to the rear of the ejection port on the right side of the slide, while current models have the logo on the same side of the slide but located closer to the muzzle. For full specifications and values, see page 304. *Images courtesy Bishop's Fine Guns*

STAR MODEL FS

The Model FS was manufactured by Star, in Eibar, Spain. The particular model shown was produced from 1942 through 1967. The Model FS features a single-action trigger, six-inch barrel, blued finish, checkered plastic grips, and adjustable sights. Chambered in .22 LR, the pistol has a ten-shot magazine. Star ceased production of all guns in 1997. For full specifications and values, see page 307. *Images courtesy Bishop's Fine Guns*

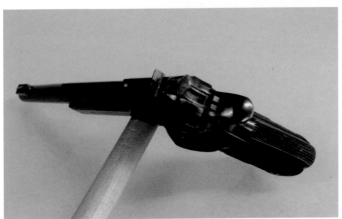

WALTHER MODEL GSP TARGET STANDARD

The GSP Target Standard is a precision target pistol chambered in either .22 LR or .32 S&W Long. This model has been manufactured by Walther, in Germany, since 1969 and was previously imported into the US by Interarms and Nygord Precision Products. Earl's Repair Service currently imports the GSP.

A letter code above the serial number on the left side of the receiver indicates the year of manufacture. This example was produced in 1985 and has been modified by a previous owner. The rear and front sights have been removed and a homemade barrel weight added toward the muzzle. Looking at the top of the receiver, it appears an optic was removed from this pistol. Due to these modifications, the value of this GSP is less than one with original sights. For full specifications and values, see page 326. *Images courtesy Bishop's Fine Guns*

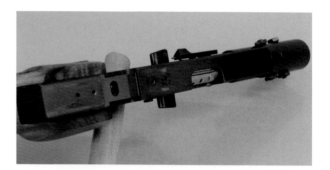

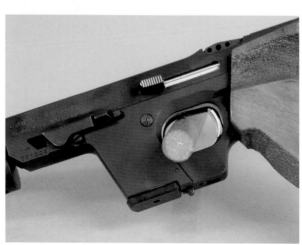

WALTHER MODEL P5

Walther designed the Model P5, in the mid-1970s, for law enforcement. Similar to the Walther P.38, the P5 uses a recoil-operated, locked-breech system and a traditional DA/SA trigger, but the P5 is compact, featuring a 3.5-inch barrel. Unlike typical semi-automatic pistols that eject empty cases from the right side of the pistol, the P5 ejects cases from the left side. The pistol was introduced in 1977 and is currently imported by Earl's Repair Service. For full specifications and values, see page 327. *Images courtesy Bishop's Fine Guns*

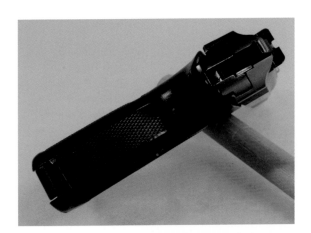

WALTHER MODEL PP SUPER

The Model PP Super was specifically designed as a law enforcement and military sidearm, in 1972. Like the Model PP, it is a .380 ACP caliber, blowback-operated pistol with a traditional DA/SA trigger. The PP Super incorporated a slide stop. Since law enforcement and militaries began adopting the 9x19mm cartridge in that era, the PP Super was dropped from production in 1979.

Only about one thousand were manufactured. A Model PP Super Ultra was chambered in 9x18mm and saw limited use with West German police. About four thousand Model PP Super Ultras were produced, making the .380 ACP PP Super more valuable. Shown is a .380 ACP PP Super model. For full specifications and values, see page 325. *Images courtesy Bishop's Fine Guns*

Handguns

A.A. (Azanza y Arrizabalaga) — Eibar, Spain

M1916 PISTOL . . . . NiB $240 Ex $140 Gd $100
Semiautomatic blowback-operated pistol. Caliber: 7.65mm, 9-rnd. magazine. 3.25-in. bbl. Wood grip, blued finish. Made 1916.

REIMS PISTOL. . . . . NiB $190 Ex $120 Gd $95
Semiautomatic blowback-operated pistol. Caliber: 6.25mm or 7.65mm. Similar to M1906 Browning pistol. Made 1914.

A.A. ARMS — Monroe, NC

AP-9 SERIES
Semiautomatic recoil-operated pistol w/polymer integral grip/frame design. Fires from a closed bolt. Caliber: 9mm Parabellum. 10- or 20-round magazine, 3- , 5- or 11-inch bbl., 11.8 inches overall w/5-inch bbl., Weight: 3.5 lbs. Fixed blade, protected post front sight adjustable for elevation, winged square notched rear. Matte phosphate/blue or nickel finish. Checkered polymer grip/frame. Made from 1988-99.
AP9 model (pre-94 w/ventilated bbl.,
  shroud) . . . . NiB $445 Ex $369 Gd $267
AP9 Mini model
  (post-94 w/o bbl., shroud) . . . . . . NiB $265 Ex $250 Gd $195
AP9 Target model
  (pre-94 w/11-inch bbl.) . . . . NiB $550 Ex $425 Gd $315
Nickel finish, add $40

ACCU-TEK — Ontario, CA

MODEL AT-9 AUTO PISTOL
Caliber: 9mm Para. 8-round magazine, Double action only. 3.2-inch bbl., 6.25 inches overall. Weight: 28 oz. Fixed blade front sight, adj. rear w/3-dot system. Firing pin block with no External safety. Stainless or black over stainless finish. Checkered black nylon grips. Announced 1992, but made from 1995-99.
Satin stainless model. . . . . NiB $347 Ex $275 Gd $210
Matte black stainless. . . . . NiB $311 Ex $250 Gd $200

MODEL AT-25 AUTO PISTOL
Similar to Model AT380 except chambered .25 ACP, 7-round magazine. Made from 1992-96.

Arrizabalaga Hijos De C 1916

Lightweight w/aluminum frame . . . NiB $164 Ex $135 Gd $115
Bright stainless (disc. 1991) . . . . . . NiB $164 Ex $135 Gd $115
Satin stainless model. . . . . NiB $164 Ex $135 Gd $115
Matte black stainless. . . . . NiB $164 Ex $135 Gd $115

MODEL AT-32 AUTO PISTOL
Similar to AT-380 except chambered .32 ACP. Made from 1990-2003.
Lightweight w/aluminum
  Frame (disc. 1991) . . . . NiB $215 Ex $160 Gd $110
Satin stainless model. . . . . NiB $215 Ex $160 Gd $110
Matte black stainless. . . . . NiB $225 Ex $170 Gd $120

MODEL AT-40 DA AUTO PISTOL
Caliber: .40 S&W. 7-round magazine, 3.2-inch bbl., 6.25 inches overall. Weight: 28 oz. Fixed blade front sight, adj. rear w/3-dot system. Firing pin block with no External safety. Stainless or black over stainless finish. Checkered black nylon grips. Announced 1992, but made from 1995-96.
Satin stainless model. . . . . NiB $290 Ex $166 Gd $129
Matte black stainless. . . . . NiB $295 Ex $177 Gd $140

MODEL AT-380 AUTO PISTOL
Caliber: .380 ACP. Five-round magazine, 2.75-inch bbl., 5.6 inches overall. Weight: 20 oz. External hammer w/slide safety. Grooved black composition grips. Alloy or stainless frame w/steel slide.

Accu-Tek Model AT .380

Accu-Tek Model BL-9

Accu-Tek HC-380SS

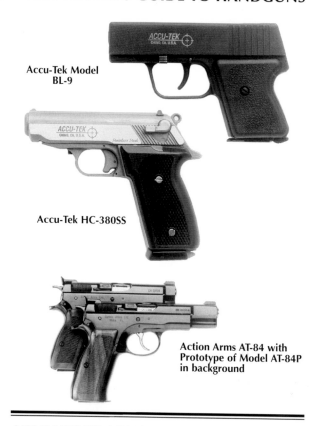

Action Arms AT-84 with Prototype of Model AT-84P in background

Black, satin aluminum or stainless finish. Made from 1992-2003.

Standard alloy frame (disc. 1992) .. NiB $291 Ex $165 Gd $145
AT-380II Satin stainless (Avail. 1990) NiB $291 Ex $165 Gd $145
Matte black stainless .... NiB $279 Ex $188 Gd $129

MODELS BL-9, BL 380 ...... NiB $200 Ex $155 Gd $130
Ultra compact DAO semiautomatic pistols. Calibers: .380 ACP, 9mm Para. 5-round magazine, 3-inch bbl., 5.6 inches overall. Weight: 24 oz. Fixed sights. Carbon steel frame and slide w/ black finish. Polymer grips. Made 1997 to 1999.

MODELS CP-9, CP-40, CP-45
Compact, double action only, semiautomatic pistols. Calibers: 9mm Parabellum, .40 S&W, .45 ACP, 8-, 7- or 6-round magazine, 3.2-inch bbl., 6.25 inches overall. Weight: 28 oz. Fixed blade front sight, adj. rear w/3-dot system. Firing-pin block with no External safety. Stainless or black/stainless finish. Checkered black nylon grips. Made1997-2002 (CP-9), 1999 (CP-40), 1996 (CP-45).
Black stainless model .... NiB $255 Ex $190 Gd $140
Satin stainless model .... NiB $255 Ex $190 Gd $140

MODEL HC-380 AUTO PISTOL .. NiB $280 Ex $235 Gd $220
Caliber: .380 ACP. 13-round magazine, 2.75-inch bbl., 6 inches overall. Weight: 28 oz. External hammer w/slide safety. Checkered black composition grips. Stainless finish. Made 1993 to 2003, Reintro. 2007.

ACTION ARMS — Philadelphia, PA
See also listings under CZ pistols. Action Arms stopped importing firearms in 1994.

AT-84S DA AUTOMATIC PISTOL NiB $530 Ex $380 Gd $320
Caliber: 9mm Para. 15-round magazine, 4.75-inch bbl., 8 inches overall. Weight: 35 oz. Fixed front sight, drift-adj. rear. Checkered walnut grips. Blued finish. Made in Switzerland from 1988 to 1989.

AT-84P DA AUTO PISTOL. ... NiB $510 Ex $365 Gd $320
Compact version of the Model AT-84. Only a few prototypes were manufactured in 1985.

AT-88P DA AUTO PISTOL. ... NiB $530 Ex $479 Gd $377
Compact version of the AT-88S w/3.7-inch bbl. Only a few prototypes of this model were manufactured in 1985. Note: The AT-88 pistol series was later manufactured by Sphinx-Muller as the AT-2000 series.

AT-88S DA AUTOMATIC. ..... NiB $550 Ex $479 Gd $377
Calibers: 9mm Para. or .41 AE, 10-round magazine, 4.6-inch bbl., 8.1 inches overall. Weight: 35.3 oz. Fixed blade front sight, adj. rear. Checkered walnut grips. Imported 1989 to 1991.

ADVANTAGE ARMS — St. Paul, MN

MODEL 422 DERRINGER. .... NiB $175 Ex $115 Gd $110
Hammerless, top-break, 4-bbl., derringer w/rotating firing pin. Calibers: .22 LR and .22 Mag., 4-round capacity, 2.5 inch bbl., 4.5 inches overall. Weight: 15 oz. Fixed sights. Walnut grips. Blued, nickel or PDQ matte black finish. Made from 1985 to 1987.

S. A. ALKARTASUNA FABRICA DE ARMAS — Guernica, Spain

"RUBY" AUTOMATIC PISTOL . NiB $355 Ex $283 Gd $225
Caliber: .32 Automatic (7.65mm), 9-round magazine, 3.63-inch bbl., 6.38 inches overall. Weight: About 34 oz. Fixed sights. Blued finish. Checkered wood or hard rubber grips. Made from 1917-22. Note: Mfd. by a number of Spanish firms, the Ruby was a secondary standard service pistol of the French Army in World Wars I and II. Specimens made by Alkartasuna bear the "Alkar" trademark.

AMERICAN ARMS — Kansas City, MO
Importer of Spanish and Italian shotguns, pistols, and rifles. Acquired by TriStar Sporting Arms, Ltd., in 2000.

BISLEY SA REVOLVER .... NiB $490 Ex $400 Gd $315
Uberti reproduction of Colt's Bisley. Caliber: .45 LC, 6-round cylinder, 4.75-, 5.5- or 7.7-inch bbl., Case-hardened steel frame. Fixed blade front sight, grooved top strap rear. Hammer block safety. Imported from 1997 to 1998

CX-22 CLASSIC DA AUTOMATIC PISTOL
Similar to Model PX-22 except w/8-round magazine, 3.33-inch bbl., 6.5 inches overall. Weight: 22 oz. Made from 1990 to 1995.

CX-22 Classic . . . . NiB $200 Ex $145 Gd $125
CXC-22 w/chrome
  Slide (disc. 1990) . . . . NiB $195 Ex $140 Gd $120

EP-380 DA AUTOMATIC PISTOL NiB $410 Ex $299 Gd $160
Caliber: .380 Automatic. 7-round magazine, 3.5-inch bbl., 6.5 inches overall. Weight: 25 oz. Fixed front sight, square notch adj. rear. Stainless finish. Checkered wood grips. Made 1989 to 1991.

ESCORT DA AUTO PISTOL. . . . NiB $315 Ex $225 Gd $155
Caliber: .380 ACP, 7-rnd. magazine, 3.38-inch bbl., 6.13 inches overall. Weight: 19 oz. Fixed, low-profile sights. Stainless steel frame, slide, and trigger. Nickel-steel bbl., Soft polymer grips. Loaded chamber indicator. Made 1995 to 1997.

MATEBA AUTO REVOLVER
Unique combination action design allows both slide and cylinder to recoil together causing cylinder to rotate. Single or double action. Caliber: .357 Mag, 6-round cylinder, 4- or 6-inch bbl., 8.77 inches overall w/4-inch bbl., Weight: 2.75 lbs. Steel/alloy frame. Ramped blade front sight, adjustable rear. Blue finish. Smooth walnut grips. Imported from 1997-99.
Mateba model (w/4-inch bbl.)NiB $1630 Ex $1130 Gd $775
Mateba model (w/6-inch bbl.)NiB $1695 Ex $1195 Gd $870

P-98 CLASSIC DA AUTO . . . . . NiB $215 Ex $140 Gd $105
Caliber: .22 LR, 8-round magazine, 5-inch bbl., 8.25 inches overall. Weight: 25 oz. Fixed front sight, square notch adj. rear. Blued finish. Serrated black polymer grips. Made 1989 to 1996.

PK-22 CLASSIC DA AUTO . . . . NiB $190 Ex $145 Gd $120
Caliber: .22 LR. 8-round magazine, 3.33-inch bbl., 6.33 inches overall. Weight: 22 oz. Fixed front sight, V-notch rear. Blued finish. Checkered black polymer grips. Made 1989 to 1996.

PX-22 DA AUTOMATIC PISTOL NiB $245 Ex $177 Gd $155
Caliber: .22 LR. 7-round magazine, 2.75-inch bbl., 5.33 inches overall. Weight: 15 oz. Fixed front sight, V-notch rear. Blued finish. Checkered black polymer grips. Made from 1989-96.

PX-25 DA AUTOMATIC PISTOL NiB $255 Ex $220 Gd $190
Same general specifications as the Model PX-22 except chambered for .25 ACP. Made from 1991-92.

REGULATOR SA REVOLVER
Similar in appearance to the Colt Single-Action Army. Calibers: .357 Mag., .44-.40, .45 Long Colt. Six-round cylinder, 4.75- or 7.5-inch bbl., blade front sight, fixed rear. Brass trigger guard/backstrap on Standard model. Casehardened steel on Deluxe model. Made from 1992 to 2000.
Standard model. . . . . NiB $279 Ex $210 Gd $125
Standard combo set (45 LC/.45 ACP
  & .44-.40/.44 Spec.) . . . . NiB $445 Ex $375 Gd $275
Deluxe model . . . . NiB $375 Ex $315 Gd $225
Deluxe combo set (.45 LC/.45
  ACP & .44-40/.44 Spl.) . . . . . . NiB $445 Ex $389 Gd $260
Stainless steel . . . . NiB $425 Ex $355 Gd $250

BUCKHORN SA REVOLVER
Similar to Regulator model except chambered .44 Mag. w/4.75-, 6- or 7.7-inch bbl., Fixed or adjustable sights. Hammer block safety. Imported 1993 to 1996.
w/standard sights . . . . NiB $425 Ex $315 Gd $255
w/adjustable sights, add $40

SPECTRE DA AUTO PISTOL
Blowback action, fires closed bolt. Calibers: 9mm Para., .40 S&W, .45 ACP, 30-round magazine, 6-inch bbl., 13.75 inches overall.

Mateba Auto Revolver

American Arms
Regulator Deluxe Model

American Derringer
Model 1

Weight: 4 lbs. 8 oz. Adj. post front sight, fixed U-notch rear. Black nylon grips. Matte black finish. Imported 1990 to 1994.
9mm Para.. . . . . NiB $545 Ex $450 Gd $260
.40 S&W (disc. 1991) . . . . NiB $515 Ex $400 Gd $300
.45 ACP. . . . . NiB $560 Ex $445 Gd $315

WOODMASTER SA AUTO PISTOL. . NiB $300 Ex $250 Gd $195
Caliber: .22 LR. 10-round magazine, 5.88-inch bbl., 10.5 inches overall. Weight: 31 oz. Fixed front sight, square-notch adj. rear. Blued finish. Checkered wood grips. Disc. 1989.

454 SSA REVOLVER . . . . NiB $795 Ex $680 Gd $530
SSA chambered 454. 6-round cylinder, 6-inch solid raised rib or 7.7-inch top-ported bbl., satin nickel finish, adj. rear sight. Hammer block safety. Imported from 1996 to 1997.

AMERICAN CLASSIC — Philippines
Manufactured in Philippines and imported by Eagle Imports, Wanamassa, New Jersey.

Amigo Series. . . . . NiB $714 Ex $690 Gd $610
Similar to Classic II except compact. Semi-automatic. SA. Caliber: .45 ACP; 8-rnd. magazine. 3.5 in.-bbl. Frame: steel. Sights: fixed, Novak style. Finish: blue, duotone, hard chrome. Grip: textured hardwood. Length: 7.25 in. Weight: 32.45 oz. Imported from 2011 to date.
hard chrome or duotone finish, add $70

COMMANDER SERIES . . . . NiB $624 Ex $560 Gd $510
1911 Commander platform. Semi-automatic. SA. Caliber: .45 ACP; 8-rnd. magazine. 5-in. bbl. Frame: steel. Sights: fixed, Novak style. Finish: blue, duotone, hard chrome. Grip: textured hardwood. Length: 7.5-in. Weight: 35.2 oz. Imported from 2011 to date.
hard chrome or duotone finish, add $70

CLASSIC SERIES . . . . NiB $589 Ex $520 Gd $480
1911 platform. Semi-automatic. SA. Caliber: .45 ACP; 8-rnd. magazine. 5-in. bbl. Frame: steel. Sights: fixed, GI style. Finish: matte blue. Grip: textured hardwood. Length: 8.25-in. Weight: 36.9 oz. Imported from 2010 to date.

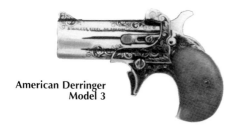

American Derringer
Model 3

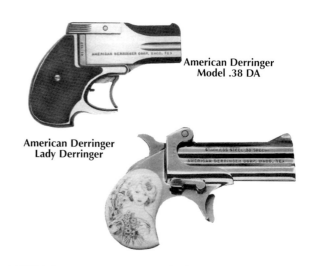

American Derringer
Model .38 DA

American Derringer
Lady Derringer

CLASSIC II SERIES . . . . **NIB $609 EX $580 GD $510**
1911 platform. Semi-automatic. SA. Caliber: 9mm or .45 ACP; 8-rnd. magazine. 5-in. bbl. Frame: steel. Sights: fixed, Novak style. Finish: blue, duotone, hard chrome. Grip: textured hardwood. Length: 8.37 in. Weight: 37.28 oz. Imported from 2010 to date.
hard chrome or duotone finish, add $70

TROPHY SERIES. . . . . **NIB $819 EX $780 GD $710**
Similar to Classic II except ambi. safety, fiber optic front sight, beavertail. Imported from 2011 to date.

AMERICAN DERRINGER CORPORATION — Waco, TX

MODEL 1 STAINLESS
Single-action similar to the Remington O/U derringer, 2-shot capacity. More than 60 calibers from .22 LR to .45-70, 3-inch bbl., 4.82 inches overall, weight: 15 oz. Automatic bbl. selection. Satin or high-polished stainless steel. Rosewood grips. Made from 1980 to date.
.45 Colt, .44-40 Win., .44
  Special, .410. . . . . **NiB $575 Ex $420 Gd $300**
.45-70, .44 Mag., 41 Mag.,
  .30-30 Win., .223 Rem. . . . . . **NiB $650 Ex $550 Gd $458**
.357 Max., .357 Mag., .45 Win.
  Mag., 9mm Para. . . . . **NiB $655 Ex $555 Gd $460**
.38 Special, .38 Super, .32 Mag.,
  .22 LR, .22 WRM. . . . . **NiB $655 Ex $560 Gd $455**

MODEL 2 STEEL "PEN" PISTOL
Calibers: .22 LR, .25 Auto, .32 Auto. Single-shot, 2-inch bbl., 5.6 inches overall (4.2 inches in pistol format). Weight: 5 oz. Stainless finish. Made from 1993 to 1994.
.22 LR . . . . **NiB $500 Ex $430 Gd $337**
.25 Auto . . . . **NiB $600 Ex $530 Gd $430**
.32 Auto . . . . **NiB $650 Ex $580 Gd $480**

MODEL 3 STAINLESS STEEL . . . . . **NiB $125 Ex $90 Gd $75**
Single-shot. Calibers: .32 Mag. or .38 Special. 2.5-inch bbl., 4.9 inches overall. Weight: 8.5 oz. Rosewood grips. Made from 1984 to 1995.

MODEL 4 DOUBLE DERRINGER
Calibers: .357 Mag., .357 Max., .44 Mag., .45 LC, .45 ACP (upper bbl., and 3-inch .410 shotshell (lower bbl.). 4.1-inch bbl, 6 inches overall. Weight: 16.5 oz. Stainless steel. Staghorn grips. Made from 1984 to date. (.44 Mag.and .45-70 disc. 2003.)
.357 Mag., .357 Max. . . . . **NiB $789 Ex $525 Gd $345**
.44 Mag., .45 LC, .45 ACP . . . . **NiB $899 Ex $555 Gd $489**
Engraved, add $150

MODEL 4 ALASKAN SURVIVAL
MODEL. . . . . **NiB $880 Ex $570 Gd $340**
Similar specifications as Model 4 except upper bbl., chambered for .45-70 or 3-inch .410 and .45 LC lower bbl. Also available in .45 Auto, .45 LC, .44 Special, .357 Mag. and .357 Max. Made from 1985 to date.

MODEL 6. . . . . **NiB $785 Ex $625 Gd $499**
Caliber: .22 Mag., .357 Mag., .45 LC, .45 ACP or .45 LC/.410 or .45 Colt. Bbl.: 6 inches, 8.2 inches overall. Weight: .22 oz. Satin or high-polished stainless steel w/rosewood grips. Made 1986 to date.
Engraved, add $150

MODEL 7
Similar as Model 1 except w/high-strength aircraft aluminum used to reduce its weight to 7.5 oz. Made from 1986 to date. (.44 Special disc. then reintroduced in 2008.)
.22 LR, .22 WMR. . . . . **NiB $575 Ex $440 Gd $280**
.44 Special, add $150

MODEL 8 . . . . **NiB $920 Ex $530 Gd $280**
Calibers: .45 LC/.410, 8-inch bbl., 9.8 inches overall. Weight: 24 oz. Rosewood grips. New 1997.
Engraved (Made from 1997 to 1998), add $1000

MODEL 10
Similar as the Model 7 except chambered for .38 Special, .45 ACP or .45 LC with aluminum grip frame
.38 Special or .45 ACP . . . . **NiB $559 Ex $365 Gd $295**
.45 LC. . . . . **NiB $500 Ex $395 Gd $279**

MODEL 11 . . . . **NiB $559 Ex $490 Gd $369**
Same general specifications as Model 7 except with a matte gray finish only, weight: 11 oz. Made from 1980 to 2003.

25 AUTOMATIC PISTOL
Calibers: .25 ACP or .250 Mag. Bbl.: 2.1 inches, 4.4 inches overall. Weight: 15.5 oz. Smooth rosewood grips. Limited production.
.25 ACP blued
  (est. production 50) . . . . **NiB $650 Ex $540 Gd $385**
.25 ACP stainless
  (est. production 400) . . . . . . **NiB $510 Ex $425 Gd $380**
.250 Mag. stainless
  (est. production 100) . . . . . . **NiB $675 Ex $530 Gd $407**

DA 38 DOUBLE ACTION DERRINGER
Hammerless, double action, double bbl (o/u). Calibers: .22LR, .357 Mag., .38 Special, 9mm Para., .40 S&W. 3-inch bbls., satin stainless with aluminum grip frame. DA trigger, hammer-block thumb safety. Weight: 14.5 oz. Made from 1990 to date.
.22LR (1996-03),
  .38 Special, 9mm Para., ... **NiB $615 Ex $415 Gd $230**
.357 Mag. or .40 cal. (Disc. 2012). . **NiB $710 Ex $445 Gd $265**
Lady Derringer (faux ivory grips, made from 1992-94), add ..$40

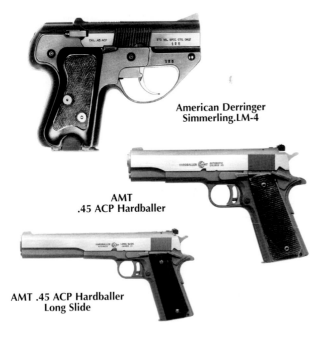

American Derringer
Simmerling.LM-4

AMT
.45 ACP Hardballer

AMT .45 ACP Hardballer
Long Slide

COP DA DERRINGER . . . . **NiB $660 Ex $510 Gd $291**
Hammerless, double-action, 4-bbl., derringer. Caliber: .357 Mag. 3.15-inch bbl., 5.5 inches overall. Weight: 16 oz. Blade front sight, open notched rear. Rosewood grips. Intro. 1990, disc. 1994.

LM-5 AUTOMATIC PISTOL
Calibers: .25 ACP, .32 H&R Mag. or .380 Automatic. Bbl.: 2 inches, 3 inches overall. Weight: 15 oz. Stainless steel construction, smooth wood grips. Limited production.
.25 ACP or 32 H&R Mag. . . . . . **NiB $650 Ex $540 Gd $385**
.380 Automatic (Disc. 1999). . . NiB $425 Ex $380 Gd $300

LADY DERRINGER . . . . **NiB $769 Ex $610 Gd $499**
Similar specifications as Model 1 except w/custom-tuned action fitted w/scrimshawed synthetic ivory grips. Calibers: .32 H&R Mag., .32 Special, .38 Special (additional calibers on request). Deluxe Grade engraved and highly polished w/French fitted jewelry box. Made from 1991 to date.
Deluxe Engraved (Disc. 1994) . NiB $699 Ex $470 Gd $355
Gold Engraved (Disc. 1994) . . . . **Rare**
Lady II (aluminum frame,
made 1999-03) . . . . **NiB $400 Ex $350 Gd $255**

MINI-COP DA DERRINGER . . . **NiB $325 Ex $200 Gd $145**
Similar general specifications as the COP except chambered for .22 WMR. Made from 1990 to 1995.

SEMMERLING LM-4
Manually operated repeater. Calibers: .45 ACP or 9mm, 4-round (.45 ACP) or 6-round magazine (9mm), 3.6-inch bbl., 5.2 inches overall. Weight: 24 oz. Made from 1997 to date. Limited availability.
Blued or Stainless steel . . . **NiB $4350 Ex $3200 Gd $2020**

TEXAS COMMEMORATIVE . . . **NiB $380 Ex $350 Gd $300**
Similar to Model 1 except w/solid brass frame, stainless bbls. and stag grips. Calibers: .22 LR, .32 Mag., .38 Special, .44-40 Win. or .45 LC. Made from 1991 to date.
.44-40 Win. or .45 LC . . . . **NiB $800 Ex $750 Gd $695**

125TH ANNIVERSARY
Same general specifications as Model 1 except w/solid brass frame, stainless bbls. and stag grips. Calibers: .38 Special, .44-40 Win. or .45 LC. Disc. 1993. Limited production.
.38 Special . . . . **NiB $337 Ex $320 Gd $295**
.44-40 Win. or .45 LC . . . . **NiB $400 Ex $395 Gd $375**

AMERICAN FIREARMS MFG. CO., INC. — San Antonio, TX

25 AUTO PISTOL
Caliber: .25 Auto. 8-round magazine, 2.1-inch bbl., 4.4 inches overall. Weight: 14.5 oz. Fixed sights. Stainless or blued ordnance steel. Smooth walnut grips. Made from 1966 to 1974.
Stainless steel model . . . . **NiB $215 Ex $190 Gd $110**
Blued steel model . . . . **NiB $200 Ex $145 Gd $110**

380 AUTO PISTOL . . . . **NiB $735 Ex $540 Gd $389**
Caliber: .380 Auto. 8-round magazine, 3.5-inch bbl., 5.5 inches overall. Weight: 20 oz. Stainless steel. Smooth walnut grips. Made from 1972 to 1974.

AMT (ARCADIA MACHINE & TOOL) —Trademark owed by Crusader Gun Company Houston, TX

Previously Galena Industries, Strugis, SD; and Irwindale Arms, Inc., Irwindale, CA

NOTE: *The AMT Backup II automatic pistol was introduced in 1993 as a continuation of the original .380 Backup with a double action trigger and a redesigned double safety. AMT Backup and Automag II line of handguns is currently marketed by High Standard Manufacturing, Houston, TX.*

45 ACP HARDBALLER . . . . **NiB $545 Ex $430 Gd $345**
Colt 1991 style. Caliber: .45 ACP, 7-round magazine, 5-inch bbl., 8.5 inches overall. Weight: 39 oz. Adj. or fixed sights. Serrated matte slide rib w/loaded chamber indicator. Extended combat safety, adj. trigger and long grip safety. Wraparound Neoprene grips. Stainless steel. Made 1978-2001.
Long slide conversion kit (disc. 1997), add. $315

45 ACP HARDBALLER LONG SLIDE
Similar to the standard Hardballer except w/7-inch bbl. and slide. Also chambered for .400 Cor-Bon. Made from 1980-2001
.45 ACP long slide. . . . . **NiB $529 Ex $435 Gd $320**
.400 Cor-Bon long
slide (Intro.1998) . . . . **NiB $535 Ex $425 Gd $300**
5-inch conversion kit (disc. 1997), add. $315

45 ACP STANDARD GOVERNMENT MODEL
AUTO PISTOL. . . . . **NiB $460 Ex $395 Gd $339**
Caliber: .45 ACP, 7-round magazine, 5-inch bbl., 8.5 inches overall. Weight: 38 oz. Fixed sights. Wraparound Neoprene grip. Made from 1979 to date.

AUTOMAG II AUTOMATIC PISTOL . . . **NiB $845 Ex $575 Gd $360**
Caliber: .22 Mag., 7- or 9-round magazine, bbl. lengths: 3.38, 4.5-, 6-inch. Weight: 32 oz. Fully adj. Millett sights. Stainless finish. Smooth black composition grips. Made from 1986 to 2001, reintro. 2004.

AUTOMAG III AUTOMATIC PISTOL . . **NiB $600 Ex $495 Gd $365**
Calibers: .30 M1 or 9mm Win. Mag., 8-round magazine., 6.38-inch bbl., 10.5 inches overall. Weight: 43 oz. Millet adj.

sights. Stainless finish. Carbon fiber grips. Made from 1992 to 2001.

AUTOMAG IV AUTOMATIC PISTOL . . NiB $610 Ex $520 Gd $395
Calibers: 10mm or .45 Win. Mag., 8- or 7-round magazine, 6.5- or 8.63-inch bbl., 10.5 inches overall. Weight: 46 oz. Millet adj. sights. Stainless finish. Carbon fiber grips. Made from 1992-2001.

AUTOMAG V AUTOMATIC PISTOL . . NiB $1000 Ex $855 Gd $775
Caliber: .50 A.E., 5-round magazine, 7-inch bbl., 10.5 inches overall. Weight: 46 oz. Custom adj. sights. Stainless finish. Carbon fiber grips. Made from 1994 to 1995.

BACKUP (SMALL FRAME) AUTOMATIC PISTOL
Caliber: .22 LR, .380 ACP, 8-round (.22LR) or 5-round (.380 ACP) magazine, 2.5-inch bbl., 5 inches overall. Weight: 18 oz. (.380 ACP). Open sights. Carbon fiber or walnut grips. Stainless steel finish. Made from 1990 to 1987.
.22 LR (disc. 1987) . . . . NiB $495 Ex $335 Gd $188
.380 ACP (disc. 2000, reintro.
    2004, disc. 2010) . . . . NiB $450 Ex $305 Gd $171

BACKUP II . . . . NiB $300 Ex $260 Gd $200
Caliber: .380 ACP, 5-round magazine, 2.5-inch bbl., 5 inches overall. Weight: 18 oz. Single action. Open sights. Stainless steel finish. Carbon-fiber grips. Made from 1993 to 1998.

BACKUP (LARGE FRAME) AUTO PISTOL
Calibers: .357 SIG, .38 Super, 9mm Para., .40 Cor-Bon, .40 S&W, .45 ACP. Six-round (.357 SIG, .38 Super 9mm) or 5-round (.40 Cor-Bon, .40 S&W, .45 ACP) magazine, 2.5-inch bbl., 5.75-inches overall. Weight: 23 oz. Double action only. Open fixed sights. Stainless steel finish. Carbon fiber grips. Made from 1992 to date.
.357 SIG, .38 Super, 9mm.40 S&W,
    .45 ACP . . . . NiB $530 Ex $400 Gd $300
.40 Cor-Bon (disc. 2010) . . . . . NiB $630 Ex $500 Gd $400

BULL'S EYE TARGET MODEL . NiB $695 Ex $550 Gd $415
Similar to the standard Hardballer. Caliber: .40 S&W, 8-round magazine, 5-inch bbl., 8.5 inches overall. Weight: 38 oz. Millet adjustable sights. Wide adj. trigger. Wraparound Neoprene grips. Made from 1990 to 1991.

JAVELINA . . . . NiB $695 Ex $550 Gd $420
Caliber: 10mm, 8-round magazine, 7-inch bbl., 10.5 inches overall. Weight: 48 oz. Long grip safety, beveled magazine well, wide adj. trigger. Millet adj. sights. Wraparound Neoprene grips. Stainless finish. Made from 1991 to 1993.

LIGHTNING AUTO PISTOL
Caliber: .22 LR. 10-round magazine, 5-, 6.5-, 8.5-, 10-inch bbl., 10.75 inches overall (6.5-inch bbl.). Weight: 45 oz. (6.5-inch bbl.). Millett adj. sights. Checkered rubber grips. Stainless finish. Made from 1984 to 1987.
Standard model. . . . . NiB $455 Ex $315 Gd $210
Bull's-Eye model
    (6.5-inch bull bbl.) . . . . NiB $520 Ex $355 Gd $240

ON DUTY DA PISTOL
Calibers: .40 S&W, 9mm Para., .45 ACP. 15-round (9mm), 13-shot (.40 S&W) or 9-round (.45 ACP) magazine, 4.5-inch bbl., 7.75 inches overall. Weight: 32 oz. Hard anodized aluminum frame. Stainless steel slide and bbl., Carbon fiber grips. Made from 1991 to 1994.
9mm or .40 S&W . . . . NiB $465 Ex $316 Gd $235
.45 ACP. . . . . NiB $515 Ex $400 Gd $265

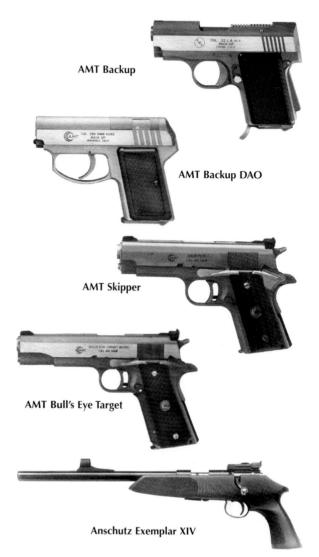

AMT Backup

AMT Backup DAO

AMT Skipper

AMT Bull's Eye Target

Anschutz Exemplar XIV

SKIPPER AUTO PISTOL. . . . . . . NiB $465 Ex $359 Gd $325
Calibers: .40 S&W or .45 ACP, 7-round magazine, 4.25-inch bbl., 7.5 inches overall. Weight: 33 oz. Millet adj. sights. Walnut grips. Matte finish stainless. Made from 1990 to 1992.

ANSCHUTZ — Ulm, Germany

Mfd. by J.G. Anschutz GmbH Jagd und Sportwaffenfabrik.
Currently imported by Champion's Choice, La Vergne, TN; previously imported by Accuracy International, Boseman, MT and AcuSport Corporation, Bellefontaine, OH

MODEL 64P
Calibers: .22 LR or .22 WMR, 5- or 4-round magazine, 10-inch bbl., 64MS action w/two-stage trigger. Target sights optional. Rynite black synthetic stock. Imported from 1998 to 2003.
.22 LR . . . . NiB $490 Ex $305 Gd $225
.22 WMR . . . . NiB $515 Ex $249 Gd $195
w/tangent sights, add $100

EXEMPLAR (1416P/1451P) BOLT-ACTION PISTOL
Caliber: .22 LR, single-shot or 5-round magazine, 7- or 10-inch bbl., 19 inches overall (10-inch bbl.). Weight: 3.33

lbs. Match 64 action. Slide safety. Hooded ramp post front sight, adjustable open notched rear. European walnut contoured grip. Exemplar made from 1987-95 and 1400 series made from 1997. Disc. 1997. Note: The .22 WMR chambering was advertised but never manufactured.

Exemplar w/7- or 10-inch bbl . . . NiB $420 Ex $295 Gd $185
Left-hand model (disc. 1997) . . NiB $535 Ex $455 Gd $365
Model 1451P (single-shot) . . . . NiB $450 Ex $365 Gd $285
Model 1416P (5-round repeater)NiB $1150 Ex $869 Gd $610

EXEMPLAR HORNET . . . . . . NiB $1015 Ex $815 Gd $700
Based on the Anschutz Match 54 action, tapped and grooved for scope mounting with no open sights. Caliber: .22 Hornet, 5-round magazine, 10-inch bbl., 20 inches overall. Weight: 4.35 lbs. Checkered European walnut grip. Winged safety. Made from 1990 to 1995.

EXEMPLAR XIV . . . . NiB $875 Ex $560 Gd $465
Same general specifications as the standard Exemplar bolt-action pistol except with 14-inch bbl., weight: 4.15 lbs. Made from 1989 to 1995.

ARMALITE, INC. — Genesco, IL
Formerly Costa Mesa, CA.

AR-24 AUTOMATIC PISTOL . . . NiB $550 Ex $380 Gd $300
Full size automatic, mfg. by Sarzsilmaz in Turkey. Caliber: 9mm Para, 15-round magazine, 4.67-inch bbl., 8.3 inches overall. Parkerized finish, checkered synthetic grips. Imported from 2007 to 2013.
AR-24-15C Combat Custom
(adj. rear sight) . . . . NiB $630 Ex $430 Gd $375
AR-24K-13 Compact
(3.89-inch bbl.) . . . . NiB $560 Ex $400 Gd $380
AR-24K-13 Combat Custom Compact (adj. rear sight,
3.89-inch bbl.) . . . . NiB $630 Ex $430 Gd $375

ARMSCOR (Arms Corp.)—Manila, Philippines
Currently imported by Armscor Precision Int'l. Pahrump, NV. Previously Imported by K.B.I., Harrisburg, PA., 1991–95 by Ruko Products, Inc., Buffalo NY., Armscor Precision, San Mateo, CA.

MODEL M1911-A1 . . . . NiB $400 Ex $320 Gd $275
Semi-automatic pistol. 1911 style. Caliber: .45 ACP. Eight-round magazine, 5-inch bbl., 8.75 inches overall. Weight: 38 oz. Blade front sight, drift adjustable rear w/3-dot system. Skeletonized tactical hammer and trigger. Extended slide release and beavertail grip safety. Parkerized finish. Checkered composition or wood stocks. Imported from 1996 to 1997. Reintro. 2001 to 2008.

MODEL M1911-A1 COMMANDER . . NiB $410 Ex $300 Gd $220
Caliber: .45 ACP. Similar to M1911-A-1 except with Commander configuration and 4-inch bbl. Rear slide serrations only. Disc. 1991.
Two-tone finish, add $50
Stainless, add $95

MODEL M1911-A1 OFFICER . . NiB $425 Ex $350 Gd $265
Caliber: .45 ACP. Similar to M1911-A-1 except with Combat configuration. Bbl.:3.5 inches. Checkered hardwood grips. Weight: 2.16 pounds. Disc. 1991.
Two-tone finish, add $50
Stainless, add $95

MODEL M1911-A1
MEDALLION SERIES . . . . NiB $495 Ex $360 Gd $285
Caliber: 9mm Para., .40 S&W, .45 ACP. Standard or Tactical, blue finish standard. Bbl.: 5 inches. Custom model with match barrel, checkered wood Pachmayr grips. Disc. 1991.
Two-tone finish (Tactical), add $200
Chrome (Tactical), add $250

MODEL 200 DC/TC DA REVOLVER . . . NiB $240 Ex $160 Gd $110
Caliber: .38 Special. Six-round cylinder, 2.5-, 4-, or 6-inch bbl.; 7.3, 8.8, or 11.3 inches overall. Weight: 22, 28, or 34 oz. Ramp front and fixed rear sights. Checkered mahogany or rubber grips. Disc. 1991.

MODEL 202A REVOLVER . . . . . NiB $165 Ex $110 Gd $95
Caliber: .38 Special. Similar to Model 200 (DC) revolver except does not have barrel shroud. Disc. 1991.

MODEL 206 REVOLVER . . . . NiB $250 Ex $203 Gd $170
Caliber: .38 Special. Similar to Model 200 (DC) revolver except has a 2.87-in. bbl. Weight: 24 oz. Disc. 1991.

MODEL 210 REVOLVER . . . . . . NiB $219 Ex $170 Gd $135
Caliber: .38 Special. Similar to Model 200 (DC) except has a 4-inch ventilated rib bbl., adj. rear sight. Weight: 28 oz. Disc. 1991.

ASAI AG — Advanced Small Arms Industries Solothurn, Switzerland
Currently imported by Magnum Research Inc., Minneapolis, MN.
See listings under Magnum Research Pistols

ASTRA — Guernica, Spain
Manufactured by Unceta y Compania. Currently not imported to U.S., previously imported by E.A.A. Corporation, Sharpes, FL.

MODEL 357 DA REVOLVER . . . NiB $385 Ex $299 Gd $230
Caliber: .357 Magnum. Six-round cylinder. 3-, 4-, 6-, 8.5-inch bbl., 11.25 inches overall (with 6-inch bbl.). Weight: 42 oz. (with 6-inch bbl.). Ramp front sight, adj. rear sight. Blued finish. Checkered wood grips. Imported from 1972 to 1988.

MODEL 44 DA REVOLVER
Similar to Astra .357 except chambered for .44 Magnum. Six- or 8.5-inch bbl., 11.5 inches overall (6-inch bbl.). Weight: 44 oz. (6-inch bbl.). Imported from 1980 to 1993.
Blued finish (disc. 1987) . . . . . . NiB $375 Ex $290 Gd $245
Stainless finish (disc. 1993) . . . . NiB $395 Ex $320 Gd $255

MODEL 41 DA REVOLVER . . . . NiB $375 Ex $295 Gd $235
Same general specifications as Model 44 except in .41 Mag. Imported from 1980-85.

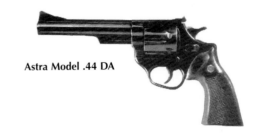

Astra Model .44 DA

MODEL 45 DA REVOLVER . . . . NiB $366 Ex $275 Gd $215
Similar to Astra .357 except chambered for .45 LC or .45 ACP. Six- or 8.5-inch bbl., 11.5 inches overall (with 6-inch bbl.). Weight: 44 oz. (6-inch bbl.). Imported from 1980-87.

MODEL 200 FIRECAT
VEST POCKET AUTO PISTOL . . NiB $320 Ex $260 Gd $205
Caliber: .25 Automatic (6.35mm). Six-round magazine, 2.25-inch bbl., 4.38 inches overall. Weight: 11.75 oz. Fixed sights. Blued finish. Plastic grips. Made 1920 to date. U.S. importation disc. in 1968.

MODEL 202 FIRECAT
VEST POCKET AUTO PISTOL . . NiB $590 Ex $475 Gd $400
Same general specifications as the Model 200 except chromed and engraved w/pearl grips. U.S. importation disc. 1968.

MODEL 400 AUTO PISTOL . . . NiB $725 Ex $595 Gd $350
Caliber: 9mm Bayard Long (.38 ACP, 9mm Browning Long, 9mm Glisenti, 9mm Para. and 9mm Steyr cartridges may be used interchangeably in this pistol because of its chamber design). Nine-round magazine., 6-inch bbl., 10 inches overall. Weight: 35 oz. Fixed sights. Blued finish. Plastic grips. Made 1922-45. Note: This pistol, as well as Astra Models 600 and 3000, is a modification of the Browning Model 1912.
Nazis Mfg. (S/N range 92,850-98,850), add 100%

MODEL 600 MIL./POLICE-TYPE
AUTO PISTOL . . . . NiB $565 Ex $425 Gd $300
Calibers: .32 Automatic (7.65mm), 9mm Para. Magazine: 10-round (.32 cal.) or 8-round (9mm)., 5.25-inch bbl., 8 inches overall. Weight: About 33 oz. Fixed sights. Blued finish. Checkered wood or plastic grips. Made from 1944 to 1945.
Nazis markings, add 100%

MODEL 800 CONDOR
MILITARY AUTO PISTOL . . NiB $2101 Ex $1754 Gd $1512
Similar to Models 400 and 600 except has an external hammer. Caliber: 9mm Para. Eight-round magazine, 5.25-inch bbl., 8.25 inches overall. Weight: 32.5 oz. Fixed sights. Blued finish. Plastic grips. Imported from 1958 to 1965.

MODEL 2000 CAMPER
AUTOMATIC PISTOL . . . . NiB $395 Ex $279 Gd $215
Same as Model 2000 Cub except chambered for .22 Short only, has 4-inch bbl., overall length, 6.25 inches, weight: 11.5 oz. Imported from 1955 to 1960.

MODEL 2000 CUB
POCKET AUTO PISTOL . . . . . . NiB $363 Ex $297 Gd $214
Calibers: .22 Short, .25 Auto. Six-round magazine, 2.25-inch bbl., 4.5 inches overall. Weight: About 11 oz. Fixed sights. Blued or chromed finish. Plastic grips. Made 1954 to date. U.S. importation disc. 1968.

MODEL 3000
POCKET AUTO PISTOL . . . . . NiB $1001 Ex $654 Gd $467
Calibers: .22 LR, .32 Automatic (7.65mm), .380 Auto (9mm Short). Ten-round magazine (.22 cal.), 7-round (.32 cal.), 6-round (.380 cal.). Four-inch bbl., 6.38 inches overall. Weight: About 22 oz. Fixed sights. Blued finish. Plastic grips. Made from 1947 to 1956.

MODEL 3003
POCKET AUTO PISTOL . . . . NiB $2420 Ex $1419 Gd $880
Same general specifications as the Model 3000 except chromed and engraved w/pearl grips. Disc. 1956.

Astra Model 3003
Pocket

Astra Model
4000 Falcon

MODEL 4000
FALCON AUTO PISTOL . . . . . . NiB $675 Ex $495 Gd $320
Similar to Model 3000 except has an External hammer. Calibers: .22 LR, .32 Automatic (7.65mm), .380 Auto (9mm Short). Ten-round magazine (.22 LR), 8-round (.32 Auto), 7-round (.380 Auto), 3.66-inch bbl., 6.5-inches overall. Weight: 20 oz. (.22 cal.) or 24.75 oz. (.32 and .380). Fixed sights. Blued finish. Plastic grips. Made from 1956 to 1971.

CONSTABLE DA AUTO PISTOL
Calibers: .22 LR, .32 Automatic (7.65mm), .380 Auto (9mm Short). Magazine capacity: 10-round (.22 LR), 8-round (.32), 7-round (.380). 3.5-inch bbl., 6.5 inches overall. Weight: about 24 oz. Blade front sight, windage adj. rear. Blued or chromed finish. Imported from 1965 to 1992.
Stainless finish. . . . . NiB $395 Ex $290 Gd $229
Blued engraved finish . . . . NiB $605 Ex $419 Gd $297
Chrome finish (disc. 1990) . . . . NiB $500 Ex $335 Gd $234

MODEL A-60 . . . . NiB $415 Ex $285 Gd $210
Similar to the Constable except in .380 only, w/13-round magazine and slide-mounted ambidExtrous safety. Blued finish only. Imported from 1980 to 1991.

MODEL A-70 COMPACT AUTO PISTOL
Calibers: 9mm Para., .40 S&W. Eight-round (9mm) or 7-round (.40 S&W) magazine., 3.5-inch bbl., 6.5 inches overall. Blued, nickel or stainless finish. Weight: 29.3 oz. Imported 1992–96.
Blued finish. . . . . NiB $414 Ex $295 Gd $210
Nickel finish . . . . NiB $424 Ex $345 Gd $229
Stainless finish. . . . . NiB $593 Ex $430 Gd $372

MODEL A-75 ULTRALIGHT . . . NiB $400 Ex $299 Gd $234
Similar to the standard Model 75 except 9mm only w/24-oz. aluminum alloy frame. Imported from 1994 to 1997.

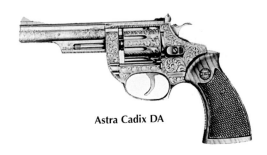

Astra Cadix DA

Astra Constable DA

Auto-Ordnance 1927 A-1
Deluxe w/drum magazine

MODEL A-80 AUTO PISTOL. . . NiB $450 Ex $404 Gd $265
Calibers: 9mm Para., .38 Super, .45 ACP. 15-round or 9-round (.45 ACP). magazine. Bbl.: 3.75 inches., 7 inches overall. Weight: 36 oz. Imported from 1982 to 1989.

MODEL A-90 DA
AUTOMATIC PISTOL. . . . . NiB $505 Ex $400 Gd $245
Calibers: 9mm Para., .45 ACP. 15-round (9mm) or 9-round (.45 ACP) magazine, 3.75-inch bbl., 7 inches overall. Weight: about 40 oz. Fixed sights. Blued finish. Checkered plastic grips. Imported 1985 to 1990.

MODEL A-100 DA AUTO PISTOL
Same general specifications as the Model A-90 except selective double action chambered for 9mm Para., .40 S&W or .45 ACP. Imported from 1991 to 1997.
Blued finish. . . . . .NiB $470 Ex $310 Gd $249
Nickel finish . . . . .NiB $495 Ex $340 Gd $287
For night sights, add $100

CADIX DA REVOLVER
Calibers: .22 LR, .38 Special. Nine-round (.22 LR) or 5-round (.38 cal.) cylinder. Four- or 6-inch bbl., Weight: About 27 oz. (6-inch bbl.). Ramp front sight, adj. rear sight. Blued finish. Plastic grips. Imported from 1960-68.
Standard model. . . . . .NiB $275 Ex $229 Gd $160

Lightly engraved model. . . . . . .NiB $380 Ex $255 Gd $200
Heavily engraved model (shown) . .NiB $700 Ex $515 Gd $395

MODEL A-75 DECOCKER AUTO PISTOL
Similar to the Model 70 except in 9mm, .40 S&W and .45 ACP w/ decocking system and contoured pebble-tExtured grips. Imported from 1993-97.
Blued finish, 9mm or .40 S&W . . . .NiB $395 Ex $320 Gd $235
Nickel finish, 9mm or .40 S&W . . .NiB $405 Ex $330 Gd $245
Stainless, 9mm or .40 S&W . . . . NiB $410 Ex $305 Gd $197
Blued finish, .45 ACP . . . . NiB $395 Ex $315 Gd $235
Nickel finish, .45 ACP. . . . . NiB $405 Ex $350 Gd $275
Stainless, .45 ACP. . . . . NiB $420 Ex $365 Gd $290

AUTAUGA ARMS — Prattville, AL

MODEL 32 (MK II)
DAO AUTOMATIC PISTOL. . . . NiB $367 Ex $309 Gd $267
Caliber: .32 ACP. Six-round magazine, 2-inch bbl., weight: 11.36 oz. Double action only. Stainless steel. Black polymer grips. Made from 1996 to 2000.

AUTO-ORDNANCE CORPORATION — Division of Kahr Arms, Worchester, MA

Previously West Hurley, New York.

1911 A1 GOVERNMENT AUTO. . . NiB $515 Ex $375 Gd $300
Copy of Colt 1911 A1 semiautomatic pistol. Calibers: 9mm Para., .38 Super, 10mm, .45 ACP. 9-round (9mm, .38 Super) or 7-round 10mm, .45 ACP) magazine. 5-in. bbl., 8.5 inches overall. Weight: 39 oz. Fixed blade front sight, rear adj. Blued, satin nickel or Duo-Tone finish. Checkered plastic grips. Made 1983 to 1999.

1911 A1 WWII . . . . NiB $588 Ex $525 Gd $300
Similar to 1911 A1 Government model except w/parkerized or matte black finish, checkered plastic or wood. 1992 to date.
1911 A1 100th Anniversary (laser engraved), add 20%

1911A1 .40 S&W PISTOL . . . . . NiB $498 Ex $399 Gd $309
Similar to the Model 1911 A1 except has 4.5-inch bbl., w/7.75-inch overall length. Eight-round magazine, weight: 37 oz. Blade front and adj. rear sights w/3-dot system. Checkered black rubber wraparound grips. Made 1991–99.

1911 A1 "THE GENERAL". . . . . NiB $441 Ex $351 Gd $253
Caliber: .45 ACP. Seven-round magazine, 4.5-inch bbl., 7.75 inches overall. Weight: 37 oz. Blued nonglare finish. Made 1992 to 1999.

1927 A-1 DELUXE SEMIAUTOMATIC PISTOL
Similar to Thompson Model 1928A submachine gun except has no provision for automatic firing and does not have detachable buttstock. Caliber: .45 ACP, 5-, 15-, 20- and 30-round detachable box magazines. 30-round drum also available. 13-inch finned bbl., 26 inches overall. Weight: About 6.75 lbs. Adj. rear sight, blade front. Blued finish. Walnut grips. Made from 1977 to 1994.
w/box magazine . . . . .NiB $1412 Ex $1078 Gd $764
w/drum magazine, add $300

ZG-51 PIT BULL PISTOL. . . . . .NiB $435 Ex $325 Gd $288
Caliber: .45 ACP. Seven-round magazine, 3.5-inch bbl., 7 inches overall. Weight: 32 oz. Fixed front sight, square-notch rear. Blued finish. Checkered plastic grips. Made from 1991 to 1999.

LES BAER — Le Claire, IA
Previously Hilldale, Illinois.

1911 CONCEPT SERIES AUTOMATIC PISTOL
Similar to Government 1911 built on steel or alloy full-size or compact frame. Caliber: .45 ACP. Seven-round magazine, 4.25- or 5-inch bbl. Weight: 34 to 37 oz. Adjustable low mount combat or BoMar target sights. Blued, matte black, Two-Tone or stainless finish. Checkered wood grips. Made from 1996 to date.

Concept models I & II . . . . . NiB $1402 Ex $1116 Gd $797
Concept models III, IV & VII . . . . NiB $1556 Ex $1414 Gd $1204
Concept models V, VI & VIII . . . NiB $1538 Ex $1369 Gd $863
Concept models IX & X . . . . NiB $1529 Ex $1237 Gd $1045

1911 PREMIER SERIES AUTOMATIC PISTOL
Similar to the Concept series except also chambered for .38 Super, 9x23 Win., .400 Cor-Bon and .45 ACP. 5- or 6-inch bbl. Weight: 37 to .40 oz. Made from 1996 to date.

Premier II
  (9x23 w/5-inch bbl.) . . . . NiB $1760 Ex $1479 Gd $1331
Premier II (.400
  Cor-Bon w/5-inch bbl.) . . NiB $1540 Ex $1369 Gd $1292
Premier II (.45 ACP
  w/5-inch bbl.). . . . . NiB $1446 Ex $1314 Gd $1098
Premier II (.45 ACP
  S/S w/5-inch bbl.) . . . . . . NiB $1531 Ex $1265 Gd $875
Premier II (.45/.400
  combo w/5-inch bbl.). . . . NiB $1749 Ex $1457 Gd $1281
Premier II (.38
  Super w/6-inch bbl.) . . . . NiB $1996 Ex $1864 Gd $1490
Premier II (.400
  Cor-Bon w/6-inch bbl.) . . NiB $1798 Ex $1529 Gd $1364
Premier II (.45 ACP
  w/6-inch bbl.). . . . . NiB $1672 Ex $1501 Gd $1408

S.R.P. AUTOMATIC PISTOL
Similar to F.B.I. Contract "Swift Response Pistol" built on a (customer-supplied) Para-Ordnance over-sized frame or a 1911 full-size or compact frame. Caliber: .45 ACP. Seven-round magazine, 5-inch bbl., weight: 37 oz. Ramp front and fixed rear sights, w/Tritium Sight insert.

SRP 1911 Government
  or Commanche model . . . NiB $2295 Ex $2084 Gd $1905
SRP P-12 model . . . . NiB $2619 Ex $2346 Gd $2199
SRP P-13 model . . . . NiB $2404 Ex $2178 Gd $2021
SRP P-14 model . . . . NiB $2320 Ex $2109 Gd $1317

1911 ULTIMATE MASTER COMBAT SERIES
Model 1911 in Combat Competition configuration. Calibers: .38 Super, 9x23 Win., .400 Cor-Bon and .45 ACP. Five- or 6-inch NM bbl., weight: 37 to 40 oz. Made from 1996 to date.

Ultimate MC (.38 or 9x23
  w/5-inch bbl.). . . . . NiB $2580 Ex $2010 Gd $1400
Ultimate MC (.400 Cor-Bon
  w/5-inch bbl.). . . . . NiB $2480 Ex $1835 Gd $1300
Ultimate MC (.45 ACP
  w/5-inch bbl.). . . . . NiB $2430 Ex $1910 Gd $1300
Ultimate MC (.38 or 9x23
  w/6-inch bbl.). . . . . NiB $2680 Ex $2025 Gd $1495
Ultimate MC (.400 Cor-Bon
  w/6-inch bbl.). . . . . NiB $2630 Ex $2060 Gd $1450
Ultimate MC (.45 ACP
  w/6-inch bbl.). . . . . NiB $2580 Ex $2010 Gd $1400
Ultimate "Steel Special"

Auto-Ordnance
ZG-51 Pit Bull

  (.38 Super Bianchi SPS) . . .NiB $2855 Ex $2310 Gd $1661
Ultimate "PARA" (.38, 9x23
  or .45 IPSC comp) . . . . . . NiB $2871 Ex $2326 Gd $1650
w/Triple-Port Compensator, add. $100

1911 CUSTOM CARRY SERIES AUTOMATIC PISTOL
Model 1911 in Combat Carry configuration built on steel or alloy full-size or compact frame. 4.5- or 5-inch NM bbl., chambered for .45 ACP. Weight: 34 to 37 oz.

Custom carry (steel frame
  w/4.24- or 5-inch bbl.). . .NiB $1728 Ex $1555 Gd $1166
Custom carry (alloy frame
  w/4.24-inch bbl.) . . . . . . .NiB $2039 Ex $2029 Gd $1521

BAUER FIREARMS CORP. — Fraser, MI

.25 AUTOMATIC PISTOL . . . . . . NiB $175 Ex $125 Gd $95
Stainless steel. Caliber: .25 Automatic. Six-round magazine, 2.13-inch bbl., 4 inches overall. Weight: 10 oz. Fixed sights. Checkered walnut or simulated pearl grips. Made from 1972 to 1984.

BAYARD — Herstal, Belgium
Mfd. by Anciens Etablissements Pieper.

MODEL 1908
POCKET AUTOMATIC PISTOL . NiB $455 Ex $300 Gd $195
Calibers: .25 Automatic (6.35mm). .32 Automatic (7.65mm), .380 Automatic (9mm Short). Six-round magazine, 2.25-inch bbl., 4.88 inches overall. Weight: About 16 oz. Fixed sights. Blued finish. Hard rubber grips. Intro. 1908. Disc. 1923.

MODEL 1923 POCKET
.25 AUTOMATIC PISTOL . . . . . NiB $480 Ex $300 Gd $170
Caliber: .25 Automatic (6.35mm). 2.13-inch bbl., 4.31 inches overall. Weight: 12 oz. Fixed sights. Blued finish. Checkered hard-rubber grips. Intro. 1923. Disc. 1930.

MODEL 1923 POCKET
AUTOMATIC PISTOL . . . . NiB $780 Ex $350 Gd $230
Calibers: .32 Automatic (7.65mm), .380 Automatic (9mm Short). Six-round magazine, 3.31-inch bbl., 5.5 inches overall. Weight: About 19 oz. Fixed sights. Blued finish. Checkered hard-rubber grips. Intro. 1923. Disc. 1940. .380 ACP, add. $80

MODEL 1930 POCKET
.25 AUTOMATIC PISTOL . . . . . NiB $480 Ex $255 Gd $195
This is a modification of the Model 1923, which it closely resembles.

Benelli MP90S

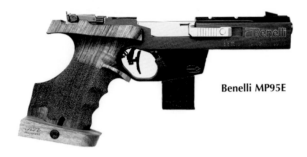

Benelli MP95E

BEEMAN PRECISION ARMS, INC. — Santa Rosa, CA

P08 AUTOMATIC PISTOL......NiB $420 Ex $335 Gd $245
Luger toggle action. Caliber: .22 LR. 10-round magazine, 3.8-inch bbl., 7.8 inches overall. Weight: 25 oz. Fixed sights. Blued finish. Checkered hardwood grips. Imported from 1969 to 1991.

MINI P08 AUTOMATIC PISTOL NiB $470 Ex $375 Gd $295
Caliber: Same general specifications as P08 except shorter 3.5-inch bbl., 7.4 inches overall. Weight: 20 oz. Imported 1986 to 1991.

SP METALLIC SILHOUETTE PISTOLS
Caliber: .22 LR. Single-shot. Bbl. lengths: 6-, 8-, 10- or 15-inches. Adj. rear sight. Receiver contoured for scope mount. Walnut target grips w/adj. palm rest. Models SP made 1985-86 and SPX 1993-94.

SP Standard w/8-or 10-inch bbl.NiB $285 Ex $235 Gd $172
SP Standard w/12-inch bbl. . . .NiB $330 Ex $266 Gd $191
SP Standard w/15-inch bbl. . . .NiB $344 Ex $286 Gd $200
SP Deluxe w/8-or 10-inch bbl. NiB $346 Ex $276 Gd $199
SP Deluxe w/12-inch bbl.. . . . .NiB $355 Ex $291 Gd $209
SP Deluxe w/15-inch bbl.. . . . .NiB $374 Ex $306 Gd $215
SPX Standard w/10-inch bbl. . .NiB $679 Ex $548 Gd $387
SPX Deluxe w/10-inch bbl.. . . .NiB $925 Ex $744 Gd $524

BEHOLLA — Suhl, Germany

Mfd. by both Becker and Holländer and Stenda-Werke GmbH.

POCKET AUTOMATIC PISTOL . NiB $272 Ex $227 Gd $191
Caliber: .32 Automatic (7.65mm). Seven-round magazine, 2.9-inch bbl., 5.5 inches overall. Weight: 22 oz. Fixed sights. Blued finish. Serrated wood or hard rubber grips. Made by Becker and Hollander 1915 to 1920, by Stenda-Werke circa 1920 to 1925. Note: Essentially the same pistol was manufactured w/

the Stenda version as the "Leonhardt" by H. M. Gering and as the "Menta" by August Menz.

BENELLI — Urbino, Italy

Imported by Larry's Guns in Gray, ME since 2003. Previously imported by EEA in Sharpes, FL; Sile Dist. New York, NY; Saco, Arlington, VA.

MP90S WORLD CUP TARGET PISTOL
Semiautomatic blowback action. Calibers: .22 Short, .22 LR, .32 W.C. Five-round magazine, 4.33-inch fixed bbl. 6.75 inches overall. Weight: 36 oz. Post front sight, adjustable rear. Blue finish. Anatomic shelf-style grip. Imported 1992 to 2001.
MP90S (.22 LR)......... NiB $1430 Ex $1221 Gd $1095
MP90S (.22 Short, disc. 1995) ... NiB $1314 Ex $1155 Gd $984
MP90S (.32 S&W) .... NiB $1562 Ex $1364 Gd $1221
w/conversion kit, add $80

MODEL B-76 .... NiB $441 Ex $326 Gd $257
Semi-auto, SA/DA. Cal.: 9 mm Para. Bbl.: 4.25 inches. 8-round mag. Weight: 34 oz. Disc. 1990.

MODEL B-765 TARGET .... NiB $604 Ex $475 Gd $665
Cal.: 9 mm Para. Similar to B-76 model but w/5.5-inch bbl., target grips, adj. rear sight. Disc. 1990.

MODEL B-77 .... NiB $405 Ex $309 Gd $220
Semi-auto, SA/DA. Cal.: .32 ACP. Bbl.: Steel, 4.25 inches. 8-round mag. Disc. 1995.

MODEL B-80 .... NiB $425 Ex $315 Gd $245
Semi-auto, SA/DA. Cal.: .30 Luger. Bbl.: Steel, 4.25 inches. 8-round mag. Weight: 34 oz. Disc. 1995.
B-80s Target, add $126

MODEL B-82 .... NiB $813 Ex $551 Gd $414
Limited production Italian police model; serial no. with "D" suffix. Cal.: .30 Luger, .32 ACP, 9 mm Ultra.

MODEL MP3S.............. NiB $603 Ex $467 Gd $336
Semi-auto, target model. Cal.: .32 S&W Long Wadcutter. Bbl.: 5.5 inches. High gloss blued finish, target grips. Adj. rear sight. Disc. 1995.

MP95E SPORT TARGET PISTOL
Similar to the MP90S except with 5- or 9-round magazine, 4.25-inch bbl., Blue or chrome finish. Checkered target grip. Imported from1994 to date.
Blue MP95 (.22 LR)......... NiB $892 Ex $708 Gd $467
Blue MP95 (.32 WC)........ NiB $981 Ex $840 Gd $640
Chrome, add...................................$80

BERETTA USA CORP. — Accokeek, MD

Beretta firearms are manufactured by Fabbrica D'Armi Pietro Beretta S. p. A. in Gardone Val Trompia (Brescia), Italy. This prestigious firm has been in business since 1526. In 1977, Beretta U.S.A. Corp., a manufacturing and importing facility, opened in Accokeek, MD. (Previously imported by Garcia Corp., J.L. Galef & Son, Inc. and Berben Corporation.) Note: Beretta holdings also owns additional firearms companies including: Benelli, Franchi, Sako, Stoeger, Tikka and Uberti.

MODEL 20 DA AUTO PISTOL. . . NiB $257 Ex $203 Gd $136
Caliber: .25 ACP. Eight-round magazine, 2.5-inch bbl., 4.9 inches overall. Weight: 10.9 oz. Plastic or walnut grips. Fixed sights. Made 1984 to 1985.

Beretta Model 21

Beretta Model 71

Beretta Model 72

Beretta Model 84

MODEL 21 DA AUTO PISTOL
Calibers: .22 LR and .25 ACP. Seven-round (.22 LR) or 8-round (.25 ACP) magazine, 2.5-inch bbl., 4.9 inches overall. Weight: About 12 oz. Blade front sight, V-notch rear. Walnut grips. Made from 1985 to date. Model 21EL disc. 2000.

Blued finish . . . . NiB $285 Ex $210 Gd $165
Nickel finish (.22 LR only) . . . . NiB $300 Ex $225 Gd $177
Model 21EL engraved model . . . . . . NiB $375 Ex $310 Gd $230

MODEL 70 AUTOMATIC PISTOL . . NiB $278 Ex $199 Gd $131
Improved version of Model 1935. Steel or lightweight alloy. Calibers: .32 Auto (7.65mm), .380 Auto (9mm Short). Eight-round (.32) or 7-round (.380) magazine, 3.5-inch bbl., 6.5 inches overall. Weight: Steel, 22.25 oz.; alloy, 16 oz. Fixed sights. Blued finish. Checkered plastic grips. Made 1959–85. Note: Formerly marketed in U.S. as "Puma" (alloy model in .32) and "Cougar" (steel model in .380). Disc.

MODEL 70S . . . . NiB $420 Ex $288 Gd $210
Similar to Model 70T except chambered for .22 Auto and .380 Auto. Longer bbl. guide and safety lever blocking hammer. Front blade and rear sight fixed on breechblock. Weight: 1 lb., 7 oz. Made 1977 to 1985.

MODEL 70T AUTOMATIC PISTOL NiB $315 Ex $231 Gd $189
Similar to Model 70. Caliber: .32 Automatic (7.65mm). Nine-round magazine, 6-in. bbl., 9.5-in. overall. Weight: 19 oz. adj. rear sight, blade front sight. Blued finish. Checkered plastic grips. Intro. in 1959. Disc.

MODEL 71 AUTOMATIC PISTOL . . NiB $268 Ex $199 Gd $142
Similar to alloy Model 70. Caliber: .22 LR. Six-inch bbl., 8-round magazine, Adj. rear sight frame. Single action. Made 1959 to 1989. Note: Formerly marketed in U.S. as the "Jaguar Plinker."

MODEL 72 . . . . NiB $315 Ex $231 Gd $190
Same as Model 71 except has 6-inch bbl., weight: 18 oz. Intro. in 1959. Disc. Note: Formerly marketed in U.S as "Jaguar Plinker."

MODEL 76 AUTO TARGET PISTOL
Caliber: .22 LR. 10-round magazine, 6-inch bbl., 8.8 inches overall. Weight: 33 oz. adj. rear sight, front sight w/interchange-able blades. Blued finish. Checkered plastic or wood grips. Made from 1966-85. Note: Formerly marketed in the U.S. as the "Sable."
Model 76 w/plastic grips . . . . NiB $790 Ex $640 Gd $510
Model 76W w/wood grips, add $35

MODEL 81 DA AUTO PISTOL . . . . NiB $341 Ex $247 Gd $199
Caliber: .32 Automatic (7.65mm). 12-round magazine, 3.8-inch bbl., 6.8 inches overall. Weight: 23.5 oz. Fixed sights. Blued finish. Plastic grips. Made principally for the European market 1975 to 1984, w/similar variations as the Model 84.

MODEL 82W DA AUTO PISTOL . . . NiB $330 Ex $231 Gd $178
Caliber: .32 ACP. Similar to the Model 81 except with a slimmer-profile frame designed to accept a single column 9-round magazine. Matte black finish. Importation disc. 1984.

MODEL 84 DA AUTO PISTOL . . . . NiB $325 Ex $222 Gd $173
Same as Model 81 except made in caliber .380 Automatic w/13-round magazine, 3.82-inch bbl., 6.8 inches overall. Weight: 23 oz. Fixed front and rear sights. Made from 1975 to 1982.

MODEL 84B DA AUTO PISTOL . . . NiB $335 Ex $230 Gd $184
Improved version of Model 84 w/strengthened frame and slide, and firing-pin block safety added. AmbidExtrous reversible magazine release. Blued or nickel finish. Checkered black plastic or wood grips. Other specifications same. Made circa 1982 to 1984.

MODEL 84(BB) DA AUTO PISTOL
Improved version of Model 84B w/further-strengthened slide, frame and recoil spring. Caliber: .380 ACP. 13-round magazine, 3.82-inch bbl., 6.8 inches overall. Weight: 23 oz. Checkered black plastic or wood grips. Blued or nickel finish. Notched rear and blade front sight. Made circa 1984-94.
Blued w/plastic grips . . . . NiB $393 Ex $241 Gd $152
Blued w/wood grips . . . . NiB $446 Ex $372 Gd $270
Nickel finish w/wood grips . . . . NiB $630 Ex $493 Gd $383

MODEL 84 CHEETAH SEMI-AUTO PISTOL
Similar to the Model 84 BB except with required design changes as mandated by regulation, including reduced magazine capacity (10-round magazine) and marked as 9mm short (.380) as a marketing strategy to counter increased availability of 9mm chamberings from other manufacturers. Made 1994–2002,, reintro. 2004.
Blued w/plastic grips . . . . NiB $650 Ex $520 Gd $360

Beretta Model 85

Beretta Model 85BB

Beretta Model 86 Cheetah

Blued w/wood grips . . . . NiB $667 Ex $551 Gd $367
Nickel finish w/wood grips. . . . NiB $735 Ex $498 Gd $372

MODEL 85 DA AUTO PISTOL . NiB $660 Ex $460 Gd $330
Similar to the Model 84 except designed with a slimmer-profile frame to accept a single column 8-round magazine, no ambidextrous magazine release. Matte black finish. Weight: 21.8 oz. Introduced in 1977 following the Model 84.

MODEL 85B DA AUTO PISTOL NiB $430 Ex $330 Gd $210
Improved version of the Model 85. Imported from 1982-85.

MODEL 85BB DA PISTOL
Improved version of the Model 85B w/strengthened frame and slide. Caliber: .380 ACP. Eight-round magazine, 3.82

inch bbl., 6.8 inches overall. Weight: 21.8 oz. Blued or nickel finish. Checkered black plastic or wood grips. Imported from 1985 to 1994.
Blued finish w/plastic grips. . . . NiB $520 Ex $395 Gd $280
Blued finish w/wood grips . . . . NiB $530 Ex $404 Gd $295
Nickel finish w/wood grips. . . . NiB $582 Ex $430 Gd $315

MODEL 85 CHEETAH SEMI-AUTO PISTOL
Similar to the Model 85BB except with required design changes as mandated by regulation and marked as 9mm short (.380). Made from 1994 to date.
Blued finish w/plastic grips. . . . NiB $656 Ex $470 Gd $310
Blued finish w/wood grips . . . . NiB $680 Ex $490 Gd $330
Nickel finish w/wood grips. . . . NiB $719 Ex $525 Gd $393

MODEL 85F DA PISTOL
Similar to the Model 85BB except has re-contoured trigger guard and manual ambidextrous safety w/decocking device. Matte black Bruniton finish. Imported in 1990 only.
plastic grips. . . . . NiB $390 Ex $315 Gd $255
wood grips . . . . NiB $420 Ex $344 Gd $283

MODEL 86 CHEETAH . . . . NiB $628 Ex $493 Gd $278
Caliber: .380 auto. Eight-round magazine, 4.4- inch bbl., 7.3 inches overall. Weight: 23.3 oz. Bruniton finish w/ wood grips. Made from 1986-89. (Reintroduced 1990 in the Cheetah series.)

MODEL 87 CHEETAH AUTOMATIC PISTOL
Similar to the Model 85 except in .22 LR w/8- or 10- round magazine (Target) and optional Extended 6-inch bbl. (Target in single action). Overall length: 6.8 to 8.8 inches. Weight: 20.1 oz. to 29.4 oz (Target). Checkered wood grips. Made from 1987 to date.
Blued finish
    (double-action) . . . . NiB $735 Ex $550 Gd $430
Target model
    (single action) . . . . NiB $765 Ex $580 Gd $467

MODEL 89 GOLD STANDARD TARGET
AUTOMATIC PISTOL . . . . NiB $703 Ex $556 Gd $467
Caliber: .22 LR. Eight-round magazine, 6-inch bbl., 9.5 inches overall. Weight: 41 oz. Adj. target sights. Blued finish. Target-style walnut grips. Made from 1988 to 2000.

MODEL 90 DA AUTO PISTOL . NiB $325 Ex $235 Gd $195
Caliber: .32 Auto (7.65mm). Eight-round magazine, 3.63-inch bbl., 6.63 inches overall. Weight: 19.5 oz. Fixed sights. Blued finish. Checkered plastic grips. Made from 1969 to 1983.

MODEL 90-TWO TYPE F . . . . . NiB $600 Ex $460 Gd $400
Similar to 92F. Caliber: 9mm Para or .40 S&W, DA/SA, 4.9-inch bbl., 8.5 inches overall. Weight: 32.5 oz. Fixed sights. Blued finish. Wrap around grip in two sizes. Accessory rail w/cover. Made from 2006-09.

MODEL 92 DA AUTO
PISTOL (1ST SERIES). . . . . NiB $824 Ex $640 Gd $445
Caliber: 9mm Para. 15-round magazine, 4.9-inch bbl., 8.5 inches overall. Weight: 33.5 oz. Fixed sights. Blued finish. Plastic grips. Initial production of 5,000 made in 1976.

MODEL 92S DA AUTO
PISTOL (2ND SERIES). . . . . NiB $700 Ex $400 Gd $260
Revised version of Model 92 w/ambidextrous slide-mounted safety modification intended for both commercial and military production. Evolved to Model 92S-1 for U.S. Military trials. Made 1980-85.

MODEL 92SB-P DA
AUTO PISTOL (3RD SERIES)... NiB $598 Ex $430 Gd $345
Same general specifications as standard Model 92 except has slide-mounted safety and repositioned magazine release. Made 1981 to 1985.

MODEL 92D DA AUTO PISTOL .... NiB $667 Ex $470 Gd $364
Same general specifications as Model 92F except DAO only w/bobbed hammer and 3-dot sight. Made from 1992 to 1998.
w/Tritium sights, add **$100**

MODEL 92F COMPACT
DA AUTOMATIC PISTOL ..... NiB $630 Ex $560 Gd $279
Caliber: 9mm Para. 12-round magazine, 4.3-inch bbl., 7.8 inches overall. Weight: 31.5 oz. Wood grips. Square-notched rear sight, blade front integral w/slide. Made from 1990-93.

MODEL 92F COMPACT L TYPE M DA AUTOMATIC PISTOL
Same general specifications as the original 92F Compact except 8-round magazine, Weight: 30.9 oz. Bruniton matte finish. Made 1998–2003.

MODEL 92F Compact L Type M NiB $660 Ex $580 Gd $390
Inox finish...............NiB $656 Ex $583 Gd $393
w/Tritium sights, add **$100**

MODEL 92F DA AUTOMATIC PISTOL
Same general specifications as Model 92 except w/slide-mounted safety and repositioned magazine release. Replaced Model 92SB. Blued or stainless finish. Made from 1992 to 1998.
Blued finish...............NiB $630 Ex $493 Gd $341
Stainless finish.............NiB $619 Ex $477 Gd $325
Model 92F-EL gold, add **$200**

MODEL 92FS DA AUTOMATIC PISTOL
Calibers: 9mm, 9mmx19 and .40 S&W. 15- round magazine, 4.9- inch bbl., 8.5 inches overall. Weight: 34.4 to 35.3 oz. Ambidextrous safety/decock lever. Chrome-lined bore w/ combat trigger guard. Bruniton finish w/plastic grips or Inox finish w/rubber grips. Made from 1999 to date. This model was adopted as the standard-issue sidearm by the U.S. Armed Forces in 1985 and renamed the M9.
matte black Bruniton finish.... NiB $630 Ex $520 Gd $325
olive drab finish (made 2004), add..................$30
Inox finish................NiB $660 Ex $550 Gd $355
Inox Tacical...................NiB $690 Ex $470 Gd $380
w/ checkered wood grips, add $25
w/B-lok (made 2003), add $25
470th Anniversary (made 1999) NiB $2205 Ex $1900 Gd $1690
"Desert Storm" edition (made 1991-92) NiB $630 Ex $500 Gd $450

MODEL 92FS BORDER MARSHAL
AUTOMATIC PISTOL........ NiB $675 Ex $485 Gd $460
Similar to 92F except commericial equivilent of I.N.S. gov't. contract pistol. Made from 1999 to 2000.

MODEL 92FS BRIGADIER AUTOMATIC PISTOL
Similar to 92FS except w/heavier slide and rubber wrap around grips. Made from 1999-2005; reintro. 2015 to date.
Matte black Bruniton ....NiB $760 Ex $556 Gd $395
Inox.....................NiB $766 Ex $630 Gd $477

MODEL 92FS CENTURION AUTOMATIC PISTOL
Similar to 92FS except w/compact barrel/slide and full size frame. Wood or plastic grips. Made from 1999-2005; reintro. 2015 to date.
Matte black Bruniton ....NiB $525 Ex $400 Gd $340

MODEL 92FS VERTEC........ NiB $640 Ex $450 Gd $400
Similar to 92FS except w/straight backstrap, thin grip panels, short-reach trigger, and accessory rail. Made from 2002 to 2005.

MODEL 92G-SD .... NiB $960 Ex $590 Gd $460
Similar to 92F except w/srping loaded decocking lever, accessory rail, 10-round magazine, Tritium sights. Made from 2003-05.

Beretta Model 92F

**Beretta Model 92
Compact L Type M**

**Beretta Model 92FS
Brigadier Inox**

Beretta Model 96
Stock

Beretta Model 950BS
Jetfire

MODEL 92G ELITE IA . . . . NiB $730 Ex $500 Gd $360
Similar to 92FS Brigadier except w/4.7-in. stainless bbl. Made
from 1999 to 2005.
Elite II (made 2000-2005) . . . . . NiB $820 Ex $540 Gd $390

MODEL 96 DA AUTO PISTOL
Similar to Model 92F except in .40 S&W. 10-round magazine (9-round in Compact model). Made from 1992 to
1998.
Model 96 D (DA only) . . . . NiB $475 Ex $355 Gd $300
Model 96 Centurion (compact) NiB $550 Ex $460 Gd $310
w/Tritium sights, add $110
w/Tritium sights system, add. $115

MODEL 96 STOCK . . . . NiB $1200 Ex $870 Gd $610
Similar to Model 96 except w/frame mounted safety. Set up
for I.D.P.A. competion. Made from 1997 to 1999.

MODEL 101 . . . . NiB $270 Ex $200 Gd $155
Same as Model 70T except caliber .22 LR, has 10-round magazine, Intro. in 1959. Disc.

MODEL 318 AUTO PISTOL . . . . . NiB $270 Ex $200 Gd $155
Caliber: .25 Automatic (6.35mm). Eight-round magazine, 2.5-
inch bbl., 4.5 inches overall. Weight: 14 oz. Fixed sights. Blued
finish. Plastic grips. Made from 1934 to c. 1939.

MODEL 418 AUTO PISTOL . . . . . NiB $270 Ex $200 Gd $155
Similar to Model 318 but with loaded chamber indicator and
grip safety. Made from 1937 to 1961.

MODEL 948 . . . NIB $400 EX $320 GD $200
Similar to Model 1934 except chambered in .22 LR.
Discontinued in mid 1950s.
w/additional extended barrel, add. 20%
engraved, add 50%

MODEL 949 OLYMPIC TARGET . . . NiB $708 Ex $577 Gd $456
Calibers: .22 Short, .22 LR. Five-round magazine, 8.75-inch
bbl., 12.5 inches overall. Weight: 38 oz. Target sights. Adj.
bbl., weight. Muzzle brake. Checkered walnut grips w/thum-
brest. Made from 1959 to 1964.

MODEL 950B AUTO PISTOL . . NiB $225 Ex $168 Gd $115
Same general specifications as Model 950CC except caliber
.25 Auto, has 7-round magazine, Made from 1959 to date.
Note: Formerly marketed in the U.S. as "Jetfire."

MODEL 950B JETFIRE SA PISTOL
Calibers: .25 ACP or .22 Short (disc.1992). Seven- or 8-round
magazine, 2.4- or 4- inch bbl. Weight: 9.9 oz. Fixed blade front
and V-notch rear sights. Matte Blue or Inox (Stainless) finish.
Checkered black plastic grips. Made from 1987 to 2002.
Blued finish. . . . . NiB $168 Ex $99 Gd $84
Nickel finish . . . . NiB $225 Ex $173 Gd $147
Inox finish. . . . . NiB $257 Ex $204 Gd $160
w/4-inch bbl., (.22 Short) . . . . . NiB $256 Ex $207 Gd $157

MODEL 950CC AUTO PISTOL NiB $157 Ex $126 Gd $104
Caliber: .22 Short. Six-round magazine, hinged 2.38-inch bbl.,
4.75 inches overall. Weight: 11 oz. Fixed sights. Blued finish.
Plastic grips. Made from 1959 to date. Note: Formerly marketed
in the U.S. as "Minx M2."

MODEL 950CC SPECIAL. . . . . . . NiB $155 Ex $103 Gd $88
Same general specifications as Model 950CC Auto except has
4-inch bbl. Made from 1959 to date. Note: Formerly marketed in the U.S. as "Minx M4."

MODEL 951 (1951) BRIGADIER
MILITARY AUTO PISTOL . . . . . NiB $560 Ex $395 Gd $295
Caliber: 9mm Para. Eight-round magazine, 4.5-inch bbl.,
8 inches overall. Weight: 31 oz. Fixed sights. Blued finish.
Plastic grips. Made   from 1952 to date. Note: Was standard
pistol of the Italian Armed Forces, also used by Egyptian and
Israeli armies and by the police in Nigeria. Egyptian and
Israeli models usually command a premium. Formerly mar-
keted in the U.S. as the "Brigadier."

MODEL 1915 AUTO PISTOL . . . NiB $1587 Ex $1386 Gd $1087
Calibers: 9mm Glisenti and .32 ACP (7.65mm). Eight-round
magazine, 4-inch bbl., 6.7 inches overall (9mm), 5.7 inches
(.32 ACP). Weight: 30 oz. (9mm), 20 oz. (.32 ACP). Fixed sights.
Blued finish. Wood grips. Made 1915-1922. An improved post-
war 1915/1919 version in caliber .32 ACP was later offered for
sale in 1922 as the Model 1922.

MODEL 1923 AUTO PISTOL . . . NiB $2136 Ex $2094 Gd $1669
Caliber: 9mm Glisenti (Luger). Eight-round magazine, 4-inch
bbl., 6.5 inches overall. Weight: 30 oz. Fixed sights. Blued finish. Plastic grips. Made circa 1923 to 1936.

MODEL 1934 AUTO PISTOL

Caliber: .380 Automatic (9mm Short). Seven-round magazine, 3.38-inch bbl., 5.88 inches overall. Weight: 24 oz. Fixed sights. Blued finish. Plastic grips. Official pistol of the Italian Armed Forces. Wartime pieces not as well made and finished as commercial models. Made from 1934 to 1959.

Commercial model . . . . NiB $2340 Ex $2100 Gd $1333
War model . . . . NiB $598 Ex $383 Gd $299

MODEL 1935 AUTO PISTOL

Caliber: .32 ACP (7.65mm). Eight-round magazine, 3.5-inch bbl., 5.75 inches overall. Weight: 24 oz. Fixed sights. Blued finish. Plastic grips. A roughly-finished version of this pistol was produced during WW II. Made from 1935 to 1959.

Commercial model . . . . NiB $1806 Ex $1465 Gd $1078
Deluxe Commercial model (engraved, gold plated, cased)
. . . . NiB $3000 Ex $2000 Gd $1500
War model . . . . NiB $598 Ex $383 Gd $299

MODEL 3032 DA SEMIAUTOMATIC TOMCAT

Caliber: .32 ACP. Seven-round magazine, 2.45-inch bbl., 5 inches overall. Weight: 14.5 oz. Fixed sights. Blued or stainless finish. Made from 1996 to date.

Matte blue . . . . NiB $329 Ex $262 Gd $180
Polished blue. . . . . NiB $386 Ex $329 Gd $252
Stainless . . . . NiB $412 Ex $365 Gd $252

MODEL 8000/8040/8045 COUGAR DA PISTOL

Calibers: 9mm, .40 S&W and .45 Auto. Eight- or 10-shot magazine, 3.6 to 3.7-inch bbl., 7- to 7.2 inches overall. Weight: 32 to 32.6 oz. Short recoil action w/rotating barrel. Fixed sights w/3-dot Tritium system. Textured black grips. Matte black Bruniton w/alloy frame. Made 1995-2005.

8000 Cougar D (9mm DAO). . . NiB $715 Ex $649 Gd $400
8000 Cougar F (9mm DA). . . . . NiB $750 Ex $644 Gd $388
8040 Cougar D (.40 S&W DAO)NiB $685 Ex $618 Gd $373
8040 Cougar F (.40 S&W DA) . NiB $685 Ex $618 Gd $373
8045 Cougar D (.45 Auto DAO)NiB $736 Ex $637 Gd $400
8045 Cougar F (.357 Sig SA/DA)NiB $685 Ex $536 Gd $386

MODEL 8000/8040/8045 MINI COUGAR DA PISTOL

Calibers: 9mm, .40 S&W and .45 Auto. Six- 8- or 10-round magazine, 3.6- to 3.7-inch bbl., 7 inches overall. Weight: 27.4 to 30.4 oz. Fixed sights w/3-dot Tritium system. AmbidExtrous safety/decocker lever. Matte black Bruniton finish w/anodized aluminum alloy frame. Made from 1995 to 2008.

8000 Mini Cougar D (9mm DAO) . . NiB $654 Ex $577 Gd $326
8000 Mini Cougar F (9mm DA). . . . . NiB $654 Ex $577 Gd $326
8040 Mini Cougar D (.40 S&W DAO) . . . NiB $654 Ex $577 Gd $326
8040 Mini Cougar F (.40 S&W DA). . . NiB $654 Ex $577 Gd $326
8045 Mini Cougar D (.45 Auto DAO) . . . NiB $654 Ex $577 Gd $326
8045 Mini Cougar F (.45 Auto DA) . . . NiB $654 Ex $577 Gd $326

MODEL 9000S SUBCOMPACT PISTOL SERIES

Calibers: 9mm, .40 S&W. 10-round magazine, 3.5-inch bbl., 6.6 inches overall. Weight: 25.7 to 27.5 oz. Single/double and double-action only. Front and rear dovetail sights w/3-dot system. Chrome-plated barrel w/Techno-polymer frame. Geometric locking system w/tilt barrel. Made from 2000–05.

Type D (9mm) . . . . NiB $432 Ex $366 Gd $304
Type D (.40 S&W). . . . . NiB $432 Ex $366 Gd $304
Type F (9mm) . . . . NiB $432 Ex $366 Gd $304
Type F (.40 S&W) . . . . NiB $432 Ex $366 Gd $304

NANO . . . . NiB $450 Ex $410 Gd $390
Semi-automatic. Striker fired. Caliber: 9mm. 6-round magazine. 3.07-in. bbl. Frame: polymer with removable trigger group. Grip: texture polymer; black, pink or FDE. Sights: low-

**Beretta
Model 3032 Tomcat**

**Beretta
Model 8000 Cougar D**

**Beretta
Model 8040 Mini Cougar D**

profile,fixed. Length: 5.63 ins. Weight: 19.8 oz. Made from 2011 to date.

PICO . . . . NiB $400 Ex $390 Gd $350
Semi-automatic. Striker fired. Caliber: .380 ACP, 6-rnd magazine. 2.7-in. bbl. Frame: polymer with removable trigger group. Grip: texture polymer, black. Sights: low-profile, fixed. Length: 5.1 ins. Weight: 11.5 oz. Made from 2013 to date.

PX4 STORM . . . . NiB $575 Ex $490 Gd $440
SA/DA semi-automatic pistol. Rotating barrel system. Polymer frame. Calibers: 9mm, .40 S&W or .45 ACP. 9-17 rnd. magazine. Bbl lengths: 3.2 or 4 inches. Finish: matte black, Pronox or Super Luminova. Made from 2005 to date.

Inox finish, add 90%
Storm Special Duty . . . . NiB $1145 Ex $980 Gd $830

Beretta Stampede

**Bernardelli
Model 60 Pocket**

Bernardelli Model 68

**Bernardelli
Model 80 Pocket**

LARAMIE SA REVOLVER . . . . **NiB $1030 Ex $760 Gd $550**
Reproduction of S&W Model 1870 Schofield. Calibers: .38 Special, .45 Long Colt. 6-round cylinder, Bbl length: 5, 6.5 inches. Blued finish. Built by Uberti from 2005 to 2008.

STAMPEDE SA REVOLVER
Calibers: .357 Magnum, .44-40, .45 Long Colt. 6-round cylinder, Bbl length: 4.75, 5.5, 7.5 inches. Built by Uberti from 2003-11.
Blued finish . . . . **NiB $490 Ex $345 Gd $265**

Brushed nickel finish. . . . . NiB $510 Ex $355 Gd $275
Deluxe finish. . . . . NiB $520 Ex $425 Gd $325
Old west finish . . . . NiB $515 Ex $405 Gd $305
Bisley model . . . . NiB $510 Ex $355 Gd $275

U22 NEOS . . . . **NiB $295 Ex $240 Gd $210**
SA semi-automatic pistol. .22 LR w/10-rnd. magazine. Bbl length: 4.5 or 6 in. Modular design. Finishes: aqua, black/blue or gray. Weight: 31.5-36 oz. made from 2002 to date.
DLX (adj. trigger, interchangable sights) add $40

BERNARDELLI, VINCENZO S.P.A. — Gardone V. T. (Brescia), Italy

MODEL 60 POCKET
AUTOMATIC PISTOL . . . . **NiB $247 Ex $221 Gd $190**
Calibers: .22 LR, .32 Auto (7.65mm), .380 Auto (9mm Short). Eight-round magazine (.22 and .32), 7-round (.380). 3.5-inch bbl., 6.5 inches overall. Weight: About 25 oz. Fixed sights. Blued finish. Bakelite grips. Made from 1959 to 1990.

MODEL 68 AUTOMATIC PISTOL . . .**NiB $180 Ex $128 Gd $92**
Caliber: 6.35. Five- and 8-round magazine, 2.13-inch bbl., 4.13 inches overall. Weight: 10 oz. Fixed sights. Blued or chrome finish. Bakelite or pearl grips. This model, like its .22-caliber counterpart, was known as the "Baby" Bernardelli. Disc. 1970.

MODEL 69 AUTOMATIC
TARGET PISTOL . . . . **NiB $693 Ex $570 Gd $383**
Caliber: .22 LR. 10-round magazine, 5.9-inch bbl., 9 inches overall. Weight: 2.2 lbs. Fully adj. target sights. Blued finish. Stippled right- or left-hand wraparound walnut grips. Made from 1987 to date. This was previously Model 100; not imported to the U.S.

MODEL 80 . . . . **NiB $204 Ex $128 Gd $92**
Calibers: .22 LR, .32 ACP (7.65mm), .380 Auto (9mm Short). Magazine capacity: 10-round (.22), 8-round (.32), 7-round (.380). 3.5-inch bbl., 6.5 inches overall. Weight: 25.6 oz. adj. rear sight, white dot front sight. Blued finish. Plastic thumbrest grips. Note: Model 80 is a modification of Model 60 designed to conform w/U.S. import regulations. Made from 1968 to 1988.

MODEL 90 SPORT TARGET . . . **NiB $245 Ex $199 Gd $148**
Same as Model 80 except has 6-inch bbl., 9 inches overall, weight: 26.8 oz. Made from 1968 1990.

MODEL 100 TARGET PISTOL . . **NiB $428 Ex $362 Gd $291**
Caliber: .22 LR. 10-round magazine, 5.9-inch bbl., 9 inches overall. Weight: 37.75 oz. Adj. rear sight, interchangeable front sights. Blued finish. Checkered walnut thumbrest grips. Made from 1969-86. Note: Formerly Model 69.

MODEL AMR AUTO PISTOL . . . **NiB $433 Ex $321 Gd $270**
Simlar to Model USA except with 6-inch bbl. and target sights. Imported from 1992 to 1994.

"BABY" AUTOMATIC PISTOL . **NiB $321 Ex $235 Gd $179**
Calibers: .22 Short, .22 Long. Five-round magazine, 2.13-inch bbl., 4.13 inches overall. Weight: 9 oz. Fixed sights. Blued finish. Bakelite grips. Made from 1949 to 1968.

MODEL P010 . . . . **NiB $712 Ex $520 Gd $341**
Caliber: .22 LR. Five- and 10-round magazine, 5.9-inch bbl. w/7.5-inch sight radius. Weight: 40 oz. Interchangeable front sight, adj. rear. Blued finish. Textured walnut grips. Made from 1988 to 1992 and 1995 to 1997.

P018 COMPACT MODEL . . . . . **NiB $571 Ex $461 Gd $385**
Slightly smaller version of the Model P018 standard DA automatic except has 14-round magazine and 4-inch bbl., 7.68 inches overall. Weight: 33 oz. Walnut grips only. Imported from 1987 to 1996.

P018 DOUBLE-ACTION AUTOMATIC PISTOL
Caliber: 9mm Para. 16-round magazine, 4.75-inch bbl., 8.5 inches overall. Weight: 36 oz. Fixed combat sights. Blued finish. Checkered plastic or walnut grips. Imported from 1987 to 1996.
w/plastic grips . . . . **NiB $510 Ex $405 Gd $305**
w/walnut grips . . . . **NiB $551 Ex $428 Gd $342**

P-ONE DA AUTO PISTOL
Caliber: 9mm Para. or .40 S&W. 10- or 16-round magazine, 4.8-inch bbl., 8.35 inches overall. Weight: 34 oz. Blade front sight, adjustable rear w/3-dot system. Matte black or chrome finish. Checkered walnut or black plastic grips. Imported from 1993 to 1997. **Model P-One blue finish** . **NiB $622 Ex $525 Gd $357**
Model P-One chrome finish . . . **NiB $693 Ex $556 Gd $393**
w/walnut grips, add **$50**

P-ONE PRACTICAL VB AUTO PISTOL
Similar to Model P One except chambered for 9x21mm w/2-, 4- or 6-port compensating system for IPSC competition. Imported 1993 to 1997.
Model P One
  Practical (2 port) . . . . **NiB $1148 Ex $1068 Gd $785**
Model P One
  Practical (4 port) . . . . **NiB $1259 Ex $1054 Gd $782**
Model P One
  Practical (6 port) . . . . **NiB $1678 Ex $1393 Gd $995**
w/chrome finish, add **$75**

SPORTER AUTOMATIC PISTOL . **NiB $332 Ex $245 Gd $133**
Caliber .22 LR. Eight-round magazine, bbl., lengths: 6-, 8- and 10-inch, 13 inches overall (10-inch bbl.). weight: About 30 oz. (10-inch bbl.) Target sights. Blued finish. Walnut grips. Made 1949 to 1968.

MODEL USA AUTO PISTOL
Single-action, blowback. Calibers: .22 LR, .32 ACP, .380 ACP. Seven-round magazine or 10-round magazine (.22 LR). 3.5-inch bbl., 6.5 inches overall. Weight: 26.5 oz. Ramped front sight, adjustable rear. Blue or chrome finish. Checkered black bakelite grips w/thumbrest. Imported from 1991 to 1997.
Model USA blue finish . . . . **NiB $420 Ex $330 Gd $265**
Model USA chrome finish . . . . . **NiB $469 Ex $385 Gd $219**

VEST POCKET
AUTOMATIC PISTOL . . . . **NiB $275 Ex $199 Gd $148**
Caliber: .25 Auto (6.35mm). Five- or 8-round magazine, 2.13-inch bbl., 4.13 inches overall. Weight: 9 oz. Fixed sights. Blued finish. Bakelite grips. Made 1945 to 1968.

Bernardelli P010

Bernardelli P018

Bersa Model 85

BERSA — Argentina
Currently imported by Eagle Imports, Wanamassa, NJ. Previously by Interarms & Outdoor Sports.

MODEL 83 DA AUTO PISTOL
Similar to the Model 23 except for the following specifications: Caliber: .380 ACP. Seven-round magazine, 3.5-inch bbl., Front blade sight integral on slide, square-notch rear adj. for windage. Blued or satin nickel finish. Custom wood grips. Imported from 1988 to 1994.
Blued finish . . . . **NiB $275 Ex $201 Gd $126**
Satin nickel . . . . **NiB $321 Ex $271 Gd $194**

MODEL 85 DA AUTO PISTOL
Same general specifications as Model 83 except 13-round magazine, Imported from 1988 to 1994.
Blued finish . . . . **NiB $326 Ex $235 Gd $128**
Satin nickel . . . . **NiB $377 Ex $286 Gd $179**

Bersa Model 383

Bersa Thunder .380

MODEL 86 DA AUTO PISTOL
Same general specifications as Model 85 except available in matte blued finish and w/Neoprene grips. Imported from 1992 to 1994.
Matte blued finish . . . . NiB $347 Ex $270 Gd $219
Nickel finish . . . . NiB $362 Ex $262 Gd $199

MODEL 95 (THUNDER SERIES) DA AUTOMATIC PISTOL
Caliber: .380 ACP. Seven-round magazine, 3.5-inch bbl., weight: 23 oz. Grip: checkered polymer panels or wrap around rubber. Blade front and rear notch sights. Imported from 1995 to date.
Blued finish . . . . NiB $329 Ex $214 Gd $158
Nickel finish . . . . NiB $318 Ex $204 Gd $143
Thunder Combat series (smaller beavertail, 8- or 15-rnd. magazine), add $10
Thunder Plus series (15-rnd. magazine), add $10
Thunder Conceal Carry series (bobbed hammer), add . . . $10

MODEL 97 AUTO PISTOL . . . . NiB $389 Ex $332 Gd $219
Caliber: .380 ACP. Seven-round magazine, 3.3-inch bbl., 6.5 inches overall. Weight: 28 oz. Intro. 1982. Disc.

MODEL 223
Same general specifications as Model 383 except in .22 LR w/10-round magazine capacity. Disc. 1987.
Double-action . . . . NiB $243 Ex $213 Gd $143
Single-action . . . . NiB $224 Ex $168 Gd $125

MODEL 224
Caliber: .22 LR. 10-round magazine, 4-inch bbl., weight: 26 oz. Front blade sight, square-notched rear adj. for windage. Blued finish. Checkered nylon or custom wood grips. Made 1984. SA. disc. 1986.
Double-action . . . . NiB $240 Ex $204 Gd $143
Single-action . . . . NiB $204 Ex $179 Gd $122

MODEL 226
Similar as Model 224 but w/6-inch bbl. Disc. 1987.
Double-action . . . . NiB $240 Ex $204 Gd $143
Single-action . . . . NiB $204 Ex $179 Gd $122

MODEL 383 AUTO PISTOL
Caliber: .380 Auto. Seven-round magazine, 3.5-inch bbl. Front blade sight integral on slide, square-notched rear sight adj. for windage. Custom wood grips on double-action, nylon grips on single action. Blued or satin nickel finish. Made 1984. SA. disc. 1989.
Double-action . . . . NiB $235 Ex $150 Gd $102
Single-action . . . . NiB $219 Ex $158 Gd $122

MODEL 622 AUTO PISTOL . . . NiB $204 Ex $138 Gd $100
Caliber: .22 LR. Seven-round magazine, 4- or 6-inch bbl., 7 or 9 inches overall. Weight: 2.25 lbs. Blade front sight, square-notch rear adj. for windage. Blued finish. Nylon grips. Made from 1982 to 1987.

MODEL 644 AUTO PISTOL . . . NiB $286 Ex $240 Gd $168
Caliber: .22 LR. 10-round magazine, 3.5-inch bbl., weight: 26.5 oz. 6.5 inches overall. Adj. rear sight, blade front. Contoured black nylon grips. Made from 1980 to 1988.

MODEL BPCC . . . . NiB $410 Ex $310 Gd $230
Semi-automatic. Striker-fired. Caliber: .380 ACP, 9mm or .40 S&W; 8-rnd. magazine. 3.3-in bbl. Frame: polymer. Sights: fixed, 3-dot. Finish: numerous. Grip: textured polymer. Length: 6.83-in. Weight: 21.5 oz. Made from 2010 to date.

THUNDER PRO . . . . NiB $470 Ex $360 Gd $260
Semi-automatic. DA/SA. Caliber: 9mm or .40 S&W; 13- or 17-rnd. magazine. 4.25-in. bbl. Frame: alloy. Sights: fixed, low-profile. Finish: two-tone or matte black. Grip: textured polymer. Length: 7.56-in. Weight: 30.7 oz. Made from 2004 to date.
Ultra Compact model (3.2-in. bbl.), subtract $10
XT model (adj. sights) add, ... $20

THUNDER 9 AUTO PISTOL . . . NiB $408 Ex $272 Gd $168
Caliber: 9mm Para. 15-round magazine, 4-inch bbl., 7.38 inches overall. Weight: 30 oz. Blade front sight, adj. rear w/3-dot system. AmbidExtrous safety and decocking device. Matte blued finish. Checkered black polymer grips. Made from 1993 to 1996.

THUNDER .22 AUTO PISTOL (MODEL 23)
Caliber: .22 LR, 10-round magazine, 3.5-inch bbl., 6.63 inches overall. Weight: 24.5 oz. Notched-bar dovetailed rear, blade integral w/slide front. Black polymer grips. Made from 1988 to 1998.
Blued finish . . . . NiB $254 Ex $214 Gd $168
Nickel finish . . . . NiB $260 Ex $220 Gd $177

THUNDER .380 AUTO PISTOL
Caliber: .380 ACP. Seven-round magazine, 3.5-inch bbl., 6.63 inches overall. Weight: 25.75 oz. Notched-bar dovetailed rear, blade integral w/slide front. Blued, satin nickel, or Duo-Tone finish. Made from 1995 to 1998.
Blued finish . . . . NiB $306 Ex $230 Gd $183
Satin nickel finish . . . . NiB $333 Ex $255 Gd $204
Duo-Tone finish . . . . NiB $306 Ex $230 Gd $168

THUNDER .380 PLUS AUTO PISTOL

Same general specifications as standard Thunder .380 except has 10-round magazine and weight: 26 oz. Made 1995-97.

Matte finish. . . . . NiB $306 Ex $230 Gd $168
Satin nickel finish . . . . NiB $321 Ex $245 Gd $194
Duo-Tone finish, add. $40

BOBERG ARMS CORP — White Bear Lake, MN

Boberg purchased by Bond Arms in 2016.

MODEL XR9-S . . . . NiB $942 Ex $860 Gd $660
DAO. Semi-automatic. Reverse feed system. Caliber: 9mm; 6-rnd. magazine. 3.5-in. bbl. Frame: polymer. Sights: fixed, low-profile, 3-dot. Finish: two-tone. Grip: textured polymer. Length: 8.3-in. Weight: 17.4 oz. Made from 2013 to 2016.
L model (4.2-in. bbl.), add $10

MODEL XR45-S . . . . NiB $1199 Ex $1060 Gd $810
Similar to XR9-S except in .45 ACP. Made from 2014 to 2016.

BREN 10 — Huntington Beach, CA

Original mfg. by Dornaus & Dixon Ent., Inc. (1983-86) in Huntington Beach, CA.

STANDARD. . . . . NiB $2460 Ex $1880 Gd $980
Semi-automatic. Selective DA trigger. Caliber: 10mm; 11-rnd. magazine. 5-in. bbl. Sights: fixed, low-profile, 3-dot. Finish: two-tone. Serial number prefix: 83SM. Made from 1984 to 1986.
Military/Police model (DA/SA trigger, Serial # prefix: 83MP,
Made 1984–86.), add $200
Special Forces Model D (DA/SA trigger, 4-in. brrl., dark finish,
Serial # prefix: SFD, Made 1986.), add. $225
Special Forces Model L (DA/SA trigger, 4-in. brrl., light finish,
Serial # prefix: SFL, Made 1986.), add $225

Recent mfg. by Vltor Mfg. (2010-11).
SM SERIES. . . . . NiB $1100 Ex $880 Gd $660
Semi-automatic. DA/SA trigger. Caliber: 10mm or .45 ACP; 10- or 15-rnd. magazine. 5-in. bbl. Sights: fixed, low-profile, 3-dot. Finish: blue slide/stainless frame. Rare, few manufactured. Made from 2010-11.
SMV Series (stainless frame/hard chrome slide), add $80

BROLIN ARMS — La Verne, CA

"LEGEND SERIES" SA AUTOMATIC PISTOL

Caliber: .45 ACP. Seven-round magazine, 4- or 5-inch bbl., weight: 32-36 oz. Walnut grips. Single action, full size, compact, or full size frame compact slide. Matte blued finish. Lowered and flared ejection port. Made from 1995 to 1998.

Model L45. . . . . NiB $469 Ex $398 Gd $306
Model L45C . . . . NiB $487 Ex $366 Gd $305
Model L45T. . . . . NiB $487 Ex $366 Gd $305

"PATRIOT SERIES" SA AUTOMATIC PISTOL

Caliber: .45 ACP. Seven-round magazine, 3.25- and 4-inch bbl., weight: 33-37 oz. Wood grips. Fixed rear sights. Made 1996 to 1997.

Model P45 . . . . NiB $627 Ex $469 Gd $301
Model P45C (disc. 1997) . . . . . NiB $638 Ex $479 Gd $311
Model P45T (disc. 1997). . . . . . NiB $658 Ex $551 Gd $372

"PRO-STOCK AND PRO-COMP" SA PISTOL

Caliber: .45 ACP. Eight-round magazine, 4- or 5-inch bbl., weight: 37 oz. Single action, blued or two-tone finish. Wood grips. Bomar adjustable sights. Made from 1996 to 1997.

Model Pro comp . . . . NiB $872 Ex $663 Gd $566
Model Pro stock . . . . NiB $714 Ex $551 Gd $475

TAC SERIES

Caliber: .45 ACP. Eight-round magazine, 5-inch bbl., 8.5 inches overall. Weight: 37 oz. Low profile combat or Tritium sights. Beavertail grip safety. Matte blue, chrome or two-tone finish. Checkered wood or contoured black rubber grips. Made from 1997 to 1998.

Model TAC 11 service . . . . NiB $643 Ex $510 Gd $398
Model TAC 11 compact . . . . . . NiB $653 Ex $531 Gd $419
w/Tritium sights, add $100

BANTAM MODEL . . . . NiB $403 Ex $283 Gd $ 204
Caliber: 9mmPara., .40 S&W. Single or double-action, super compact size, concealed hammer, all steel construction; 3-dot sights; royal blue or matte finish. Manufactured 1999 only.

BRONCO — Eibar, Spain

Manufactured by Echave y Arizmendi.

MODEL 1918 POCKET

AUTOMATIC PISTOL . . . . NiB $204 Ex $129 Gd $92
Caliber: .32 ACP (7.65mm). Six-round magazine 2.5-inch bbl., 5 inches overall. Weight: 20 oz. Fixed sights. Blued finish. Hard rubber grips. Made circa 1918- to 1925.

VEST POCKET AUTO PISTOL . . . NiB $203 Ex $128 Gd $66
Caliber: .25 ACP, 6-round magazine, 2.13-inch bbl., 4.13 inches overall. Weight: 11 oz. Fixed sights. Blued finish. Hard rubber grips. Made from 1919 to 1935.

BROWNING — Morgan, UT

The following Browning pistols have been manufactured by Fabrique Nationale d'Armes de Guerre (now Fabrique Nationale Herstal) of Herstal, Belgium, by Arms Technology Inc. of Salt Lake City and by J. P. Sauer & Sohn of Eckernforde, W. Germany. See also FN Browning and J.P. Sauer & Sohn listings.

**Browning
Model 25 Automatic**

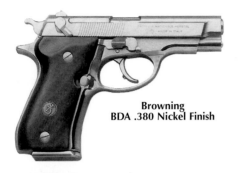

**Browning
BDA .380 Nickel Finish**

**Browning
Buck Mark 5.5 Field**

**Browning
Buck Mark Bullseye**

**Browning
Buck Mark Plus**

**Browning
BDM 9mm DA**

1911-22 SERIES . . . . NiB $599 EX $530 GD $520
1911 style platform. Semi-automatic. SA. Caliber: .22 LR, 10-rnd. magazine. 4.25-in. bbl. Frame: alloy. Sights: fixed. Finish: matte black. Grip: checkered walnut. Length: 7.37 in. Weight: 15 oz. Made from 2011 to date.
Compact (3.62-in. bbl.). . . . . . NiB $599 Ex $530 Gd $520
Black Label Series . . . . NiB $639 Ex $600 Gd $580
**Black Label Series Compact
(3.62-in. bbl.)** . . . . NiB $639 Ex $600 Gd $580
Black Label Series Suppressor Ready, add. $90

.25 AUTOMATIC PISTOL
Same general specifications as FN Browning Baby (see separate listing). Standard Model, blued finish, hard rubber grips. Light Model, nickel-plated, Nacrolac pearl grips. Renaissance Engraved Model, nickel-plated, Nacrolac pearl grips. Made by FN from 1955 to 1969.
Standard model. . . . . NiB $587 Ex $534 Gd $283
Lightweight model . . . . NiB $592 Ex $540 Gd $294
Renaissance model . . . . NiB $1121 Ex $867 Gd $539

.32 AND .380 AUTOMATIC PISTOL, 1955 TYPE
Same general specifications as FN Browning .32 (7.65mm) and .380 Pocket Auto. Standard Model, Renaissance Engraved Model as furnished in .25 Automatic. Made by FN from 1955 to 1969.
Standard model (.32 ACP). . . . . NiB $507 Ex $386 Gd $291
Standard model (.380 ACP). . . . NiB $454 Ex $376 Gd $283
Renaissance model . . . . NiB $1121 Ex $918 Gd $740

.380 AUTOMATIC PISTOL, 1971 TYPE
Same as .380 Automatic, 1955 Type except has longer slide, 4.44-inch bbl., is 7.06 inches overall, weight: 23 oz. Rear sight adj. for windage and elevation, plastic thumbrest grips. Made 1971 to 1975.
Standard model. . . . . NiB $509 Ex $387 Gd $294
Renaissance model . . . . NiB $1132 Ex $913 Gd $616

BDA .380 DA AUTOMATIC PISTOL
Caliber: .380 Auto. 10- or 13-round magazine, bbl. length: 3.81 inches., 6.75 inches overall. Weight: 23 oz. Fixed blade front sight, square-notch drift-adj. rear sight. Blued or nickel finish. Smooth walnut grips. Made from 1982 to 1997 by Beretta.
Blued finish . . . . NiB $602 Ex $454 Gd $284
Nickel finish, add. $80

BDA DA AUTOMATIC PISTOL
Similar to SIG-Sauer P220. Calibers: 9mm Para., .38 Super Auto, .45 Auto. Nine-round magazine (9mm and .38), 7-round (.45 cal), 4.4-inch bbl., 7.8 inches overall. Weight: 29.3 oz. Fixed sights. Blued finish. Plastic grips. Made from 1977 to 1980 by J. P. Sauer.
9mm, .45 ACP. . . . . NiB $611 Ex $464 Gd $326
.38 Super . . . . NiB $741 Ex $465 Gd $437
Nickel finish . . . . NiB $692 Ex $524 Gd $377

BDM SERIES AUTOMATIC PISTOLS
Calibers: 9mm Para., 10-round magazine, 4.73-inch bbl., 7.85 inches overall. Weight: 31 oz., windage adjustable sights w/3-dot system. Low profile removable blade front sights. Matte blued, Bi-Tone or silver chrome finish. Selectable shooting mode and decocking safety lever. Made from 1991 to 1997.
Standard . . . . NiB $622 Ex $499 Gd $333
Practical . . . . NiB $598 Ex $490 Gd $373
Silver Chrome finish . . . . NiB $693 Ex $509 Gd $384

BUCK MARK AUTOMATIC PISTOL
Caliber: .22 LR. 10-round magazine, 5.5-inch bbl., 9.5 inches overall. Weight: 32 oz. Black molded grips. Adj. rear sight. Blued or nickel finish. Made from 1985 to date.
Blued finish. . . . . NiB $342 Ex $221 Gd $143
Nickel finish . . . . NiB $403 Ex $285 Gd $203

BUCK MARK BULLSEYE PISTOL

Same general specifications as the standard Buck Mark 22 except w/7.25-inch fluted barrel, 11.83 inches overall. Weight: 36 oz. Adjustable target trigger. Undercut post front sight, click-adjustable Pro-Target rear. Laminated, Rosewood, black rubber or composite grips. Made from 1996 to 2006.

Standard model (composite grips)...NiB $487 Ex $344 Gd $249
Target model . . . . NiB $475 Ex $316 Gd $219

BUCK MARK

BULLSEYE TARGET . . . . NiB $487 Ex $344 Gd $249
Caliber: .22 LR. 10-round magazine, 7.25-inch fluted bbl., 11.83 inches overall. Weight: 31 oz. Rosewood wrap-around finger groove grips w/matte blued finish. Made 1996-2005.

BUCK MARK CAMPER . . . . NiB $300 Ex $210 Gd $150
Similar to Buckmark except w/5.5-inch heavy bbl., matte blued or satin nickel finish. Black polymer grips. Made from 1999 to 2012.
Stainless . . . . NiB $320 Ex $230 Gd $17

BUCK MARK CHALLENGER . . NiB $345 Ex $220 Gd $165
Similar to Buckmark except w/smaller grip. 5.5-inch bbl., matte blued finish. Made from 1999 to 2010.
Micro Challenge (4-in. bbl.) . . . . NiB $300 Ex $210 Gd $155

BUCK MARK 5.5 FIELD . . . . . . NiB $487 Ex $344 Gd $249
Similar to Buck Mark 5.5 Target except w/standard sights. Made from 1991 to 2011.

BUCK MARK LITE SPLASH URX . . . NiB $375 Ex $235 Gd $200
Similar to Buck Mark except w/5.5- or 7.25-in. round aluminum bbl. sleeve. TruGlo fibrtr optic sights. Made from 2006 to 2009.

BUCK MARK MICRO AUTOMATIC PISTOL

Same general specifications as standard Buck Mark except w/4-inch bbl., 8 inches overall. Weight: 32 oz. Molded composite grips. Ramp front sight, Pro Target rear sight. URX grip introduced in 2007. Made from 1992 to 2013.
Blued finish . . . . NiB $367 Ex $271 Gd $181
Nickel finish . . . . NiB $418 Ex $321 Gd $244
Stainless finish . . . . NiB $367 Ex $271 Gd $181

BUCK MARK MICRO PLUS AUTO PISTOL

Same specifications as the Buck Mark Micro except ambidextrous, laminated wood grips. Made from 1996 to 2001.
Blued finish . . . . NiB $285 Ex $234 Gd $192
Nickel finish . . . . NiB $382 Ex $321 Gd $204

BUCK MARK PLUS AUTO PISTOL

Same general specifications as standard Buck Mark except for black molded, impregnated hardwood grips. Made from 1987-2001.
Blued finish . . . . NiB $383 Ex $321 Gd $204
Nickel finish . . . . NiB $404 Ex $329 Gd $223

BUCK MARK 5.5 TARGET AUTO PISTOL

Caliber: .22 LR. 10-round magazine, 5.5-inch bbl., 9.6 inches overall. Weight: 35.5 oz. Pro target sights. Wrap-around walnut or contoured finger groove grips. Made from 1990 to 2009.
Matte blue finish . . . . NiB $455 Ex $374 Gd $223
Nickel finish (1994 to date) . . . NiB $499 Ex $395 Gd $245
Gold finish (1991-99) . . . . NiB $385 Ex $270 Gd $184

BUCK MARK SILHOUETTE . . . . NiB $544 Ex $372 Gd $220
Similar to standard Buck Mark except for 9.88-inch bbl. Weight: 53 oz. Target sights mounted on full-length scope base, and laminated hardwood grips and forend. Made from 1987 to 1999.

Browning
Buck Mark Silhouette

Browning
Buck Mark 5.5 Target

Browning
Buck Mark Micro Plus

Browning Challenger
Standard Model

Browning Challenger
Renaissance Model

**Browning
Challenger III Sporter**

**Browning
9mm Hi-Power w/Molded Grips**

**Browning
9mm Hi-Power AmbidExtrous Safety**

**Browning
Hi-Power Captain**

BUCK MARK UNLIMITED

SILHOUETTE. . . . . NiB $547 Ex $431 Gd $285
Same general specifications as standard Buck Mark Silhouette except w/14-inch bbl., 18.69 inches overall. Weight: 64 oz. Interchangeable post front sight and Pro Target rear. Nickel finish. Made from 1991 to 1999.

BUCK MARK VARMINT

AUTO PISTOL. . . . . NiB $346 Ex $282 Gd $230
Same general specifications as standard Buck Mark except for 9.88-inch bbl. Weight: 48 oz. No sights, full-length scope base, and laminated hardwood grips. Made from 1987 to 1999.

CHALLENGER AUTOMATIC PISTOL

Semi-automatic pistol. Caliber: .22 LR. 10-round magazine, bbl. lengths: 4.5 and 6.75-inches. 11.44 inches overall (with 6.75-inch bbl.). Weight: 38 oz. (6.75-inch bbl.). Removable blade front sight, screw adj. rear. Standard finish, blued, also furnished gold inlaid (Gold model) and engraved and chrome-plated (Renaissance model). Checkered walnut grips. Finely figured and carved grips on Gold and Renaissance models. Standard made by FN 1962-75, higher grades. Intro. 1971. Disc.

Standard model. . . . . NiB $590 Ex $427 Gd $285
Gold model. . . . . NiB $3172 Ex $2448 Gd $1742
Renaissance model . . . . NiB $3058 Ex $2445 Gd $1744

CHALLENGER II . . . . NiB $363 Ex $259 Gd $164
Same general specifications as Challenger Standard model w/6.75-inch bbl. except changed grip angle and impregnated hardwood grips. Original Challenger design modified for lower production costs. Made by ATI from 1976 to 1983.

CHALLENGER III . . . . NiB $295 Ex $217 Gd $153
Same general description as Challenger II except has 5.5 inch bull bbl., alloy frame and new sight system. Weight: 35 oz. Made from 1982-84. Sporter Model w/6.75-inch bbl. Made from 1982-85.

HI-POWER AUTOMATIC PISTOL

Same general specifications as FN Browning Model 1935 except chambered for 9mm Para., .30 Luger or .40 S&W. 10- or 13-round magazine, 4.63-inch bbl., 7.75 inches overall. Weight: 32 oz. (9mm) or 35 oz. (.40 S&W). Fixed sights, also available w/rear sight adj. for windage and elevation, and ramp front sight. AmbidExtrous safety added after 1989. Standard model blued, chrome-plated or Bi-Tone finish. Checkered walnut, contour-molded Polyamide or wraparound rubber grips. Renaissance Engraved model chrome-plated, w/ Nacrolac pearl grips. Made by FN from 1954 to 2002.

Standard model,
fixed sights, 9mm . . . . NiB $895 Ex $689 Gd $510
Standard model, fixed sights,
.40 S&W (intro. 1995). . . . . . NiB $784 Ex $683 Gd $582
Standard model,
.30 Luger (1986-89) . . . . NiB $942 Ex $702 Gd $489
Renaissance model,
fixed sights . . . . NiB $4098 Ex $3651 Gd $2688
w/adjustable rear sight, add $75
w/ambidextrous safety, add $110
w/moulded grips, deduct $50
w/tangent rear sight (1965-78), add* $315
w/T-Slot grip & tangent sight (1965-78), add* $620
*Check with FN to certify serial number.

HI-POWER CAPTAIN . . . . NiB $804 Ex $605 Gd $429
Similar to the standard Hi-Power except fitted w/adj. 500-meter tangent rear sight and rounded hammer. Made from 1993 to 2000.

Browning
Hi-Power Mark III

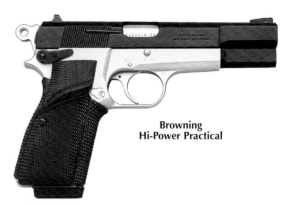

Browning
Hi-Power Practical

HI-POWER MARK III
AUTOMATIC PISTOL . . . . **NiB $793 Ex $498 Gd $398**
Calibers: 9mm or .40 S&W. 10-round magazine, 4.75-inch bbl., 7.75 inches overall. Weight: 32 oz. Fixed sights with molded grips. Durable non-glare matte blue or black epoxy finish. Made from 1985 to 2000; reintro. 2002 to date.

HI-POWER PRACTICAL AUTOMATIC PISTOL
Similar to standard Hi-Power except has silver-chromed frame and blued slide w/Commander-style hammer. Made from 1991 to 2006.
w/fixed sights . . . . **NiB $729 Ex $533 Gd $385**
w/adj. sights, add **$75**

HI-POWER SILVER CHROME . . **NiB $792 Ex $650 Gd $407**
Calibers: 9mm or .40 S&W. 10-round magazine, 4.75-inch bbl., 7.75 inches overall. Weight: 36 oz. Adjustable sights with Pachmayer grips. Silver-chromed finish. Made from 1991 to 2000.

Browning
Hi-Power Silver Chrome

HI-POWER 9MM CLASSIC
Limited Edition 9mm Hi-Power, w/silver-gray finish, high-grade engraving and finely-checkered walnut grips w/double border. Proposed production of the Classic was 5000 w/less than half that number produced. Gold Classic limited to 500 w/two-thirds proposed production in circulation. Made 1985-86.
Gold classic . . . . **NiB $5401 Ex $4999 Gd $3495**
Standard classic . . . . **NiB $1900 Ex $1200 Gd $1000**

INTERNATIONAL MEDALIST EARLY MODEL
TARGET PISTOL . . . . **NiB $1197 Ex $992 Gd $804**
Modification of Medalist to conform w/International Shooting Union rules. 5.9-inch bbl., Smaller grip with no forearm. Weight: 42 oz. Made from 1970-73. Subtract 30% for post 1974 models.

MEDALIST AUTOMATIC TARGET PISTOL
Caliber: .22 LR. 10-round magazine, 6.75-inch bbl. w/vent rib, 11.94 inches overall. Weight: 46 oz. Removable blade front sight, click-adj. micrometer rear. Standard finish, blued also furnished gold-inlaid (Gold Model) and engraved and chrome-plated (Renaissance Model). Checkered walnut grips w/thumbrest (for right- or left-handed shooter). Finely figured and carved grips on Gold and Renaissance Models. Made by FN from 1962 to 1975. Higher grades. Intro. 1971.
Standard model. . . . . **NiB $1552 Ex $1333 Gd $1072**
Gold model. . . . . **NiB $3900 Ex $2500 Gd $1032**
Renaissance model . . . . **NiB $4200 Ex $2750 Gd $2100**

NOMAD AUTOMATIC PISTOL. . . **NiB $486 Ex $328 Gd $227**
Caliber: .22 LR. 10-round magazine, bbl. lengths: 4.5 and 6.75-inches, 8.94 inches overall (4.5-inch bbl.). Weight: 34

Browning
Hi-Power 9mm Classic

Browning
Medalist International

**Browning
Medalist Automatic Target**

**Browning Medalist
Renaissance**

oz. (with 4.5-inch bbl.). Removable blade front sight, screw adj. rear. Blued finish. Plastic grips. Made by FN from 1962 to 1974.

RENAISSANCE 9MM, .25 AUTO AND .380 AUTO (1955) ENGRAVED, CASED SET . . . NiB $9500 Ex $5700 Gd $5000
One pistol of each of the three models in a special walnut or black vinyl carrying case, all chrome-plated w/Nacrolac pearl grips. Made by FN from 1954 to 1969. Options and engraving varies.

BRYCO ARMS INC. — Irvine, CA

Distributed by Jennings Firearms. Inc. Carson City, NV.

MODELS J22, J25 AUTO PISTOL
Calibers: .22 LR, .25 ACP. Six-round magazine, 2.5-inch bbl., about 5 inches overall. Weight: 13 oz. Fixed sights. Chrome, satin nickel or black Teflon finish. Walnut, grooved black Cycolac or resin-impregnated wood grips. Made 1981-85.
Model J-22 (disc. 1985) . . . . NiB $73 Ex $56 Gd $45
Model J-25 (disc. 1995) . . . . NiB $123 Ex $90 Gd $75

MODELS M25, M32, M38 AUTO PISTOL
Calibers: .25 ACP, .32 ACP, .380 ACP. Six-round magazine, 2.81-inch bbl., 5.31 inches overall. Weight: 11oz. to 15 oz. Fixed sights. Chrome, satin nickel or black Teflon finish. Walnut, grooved, black Cycolac or resin-impregnated wood grips. Made from 1988 to 2000.
Model M25 (disc.) . . . . NiB $119 Ex $92 Gd $74
Model M32 . . . . NiB $143 Ex $102 Gd $77
Model M38 . . . . NiB $147 Ex $108 Gd $91

MODEL M48 AUTO PISTOL. . . . NiB $128 Ex $102 Gd $81
Calibers: .22 LR, .32 ACP, .380 ACP. Seven-round magazine, 4-inch bbl., 6.69 inches overall. Weight: 20 oz. Fixed sights. Chrome, satin nickel or black Teflon finish. Smooth wood or black Teflon grips. Made from 1989 to 1995.

MODEL M58. . . . . NiB $132 Ex $108 Gd $90
Caliber: .380 ACP. 10-round magazine, 3.75-inch bbl., 5.5 inches overall. Weight: 30 oz. Fixed sights. Chrome, satin nickel, blued or black Teflon finish. Smooth wood or black Teflon grips. Made 1993 to 1995.

MODEL M59 AUTO PISTOL. . . . NiB $128 Ex $102 Gd $82
Caliber: 9mm Para. 10-round magazine, 4-inch bbl., 6.5 inches overall. Weight: 33 oz. Fixed sights. Chrome, satin nickel, blued or black Teflon finish. Smooth wood or black Teflon grips. Made 1994 to 1996.

MODEL NINE. . . . . NiB $171 Ex $136 Gd $112
Similar to Bryco/Jennings Model M59 except w/redesigned slide w/loaded chamber indicator and frame mounted ejector. Weight: 30 oz. Made from 1997 to 2003.

MODEL 5 AUTO PISTOL . . . . NiB $102 Ex $69 Gd $46
Caliber: .380 ACP, 9mm Para.; 10- or 12-shot magazine. Bbl: 3.25 inches. Blue or nickel finish, black synthetic grips. Weight: 36 oz. Disc. 1995.

BUDISCHOWSKY — Mt. Clemens, MI
Mfd. by Norton Armament Corporation

TP-70 DA AUTOMATIC PISTOL
Calibers: .22 LR, .25 Auto. Six-round magazine, 2.6-inch bbl., 4.65 inches overall. Weight: 12.3 oz. Fixed sights. Stainless steel. Plastic grips. Made from 1973 to 1977.
.22 LR . . . . NiB $487 Ex $361 Gd $372
.25 ACP. . . . . NiB $362 Ex $249 Gd $192

CALICO LIGHT WEAPONS SYSTEM — Hillsboro, OR

MODEL 110 AUTO PISTOL . . . NiB $635 Ex $576 Gd $486
Caliber: .22 LR. 100-round magazine, 6-inch bbl., 17.9 inches overall. Weight: 3.75 lbs. Adj. post front sight, fixed U-notch rear. Black finish aluminum frame. Molded composition grip. Made from 1986 to 1994.

MODEL M-950 AUTO PISTOL . NiB $850 Ex $479 Gd $362
Caliber 9mm Para. 50- or 100-round magazine, 7.5-inch bbl., 14 inches overall. Weight: 2.25 lbs. Adj. post front sight, fixed U-notch rear. Glass-filled polymer grip. Made 1989-94.

CANIK — Turkey
See Century Arms.

CARACAL — Abu Dhabi, UAE

MODEL C . . . . NiB $560 Ex $460 Gd $340
Semi-automatic. Striker-fire. Glock style trigger safety. Caliber: 9mm, 15-rnd. magazine, 3.5-in. bbl., 6.6 inches overall. Weight: 24.6 oz. Fixed sights. Finish: Matte black. Polymer frame. Made from 2006 to date.
Model SC (subcompact version) NiB $560 Ex $460 Gd $340

MODEL F . . . . NiB $560 Ex $460 Gd $340
Semi-automatic. Striker-fire. Glock style trigger safety. Caliber: 9mm, 18-rnd. magazine, 4.1-in. bbl., 7 inches overall. Weight: 26 oz. Fixed sights. Finish: Matte black. Polymer frame. Made from 2006 to date.

**Charter Arms
Bonnie**

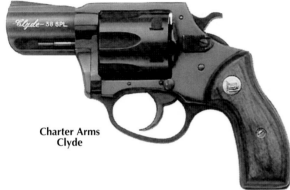

**Charter Arms
Clyde**

**Charter Arms
Bulldog Police**

CENTURY ARMS — Delray Beach, FL
Formerly Century Arms International, importer of military surplus firearms. In 2015 named changed to Century Arms with continued import of new firearms and U.S.-made AK-47 platform firearms.

TP9 (CANIK55) . . . . **NiB $350 Ex $320 Gd $300**
Similar to Walther P99 platform. Semi-automatic. DAO. Caliber: 9mm, 17-rnd. magazine, 4.07-in. bbl., 6.75 inches overall. Weight: 29 oz. Fixed sights. Finish: Matte black. Polymer frame. Made from 2013 to 2015.
TP9v2 (improved version) . . . . . **NiB $350 Ex $320 Gd $300**

PAP M85 NP . . . . **NiB $630 Ex $560 Gd $370**
Similar to AK-47 platform. Semi-automatic. Caliber: 5.56x45mm, 30-rnd. magazine, 10-in. bbl., 19.7 inches overall. Weight: 6.4 lbs. Finish: blued. Krinkov style muzzle brake and hinged dust cover. Stamped receiver. Made in U.S. from 2013 to date.

PAP M92 PV . . . . **NiB $530 Ex $550 Gd $350**
Similar to AK-47 platform. Semi-automatic. Caliber: 7.62x39mm, 30-rnd. magazine, 10-in. bbl., 19.7 inches overall. Weight: 6.4 lbs. Fixed sights. Finish: blued. Krinkov style muzzle brake. Stamped receiver. Made in U.S. from 2013 to date.

CHARLES DALY — Dayton, OH
See Daly, Charles.

CHARTER ARMS — Shelton, CT
Formerly Charter 2000 and ChartArmsms Corp. (Ansonia, CT). Established in 1962 Charter Arms has gone through several names changes. Models name and features are similar; recent manufacture noted.

MODEL 40 AUTOMATIC PISTOL . **NiB $283 Ex $224 Gd $171**
Caliber: .22 LR. Eight-round magazine, 3.3-inch bbl., 6.3 inches overall. Weight: 21.5 oz. Fixed sights. Checkered walnut grips. Stainless steel finish. Made from 1985 to 1986.

**MODEL 79K DA
AUTOMATIC PISTOL** . . . . **NiB $362 Ex $286 Gd $230**
Calibers: .380 or .32 Auto. Seven-round magazine, 3.6-inch bbl., 6.5 inches overall. Weight: 24.5 oz. Fixed sights. Checkered walnut grips. Stainless steel finish. Made from 1985 to 1986.

BONNIE AND CLYDE SET . . . . **NiB $454 Ex $342 Gd $297**
Matching pair of shrouded 2.5-inch bbl., revolvers chambered for .32 Magnum (Bonnie) and .38 Special (Clyde). Blued finish w/scrolled name on bbls. Made 1989 to 1990 and 1999.

BULLDOG .44 DA REVOLVER
SA/DA revolver. Caliber: .44 Special. Five-round cylinder, 2.5- or 3-inch bbl., 7 or 7.5 inches overall. Weight: 19 or 19.5 oz. Fixed sights. Blued, nickel-plated or stainless finish. Checkered walnut Bulldog or square buttgrips. Made from 1973 to 1996.
**Blued finish/
  Pocket Hammer (2.5-inch)** . . . **NiB $260 Ex $192 Gd $134**
**Blued finish/Bulldog grips
  (3-inch disc. 1988)** . . . . **NiB $244 Ex $206 Gd $147**
Electroless nickel. . . . . **NiB $274 Ex $223 Gd $146**
**Stainless steel/
  Bulldog grips (disc. 1992).** . . . **NiB $220 Ex $193 Gd $132**
Neoprene grips/Pocket Hammer. . **NiB $242 Ex $203 Gd $148**

NOTE: *In 1999 the Bulldog was reintroduced. Simialr to other Bulldog models but with 2.5-inch barrel, shrouded ejector rod, blued finish, and checkered rubber grips. Other older model were also reintroduced as noted. Recent models offered in numerous color finishes and patterns.*

- Recent Manufacture (1999 to date) -
Standard . . . . **NiB $409 Ex $355 Gd $315**
stainless finish, add **$20**
Classic. . . . . **NiB $436 Ex $400 Gd $395**
DAO . . . . **NiB $426 Ex $370 Gd $345**
**On Duty (shrouded hammer,
  stainless finish)** . . . . **NiB $432 Ex $380 Gd $355**
Police (4.2-in. bbl., stainless) . . . . **NiB $408 Ex $360 Gd $320**
**Target (4.2-in. bbl., adj. sights,
  stainless)** . . . . **NiB $475 Ex $420 Gd $370**

**Charter Arms
Bulldog Pug**

**Charter Arms
Bulldog Target**

**Charter Arms
Explorer II**

BULLDOG .357 DA REVOLVER... NiB $214 Ex $169 Gd $129
Caliber: .357 Magnum. Five-round cylinder, 6-inch bbl., 11 inches overall. Weight: 25 oz. Fixed sights. Blued finish. Square, checkered walnut grips. Made from 1977 to 1996.

BULLDOG NEW POLICE DA REVOLVER
Same general specifications as Bulldog Police except chambered for .44 Special. Five-round cylinder, 2.5- or 3.5-inch bbl. Made from 1990 to 1992.
Blued finish................NiB $263 Ex $201 Gd $148
Stainless finish (2.5-inch bbl. only) NiB $202 Ex $166 Gd $114

BULLDOG POLICE DA REVOLVER
Caliber: .38 Special or .32 H&R Magnum. Six-round cylinder, 4-inch bbl., 8.5 inches overall. Weight: 20.5 oz. Adj. rear sight, ramp front. Blued or stainless finish. Square checkered walnut grips. Made from 1976-93. No shroud on new models.
Blued finish................NiB $272 Ex $204 Gd $158
Stainless finish.............NiB $234 Ex $194 Gd $147
.32 H&R Magnum (disc.1992)...NiB $270 Ex $204 Gd $142

BULLDOG PUG DA REVOLVER
Caliber: .44 Special. Five-round cylinder, 2.5 inch bbl., 7.25 inches overall. Weight: 20 oz. Blued or stainless finish. Fixed ramp front sight, fixed square-notch rear. Checkered Neoprene or walnut grips. Made from 1988 to 1993.
Blued finish................NiB $262 Ex $224 Gd $183
Stainless finish.............NiB $224 Ex $172 Gd $121

BULLDOG TARGET.......... NiB $207 Ex $134 Gd $102
Calibers: .357 Magnum, .44 Special (latter intro. in 1977). Four-inch bbl., 8.5 inches overall. Weight: 20.5 oz. in .357. Adj. rear sight, ramp front. Blued finish. Square checkered walnut grips. Made 1976 to 1992.
Stainless steel.............NiB $271 Ex $203 Gd $147

BULLDOG TRACKER ....NiB $207 Ex $134 Gd $102
DA reviolver. Caliber: .357 Mag. Five-round cylinder, 2.5-, 4- or 6-inch bbl., 11 inches overall (6-inch bbl.). Weight: 21 oz. (2.5-inch bbl.). Adj. rear sight, ramp front. Checkered walnut grips. Blued finish. 4- or 6-inch bbl., Disc.1986. Reintro. 1989 to 1992.

EXPLORER II SEMIAUTO SURVIVAL PISTOL
Caliber: .22 LR, 8-round magazine, 6-, 8- or 10-inch bbl., 13.5 inchesoverall (6-inch bbl.). Weight: 28 oz. finishes: Black, heat cured, semigloss textured enamel or silvertone anticorrosion. Disc. 1987.
Standard model.............NiB $158 Ex $100 Gd $66
Silvertone (w/optional
  6- or 10-inch bbl.).........NiB $143 Ex $123 Gd $83

MAG PUG................. NiB $397 Ex $345 Gd $305
SImilar to Bulldog .357 except w/2.5-in. bbl. w/ejector shroud and rubber grips. Made from 2001 to date.

OFF-DUTY DA REVOLVER
Calibers: .22 LR or .38 Special. Six-round (.22 LR) or 5-round (.38 Special) cylinder. Two-inch bbl., 6.25 inches overall. Weight: 16 oz. Fixed rear sight, Partridge-type front sight. Plain walnut grips. Matte black, nickel or stainless steel finish. Made from 1992 to 1996.
Matte black finish ....NiB $185 Ex $153 Gd $112
Nickel finish ....NiB $230 Ex $194 Gd $150
Stainless steel ....NiB $260 Ex $194 Gd $128
- Recent Manufacture (1999 to date) -
Standard (2-in. bbl., hammerless, aluminum frame, matte
  black finish)..............NiB $419 Ex $360 Gd $315
two-tone finish, add $20

ON DUTY................ NiB $402 Ex $355 Gd $310
SImilar to Mag Pug or Undercover depending on caliber except w/shrouded hammer. Matte stainless finsih. Made 2009 to date.

PATHFINDER DA REVOLVER
Calibers: .22 LR, .22 WMR. Six-round cylinder, bbl. lengths: 2-, 3-, 6-inches, 7.13 inches overall (in 3-inch bbl.), and regular grips. Weight: 18.5 oz. (3-inch bbl.). Adj. rear sight, ramp front. Blued or stainless finish. Plain walnut regular, checkered Bulldog or square buttgrips. Made 1970 to date. Note: Originally designated "Pocket Target," name was changed in 1971 to "Pathfinder." Grips changed in 1984.
Blued finish................NiB $203 Ex $148 Gd $112
Stainless finish.............NiB $240 Ex $192 Gd $128
- Recent Manufacture (1999 to date) -
Standard (2-in. bbl., .22 LR or .22 Mag., 6-shot cylinder,
  stainless finish) ....NiB $365 Ex $320 Gd $280
two-tone colores finish, add......................$20

PATRIOT .... NiB $345 Ex $305 Gd $255
SImilar to Bulldog .357 except in .327 Federal. Made 2009 to 2012.

PIT BULL DA REVOLVER
Calibers: 9mm, .357 Magnum, .38 Special. Five-round cylinder, 2.5-, 3.5- or 4-inch bbl., 7 inches overall (2.5-inch bbl.). Weight: 21.5 to 25 oz. All stainless steel frame. Fixed ramp

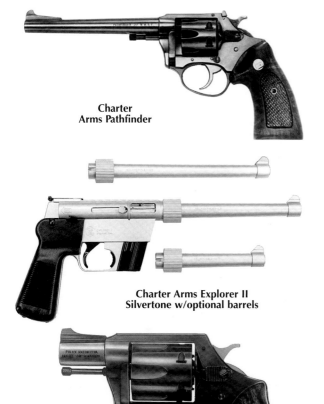

Charter Arms Pathfinder

Charter Arms Explorer II Silvertone w/optional barrels

Charter Arms Police Undercover .32 H&R Magnum

chambered for .32 H&R Magnum or .32 S&W Long, has 6-round cylinder and 2.5-inch bbl.

.32 H&R Magnum (blued)	NiB $316	Ex $253	Gd $170
.32 H&R Magnum nickel	NiB $212	Ex $171	Gd $109
.32 H&R Magnum (stainless)	NiB $332	Ex $268	Gd $187
.32 S&W Long (blued) disc. 1989	NiB $303	Ex $225	Gd $179

UNDERCOVER LITE . . . . NiB $397 Ex $345 Gd $305
SImilar to Undercover except w/aluminum frame. Caliber: .38 Special. Five-round cylinder,. bbl., lengths: 2-in. Rubber grips. Weight: 12 oz. Fixed sights. Matte aluminum finsh. Made from 1991 to date.
colored finishes, add $20

UNDERCOVER POCKET POLICE DA REVOLVER
Same general specifications as standard Undercover except has 6-round cylinder and pocket-type hammer. Blued or stainless steel finish. Made from 1969 to 1981.
Blued finish . . . . NiB $342 Ex $283 Gd $ 214
Stainless steel . . . . NiB $356 Ex $290 Gd $219

UNDERCOVER POLICE DA REVOLVER
Same general specifications as standard Undercover except has 6-round cylinder. Made from 1984 to 1989. Reintroduced 1993.
Blued, .38 Special . . . . NiB $337 Ex $ 279 Gd $204
Stainless, .38 Special . . . . NiB $270 Ex $204 Gd $158
.32 H&R Magnum . . . . NiB $250 Ex $200 Gd $143

UNDERCOVERETTE
DA REVOLVER . . . . NiB $179 Ex $130 Gd $101
Same as Undercover except w/2-in. bbl., caliber .32 S&W Long, 6-round cylinder, blued finish only. Weight: 16.5 oz. Made 1972 to 1983.
- Recent Manufacture (1999 to date) -
Standard (2-in. bbl., .32 H&R Mag.,
    stainless finish) . . . . NiB $375 Ex $330 Gd $290
two-tone colores finish, add $20

CHIAPPA FIREARMS LTD. — DAYTON, OH
Chiappa owns ARMI SPORT REPLICA FIREARMS MFG. and manufactures Cimarron, Legacy Sports, Taylor's & Co. Imported currently, manufactured in Italy.

1892 Mare's Leg . . . . NiB $515 Ex $460 Gd $360
Lever-action pistol. SA. Caliber: .357 Mag., .44 Mag., or .45 Long Colt, 4-rnd. magazine. 9- or 12-in. bbl. Sights: adj rear. Finish: case-hardened receiver, blue bbl. Imported from 2013 to date.

1911-45 Custom . . . . NiB $560 Ex $450 Gd $340
1911 full size platform. Semi-automatic. SA. Caliber: .45 ACP, 8-rnd. magazine. 5-in. bbl. Sights: Novak style. Grip: checkered olive wood. Finish: black. Imported from 2013 to date.

1911-22 Standard . . . . NiB $278 Ex $230 Gd $200
1911 style. Semi-automatic. SA. Caliber: .22 LR, 10-rnd. magazine. 5-in. bbl. Sights: fixed front, adj. rear. Grip: checkered wood. Finish: black, OD/black, tan/black. Length: 8.6 in. Weight: 33 oz. Imported from 2010 to date.
Compact model, add $50
Custom model, add $100
Target model, add $30

MFour Pistol . . . . NiB $515 Ex $460 Gd $360
AR15 style. Semi-automatic, blowback. SA. Caliber: .22 LR, 10- or 28-rnd. magazine. 6-in. bbl. Sights: adj. Imported from 2011 to 2013.

front sight, fixed square-notch rear. Checkered Neoprene grips. Blued or stainless finish. Made from 1989 to 1991.
Blued finish . . . . NiB $261 Ex $223 Gd $137
Stainless finish . . . . NiB $270 Ex $ 230 Gd $143
- Recent Manufacture (2010 to date) -
Standard (2-in. bbl., 9mm, .40 S&W or .45 ACP, 5-shot cylinder,
    stainless finish) . . . . NiB $502 Ex $420 Gd $380
.40 S&W or .45 ACP, deduct $10

SOUTHPAW . . . . NiB $419 Ex $365 Gd $330
SImilar to Undercover except true left hand design. Made 2008 to date.

UNDERCOVER DA REVOLVER
Caliber: .38 Special. Five-round cylinder,. bbl., lengths: 2-, 3-, 4-inches, 6.25 inches overall (2-inch bbl.), and regular grips. Weight: 16 oz. (2-inch bbl.). Fixed sights. Plain walnut, checkered Bulldog or square buttgrips. Made from 1965 to 1996.
Blued or nickel-plated finish . . . NiB $216 Ex $120 Gd $101
Stainless finish . . . . NiB $281 Ex $230 Gd $148
- Recent Manufacture (1999 to date) -
Standard (2-in. bbl., blued finish) . . NiB $346 Ex $290 Gd $255
stainless finish, add $10
DAO (2-in. bbl., blued finish) . . NiB $352 Ex $300 Gd $265

UNDERCOVER DA REVOLVER
Same general specifications as standard Undercover except

**Charter Arms
Undercover Stainless**

**Cimarron
El Pistolero**

M9 . . . . NiB $520 Ex $320 Gd $240
Beretta M9 style. Semi-automatic. DA/SA. Caliber: 9mm, 10- or 15-rnd. magazine. 4.9-in. bbl. Sights: fixed. Grip: checkered polymer or wood. Finish: black. Imported from 2013 to 2015.

M9-22 Standard . . . . NiB $370 Ex $320 Gd $240
Beretta M9 style. Semi-automatic. DA/SA. Caliber: .22 LR, 10-rnd. magazine. 5-in. bbl. Sights: fixed front, adj. rear. Grip: checkered polymer or wood. Finish: black. Length: 8.6 in. Weight: 37 oz. Imported from 2013 to date.
checkered wood grip, add $25

RHINO SERIES
Revolver. Bore aligns with bottom chamber of cylinder. DA/SA. Caliber: .357 Mag., 9mm, or .40 S&W, 6-rnd. cylinder. 2-, 4-, 5-, or 6-in. bbl. Frame: aluminum. Sights: fixed front, adj. rear. Grip: checkered wood or rubber. Finish: black or nickel. Weight: 24-33.2 oz. depending on bbl. length. Imported from 2010 to date.
200D (2-in. bbl., rubber grip) . . NiB $990 Ex $880 Gd $660
200DS (2-in. bbl., wood grip) . . NiB $990 Ex $880 Gd $660
200DS Polymer (2-in. bbl., wood grip,
   polymer frame) . . . . NiB $750 Ex $660 Gd $510
40DS (4-in. bbl., wood grip) . . NiB $1073 Ex $960 Gd $710
50DS (5-in. bbl., wood grip) . NiB $1075 Ex $960 Gd $710
60DS (6-in. bbl., wood grip) . . NiB $1099 Ex $980 Gd $720

CIMARRON F.A. CO. — Fredricksburg, TX

Currently imports, distrbutes and retails black powder and cartridge firearms manufactured by Armi-Sport, Chiappa, Pedersoli, Pietta, and Uberti.

1872 OPEN-TOP SA REVOLVER . . . NiB $510 Ex $345 Gd $270
Reproduction of Colt Navy and Army open-top conversion revolvers. Calibers: .38 Long Colt, .38 Spl., .44-40, .44 Spl., 44 Russian, .45 Schofield or .45 Long Colt. Six-round cylinder. 4.75- 5.5- or 7.5-inch bbl., brass backstrap and triggerguard, blued finish. Made from 1999 to date.
Silver plated backstrap (2010) . . . . NiB $550 Ex $385 Gd $310
Engraved, add $1000

BADLAND SA REVOLVER . . . . . NiB $280 Ex $210 Gd $180
Calibers: .357 Mag., .45 Colt. 6-round cylinder, 4.75-in. bbl., brass backstrap and triggerguard, wood grip. Made 2005-07.

BADLAND SA REVOLVER . . . . . NiB $400 Ex $315 Gd $200
Calibers: .44 Spl./.44 Mag. 6-round cylinder, 4.75-, 6- or 7.5-in. bbl., brass or steel backstrap and triggerguard, wood grip. Made from 1984 to 1993.
Buntline . . . . NiB $415 Ex $330 Gd $220
Bisley . . . . NiB $615 Ex $500 Gd $440
Mfg. by Uberti. See listing under Uberti. Imported 2002 to date.

EL PISTOLERO SA REVOLVER . . NiB $444 Ex $336 Gd $260
Calibers: .357 Mag., .45 Colt. Six-round cylinder, 4.75- 5.5- or 7.5-inch bbl., polished brass backstrap and triggerguard. Otherwise, same as Colt Single-Action Army revolver w/parts being interchangeable. Made from 1997 to 1998; reitro. 2007 to 2013.

EVIL ROY SAA . . . . NIB $740 EX $630 GD $530
Calibers: .38 Spl./.357 Mag., .44-40, .45 Colt. 6-round cylinder, 4.75- or 5.5-in. bbl., tuned action, wide sights, smooth or checkered wood grip. Case hardened frame, blue grip frame. Engraved with Evil Roy signature. Made from 2005 to date.

FRONTIER SIX SHOOTER . . . . . NiB $730 Ex $580 Gd $450
Calibers: .22 LR, .22 Mag., .38 Spl./.357 Mag., .38-40, .44 Spl., .44-40 or .45 Long Colt. 6-round cylinder, 4.75-, 5.5- or 7.5-in. bbl., steel backstrap. Original Colt-like finish. Made from 2008 to 2010.
Sheriff's model (3- or 4-in. bbl.) . . . NiB $400 Ex $300 Gd $220
Target model (adj. rear sight) . . NiB $360 Ex $270 Gd $200

FRONTIER SAA . . . . NiB $500 Ex $430 Gd $380
Mfg. by Pietta. Calibers: .357 Mag., .44-40, .45 Colt. 6-round cylinder. 3.5-, 4.75-, 5.5-, or 7.5-in. bbl. Finish: blue or charcoal blue. Imported from 2011 to date.

"HAND OF GOD" HOLY SMOKER
   SAA . . . . NiB $760 Ex $660 Gd $580
Hollywood Series. Mfg. by Pietta or Uberti. Calibers: .45 Colt. 6-round cylinder, 4.75- in. bbl., blue finish, one-piece walnut grip with gold cross inlay on both sides. Made from 2005 to date.

JUDGE ROY BEAN COMMEMORATIVE
   SAA . . . . NiB $1600 Ex $1400 Gd $1100
Disc. 1996.

LIGHTNING SAA . . . . NiB $500 Ex $430 Gd $380
Patterned after Colt Lightning revolver with bird's head grip expect SA. Mfg. by Uberti. Calibers: .22 LR, .38 Colt, .38 Spl., or .41 Colt. 6-round cylinder, 3.5-, 4.75-, 5.5-, or 6.5-in. bbl., blue finish, one-piece smooth walnut grip. Made from 1999 to 2001, reintro. 2003.

"MAN WITH NO NAME"
   CONVERSION . . . . NiB $817 Ex $690 Gd $590
Hollywood Series. Mfg. by Uberti. Navy cartridge conversion. Calibers: .38 Spl. 6-round cylinder, 7.5-in. bbl., Finish: case-hardened and blue, brass grip frame and trigger guard. Grip: one-piece walnut with silver rattlesnake inlay.

"MAN WITH NO NAME" SAA . . . NiB $775 Ex $680 Gd $580
Hollywood Series. Mfg. by Uberti. Calibers: .45 Colt. 6-round cylinder, 4.75- or 5.5-in. bbl., blue finish, one-piece walnut grip with silver rattlesnake inlay.

Colt
Model 1902 Military

MODEL P SAA . . . . NiB $550 Ex $480 Gd $420
Patterned after Colt Model P revolver. Calibers: .32-20, .38-40, .357 Mag., .44-40 or .45 Colt. 6-round cylinder. 4.75-, 5.5-, or 7.5-in. bbl. Available with pinched frame, Old Model or Pre-War models. Finish: blue, charcoal blue. Imported from 1996 to date.
Model P Jr. (smaller frame size). . . NiB $450 Ex $390 Gd $340
Model P Jr. Black Stallion
(.22 LR/.22 WMR) . . . . NiB $520 Ex $460 Gd $390

NEW SHERIFF SAA. . . . . NiB $550 Ex $480 Gd $420
Mfg. by Pietta or Uberti. Calibers: .357 Mag., .44-40 or .45 Colt. 6-round cylinder. 3.5-in. bbl. Finish: case-hardened and blue. Grip: smooth walnut. With ejector rod. Imported from 2011 to date.

PLINKERTON SAA . . . . NiB $180 Ex $155 Gd $130
Mfg. by Chiappa. Calibers: .22 LR. 6-round cylinder. 4.75-in. bbl. Finish: matte black. Grip: checkered black plastic. Imported from 2007 to date.

"ROOSTER SHOOTER" SAA. . . NiB $910 Ex $780 Gd $680
Hollywood Series. Mfg. by Pietta or Uberti. Calibers: .357 Mag., .44-40, or .45 Colt. 6-round cylinder, 4.75-in. bbl., antique finish, one-piece faux ivory grip with finger grooves. Imported from 2010 to date.

SCHOFIELD MODEL NO. 3 . . . NiB $850 Ex $740 Gd $650
Patterned after Smith & Wesson Schofield revolver. Mfg. by San Marco or Uberti. Calibers: .38 Spl., .38-40, .44 Russian, .44 Spl., .44-40, .45 Schofield, .45 ACP, or .45 Colt. 6-round cylinder. 3.5-(Wells Fargo model), 5-, or 7-in. bbl. Finish: blue, case hardened, or nickel. Grip: checkered or smooth walnut. Imported from 1996 to date.
Model No. 3 Russian (.44 Russian or .45 Colt, trigger guard
spur) . . . . NiB $1080 Ex $930 Gd $830

THUNDERER SAA. . . . . NiB $500 EX $430 Gd $380
Patterned after Colt Thundered revolver with bird's head grip expect SA. Mfg. by Uberti. Calibers: .357 Mag., .44 Spl., .44-40, or .45 Colt. 6-round cylinder. 3.5-, 4.75-, or 5.5-in. bbl. Finish: blue, case hardened, stainless, or nickel. Grip: checkered or smooth walnut. Imported from 1994 to date.
Thunderer Long Tom (7.5-in. bbl.,
1997-2009) . . . . NiB $540 Ex $390 Gd $340
Thunderer Doc Holliday (3.5-in. bbl.,
2008-present) . . . . NiB $1690 Ex $1400 Gd $1100

U.S.V. ARTILLERY
"ROUGH RIDER" SAA . . . . . NiB $595 Ex $500 Gd $460
Patterned after Colt U.S. Artillery revolver. Mfg. by Pietta or Uberti. Calibers: .45 Colt. 6-round cylinder. 5.5-in. bbl. Finish: blue, and case hardened. Grip: smooth walnut with cartouche. Imported from 1996 to date.

U.S. 7TH CAVALRY CUSTER
MODEL SAA . . . . NiB $600 Ex $520 Gd $460
Patterned after Colt U.S. Military cavalry contract revolver. Mfg. by Pietta or Uberti. Calibers: .45 Colt. 6-round cylinder. 7.5-in. bbl. Finish: blue, and case hardened. Grip: one-piece smooth walnut with cartouche. Imported from 1990 to date.

COLT'S MANUFACTURING CO., INC. — Hartford, CT

Previously Colt Industries, Firearms Division. Production of some Colt handguns spans the period before World War II to the postwar years. Values shown for these models are for earlier production. Those manufactured c. 1946 and later generally are less desirable to collectors and values are approximately 30 percent lower.

NOTE: *For ease in finding a particular firearm, Colt handguns are grouped into three sections: Automatic Pistols, Single-Shot Pistols & Derringers, and Revolvers. For a complete listing, please refer to the Index.*

- AUTOMATIC PISTOLS -

MODEL 1900 .38 AUTOMATIC PISTOL
Caliber: .38 ACP (modern high-velocity cartridges should not be used in this pistol). Seven-round magazine, 6-inch bbl., 9 inches overall. Weight: 35 oz. Fixed sights. Blued finish. Hard rubber and plain or checkered walnut grips. Sharp-spur hammer. Combination rear sight and safety unique to the Model 1900 (early production). In mid-1901 a solid rear sight was dovetailed into the slide. (S/N range 1-4274) Made 190003. Note: 250 models were sold to the military (50 Navy and 200 Army).
Early commercial model
(w/sight/safety) . . . NiB $15,810 Ex $14,586 Gd $11,220
Late commercial model
(w/dovetailed sight). . . NiB $15,810 Ex $14,586 Gd $11,220
Army Model w/U.S. inspector marks (1st Series - S/N 90-150
w/inspector mark J.T.T.). . . NiB $32,130 Ex $27,540 Gd $22,185
(2nd Series - S/N 1600-1750
w/inspector mark R.A.C.). . . NiB $11,577 Ex $9736 Gd $6700
Navy model (Also marked
w/USN-I.D. number) . . . NiB $18,967 Ex $13,107 Gd $10,200

MODEL 1902 MILITARY .38 AUTOMATIC PISTOL
Caliber: .38 ACP (modern high-velocity cartridges should not be used in this pistol). Eight-round magazine, 6-inch bbl., 9 inches overall. Weight: 37 oz. Fixed sights w/blade front and V-notch rear. Blued finish. Checkered hard rubber grips. Round back hammer, changed to spur type in 1908. No safety but fitted w/standard military swivel. About 18,000 produced with split S/N ranges. The government contract series (15,001-15,200) and the commercial sales series (15,000 receding to 11,000) and (30,200-47,266). Made from 1902 to 1929.
Early military model (w/front
slide serrations) . . . . NiB $6,120 Ex $3871 Gd $3528
Late military model (w/rear
slide serrations) . . . . NiB $6115 Ex $3732 Gd $2525
MARKED "U.S. ARMY"
(S/N 15,001-15,200). . . NiB $19,635 Ex $17,340 Gd $15,402

MODEL 1902 SPORTING
.38 AUTOMATIC PISTOL . . NiB $5750 Ex $4250 Gd $2500
Caliber: .38 ACP (modern high-velocity cartridges should not be used in this pistol). Seven-round magazine, 6-inch bbl., 9

Colt
1903 Early Hammer

Colt
Model 1903 Pocket Hammerless

inches overall. Weight: 35 oz. Fixed sights w/blade front and V-notch rear. Blued finish. Checkered hard rubber grips. Round back hammer was standard but some spur hammers were installed during late production. No safety and w/o swivel as found on military model. Total production about 7,500 w/split S/N ranges (4275-10,999) and (30,000-30,190) Made from 1902 to 1908.

MODEL 1903 POCKET .32 AUTOMATIC PISTOL
FIRST ISSUE - COMMERCIAL SERIES
Caliber: .32 Auto. Eight-round magazine, 4-inch bbl., 7 inches overall. Weight: 23 oz. Fixed sights. Blued or nickel finish. Checkered hard rubber grips. Hammerless (concealed hammer). Slide lock and grip safeties. Fitted w/barrel bushing but early models have no magazine safety. Total production of the Model 1903 reached 572,215. The First Issue maded from 1903 to 1908 (S/N range 1-72,000).
Blued finish. . . . . NiB $1132 Ex $806 Gd $587
Nickel finish . . . . NiB $1153 Ex $826 Gd $602

MODEL 1903 POCKET .32 AUTOMATIC PISTOL
SECOND ISSUE - COMMERCIAL SERIES
Same as First Issue but with 3.75-inch bbl. and small Extractor. Made from 1908 to 1910 (S/N range 72,001 -105,050).
Blued finish. . . . . NiB $816 Ex $602 Gd $474
Nickel finish . . . . NiB $842 Ex $689 Gd $498

MODEL 1903 POCKET .32 AUTOMATIC PISTOL,
THIRD ISSUE - COMMERCIAL SERIES
Caliber: .32 Auto. Similar to Second Issue w/3.75-inch bbl. except with integral barrel bushing and locking lug at muzzle end of bbl. Production occurred 1910 to 1926 (S/N range 105,051-468,096).
Blued finish. . . . . NiB $1326 Ex $1030 Gd $813
Nickel finish . . . . NiB $1474 Ex $1234 Gd $918

MODEL 1903 POCKET .32 AUTOMATIC PISTOL
FOURTH ISSUE - COMMERCIAL SERIES
Caliber: .32 Auto. Similar to Third Issue except a slide lock safety change was made when a Tansley-style disconnector was added on all pistols above S/N 468,097, which prevents firing of cartridge in chamber when the magazine is removed. Blued or nickel finish. Checkered walnut grips. These design changes were initiated 1926 to 1945 (S/N range 105,051-554,446).
Blued finish . . . . NiB $1331 Ex $1020 Gd $804
Nickel finish . . . . NiB $1535 Ex $1132 Gd $945

MODEL 1903 POCKET (HAMMER) .38 AUTOMATIC PISTOL
Caliber: .38 ACP (modern high-velocity cartridges should not be used in this pistol). Similar to Model 1902 Sporting .38 but w/shorter frame, slide and 4.5-inch bbl. Overall dimension reduced to 7.5 inches. Weight: 31 oz. Fixed sights w/blade front and V-notch rear. Blued finish. Checkered hard rubber grips. Round back hammer, changed to spur type in 1908. No safety. (S/N range 16,001-47,226 with some numbers above 30,200 assigned to 1902 Military). Made from 1903 to 1929.
Early model
(round hammer) . . . . NiB $2030 Ex $1713 Gd $1418
Late model
(spur hammer) . . . . NiB $2254 Ex $1953 Gd $1641

MODEL 1903 POCKET HAMMERLESS (CONCEALED HAMMER)
.32 AUTOMATIC PISTOL - MILITARY
Caliber: .32 ACP. Eight-round magazine, Similar to Model 1903 Pocket .32 except concealed hammer and equipped w/ magazine safety. Parkerized or blued finish. (S/N range with "M" prefix M1-M200,000) Made from 1941 to 1945.
Blued service model (marked
"U.S. Property") . . . . NiB $1333 Ex $1179 Gd $852
Parkerized service model (marked
"U.S. Property") . . . . NiB $2162 Ex $1821 Gd $1520
Blued documented
Officer's model. . . . . NiB $3182 Ex $2880 Gd $1760
Parkerized documented
Officer's model. . . . . NiB $3182 Ex $2880 Gd $1760

MODEL 1905 .45 AUTOMATIC PISTOL
Caliber: .45 (Rimless) Automatic. Seven-round magazine, 5-inch bbl., 8 inches overall. Weight: 32.5 oz. Fixed sights w/ blade front and V-notch rear. Blued finish. Checkered walnut, hard rubber or pearl grips. Predecessor to Model 1911 Auto Pistol and contributory to the development of the .45 ACP cartridge. (S/N range 1-6100) Made from 1905 to 1911.
Commercial model . . . . NiB $7461 Ex $5579 Gd $3784
w/slotted backstrap
(500 produced). . . . . . . NiB $10,761 Ex $8966 Gd $7359
w/shoulder stock/holster, add. . . . . $7650 to $10,200

MODEL 1905 .45 (1907)
CONTRACT PISTOL . NiB $22,440 Ex $17,340 Gd $10,200
Variation of the Model 1905 produced to U.S. Military specifications, including loaded chamber indicator, grip safety and lanyard loop. Only 201 were produced, but 200 were delivered and may be identified by the chief inspector's initials "K.M." (S/N range 1-201) Made from 1907 to 1908.

MODEL 1908 POCKET .25 HAMMERLESS AUTO PISTOL
Caliber: .25 Auto. Six-round magazine, 2-inch bbl., 4.5 inches overall. Weight: 13 oz. Flat-top front, square-notch rear sight in groove. Blued, nickel or Parkerized finish. Checkered hard rubber grips on early models, checkered walnut on later type, special pearl grips illustrated. Both a grip safety and slide lock safety are included on all models. The Tansley-style safety disconnector was added in 1916 at pistol No. 141000. (S/N

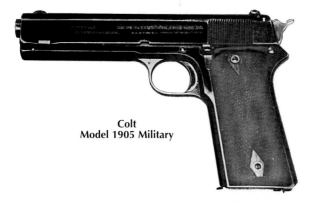

**Colt
Model 1905 Military**

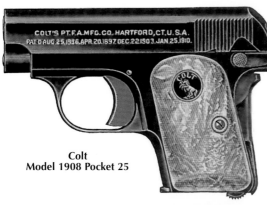

**Colt
Model 1908 Pocket 25**

**Colt
Model 1911**

range 1-409,061) Made 1908 to 1941.
Blued finish. . . . . NiB $1734 Ex $1415 Gd $1137
Nickel finish, add $125
**Marked "U.S. Property"
(w/blued finish)** . . . . NiB $3213 Ex $2861 Gd $2560

MODEL 1908 POCKET .380 AUTOMATIC PISTOL
Similar to Pocket .32 Auto w/3.75-inch bbl. except chambered for .380 Auto w/seven-round magazine. Weight: 23 oz. Blue, nickel or Parkerized finish. (S/N range 1-138,009) Made from 1908 to 1945.
**First Issue (made 1908-11, w/bbl., lock and bushing,
w/S/N 1-6,250)**. . . . . NiB $1734 Ex $1528 Gd $1312
**Second Issue (made 1911-28,w/o bbl., lock and bushing,
w/S/N 6,251-92,893)** . . . NiB $2017 Ex $1693 Gd $1528
**Third Issue (made 1928-45, w/safety disconnector,
w/S/N 92,894-138,009)**. . . . NiB $1734 Ex $1528 Gd $1312

**Parkerized service model (Marked "U.S. Property" made
1942-45, w/S/N "M" prefix.)** . . . NiB $2649 Ex $1972 Gd $1723
**Documented officer's model (service model w/military
assignment papers)** . . . . . NiB $3162 Ex $2557 Gd $1804

NOTE: *During both World Wars, Colt licensed other firms to make these pistols under government contract, including Ithaca Gun Co., North American Arms Co., Ltd. (Canada), Remington-Rand Co., Remington-UMC, Singer Sewing Machine Co., and Union Switch & Signal Co. M1911 also produced at Springfield Armory.*

MODEL 1911 AUTOMATIC PISTOL (COMMERCIAL)
Caliber: .45 Auto. Seven-round magazine, 5-inch bbl., 8.5 inches overall. Weight: 39 oz. Fixed sights. Blued finish on Commercial model. Parkerized or similar finish on most military pistols. Checkered walnut grips (early production), plastic grips (later production). Checkered, arched mainspring housing and longer grip safety spur adopted in 1923 on M1911A1. C-series.
**Model 1911 commercial (mfg. 1912-1925, S/N range:
C1-C138532)**. . . . . NiB $15,300 Ex $13,255 Gd $11,424
**Model 1911A1 commercial Pre-WWII ("C" prefix serial number,
mfg. 1925-1942, S/N range: C138533-
C215000)** . . . . NiB $3886 Ex $3172 Gd $2240
**Model 1911A1 commercial Post-WWII (changed to "C" suffix S/N
in 1950, mfg. 1946-1970)** NiB $3886 Ex $3172 Gd $2240

MODEL 1911 U.S. MILITARY GOVERNMENT
These are U.S. Military pistols made between 1912 through 1918 by a variety of manufacturers. Typical characteristics include: Straight mainspring housing, checkered wood grips, lanyard loop, and long trigger.
Colt manufacture
(mfg. 1912) . . . . NiB $10,353 Ex $8975 Gd $6849
(mfg. 1913-1915) . . . . . . NiB $5500 Ex $4800 Gd $4300
(mfg. 1916) . . . . NiB $5700 Ex $5100 Gd $4300
(mfg. 1917-1918, blue
finish) . . . . NiB $4300 Ex $3300 Gd $2100
(mfg. 1917-1918, black Army
finish) . . . . .NiB $4300 Ex $3300 Gd $2100
(mfg. 1919-1925) . . . . . . NiB $4300 Ex $3300 Gd $2100
**Marine Model M1911 type (stamped: "MODEL OF 1911
U.S. ARMY" on r. of slide)** NiB $8771 Ex $6654 Gd $4995
**Navy Model M1911 type (stamped: "MODEL OF 1911 U.S.
NAVY" on right of slide)** . NiB $8771 Ex $6654 Gd $4995
**North American Arms Co. manufacture (1918)
under 100 produced**. . . NiB $36,720 Ex $29,580 Gd $24,990
**Remington-UMC manufacture (1918-1919)
S/N range: 1-21676** . . . . . NiB $6120 Ex $4070 Gd $2458
**Springfield manufacture (1914-1915)
S/N ranges: 72751-83855, 102597-107596, 113497-120566,
125567-133186**. . . . . NiB $6120 Ex $4070 Gd $2458

MODEL 1911 FOREIGN MILITARY CONTRACTS
Simialr to U.S. Military M1911s except exported to foreign goverments.
**Argentine type (Arg. seal stamped on top of slide, S/N w/"C"
prefix, mfg. 1914-19)** . . . NiB $3900 Ex $3600 Gd $3200
**British type (stamped: "CALIBRE 455",
mfg. 1915-1919)** . . . . NiB $5800 Ex $4800 Gd $3000
**Norwegian 1914 type (w/extended slide release,
mfg. 1918-1947)** . . . . NiB $2400 Ex $1900 Gd $1600
**Russian type (w/Cyrillis markings on left side of receiver,
mfg. 1916-1917)** . . . . NiB $8800 Ex $4600 Gd $4100

M1911 SERIES 70 WWI MODEL 1918
REPRODUCTION. . . . . NiB $1500 Ex $950 Gd $700

Colt
1991 A1

Colt Cadet .22

Colt All American
Model 2000

Reproduction of Model 1911 (see above) w/black finish, original WWI rollmarks. Made from 2008 to 2009.

M1911 MODEL O SERIES 70
REPRODUCTION . . . . NiB $1500 Ex $950 Gd $700
Reproduction of Model 1911 (see above) w/original 1911 U.S. Military rollmarks, carbonia blue finish. Made 2003-09.

MODEL 1911A1 U.S. MILITARY GOVERNMENT
These are U.S. Military pistols made between 1924 through 1945 by a variety of manufacturers. Simialr to M1911 except w/arched main spring housing, blued or parkerized (mot common) finsih, cheched plastic grips, short trigger, longer grip safety, finger groove cut out in frame.
Colt manufacture . . . . NiB $4600 Ex $3900 Gd $3000
Ithaca manufacture . . . . . . NiB $2300 Ex $1900 Gd $1600

Remington-Rand manufacture. . NiB $2600 Ex $2200 Gd $200
Singer manufacture. . NiB $65,900 Ex $50,015 Gd $40,455
Union Switch &
   Signal manufacture. . . . . NiB $6227 Ex $5247 Gd $4047

MODEL 1911A1 FOREIGN MILITARY CONTRACTS
Simialr to U.S. Military M1911A1s except exported to foreign goverments.
Argentine contract (stamped w/Argentine crest and
   "Model 1927") . . . . NiB $1600 Ex $1400 Gd $1200
Argentine manufacture (stamped w/crest and two lines on r.
   side of slide: "EJERCITO ARGENTINO / SIST. COLT. CAL.
   11.25mm MOD. 1927") NiB $1500 Ex $1300 Gd $1100
Brazilian contract (stamped w/crest and two lines on
   right side of slide: "EXERCITO BRASILEIRIO / 1937", mfg.
   1937-1941) . . . . NiB $4900 Ex $4100 Gd $3800
Mexican contract (stamped w/seal and one line on right
   side of "EJERCITO NACIONAL", S/N w/"C" prefix
   mfg. 1921-1927) . . . . NiB $3900 Ex $3000 Gd $2700

M1911A1 MODEL O SERIES 70 WWII
REPRODUCTION . . . . NiB $1300 Ex $850 Gd $680
Reproduction of Model 1911A1 (see above) w/pakerized finish, original WWII rollmarks. Made from 2001 to 2004.

1991 SERIES GOVERNEMNT MODEL SERIES 70 MODEL O
Reissue of Series 70 action. Caliber: .38 Super, .45 ACP. Seven-round magazine, 5-inch bbl., 8.5 inches overall. Weight: 39 oz. Fixed blade front sight, square notch rear. Blued or stainless finish. Made from 2003 to date.
Blued. . . . . NiB $1080 Ex 900 Gd $600
Stainless . . . . NiB $1120 Ex $940 Gd $650
.38 Super (stainless) . . . . NiB $800 Ex $700 Gd $600
.38 Super (bright stainless) . . . NiB $1200 Ex $900 Gd $600

1991 SERIES GOVERNMENT MODEL SERIES 80 MODEL O
Similar to Series 80 model except w/9mm or .45 ACP. Seven-round magazine, 5-inch bbl., 8.5 inches overall. Weight: 39 oz. Fixed sights. Rollmarked "Colt M1991A1" on slide. Blued, stainless or parkerized finish. Made from 1991 to date.
Blued. . . . . NiB $975 Ex $600 Gd $300
Parkerized . . . . NiB $975 Ex $600 Gd $300
Stainless . . . . NiB $1040 Ex $750 Gd $380
Commander model . . . . NiB $995 Ex $560 Gd $380
Officer's Compact model . . . . . NiB $620 Ex $430 Gd $380

.22 CADET AUTOMATIC PISTOL . NiB $479 Ex $343 Gd $270
Caliber: 22 LR. 10-round magazine, 4.5-inch vent rib bbl., 8.63 inches overall. Weight: 33.5 oz. Blade front sight, dovetailed rear. Stainless finish. TExtured black polymer grips w/ Colt medallion. Made 1993 to 1995. Note: The Cadet Model name was disc. under litigation but the manufacturer continued to produce this pistol configuration as the Model "Colt 22". For this reason the "Cadet" model will command slight premiums.

.22 SPORT AUTOMATIC PISTOL . NiB $485 Ex $345 Gd $270
Same specifications as Cadet Model except renamed Colt .22 w/ composition monogrip or wraparound black rubber grip. Made 1994 to 1998.

.22 TARGET PISTOL . . . . NiB $464 Ex $321 Gd $204
Similar to Colt 22 Sport Model except w/6-inch vent rib bbl., 10.12 inches overall. Weight: 40.5 oz. Partridge style front sight, adjustable white outline rear on full length grooved rib. Made from 1995 to 1999.

ACE AUTOMATIC PISTOL
Caliber: .22 LR (regular or high speed). 10-round magazine. Built on the same frame as the Government Model .45 Auto w/ same safety features, etc. Hand-honed action, target bbl., adj. rear sight. 4.75-inch bbl., 8.25. inches overall. Weight: 38 oz. Made 1930 to 1940.Commercial model NiB $4650 Ex $3783 Gd $3264
Service model (1938-42)...NiB $7710 Ex $5498 Gd $4769
Post-War model (1978-89)..NiB $1500 Ex $1000 Gd $800

ALL AMERICAN
MODEL 2000 DA PISTOL.....NiB $785 Ex $566 Gd $408
Hammerless semiautomatic w/blued slide and polymer or alloy receiver fitted w/roller-bearing trigger. Caliber: 9mm Para. 15-round magazine, 4.5-inch bbl., 7.5 inches overall. Weight: 29 oz. (Polymer) or 33 oz (Alloy). Fixed blade front sight, square-notch rear w/3-dot system. Matte blued slide w/ black polymer or anodized aluminum receiver. Made from 1992 to 1994.

AUTOMATIC .25 PISTOL
As a result of the 1968 Firearms Act restricting the importation of the Colt Pocket Junior that was produced in Spain, Firearms International was contracted by Colt to manufacture a similar blowback action with the same Exposed hammer configuration. Both the U.S. and Spanish-made. .25 automatics were recalled to correct an action malfunction. Returned firearms were fitted with a rebounding firing pin to prevent accidental discharges. Caliber: .25 ACP. Six-round magazine, 2.25-inch bbl., 4.5 inches overall. Weight: 12.5 oz. Integral blade front, square-notch rear sight groove. Blued finish. Checkered wood grips w/Colt medallion. Made from 1970 to 1975.
Model as issued............NiB $386 Ex $316 Gd $198
Model recalled & refitted.....NiB $386 Ex $316 Gd $198

COLT 22 ....NiB $430 Ex $260 Gd $200
Semi-automatic. SA. Caliber: .22 LR, 10-rnd. magazine. 4.5-in. vent rib bbl. Weight: 33.5 oz. Sights: fixed. Finish: stainless. Pachmayr rubber grips. Made from 1994 to 1998.

COLT 22 TARGET ....NiB $430 Ex $260 Gd $200
Similar to Colt 22 model except w/6-in. vent rib bbl. Weight: 40.5 oz. Sights: adj. rear. Made from 1995 to 1999.

CHALLENGER.............NiB $1100 Ex $800 Gd $400
Similar as Second Series Woodsman Target model but 4.5- or 6-inch bbl., 9 to 10.5 inches overall. Weight: 30 oz. (4.5-inch bbl.) or 31.5 oz. (6-inch bbl.) Blued finish. Checkered plastic grips. Made from 1950 to 1955.

COMMANDER (pre-Series 70) AUTOMATIC PISTOL
Same basic design as Government Model except w/shorter 4.25-inch bbl., and a special lightweight "Coltalloy" receiver and mainspring housing. Calibers: .45 Auto, .38 Super Auto, 9mm Para. Seven-round magazine (.45 cal.), nine-round (.38 Auto and 9mm), 8 inches overall. Weight: 26.5 oz. Fixed sights. Round spur hammer. Improved safety lock. Blued finish. Checkered plastic or walnut grips. Made from 1950 to 1969.
9mm Para...............NiB $1350 Ex $1000 Gd $700
.38 Super, .45 ACP.......NiB $1450 Ex $1150 Gd $900

SERIES 70 COMBAT COMMANDER AUTOMATIC PISTOL
Similar to Lightweight Commander except w/steel frame, blued or nickel-plated finish. Made from 1971 to 1980.
9mm Para................NiB $736 Ex $590 Gd $444
.38 Super, .45 ACP.........NiB $852 Ex $691 Gd $486

SERIES 70 LIGHTWEIGHT COMMANDER AUTOMATIC PISTOL
Same as Commander except w/blued or nickel-plated finish. Made from 1970 to 1983.
9mm Para...............NiB $1350 Ex $1000 Gd $700
.38 Super, .45 ACP.........NiB $1150 Ex $870 Gd $620

CONVERSION UNIT—.22-.45...NiB $306 Ex $255 Gd $179
Converts Service Ace .22 to National Match .45 Auto. Unit consists of match-grade slide assembly and bbl., bushing, recoil spring, recoil spring guide and plug, magazine and slide stop. Made from 1938 to 1942.

CONVERSION UNIT — .45-.22...NiB $617 Ex $489 Gd $362
Converts Government Model .45 Auto to a .22 LR target pistol. Unit consists of slide assembly, bbl., floating chamber (as in Service Ace), bushing, ejector, recoil spring, recoil spring guide and plug, magazine and slide stop. The component parts differ and are not interchangable between post war, series 70, series 80, ACE I and ACE II units. Made from 1938 to 1984.

DEFENDER.............. NiB $1100 Ex $700 Gd $480
Caliber: 9mm, .40 S&W or .45 ACP. 3-inch bbl. 7-round magazine, Three-dot, sights. rubber finger-groove wrap around grips. Matte stainless finish. Made from 1998 to date.
Defender Plus (2002-03).....NiB $880 Ex $660 Gd $5801

DELTA ELITE SEMIAUTO PISTOL
Caliber: 10mm. Five-inch bbl., 8.5 inches overall. Eight-round magazine, Weight: 38 oz. Checkered Neoprene combat grips w/Delta medallion. Three-dot, high-profile front and rear combat sights. Blued or stainless finish. Made from 1987 to 1996.
First Edition
(500 Ltd. edition).........NiB $975 Ex $784 Gd $551
Blued finish................NiB $923 Ex $626 Gd $468
Matte stainless finish........NiB $975 Ex $784 Gd $551
Ultra bright stainless finish, add..................$100

DELTA ELITE (CURRENT MFG.)
SEMIAUTOMATIC PISTOL...NiB $1115 Ex $830 Gd $520
Updated model similar to earlier Delta Elite except stainless finish only. Made from 2008 to date.

DELTA GOLD CUP SEMIAUTO PISTOL
Same general specifications as Delta Elite except w/Accro adjustable rear sight. Made 1989 to 1993; 1995 to 1996.
Blued finish (disc. 1991)......NiB $997 Ex $693 Gd $474
Stainless steel finish........NiB $1076 Ex $792 Gd $576

GOLD CUP TROPHY NATIONAL
MATCH .45 AUTO ....NiB $1250 Ex $900 Gd $640
Similar to MK IV Series 80 Gold Cup National Match except w/aluminum trigger, Bo-Mar raer adj. sight, black checkered rubber wrap around grips, 7 or 8-round magazine. Weight: 39 oz. Made 1997 to 2010.

GOLD CUP
NATIONAL MATCH..........NiB $1220 Ex $880 Gd $700
Similar to Gold Cup Trophy National Match. Made 2010 to date.
Stainless steel finish........NiB $1240 Ex $750 Gd $530

GOVERNMENT MODEL 1911/1911A1
See Colt Model 1911.

HUNTSMAN ....NiB $900 Ex $650 Gd $350
Similar to Third Series Woodsman Target and Sport models, except 4.5- or 6-in. bbl., fixed rear sight, no automatic slide stop. Early versions had black plastic grips. Later versions,

**Colt
National Match**

**Colt MK II/Series 90
Double Eagle**

**Colt MK IV/
Series 80 .380**

**Colt Series 70 Combat
Commander**

beginning in 1960, had walnut stocks. No thumbrest. Made from 1955 to 1977.

MK I & II/SERIES 90 DOUBLE EAGLE
COMBAT COMMANDER . . . . NiB $860 Ex $500 Gd $380
SA/DA trigger. Calibers: .40 S&W, .45 ACP. Seven-round magazine, 4.25-inch bbl., 7.75 inches overall. Weight: 36 oz. Fixed blade front sight, square-notch rear. Checkered Xenoy grips. Stainless finish. Made from 1991 to 1996.

MK II/SERIES 90 DOUBLE EAGLE SEMIAUTO
PISTOL . . . . NiB $860 Ex $510 Gd $380
SA/DA trigger. Calibers: .38 Super, 9mm, 10mm, .45 ACP. Seven-round magazine. Five-inch bbl., 8.5 inches overall. Weight: 39 oz. Fixed or Accro adj. sights. Matte stainless finish. Checkered Xenoy grips. Made from 1990 to 1996.
.38 Super, 9mm, add. $100
10mm , add. $25

MK II/SERIES 90 DOUBLE EAGLE
OFFICER'S MODEL . . . . NiB $860 Ex $510 Gd $380
Same general specifications as Double Eagle except chambered for .45 ACP only, 3.5-inch bbl., 7.25 inches overall. Weight: 35 oz. Also available in lightweight (25 oz.) w/blued finish (same price). Made from 1990 to 1991.

MK II/MK III NATIONAL MATCH
MID-RANGE . . . . NiB $1241 Ex $1020 Gd $704
Similar to Gold Cup National Match .45 Auto except chambered for .38 Special Mid Range. Five-round magazine, Made 1961 to 1974.

MK IV/SERIES 70 COMBAT COMMANDER
Same general specifications as the Lightweight Commander except made from 1970 to 1983.
Blued finish. . . . . NiB $1020 Ex $903 Gd $750
Nickel finish . . . . NiB $1193 Ex $974 Gd $815

MK IV/SERIES 70 GOLD CUP
NATIONAL MATCH. . . . . NiB $1743 Ex $1356 Gd $1153
Match version of MK IV/Series '70 Government Model. Caliber: .45 Auto only. Flat mainspring housing. Accurizor bbl., and bushing. Solid rib, Colt-Elliason adj. rear sight undercut front sight. Adj. trigger, target hammer. 8.75 inches overall. Weight: 38.5 oz. Blued finish. Checkered walnut grips. Made from 1970 to 1984.

MK IV/SERIES 70
GOVERNMENT. . . . . NiB $1120 Ex $815 Gd $570
Calibers: .45 Auto, .38 Super Auto, 9mm Para. Seven-round magazine in .45, 9-round in .38 and 9mm. Five-inch bbl., 8.38 inches overall. Weight: 38 oz., (.45); 39 oz. in .38 and 9mm. Fixed rear sight and ramp front sight. Blued or nickel-plated finish. Checkered walnut grips. Made from 1970 to 1984.

MK IV/SERIES 80 .380 GOVERNMENT AUTOMATIC
PISTOL
Caliber: .380 ACP, 3.29-inch bbl., 6.15 inches overall. Weight: 21.8 oz. Composition grips. Fixed sights. Made since 1983 to 1996.
Blued finish (disc.1997) . . . . . NiB $1132 Ex $918 Gd $712
Bright nickel (disc.1995). . . . . NiB $1181 Ex $974 Gd $729
Satin nickel Coltguard (disc.1989)NiB$1219 Ex$1016 Gd$751
Stainless finish. . . . . NiB $1173 Ex $974 Gd $755

MK IV/SERIES 80 COMBAT COMMANDER
Simialr specifications as MK IV/Series 80 Governemnt except

Colt MK IV/Series 80 Gold Cup National Match

Colt MK IV/Series 80 Government Model

Colt MK IV/Series 80 Mustang Plus II

Colt MK IV/Series 80 Mustang Pocketlite

w/ steel frame, 4.25-in. bbl. Made 1983 to 1993.

Blued finish (disc.1996) . . . . . . NiB $950 Ex $620 Gd $470
Satin nickel (disc.1987). . . . . . NiB $975 Ex $650 Gd $580
Stainless finish (disc.1998) . . . . NiB $860 Ex $570 Gd $450
Two-tone finish (disc.1998). . . . NiB $810 Ex $600 Gd $450
Gold Cup (disc.1993) . . . . NiB $1200 Ex $930 Gd $830

MK IV/SERIES 80 COMBAT
GOVERNMENT . . . . NiB $960 Ex $670 Gd $480
Same general specifications as MK IV/Series 80 Government except w/matte black finish. Calibers: .45 ACP. Made from 1983 to 1998.

Combat Elite (.38 Super). . . . . . NiB $980 Ex $700 Gd $600
Combat Target (adj. sights) . . . . NiB $770 Ex $530 Gd $460

MK IV/SERIES 80 GOLD CUP NATIONAL MATCH
Same general specifications as Match Series 70 except w/ additional finishes and "pebbled" wraparound Neoprene grips. Made from 1983 to 1996.

Blued finish. . . . . NiB $1071 Ex $714 Gd $490
Bright blued finish . . . . NiB $1071 Ex $714 Gd $490
Stainless finish. . . . . NiB $1148 Ex $867 Gd $638

MK IV/SERIES 80 GOVERNMENT MODEL
Similar specifications as Government Model Series 70 except w/firing pin safety feature. Made 1983 to 1997.

Blued finish. . . . . NiB $1117 Ex $755 Gd $520
Nickel finish . . . . NiB $1150 Ex $800 Gd $570
Stain nickel/blue finish . . . . . . NiB $1150 Ex $800 Gd $570
Matte stainless finish. . . . . . . NiB $1100 Ex $730 Gd $490
Bright stainless finish . . . . . . NiB $1410 Ex $1010 Gd $580

MK IV/SERIES 80 LIGHT-
WEIGHT COMMANDER . . . . NiB $1071 Ex $714 Gd $490
Updated version of the MK IV/Series 70.

MK IV/SERIES 80
MUSTANG .380 AUTOMATIC
Caliber: .380 ACP. Five- or 6-round magazine, 2.75-inch bbl., 5.5 inches overall. Weight: 18.5 oz. Blued, nickel or stainless finish. Black composition grips. Made from 1983 to 1998.

Blued finish. . . . . NiB $638 Ex $437 Gd $296
Nickel finish (disc.1994). . . . . . NiB $770 Ex $479 Gd $308
Satin nickel
 Coltguard (disc.1988). . . . . . NiB $740 Ex $474 Gd $306
Stainless finish. . . . . NiB $709 Ex $397 Gd $306

MK IV/SERIES 80 MUSTANG PLUS II
Caliber: .380 ACP, 7-round magazine, 2.75-inch bbl., 5.5 inches overall. Weight: 20 oz. Blued or stainless finish w/checkered black composition grips. Made from 1988 to 1996.

Blued finish. . . . . NiB $693 Ex $407 Gd $302
Stainless finish. . . . . NiB $693 Ex $407 Gd $302

MK IV/SERIES 80 MUSTANG POCKETLITE
Same general specifications as the Mustang 30 except weight: 12.5 oz. w/aluminum alloy receiver. Blued, chrome or stainless finish. Optional wood grain grips. Made since 1987.

Blued finish. . . . . NiB $683 Ex $405 Gd $305
Lady Elite (two-tone) finish. . . . NiB $683 Ex $405 Gd $305
Stainless finish. . . . . NiB $683 Ex $405 Gd $305
Teflon/stainless finish . . . . NiB $683 Ex $405 Gd $305

MK IV/SERIES 80 OFFICER'S ACP AUTOMATIC PISTOL
Caliber: .45 ACP, 3.63-inch bbl., 7.25 inches overall. 6-round magazine. Weight: 34 oz. Made from 1984 to 1998.

**Colt MK IV/Series 80
Officer's ACP**

Colt Pocket Junior

Colt Super Match .38

Blued finish (disc.1996) . . . . . . NiB $605 Ex $500 Gd $357
Matte finish (disc.1991) . . . . . . NiB $581 Ex $474 Gd $349
Satin nickel finish (disc.1985) . . NiB $669 Ex $544 Gd $378
Stainless steel (disc.1997) . . . . . NiB $630 Ex $514 Gd $367
Lightweight (disc.1997) . . . . . . NiB $900 Ex $710 Gd $520
Conceal Carry (disc.1998) . . . . NiB $900 Ex $710 Gd $520
General's Officer (disc.1996) NiB $1350 Ex $1040 Gd $680

**MK IV/SERIES 80 SA LIGHTWEIGHT CONCEALED
CARRY OFFICER** . . . . NiB $741 Ex $581 Gd $415
Caliber: .45 ACP. Seven-round magazine, 4.25-inch bbl., 7.75
inches overall. Weight: 35 oz. Aluminum alloy receiver w/
stainless slide. Dovetailed low-profile sights w/3-dot system.
Matte stainless finish w/blued receiver. Wraparound black rubber grip w/finger grooves. Made in 2000.

**MK IV/SERIES 80 SPECIAL COMBAT GOVERNMENT SEMI-
AUTOMATIC PISTOL** . . . . . . NiB $2100 Ex $1450 Gd $800
Calibers: .38 Super or .45 ACP, 5-inch bbl., custom tuned for
competition. Blued, hard crome or two-tone finsh. Made from
1992 to date.
Carry (1992-00, reintro. 1996) . . . NiB $2095 Ex $1450 Gd $800
CMC Marine Pistol . . . . NiB $2160 Ex $1200 Gd $820

**MK IV/SERIES 90 DEFENDER
SA LIGHTWEIGHT** . . . . NiB $918 Ex $576 Gd $398
Caliber: .45 ACP. Seven-round magazine, 3-inch bbl., 6.75
inches over-all. Weight: 22.5 oz. Aluminum alloy receiver
w/stainless slide. Dovetailed low-profile sights w/3-dot
system. Matte stainless finish w/Nickel-Teflon receiver.
Wraparound black rubber grip w/finger grooves. Made since
1998.

**MK IV/SERIES 90
PONY DAO PISTOL** . . . . NiB $772 Ex $567 Gd $396
Caliber: .380 ACP. Six-round magazine, 2.75-inch bbl., 5.5
inches overall. Weight: 19 oz. Ramp front sight, dovetailed
rear. Stainless finish. Checkered black composition grips. Made
1997 to 1998.

**MK IV/SERIES 90
PONY POCKETLITE** . . . . NiB $794 Ex $577 Gd $396
Similar to standard weight Pony Model except w/aluminum
frame. Brushed stainless and Teflon finish. Made 1997-99.

NATIONAL MATCH (PRE-WWWII)
Identical to the Government Model .45 Auto but w/hand-
honed action, match-grade bbl., adj. rear and ramp front sights
or fixed sights. Made from 1932 to 1940.
w/adjustable sights . . . . . NiB $10,000 Ex $8000 Gd $4300
w/fixed sights . . . . NiB $8500 Ex $7000 Gd $4000

**NATIONAL MATCH (WWII & POST-WWII)
AUTOMATIC PISTOL** . . . . . NiB $2500 Ex $1600 Gd $900
Similar to Pre-WWII National Match except in .45 Auto only.
Made from 1957 to 1970.

NEW AGENT . . . . NiB $1080 Ex $800 Gd $500
Series 80 system. Similar to Defender except in 9mm
or .45 ACP w/trench style sights, hammerless. Made 2008 to
2013.

**NRA CENTENNIAL .45 GOLD CUP
NATIONAL MATCH** . . . . NiB $1321 Ex $1024 Gd $841
Only 2500 produced in 1971.

**POCKET JUNIOR MODEL
AUTOMATIC PISTOL** . . . . NiB $464 Ex $344 Gd $260
Made in Spain by Unceta y Cia (Astra). Calibers: .22 Short,
.25 Auto. Six-round magazine, 2.25 inch bbl., 4.75 inches
overall. Weight: 12 oz. Fixed sights. Checkered walnut grips.
Note: In 1980, this model was subject to recall to correct
an action malfunction. Returned firearms were fitted with a
rebounding firing pin to prevent accidental discharges. Made
from 1958 to 1968.

SUPER .38 AUTOMATIC PISTOL
Identical to Government Model .45 Auto except for caliber
and magazine capacity. Caliber: .38 Automatic. Nine-round
magazine, Made from 1928 to 1970.
Pre-war . . . . NiB $6125 Ex $4429 Gd $3010
Post-war . . . . NiB $2709 Ex $2199 Gd $2008

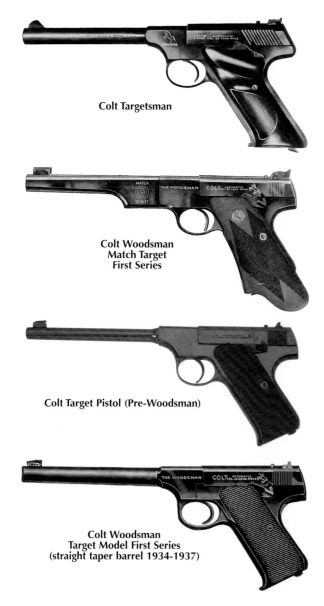

Colt Targetsman

Colt Woodsman
Match Target
First Series

Colt Target Pistol (Pre-Woodsman)

Colt Woodsman
Target Model First Series
(straight taper barrel 1934-1937)

**COLT AUTOMATIC TARGET PISTOL
(PRE-WOODSMAN)** ...... **NiB $3000 Ex $2000 Gd $700**
Semi-automatic. SA. Caliber: .22 LR (reg. velocity).
10-rnd. magazine w/ bottom release. 6-5/8-in. bbl., 10.5
in. overall. Weight: 28 oz. Adj. front and rear sights. Blued
finish. Checkered walnut grips. Serial number range:
1-54000. Made 1915 to 1922.

NOTE: *The earliest model of what would come to be known
as the Woodsman originally came in only one version and was
known simply as "Colt Automatic Target Pistol." Usually called
Pre-Woodsman by collectors today.Note: The mainspring
housing of this model is not strong enough to permit safe
use of high-speed cartridges. Change to a new heat-treated
mainspring housing was made at pistol No. 83,790. Many
of the old models were converted by installation of new
housings. The new housing may be distinguished from
the earlier type by the checkering in the curve under the
breech. The new housing is grooved straight across, while
the old type bears a diagonally-checkered oval.*

**FIRST SERIES WOODSMAN TARGET
MODEL**................**NiB $2600 Ex $1500 Gd $500**
Similar to late pre-Woodsman except "THE WOODSMAN" is
marked on side of receiver. Made from 1927 to 1947.

NOTE: *There are three series of Woodsman pistols, corresponding to three basic frame designs. First Series refers to all those
built on the S frame as it existed prior to and during World War
Two. Second Series includes all versions built on the second S
frame design from late 1947 until mid 1955, and Third Series
means the third S frame design as used from 1955 to the end of
regular production in 1977. Each series had a Sport Model with
a 4-1/2 inch round barrel, a Target Model with a 6 or 6-5/8 inch
round barrel, and a Match Target Model with a heavy, flat sided
barrel. The very similar Challenger, Huntsman, and Targetsman
were made during the post-WWII years only.*

**FIRST SERIES WOODSMAN MATCH TARGET
MODEL**...............**NiB $4500 Ex $2600 Gd $1500**
Same basic design as other First Series Woodsman Target
model. Caliber: .22 LR. 10-rnd. magazine, 6-5/8-in. bbl.
slightly tapered w/flat sides, 11 inches overall. Weight: 36 oz.
Adjustable rear sight. Blued finish. Checkered walnut one-
piece grip w/extended sides known as "Elephant Ear" grips.
Made from 1938 to 1943.

**FIRST SERIES WOODSMAN SPORT
MODEL** .... **NiB $2800 Ex $1700 Gd $600**
Similar as Firts Series Woodsman Target model except has 4.5-
inch bbl., fixed front sight. Weight: 27 oz., 8.5 inches overall.
Note: Some of the early Sport Models had a lighter, medium
weight barrel, and some of the later pre-WWII Sport Models
had an optional elevation adjustable front sight. Made from
1933 to 1947.

NOTE: *The Second Series Woodsmans are the only models that
have a push button thumb magazine release, similar to Colt
Government Model 1911 pistols.*

**SECOND SERIES WOODSMAN MATCH TARGET
MODEL**................**NiB $2400 Ex $1600 Gd $800**
Same basic design as First Series Woodsman Target model
except: Caliber: .22 LR (reg. or high speed). 10-round magazine.
4.5- or 6-in. bbl. Grips: plastic with left panel thumbrest. Made
from 1947 to 1955.

SUPER MATCH .38 AUTOMATIC PISTOL
Identical to Super .38 Auto but w/hand-honed action, match grade
bbl., adjustable rear sight and ramp front sight or fixed sights. Made
from 1933 to 1946.
w/adjustable sights . . . . . **NiB $11,595 Ex $6125 Gd $3162**
w/fixed sights . . . . **NiB $10,125 Ex $5125 Gd $2125**

TARGETSMAN MODEL.......**NiB $950 Ex $700 Gd $400**
Similar to Third Series Woodsman Target model except w/
6-in. bbl. only, economy adj. rear sight, lacks automatic slide
stop. Grip: Early versions had black plastic stocks, later versions, beginning in 1960, had walnut stocks, standard with
left panel thumbrest. Made from 1959 to 1977.

USMC M45 CQBP . . . . . . **NiB $1995 Ex $1500 Gd $1000**
Caliber: .45 ACP. Same general specifications as MK IV/Series
80 Rail Gun except w/Cerakote desert tan finish, stainless barrel, G10 grips. Made from 2013 to date.

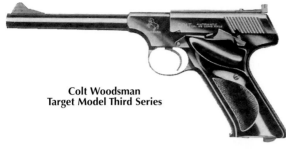

**Colt Woodsman
Target Model Third Series**

**Colt Woodsman
Sport Model Third Series**

**Colt World War II
D-Day Invasion
Commemorative**

**Colt World
War II
50th Anniversary
Commemorative**

**SECOND SERIES WOODSMAN SPORT
MODEL**. . . . . NiB $2100 Ex $453 Gd $316
Same as Second Series Match Target model except w/4.5-inch bbl., 9 inches overall. Weight: 36 oz. Grips: standard was plastic, before mid-1949 no thumbrest, after mid-1949 left panel thumbrest. Made from 1948 to 1955.

**SECOND SERIES WOODSMAN TARGET
MODEL**. . . . . NiB $1900 Ex $800 Gd $750
Same as Second Series Woodsman Match Target model except 6-in. bbl. only, 9 inches overall. Weight: 30 oz. Grips: standard with plastic and left panel thumbrest. Made 1948-55.

NOTE: The Third Series replaced the Second Series in mid 1955. The most obvious change was the replacement of the push button magazine release with a snap catch at the butt. The Challenger was replaced in the third series with the very similar Huntsman.

**THIRD SERIES WOODSMAN TARGET
MODEL**. . . . . NiB $1400 Ex $950 Gd $500
Same basic design as Second Series Woodsman Target model but w/6-in. bbl. only. Grip: early versions had black plastic stocks, later versions, beginning in 1960, had walnut stocks. NOTE: All Second and Third Series Target models were standard with left panel thumbrest. Made from 1955 to 1977.

**THIRD SERIES WOODSMAN SPORT
MODEL**. . . . . NiB $1450 Ex $1000 Gd $500
Same basic design as Third Series Woodsman Target model but w/4.5-in. bbl. only. Grip: standard with left panel thumbrest, early versions had black plastic stocks, later versions, beginning in 1960, had walnut stocks. Made from 1955 to 1977.

**THIRD SERIES WOODSMAN MATCH TARGET
MODEL**. . . . . NiB $900 Ex $650 Gd $350
Same basic design as Third Series Woodsman Target model but w/4.5- or 6-in. bbl. Grip: early versions had black plastic stocks, later versions, beginning in 1960, had walnut stocks. NOTE: All Second and Third Series Target models were standard with left panel thumbrest. Made from 1955 to 1977.

**WORLD WAR I 50TH ANNIVERSARY
COMMEMORATIVE SERIES**
Limited production replica of Model 1911 .45 Auto engraved w/battle scenes, commemorating Battles at Chateau Thierry, Belleau Wood Second Battle of the Marne, Meuse Argonne. In special presentation display cases. Production: 7,400 Standard model, 75 Deluxe, 25 Special Deluxe grade. Match numbered sets offered. Made 1967 to 1969. Values indicated are for commemoratives in new condition.
Standard grade . . . . NiB $1046 Ex $780 Gd $638
Deluxe grade . . . . NiB $2152 Ex $1743 Gd $1220
Special Deluxe grade . . . . . NiB $4687 Ex $3890 Gd $2448

**WORLD WAR II COMMEMORATIVE
.45 AUTO** . . . . NiB $1047 Ex $774 Gd $562
Limited production replica of Model 1911A1 .45 Auto engraved w/respective names of locations where historic engagements occurred during WW II, as well as specific issue and theater identification. European model has oak leaf motif on slide, palm leaf design frames the Pacific issue. Cased. 11,500 of each model were produced. Made in 1970. Value listed is for gun in new condition.

**WORLD WAR II 50TH ANNIVERSARY
COMMEMORATIVE** . . . . . . NiB $2647 Ex $2064 Gd $1629
Same general specifications as the Colt World War II Commemorative .45 Auto except slightly different scroll engraving, 24-karat gold-plate trigger, hammer, slide stop, magazine catch, magazine catch lock, safety lock and four grip screws. Made in 1995 only.

**WORLD WAR II D-DAY
INVASION COMMEMORATIVE** . . NiB $1550 Ex $1436 Gd $1138
High-luster and highly decorated version of the Colt Model 1911A1. Caliber: .45 ACP. Same general specifications as the Colt Model 1911 except for 24-karat gold-plated hammer, trigger, slide stop, magazine catch, magazine catch screw, safety lock and four grip screws. Also has scrolls and inscription on slide. Made in 1991 only.

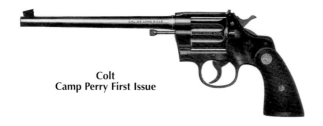

Colt
Camp Perry First Issue

Colt Agent
First Issue

Colt
Camp Perry Second Issue

WORLD WAR II GOLDEN ANNIVERSARY V-J DAY

TRIBUTE .45 AUTO . . . . **NiB $2662 Ex $2239 Gd $1658**
Basic Colt Model 1911A1 design w/highly-polished bluing and decorated w/specialized tributes to honor V-J Day. Two 24-karat gold scenes highlight the slide. 24-karat gold-plated hammer. Checkered wood grips w/gold medallion on each side. Made 1995.

XSE SERIES MODEL O SEMI-AUTOMATIC PISTOL

Caliber: .45 Auto. 8-round magazine, 4.24- or 5-in. bbl. Novak sights, front/rear slide serrations, extanded ambi. thumb safety. Checkered rosewood grips. Made 2000 to date.

Combat Elite	NiB $1100	Ex $700	Gd $500
Commander	NiB $1200	Ex $730	Gd $530
Government	NiB $1100	Ex $700	Gd $500
Ligthweight Commander	NiB $1100	Ex $700	Gd $500
Ligthweight Government	NiB $1100	Ex $700	Gd $500
Rail Gun	NiB $1200	Ex $730	Gd $530

- SINGLE-SHOT PISTOLS & DERRINGERS -

CAMP PERRY MODEL SINGLE-

SHOT PISTOL, FIRST ISSUE . . . **NiB $2410 Ex $1960 Gd $1660**
Built on Officers' Model frame. Caliber: .22 LR (embedded head chamber for high-speed cartridges after 1930). 10 inch bbl., 13.75 inches overall. Weight: 34.5 oz. Adj. target sights. Hand-finished action. Blued finish. Checkered walnut grips. Made 1926 to 1934.

CAMP PERRY MODEL

SECOND ISSUE . . . . **NiB $3374 Ex $2744 Gd $2324**
Same general specifications as First Issue except has shorter hammer fall and 8-inch bbl., 12 inches overall. Weight: 34 oz. Made from 1934 to 1941 (about 440 produced).

CIVIL WAR CENTENNIAL MODEL PISTOL

Single-shot replica of Colt Model 1860 Army Revolver. Caliber: .22 Short. Six-inch bbl., weight: 22 oz. Blued finish w/gold-plated frame, grip frame, and trigger guard, walnut grips. Cased. 24,114 were produced. Made in 1961.
Single pistol . . . . **NiB $362 Ex $265 Gd $204**
Pair w/consecutive
 serial numbers . . . . **NiB $689 Ex $541 Gd $408**

DERRINGER NO. 4

Replica of derringer No. 3 (1872 Thuer Model). Single-shot w/sideswing bbl., Caliber: .22 Short, 2.5-inch bbl., 4.9 inches overall. Weight: 7.75 oz. Fixed sights. Gold-plated frame w/blued bbl., and walnut grips or completely nickel- or gold-plated w/simulated ivory or pearl grips. Made 1959 to 1963. 112,000 total production. (S/N w/D or N suffix)
Single pistol (gun only) . . . . **NiB $128 Ex $88 Gd $61**
Single pistol (cased w/accessories) . . . **NiB $408 Ex $281 Gd $189**

DERRINGER NO. 4 COMMEMORATIVE MODELS

Limited production version of .22 derringers issued, w/appropriate inscription, to commemorate historical events. Additionally, non-firing models (w/unnotched bbls.) were furnished in books, picture frames and encased in plExiglass as singles or in cased pairs.
No. 4 Presentation Derringers
(Non-firing w/accessories) . . . . **NiB $408 Ex $281 Gd $189**
Ltd. Ed. Book Series(w/nickel-plated
 derringers) . . . . **NiB $388 Ex $255 Gd $143**
1st Presentation Series
 (Leatherette covered metal case) . . **NiB $408 Ex $281 Gd $189**
2nd Presentation Series
 (Single wooden case) . . . . **NiB $408 Ex $281 Gd $189**
2nd Presentation Series
 (Paired wooden case) . . . . **NiB $423 Ex $291 Gd $198**
1961 Issue Geneseo, Illinois,
 125th Anniversary (104 produced) . . **NiB $729 Ex $556 Gd $388**
1962 Issue Fort McPherson, Nebraska, Centennial
 (300 produced) . . . . **NiB $729 Ex $556 Gd $388**

LORD AND LADY DERRINGERS (NO. 5)

Same as Derringer No. 4. Lord model with blued bbl., w/gold-plated frame and walnut grips. Lady model is gold-plated w/simulated pearl grips. Sold in cased pairs. Made from 1970 to 1972. (S/N w/Der suffix)
Lord derringer, pair in case . . . . **NiB $577 Ex $408 Gd $301**
Lady derringer, pair in case . . . . **NiB $577 Ex $408 Gd $301**
Lord and Lady derringers,
 one each, in case . . . . **NiB $577 Ex $408 Gd $301**

ROCK ISLAND ARSENAL

CENTENNIAL PISTOL . . . . **NiB $520 Ex $489 Gd $332**
Limited production (550 pieces) version of Civil War Centennial Model single-shot .22 pistol, made Exclusively for Cherry's Sporting Goods, Geneseo, Illinois, to commemorate the cen-

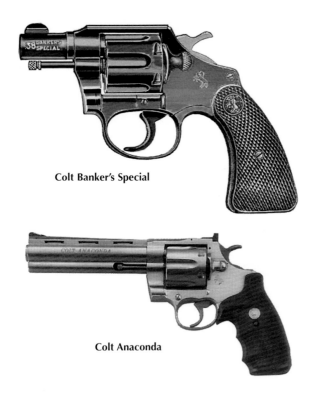

Colt Banker's Special

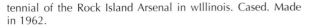

Colt Anaconda

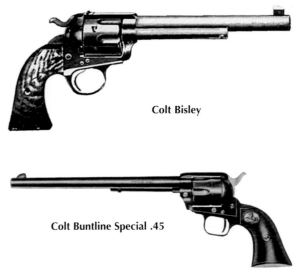

Colt Bisley

Colt Buntline Special .45

tennial of the Rock Island Arsenal in wIllinois. Cased. Made in 1962.

NOTE: *This section of Colt handguns contains only revolvers (single action and double action) by model name in alphabetical order. For automatic pistols or single-shot pistols and derringers, please see the two sections that precede this. For a complete listing, refer to the Index.*

- REVOLVERS -

MODEL 1877 LIGHTNING NiB $4197 Ex $3264 Gd $2973
DA revolver w/fixed cyilnder. Also called Thunderer Model. Calibers: .38 and .41 centerfire. Six-round cylinder, bbl. lengths: 2.5-, 3.5-, 4.5- and 6-inch without ejector, 4.5- and 6-inch w/ejector, 8.5 inches overall (3.5-inch bbl.). Weight: 23 oz. (.38 cal., with 3.5-inch bbl.) Fixed sights. Blued or nickel finish. Hard rubber bird's-head grips. Made 1877 to 1909.

MODEL 1877 THUNDERER NiB $4210 Ex $3210 Gd $2260
Similar to Lightning except in .41 Colt only. Made 1877 to 1909.

MODEL 1878
DA REVOLVER . . . . NiB $5780 Ex $5260 Gd $3250
DA. Calibers: .32-20, .38 Colt, .38-40, .41 LC, .44 Russian, .44 S&W, .44-40, .45 LC, .450 Eley, .455 Eley or .476 Eley. Six-round fixed cylinder. Bbl. Lengths: 2.5-, 3.5-, 4- w/o ejector rod and 4.75-, 5.5-, 7.5-, 8.5-, 9-, 10- or 12-in. w/ejctor rod. Fixed sights. Finish: blued, case hardened or nickel. Checkered hard rubber bird's-head grips. Made 1878 to 1905.

.357 MAGNUM . . . . NiB $910 Ex $810 Gd $735
DA. Simialr to Trooper model. Caliber: .357 Mag. Six-round cylinder, 4- or 6-in. bbl. Accro target sights. Finish: blued or nickel. Grips: checkered walnut. Made from 1953 to 1961.

.38 DS II REVOLVER . . . . NiB $660 Ex $560 Gd $430
Similar to Detective Special. Caliber: .38 Special or .357 Mag. Six-round cylinder, 2-inch bbl., 7 inches overall. Weight: 21 oz. Ramp front sight, fixed notch rear. Satin stainless finish. Black rubber combat grip w/finger grooves. Made from 1997 to 1998.

.38 SF-VI . . . . NiB $660 Ex $560 Gd $430
DA. Caliber: .38 Special only. Six-round cylinder, 2- or 4-in. bbl. Ramp front sight, fixed notch rear. Finish: Satin, polished or black. Grip: black rubber. Made from 1995 to 1996.

AGENT FIRST ISSUE . . . . NiB $800 Ex $710 Gd $510
Same as Cobra, first issue except has short-grip frame .38 Special only, weight: 14 oz. Made from 1955 to 1972.

AGENT (LW) SECOND ISSUE . . NiB $630 Ex $530 Gd $430
Same as Colt Agent, first issue except has shrouded ejector rod and alloy frame. Made from 1973 to 1986.

AIRCREWMAN . . . . NiB $4010 Ex $3510 Gd $2760
DA revolver made for U.S. Air Force. Caliber: .38 Special only. Six-round swing-out cylinder, 2-in. bbl. Aluminum frame. Weight: 11 oz. Fixed sights. Grip: checkered walnut that overlapped the frame above the grip w/silver U.S. Air Force medallions. Satmped "Property of U.S. Air Force" on back strap and an U.S. Air Force issue number on the butt. S/N range: 2,901LW to about 7,775LW. Made 1951.

ANACONDA DA REVOLVER
Calibers: .44 Mag., .45 Colt., bbl. lengths: 4, 6 or 8 inches; 11.63 inches overall (with 6-inch bbl.). Weight: 53 oz. (6-inch bbl.). Adj. white outline rear sight, red insert ramp-style front. Matte stainless or Realtree gray camo finish. Black Neoprene combat grips w/finger grooves. Made 1990 to 1999 and 2002 to 2006.
Matte stainless . . . . NiB $1000 Ex $714 Gd $487
Realtree gray camo
** finish (disc. 1996) . . . . NiB $1632 Ex $1357 Gd $1151**
Custom model
** (.44 Mag. w/ported bbl.) . . . NiB $1510 Ex $816 Gd $587**
First Edition model
** (Ltd. Edition 1000) . . . . . . NiB $1800 Ex $1460 Gd $1160**
Hunter model
** (.44 Mag. w/2x scope) . . . NiB $1652 Ex $1357 Gd $1151**

Colt Commando Special

**Colt Cobra
Round Butt First Issue**

.38 caliber. . . . . NiB $2260 Ex $1860 Gd $1260
.22 caliber. . . . . NiB $3210 Ex $2510 Gd $1860

BOA . . . . NiB $3860 Ex $3360 Gd $2810
DA. Uses Mark V action. Caliber: .357 Mag. 4- or 6-in. bbl.
w/full ejector shroud. Lew Horton distributor. Made 1985.
Two gun set. . . . . NiB $7960 Ex $6885 Gd $5510

COBRA (ROUND BUTT)
FIRST ISSUE . . . . NiB $810 Ex $660 Gd $610
Similar to Detective Special model except w/Colt-alloy lightweight frame. Two-inch bbl., calibers: .22 LR, .38 Special,
.38 New Police, .32 New Police. Weight: 15 oz., (.38 cal.).
Blued finish. Checkered plastic or walnut grips. Made 1950
to 1972.
.22 LR, add **20%**
nickel finish, add. **20%**

COBRA SECOND ISSUE . . . . . . NiB $960 Ex $835 Gd $735
Similar to Cobra First Issue except w/shrouded ejector rod.
Made from 1973 to 81.

COBRA (SQUARE BUTT)
FIRST ISSUE . . . . NiB $530 Ex $425 Gd $304
Similar to Cobra First Issue except w/4-inch bbl., Calibers: .38
Special, .38 New Police, .32 New Police. Weight: 17 oz. in
.38 caliber. Blued finish. Checkered plastic or walnut grips.
Early models.

COMMANDO SPECIAL . . . . . . NiB $546 Ex $423 Gd $329
Similar to Detective Special. Caliber: .38 Special. Six-round
cylinder, 2-inch bbl., 6.88 inches overall. Weight: 21.5 oz.
Fixed sights. Low-luster blued finish. Rubber grips. Made from
1984 to 1986.

COURIER . . . . NiB $1310 Ex $1110 Gd $960
Aluminum "D" frame, similar to Cobra. Caliber: .22 LR or .32
S&W. Six-round swing-out cylinder, 3-in. bbl. Fixed sights.

ANACONDA TITANIUM DA REVOLVER
Same general specifications as the standard Anaconda except
chambered .44 Mag. only w/titanium-plated finish, gold-plated
trigger, hammer and cylinder release. Limited edition of 1,000
distributed by American Historical Foundation w/personalized
inscription. Made in 1996.
One of 1000 . . . . NiB $2744 Ex $2242 Gd $1624
Presentation case, add $255

ARMY SPECIAL
DA REVOLVER . . . . NiB $1300 Ex $1000 Gd $760
.41-caliber frame. Calibers: .32-20, .38 Special (.41 Colt).
Six-round cylinder, right revolution. Bbl., lengths: 4-, 4.5, 5-,
and 6-inches, 9.25 inches overall (4-inch bbl.). Weight: 32 oz.
(4-inch bbl.). Fixed sights. Blued or nickel-plated finish. Hard
rubber grips. Made 1908-27. Note: This model has a somewhat
heavier frame than the New Navy, which it replaced. S/N begin
w/300,000. The heavy .38 Special High velocity loads should
not be used in .38 Special arms of this model. Made from 1908
to 1927.

BANKER'S SPECIAL DA REVOLVER
This is the Police Positive w/a 2-inch bbl., otherwise specifications
same as that model, rounded butt intro. in 1933. Calibers: .22 LR
(embedded head-cylinder for high speed cartridges intro. 1933), .38
New Police. 6.5 inches overall. Weight: 23 oz. (.22 LR), 19 oz. (.38).
Made from 1926 to 1940.

**Colt
Detective Special First Issue**

Bright blue-black anodized finish. Checkered wood grips. Made from 1953 to 1956.

DETECTIVE SPECIAL DA REVOLVER, FIRST ISSUE
Similar to Police Positive Special except w/2-inch bbl., otherwise specifications same as that model, rounded butt intro. 1933. .38 Special only in pre-war issue. Blued or nickel-plated finish. Weight: 17 oz. 6.75 inches overall. Made from 1927 to 46.

Blued finish. . . . . NiB $2155   Ex $1855   Gd $1630
Nickel finish, add. 20%

DETECTIVE SPECIAL SECOND ISSUE
Similar to Detective special first issue except w/2- or 3-inch bbl., and also chambered .32 New Police, .38 New Police. Wood, plastic or over-sized grips. Post-WWII manufacture, made from 1947 to 1972.

Blued finish. . . . . NiB $1355   Ex $1155   Gd $955
Nickel finish, add 20%
w/three-inch bbl., add 15%

DETECTIVE SPECIAL THIRD ISSUE
"D" frame, shrouded ejector rod. Caliber: .38 Special. Six-round cylinder, 2-inch bbl., 6.88 inches overall. Weight: 21.5 oz. Fixed rear sight, ramp front. Blued or nickel-plated finish. Checkered walnut wraparound grips. Made from 1973 to 1986.

Blued finish. . . . . NiB $980   Ex $860   Gd $760
Nickel finish . . . . NiB $571   Ex $464   Gd $342
w/three-inch bbl., add $90

DETECTIVE SPECIAL DA REVOLVER, FOURTH ISSUE
Similar to Detective Special, Third Issue except w/alloy frame. Blued or chrome finish. Wraparound black neoprene grips w/ Colt medallion. Made from 1993 to 1995.

Blued finish. . . . . NiB $700   Ex $662   Gd $596
Chrome finish, add 10%
DAO model (bobbed hammer) . . . NiB $855   Ex $730   Gd $610

DIAMONDBACK DA REVOLVER
"D" frame, shrouded ejector rod. Calibers: .22 LR, .22 WRF, .38 Special. Six-round cylinder, 2.5-, 4- or 6-inch bbl., w/vent rib, 9 inches overall (with 4-inch bbl). Weight: 31.75 oz. (.22 cal., 4-inch bbl.), 28.5 oz. (.38 cal.). Ramp front sight, adj. rear. Blued or nickel finish. Checkered walnut grips. Made from 1966 to 1984.

Blued finish. . . . . NiB $1336   Ex $1127   Gd $826
Nickel finish . . . . NiB $1545   Ex $1231   Gd $986
.22 Mag. model. . . . . NiB $2118   Ex $1937   Gd $1754
w/2.5-inch bbl., add $100

DA ARMY (1878) . . . . NiB $6140   Ex $4524   Gd $3177
Also called DA Frontier. Similar in appearance to the smaller Lightning Model but has heavier frame of different shape, round disc on left side of frame, lanyard loop in butt. Calibers: .38-40, .44-40, .45 Colt. Six-round cylinder, bbl. lengths: 3.5- and 4-inches (w/o ejector), 4.75-, 5.5- and 7.5-inches w/ejector. 12.5 inches overall (7.5-inch bbl.). Weight: 39 oz. (.45 cal., 7.5-inch bbl.). Fixed sights. Hard rubber bird's-head grips. Blued or nickel finish. Made from 1878 to 1905.

FRONTIER SCOUT REVOLVER
SA Army replica, smaller scale. Calibers: .22 Short, Long, LR or .22 WMR (interchangeable cylinder available). Six-round cylinder, 4.75-inch bbl., 9.9 inches overall. Weight: 24 oz. Fixed sights. Plastic grips. Originally made w/bright alloy frame. Since 1959 w/steel frame and blued finish or all-nickel finish w/composition, wood or Staglite grips. Made 1958 to 1971.

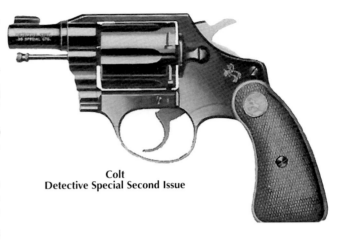

Colt
Detective Special Second Issue

Colt
Diamondback

Blued finish, plastic grips . . . . . NiB $464   Ex $395   Gd $272
Nickel finish, wood grips . . . . . NiB $499   Ex $407   Gd $286
Buntline model, add $75
Extra interchangeable cylinder, add $100

FRONTIER SCOUT REVOLVER COMMEMORATIVE MODELS
Limited production versions of Frontier Scout issued, w/appropriate inscription, to commemorate historical events. Cased, in new condition.

1961 ISSUES
Kansas Statehood Centennial (6201 produced) . . . NiB $536
Pony Express Centennial
   (1007 produced) . . . . NiB $638

1962 ISSUES
Columbus, Ohio, Sesquicentennial
   (200 produced) . . . . NiB $638
Fort Findlay, Ohio,
   Sesquicentennial (130 produced) . . . . NiB $913
Fort Findlay Cased Pair, .22 Long
   Rifle and .22 Magnum (20 produced) . . . . NiB $2627
New MExico Golden Anniversary . . . . NiB $638
West Virginia Statehood
   Centennial (3452 produced) . . . . NiB $6130

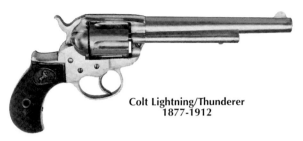

Colt Lightning/Thunderer
1877-1912

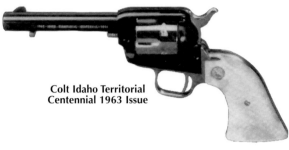

Colt Idaho Territorial
Centennial 1963 Issue

Colt New Jersey Tercentenary 1964 issue

Colt General Hood
Centennial 1964 issue

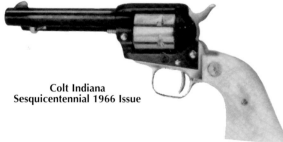

Colt Indiana
Sesquicentennial 1966 Issue

1963 ISSUES
Arizona Territorial Centennial
    (5355 produced) . . . . NiB $638
Battle of Gettysburg Centennial
    (1019 produced) . . . . NiB $638
Carolina Charter Tercentenary (300 produced) . . NiB $2270
Fort Stephenson, Ohio,
    Sesquicentennial (200 produced) . . . . NiB $638
General John Hunt Morgan Indiana Raid . . . . NiB $689
Idaho Territorial Centennial (902 produced) . . . . . NiB $638

1964 ISSUES
California Gold Rush (500 produced) . . . . NiB $638
Chamizal Treaty (450 produced) . . . . NiB $638
General Hood Centennial (1503 produced) . . . . . NiB $638
Montana Territorial Centennial (2300 produced) . . NiB $638
Nevada "Battle Born" (981 produced) . . . . NiB $597
Nevada Statehood Centennial (3984 produced) . . NiB $2678
New Jersey Tercentenary (1001 produced) . . . . . . NiB $577
St. Louis Bicentennial (802 produced) . . . . NiB $638
Wyoming Diamond Jubilee (2357 produced) . . . . . NiB $638

1965 ISSUES
Appomattox Centennial (1001 produced) . . . . NiB $577
Forty-Niner Miner (500 produced) . . . . NiB $638
General Meade Campaign (1197 produced) . . . . . NiB $1647
Kansas Cowtown Series—Wichita (500 produced) . . . . . . NiB $577
Old Fort Des Moines Reconstruction (700 prod.) . NiB $2280
Oregon Trail (1995 produced) . . . . NiB $638
St. Augustine Quadricentennial (500 produced) . . . NiB $638

1966 ISSUES
Colorado Gold Rush (1350 produced) . . . . NiB $638
Dakota Territory (1000 produced) . . . . NiB $638
Indiana Sesquicentennial (1500 produced) . . . . . . NiB $638
Kansas Cowtown Series—Abilene (500 produced) . . NiB $577
Kansas Cowtown Series—Dodge City
    (500 produced) . . . . NiB $577
Oklahoma Jubilee (1343 produced) . . . . NiB $638

1967 ISSUES
Alamo (4500 produced) . . . . NiB $577
Kansas Cowtown Series—Coffeyville
    (500 produced) . . . . NiB $561
Kansas Trail Series—Chisholm Trail (500 produced) NiB $577
Lawman Series—Bat Masterson (3000 produced) . . NiB $570

1968 ISSUES
Kansas Cowtown Series—Santa Fe
    Trail (501 produced) . . . . NiB $577
Kansas Trail Series—Pawnee Trail (501 produced) . NiB $577
Lawman Series—Pat Garrett (3000 produced) . . . . NiB $638
Nebraska Centennial (7001 produced) . . . . NiB $577

1969 ISSUES
Alabama Sesquicentennial (3001 produced) . . . . . . NiB $577
Arkansas Territory Sesquicentennial
    (3500 produced) . . . . NiB $561
California Bicentennial (5000 produced) . . . . NiB $577
General Nathan Bedford Forrest (3000 produced) . . . . NiB $577
Golden Spike (11,000 produced) . . . . NiB $577
Kansas Trail Series—Shawnee Trail
    (501 produced) . . . . NiB $577
Lawman Series—Wild Bill Hickock
    (3000 produced) . . . . NiB $638

Colt Golden Spike
Centennial 1969 Issue

Colt King Cobra

Colt Lawman
MK V

1970 ISSUES
Kansas Fort Series—Fort Larned (500 produced) ... NiB $577
Kansas Fort Series—Fort Hays (500 produced) ... NiB $577
Kansas Fort Series—Fort Riley (500 produced) .... NiB $577
Lawman Series—Wyatt Earp (3000 produced) ... NiB $780
Maine Sesquicentennial (3000 produced)........ NiB $577
Missouri Sesquicentennial (3000 produced) ..... NiB $577

1971 ISSUES
Kansas Fort Series—Fort Scott (500 produced) .... NiB $577

1972 ISSUES
Florida Territory Sesquicentennial
 (2001 produced) .... NiB $638

1973 ISSUES
Arizona ranger (3001 produced) .... NiB $638

KING COBRA REVOLVER
Caliber: .357 Mag., bbl. lengths: 2.5-, 4-, 6- or 8-inches, 9 inches overall (with 4-inch bbl.). Weight: 42 oz., average. Matte stainless steel or blued finish. Black Neoprene combat grips. Made 1986 to date. 2.5-inch bbl. and "Ultimate" bright or blued finish. Made from 1988 to 1992.
Blued................. NiB $1260 Ex $1145 Gd $970
Matte stainless .... NiB $1210 Ex $1085 Gd $910
Ultimate bright stainless, add 15%
2.5-in. bbl., add 20%

LAWMAN MK III DA REVOLVER
Shrouded ejector rod on 2-inch bbl., only. Caliber: .357 Magnum. Six-round cylinder, bbl. lengths: 2-, 4-inch. 9.38 inches overall (w/4-inch bbl.), Weight: (with 4-inch bbl.), 35 oz. Fixed rear sight, ramp front. Service trigger and hammer or target trigger and wide-spur hammer. Blued or nickel-plated finish. Checkered walnut service or target grips. Made from 1969 to 1983.
Blued finish............... NiB $560 Ex $465 Gd $380
Nickel finish .... NiB $660 Ex $565 Gd $480

LAWMAN MK V DA REVOLVER
Similar to Trooper MK V. Caliber: .357 Mag. Six-round cylinder, 2- or 4-inch bbl., 9.38 inches overall (4-inch bbl.). Weight: 35 oz. (4-inch bbl.). Fixed sights. Checkered walnut grips. Made 1984 and 1991.
Blued finish............... NiB $655 Ex $555 Gd $455
Nickel finish .... NiB $680 Ex $580 Gd $480

MAGNUM CARRY
DA REVOLVER .... NiB $900 Ex $800 Gd $790
Similar to Model DS II except chambered for .357 Magnum. Made from 1998 to date.

MARINE CORPS MODEL (1905) DA REVOLVER
General specifications same as New Navy Second Issue except has round butt, was supplied only in .38 caliber (.38 Short & Long Colt, .38 Special) w/6-inch bbl. (S/N range 10,001-10,926) Made 1905 to 1909.
Marine Corps model ... NiB $15,606 Ex $14,050 Gd $13,260
Marked "USMC"......... NiB $7803 Ex $5636 Gd $3886

METROPOLITAN MK III ...... NiB $630 Ex $530 Gd $430
Same as Official Police MK III except has 4-inch bbl. w/service or target grips. Weight: 36 oz. Made from 1969 to 1972.

NEW FRONTIER BUNTLINE SPECIAL
Same as New Frontier SA Army except has 12-inch bbl.,
Second generation (1962-75)... NiB $2570 Ex $2028 Gd $1392
Third generation (1976-92) ... NiB $1352 Ex $1120 Gd $861

NEW FRONTIER SA ARMY REVOLVER
Same as SA Army except has flat-top frame, adj. target rear sight, ramp front sight, smooth walnut grips. 5.5- or 7.5-inch bbl., Calibers: .357 Magnum, .44 Special, .45 Colt. Made 1961 to 1992.
Second generation (1961-75)... NiB $2902 Ex $2647 Gd $2458
Third generation (1976-92).. NiB $1362 Ex $1118 Gd $857

NEW FRONTIER
SA .22 REVOLVER........... NiB $532 Ex $342 Gd $235
Same as Peacemaker .22 except has flat-top frame, adj. rear sight, ramp front sight. Made from 1971-76; reintro. 1982-86.

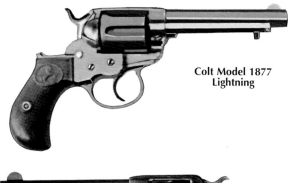

**Colt Model 1877
Lightning**

Colt New Navy

Colt New Service

NEW NAVY (1889) DA, FIRST ISSUE
Also called New Army. Calibers: .38 Short & Long Colt, .41 Short & Long Colt. Six-round cylinder, left revolution. Bbl. lengths: 3-, 4.5- and 6-inches, 11.25 inches overall (with 6-inch bbl.). Weight: 32 oz. with 6-inch bbl. Fixed sights, knife-blade and V-notch. Blued or nickel-plated finish. Walnut or hard rubber grips. Made 1889 to 1994. Note: This model, which was adopted by both the Army and Navy, was Colt's first revolver of the solid frame, swing-out cylinder type. It lacks the cylinder-locking notches found on later models made on this .41 frame; ratchet on the back of the cylinder is held in place by a double projection on the hand.
First issue . . . . NiB $2260 Ex $1860 Gd $1460
First issue w/3-inch bbl., add 40%
Navy contract (marked U.S.N. on butt,
  S/N range: 1-1500) . . . . . . NiB $3682 Ex $2981 Gd $2121

NEW NAVY (1892) DA, SECOND ISSUE
Also called New Army. General specifications same as First Issue except double cylinder notches and double locking bolt. Calibers: .38 Special added in 1904 and .32-20 in 1905. Made 1892 to 1907. Note: The heavy .38 Special High Velocity loads should not be used in .38 Special arms of this model.
Second issue . . . . NiB $1950 Ex $1446 Gd $1020

NEW POCKET
DA REVOLVER . . . . NiB $1360 Ex $1150 Gd $900
Caliber: .32 Short & Long Colt. Six-round cylinder. bbl. lengths: 2.5, 3.5- and 6-inches. 7.5 inches overall w/3.5-inch bbl., Weight: 16 oz., with 3.5-inch bbl. Fixed sights, knife-blade and V-notch. Blued or nickel finish. Rubber grips. Made from 1893 to 1905.

NEW POLICE
DA REVOLVER . . . . NiB $1260 Ex $960 Gd $760
Built on New Pocket frame but w/larger grip. Calibers: .32 Colt New Police, .32 Short & Long Colt. Bbl. lengths: 2.5-, 4- and 6-inches; 8.5 inches overall (with 4-inch bbl.). Weight: 17 oz., with 4-inch bbl. Fixed knife-blade front sight, V-notch rear. Blued or nickel finish. Rubber grips. Made from 1896 to 1907.

NEW POLICE TARGET
DA REVOLVER . . . . NiB $1860 Ex $1660 Gd $1110
Target version of the New Police except w/target sights. Six-inch bbl., blued finish only. Made 1896 to 1905.

NEW SERVICE DA REVOLVER
Calibers: .38 Special, .357 Magnum (intro. 1936), .38-40, .44-40, .44 Russian, .44 Special, .45 Auto, .45 Colt, .450 Eley, .455 Eley, .476 Eley. Six-round cylinder, bbl. lengths: 4-, 5- and 6-inch in .38 Special and .357 Magnum, 4.5-, 5.5- and 7.5 inches in other calibers; 9.75 inches overall (with 4.5-inch bbl.). Weight: 39 oz. (.45 cal. with 4.5-inch bbl.). Fixed sights. Blued or nickel finish. Checkered walnut grips. Made 1898-42. Note: More than 500,000 of this model in caliber .45 Auto (designated "Model 1917 Revolver") were purchased by the U.S. Gov't. during WW I. These arms were later sold as surplus to National Rifle Association members through the Director of Civilian Marksmanship. Price was $16.15 plus packing charge. Supply Exhausted during the early 1930s. Made from 1898 to 1927.

1909 Army	NiB $3300	Ex $2900	Gd $2500
1909 Navy	NiB $3600	Ex $3200	Gd $2700
1909 USMC	NiB $4100	Ex $3700	Gd $3200
1917 Army	NiB $2000	Ex $1680	Gd $1500
1917 Commercial	NiB $1600	Ex $1300	Gd $1000
Commercial model	NiB $2888	Ex $2483	Gd $2197
Magnum	NiB $1223	Ex $1018	Gd $729
RNWMP/RCMP model	NiB $2000	Ex $1483	Gd $1197

**Shooting Master (various calibers, 6-in. bbl., round or square
  butt, checkered grips straps) . . . NiB $2000 Ex $1900 Gd $1700**
Shooting Master (.357 Mag.), add $1000
Shooting Master (.45 ACP or .45 LC), add $2000
Shooting Master (.44 Spl.), add $3000

NEW SERVICE TARGET . . . . NiB $3500 Ex $3350 Gd $2800
Target version of the New Service. Calibers: Originally chambered for .44 Russian, .450 Eley, .455 Eley and .476 Eley, later models in .44 Special, .45 Colt and .45 Auto. Six- or 7.5-inch bbl., 12.75 inches overall (7.5-inch bbl.). Adj. target sights. Hand-finished action. With blued finish. Checkered walnut grips. Made 1900 to 1940.

OFFICER'S MODEL
FIRST ISSUE . . . . NiB $1860 Ex $1499 Gd $1260
DA/SA. Caliber: .38 Spl. or .38 LC. Six-inch bbl., flat top frame, hand-finished action, adj. target sights. Checkered with walnut grips w/o medalion. Made 1904 to 1908.

Colt Officers' Match

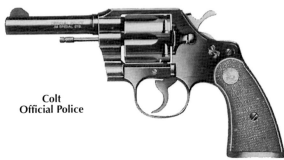

**Colt
Officers' Target Second Issue**

**Colt
Official Police**

**Colt
Peacekeeper**

OFFICER'S MODEL SECOND
ISSUE . . . . NiB $1760 Ex $1550 Gd $1150
Similar to Officer's Modle First Issue except using improved Army Special action and more bbl. lengths: 4-, 4.5-, 5-, 6- and 7.5-inch. Made from 1908 to 1926.

OFFICER'S MODEL TARGET THIRD
ISSUE . . . . NiB $1460 Ex $1250 Gd $1000
Calibers: .22 LR (intro. 1930, embedded head-cylinder for high-speed cartridges after 1932), .32 Police Positive (made 1932-1942), .38 Special. Six-round cylinder, bbl. lengths: 4-, 4.5-, 5-, 6- and 7.5-inch (in .38 Special) or 6-inch only (.22 LR and .32 PP), 11.25 inches overall (6-inch bbl. in .38 Special). Adj. target sights. Blued finish. Checkered walnut grips. Hand-finished action. General features same as Army Special and Official Police of same date. Made from 1908 to 1949 (w/ exceptions noted).

.38 caliber . . . . NiB $1130 Ex $930 Gd $653
.32 caliber . . . . NiB $1744 Ex $1426 Gd $984
.22 caliber . . . . NiB $1232 Ex $1018 Gd $729
w/shorter bbls. (4-, 4.5- or 5-inches), add 50%

OFFICER'S MODEL SPECIAL
(FOURTH ISSUE) . . . . NiB $1030 Ex $930 Gd $830
Post WWII model. Similar Officers' Model Third Issue excpt w/ extra heavy, nontapered bbl. Redesigned hammer. Ramp front sight, "Coltmaster" rear sight adj. for windage and elevation. Blued finish. Checkered plastic reddish-brown "Coltwood" grips. Made from 1949 to 1952.

OFFICER'S MODEL MATCH
(FIFTH ISSUE) . . . . NiB $960 Ex $900 Gd $810
Same general design as Officers' Model Special except w/ tapered heavy bbl., wide hammer spur, Adjustable rear sight ramp front sight, large target grips of checkered walnut w/medalion. Calibers: .22 LR, .22 Mag., .38 Special. Six-inch bbl., 11.25 inches overall. Weight: 43 oz. (in .22 cal.), 39 oz. (.38 cal.). Blued finish. Made from 1953 to 1969.
.22 Mag., add $1000

OFFICER'S MODEL MATCH MK III
(SIXTH ISSUE) . . . . NiB $1900 Ex $1525 Gd $1400
Similar to Officers' Model Match Fifth Issue except .38 Special only. Made from 1969 to 1971.

OFFICIAL POLICE DA REVOLVER
Calibers: .22 LR (intro. 1930, embedded head-cylinder for high-speed cartridges after 1932), .32-20 (disc. 1942), .38 Special, .41 Long Colt (disc. 1930). Six-round cylinder, bbl. lengths: 4-, 5-, and 6-inch or 2-inch and 6-inch heavy bbl. in .38 Special only; .22 LR w/4- and 6-inch bbls. only; 11.25 inches overall. Weight: 36 oz. (standard 6-inch bbl.) in .38 Special. Fixed sights. Blued or nickel-plated finish. Checkered walnut grips on all revolvers of this model except some of postwar production had checkered plastic grips. Made 1927-69. Note: This model is a refined version of the Army Special, which it replaced in 1928 at about serial number 520,000. The Commando .38 Special was a wartime adaptation of the Official Police made to government specifications. Commando can be identified by its sandblasted blued finish and stamped "COLT COMMANDO". Serial numbers start w/number 1-50,000 (made 1942 to 1945). Marshal Model marked "COLT MARSHAL" has S/N w/"M" suffix (made 1954 to 1956).
Commercial model (pre-war) . . NiB $960 Ex $850 Gd $560
Commercial model (post-war) . . . NiB $860 Ex $700 Gd $550
Commando model . . . . NiB $1950 Ex $1700 Gd $1450
Marshal model . . . . NiB $2000 Ex $1750 Gd $1500

OFFICIAL POLICE MK III . . . . . NiB $560 Ex $510 Gd $460
"J" frame, without shrouded ejector rod. Caliber: .38 Special. Six-round cylinder. bbl., lengths: 4-, 5-, 6-inches, 9.25 inches overall w/4-inch bbl., weight: 34 oz. (4-inch bbl.). Fixed rear sight, ramp front. Service trigger and hammer or target trigger and wide-spur hammer. Blued or nickel-plated finish. Checkered walnut service grips. Made 1969 to 1975.

PEACEKEEPER DA REVOLVER . . . NiB $580 Ex $455 Gd $330
Caliber: .357 Mag. Six-round cylinder, 4- or 6-inch bbl., 11.25 inches overall (6-inch bbl.). Weight: 46 oz. (with 6-inch bbl.). Adj. white outline rear sight, red insert ramp-style front. Non-reflective matte blued finish. Made from 1985 to 1989.

**Colt
Pocket Positive**

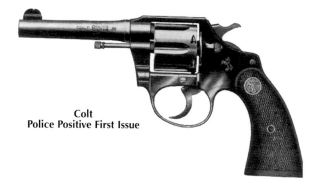

**Colt
Police Positive First Issue**

Colt SA Army

PEACEMAKER .22 SECOND AMENDMENT
COMMEMORATIVE . . . . **NiB $660 Ex $544 Gd $286**
Caliber: .22, revolver w/7.5-inch bbl., nickel-plated frame, bbl. ejector rod assembly, hammer and trigger, blued cylinder, backstrap and trigger guard. Black pearlite grips. bbl., inscribed "The Right to Keep and Bear Arms." Presentation case. Limited edition of 3000 issued in 1977. Top value is for revolver in new condition.

PEACEMAKER .22
SA REVOLVER . . . . **NiB $423 Ex $332 Gd $275**
Calibers: .22 LR and .22 WMR. Furnished w/cylinder for each caliber, 6-round. Bbl.: 4.38-, 6- or 7.5-inches, 11.25 inches overall (with 6-inch bbl.). Weight: 30.5 oz. (with 6-inch bbl.). Fixed sights. Black composite grips. Made from 1971 to 1976.

POCKET POSITIVE DA REVOLVER FIRST & SECOND ISSUES
General specifications same as New Pocket except this model has positive lock feature (see Police Positive). Calibers: .32 Short & Long Colt (disc. 1914), .32 Colt New Police (.32 S&W Short & Long). Fixed sights, flat top and square notch. Blue or nickel finish. Made from 1905 to 1940.
Blue finish . . . . **NiB $1300 Ex $1000 Gd $760**
Nickel finish, add **20%**

POLICE POSITIVE FIRST ISSUE
Improved version of the New Police w/the "Positive Lock," which prevents the firing pin coming in contact w/the cartridge except when the trigger is pulled. Calibers: .32 Short & Long Colt (disc. 1915), .32 Colt New Police (.32 S&W Short & Long), .38 New Police (.38 S&W). Six-round cylinder, bbl. lengths: 2.5- (.32 cal. only), 4- 5- and 6-inches; 8.5 inches overall (with 4-inch bbl.). Weight 20 oz. (with 4-inch bbl.). Fixed sights. Blued or nickel grips. Rubber or checkered walnut grips. Made from 1907 to 1927.

Blue finish . . . . **NiB $800 Ex $660 Gd $560**
Nickel finish, add **20%**

POLICE POSITIVE SECOND ISSUE
Same as Detective Special second issue except has 4-inch bbl., 9 inches overall, weight: 26.5 oz. Intro. in 1977. Note: Original Police Positive (First Issue) has a shorter frame, is not chambered for .38 Special. Made 1928 to 1947.
Blue finish . . . . **NiB $860 Ex $760 Gd $530**

POLICE POSITIVE SPECIAL FIRST & SECOND ISSUES
DA REVOLVER . . . . **NiB $810 Ex $660 Gd $460**
Based on the Police Positive w/frame lengthened to permit longer cylinder. Calibers: .32-20 (disc. 1942), .38 Special, .32 New Police and .38 New Police (intro. 1946). Six-round cylinder; bbl. lengths: 4-(only length in current production), 5- and 6-inch; 8.75 inches overall (with 4-inch bbl.). Weight: 23 oz. (with 4-inch bbl. in .38 Special). Fixed sights. Checkered grips of hard rubber, plastic or walnut. Made 1907 to 1927 (First Issue) and 1928 to 1946 (Second Issue).

POLICE POSITIVE SPECIAL THIRD & FOURTH ISSUES
Based on Detective Special Second Issue but w/4-, 5- or 6-in. bbl. in .38 Spl. only. Made from 1947 to 1976 (Third Issue), 1977 to 1978 (Fourth Issue).
Third Issue . . . . **NiB $560 Ex $460 Gd $360**
Fourth Issue, deduct **10%**

POLICE POSITIVE MK V FIFTH ISSUE
DA REVOLVER . . . . **NiB $450 Ex $380 Gd $330**
.38 Spl. only. 4-in. bbl. w/ejector shroud. Finish: blued. Grips: rubber. Made from 1994 to 1995.

POLICE POSITIVE TARGET FIRST AND SECOND ISSUES
DA REVOLVER . . . . **NiB $1310 Ex $1110 Gd $860**
Target version of the Police Positive. Calibers: .22 LR (intro. 1910, embedded-head cylinder for high-speed cartridges after 1932), .22 WRF (1910-35), .32 Short & Long Colt, (1915), .32 New Police (.32 S&W Short & Long). Six-inch bbl., blued finish only, 10.5 inches overall. Weight: 26 oz. in .22 cal. Adj. target sights. Hard rubber grips until 1923 then checkered walnut grips. Second Issue had heavier fram. Made from 1907 to 1925 (First Issue), 1926 to 1941 (Second Issue).
Second Issue, deduct **10%**

PYTHON DA REVOLVER
"I" frame, shrouded ejector rod. Calibers: .357 Magnum, .38 Special. Six-round cylinder, 2.5-, 4-, 6- or 8-inch vent rib bbl., 11.25 inches overall (with 6-inch bbl.). Weight: 44 oz. (6-inch

**Colt
Police Positive Target**

Colt Python

bbl.). Adj. rear sight, ramp front. Blued, nickel or stainless finish. Checkered walnut target grips. Made from 1955 to 1996. Ultimate stainless finish made in 1985.

Blued or Royal

Blued finish.	NiB $2100	Ex $1900	Gd $1500
Nickel finish	NiB $1910	Ex $1510	Gd $1275
Stainless finish.	NiB $2310	Ex $2010	Gd $1610
Ultimate stainless finish	NiB $2210	Ex $1960	Gd $1660
2.5-in. bbl., add			100%
Elite model (mfg. 2002-06).	NiB $2760	Ex $2410	Gd $2010

Grizzly model (ported bbl., non-fluted cylinder,
Pachmayer grips) . . . . . . NiB $4000 Ex $3610 Gd $3260
Hunter model (w/2x scope) NiB $3500 Ex $3230 Gd $2960
Silhouette model (w/2x scope)NiB $3760 Ex $3360 Gd $3060
Ten Pointer model (w/3x scope, carrying case, two sets
of grips, 8-in. bbl.) . . . . . NiB $3000 Ex $2810 Gd $2760
Whitetailer model (w/2x scope, 8-in. bbl., aluminum
case). . . . . NiB $1860 Ex $1610 Gd $1385
Whitetailer II model (w/1.5-4x scope, 8-in. bbl., bright
satinless finish) . . . . NiB $2210 Ex $2010 Gd $1960
Ultimate model (custom shop tuned, two sets of sights, two
sets of grips, 1991-93) . . NiB $2310 Ex $2060 Gd $1935

SHOOTING MASTER DA REVOLVER

Deluxe target arm based on the New Service model. Calibers: Originally made only in .38 Special, .44 Special, .45 Auto and .45 Colt added in 1933, .357 Magnum in 1936. Six-inch bbl., 11.25 inches overall. Weight: 44 oz., in (.38 cal.), adj. target sights. Hand-finished action. Blued finish. Checkered walnut grips. Rounded butt. Made from 1932 to 1941.

Shooting Master
.38 Special . . . . NiB $1507 Ex $1344 Gd $915
Shooting Master
.357 Mag. . . . . NiB $1533 Ex $1269 Gd $908
Shooting Master
.44 Special, .45 ACP, .45LCNiB $4092 Ex $3773 Gd $2285

TROOPER MK III . . . . NiB $587 Ex $418 Gd $225
DA revolver. "J" frame, shrouded ejector rod. Calibers: .22 LR, .22 Magnum, .38 Special, .357 Magnum. Six-round cylinder. bbl. lengths: 4-, 6-inches. 9.5 inches overall (with 4-inch bbl.). Weight: 39 oz. (4-inch bbl.). Adj. rear sight, ramp front. Target trigger and hammer. Blued or nickel-plated finish. Checkered walnut target grips. Made 1969 to 1978.

Nickel finish . . . . NiB $643 Ex $452 Gd $224

TROOPER MK V REVOLVER

Re-engineered Mark III for smoother, faster action. Caliber: .357 Magnum. Six-round cylinder, bbl. lengths: 4-, 6-, 8-inch w/vent rib. Adj. rear sight, ramp front, red insert. Checkered walnut grips. Made from 1982 to 1986.
Blued finish. . . . . NiB $562 Ex $437 Gd $321
Nickel finish . . . . NiB $577 Ex $499 Gd $316

VIPER DA REVOLVER . . . . . NiB $1500 Ex $1400 Gd $1200
Same as Cobra, Second Issue except has 4-in. bbl., 9 in. overall, weight: 20 oz. Made from 1977 to 1984.

SINGLE ACTION ARMY (SAA) REVOLVER

Also called Frontier Six-Shooter and Peacemaker. Available in more than 30 calibers including: .22 Rimfire (Short, Long, LR), .22 WRF, .32 Rimfire, .32 Colt, .32 S&W, .32-20, .38 Colt, .38 S&W, .38 Special, .357 Magnum, .38-40, .41 Colt, .44 Rimfire, .44 Russian, .44 Special, .44-40, .45 Colt, .45 Auto, .450 Boxer, 450 Eley, .455 Eley, .476 Eley. Six-round cylinder. Bbl. lengths: 4.75, 5 .5 and 7.5 inches w/ejector or 3 and 4 inches w/o ejector. 10.25 inches overall (with 4.75-inch bbl.). Weight: 36 oz. (.45 cal. w/4.75-inch bbl.). Fixed sights. Also made in Target Model w/flat top-strap and target sights. Blued finish w/casehardened frame or nickel-plated. One-piece smooth walnut or checkered black rubber grips. Note: S.A. Army Revolvers w/serial numbers above 165,000 (circa 1896) are adapted to smokeless powder and cylinder pin screw was changed to spring catch at about the same time. The "First Generation" of SA Colts included both blackpowder and smokeless configurations and were manufactured from 1873 to 1940. Production resumed in 1955 w/ serial number 1001SA and continued through 1975 to complete the second series, which is referred to as the "Second Generation." In 1976, the "Third Generation" of production began and continues to to date. However, several serial number rollovers occurred at 99,999. For Example, in 1978 the "SA" suffix became an "SA" prefix and again in 1993, when the serial number SA99,999 was reached, the serialization format was changed again to include both an "S" prefix and an "A" suffix. Although the term "Fourth Generation" is frequently associated with this rollover, no series change actually occurred, therefore, the current production is still a "Third Generation" series. Current calibers: .357 Magnum, .44 Special, .45 Long Colt.

Pinched frame
(1873 only) . . . . .Ex $250,000 Gd $175,000
Early commercial
(1873-77) . . . . .Ex $90,000 Gd $70,000
Early U.S. Military
(1873-77) . . . . Ex $175,000-$87,000 Gd $80,000-$42,000
Large bore rimfire
(1875-80) . . . . .Ex $75,000 Gd $60,000
Small bore
rimfire (1875-80) . . . . Ex $40,000 Gd $25,000
Frontier six-shooter, .44-40
(1878-82) . . . . . Ex $52,000-$42,000 Gd $26,000-$20,000
Storekeeper's model, no ejector
(1883-98) . . . . . Ex $95,000-$75,000 Gd $35,000-$32,000
Sheriff's model
(1883-98) . . . . . Ex $95,000-$75,000 Gd $35,000-$32,000
Target model, flat top strap,
target sights . . . . .Ex $25,000 Gd $11,000
U.S. Artillery model, .45
(1895-1903) . . . . .Ex $16,000 Gd $7,500

Colt SA Army — 125th Anniversary

Colt 150th Anniversary Deluxe

Colt 150th Anniversary Engraving Sampler

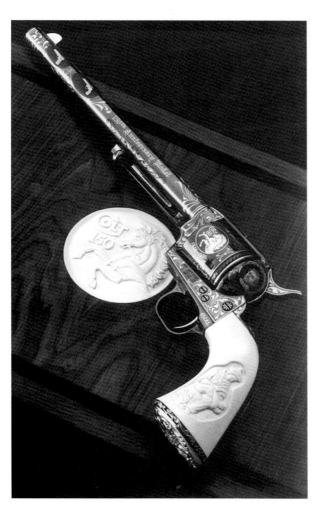

Note: *In the previous section the GTG deviates from the observed practice of listing only the value of firearms produced after 1900. This deliberate departure from the standard format is intended to provide a general reference and establish proper orientation for the reader, because the Colt SSA had its origins in the last quarter of the 19th century. Consequently, antique firearms produced prior to 1898 have been listed as a preface and introduction to the first series of production (what is now recognized as "1st Generation") in order to systematically demonstrate the progressive and sequential development of the multi-generation Colt SAA. Therefore, the previous general values have been provided to establish a point of reference to allow a more comprehensive Examination of the evolution of the Colt SAA. However, please note that the following values apply only to original models, not to similar S.A.A. revolvers of more recent manufacture.*

1st generation (mfg. 1873-1940)
SAA (COMMERICAL) . . . . Ex $250,000 Gd $10,000
Variation of the SAA military model developed for commercial market.

SAA (U.S. MILITARY) . . . . Ex $175,000 Gd $11,000
Original SAA revolver model developed for U.S. military. Mfg. 1873 to 1909.

SAA BISLEY . . . . NiB $10,000 Ex $8600 Gd $7600
Variation of the SAA commercial developed for target shooting w/modified grips, trigger and hammer. Made 1894 to 1915.
Flattop Target Bisley (w/flattop frame, adj. rear sight,
 7.5-in. bbl., mfg. 1894-1913) . . . NiB $20,000 Ex $18,000
 Gd $15,000

SAA FLATTOP
TARGET . . . . NiB $25,000 Ex $20,000 Gd $16,500
Similar to the SAA Commercial model developed for target shooting w/flattop frame w/adj. rear sight. 925 mfg. Made 1888 to 1896.

SAA LONG FLUTE . . . . . NiB $17,600 Ex $9,999 Gd $6,200
Similar to the SAA Commercial model except w/modified long fluted cylinders from 1878 DA revolvers. Made 1913 to 1915.

SAA SHERIFF . . . . **EX $95,000 TO $25,500**
Similar to the Single-Action Army except commercial model w/o an ejector rod.

2nd generation (mfg. 1956-1975)
SAA (STANDARD MODEL)
Variation of the 1st Gen. SAA commercial w/slight changes to mechanism. Calibers: .38 Spl., .357 Mag., .44 Spl. or .45 LC. Bbl. length: 4.75-, 5.5- or 7.5-in. Finish: blued or nickel.
.38 Spl. . . . . **NiB $3000 Ex $2600 Gd $1800**
.357 Mag. . . . . **NiB $2600 Ex $2000 Gd $1250**
.44 Spl. . . . . **NiB $3260 Ex $2650 Gd $1900**
.45 LC . . . . **NiB $3200 Ex $2950 Gd $2600**
4.75-in. bbl., add **15%**
nickel finish, add. **10%**
factory engraved w/ factory letter, add **75-100%**

BUNTLINE SPECIAL . . . . . . **NiB $2448 Ex $1960 Gd $1260**
Same as standard 2nd Gen. SAA except w/12-in. bbl., caliber .45 Long Colt only. Made from 1957 to 1975.

NEW FRONTIER . . . . **NiB $1420 Ex $1220 Gd $1120**
Similar to 2nd Gen. SAA except w/adj. rear sight and ramp blade front sight. Calibers: .38 Spl., .357 Mag., .44 Spl. or .45 LC. Bbl. length: 4.75-, 5.5- or 7.5-in. Finish: blued or nickel. Grip: smooth walnut w/medalion. Made from 1961 to 1975.
.38 Spl., add **270%**
4.75-in. bbl., add **50%**
5.5-in. bbl., add **25%**
Buntline (12-in. bbl.,
   .45 LC) . . . . **NiB $2520 Ex $2200 Gd $1895**

SHERIFF MODEL . . . . **NiB $2260 Ex $2060 Gd $1780**
Same as standard 2nd Gen. SAA except w/3-in. bbl. w/o ejector rod. Caliber .45 Long Colt. Finish: blued and case hardened or nickel.
nickel finish, add. **350%**

3rd Generation (1976 to date)

SAA (STANDARD MODEL) . . . **NiB $1420 Ex $1230 Gd $1000**
Variation of the 2nd Gen. SAA standard w/slight changes to mechanism. Calibers: .32-20, .38-40, .38 Spl., .357 Mag., .44 Spl., .44-40 or .45 LC. Bbl. length: 4-, 4.75-, 5-, 5.5- or 7.5-in. Finish: blued or nickel. Grip: smooth wood or black plastic w/eagle.
.38 Spl., add **25%**
nickel finish, add. **20%**
black powder frame (pre-1996), add. **15%**
factory ivory grip, add **70%**
factory Class A engraving, add **$1200**
factory Class B engraving, add **$2400**
factory Class C engraving, add **$3500**
factory Class D engraving, add. **$4700**

Colt New Frontier

COWBOY SAA . . . . **NiB $800 Ex $660 Gd $510**
SA revolver with transfer-bar safety system. Caliber: .45 Long Colt only. Bbl.: 4.75-, 5.5- or 7.5-in. Blued and case hardened finish. Grip: checkered composite. Made 1999 to 2003.

BUNTLINE SPECIAL . . . . **NiB $1300 Ex $1070 Gd $900**
Same as standard 3rd Gen. SAA except w/12-in. bbl. Caliber: .44-40 or .45 Long Colt. Blued and case hardened finish. Grip: smooth walnut.

NEW FRONTIER . . . . **NiB $1560 Ex $1120 Gd $900**
Similar to 2nd Gen. New Frontier except w/adj. rear sight and ramp blade front sight. Calibers: .357 Mag., .44 Spl., .44-40 or .45 LC. Bbl. length: 4.75-, 5.5- or 7.5-in. Finish: blued. Grip: smooth walnut w/medalion. Made 1978 to 1981 and 2008 to 2010, reintro. 2011 to date.
Buntline (12-in. bbl.,
   .45 LC) . . . . **NiB $2520 Ex $2200 Gd $1895**

SHERIFF MODEL . . . . **NiB $1300 Ex $1060 Gd $900**
Same as standard 2nd Gen. Sheriff except w/3-in. bbl. w/o ejector rod. Caliber .44 Spl., .44-40 or .45 LC. Finish: blued and case hardened, royal blue or nickel.
extra convertiable cylinder, add **10%**
factory ivory grip, add **70%**
nickel finish, add. **10%**
Royal blue finish, deduct **15%**

STOREKEEPERS MODEL . . . **NiB $1810 Ex $1660 Gd $1510**
Similar to 3rd Gen. Sheriff except w/4-in. bbl. w/o ejector rod. Caliber: .45 LC only. Finish: blued and case hardened or nickel. Grips: ivory. Made from 1984 to 1985 and 2008 to 2010.
nickel finish, add. **10%**

SAA 125TH ANNIVERSARY . . . **NiB $1668 Ex $1438 Gd $1239**
Limited production deluxe version of SAA issued in commemoration of Colt's 125th Anniversary. Caliber: .45 Long Colt., 7.5-inch bbl., cold-plated frame trigger, hammer, cylinder pin, ejector rod tip, and grip medallion. Presentation case w/anniversary medallion. Serial numbers "50AM." 7368 were made in 1961.

SAA COMMEMORATIVE MODELS
Limited production versions of SAA .45 issued, w/appropriate inscription to commemorate historical events. Cased. Note: Values indicated are for commemorative revolvers in new condition.
1963 ISSUES
Arizona Territorial Centennial (1280 produced) . . **NiB $1663**
West Virginia Statehood Centennial
   (600 produced) . . . . **NiB $1663**

1964 ISSUES
Chamizal Treaty (50 produced) . . . . **NiB $1867**
Colonel Sam Colt Sesquicentennial
   Presentation (4750 produced) . . . . **NiB $1663**
Deluxe Presentation (200 produced) . . . . **NiB $3621**
Special Deluxe Presentation (50 produced) . . . . . **NiB $5687**
Montana Territorial Centennial (851 produced) . . **NiB $1724**
Nevada "Battle Born" (100 produced) . . . . **NiB $2672**
Nevada Statehood Centennial (1877 produced) . . **NiB $2275**
New Jersey Tercentenary (250 produced) . . . . **NiB $1663**
Pony Express Presentation (1004 produced) . . . . . **NiB $1836**
St. Louis Bicentennial (450 produced) . . . . **NiB $1663**
Wyatt Earp Buntline (150 produced) . . . . **NiB $2809**

Colt Trooper

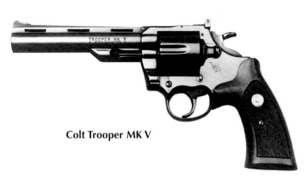

Colt Trooper MK V

1965 ISSUES
Appomattox Centennial (500 produced) .... NiB $1454
Old Fort Des Moines Reconstruction
(200 produced)......................... NiB $1454

1966 ISSUES
Abercrombie & Fitch Trailblazer—Chicago
(100 produced) ....NiB $1423
Abercrombie & Fitch Trailblazer—New York
(200 produced) ....NiB $1423
Abercrombie & Fitch Trailblazer—San Francisco
(100 produced) ....NiB $1423
California Gold Rush (130 produced) .... NiB $1423
General Meade (200 produced) ....NiB $1663
Pony Express Four Square (4 guns) ....NiB $7268

1967 ISSUES
Alamo (1000 produced) .... NiB $1663
Lawman Series—Bat Masterson
(500 produced)......................... NiB $1760

1968 ISSUES
Lawman Series—Pat Garrett (500 produced) ....NiB $1663

1969 ISSUES
Lawman Series—Wild Bill Hickok
(500 produced)......................... NiB $1663

1970 ISSUES
Lawman Series—Wyatt Earp (501 produced) .....NiB $2907
Texas Ranger (1000 produced) ....NiB $2351

1971 ISSUES
NRA Centennial, .357 or .45 (5001 produced) ....NiB $1525

1975 ISSUES
Peacemaker Centennial .45 (1501 produced) ... NiB $1872
Peacemaker Centennial .44-40
(1501 produced)........................ NiB $1872
Peacemaker Centennial Cased Pair
(501 produced)......................... NiB $1872
Missouri Sesquicentennial
(501 produced)......................... NiB $1627
1975 ISSUES
Peacemaker Centennial .45 (1501 produced) ... NiB $1872
Peacemaker Centennial .44-40 (1501 produced)... NiB $1872
Peacemaker Centennial Cased
Pair (501 produced) .... NiB $1872

1979 ISSUES
Ned Buntline .45 (3000 produced)........... NiB $1367

1986 ISSUES
Colt 150th Anniversary (standard) .... NiB $2064
Colt 150th Anniversay (engraved)............. NiB $3647

COLT COWBOY REVOLVER . . . NiB $632 Ex $468 Gd $363
SA variant designed for "Cowboy Action Shooting" w/ safety transfer bar system. Caliber: .45 Colt. Six-round cylinder, 5.5-inch bbl., 11 inches overall. Weight: 42 oz. Blade front sight, fixed V-notch rear. Blued finish w/color casehardened frame. Smooth walnut grips. Made from 1999 to 2003.

SA SHERIFF'S MODEL .45
Limited edition replica of Storekeeper's Model in caliber .45 Colt, made Exclusively for Centennial Arms Corp. Chicago, Illinois. Numbered "1SM." Blued finish w/casehardened frame or nickel-plated. Walnut grips. Made in 1961.
Blued finish
(478 produced)........NiB $2152 Ex $1780 Gd $1454
Nickel finish
(25 produced).........NiB $8155 Ex $5763 Gd $4024

THREE-FIFTY-SEVEN DA REVOLVER
Heavy frame. Caliber: .357 Magnum. Six-shot cylinder, 4 or 6-inch bbl. Quickdraw ramp front sight, Accro rear sight. Blued finish. Checkered walnut grips. 9.25 or 11.25 inches overall. Weight: 36 oz. (4-inch bbl.), 39 oz. (6 inch bbl.). Made from 1953 to 1961.
w/standard hammer and
service grips ....NiB $711 Ex $601 Gd $431
w/wide-spur hammer and
target grips ....NiB $733 Ex $612 Gd $444

TROOPER DA REVOLVER
Similar specifications as Officers' Model Match except has 4-inch bbl. w/quick-draw ramp front sight, weight: 34 oz. Claiber: .22 LR, .38 Spl. or .357 Mag. Made from 1953 to 1969.
w/standard hammer and
service grips ....NiB $810 Ex $710 Gd $635
w/wide-spur hammer and
target grips ....NiB $835 Ex $735 Gd $660

U.S. BICENTENNIAL COMMEMORATIVE SET . . . NiB $3290
Replica Colt 3rd Model Dragoon revolver w/accessories, Colt SA Army revolver, and Colt Python revolver. Matching roll-engraved unfluted cylinders, blued finish and rosewood grips w/Great Seal of the United States silver medallion. Dragoon revolver has silver grip frame. Serial numbers 0001 to 1776. All revolvers in set have same number. Deluxe drawer-style presentation case of walnut w/book compartment containing

Colt U.S. Bicentennial Commemorative Set

a reproduction of "Armsmear." Issued in 1976. Value is for revolvers in new condition.

COONAN ARMS, INC. — Blaine, MN

Formerly Maplewood, Minnesota and St. Paul, Minnesota.

MODEL .357 MAGNUM SEMI-AUTO PISTOL

Caliber: .357 Mag. Seven-round magazine, 5- or 6-inch bbl., 8.3 inches overall (with 5-inch bbl.). Weight: 42 oz. Front ramp interchangeable sight, fixed rear sight, adj. for windage. Black walnut grips. Made from 1983 to 1999; reintro. 2010.

Model A Std. grade w/o grip
safety (disc. 1991). . . . . NiB $1221 Ex $1056 Gd $869
Model B Std. grade
   w/5-inch bbl., ... NiB $944 Ex $703 Gd $500
Model B Std. grade
   w/6-inch bbl., ... NiB $714 Ex $601 Gd $437
Model B w/5-inch compensated bbl.,
   (Classic). . . . . NiB $1336 Ex $1122 Gd $923
Model B w/6-inch
   compensated bbl . . . . NiB $1016 Ex $789 Gd $561

.357 MAGNUM CADET COMPACT

Similar to the standard .357 Magnum model except w/3.9-inch bbl., on compact frame. Six-round (Cadet), 7- or 8-round magazine (Cadet II). Weight: 39 oz., 7.8 inches overall. Made 1993 to 1999; reintro. 2010.

Cadet model . . . . NiB $897 Ex $653 Gd $497
Cadet II model . . . . NiB $897 Ex $653 Gd $497

CZ (CESKA ZBROJOVKA), INC. — Uhersky Brod, Czech Republic

Formerly Strakonice, Czechoslovakia. Mfd. by Ceska Zbrojovka-Nardoni Podnik formerly Bohmische Waffenfabrik

A. G. Currently imported by CZ-USA (cz-usa.com), Kansas City, KS. Previously by Magnum Research and Action Arms. Vintage importation is by Century International Arms. Also, see Dan Wesson Firearms listings.

CZ P-01. . . . . NiB $658 Ex $406 Gd $305
Caliber: 9mm Para. Based on CZ-75 design but with improved metals, aluminum alloy frame, hammer forged bbl. (3.8 inches), checkered rubber grips, matte black polycoat finish. Imported 2003.

CZ P-06. . . . . NiB $680 Ex $580 Gd $490
Similar to P-01 except in .40 S&W. Imported from 2008 to date.

CZ P-07 DUTY . . . . NiB $440 Ex $330 Gd $270
Caliber: 9mm Para. or .40 S&W. Polymer frame in black or OD green, 3.8-in. bbl. Made from 2009 to 2013.

CZ P-09. . . . . NiB $510 Ex $450 Gd $380
Semi-automatic. DA/SA. Based on CZ P-07 Duty. Caliber: 9mm or .40 S&W; 10-, 12- or 14-rnd. magazine depending on caliber. 3.8-in. bbl. Frame: polymer. Sights: fixed 3-dot. Finish: matte black. Grip: textured polymer w/modular backstraps. Made from 2014 to date.

CZ P-09 DUTY . . . . NiB $530 Ex $480 GD $400
Semi-automatic. DA/SA. Full size version of CZ P-09. Caliber: 9mm or .40 S&W; 15- or 14-rnd. magazine depending on caliber. 4.5-in. bbl. Frame: polymer. Sights: fixed 3-dot. Finish: matte black. Grip: textured polymer. Made from 2013 to date.
CZ P-09 Duty FDE (FDE finish) add $60

CZ 2075 RAMI P. . . . . NiB $440 Ex $330 Gd $270
Caliber: 9mm Para. or .40 S&W. Polymer frame in black, 3-in. bbl. Made from 2006 to 2011.

CZ 40 . . . . NiB $530 Ex $372 Gd $321
Caliber: .40 S&W. M1911-style frame, CZ-75B operating mechanism; single or double-action; black polycoat finish. Fixed sights; 10-round mag.

MODEL 27 AUTO PISTOL . . . . NiB $653 Ex $555 Gd $385
Caliber: .32 Automatic (7.65mm). Eight-round magazine, 4-inch bbl., 6 inches overall. Weight: 23.5 oz. Fixed sights. Blued finish. Plastic grips. Made from 1927 to 1951. Note: After the German occupation (March 1939), Models 27 and 38 were marked w/manufacturer code "fnh." Designation of Model 38 was changed to "Pistole 39(t)."

**CZ 2075 Rami P shown w/
extended magazine**

MODEL 38 AUTO PISTOL (VZ SERIES)
Caliber: .380 Automatic (9mm). Nine-round magazine, 3.75-inch bbl., 7 inches overall. Weight: 26 oz. Fixed sights. Blued finish. Plastic grips. After 1939 designated as T39. Made 1938 to 1945.
CZ DAO model . . . . NiB $518 Ex $442 Gd $358
CZ SA/DA model . . . . NiB $1451 Ex $1144 Gd $825

MODEL 50 DA AUTO PISTOL . NiB $265 Ex $191 Gd $153
Similar to Walther Model PP except w/frame-mounted safety and trigger guard not hinged. Caliber: .32 ACP (7.65mm), 8-round magazine, 3.13-inch bbl., 6.5 inches overall. Weight: 24.5 oz. Fixed sights. Blued finished. Intro. in 1950. disc.
Note: "VZ50" is the official designation of this pistol used by the Czech National Police (Models with crossed swords marking indicates a government-issued pistol).

MODEL 52
SA AUTO PISTOL . . . . NiB $248 Ex $202 Gd $137
Roller-locking breech system. Calibers: 7.62mm or 9mm Para. Eight-round magazine, 4.7-inch bbl., 8.1 inches overall. Weight: 31 oz. Fixed sights. Blued finish. Grooved composition grips. Made 1952 to 1956.

MODEL 70
DA AUTO PISTOL. . . . . NiB $530 Ex $420 Gd $296
Similar to Model 50 but redesigned to improve function and dependability. Made from 1962 to 1983.

MODEL 75 DA/DAO AUTOMATIC PISTOL
Calibers: 9mm Para. or .40 S&W w/selective action mode. 10-, 13- or 15-round magazine, 3.9-inch bbl., (Compact) or 4.75-inch bbl., 8 inches overall (Standard). Weight: 35 oz. Fixed sights. Blued, nickel, Two-Tone or black polymer finish. Checkered wood or high-impact plastic grips. Made from 1994 to date.
Black polymer finish . . . . NiB $459 Ex $385 Gd $284
High-polish blued finish . . . . . . NiB $526 Ex $453 Gd $347
Matte blued finish. . . . . NiB $499 Ex $398 Gd $295
Nickel finish . . . . NiB $541 Ex $442 Gd $330
Two-tone finish . . . . NiB $530 Ex $431 Gd $325
w/.22 Kadet conversion, add $281
Compact model, add. $65
Champion (1999-04,
    2006-09). . . . . NiB $1430 Ex $1055 Gd $610

MODEL 75 SHADOW AUTOMATIC PISTOL
Competition variant of the Model 75 except w/DA/SA or SAO trigger and Model 85 style trigger. Caliber: 9mm Para. Made from 2011 to 2013.
DA/SA. . . . . NiB $920 Ex $730 Gd $580
SAO . . . . NiB $850 Ex $660 Gd $460
CTS LS-P (long slide). . . . . . . NiB $1300 Ex $1030 Gd $780

MODEL 75 SP-01 PHANTOM. . NiB $530 Ex $380 Gd $280
Caliber: 9mm Para. Polymer black frame. Made from 2009 to 2013.

MODEL 75 B DA/DAO AUTOMATIC PISTOL
Similar to Model 75 except w/firing pin safety block. Made from 1998 to date.
Military (2000-02) . . . . NiB $370 Ex $275 Gd $230
Target SA (2010) . . . . NiB $1055 Ex $800 Gd $530

MODEL 82 DA AUTO PISTOL. . . NiB $407 Ex $306 Gd $221
Similar to the standard CZ 83 model except chambered in 9x18 Makarov. This model currently is the Czech military sidearm since 1983.

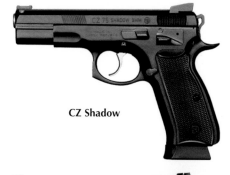

CZ Shadow

CZ Model 75 Compact

CZ Model 75 Kadet

CZ Model 83

MODEL 83 DA AUTOMATIC PISTOL
Calibers: .32 ACP, .380 ACP. 15-round (.32 ACP) or 13-round (.380 ACP) magazine, 3.75-inch bbl., 6.75 inches overall. Weight: 26.5 oz. Fixed sights. Blued (standard); chrome and nickel (optional special edition) w/brushed, matte or polished finish. Checkered black plastic grips. Made 1985-2012.
Standard finish . . . . NiB $434 Ex $357 Gd $221
Special edition . . . . NiB $580 Ex $453 Gd $322
Engraved . . . . NiB $1234 Ex $1017 Gd $718

GRADING: NiB = New in Box   Ex = Excellent or NRA 95%   Gd = Good or NRA 68%

CZ Model 85 Combat

CZ Model 97B

CZ Model 100

Daewoo DH40

CZ VZ 61 Skorpion

MODEL 85 AUTOMATIC DA PISTOL
Same as CZ 75 except w/ambidExtrous slide release and safety. Calibers: 9mm Para., 7.65mm. Made 1986 to date.

Black polymer finish	NiB $478	Ex $388	Gd $274
High-polish blued finish	NiB $576	Ex $477	Gd $319
Matte blued finish	NiB $529	Ex $372	Gd $267

MODEL 85 COMBAT DA AUTOMATIC PISTOL
Similar to the standard CZ 85 model except w/13-round magazine, combat-style hammer, fully adj. rear sight and walnut grips. Made from 1986 to date.

Black polymer finish	NiB $569	Ex $489	Gd $306
High-polished blued finish	NiB $610	Ex $498	Gd $373
Matte blued finish	NiB $614	Ex $486	Gd $366

MODEL 97B DA . . . . NiB $629 Ex $540 Gd $344
Similar to the CZ Model 75 except chambered for the .45 ACP cartridge. 10-round magazine, Frame-mounted thumb safety that allows single-action, cocked-and-locked carry. Made from 1998 to date.

MODEL 100 DA . . . . NiB $488 Ex $398 Gd $265
DA semi-automatic. Caliber: 9mm, .40 S&W. 10-round magazine, 3.8-inch bbl., Weight: 25 oz. Polymer grips w/ fixed low-profile sights. Made from 1996 to 2007. Reintro. 2009.

MODEL 1945 DA POCKET . . . . NiB $328 Ex $241 Gd $183
Caliber: .25 Auto (6.35mm). Eight-round magazine, 2.5-inch bbl., 5 inches overall. Weight: 15 oz. Fixed sights. Blued finish. Plastic grips. Intro. 1945. disc.

CZ VZ 61 SKORPION . . . . NiB $599 Ex $340 Gd $300
Semi-automatic version of VZ 61 Skorpion submachine gun. Caliber: .32 ACP. 20-round magazine, 4.5-in. bbl. Made from 2009 to 2010.

SCORPION EVO 3 S1 . . . . NiB $850 Ex $790 Gd $700
Semi-automatic. SA. Caliber: 9mm; 20-rnd. magazine. 7.72-in. bbl. Frame: polymer. Sights: low profile adj. aperture. Finish: matte black. Grip: textured polymer, adj. for reach. Weight: 5 lbs. Length: 16 in. Made from 2015 to date.

DUO POCKET AUTO PISTOL . NiB $328 Ex $252 Gd $174
Caliber: .25 Automatic (6.35mm). Six-round magazine, 2.13 inch bbl., 4.5 inches overall. Weight: 14-.5 oz. Fixed sights. Blued or nickel finish. Plastic grips. Made circa 1926 to 1960.

DAEWOO — Seoul, Korea
Mfd. by Daewoo Precision Industries Ltd. Imported by Daewoo Precision Industries, Southhampton, PA, Previously by Nationwide Sports Distributors and KBI, Inc.

DH40 AUTO PISTOL . . . . NiB $357 Ex $255 Gd $172
Caliber: .40 S&W. 12-round magazine, 4.25-inch bbl., 7 inches overall. Weight: 28 oz. Blade front sight, dovetailed rear w/3-dot system. Blued finish. Checkered composition grips. DH/DP series feature a patented "fastfire" action w/5-6 lb. trigger pull. Made from 1994 to 1996.

DH45 AUTO PISTOL . . . . NiB $346 Ex $248 Gd $189
Caliber: .45 ACP. 13-round magazine, 5-inch bbl., 8.1 inches over all. Weight: 35 oz. Blade front sight, dovetailed rear w/3-dot system. Blued finish. Checkered composition grips. Announced 1994, but not imported.

DP51 AUTO PISTOL . . . . NiB $330 Ex $221 Gd $148
Caliber: 9mm Para. 13-round magazine, 4.1-inch bbl., 7.5 inches overall. Weight: 28 oz. Blade front and square-notch rear sights. Matte black finish. Checkered composition grips. Made from 1991 to 1996.

DP52 AUTO PISTOL . . . . NiB $358 Ex $255 Gd $172
Caliber: .22 LR. 10-round magazine, 3.8-inch bbl., 6.7 inches overall. Weight: 23 oz. Blade front sight, dovetailed rear w/3-dot system. Blued finish. Checkered wood grips. Made from 1994 to 1996.

DAKOTA/E.M.F. CO. — Santa Ana, CA

MODEL 1873 SA REVOLVER
Calibers: .22 LR, .22 Mag., .357 Mag., .45 Long Colt, .30 M1 carbine, .38-40, .32-20, .44-40. Bbl. lengths: 3.5, 4.75, 5.5, 7.5 inches. Blued or nickel finish. Engraved models avail.
Standard model . . . . NiB $347 Ex $305 Gd $229
Nickel finish, add 40%

MODEL 1875 OUTLAW . . . . . NiB $525 Ex $420 Gd $293
Calibers: .45 Long Colt, .357 Mag., .44-40. 7.5-inch bbl. Casehardened frame, blued finish. Walnut grips. Exact replica of the Remington Number 3 SA revolver produced 1875 to 1889.

MODEL 1890 REMINGTON POLICE
Calibers: .357 Mag., .44-40, .45 Long Colt, 5.75-inch bbl., blued or nickel finish. Similar to 1875 Outlaw w/lanyard ring and no bbl. web.
Standard model . . . . NiB $560 Ex $441 Gd $332
Nickel model . . . . NiB $637 Ex $523 Gd $371
Engraved model . . . . NiB $780 Ex $603 Gd $444

BISLEY SA REVOLVER
Calibers: .44-40, .45 Long Colt, .357 Mag, 5.5- or 7.5-inch bbl., disc. 1992. Reintroduced 1994.
Standard model . . . . NiB $459 Ex $378 Gd $272
Engraved model . . . . NiB $638 Ex $509 Gd $283

HARTFORD SA REVOLVER
Calibers: .22 LR, .32-20, .357 Mag., .38-40, .44-40, .44 Special, .45 Long Colt. These are Exact replicas of the original Colts w/steel backstraps, trigger guards and forged frames. Blued or nickel finish. Imported from 1990 to 2008.
Standard model . . . . NiB $444 Ex $367 Gd $274
Engraved model . . . . NiB $734 Ex $546 Gd $499
Hartford Artillery, U.S. Cavalry
models . . . . NiB $484 Ex $401 Gd $267

SHERIFF'S MODEL . . . . NiB $437 Ex $377 Gd $271
SA revolver. Calibers: .32-20, .357 Mag., .38-40, .44 Special, .44-40, .45 LC. 3.5-inch bbl. Reintroduced 1994.

**Dakota Hartford
Engraved Model**

TARGET SA REVOLVER . . . . . . NiB $478 Ex $351 Gd $279
SA revolver. Calibers: .45 Long Colt, .357 Mag., .22 LR; 5.5- or 7.5-inch bbl. Polished, blued finish, casehardened frame. Walnut grips. Ramp front, blade target sight, adj. rear sight.

DALY, CHARLES — Dayton, OH
Mfd. by Flli. Pietta (SAA models) Armscor (1911 series) and Bul Transmark (M-5 series).

MODEL 1873 CLASSIC SERIES NiB $520 Ex $370 Gd $315
SA revolver based on Colt SAA. Caliber: .357 Mag. or .45 LC. 6-rnd. cylinder. Bbbl. length: 4.75-, 5.5- or 7.5-in. Brass or steel backstrap/trigger guard. Imported from 2004 to 2007.
Birdshead model (birdshead grip, .45 LC only), add $30
Lightning model, add $30
Sonora model (matte blue finish), add $100

MODEL 1911-A1 SERIES. . . . . NiB $480 Ex $420 Gd $360
SA semi-auto. 1911 style. Various bbl. lenghts depending on model.Caliber: .38 Super, .40 S&W or .45 ACP. 8- or 10-rnd. magazine, 5-in. bbl. Weight: 39.5 oz. Blued finish. Imported from 1998 to 2008.
Satinless finish, add. $100
Target model, add. $80
Empire ECMT Custom Match model, add $275
Commander model . . . . NiB $480 Ex $420 Gd $360
Officer's model . . . . NiB $480 Ex $420 Gd $360
Polymer Frame PC model . . . . . NiB $470 Ex $410 Gd $350

MODEL M1911-A1 FIELD FS AUTOMATIC PISTOL
Caliber: .45 ACP. Eight- or 10-round magazine (Hi-Cap), 5-inch bbl., 8.75 inches overall. Weight: 38 oz. Blade front sight, drift adjustable rear w/3-dot system. Skeletonized tactical hammer and trigger. Extended slide release and beavertail grip safety. Matte blue, stainless or Duo finish. Checkered composition or wood stocks. Imported from 1999 to 2000.
Matte blue (Field FS) . . . . NiB $525 Ex $479 Gd $326
Stainless (Empire EFS) . . . . NiB $560 Ex $459 Gd $361
Duo (Superior FS) . . . . NiB $653 Ex $497 Gd $363
w/.22 conversion kit, add $204

MODEL DDA
10-45 FS PISTOL . . . . NiB $455 Ex $400 Gd $345
SA/DA semi-automatic polymer pistol. Calibers: .40 S&W or .45 ACP. 10-rnd. magazine. 4.3-in. bbl. Weight: 28.5 oz. Finish: matte black or two-tone. Imported from 2000 to 2002.

FIELD HP HI-POWER . . . . NiB $390 Ex $340 Gd $295
Similar to Browning HP pistol. 9mm. 10- or 13-rnd. magazine. 4.75-in. bbl. Finish: matte blued. Made in U.S. from 2003 to 2006.
Hard Chrome finish, add $100

M-5 FS
SEMI-AUTOMATIC PISTOL . . . . NiB $670 Ex $585 Gd $505
Based on 1911 pistol w/polymer frame. Caliber: 9mm, .40 S&W or .45 ACP. 10-, 14- or 17-rnd. magazine. 3.1-, 4.2- or 5-in. bbl. Finish: blued or chrome. Weight: 31-33 oz. Imported from 2004 to 2009.
IPSC model (2004-07) . . . . . . NiB $1255 Ex $1100 Gd $945

DAN WESSON — Kansas City, KS
Currently owned by CZ-USA. Listsing below are for recent production of pistols and revolvers. Also see Wesson Fireams Company for older production revolvers.

MODEL 44-AGS (ALASKA GUIDE SPECIAL)
REVOLVER . . . . **NiB $1295 Ex $1080 Gd $960**
Caliber: .445 Super Mag., 6-shot cylinder. 4-in. heavy w/VR bbl. Finish: black teflon. Grip: rubber finger groove. Made 2002-04, and 2006-07.

MODEL 715 SEREIS . . . . **NiB $710 Ex $630 Gd $560**
Small frame revolver. Caliber: .357 Mag., 6-shot cylinder. 2.5-, 4-, 6-, 8-, or 10-in. heavy w/VR interchangeable bbls. Finish: stainless. Grip: rubber finger groove. Made 2002 to 2004, and 2011 to 2012.
2011-2012 mfg. (6-in. bbl.). . NiB $1168 Ex $1030 Gd $910

MODEL 741 SEREIS . . . . **NiB $830 Ex $730 Gd $660**
Large frame revolver. Caliber: .44 Mag., 6-shot cylinder. 4-, 6-, 8-, or 10-in. heavy w/VR interchangeable bbls. Finish: stainless. Grip: rubber finger groove. Made 2002 to 2004.

MODEL 7445 SEREIS . . . . **NiB $830 Ex $730 Gd $660**
Supermag frame revolver. Caliber: .445 Super Mag., 6-shot cylinder. 4-, 6-, 8-, or 10-in. heavy w/VR interchangeable bbls. Finish: stainless. Grip: rubber finger groove. Made 2002 to 2004, and 2006 to 2007.

MODEL 7460 SEREIS . . . . **NiB $1070 Ex $810 Gd $730**
Supermag frame revolver. Caliber: .45 ACP, .45 Auto Rim, .445 Super Mag., .45 Win. Mag., or .450 Rowland, 6-shot cylinder. Made 1999.

COMMANDER
CLASSIC BOBTAIL. . . . . **NiB $1050 Ex $780 Gd $610**
1911 platform. Caliber: 10mm or .45 Auto. 4.25-in. bbl., bobbed frame. Series 70. Made 2005 to 2009.

GLOBAL . . . . **NiB $1000 Ex $790 Gd $610**
1911 platform. Caliber: 10mm or .45 Auto. 5- or 6-in. bbl., accessory rail or full length dust cover frame. Series 70. Made 2005.

PATRIOT . . . . **NiB $830 Ex $660 Gd $480**
1911 platform. Caliber: 10mm or .45 Auto. 4.25- or 5-in. bbl., blued or stainless. Series 70. Made 2001 to 2005.

POINTMAN SEVEN . . . . **NiB $1050 Ex $780 Gd $610**
1911 platform. Caliber: .40 S&W, 10mm or .45 Auto. 5-in. bbl., blued or stainless, adj. target sights. Series 70. Made 2005 to 2009.

DAVIS INDUSTRIES, INC. — Chino, CA

MODEL D DERRINGER
Single-action double derringer. Calibers: .22 LR, .22 Mag., .25 ACP, .32 Auto, .32 H&R Mag., 9mm, .38 Special. Two-round capacity, 2.4-inch or 2.75-inch bbl., 4 inches overall (2.4-inch bbl.). Weight: 9 to 11.5 oz.
Laminated wood grips. Black Teflon or chrome finish. Made from 1987 to 2001.
.22 LR or .25 ACP . . . . **NiB $192 Ex $109 Gd $88**
.22 Mag., .32 H&R
  Mag., .38 Spec. . . . . **NiB $204 Ex $128 Gd $91**
.32 Auto . . . . **NiB $214 Ex $115 Gd $91**
9mm Para. . . . . **NiB $170 Ex $122 Gd $96**

LONG BORE DERRINGER . . . . . **NiB $219 Ex $122 Gd $97**
Similar to Model D except in calibers .22 Mag., .32 H&R Mag., .38 Special, 9mm Para. 3.75-inch bbl., weight: 16 oz. Made from 1995 to 2001.

MODEL P-.32 . . . . **NiB $152 Ex $101 Gd $78**
Caliber: .32 Auto. Six-round magazine, 2.8-inch bbl., 5.4 inches overall. Weight: 22 oz. Black Teflon or chrome finish. Laminated wood grips. Made from 1987 to 2001.

MODEL P-.380 . . . . **NiB $192 Ex $115 Gd $89**
Caliber: .380 Auto. Five-round magazine, 2.8-inch bbl., 5.4 inches overall. Weight: 22 oz. Black Teflon or chrome finish. Made from 1990 to 2001.

DESERT INDUSTRIES, INC. — Las Vegas, NV
Previously Steel City Arms, Inc.

DOUBLE DEUCE DA PISTOL . . **NiB $386 Ex $286 Gd $225**
Caliber: .22 LR. Six-round magazine, 2.5-inch bbl., 5.5 inches overall. Weight: 15 oz. Matte-finish stainless steel. Rosewood grips.

TWO-BIT SPECIAL PISTOL . . . . **NiB $431 Ex $326 Gd $237**
Similar to the Double Deuce model except chambered in .25 ACP w/5-shot magazine.

DETONICS FIREARMS IND. — Phoenix, AZ
Previously Detonics Firearms Industries, Bellevue, WA.

COMBAT MASTER
Calibers: .45 ACP, .451 Detonics Mag. Six-round magazine, 3.5-inch bbl., 6.75 inches overall. Combat-type w/fixed or adjustable sights. Checkered walnut grip. Stainless steel. Disc. 1992.
MK I, matte stainless,
  fixed sights (disc. 1981) . . . . **NiB $1097 Ex $963 Gd $893**
MK II polished finish,
  (disc. 1979). . . . . **NiB $1494 Ex $1370 Gd $1133**
MK III chrome, (disc. 1980) . . . **NiB $551 Ex $443 Gd $328**
MK IV polished blued,
  adj. sights, (disc. 1981). . . . . . **NiB $612 Ex $500 Gd $373**
MK V matte stainless,
  fixed sights, (disc. 1985). . . . . **NiB $762 Ex $621 Gd $499**
MK VI polished stainless, fixed
  sights, (disc. 1985) . . . . **NiB $831 Ex $666 Gd $509**
MK VI in .451 Magnum,
  (disc. 1986) . . . . **NiB $1199 Ex $979 Gd $695**
MK VII matte stainless steel,
  no sights, (disc. 1985) . . . . . **NiB $1037 Ex $845 Gd $591**
MK VII in .451 Magnum,
  (disc. 1980) . . . . **NiB $1380 Ex $1131 Gd $806**

POCKET 9 . . . . **NiB $668 Ex $541 Gd $426**
Calibers: 9mm Para., .380. Six-round magazine, three-inch bbl., 5.88 inches overall. Fixed sights. Double- and single-action trigger mechanism. Disc. 1986.

Detonics Combatmaster

Detonics Scoremaster

Dreyse Model 1907

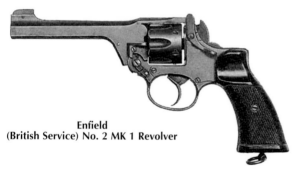

**Enfield
(British Service) No. 2 MK 1 Revolver**

SCOREMASTER.........NiB $1550 Ex $1257 Gd $1120
Calibers: .45 ACP, .451 Detonics Mag. Seven-round magazine. Five- or 6-inch heavyweight match bbl., 8.75 inches overall. Weight: 47 oz. Stainless steel construction, self-centering bbl., system. Disc. 1992.

SERVICEMASTER..........NiB $1117 Ex $780 Gd $530
Caliber: .45 ACP. Seven-round magazine, 4.25-inch bbl., weight: 39 oz. Interchangeable front sight, Millett rear sight. Disc. 1986.

SERVICEMASTER II........NiB $1117 Ex $780 Gd $530
Same general specifications as standard Service Master except comes in polished stainless steel w/self-centering bbl., system. Disc. 1992.

DIAMONDBACK FIREARMS — COCOA, FL

DB9.....................NiB $431 Ex $380 Gd $280
Semi-automatic. Striker fire. Caliber: 9mm, 6-rnd. magazine. 3-in. bbl. Frame: polymer. Sights: fixed. Finish: matte black, FDE, pink, or two-tone. Grip: textured polymer. Weight: 11 oz. Length: 5.6 in. Made from 2011 to date.

FDE or pink, add................................$10
Two-tone, add..................................$30

MODEL DB FS 9...........NiB $483 Ex $400 Gd $380
Semi-automatic. Striker fire. Caliber: 9mm, 15-rnd. magazine. 4.75-in. bbl. Frame: polymer. Sights: fixed. Finish: matte black. Grip: textured polymer. Weight: 21.5 oz. Length: 7.8 in. Made from 2014 to date.

MODEL DB15PODG7.......NiB $914 Ex $890 Gd $810
AR15 platform. Semi-automatic. SA. Caliber: 5.56 NATO, 30-rnd. magazine. 7.5-in. bbl. Frame: forged aluminum. Sights: none. Finish: matte black. Grip: textured polymer. Made from 2014 to date.

MODEL DB380...........NIB $394 EX $430 GD $330
Similar to DB9 except chambered in .380 ACP.

DOUBLETAP DEFENSE — ST. LOUIS, MO

DOUBLETAP..............NIB $499 EX $460 GD $390
O/U derringer, break action, dbl. bbl. DAO. Caliber: 9mm or .45 ACP. 3-in. bbl., allows bbls. to be swapped. Frame: aluminum. Sights: fixed. Finish: matte black. Grip: textured aluminum w/storage for 2 extra cartridges. Weight: 15 oz. Length: 5.5 in. Made from 2012 to date.
Ported brls., add..............................$70
Titanium frame, add...........................$240

DOWNSIZER CORPORATION — Santee, CA

MODEL WSP DAO PISTOL....NiB $499 Ex $381 Gd $264
Single-round, tip-up pistol. Calibers: .22 Mag., .32 Mag., .380 ACP. 9mm Parabellum, .357 Mag., .40 S&W, .45 ACP. Six-round cylinder, 2.10-inch bbl. w/o Extractor, 3.25 inches overall. Weight: 11 oz. No sights. Stainless finish. Synthetic grips. Made from 1994 to 2007.

DREYSE — Sommerda, Germany
Mfd. by Rheinische Metallwaren und Maschinenfabrik ("Rheinmetall").

MODEL 1907
AUTOMATIC PISTOL........NiB $273 Ex $224 Gd $179
Caliber: .32 Auto (7.65mm). Eight-round magazine, 3.5-inch bbl., 6.25 inches overall. Weight: About 24 oz. Fixed sights. Blued finish. Hard rubber grips. Made circa 1907 to 1914.

VEST POCKET
AUTOMATIC PISTOL........NiB $357 Ex $293 Gd $204
Conventional Browning type. Caliber: .25 Auto (6.35mm). Six-round magazine, 2-inch bbl., 4.5 inches overall. Weight: About 14 oz. Fixed sights. Blued finish. Hard rubber grips. Made 1909 to 1914.

DWM — Berlin, Germany
Mfd. by Deutsche Waffen-und-Munitionsfabriken.

POCKET AUTOMATIC PISTOL...NiB $1050 Ex $918 Gd $713
Similar to the FN Browning Model 1910. Caliber: .32 Automatic (7.65mm). 3.5-inch bbl., 6 inches overall. Weight: About 21 oz. Blued finish. Hard rubber grips. Made circa 1921 to 1931.

ED BROWN — Perry, MT
Manufacturer of custom 1911 style pistols.

CLASS A LTD. . . . . NiB $2312 Ex $2152 Gd $1041
Caliber: .38 Super, 9mm, 9x23, .45 ACP. Seven-round magazine, 4.25- or 5-inch bbl., weight: 34-39 oz. Rubber checkered or optional Hogue Exotic wood grip. M1911 style single action pistol. Fixed front and rear Novak Lo-mount or fully adjustable sights.

CLASSIC CUSTOM . . . . NiB $3231 Ex $2553 Gd $1527
Caliber: .45 ACP. Seven-round magazine, 4.25- or 5-inch bbl., weight: 39 oz. Exotic Hogue wood grip w/modified ramp or post front and rear adjustable sights.

SPECIAL FORCES . . . . NiB $2240 Ex $1918 Gd $1437
Caliber: .45 ACP. Seven-round magazine, 4.25- or 5-inch bbl., weight: 34-39 oz. Rubber checkered, optional exotic wood grips. Single action M1911 style pistol.

E.M.F. Co., In. — Santa Anna, CA
Importer, distrributor and retailer of numerous reproduction and new deisgn pistols and revolvers. See Davide Pedersoli & Co., F.A.P F.LLI. Pietta, and Uberti.

ENFIELD — Enfield Lock, Middlesex, England
Mfd. by Rheinische Metallwaren und Manufactured by Royal Small Arms Factory.

NO. 2 MK 1 DA REVOLVER . . . NiB $362 Ex $271 Gd $221
British Military Service. Webley pattern. Hinged frame. Double action. Caliber: .380 British Service (.38 S&W w/200-grain bullet). Six-round cylinder, 5-inch bbl., 10.5 inches overall. Weight: About 27.5 oz. Fixed sights. Blued finish. Vulcanite grips. First issued in 1932, this was the standard revolver of the British Army in WW II. Now obsolete. Note: This model also produced w/spurless hammer as No. 2 Mk 1* and Mk 1**.

ENTREPRISE ARMS — Irwindale, CA

ELITE SERIES SA AUTO PISTOL . . . NiB $661 Ex $498 Gd $401
Single action M1911 style pistol. Caliber: .45 ACP. 10-round magazine, 3.25-, 4.25-, 5-inch bbl., (models P325, P425, P500). Weight: 36-40 oz. Ultraslim checkered grips, Tactical 2 high profile sights w/3-dot system. Lightweight adjustable trigger. Blued or matte black oxide finish. Made from 1997 to date.

MEDALIST SA AUTOMATIC PISTOL
Similar to Elite model except machined to match tolerances and target configuration. Caliber: .45 ACP, .40 S&W. 10-round magazine, 5-inch compensated bbl. w/dovetail front and fully adjustable rear Bo-Mar sights. Weight: 40 oz. Made from 1997 to date.
.40 S&W model. . . . . NiB $1015 Ex $862 Gd $689
.45 ACP model . . . . NiB $893 Ex $740 Gd $577

TACTICAL SA AUTOMATIC PISTOL
Similar to Elite model except in combat carry configuration. De-horned frame and slide w/ambidExtrous safety. Caliber: .45 ACP. 10-round magazine, 3.25-, 4.25-, 5-inch bbl., weight: 36-40 oz. Tactical 2 Ghost Ring or Novak Lo-mount sights.
Tactical 2 ghost
ring sights. . . . . NiB $917 Ex $724 Gd $571
Novak Lo-Mount. . . . . NiB $917 Ex $724 Gd $571

Erma
Model ER-772 Match Revolver

Erma-Werke
Model KGP69

Model ESP-85A
Competition Pistol

Tactical plus model . . . . NiB $917 Ex $724 Gd $571

BOXER . . . . NiB $1243 Ex $1122 Gd $831
Similar to Medalist model except w/profiled slide configuration and fully adjustable target sights. weight: 42 oz. Made from 1997 to date.

TOURNAMENT SHOOTER MODEL SA AUTOMATIC PISTOL
Similar to Elite model except in IPSC configuration. Caliber: .45 ACP, .40 S&W. 10-round magazine, 5-inch compensated bbl., w/dovetail front and fully adjustable rear Bo-Mar sights. Weight: 40 oz. Made from 1997 to date.
TSM I model . . . . NiB $2145 Ex $1986 Gd $1637
TSM II model . . . . NiB $1834 Ex $1687 Gd $1331
TSM III model. . . . . NiB $2575 Ex $1403 Gd $1661

ERMA-WERKE — Dachau, Germany

MODEL ER-772. . . . . NiB $1132 Ex $1071 Gd $655
Revolver. Caliber: .22 LR. Six-round cylinder, 6-inch bbl., 12 inches overall. Weight: 47.25 oz. Adjustable micrometer rear sight and front sight blade. Adjustable trigger. Interchangeable walnut sporter or match grips. Polished blued finish. Made from 1991 to 1994.

European American Armory Big Bore Bounty Hunter shown w/optional scope

MODEL ER-773 MATCH . . . . . . NiB $957 Ex $831 Gd $587
Same general specifications as Model 772 except chambered for .32 S&W. Made from 1991 to 1995.

MODEL ER-777 MATCH . . . . . . NiB $923 Ex $785 Gd $623
Revolver. Caliber: .357 Magnum. Six-round cylinder. 4- or 5.5-inch bbl., 9.7 to 11.3 inches overall. Weight: 43.7 oz. (with 5.5-inch bbl.). Micrometer adj. rear sight. Checkered walnut sporter or match-style grip (interchangeable). Made from 1991 to 1995.

MODEL ESP-85A COMPETITION PISTOL
Calibers: .22 LR and .32 S&W Wadcutter. Eight- or 5-round magazine, 6-inch bbl., 10 inches overall. Weight: 40 oz. Adj. rear sight, blade front sight. Checkered walnut grip w/thumbrest. Made from 1991 to 1997.
Match model . . . . NiB $1280 Ex $1128 Gd $716
Chrome match . . . . NiB $1540 Ex $1330 Gd $998
Sporting model . . . . NiB $1251 Ex $1049 Gd $735
Conversion unit .22 LR . . . . NiB $1566 Ex $1212 Gd $1030
Conversion unit .32 S&W . . NiB $1566 Ex $1212 Gd $1030

MODEL KGP68
AUTOMATIC PISTOL . . . . NiB $484 Ex $306 Gd $239
Luger type. Calibers: .32 Auto (7.65mm), .380 Auto (9mm Short). Six-round magazine (.32 Auto), 5-round (.380 Auto), 4-inch bbl., 7.38 inches overall. Weight: 22.5 oz. Fixed sights. Blued finish. Checkered walnut grips. Made from 1968 to 1993.

MODEL KGP69
AUTOMATIC PISTOL . . . . NiB $357 Ex $291 Gd $214
Luger type. Caliber: .22 LR. Eight-round magazine, 4-inch bbl., 7.75 inches overall. Weight: 29 oz. fixed sights. Blued finish. Checkered walnut grips. Imported from 1969 to 1993.

EUROPEAN AMERICAN ARMORY (EAA) — Rockledge, FL
See also listings under Astra Pistols.

EUROPEAN MODEL AUTO PISTOL
Calibers: .32 ACP (SA only), .380 ACP (SA or DA), 3.85-inch bbl., 7.38 overall, 7-round magazine, Weight: 26 oz. Blade front sight, drift-adj.
rear. Blued, chrome, blue/chrome, blue/gold, Duo-Tone or Wonder finish. Imported 1991 to date.
Blued .32 ACP (disc. 1995) . . . . NiB $140 Ex $101 Gd $81
Blue/chrome .32 caliber
  (disc. 1995) . . . . NiB $204 Ex $117 Gd $81
Chrome .32 caliber
  (Disc. 1995) . . . . NiB $137 Ex $101 Gd $81

Blued .380 caliber. . . . . NiB $158 Ex $116 Gd $88
Blue/chrome .380 caliber
  (disc. 1993) . . . . NiB $204 Ex $136 Gd $91
DA .380 caliber (disc. 1994) . . . NiB $398 Ex $267 Gd $167
Lady .380 caliber (disc. 1995) . NiB $270 Ex $203 Gd $143
Wonder finish .380 caliber . . . . NiB $275 Ex $186 Gd $131

BIG BORE BOUNTY HUNTER SA REVOLVER
Calibers: .357 Mag., .41 Mag., .44-40, .44 Mag., .45 Colt. Bbl., lengths: 4.63, 5.5, 7.5 inches. Blade front and grooved topstrap rear sights. Blued or chrome finish w/color casehardened or gold-plated frame. Smooth walnut grips. Imported 1992.
Blued finish . . . . NiB $377 Ex $255 Gd $189
Blued w/color-
  casehardened frame . . . . NiB $388 Ex $265 Gd $190
Blued w/gold-plated frame . . . . NiB $403 Ex $281 Gd $214
Chrome finish . . . . NiB $408 Ex $286 Gd $219
Gold-plated frame, add. $110

BOUNTY HUNTER SA REVOLVER
Calibers: .22 LR, .22 Mag. Bbl. lengths: 4.75, 6 or 9 inches. Blade front and dovetailed rear sights. Blued finish or blued w/ gold-plated frame. European hardwood grips. Imported from 1997 to date.
Blued finish (4.75-inch bbl.) . . . NiB $281 Ex $191 Gd $128
Blued .22 LR/.22 WRF combo
  (4.75-inch bbl.) . . . . NiB $281 Ex $191 Gd $128
Blued .22 LR/.22 WRF combo
  (6-inch bbl.) . . . . NiB $281 Ex $191 Gd $128
Blued .22 LR/.22 WRF combo
  (9-inch bbl.) . . . . NiB $281 Ex $191 Gd $128

EA22 TARGET . . . . NiB $398 Ex $281 Gd $214
Caliber: .22 LR. 12-round magazine, 6-inch bbl., 9.10 inches overall. Weight: 40 oz. Ramp front sight, fully adj. rear. Blued finish. Checkered walnut grips w/thumbrest. Made from 1991 to 1994.

FAB 92 AUTO PISTOL
Similar to the Witness model except chambered in 9mm only w/slide-mounted safety and no cock-and-lock provision. Imported 1992 to 1995.
FAB 92 standard . . . . NiB $437 Ex $342 Gd $223
FAB 92 compact . . . . NiB $437 Ex $342 Gd $223

SARGUN . . . . NiB $604 Ex $580 Gd $500
Semi-automatic. SA. Caliber: 9mm, .40 S&W or .45 ACP; 17- or 15-rnd. magazine depending on caliber. 4.5-in. bbl. Frame: polymer. Sights: low profile adj. Finish: matte black, two-tone. Grip: textured polymer. Weight: 30.5 oz. Length: 7.8

European American Armory Windicator Target

European American Armory Witness

in. Ambidextrous controls. Imported from Turkey from 2013 to date.

STANDARD GRADE REVOLVER

Calibers: .22 LR, .22 WRF, .32 H&R Mag., .38 Special. Two-, 4- or 6-inch bbl., blade front sight, fixed or adj. rear. Blued finish. European hardwood grips w/finger grooves. Imported 1991 to date.

.22 LR (4-inch bbl.)	NiB $215	Ex $171	Gd $128
.22 LR (6-inch bbl.)	NiB $228	Ex $181	Gd $133
.22 LR combo (4-inch bbl.)	NiB $301	Ex $237	Gd $171
.22 LR combo (6-inch bbl.)	NiB $337	Ex $265	Gd $187
.32 H&R, .38 Special (2-inch bbl.)	NiB $231	Ex $174	Gd $128
.38 Special (4-inch bbl.)	NiB $235	Ex $187	Gd $132
.357 Mag.	NiB $242	Ex $206	Gd $144

TACTICAL GRADE REVOLVER

Similar to the Standard model except chambered in .38 Special only. Two- or 4-inch bbl., fixed sights. Available w/compensator. Imported from 1991-93.

Tactical revolver	NiB $229	Ex $185	Gd $109
Tactical revolver w/compensator	NiB $316	Ex $270	Gd $192

WINDICATOR TARGET

REVOLVER	NiB $444	Ex $381	Gd $255

Calibers: .22 LR, .38 Special, .357 Magnum. Eight-round cylinder in .22 LR, 6-round in .38 Special and .357 Magnum. Six-inch bbl. w/bbl. weights. 11.8 inches overall. Weight: 50.2 oz. Interchangeable blade front sight, fully adj. rear. Walnut competition-style grips. Imported from 1991-93.

WITNESS DA AUTO PISTOL

Similar to the Brno CZ-75 w/a cocked-and-locked system. Double or single action. Calibers: 9mm Para. .38 Super, .40 S&W, 10mm; .41 AE and .45 ACP. 16-round magazine (9mm), 12 shot (.38 Super/.40 S&W), or 10-round (10mm/.45 ACP), 4.75-inch bbl., 8.10 inches overall. Weight: 35.33 oz. Blade front sight, rear sight adj. for windage w/3-dot sighting system. Steel or polymer frame. Blued, satin chrome, blue/chrome, stainless or Wonder finish. Checkered rubber grips. EA Series imported 1991 to date.

9mm blue	NiB $475	Ex $337	Gd $249
9mm chrome or blue/chrome	NiB $475	Ex $337	Gd $249
9mm stainless	NiB $469	Ex $337	Gd $283
9mm Wonder finish	NiB $500	Ex $356	Gd $265
.38 Super and .40 S&W blued	NiB $475	Ex $337	Gd $237
.38 Super and .40 S&W chrome or blue/chrome	NiB $469	Ex $388	Gd $273
.38 Super and .40 S&W stainless	NiB $546	Ex $425	Gd $292
.38 Super and .40 S&W Wonder finish	NiB $577	Ex $340	Gd $296
10mm, .41 AE and .45 ACP blued	NiB $474	Ex $346	Gd $235
10mm, .41 AE and .45 ACP chrome or blue/chrome	NiB $546	Ex $437	Gd $316
10mm, .41 AE and .45 ACP stainless	NiB $577	Ex $464	Gd $337
10mm, .41 AE and .45 ACP Wonder finish	NiB $562	Ex $439	Gd $321

WITNESS COMPACT DA AUTO PISTOL (L SERIES)

Similar to the standard Witness series except more compact w/ 3.625-inch bbl., and polymer or steel frame. Weight: 30 oz. Matte blued or Wonder finish. Imported 1999 to date.

9mm blue	NiB $468	Ex $330	Gd $235
9mm Wonder finish	NiB $468	Ex $330	Gd $235
.38 Super and .40 S&W blued	NiB $468	Ex $330	Gd $235
.38 Super and .40 S&W Wonder finish	NiB $468	Ex $330	Gd $235
10mm, .41 AE and .45 ACP blued	NiB $549	Ex $369	Gd $273
10mm, .41 AE and .45 ACP Wonder fin.	NiB $549	Ex $369	Gd $273
w/ported bbl., add			$50

WITNESS CARRY COMP

Double/Single action. Calibers: .38 Super, 9mm Parabellum, .40 S&W, 10mm, .45 ACP. 10-, 12- or 16-round magazine, 4.25-inch bbl., w/1-inch compensator. Weight: 33 oz., 8.10 inches overall. Black rubber grips. Post front sight, drift adjustable rear w/3-dot system. Matte blue, Duo-Tone or Wonder finish. Imported 1992 to 2004.

9mm, .40 S&W	NiB $453	Ex $359	Gd $273
.38 Super, 10mm, .45 ACP	NiB $453	Ex $359	Gd $273
w/Duo-Tone finish (disc.), add			$40
w/Wonder finish, add			$20

WITNESS LIMITED CLASS	NiB $909	Ex $734	Gd $559

Single action. Semi-automatic. Calibers: .38 Super, 9mm Parabellum, .40 S&W, .45 ACP. 10-round magazine, 4.75-inch bbl., Weight: 37 oz. Checkered competition-style walnut grips. Long slide w/post front sight, fully adj. rear. Matte blue finish. Imported 1994 to 1998.

WITNESS SUBCOMPACT DA AUTO PISTOL

Calibers: 9mm Para., .40 S&W, 41 AK, .45 ACP. 13-round magazine in 9mm, 9-round in .40 S&W, 3.66-inch bbl., 7.25 inches overall. Weight: 30 oz. Blade front sight, rear sight adj. for windage. Blued, satin chrome or blue/chrome finish. Imported from 1995 to 1997.

9mm blue	NiB $408	Ex $281	Gd $204
9mm chrome or blue/chrome	NiB $453	Ex $306	Gd $225
.40 S&W blue	NiB $453	Ex $306	Gd $225
.40 S&W chrome or blue/chrome	NiB $497	Ex $366	Gd $229
.41 AE blue	NiB $525	Ex $429	Gd $308
.41 AE chrome or blue/chrome	NiB $577	Ex $448	Gd $319
.45 ACP blued	NiB $525	Ex $336	Gd $308
.45 ACP chrome or blue/chrome	NiB $500	Ex $439	Gd $321

WITNESS TARGET PISTOLS

Similar to standard Witness model except fitted w/2- or 3-port compensator, competition frame and S/A target trigger. Calibers: 9mm

Feather Guardian Angel Derringer

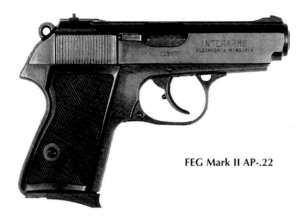

FEG Mark II AP-.22

Para., 9x21, .40 S&W, 10mm and .45 ACP, 5.25-inch match bbl., 10.5 inches overall. Weight: 38 oz. Square post front sight, fully adj. rear or drilled and tapped for scope. Blued or hard chrome finish. Low-profile competition grips. Imported 1992 to date.
Silver Team (blued w/2-port
    compensator) . . . . NiB $895 Ex $785 Gd $561
Gold Team (chrome
    w/3-port compensator) . . . NiB $1810 Ex $1632 Gd $1331

FAS — Malino, Italy
Currently imported by Nygord Precision Products. Previously by Beeman Precision Arms and Osborne's, Cheboygan, MI.

OP601 SEMIAUTOMATIC MATCH TARGET PISTOL
Caliber: .22 Short. Five-round top-loading magazine, 5.6-inch ported and ventilated bbl., 11 inches overall. Weight: 41.5 oz. Removable, adj. trigger group. Blade front sight, open-notch fully adj. rear. Stippled walnut wraparound or adj. target grips.
Right-hand model . . . . NiB $1076 Ex $930 Gd $714
Left-hand model . . . . NiB $1153 Ex $985 Gd $755

602 SEMIAUTOMATIC MATCH TARGET PISTOL
Similar to Model FAS 601 except chambered for .22 LR. Weight: 37 oz.
Right-hand model . . . . NiB $960 Ex $705 Gd $581
Left-hand model . . . . NiB $1030 Ex $830 Gd $691

CF603 SEMIAUTOMATIC
MATCH TARGET PISTOL . . . . NiB $1030 Ex $816 Gd $647
Similar to Model FAS 601 except chambered for .32 S&W (wadcutter).

SP607 SEMIAUTOMATIC
MATCH TARGET PISTOL . . . . NiB $1030 Ex $804 Gd $658
Similar to Model FAS 601 except chambered for .22 LR, w/ removable bbl. weights. Imported 1995 to date.

FEATHER INDUSTRIES — Boulder, CO

GUARDIAN ANGEL DERRINGER
Double-action over/under derringer w/interchangeable drop-in loading blocks. Calibers: .22 LR, .22 WMR, 9mm, .38 Spec. Two-round capacity, 2-inch bbl., 5 inches overall. weight: 12 oz. Stainless steel. Checkered black grip. Made 1988 to 1995.
.22 LR, .22 WMR . . . . NiB 165 Ex $101 Gd $81
9mm, .38 Special (disc. 1989) . . . NiB $233 Ex $189 Gd $150

FEG (FEGYVERGYAN) — Budapest, Soroksariut, Hungary
Currently imported by KBI, Inc. and Century International Arms. Previously by Interarms.

MARK II AP-.22 DA
AUTO PISTOL . . . . NiB $271 Ex $219 Gd $179
Caliber: .22 LR. 8-round magazine, 3.4-inch bbl., Weight: 23 oz. Drift-adj. sights. Double action, all-steel pistol. Imported 1997 to 1998.

MARK II AP-.380 DA AUTO
PISTOL . . . . NiB $271 Ex $219 Gd $179
Caliber: .380. 7-round magazine, 3.9-inch bbl., weight 27 oz. Drift-adj. sights. Double action, all-steel pistol. Imported 1997 to 1998.

MARK II APK-.380 DA AUTO
PISTOL . . . . NiB $271 Ex $219 Gd $179
Caliber: .380. 7-round magazine, 3.4-inch bbl., weight: 25 oz. Drift-adj. sights. Double action, all-steel pistol. Imported 1997 to 1998.

MODEL GKK-9 (92C)
AUTO PISTOL . . . . NiB $321 Ex $240 Gd $204
Improved version of the double-action FEG Model MBK. Caliber: 9mm Para. 14-round magazine, 4-inch bbl., 7.4 inches overall. Weight: 34 oz. Blade front sight, rear sight adj. for windage. Checkered wood grips. Blued finish. Imported from 1992 to 1993.

MODEL GKK-.45 AUTO PISTOL
Improved version of the double-action FEG Model MBK. Caliber: .45 ACP. Eight-round magazine, 4.1-inch bbl., 7.75 inches overall. Weight: 36 oz. Blade front sight, adj. rear sight w/3-dot system. Checkered walnut grips. Blued or chrome finish. Imported 1993 to 1996.
Blued model (disc. 1994) . . . . . NiB $325 Ex $265 Gd $204
Chrome model . . . . NiB $362 Ex $281 Gd $220

MODEL MBK-9HP
AUTO PISTOL . . . . NiB $469 Ex $306 Gd $281

GRADING: **NiB** = New in Box   **Ex** = Excellent or NRA 95%   **Gd** = Good or NRA 68%   **195**

FEG Model PJK-9HP

F.I.E. Model A27BW

F.I.E. Arminius

Similar to the double-action Browning Hi-Power. Caliber: 9mm Para. 14-round magazine, 4.6-inch bbl., 8 inches overall. Weight: 36 oz. Blade front sight, rear sight adj. for windage. Checkered wood grips. Blued finish. Imported 1992 to 1993.

MODEL PA-63 AUTO PISTOL . . . . **Ex $175 Gd $95**
Hungary's military pistol. Similar to the Walther PP. Caliber: 9x18mm Makarov. 7-round magazine, 3.95-inch bbl., 6.9 inches overall. Weight: 21 oz. Fixed sights. Two-tone finish; blued slide natutal aluminum frame. Checkered plasic grips. Military surplus.

MODEL PJK-9HP AUTO PISTOL
Similar to the single-action Browning Hi-Power. Caliber: 9mm Para. 13-round magazine, 4.75-inch bbl., 8 inches overall. Weight: 21 oz. Blade front sight, rear sight adj. for windage w/3-dot system. Checkered walnut or rubber grips. Blued or chrome finish. Imported 1992 to 2003.
Blued model . . . . .NiB $469 Ex $388 Gd $265
Chrome model . . . . .NiB $500 Ex $408 Gd $316

MODEL PSP-.25 AUTO PISTOL
Similar to the Browning .25. Caliber: .25 ACP. Six-round magazine, 2.1-inch bbl., 4.1 inches overall. Weight: 9.5 oz. Fixed sights. Checkered composition grips. Blued or chrome finish.
Blued model . . . . .NiB $316 Ex $204 Gd $150
Chrome model . . . . .NiB $316 Ex $204 Gd $150

MODEL SMC-.22 . . . . .NiB $222 Ex $130 Gd $79
Same general specifications as FEG Model SMC-.380 except in .22 LR. Eight-round magazine, 3.5-inch bbl., 6.1 inches overall. Weight: 18.5 oz. Blade front sight, rear sight adj. for windage. Checkered composition grips w/thumbrest. Blued finish.

MODEL SMC-.380 . . . . .NiB $222 Ex $130 Gd $79
Similar to the Walther DA PPK w/alloy frame. Caliber: .380 ACP. Six-round magazine, 3.5-inch bbl., 6.1 inches overall. Weight: 18.5 oz. Blade front sight, rear sight adj. for windage. Checkered composition grips w/ thumbrest. Blued finish. Imported 1993 to 1997.

MODEL SMC-918 . . . . .NiB $203 Ex $120 Gd $90
Same general specifications as FEG Model SMC-.380 except chambered in 9x18mm Makarov. Imported from 1994 to 1997.

FIALA OUTFITTERS, INC. — New York, NY

REPEATING PISTOL . . . . .NiB $689 Ex $479 Gd $365
Hand-operated, not semi-auto. Caliber: .22 LR. 10-round magazine, bbl. lengths: 3-, 7.5- and 20-inch. 11.25 inches overall (with 7.5-inch bbl.). Weight: 31 oz. (with 7.5-inch bbl.). Target sights. Blued finish. Plain wood grips. Shoulder stock was originally supplied for use w/20-inch bbl. Made from 1920 to 1923. Value shown is for pistol w/one bbl., no shoulder stock. Three bbl. cased sets start at $3,030.

F.I.E. CORPORATION — Hialeah, FL
The F.I.E. Corporation became QFI (Quality Firearms Corp.) of Opa Locka, Fl., about 1990, when most of F.I.E.'s models were discontinued.

MODEL A27 "THE BEST"
SEMI-AUTO . . . . NiB $140 Ex $95 Gd $55
Caliber: .25 ACP. Six-round magazine, 2.5-inch bbl., 6.75 inches overall. Weight: 13 oz. Fixed sights. Checkered walnut grip. Discontinued in 1990.

ARMINIUS DA STANDARD REVOLVER
Calibers: .22 LR, .22 combo w/interchangeable cylinder, .32 S&W, .38 Special, .357 Magnum. Six, 7 or 8 rounds depending on caliber. Swing-out cylinder. bbl., lengths: 2-, 3-, 4, 6-inch. Vent rib on calibers other than .22, 11 inches overall (with 6-inch bbl.). Weight: 26 to 30 oz. Fixed or micro-adj. sights. Checkered plastic or walnut grips. Blued finish. Made in Germany. Disc.
.22 LR . . . . .NiB $130 Ex $89 Gd $67
.22 Combo . . . . .NiB $198 Ex $148 Gd $101
.32 S&W .NiB $207 Ex $149 Gd $101
.38 Special . . . . .NiB $161 Ex $95 Gd $70
.357 Magnum . . . . .NiB $240 Ex $179 Gd $135

BUFFALO SCOUT SA REVOLVER
Calibers: .22 LR, .22 WRF, .22 combo w/interchangeable cylinder. 4.75-inch bbl., 10 inches overall. Weight: 32 oz. Adjustable sights. Blued or chrome finish. Smooth walnut or black checkered nylon grips. Made in Italy. Disc.

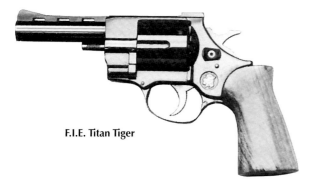

F.I.E. Titan Tiger

F.I.E. Titan II

F.I.E. Model TZ75

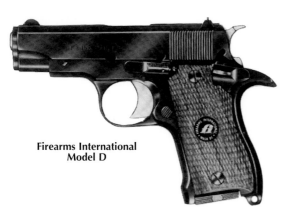

**Firearms International
Model D**

Blued standard . . . . NiB $84 Ex $62 Gd $40
Blued convertible . . . . NiB $91 Ex $62 Gd $40
Chrome standard . . . . NiB $91 Ex $62 Gd $40
Chrome convertible . . . . NiB $91 Ex $62 Gd $40

HOMBRE SA REVOLVER. . . . . . NiB $230 Ex $179 Gd $105
Calibers: .357 Magnum, .44 Magnum, .45 Colt. Six-round cylinder. bbl. lengths: 6 or 7.5 inches, 11 inches overall (with -inch bbl.). Weight: 45 oz. (6-inch bbl.). Fixed sights. Blued bbl., w/color-casehardened receiver. Smooth walnut grips. Made from 1979 to 1990.

SUPER TITAN II
Caliber: .32 ACP or .380 ACP, 3.25-inch bbl., weight: 28 oz. Blued or chrome finish. Disc. 1990.
.32 ACP blue; . . . . NiB $138 Ex $95 Gd $70
.32 ACP chrome. . . . . NiB $138 Ex $95 Gd $70
.380 ACP blue; . . . . NiB $138 Ex $95 Gd $70
.380 ACP chrome. . . . . NiB $138 Ex $95 Gd $70

TEXAS RANGER SINGLE-ACTION REVOLVER
Calibers: .22 LR, .22 WRF, .22 combo w/interchangeable cylinder. bbl., lengths: 4.75-, 6.5-, 9-inch. 10 inches overall (with 4.75-inch bbl.). Weight: 32 oz. (with 4.75-inch bbl.). Fixed sights. Blued finish. Smooth walnut grips. Made 1983 to 1990.
Standard . . . . NiB $97 Ex $75 Gd $55
Convertible. . . . . NiB $97 Ex $75 Gd $55

LITTLE RANGER SA REVOLVER
Same as the TExas Ranger except w/3.25-inch bbl. and bird's-head grips. Made from 1986 to 1990.
Standard . . . . NiB $97 Ex $75 Gd $55
Convertible. . . . . NiB $109 Ex $81 Gd $61

TITAN TIGER DA REVOLVER . . . . . NiB $78 Ex $47 Gd $35
Caliber: .38 Special. Six-round cylinder, 2- or 4-inch bbl., 8.25 inches overall (with 4-inch bbl.). Weight: 30 oz. (4-inch bbl.). Fixed sights. Blued finish. Checkered plastic or walnut grips. Made in the U.S. Disc. 1990.

TITAN II SEMIAUTOMATIC
Caiibers: .22 LR, .32 ACP, .380 ACP. 10-round magazine, integral tapered post front sight, windage-adjustable rear sight. European walnut grips. Blued or chrome finish. Disc. 1990.
.22 LR in blue . . . . NiB $140 Ex $108 Gd $88
.32 ACP in blued. . . . . NiB $211 Ex $170 Gd $128
.32 ACP in chrome . . . . NiB $221 Ex $176 Gd $141
.380 ACP in blue. . . . . NiB $221 Ex $176 Gd $141
.380 ACP in chrome . . . . NiB $235 Ex $181 Gd $158

MODEL TZ75 DA SEMIAUTOMATIC
Double action. Caliber: 9mm. 15-round magazine, 4.5-inch bbl., 8.25 inches overall. Weight: 35 oz. Ramp front sight, windage-adjustable rear sight. European walnut or black rubber grips. Imported from 1988 to 1990.
Blued finish. . . . . NiB $387 Ex $302 Gd $214
Satin chrome. . . . . NiB $425 Ex $321 Gd $255

YELLOW ROSE SA REVOLVER
Same general specifications as the Buffalo Scout except in .22 combo w/interchangeable cylinder and plated in 24-karat gold. Limited Edition w/scrimshawed ivory polymer grips and American walnut presentation case. Made from 1987 to 1990.
Yellow Rose .22 combo. . . . . NiB $140 Ex $93 Gd $59
Yellow Rose Limited Edition . . . NiB $292 Ex $229 Gd $188

**Firearms
International Regent**

**FN Browning
6.35mm Pocket**

**FN Browning
1900 Pocket**

**FN Browning 1910
Pocket**

FIREARMS INTERNATIONAL CORP. — Washington, D.C.

MODEL D AUTOMATIC PISTOL NiB $219 Ex $179 Gd $95
Caliber: .380 Automatic. Six-round magazine, 3.3-inch bbl., 6.13 inches overall. Weight: 19.5 oz. Blade front sight, windage-adjustable rear sight. Blued, chromed, or military finish. Checkered walnut grips. Made from 1974 to 1977.

REGENT DA REVOLVER . . . . . . NiB $189 Ex $130 Gd $101
Calibers: .22 LR, .32 S&W Long. Eight-round cylinder (.22 LR), or 7-round (.32 S&W). Bbl. lengths: 3-, 4-, 6-inches (.22 LR) or 2.5-, 4-inches (.32 S&W). Weight: 28 oz.(with 4-inch bbl.). Fixed sights. Blued finish. Plastic grips. Made 1966-72.

FN BROWNING — Liege, Belgium.

Mfd. by Fabrique Nationale Herstal

See also Browning handguns

6.35MM POCKET AUTO PISTOL
See FN Browning Baby Auto Pistol.

MODEL 1900 POCKET
AUTO PISTOL. . . . . NiB $1200 Ex $900 Gd $600
Caliber: .32 Automatic (7.65mm). Seven-round magazine, 4-inch bbl., 6.75 inches overall. Weight: 22 oz. Fixed sights. Blued finish. Hard rubber grips. Made from 1899 to 1910.
Imperial Russian contract model, add $1200
Imperial German contract model, add $110

MODEL 1903 MILITARY AUTO PISTOL
Caliber: 9mm Browning Long. Seven-round magazine, 5-inch bbl., 8 inches overall. Weight: 32 oz. Fixed sights. Blued finish. Hard rubber grips. Note: Aside from size, this pistol is of the same basic design as the Colt Pocket .32 and .380 Automatic pistols. Made from 1903 to 1939.
Standard. . . . . NiB $2000 Ex $1500 Gd $1000
w/slotted backstrap. . . . . . . NiB $4000 Ex $3000 Gd $2000
w/slotted backstrap, shoulder stock
**   and extended magazine . . NiB $5525 Ex $5270 Gd $4790**

MODEL 1910 (MODEL 1955 OR 1910/55)
POCKET AUTO PISTOL . . . . . . NiB $630 Ex $330 Gd $260
Calibers: .32 Auto (7.65mm), .380 Auto (9mm). Seven-round magazine (.32 cal.), or 6-round (.380 cal.), 3.5-inch bbl., 6 inches overall. Weight: 20.5 oz. Fixed sights. Blued finish. Hard rubber grips. Made from 1910 to 1983.

MODEL 1922 (10/22) POLICE/MILITARY AUTO
Calibers: .32 Auto (7.65mm), .380 Auto (9mm). Nine-round magazine (.32 cal.), or 8-round (.380 cal.), 4.5-inch bbl., 7 inches overall. Weight: 25 oz. Fixed sights. Blued finish. Hard rubber grips. Made from 1922 to 1959.
Commercial model . . . . NiB $530 Ex $380 Gd $280
Military contract, add. $120
w/Nazis proofs, add....10% . . . NiB $414 Ex $326 Gd $265

MODEL 1935 MILITARY HI-POWER PISTOL
Variation of the Browning-Colt .45 Auto design. Caliber: 9mm Para.13-round magazine, 4.63-inch bbl., 7.75 inches overall. Weight: About 35 oz. Adjustable rear sight and fixed front, or both fixed. Blued finish (Canadian manufacture Parkerized). Checkered walnut or plastic grips. Note: Above specifications in general apply to both the original FN production and the pistols made by John Inglis Company of Canada for the Chinese govern-

**FN Browning 1922
Police/Military**

**FN Browning 1935
Military Hi-Power**

**FN Browning
Baby**

ment. A smaller version, w/shorter bbl. and slide and 10-round magazine, was made by FN for the Belgian and Rumanian Governments about 1937 to 191940. Both types were made at the FN plant during the German occupation of Belgium.

Pre-war commercial
(w/fixed sights) . . . . NiB $1152 Ex $918 Gd $729
Pre-war commercial
(w/tangent sight only) . . . . NiB $2040 Ex $1347 Gd $712
Pre-war commercial
(w/tangent sight, slotted
backstrap) . . . . NiB $3014 Ex $2652 Gd $1448
Pre-war Belgian military
contract . . . . NiB $1234 Ex $1020 Gd $704
Pre-war Foreign military
contract . . . . NiB $2212 Ex $1785 Gd $1225
War production
(w/fixed sights) . . . . NiB $861 Ex $674 Gd $485
War production
(w/tangent sight only) . . . . NiB $1405 Ex $1133 Gd $783

War production (w/tangent sight and slotted
backstrap) . . . . NiB $3488 Ex $2770 Gd $1913
Post-war/pre-BAC
(w/fixed sights) . . . . NiB $880 Ex $577 Gd $430
Post-war/pre-BAC
(w/tangent sight only) . . . . . NiB $893 Ex $577 Gd $492
Post-war/pre-BAC (w/tangent sight,
slotted backstrap) . . . . NiB $663 Ex $784 Gd $756
Inglis manufacture Canadian military
(w/fixed sights) . . . . NiB $1015 Ex $743 Gd $571
Canadian military
(w/fixed sight, slotted) . . . . NiB $1871 Ex $1494 Gd $1021
Canadian military
(w/tangent sight, slotted) . . . NiB $1533 Ex $1235 Gd $884
Canadian military
(marked w/Inglis logo) . . . . NiB $2654 Ex $2149 Gd $1462
Chinese military contract
(w/tangent sight, slotted) . . NiB $3500 Ex $2754 Gd $1876
Canadian military
(w/fixed sight, slotted backstrap) . . . NiB $1879 Ex $1503
Gd $1029
Canadian military (marked
w/Inglis logo) . . . . NiB $3500 Ex $2760 Gd $1750
w/issue wooden holster, add. $500

BABY AUTO PISTOL. . . . . NiB $638 Ex $530 Gd $377
Caliber: .25 Automatic (6.35mm). Six-round magazine, 2.13-inch bbl., 4 inches overall. Weight: 10 oz. Fixed sights. Blued finish. Hard rubber grips. Made from 1931 to 1983.

FNH USA — Liege, Belgium

FIVE-SEVEN . . . . NiB $1329 Ex $1150 Gd $850
Semi-automatic. SA. Caliber: 5.7x28mm, 10- or 20-rnd. 4.8-in. bbl. Frame: polymer. Sights: adj. rear. Finish: matte black, two-tone, or FDE. Grip: textured polymer. Ambi. safety. Imported from 2000 to date.

FNP-9 . . . . NiB $649 Ex $580 Gd $440
Semi-automatic. DA/SA. Caliber: 9mm, 10- or 16-rnd. 4-in. bbl. Frame: polymer. Sights: low profile fixed. Finish: matte black, two-tone, or FDE. Grip: textured polymer w/inserts. Ambidextrous decocker. Imported from 2006 to 2011.
FNP-9M (3.8-in. bbl.), subtract. $20
FNP-40 (.40 S&W) . . . . NiB $649 Ex $580 Gd $440
FNP-45 (.45 ACP) . . . . NiB $795 Ex $730 Gd $580
FNP-45 Competition, add $300
FNP-45 Tactical, add. $400

FNS-9 . . . . NiB $699 Ex $630 Gd $560
Semi-automatic. Striker fire. Caliber: 9mm, 17-rnd. 4-in. bbl. Frame: polymer. Sights: low profile fixed. Finish: matte black or two-tone. Grip: textured polymer w/interchangeable backstraps. Ambidextrous slide stop and magazine release. Imported from 2012 to date.
FNS-9 Compact (3.6-in. bbl.) . . NiB $599 Ex $550 Gd $520
FNS-9 Longslide (5-in. bbl.) . . . NiB $749 Ex $680 Gd $580
FNS-40 (.40 S&W) . . . . NiB $699 Ex $630 Gd $560
FNS-40 Compact (3.6-in. bbl.) . NiB $599 Ex $550 Gd $520
FNS-40 Longslide (5-in. bbl.) . . NiB $749 Ex $680 Gd $580

FNX-9 . . . . NiB $699 Ex $630 Gd $460
Semi-automatic. DA/SA. Caliber: 9mm, 10- or 17-rnd. 4-in. bbl. Frame: polymer w/replaceable steel inserts. Sights: 3-dot

fixed. Finish: two-tone, or FDE. Grip: textured polymer w/ inserts. Ambidextrous decocker. Imported from 2010 to date.

FNX-40 (.40 S&W) . . . . NiB $699 Ex $630 Gd $460

FNX-45 . . . . NiB $824 Ex $745 Gd $555
Semi-automatic. DA/SA. Caliber: .45 ACP, 10- or 12-rnd. 4.5-in. bbl. Frame: polymer w/replaceable steel inserts. Sights: 3-dot fixed. Finish: matte black, two-tone, or FDE. Grip: textured polymer w/inserts. Ambidextrous decocker. Imported from 2012 to date.

FNX-45 Tactical. . . . . NiB $1399 Ex $1200 Gd $880
Similar to FNX-45 except w/threaded bbl., 15-rnd. magazine, slide accepts reflex sight, high-profile sights.

FOREHAND & WADSWORTH — Worcester, MA
See listings of comparable Harrington & Richardson and Iver Johnson revolvers for values.

FORT WORTH FIREARMS — Fort Worth, TX

MATCH MASTER STANDARD . . . NiB $499 Ex $283 Gd $225
Semi-automatic. Caliber: .22LR. Equipped with 3 7/8-, 4 1/2-, 5 1/2-, 7 1/2- or 10-inch bull bbl., double Extractors, includes upper push button and standard magazine release, angled grip, low profile frame. Made from 1995 to 2000.

MATCH MASTER DOVETAIL . . . . NiB $500 Ex $408 Gd $321
Similar to Match Master except has 3 7/8-, 4 1/2-, or 5 1/2-inch bbl. with dovetail rib.

MATCH MASTER DELUXE . . . . NiB $581 Ex $464 Gd $367
Similar to Match master Standard except has Weaver rib on bbl.
w/10-in. bbl., add. $128

SPORT KING. . . . . NiB $601 Ex $321 Gd $270
Semi-automatic. Caliber: .22 LR. Equipped with 4 1/2- or 5 1/2-inch bbl., blued finish, military grips, drift sights, 10 round magazine. Made from 1995 to 2000.

CITATION . . . . NiB $439 Ex $319 Gd $265
Semi-automatic. Caliber: .22 LR. Equipped with 5 1/2-inch bull bbl. or 7 1/2-inch fluted bbl., military grips, 10-round magazine.

TROPHY . . . . NiB $433 Ex $332 Gd $270
Semi-automatic. Caliber: .22 LR. Equipped with 5 1/2- or 7 1/2-inch bull bbl. blued finish, military grips, 10-round magazine.
w/LH action (5 1/2-inch bbl. only), add $65

VICTOR . . . . NiB $499 Ex $398 Gd $301
Semi-automatic. Caliber: .22LR. Equipped with 3 7/8-, 4 1/2-(VR or Weaver rib), 8- (Weaver rib) or 10-inch (Weaver rib) bbls.; blued finish, military grips, 10-round magazine.
w/4 1/2- or 4 1/2-inch Weaver rib bbls, add $100
w/8- or 10-inch Weaver rib bbls, add $190

OLYMPIC . . . . NiB $668 Ex $525 Gd $410
Semi-automatic. Caliber: .22 LR or Short. Equipped with 6 1/2-inch fluted bbl., blued finish, military grips, 10-round magazine.

Freedom Arms Model 83
Varmint Class

SHARPSHOOTER . . . . NiB $499 Ex $365 Gd $259
Semi-automatic. Caliber: .22 LR. Equipped with 5 1/2-inch bull bbl.,blued finish, military grips, 10-round magazine.

LE FRANCAIS — St. Etienne, France
Produced by Manufacture Francaise d'Armes et Cycles.

**ARMY MODEL
AUTOMATIC PISTOL** . . . . . . NiB $1749 Ex $1305 Gd $842
Similar in operation to the Le Francais .25 Automatics. Caliber: 9mm Browning Long. Eight-round magazine, 5-inch bbl., 7.75 inches overall. Weight: About 34 oz. Fixed sights. Blued finish. Checkered walnut grips. Made from 1928 to 1938.

**POLICEMAN MODEL
AUTOMATIC PISTOL** . . . . NiB $1020 Ex $917 Gd $416
DA. Hinged bbl., Caliber: .25 Automatic (6.35mm). Seven-round magazine, 3.5-inch bbl., 6 inches overall. Weight: About 12 oz. Fixed sights. Blued finish. Hard rubber grips. Introduced in 1914. disc.

**STAFF OFFICER MODEL
AUTOMATIC PISTOL** . . . . NiB $388 Ex $301 Gd $205
Caliber: .25 Automatic. Similar to the "Policeman" model except no cocking-piece head, barrel, is about an inch shorter and weight is an ounce less. Introduced in 1914. disc.

FREEDOM ARMS — Freedom, WY

MODEL 97 PREMIER GRADE SA REVOLVER
Calibers: .17 HMR, .22 LR, .224-32 F.A., .327 Fed., .32 H&R Mag., .357 Mag., .41 Mag. or .45 LC. Five- or 6-round cylinder, 4.25, 5, 5.5, 6 or 7.5-inch bbl., removable front blade with adjustable or fixed rear sight. Hardwood or black Micarta grips. Satin stainless finish. Made from 1997 to date.
Premier grade 97 . . . . NiB $2178 Ex $1775 Gd $890
w/extra cylinder, add $225
w/fixed sights, deduct. $150

**MODEL 83 FIELD GRADE VARIANTS
SA REVOLVER** . . . . NiB $2283 Ex $1825 Gd $870
Calibers: .22LR, .357 Mag., .41 Mag., .44 Mag., .454 Casull, .475 Linebaugh , .50 AE or .500 Wyoming Express. Five-round cylinder, bbl. lengths: 4.75-, 6-, 7.5-, 9- or 10-in. Adj. sight or fixed. Impregnated hardwood grips. Brushed matte stainless steel finish. Made from 1988 to date.

**MODEL 83 FIELD GRADE HUNTER PACK
SA REVOLVER** . . . . NiB $1160 Ex $900 Gd $710
Similar to Model 83 Field Grade except calibers: .357 Mag., .44 Mag., or .454 Casull only. 7.5-in. bbl., sling studs. Made from 1990 to 1993.

MODEL 83 PREMIER GRADE
SA REVOLVER . . . . NiB $2686 Ex $2175 Gd $1000
Calibers: .357 Mag., .41 Mag., .44 Mag., .454 Casull, .475 Linebaugh, .50 AE or .500 Wyoming Express.Adjustable sight or fixed. Impregnated hardwood grips. Brushed bright stainless steel finish. Made from 1983 to date.

MODEL 83 PREMIER GRADE HUNTER PACK
SA REVOLVER . . . . NiB $1400 Ex $930 Gd $760
Similar to Model 83 Field Grade except calibers: .357 Mag., .44 Mag., or .454 Casull only. 7.5-in. bbl., sling studs. Made from 1990 to 1993.

MODEL 83 RIMFIRE GRADE
SA REVOLVER . . . . NiB $2484 Ex $1525 Gd $800
Calibers: .22 LR. Bbl. length: 10-in. Adjustable sights. Brushed matte stainless finish. Rosewood grips. Made from 1991 to date.

MODEL 83 SILHOUETTE GRADE (RIMFIRE)
SA REVOLVER . . . . NiB $2603 Ex $1875 Gd $830
Calibers: .22 LR. Bbl. lengths: 5.13 or 10 inches. Adjustable competition silhouette sights. Brushed or matte stainless finish. Black Micarta grips. Made from 1991 to date.

MODEL 83 SILHOUETTE GRADE (CENTERFIRE)
SA REVOLVER . . . . NiB $2318 Ex $1975 Gd $1000
Calibers: .357 Mag., .41 Mag., or .44 Mag. Bbl. lengths: 9- or 10-in. Removable blade front sight w/hood, adjustable rear. Brushed matte stainless finish. Wood grips.
.454 Casull . . . . NiB $1600 Ex $1080 Gd $850

MODEL U.S. DEPUTY MARSHAL
SA REVOLVER . . . . NiB $1330 Ex $780 Gd $540
Bbl. lengths: 3-in. Adj. or fixed sights. No ejector rod. Brushed matte stainless. Made from 1990 to 1993.

MODEL FA-L-22LR
MINI-REVOLVER. . . . . NiB $204 Ex $159 Gd $103
Caliber: .22 LR, 1.75-inch contoured bbl., partial high-gloss stainless steel finish. Bird's-head-type grips. Disc. 1987.

MODEL FA-S-22LR
MINI-REVOLVER. . . . . NiB $214 Ex $189 Gd $105
Caliber: .22 LR. One-inch contoured bbl., partial high-gloss stainless steel finish. Disc. 1988.
w/1.75-in. bbl . . . . NiB $204 Ex $159 Gd $103
w/3-in. bbl . . . . NiB $237 Ex $165 Gd $128

MODEL FA-S-22M
MINI-REVOLVER. . . . . NiB $189 Ex $135 Gd $101
Same general specifications as Model FA-S-22LR except in caliber .22 WMR. Disc. 1988.

FRENCH MILITARY PISTOLS — Cholet, France
Manufactured originally by Société Alsacienne de Constructions Mécaniques (S.A.C.M.). Currently made by Manufacture d'Armes Automatiques, Lotissement Industriel des Pontots, Bayonne.

MODEL 1935A
AUTOMATIC PISTOL . . . . NiB $377 Ex $274 Gd $143
Caliber: 7.65mm Long. Eight-round magazine, 4.3-inch bbl., 7.6 inches overall. Weight: 26 oz. Two-lug locking system similar to the Colt U.S. M1911A1. Fixed sights. Blued finish. Checkered grips. Made 1935-45. Note: This pistol was used by French troops during WW II and in Indo-China 1945 to 1954.

MODEL 1935S
AUTOMATIC PISTOL . . . . NiB $342 Ex $281 Gd $135
Similar to Model 1935A except 4.1-inch bbl., 7.4 inches overall and 28 oz. Single-step lug locking system.

MODEL 1950
AUTOMATIC PISTOL . . . . NiB $485 Ex $397 Gd $270
Caliber: 9mm Para. Nine-round magazine, 4.4-inch bbl., 7.6 inches overall. Weight: 30 oz. Fixed sights, tapered post front and U-notched rear. Similar in design and function to the U.S. .45 service automatic except no bbl. bushing.

MODEL MAB F1
AUTOMATIC PISTOL . . . . NiB $653 Ex $587 Gd $270
Similar to Model MAB P-15 except w/6-inch bbl. and 9.6 inches overall. Adjustable target-style sights. Parkerized finish.

MODEL MAB P-8
AUTOMATIC PISTOL . . . . NiB $576 Ex $464 Gd $342
Similar to Model MAB P-15 except w/8-round magazine,

MODEL MAB P-15
AUTOMATIC PISTOL . . . . NiB $632 Ex $474 Gd $385
Caliber: 9mm Para. 15-round magazine, 4.5-inch bbl., 7.9 inches overall. Weight: 38 oz. Fixed sights, tapered post front and U-notched rear.

FROMMER — Budapest, Hungary
Manufactured by Fémáru-Fegyver-és Gépgyár R.T.

LILIPUT POCKET
AUTOMATIC PISTOL . . . . NiB $437 Ex $362 Gd $240
Caliber: .25 Automatic (6.35mm). Six-round magazine, 2.14-inch bbl., 4.33 inches overall. Weight: 10.13 oz. Fixed sights. Blued finish. Hard rubber grips. Made during early 1920s. Note: Although similar in appearance to the Stop and Baby, this pistol is designed for blowback operation.

STOP POCKET
AUTOMATIC PISTOL . . . . NiB $414 Ex $321 Gd $165
Locked-breech action, outside hammer. Calibers: .32 Automatic (7.65mm), .380 Auto (9mm short). Seven-round (.32 cal.) or 6-round (.380 cal.) magazine, 3.88-inch bbl., 6.5 inches

Frommer Stop

overall. Weight: About 21 oz. Fixed sights. Blued finish. Hard rubber grips. Made 1912 to 1920.

BABY POCKET
AUTOMATIC PISTOL . . . . **NiB $321 Ex $262 Gd $143**
Similar to Stop model except has 2-inch bbl., 4.75 inches overall. Weight 17.5 oz. Magazine capacity is one round less than Stop Model. Intro. shortly after WW I.

GALENA INDUSTRIES INC. — Sturgis, SD

Galena Industries purchased the rights to use the AMT trademark in 1998. Many, but not all, original AMT designs were included in the transaction.

AMT BACKUP . . . . **NiB $474 Ex $291 Gd $219**
Caliber: .380 (small frame, 2.5-inch bbl. only), .38 Super, .357 Sig, .40 S&W, .400 CorBon, .45 ACP, 9mm; magazine capacity: 5 or 6 rounds. Double action, 3-inch bbl., weight: 18 oz. (in .380), or 23 oz.
.38 Super, .357 Sig, .400 CorBon, add. **$75**

AUTOMAG II SEMI AUTO . . . . **NiB $831 Ex $587 Gd $321**
Caliber: .22 WMR, 9-round magazine (except 7-round in 3.38-inch bbl.); 3.38- 4.5- or 6-inch bbls.; weight: About 32 oz.

AUTOMAG III . . . . **NiB $561 Ex $500 Gd $377**
Similar to Automag II except chambered for the .30 Carbine cartridge, 6.38-inch bbl., stainless steel finish, weight: About 43 oz.

AUTOMAG IV. . . . . **NiB $561 Ex $500 Gd $377**
Caliber: .45 Winchester Magnum; 7-round magazine, 6.5-inch bbl., weight: 46 oz.

AUTOMAG .440 CORBON. . . . . **NiB $816 Ex $689 Gd $571**
Semiautomatic, 7.5-inch bbl., 5-round magazine, checkered walnut grips, matte black finish, weight: 46 oz. Intro. in 2000.

COMMANDO. . . . . **NiB $474 Ex $326 Gd $220**
Similar to Hardballer model except caliber: .40 S&W, 4-inch bbl., 8-round magazine capacity, stainless steel finish, weight: About 38 ounces.

HARDBALLER II . . . . **NiB $505 Ex $347 Gd $235**
Based on the Colt Model 1911 frame. Caliber: .45 ACP, .40 S&W, .400 CorBon, 7-round magazine capacity, 5-inch bbl., weight: About 38 oz.

HARDBALLER II LONGSLIDE. . **NiB $530 Ex $431 Gd $342**
Similar to Hardballer model except caliber: .45 ACP, 7-inch bbl., 7-round magazine capacity, stainless steel finish, weight: About 46 ounces.

HARDBALLER ACCELERATOR . . **NiB $587 Ex $437 Gd $332**
Similar to Hardballer model except caliber: .400 CorBon, 7-inch bbl., 7-round magazine capacity, stainless steel finish, weight: About 46 ounces.

Galesi
Model 6 Pocket

Glock Model 19
Gen 1

Glock Model 30
Gen 3

GALESI — Collebeato (Brescia), Italy

Manufactured by Industria Armi Galesi.

MODEL 6
POCKET AUTOMATIC PISTOL . **NiB $227 Ex $179 Gd $128**
Calibers: .22 Long, .25 Automatic (6.35mm). Six-round magazine, 2.25-inch bbl., 4.38 inches overall. Weight: About 11 oz. Fixed sights. Blued finish. Plastic grips. Made from 1930 disc.

MODEL 9 POCKET AUTOMATIC PISTOL
Calibers: .22 LR, .32 Auto (7.65mm), .380 Auto (9mm Short). Eight-round magazine, 3.25-inch bbl., 5.88 inches overall. Weight: About 21 oz. Fixed sights. Blued finish. Plastic grips. Made from 1930 disc.

AUTOMATIC PISTOL

Note: Specifications vary, but those shown for .32 Automatic are common.

.22 LR or
.380 Auto . . . . NiB $273 Ex $191 Gd $135
.32 Auto . . . . NiB $265 Ex $180 Gd $110

GIRSAN — Giresun, Turkey

Mfg. of pistols currently imported by Zenith Firearms, Afton, VA.

MC 14 . . . . NiB $379 Ex $350 Gd $300
Semi-automatic. DA/SA. Caliber: .380 ACP, 13-rnd. magazine. 3.4-in. bbl. Frame: alloy. Sights: fixed. Finish: matte black. Grip: textured polymer. Ambidextrous thumb safety. Imported from 2016 to date.

MC 28 SAC . . . . NiB $320 Ex $330 Gd $280
Semi-automatic. Striker fired. Caliber: 9mm, 15-rnd. magazine. 3.8-in. bbl. Frame: polymer. Sights: fixed. Finish: numerous. Grip: textured polymer. Imported from 2016 to date.
MC 28 SA (4.25-in, brrl . . . . NiB $320 Ex $330 Gd $280

MC 39 . . . . NiB $450 Ex $430 Gd $370
Beretta 92 style platform. Semi-automatic. DA/SA. Caliber: 9mm, 15-rnd. magazine. 4.3-in. bbl. Frame: alloy. Sights: fixed. Finish: matte black. Grip: textured polymer. Ambidextrous thumb safety. Imported from 2016 to date.
Regard MC (4.92-in. brrl.) . . . . NiB $450 Ex $430 Gd $370
Regard MCCompact (4.33-in. brrl.) . NiB $450 Ex $430 Gd $370

MC 1911 S . . . . NiB $480 Ex $460 Gd $390
1911 style platform. Semi-automatic. SA. Caliber: .45 ACP, 8-rnd. magazine. 5-in. bbl.Frame: alloy. Sights: fixed. Finish: matte black. Grip: checkered wood. Accessory rail. Imported from 2016 to date.
MC 1911 S (4.36-in, brrl.) . . . . NiB $480 Ex $460 Gd $390

GLISENTI — Carcina (Brescia), Italy
Mfd. by Societa Siderurgica Glisenti.

MODEL 1910 ITALIAN
SERVICE AUTOMATIC . . . . NiB $1397 Ex $1214 Gd $1015
Caliber: 9mm Glisenti. Seven-round magazine, 4-inch bbl., 8.5 inches overall. Weight: About 32 oz. Fixed sights. Blued finish. Hard rubber or plastic grips. Adopted 1910 and used through WWII.

BRIXIA MODEL . . . . NiB $1627 Ex $1122 Gd $943
Similar to Glisenti Model 1910 except mass produced using simplified mfg. techniques for the civilian market.

SOSSO MODEL . . . . **EXTREMELY RARE**
Experimental semi-auto. Cal.: 9 mm Para. Double action (marked "Sosso"), later single action. Mag.: 19 or 21 rounds. Made by FNA. Fewer than 10 made.

GLOCK, INC. — Austria

Manufactured in Austria and since 2005 in Smyrna, Georgia. NOTE: From 1986 to 1988 Generation 1 models were produced with a pepple texture grip; from 1988 to 1997 Generation 2 models were produced with a checkered grenade type grip texture with horizontal serrations on the front and back grips straps; from 1995 to 2014 Generation 3 models

were first produced w/finger grooves in the front grip strap and thumbrests, they then transitioned into finger grooves with thumbrests and checkered finished frame with a front accessory rail. Generation 4 production began from 2010 to date and have interchangable backstraps. The "C" suffix added to model numbers indicated a compensated model. All use a striker-fired system and generally differ in barrel length, overal size, caliber and magazine capacity.

MODEL 17 . . . . NiB $505 Ex $385 Gd $301
Striker-fire action. Caliber: 9mm Parabellum. 10-, 17- or 19-round magazine, 4.5-inch bbl., 7.2 inches overall. Weight: 22 oz. w/o magazine, Polymer frame, steel bbl., slide and springs. Fixed or adj. rear sights. Matte, nonglare finish. Made of only 35 components, including three internal safety devices. Imported from 1985 to date.
Model 17C (compensated bbl.) . . NiB $672 Ex $562 Gd $398
w/adjustable sights, add $75
w/Meprolight sights, add $100
w/Trijicon sights, add $120
Gen4 variant, add $50

MODEL 17L . . . . NiB $714 Ex $577 Gd $396
Same general specifications as Model 17 except w/long slide and with 6-in. bbl., 8.85 inches overall., weight: 23.35 oz. Imported 1988 to 1999, Gen 3 1998 to date.
w/ported bbl., (early production), add $75
w/adjustable sights, add $50

MODEL 19 COMPACT . . . . NiB $499 Ex $395 Gd $255
Same general specifications as Model 17 except smaller compact version with 4-inch bbl., 6.85 inches overall and weight: 21 oz. Imported from 1988 to date.
Model 20C (compensated bbl.) . . NiB $602 Ex $498 Gd $362
w/adjustable sights, add $75
w/Meprolight sights, add $95
w/Trijicon sights, add $120
Gen4 variant, add $50

MODEL 20 . . . . NiB $530 Ex $377 Gd $270
Caliber: 10mm. 15-round, hammerless, 4.6-inch bbl., 7.59 inches overall. Weight: 26.3 oz. Fixed sights. Matte, non-glare finish. Made from 1990 to date.
Model 19C (compensated bbl.) . . NiB $632 Ex $485 Gd $377
w/adjustable sights, add $75
w/Meprolight sights, add $95
w/Trijicon sights, add $120
Gen4 variant, add $50

MODEL 21 . . . . NiB $530 Ex $377 Gd $270
Caliber: .45 ACP. 13-round magazine, 7.59 inches overall. Weight: 25.2 oz. Imported from 1990 to date.
Model 21C (compensated bbl.) . . NiB $632 Ex $485 Gd $377
w/adjustable sights, add $75
w/Meprolight sights, add $95
w/Trijicon sights, add $120
Gen4 variant, add $50

MODEL 22 . . . . NiB $505 Ex $348 Gd $270
Similar to Model 17 except chambered for .40 S&W. 15-round magazine, 7.4 inches overall. Imported from 1990 to date.
Model 22C (compensated bbl.) . . . NiB $612 Ex $362 Gd $281
w/adjustable sights, add $75
w/Meprolight sights, add $95
w/Trijicon sights, add $120
Gen4 variant, add $50

MODEL 23 COMPACT...... NiB $505 Ex $348 Gd $270
Same general specifications as Model 19 except chambered for .40 S&W. 13-round magazine, 6.97 inches overall, fixed sights. Imported from 1990 to date.
Model 23C (compensated bbl.)....NiB $586 Ex $434 Gd $357
w/adjustable sights, add $50
w/Meprolight sights, add $80
w/Trijicon sights, add $105
Gen4 variant, add................................$50

MODEL 24 COMPETITION... NiB $617 Ex $530 Gd $431
Caliber: .40 S&W, 10- and 15-round magazine, 6.02-in. bbl., 8.85 inches overall. Weight: 26.5 oz., fixed sights. Made from 1994-99.
Model 24C (compensated bbl.)...NiB $816 Ex $648 Gd $500
w/adjustable sights, add $75

MODEL 26 SUB-COMPACT... NiB $505 Ex $357 Gd $306
Caliber: 9mm, 10-round magazine, 3.47-inch bbl., 6.3 inches overall. Weight: 19.77 oz., fixed sights. Imported from 1995 to date.
w/adjustable sights, add $75
Gen4 variant, add................................$50

MODEL 27 SUB-COMPACT ....NiB $505 Ex $389 Gd $290
Similar to the Model 22 except subcompact. Caliber: .40 S&W, 10-round magazine, 3.5-inch bbl., Weight: 21.7 oz. Polymer stocks, fixed sights. Imported from 1995 to date.
w/adjustable sights, add $75
w/Meprolight sights, add $95
w/Trijicon sights, add $120

MODEL 29 SUB-COMPACT... NiB $546 Ex $365 Gd $270
Similar to the Model 20 except subcompact. Caliber: 10mm. 10-round magazine, 3.8-inch bbl., weight: 27.1 oz. Polymer stocks, fixed sights. Imported from 1997 to date.
w/adjustable sights, add $75
w/Meprolight sights, add $95
w/Trijicon sights, add $120
Gen4 variant, add............................... $50

MODEL 30 SUB-COMPACT... NiB $546 Ex $365 Gd $270
Similar to the Model 21 except subcompact. Caliber: .45 ACP. 10-round magazine, 3.8-inch bbl., weight: 26.5 oz. Polymer stocks, fixed sights. Imported from 1997 to date.
w/adjustable sights, add $75
w/Meprolight sights, add $90
w/Trijicon sights, add $120
Gen4 variant, add................................$50

MODEL 31............... NiB $546 Ex $357 Gd $270
Caliber: .357 Sig. 10- 15- or 17-round magazine, 4.49-inch bbl., weight: 23.28 oz., fixed sights. Imported from 1998 to date.
Model 31C (compensated bbl.). NiB $612 Ex $464 Gd $270
w/adjustable sights, add $75
w/Meprolight sights, add $95
w/Trijicon sights, add $120
Gen4 variant, add................................$50

MODEL 32 COMPACT...... NiB $546 Ex $357 Gd $270
Caliber: .357 Sig., safe action system. 10- 13- or 15-round magazine, 4.02-inch bbl., weight: 21.52 oz. Imported from 1998 to date.Model 32C ..... NiB $648 Ex $485 Gd $395
w/adjustable sights, add $75
w/Meprolight sights, add $95

w/Trijicon Sights, add........................... $120
Gen4 variant, add................................$50

MODEL 33 SUB-COMPACT... NiB $530 Ex $357 Gd $286
Caliber: .357 Sig., safe action system. Nine- or 11-round magazine, 3.46-inch bbl. Weight: 19.75 oz. Imported from 1998 to date.
w/adjustable sights, add $75
w/Meprolight sights, add $95
w/Trijicon sights, add $120
Gen4 variant, add................................ $50

MODEL 34 COMPETITION .... NiB $577 Ex $485 Gd $377
Similar to Model 17 except w/longer slide and extended slide-stop lever and magazine release. 10-, 17- or 19-round magazine, 5.31-in. bbl. Weight: 22.9 oz., adj. sights. Imported from 1998 to date.
Gen4 variant, add................................$50

MODEL 35 COMPETITION ...NiB $581 Ex $469 Gd $362
Similar to Model 34 except .40 S&W. Imported from 1998 to date.
Gen4 variant, add................................$50

MODEL 36 SUB-COMPACT ....NiB $536 Ex $444 Gd $342
Similar to Model 30 sub-compact except w/6-round single stackmagazine. Weight: 20.11 oz. Imported from 1999 to date.
w/adjustable sights, add $75
w/Meprolight sights, add $95
w/Trijicon sights, add $120

MODEL 37............... NiB $614 Ex $450 Gd $290
Similar to Model 21 except chambered in .45 G.A.P. Made from 2003 to date.
Gen4 variant, add................................$50

MODEL 38 COMPACT...... NiB $614 Ex $450 Gd $290
Similar to Model 37 except more compact w/4-in. bbl. Made from 2005 to date.
Gen4 variant, add................................$50

MODEL 39 SUB-COMPACT... NiB $614 Ex $450 Gd $290
Similar to Model 37 except more sub-compact w/3.4-in. bbl. Made from 2005 to date.
Gen4 variant, add................................$50

MODEL 41............... NiB $599 Ex $395 Gd $340
Similar to Model 21 except w/long slide and 5.3-in. bbl. Made 2014 to date.

MODEL 42 SUB-COMPACT... NiB $599 Ex $395 Gd $340
Caliber: .380 ACP; 3.25-inch bbl. Weight: 13.7 ozs. Made 2014 to date.

DESERT STORM
COMMEMORATIVE ......NiB $1525 Ex $1375 Gd $1225
Same specifications as Model 17 except "Operation Desert Storm, January 16-February 27, 1991" engraved on side of slide w/list of coalition forces. Limited issue of 1,000 guns. Made in 1991.

GRAND POWER — Slovenská Ľupča, Slovakia

Manufactured in Slovenia and imported by Eagle Imports, Wanamassa, New Jersey. In 2002 STI partnered with Grand Power and imported GP 6 (K100 MK6) pistols in 2008.

K22S Series . . . . NiB $528 Ex $480 Gd $400
Semi-automatic. DA/SA. Caliber: .22 LR; 10-rnd. magazine. 5-in. bbl. threaded. Frame: steel. Sights: fixed, low-profile. Finish: black. Grip: textured polymer w/modular backstraps. Length: 8-in. Weight: 24.5 oz. Imported from 2016 to date.
K22 X-TRIM (scalloped slide) . . . NiB $788 Ex $700 Gd $680

K100 Series . . . . NiB $629 Ex $600 Gd $580
Semi-automatic. Rotary locking bbl. system. DA/SA. Caliber: 9mm; 15-rnd. magazine. 4.3-in. bbl. Frame: steel. Sights: fixed, low-profile. Finish: black. Grip: textured polymer w/modular backstraps. Length: 8-in. Weight: 26.1 oz. Imported from 2014 to date.

K100 X-Caliber . . . . NiB $999 Ex $950 Gd $820
Similar to X-TRIM except w/extra scalloping on slide, adj. rear sight/fiber optic front, over sized controls. Imported from 2015 to date.

K100 X-TRIM . . . . NiB $865 Ex $820 Gd $780
Similar to K100 except w/scalloped slide, adj. rear sight/fiber optic front. Imported from 2014 to date.

P1 Series . . . . NiB $629 Ex $600 Gd $580
Similar to K100 except more compact w/3.7-in. bbl. Imported from 2014 to date.
P1 Ultra (scalloped slide) . . . . . NiB $789 Ex $740 Gd $680
P11 (sub compact) . . . . NiB $615 Ex $570 Gd $500
CP 380 (similar to P11
except .380 ACP) . . . . NiB $528 Ex $480 Gd $400

P40 Series . . . . NiB $819 Ex $780 Gd $690
Similar to K100 except chambered in .40 S&W. Imported from 2014 to date.

P45 Series . . . . NiB $819 Ex $780 Gd $690
Similar to K100 except chambered in .45 ACP. Imported from 2014 to date.

Q100 Series . . . . NiB $574 Ex $540 Gd $500
Semi-automatic. Rotary locking bbl. system. Striker fire. Caliber: 9mm; 15-rnd. magazine. 4.3-in. bbl. Frame: steel. Sights: fixed, low-profile. Finish: black. Grip: textured polymer w/modular backstraps. Length: 8-in. Weight: 26.1 oz. Imported from 2016 to date.

GREAT WESTERN ARMS CO. — North Hollywood, CA

NOTE: *Values shown are for improved late model revolvers early Great Westerns are variable in quality and should be evaluated accordingly. It should also be noted that, beginning about July 1956, these revolvers were offered in kit form. Values of guns assembled from these kits will, in general, be of less value than factory-completed weapons.*

DOUBLE BARREL DERRINGER . . NiB $884 Ex $780 Gd $536
Replica of Remington Double Derringer. Caliber: .38 S&W, .38 S&W Spl. . Double bbls. (superposed), 3-inch bbl. Overall length: 5 inches. Fixed sights. Blued finish. Checkered black plastic grips. Made 1953 to 1962 in various configurations.

SA FRONTIER REVOLVER . . . . . NiB $793 Ex $530 Gd $388
Replica of the Colt Single Action Army Revolver. Calibers: .22 LR, .22 WMR, .357 Magnum, .38 Special, .44 Special, .44 Magnum .45 Colt. Six-round cylinder, bbl. lengths: 4.75-, 5.5 and 7.5-inches. Weight: 40 oz. in .22 cal. w/5.5-inch bbl.

Grendel Model P-12

Overall length: 11.13 inches w/5.5-inch bbl. Fixed sights. Blued finish. Imitation stag grips. Made from 1951 to 1962.

SHERIFF'S MODEL . . . . NiB $791 Ex $638 Gd $500
Reportedly made from old Colt parts inventory. Cal.: .45 Long Colt. Blue, nickel, or case-colored finish. Plastic staghorn grips.

FAST DRAW MODEL . . . . NiB $714 Ex $601 Gd $439
Similar to Frontier model. Bbl.: 4.75 inches. Brass backstrap and trigger guard; blue finish; plastic staghorn grips. Longer, turned-up hammer spur.

TARGET MODEL . . . . NiB $740 Ex $616 Gd $474
Similar to Frontier model. Cal.: .22 LR. Adj. rear sights, Micro front blade. Blue or case colored frame. Bbl.: Various lengths.

DEPUTY MODEL . . . . NiB $831 Ex $709 Gd $500
Cal.: .22 LR, .38 Spl., .357 Mag. Bbl.: 4 inches. Deluxe blue finish, walnut grips. Adj. rear sight. Fewer than 100 made.

GRENDEL, INC. — Rockledge, FL

MODEL P-10 AUTOMATIC PISTOL
Hammerless, blow-back action. DAO with no external safety. Caliber: .380 ACP. 10-round box magazine integrated in grip. Three-inch bbl., 5.3 inches overall. Weight: 15 oz. Matte blue, nickel or green Teflon finish. Made from 1988 to 1991.
Blued finish . . . . NiB $219 Ex $160 Gd $105
Nickel finish . . . . NiB $227 Ex $179 Gd $120
Green finish . . . . NiB $227 Ex $179 Gd $105
w/compensated bbl., add $65

MODEL P-12 DA AUTOMATIC PISTOL
Caliber: .380 ACP. 11-round Zytel magazine, 3-inch bbl., 5.3 inches overall. Weight: 13 oz. Fixed sights. Polymer DuPont ST-800 grip. Made from 1991 to 1995.
Standard model . . . . NiB $214 Ex $135 Gd $105
Electroless nickel . . . . NiB $219 Ex $135 Gd $105

MODEL P-30 AUTOMATIC PISTOL
Caliber: .22 WMR. 30-round magazine, 5-or 8-inch bbl., 8.5 inches overall w/5-inch bbl., weight: 21 oz. Blade front sight, fixed rear sight. Made from 1991 to 1995.
w/5-inch bbl., ... NiB $337 Ex $255 Gd $214
w/8-inch bbl., ... NiB $337 Ex $255 Gd $214

MODEL P-31
AUTOMATIC PISTOL . . . . NiB $474 Ex $352 Gd $281
Caliber: .22 WMR. 30-round Zytel magazine, 11-inch bbl.,

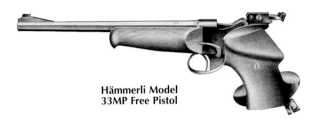

Hämmerli Model
33MP Free Pistol

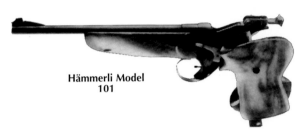

Hämmerli Model
101

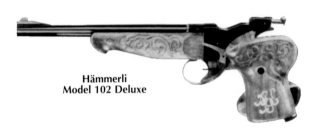

Hämmerli
Model 102 Deluxe

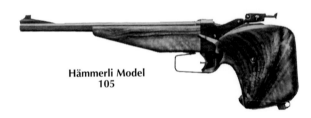

Hämmerli Model
105

Hämmerli
Model 106

17.3 inches overall. Weight: 48 oz. Adjustable blade front sight, fixed rear. Checkered black polymer DuPont ST-800 grip and forend. Made from 1991 to 1995.

GUNSITE — Paulden, AZ

"ADVANCED TACTICAL" SA AUTO PISTOL
Manufactured w/Colt 1911 or Springfield 1911 parts. Caliber:

.45 ACP. Eight-round magazine, 3.5-, 4.25-, 5-inch bbl. Weight: 32-38 oz. Checkered or laser-engraved walnut grips. Fixed or Novak Lo-mount sights.

Stainless finish. . . . . NiB $1193 Ex $974 Gd $704
Blued finish. . . . . NiB $1030 Ex $836 Gd $621

"CUSTOM CARRY" SA AUTO PISTOL
Caliber: .45 ACP. Eight-round magazine, 3.5-, 4.25-, 5-inch bbl., Weight: 32-38 oz. Checkered or laser-engraved walnut grips. Fixed Novak Lo-mount sights. Single action, manufactured based on enhanced colt models.

Stainless finish. . . . . NiB $1219 Ex $990 Gd $740
Blued finish. . . . . NiB $1151 Ex $927 Gd $709

H&R 1871, INC. — Gardner, MA

NOTE: *In 1991, H&R 1871, Inc. was formed from the residual of the parent company, Harrington & Richardson, and then took over the New England Firearms facility. H&R 1871 produced firearms under both their logo and the NEF brand name until 1999, when the Marlin Firearms Company acquired the assets of H&R 1871. See listings under Harrington & Richardson, Inc.*

HÄMMERLI — Lenzburg, Switzerland

Currently imported by Sigarms, Inc., Exeter, NH. Previously by Hämmerli, USA; Beeman Precision Arms & Mandall Shooting Supplies.

MODEL 33MP FREE PISTOL . . . NiB $964 Ex $863 Gd $577

System Martini single-shot action, set trigger. Caliber: .22 LR. 11.5-inch octagon bbl., 16.5 inches overall. Weight: 46 oz. Micrometer rear sight, interchangeable front sights. Blued finish. Walnut grips, forearm. Imported from 1933 to 1949.

MODEL 100 FREE PISTOL
Same general specifications as Model 33MP. Improved action and sights, redesigned stock. Standard model has plain grips and forearm, deluxe model has carved grips and forearm. Imported 1950 to 1956.
Standard model. . . . . NiB $938 Ex $775 Gd $556
Deluxe model . . . . NiB $1020 Ex $893 Gd $612

MODEL 101 . . . . NiB $913 Ex $791 Gd $612
Similar to Model 100 except has heavy round bbl. w/matte finish, improved action and sights, adj. grips. Weight: About 49 oz. Imported from 1956 to 1960.

MODEL 102
Same as Model 101 except bbl., has highly polished blued finish. Deluxe model (illustrated) has carved grips and forearm. Made from 1956 to 1960.
Standard model. . . . . NiB $928 Ex $760 Gd $561
Deluxe model . . . . NiB $1035 Ex $791 Gd $602

MODEL 103 . . . . NiB $969 Ex $826 Gd $536
Same as Model 101 except has lighter octagon bbl. (as in Model 100) w/highly polished blued finish, grips and forearm of select French walnut. Weight: About 46 oz. Imported 1956 to 1960.

MODEL 104 . . . . NiB $804 Ex $673 Gd $439
Similar to Model 102 except has lighter round bbl., improved action redesigned grips and forearm. Weight: 46 oz. Imported 1961 to 1965.

**Hämmerli
Model 107 Deluxe**

**Hämmerli
Model 120 Heavy Barrel**

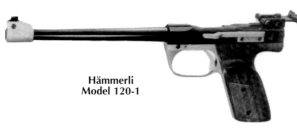

**Hämmerli
Model 120-1**

**Hämmerli
Model 150**

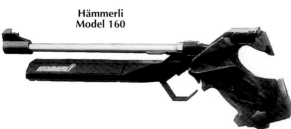

**Hämmerli
Model 160**

MODEL 105 . . . . NiB $960 Ex $779 Gd $500
Similar to Model 103 except has improved action, redesigned grips and forearm. Imported from 1961 to 1965.

MODEL 106 . . . . NiB $933 Ex $796 Gd $464
Similar to Model 104 except has improved trigger and grips. Made from 1966 to 1971.

MODEL 107
Similar to Model 105 except has improved trigger and stock. Deluxe model (illustrated) has engraved receiver and bbl., carved grips and forearm. Imported from 1966 to 1971.
Standard model. . . . . NiB $1034 Ex $831 Gd $462
Deluxe model . . . . NiB $1025 Ex $826 Gd $474

MODEL 120 HEAVY BARREL
Same as Models 120-1 and 120-2 except has 5.7-inch heavy bbl., weight: 41 oz. Avail. w/standard or adj. grips. 1,000 made. Imported from 1972.
w/standard grips. . . . . NiB $627 Ex $459 Gd $388
w/adj. grips. . . . . NiB $761 Ex $588 Gd $377

MODEL 120-1 SINGLE-
SHOT FREE PISTOL. . . . . NiB $658 Ex $536 Gd $385
Side lever-operated bolt action. Adj. single-stage or two-stage trigger. Caliber: .22 LR, 9.9-inch bbl., 14.75 inches overall. Weight: 44 oz. Micrometer rear sight, front sight on high ramp. Blued finish bbl., and receiver, lever and grip frame anodized aluminum. Checkered walnut thumbrest grips. Imported from 1972 to date.

MODEL 120-2. . . . . NiB $734 Ex $648 Gd $377
Same as Model 120-1 except has hand-contoured grips w/adj. palm rest (available for right or left hand). Imported from 1972 to date.

MODELS 150/151 FREE PISTOLS
Improved Martini-type action w/lateral-action cocking lever. Set trigger adj. for weight, length and angle of pull. Caliber: .22 LR, 11.3-inch round free-floating bbl., 15.4 inches overall. Weight: 43 oz. (w/Extra weights, 49.5 oz.). Micrometer rear sight, front sight on high ramp. Blued finish. Select walnut forearm and grips w/adj. palm shelf. Imported 1972-93.
Model 150 (disc. 1989). . . . NiB $1938 Ex $1709 Gd $1020
Model 151 (disc. 1993). . . . NiB $1938 Ex $1709 Gd $1020

MODEL 152 ELECTRONIC PISTOL
Same general specifications as Model 150 except w/electronic trigger. Made from 1990 to 1992
Right hand . . . . NiB $1812 Ex $1700 Gd $1036
w/adj. grips, add. $306

MODELS 160/162 FREE PISTOLS
Caliber: .22 LR. Single-shot. 11.31-inch bbl., 17.5 inches overall. Weight: 46.9 oz. Interchangeable front sight blades, fully adj. match rear. Match-style stippled walnut grips w/adj. palm shelf and poly-carbon fiber forend. Imported from 1993 to 2002.
Model 160 w/mechanical
   set trigger (disc. 2000). . . NiB $1812 Ex $1681 Gd $1005
Model 162 w/electronic trigger NiB $1982 Ex $1622 Gd $1132

MODEL 208 STANDARD
AUTO PISTOL. . . . . NiB $1802 Ex $1488 Gd $959
Caliber: .22 LR. Eight-round magazine, 5.9-inch bbl., 10 inches overall. Weight: 35 oz. (bbl. weight adds 3 oz.). Micrometer rear sight, ramp front. Blued finish. Checkered walnut grips w/ adj. heel plate. Imported from 1966 to 1988.

MODEL 208S
TARGET PISTOL . . . . NiB $2540 Ex $2232 Gd $2066
Caliber: .22 LR. Eight-round magazine, 6-inch bbl., 10.2 inches overall. Weight: 37.3 oz. Micrometer rear sight, ramp front sight. Blued finish. Stippled walnut grips w/adj. heel plate. Imported from 1988 to 2000.

MODEL 211 . . . . NiB $1601 Ex $1458 Gd $847
Same as Model 208 except has standard. Thumbrest grips. Imported from 1966 to 1990.

Hämmerli
Model 208

Hämmerli
Model 215

Hämmerli
International Model 206

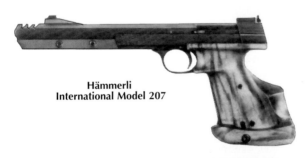

Hämmerli
International Model 207

Hämmerli
Model 232 Rapid Fire

MODEL 212
HUNTER'S PISTOL . . . . **NiB $2146 Ex $1816 Gd $1436**
Caliber: .22 LR, 4.88-inch bbl., 8.5 inches overall. Weight: 31 oz. Blade front sight, square-notched fully adj. rear. Blued finish. Checkered walnut grips. Imported 1984-93.

MODEL 215 . . . . **NiB $2368 Ex $2035 Gd $1734**
Similar to the Model 208 except w/heavier bbl. and fewer deluxe features. Imported from 1990 to 1993.

MODEL 230-1 RAPID FIRE
AUTO PISTOL. . . . . **NiB $755 Ex $576 Gd $478**
Caliber: .22 Short. Five-round magazine, 6.3-inch bbl., 11.6 inches overall. Weight: 44 oz. Micrometer rear sight, post front. Blued finish. Smooth walnut thumbrest grips. Imported from 1970 to 1983.

MODEL 230-2 RAPID FIRE
AUTO PISTOL. . . . . **NiB $785 Ex $601 Gd $444**
Same as Model 230-1 except has checkered walnut grips w/ adj. heel plate. Imported from 1970 to 1983.

MODEL 232 RAPID FIRE
AUTO PISTOL. . . . . **NiB $1454 Ex $1256 Gd $780**
Caliber: .22 Short. Six-round magazine, 5.1-inch ported bbl., 10.5 inches overall. Weight: 44 oz. Fully adj. target sights. Blued finish. Stippled walnut wraparound target grips. Imported 1984 to 1993.

INTERNATIONAL MODEL 206
AUTO PISTOL. . . . . **NiB $709 Ex $469 Gd $306**
Calibers: .22 Short, .22 LR. Six-round (.22 Short) or 8-round (.22 LR) magazine, 7.1-inch bbl. w/muzzle brake, 12.5 inches overall. Weight: 33 oz. (.22 Short), 39 oz. (.22 LR) (supplementary weights add 5 and 8 oz.). Micrometer rear sight, ramp front. Blued finish. Standard thumbrest grips. Imported from 1962 to 1969.

INTERNATIONAL MODEL 207
AUTO PISTOL. . . . . **NiB $760 Ex $621 Gd $469**
Same as Model 206 except has grips w/adj. heel plate, weight: 2 oz. more. Made from 1962 to 1969.

INTERNATIONAL MODEL 209
AUTO PISTOL. . . . . **NiB $825 Ex $672 Gd $562**
Caliber: .22 Short. Five-round mag., 4.75-inch bbl., w/muzzle brake and gas-escape holes, 11 inches overall. Weight: 39 oz. (interchangeable front weight adds 4 oz.). Micrometer rear sight, post front. Blued finish. Standard thumbrest grips of checkered walnut. Imported from 1966 to 1970.

INTERNATIONAL MODEL 210 . . **NiB $827 Ex $676 Gd $530**
Same as Model 209 except has grips w/adj. heel plate, is 0.8-inch longer and weighs 1 ounce more. Made from 1966 to 1970.Model 280 Target Pistol Carbon-reinforced synthetic frame and bbl., housing. Calibers: .22 LR, .32 S&W Long WC. Six-round (.22 LR) or 5-round (.32 S&W) magazine, 4.5-inch bbl. w/interchangeable metal or carbon fiber counterweights. 11.88 inches overall. Weight: 39 oz. Micro-adj. match sights w/interchangeable elements. Imported from 1988 to 2000.
.22 LR . . . . **NiB $1550 Ex $1295 Gd $627**
.32 S&W Long WC . . . . **NiB $1729 Ex $1550 Gd $842**
.22/.32 Conversion kit, add **$816**

Hämmerli
International Model 210

Hämmerli-Walther
Olympia Model 203 1958-Type

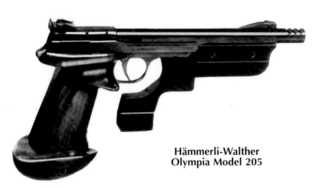

Hämmerli-Walther
Olympia Model 205

SIG-Hämmerli
Model P240 Target

5.5-inch bbl.). Weight: 40 oz. (with 5.5-inch bbl.). Fixed sights. Blued bbl. and cylinder, casehardened frame, chrome-plated grip frame and trigger guard. One-piece smooth walnut stock. Imported from 1973 to 1976 by Interarms, AlExandria, Va.

WALTHER OLYMPIA MODEL 200 AUTOMATIC
PISTOL, 1952-TYPE. . . . . NiB $704 Ex $598 Gd $479
Similar to 1936 Walther Olympia Funfkampf model. Calibers: .22 Short, .22 LR. Six-round (.22 Short) or 10-round (.22 LR) magazine, 7.5-inch bbl., 10.7 inches overall. Weight: 27.7 oz. (.22 Short, light alloy breechblock), 30.3 oz. (.22 LR). Supplementary weights provided. Adj. target sights. Blued finish. Checkered walnut thumbrest grips. Imported 1952 to 1958.

WALTHER OLYMPIA
MODEL 200,1958-TYPE . . . . . . NiB $780 Ex $632 Gd $530
Same as Model 200 1952 type except has muzzle brake, 8-round magazine (.22 LR). 11.6 inches overall. Weight: 30 oz. (.22 Short), 33 oz. (.22 LR). Imported 1958 to 1963.

WALTHER OLYMPIA
MODEL 201 . . . . NiB $704 Ex $546 Gd $437
Same as Model 200,1952-Type except has 9.5-inch bbl. Imported from 1955 to 1957.

WALTHER
OLYMPIA MODEL 202 . . . . NiB $780 Ex $632 Gd $530
Same as Model 201 except has grips w/adjustable heel plate. Imported from 1955 to 1957.

WALTHER OLYMPIA MODEL 203
Same as corresponding Model 200 (1955 type lacks muzzle brake) except has grips w/adjustable heel plate. Imported 1955 to 1963.
1955 type . . . . NiB $794 Ex $638 Gd $479
1958 type . . . . NiB $842 Ex $709 Gd $475

WALTHER OLYMPIA MODEL 204
American model. Same as corresponding Model 200 (1956-Type lacks muzzle brake) except in .22 LR only, has slide stop and micrometer rear sight. Imported from 1956 to 1963.
1956-type . . . . NiB $760 Ex $606 Gd $464
1958-type . . . . NiB $816 Ex $680 Gd $556

WALTHER OLYMPIA MODEL 205
American model. Same as Model 204 except has grips w/ adjustable heel plate. Imported from 1956 to 1963.
1956-type . . . . NiB $842 Ex $714 Gd $610
1958-type . . . . NiB $893 Ex $727 Gd $556

MODEL P240 TARGET AUTO PISTOL
Calibers: .32 S&W Long (wadcutter), .38 Special (wadcutter). Five-round magazine, 5.9-inch bbl., 10 inches overall. Weight: 41 oz. Micrometer rear sight, post front. Blued finish/smooth walnut thumbrest grips. Accessory .22 LR conversion unit available. Imported from 1975 to 1986.
.32 S&W Long . . . . NiB $1540 Ex $1329 Gd $755
.38 Special . . . . NiB $2545 Ex $2353 Gd $2025
.22 LR conversion unit, add $561

VIRGINIAN SA REVOLVER . . . NiB $780 Ex $602 Gd $ 440
Similar to Colt Single-Action Army except has base pin safety system (SWISSAFE). Calibers: .357 Magnum, .45 Colt. Six-round cylinder. 4.63-, 5.5- or 7.5-inch bbl., 11 inches overall (with

HARRINGTON & RICHARDSON, INC. — Gardner, MA
Formerly Harrington & Richardson Arms Co. of Worcester, Mass. One of the oldest and most distinguished manufacturers of handguns, rifles and shotguns, H&R suspended operations

Harrington & Richardson SL .32

Harrington & Richardson USRA Model Single-Shot Target Pistol

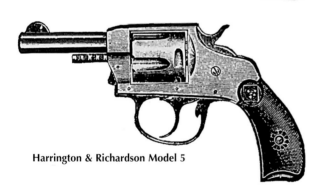

Harrington & Richardson Model 4

Harrington & Richardson Model 5

Harrington & Richardson Model 6

on January 24, 1986. In 1987, New England Firearms was established as an independent company producing selected H&R models under the NEF logo. In 1991, H&R 1871, Inc., was formed from the residual of the parent company and then took over the New England Firearms facility. H&R 1871 produced firearms under both its logo and the NEF brand name until 1999, when the Marlin Firearms Company acquired the assets of H&R 1871.

NOTE: For ease in finding a particular firearm, H&R handguns are grouped into Automatic/Single-Shot Pistols, followed by Revolvers. For a complete listing, please refer to the index.

- AUTOMATIC/SINGLE-SHOT PISTOLS -

SL .25 PISTOL . . . . NiB $587 Ex $405 Gd $290
Modified Webley & Scott design. Caliber: .25 Auto. Six-round magazine, 2-inch bbl., 4.5 inches overall. Weight: 12 oz. Fixed sights. Blued finish. Black hard rubber grips. Made from 1912 to 1916.

SL .32 PISTOL . . . . NiB $562 Ex $321 Gd $205
Modified Webley & Scott design. Caliber: .32 Auto. Eight-round magazine, 3.5-inch bbl., 6.5 inches overall. Weight: About 20 oz. Fixed sights. Blued finish. Black hard rubber grips. Made from 1916 to 1924.

USRA MODEL SINGLE-SHOT
TARGET PISTOL . . . . NiB $548 Ex $500 Gd $288
Hinged frame. Caliber: .22 LR, bbl. lengths: 7-, 8- and 10-inch. Weight: 31 oz. w/10-inch bbl., Adj. target sights. Blued finish. Checkered walnut grips. Made from 1928 to 1941.

- REVOLVERS -

MODEL 4 (1904) DA . . . . NiB $255 Ex $180 Gd $90
Solid frame. Calibers: .32 S&W Long, .38 S&W. Six-round cylinder (.32 cal.), or 5-round (.38 cal.), bbl. Lengths: 2.5-, 4.5- and 6-inch. Weight: About 16 oz. (in .32 cal.) Fixed sights. Blued or nickel finish. Hard rubber grips. Disc. prior to 1942.

MODEL 5 (1905) DA . . . . NiB $237 Ex $159 Gd $77
Solid frame. Caliber: .32 S&W. Five-round cylinder, bbl., lengths: 2.5-,4.5- and 6-inch. Weight: About 11 oz. Fixed sights. Blued or nickel finish. Hard rubber grips. Disc. prior to 1942.

MODEL 6 (1906) DA . . . . NiB $198 Ex $115 Gd $75
Solid frame. Caliber: .22 LR. Seven-round cylinder, bbl. lengths: 2.5, 4.5- and 6-inches. Weight: About 10 oz. Fixed sights. Blued or nickel finish. Hard rubber grips. Disc. prior to 1942.

.22 SPECIAL DA . . . . NiB $351 Ex $197 Gd $101
Heavy hinged frame. Calibers: .22 LR, .22 Mag. Nine-round cylinder, 6-inch bbl., weight: 23 oz. Fixed sights, front gold-plated. Blued finish. Checkered walnut grips. Recessed safety cylinder on later models for high-speed ammunition. Disc. prior to 1942.

MODEL 199 SPORTSMAN
SA Revolver . . . . NiB $347 Ex $291 Gd $158
Hinged frame. Caliber: .22 LR. Nine-round cylinder, 6-inch bbl., 11 inches overall. Weight: 30 oz. Adj. target sights. Blued finish. Checkered walnut grips. Disc. 1951.

**Harrington & Richardson
.22 Special**

**Harrington & Richardson
Model 622**

**Harrington & Richardson
Model 649**

**Harrington & Richardson
Model 199 Sportsman**

**Harrington & Richardson
Model 632**

MODEL 504 DA . . . . **NiB $255 Ex $189 Gd $143**
Caliber: .32 H&R Magnum. Five-round cylinder, 4- or 6-inch bbl., (square butt), 3- or 4-inch bbl., round butt. Made 1984 to 1986.

MODEL 532 DA . . . . **NiB $179 Ex $129 Gd $88**
Caliber: .32 H&R Magnum. Five-round cylinder, 2.5- or 4-inch bbl., weight: Approx. 20 and 25 oz. respectively. Fixed sights. American walnut grips. Lustre blued finish. Made 1984 to 1986.

MODEL 586 DA . . . . **NiB $290 Ex $188 Gd $130**
Caliber: .32 H&R Magnum. Five-round cylinder. bbl. lengths: 4.5, 5.5, 7.5, 10 inches. Weight: 30 oz. average. Adj. rear sight, blade front. Walnut finished hardwood grips. Made from 1984 to 1986.

MODEL 603 TARGET . . . . **NiB $219 Ex $158 Gd $115**
Similar to Model 903 except in .22 WMR. Six-round capacity w/unfluted cylinder. Made from 1980 to 1983.

MODEL 604 TARGET . . . . **NiB $219 Ex $158 Gd $115**
Similar to Model 603 except w/6-inch bull bbl., weight: 38 oz. Made from 1980 to 1983.

MODEL 622/623 DA . . . . **NiB $170 Ex $128 Gd $79**
Solid frame. Caliber: .22 Short, Long, LR, 6-round cylinder. bbl., lengths: 2.5-, 4-, 6-inches. Weight: 26 oz. (with 4-inch bbl.). Fixed sights. Blued finish. Plastic grips. Made from 1957

to 1986. Note: Model 623 is same except chrome or nickel finish.

**MODEL 632/633
GUARDSMAN DA REVOLVER** . . **NiB $171 Ex $128 Gd $79**
Solid Frame. Caliber: .32 S&W Long. Six-round cylinder, bbl., lengths: 2.5- or 4-inch. Weight: 19 oz. (with 2.5-inch bbl.). Fixed sights. Blued or chrome finish. Checkered Tenite grips (round butt on 2.5-inch, square butt on 4-inch). Made from 1953 to 1986. Note: Model 633 is the same except for chrome or nickel finish.

MODEL 649/650 DA . . . . **NiB $265 Ex $158 Gd $95**
Solid frame. Side loading and ejection. Convertible model w/ two 6-round cylinders. Calibers: .22 LR, .22 WMR. 5.5-inch bbl., Weight: 32 oz. Adj. rear sight, blade front. Blued finish. One-piece, Western-style walnut grip. Made from 1976 to 1986. Note: Model 650 is same except nickel finish.

MODEL 666 DA . . . . **NiB $151 Ex $104 Gd $64**
Solid frame. Convertible model w/two 6-round cylinders. Calibers: .22 LR, .22 WMR. Six-inch bbl., weight: 28 oz. Fixed sights. Blued finish. Plastic grips. Made from 1976 to 1978.

MODEL 676 DA . . . . **NiB $283 Ex $200 Gd $104**
Solid frame. Side loading and ejection. Convertible model w/two 6-round cylinders. Calibers: .22 LR, .22 WMR, bbl. lengths: 4.5, 5.5, 7.5, 12-inches. Weight: 32 oz. (with 5.5-inch bbl.). Adj. rear sight, blade front. Blued finish, color-casehardened frame. One-piece, Western-style walnut grip. Made from 1976 to 1980.

Model 686 DA . . . . NiB $306 Ex $205 Gd $128 Caliber: .22 LR and .22 WMR. Six-round magazine, 4.5, 5.5, 7.5, 10 or 12-inch bbl. Adj. rear sight, ramp and blade front. Blued, color-casehardened frame. Weight: 31 oz. (with 4.5-inch bbl.). Made from 1980 to 1986.

MODEL 732/733 DA . . . . **NiB $198 Ex $129 Gd $83**
Solid frame, swing-out 6-round cylinder. Calibers: .32 S&W, .32 S&W Long. bbl., lengths: 2.5 and 4-inch. Weight: 26 oz. (with 4-inch bbl.). Fixed sights (windage adj. rear on

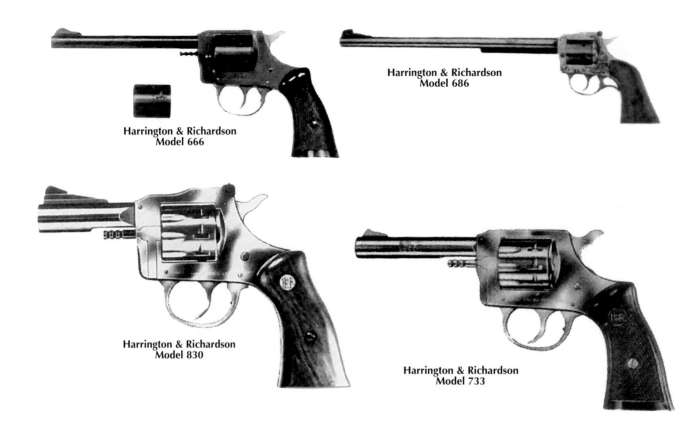

Harrington & Richardson
Model 666

Harrington & Richardson
Model 686

Harrington & Richardson
Model 830

Harrington & Richardson
Model 733

4-inch bbl. model). Blued finish. Plastic grips. Made from 1958 to 1986. Note: Model 733 is the same except with nickel finish.

MODEL 826 DA . . . . NiB $200 Ex $135 Gd $88
Caliber: .22 WMR. Six-round magazine, 3-inch bull bbl., ramp and blade front sight, adj. rear. American walnut grips. Weight: 28 oz. Made from 1981 to 1983.

MODEL 829/830 DA
Same as Model 826 except in .22 LR caliber. Nine round capacity. Made from 1981 to 1983.
Model 829, blued . . . . NiB $189 Ex $143 Gd $94
Model 830, nickel . . . . NiB $181 Ex $135 Gd $90

MODEL 832/833 DA
Same as Model 826 except in .32 SW Long. Blued or nickel finish. Made from 1981 to 1983.
Model 832, blued . . . . NiB $199 Ex $112 Gd $77
Model 833, nickel. . . . . NiB $199 Ex $112 Gd $77

MODEL 900/901 DA . . . . NiB $179 Ex $105 Gd $70
Solid frame, snap-out cylinder. Calibers: .22 Short, Long, LR. Nine-round cylinder, bbl. lengths: 2.5, 4, and 6-inches. Weight: 26 oz. (with 6-inch bbl.). Fixed sights. Blued finish. Cycolac grips. Made from 1962 to 1973. Note: Model 901 (disc. in 1963) is the same except has chrome finish and white Tenite grips.

MODEL 903 TARGET . . . . NiB $240 Ex $177 Gd $112
Caliber: .22 LR. Nine round capacity. SA/DA, 6-inch target-weight flat-side bbl., swing-out cylinder. Weight: 35 oz. Blade front sight, adj. rear. American walnut grips. Made from 1980 to 1983.

Harrington & Richardson
Model 900

MODEL 904 TARGET . . . . NiB $265 Ex $177 Gd $116
Similar to Model 903 except 4 or 6-inch bull bbl. Weight: 32 oz. with 4-inch bbl. Made from 1980 to 1986.

MODEL 905 TARGET. . . . . NiB $270 Ex $183 Gd $137
Same as Model 904 except w/4-inch bbl. only. Nickel finish. Made from 1981 to 1983.

MODEL 922 DA REVOLVER
FIRST ISSUE . . . . NiB $232 Ex $189 Gd $148
Solid frame. Caliber: .22 LR. Nine-round cylinder, 10-inch octagon bbl., (early model) or 6-inches, round bbl. (later production). Weight: 26 oz. (with 6-inch bbl.). Fixed sights. Blued finish. Checkered walnut grips. Safety cylinder on later models. Disc. prior to 1942.

Harrington & Richardson
Model 903

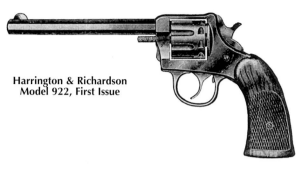

Harrington & Richardson
Model 922, First Issue

Harrington & Richardson
Model 925

Harrington & Richardson
Model 926

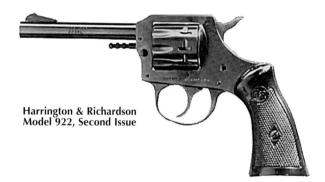

Harrington & Richardson
Model 922, Second Issue

MODEL 922/923 DA REVOLVER,
SECOND ISSUE . . . . **NiB $220 Ex $112 Gd $88**
Solid frame. Caliber: .22 LR. Nine-round cylinder, bbl. lengths: 2.5, 4, and 6-inches. Weight: 24 oz. (with 4-inch bbl.). Fixed sights. Blued finish. Plastic grips. Made 1950 to 1986. Note: Second Issue Model 922 has a different frame from that of the First Issue. Model 923 is same as Model 922, Second Issue except for nickel finish.

MODEL 925
DEFENDER . . . . **NiB $255 Ex $148 Gd $110**
DA. Hinged frame. Caliber: .38 S&W. Five-round cylinder, 2.5-inch bbl., weight: 22 oz. Adj. rear sight, fixed front. Blued finish. One-piece wraparound grip. Made from 1964 to 1978.

MODEL 926 DA . . . . **NiB $255 Ex $158 Gd $110**
Hinged frame. Calibers: .22 LR, .38 S&W. Nine-round (.22 LR) or 5-round (.38) cylinder, 4-in. bbl., weight: 31 oz. Adj. rear sight, fixed front. Blued finish. Checkered walnut grips. Made 1968 to 1978.

MODEL 929/930
SIDEKICK DA REVOLVER . . . . . **NiB $219 Ex $130 Gd $95**
Caliber: .22 LR. Solid frame, swing-out 9-round cylinder, bbl. lengths: 2.5-, 4-, 6-inches. Weight: 24 oz. (with 4-inch bbl.). Fixed sights. Blued finish. Checkered plastic grips. Made from 1956 to 1986. Note: Model 930 is same except with nickel finish.

MODEL 939/940 ULTRA SIDEKICK
DA REVOLVER . . . . **NiB $290 Ex $187 Gd $112**
Solid frame, swing-out 9-round cylinder. Safety lock. Calibers: .22 Short, Long, LR. Flat-side 6-inch bbl. w/vent rib. Weight: 33 oz. Adj. rear sight, ramp front. Blued finish. Checkered walnut grips. Made 1958 to 1986, reintroduced by H&R 1871 in 1992. Note: Model 940 is same except has round bbl.

MODEL 949/950 FORTY-NINER
DA REVOLVER . . . . **NiB $270 Ex $190 Gd $110**
Solid frame. Side loading and ejection. Calibers: .22 Short, Long, LR. Nine-round cylinder, 5.5- or 7.5 inch bbl., weight: 31 to 38 oz. Adj. rear sight, blade front. Blued or nickel finish. One-piece, Western-style walnut grip. Made 1960 to 1986, reintroduced by H&R 1871 in 1992 to 1999. Note: Model 950 is same except has nickel finish.

Harrington & Richardson
Model 939

Harrington & Richardson
Model 950

Harrington & Richardson
Model 999, First Issue

Harrington & Richardson
Model 999, Second Issue

Harrington & Richardson
Model 929

MODEL 976 DA . . . . **NiB $310 Ex $197 Gd $109**
Same as Model 949 except has color-casehardened frame, 7.5-inch bbl. Weight: 36 oz. Intro. 1977. Disc.

MODEL 999 SPORTSMAN DA REVOLVER,
FIRST ISSUE . . . . **NiB $499 Ex $316 Gd $200**
Hinged frame. Calibers: .22 LR, .22 Mag. Same specifications as Model 199 Sportsman Single Action. Disc. before 1942.

MODEL 999 SPORTSMAN DA REVOLVER
SECOND ISSUE . . . . **NiB $464 Ex $309 Gd $197**
Hinged frame. Caliber: .22 LR. Nine-round cylinder, 6-inch bbl. w/vent rib. Weight: 30 oz. Adj. sights. Blued finish. Checkered walnut grips. Made from 1950 to 1986.

(NEW) MODEL 999 SPORTSMAN
DA REVOLVER . . . . **NiB $499 Ex $316 Gd $197**
Hinged frame. Caliber: .22 Short, Long, LR. Nine-round cylinder. Six-inch bbl. w/vent rib. Weight: 30 oz. Blade front sight adj. for elevation, square-notched rear adj. for windage. Blued finish. Checkered hardwood grips. Reintroduced by H&R 1871 in 1992.

AMERICAN DA . . . . **NiB $245 Ex $115 Gd $79**
Solid frame. Calibers: .32 S&W Long, .38 S&W. Six-round (.32 cal.) or 5-round (.38 cal.) cylinder, bbl. lengths: 2.5-,4.5- and 6-inches. Weight: About 16 oz. Fixed sights. Blued or nickel finish. Hard rubber grips. Disc. prior to 1942.

AUTOMATIC EJECTING
DA REVOLVER . . . . **NiB $231 Ex $174 Gd $120**
Hinged frame. Calibers: .32 S&W Long, .38 S&W. Six-round (.32 cal.) or 5-round (.38 cal.) cylinder, bbl. lengths: 3.25-, 4-, 5- and 6-inches. Weight: 16 oz. (.32 cal.), 15 oz. (.38 cal.). Fixed sights. Blued or nickel finish. Black hard rubber grips. Disc. prior to 1942.

BOBBY DA . . . . **NiB $316 Ex $219 Gd $160**
Hinged frame. Calibers: .32 S&W, .38 S&W. Six-round cylinder (.32 cal.) or 5-round (.38 cal.). Four-inch bbl., 9 inches overall. Weight: 23 oz. Fixed sights. Blued finish. Checkered walnut grips. Disc. 1946. Note: Originally designed and produced for use by London's bobbies.

DEFENDER .38 DA . . . . **NiB $346 Ex $219 Gd $110**
Hinged frame. Based on the Sportsman design. Caliber: .38 S&W. Bbl. lengths: 4- and 6-inches, 9 inches overall (with 4-inch bbl.). Weight: 25 oz. with 4-inch bbl. Fixed sights. Blued finish. Black plastic grips. Disc. 1946. Note: This model was manufactured during WW II as an arm for plant guards, auxiliary police, etc.

EXPERT MODEL DA . . . . **NiB $499 Ex $283 Gd $110**
Same specifications as .22 Special except has 10-inch bbl., weight: 28 oz. Disc. prior to 1942.

HAMMERLESS DA,
LARGE FRAME . . . . **NiB $206 Ex $137 Gd $115**
Hinged frame. Calibers: .32 S&W Long 38 S&W. Six-round (.32

**Harrington & Richardson
Automatic Ejecting**

**Harrington & Richardson
Premier**

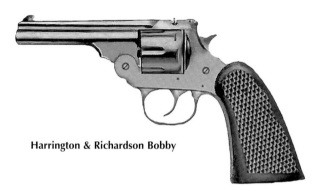

Harrington & Richardson Bobby

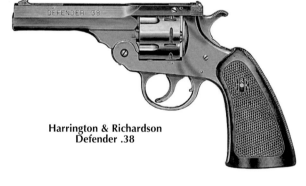

**Harrington & Richardson
Defender .38**

**Harrington & Richardson
Hammerless, Small Frame**

cal.), or 5-round (.38 cal.) cylinder, bbl. lengths: 3.25, 4, and 6-inches. Weight: About 17 oz. Fixed sights. Blued or nickel finish. Hard rubber grips. Disc. prior to 1942.

**HAMMERLESS DA,
SMALL FRAME** . . . . NiB $189 Ex $130 Gd $101
Hinged frame. Calibers: .22 LR, .32 S&W. Seven-round (.22 cal.) or 5-round (.32 cal.) cylinder, bbl. lengths: 2, 3, 4, 5 and 6-inches. Weight: About 13 oz. Fixed sights. Blued or nickel finish. Hard rubber grips. Disc. prior to 1942.

HUNTER MODEL DA . . . . NiB $601 Ex $410 Gd $309
Solid frame. Caliber: .22 LR. Nine-round cylinder, 10-inch octagon bbl., weight: 26 oz. Fixed sights. Blued finish. Checkered walnut grips. Safety cylinder on later models. Note: An earlier Hunter Model was built on the smaller 7-round frame. Disc. prior to 1942.

NEW DEFENDER DA . . . . NiB $346 Ex $244 Gd $189
Hinged frame. Caliber: .22 LR. Nine-round cylinder, 2-inch bbl., 6.25 inches overall. Weight: 23 oz. Adj. sights. Blued finish. Checkered walnut grips, round butt. Note: Basically, this is the Sportsman DA w/a short bbl., Disc. prior to 1942.

PREMIER DA . . . . NiB $306 Ex $198 Gd $109
Small hinged frame. Calibers: .22 LR, .32 S&W. Seven-round (.22 LR) or 5-round (.32) cylinder. Bbl. Lengths: 2, 3, 4, 5, and 6-inches. Weight: 13 oz. (in .22 LR), 12 oz. (in .32 S&W). Fixed sights. Blued or nickel finish. Black hard rubber grips. Disc. prior to 1942.

**STR 022
BLANK REVOLVER** . . . . NiB $143 Ex $90 Gd $70
Caliber: .22 RF blanks. Nine-round cylinder, 2.5-inch bbl. Weight: 19 oz. Satin blued finish.

**STR 032
BLANK REVOLVER** . . . . NiB $148 Ex $95 Gd $75
Same general specifications as STR 022 except chambered for .32 S&W blank cartridges.

TARGET MODEL DA . . . . NiB $237 Ex $166 Gd $120
Small hinged frame. Calibers: .22 LR, .22 W.R.F. Seven-round cylinder, 6-inch bbl., weight: 16 oz. Fixed sights. Blued finish. Checkered walnut grips. Disc. prior to 1942.

Harrington & Richardson Target

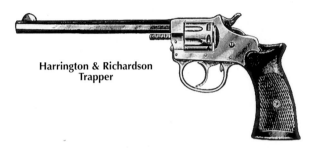

Harrington & Richardson Trapper

Harrington & Richardson Ultra Sportsmen

Harrington & Richardson Vest Pocket

Harrington & Richardson Young American

TRAPPER MODEL DA . . . . **NiB $388 Ex $219 Gd $130**
Solid frame. Caliber: .22 LR. Seven-round cylinder, 6-inch octagon bbl., weight: 12.5 oz. Fixed sights. Blued finish. Checkered walnut grips. Safety cylinder on later models. Disc. prior to 1942.

ULTRA SPORTSMAN . . . . **NiB $321 Ex $219 Gd $165**
SA. Hinged frame. Caliber: .22 LR. Nine-round cylinder, 6-inch bbl., weight: 30 oz. Adj. target sights. Blued finish. Checkered walnut grips. This model has short action, wide hammer spur, cylinder is length of a .22 LR cartridge. Disc. prior to 1942.

VEST POCKET DA . . . . **NiB $138 Ex $95 Gd $70**
Solid frame. Spurless hammer. Calibers: .22 Rimfire, .32 S&W. Seven-round (.22 cal.) or 5-round (.32 cal.) cylinder, 1.13-inch bbl., weight: About 9 oz. Blued or nickel finish. Hard rubber grips. Disc. prior to 1942.

YOUNG AMERICA DA . . . . **NiB $241 Ex $109 Gd $81**
Solid frame. Calibers: .22 Long, .32 S&W. Seven-round (.22 cal.) or 5-round (.32 cal.) cylinder. Bbl. lengths: 2-, 4.5- and 6-inches. Weight: About 9 oz. Fixed sights. Blued or nickel finish. Hard rubber grips. Disc. prior to 1942.

HARTFORD ARMS & EQUIPMENT CO. — Hartford, CT
Hartford pistols were the forebearer of the original High Standard line. High Standard Mfg. Corp. acquired Hartford Arms & Equipment Co. in 1932. The High Standard Model B is essentially the same as the Hartford Automatic.

AUTOMATIC
TARGET PISTOL . . . . **NiB $648 Ex $534 Gd $431**
Caliber. .22 LR. 10-round magazine, 6.75-inch bbl., 10.75 inches overall. Weight: 31 oz. Target sights. Blued finish. Black rubber grips. This gun closely resembles the early Colt Woodsman and High Standard pistols. Made 1929 to 1930.

REPEATING PISTOL . . . . **NiB $785 Ex $576 Gd $342**
Check for authenticity. This model is a hand-operated repeating pistol similar to the Fiala and Schall pistols Made from 1929 to 1930.

SINGLE-SHOT
TARGET PISTOL . . . . **NiB $785 Ex $577 Gd $342**
Similar in appearance to the Hartford Automatic. Caliber: .22 LR, 6.75-inch bbl., 10.75 inches overall. Weight: 38 oz. Target sights. Mottled frame and slide, blued bbl., Black rubber or walnut grips. Made from 1929 to 1930.

HASKELL MANUFACTURING — Lima, OH
See listings under Hi-Point.

HAWES FIREARMS — Van Nuys, CA

DEPUTY MARSHAL SA REVOLVER
Calibers: .22 LR, also .22 WMR in two-cylinder combination. Six-round cylinder, 5.5-inch bbl., 11 inches overall. Weight: 34

oz. Adj. rear sight, blade front. Blued finish. Plastic or walnut grips. Imported 1973 to 1981.

.22 LR (plastic grips). . . . . NiB $219 Ex $120 Gd $88
Combination, .22 LR/.22 WMR
   (plastic). . . . . NiB $293 Ex $219 Gd $130
Walnut grips, add $20

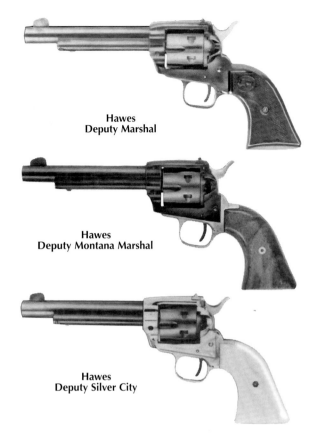

**Hawes
Deputy Marshal**

DEPUTY DENVER MARSHAL
Same as Deputy Marshal SA except has brass frame. Imported 1973 to 1981.

.22 LR (plastic grips). . . . . NiB $265 Ex $212 Gd $110
Combination, .22 LR/.22 WMR
   (plastic). . . . . NiB $293 Ex $219 Gd $130
Walnut grips add $10

DEPUTY MONTANA MARSHAL
Same as Deputy Marshal except has brass grip frame. Walnut grips only. Imported from 1973 to 1981.

.22 LR . . . . NiB $283 Ex $198 Gd $118
Combination, .22 LR/.22 WMR. . . NiB $321 Ex $235 Gd $128

**Hawes
Deputy Montana Marshal**

DEPUTY SILVER CITY MARSHAL
Same as Deputy Marshal except has chrome-plated frame, brass grip frame, blued cylinder and bbl., Imported from 1973 to 1981.

.22 LR (plastic grips). . . . . NiB $281 Ex $209 Gd $158
Combination, .22 LR/.22 WMR
   (plastic). . . . . NiB $306 Ex $205 Gd $115
Walnut grips, add $15

**Hawes
Deputy Silver City**

DEPUTY TEXAS MARSHAL
Same as Deputy Marshal except has chrome finish. Imported 1973 to 1981.

.22 LR (plastic grips). . . . . NiB $293 Ex $205 Gd $110
Combination, .22 LR/.22 WMR
   (plastic). . . . . NiB $306 Ex $190 Gd $110
Walnut grips, add $15

FAVORITE SINGLE-SHOT
TARGET PISTOL. . . . . NiB $219 Ex $128 Gd $90
Replica of Stevens No. 35. Tip-up action. Caliber: .22 LR. Eight-inch bbl., 12 inches overall. Weight: 24 oz. Target sights. Chrome-plated frame. Blued bbl., Plastic or rosewood grips (add $5). Imported 1972- to 1976.

**Hawes
Deputy Texas Marshal**

SAUER CHIEF MARSHAL SA TARGET REVOLVER
Same as Western Marshal except has adjustable rear sight and front sight, oversized rosewood grips. Not made in .22 caliber. Imported from 1973 to 1981.

.357 Magnum or .45 Colt . . . . . NiB $326 Ex $254 Gd $189
.44 Magnum . . . . NiB $362 Ex $282 Gd $214
Combination .357 Magnum and 9mm Para.
   .45 Colt and .45 Auto. . . . . . . NiB $362 Ex $282 Gd $214
Combination
   .44 Magnum and .44-40 . . . . . NiB $369 Ex $290 Gd $225

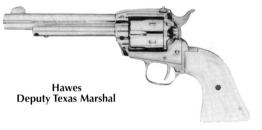

**Hawes Sauer Chief
Marshal**

SAUER FEDERAL MARSHAL
Same as Western Marshal except has color-casehardened frame, brass grip frame, one-piece walnut grip. Not made in .22 caliber. Imported from 1973 to 1981.

.357 Magnum or .45 Colt . . . . . NiB $321 Ex $235 Gd $198
.44 Magnum . . . . NiB $362 Ex $235 Gd $198
Combination .357 Magnum and 9mm Para.,
   .45 Colt and .45 Auto. . . . . . . NiB $362 Ex $290 Gd $198

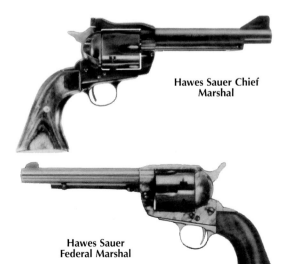

**Hawes Sauer
Federal Marshal**

Hawes Sauer
Montana Marshal .22

Hawes Sauer
Silver City Marshal

Hawes Sauer
Texas Marshal

Hawes Sauer
Western Marshal

Combination .44 Magnum
and .44-40 . . . . NiB $369 Ex $305 Gd $189

SAUER MONTANA MARSHAL
Same as Western Marshal except has brass grip frame.
Imported from 1973 to 1981.
.357 Magnum or .45 Colt . . . . . NiB $326 Ex $270 Gd $190
.44 Magnum . . . . NiB $357 Ex $281 Gd $214
Combination .357 Magnum and 9mm Para.,
.45 Colt and .45 Auto. . . . . . . NiB $377 Ex $301 Gd $219
Combination .44 Magnum
and .44-40 . . . . NiB $385 Ex $309 Gd $220
.22 LR . . . . NiB $306 Ex $240 Gd $180
Combination .22 LR
and .22 WMR . . . . NiB $332 Ex $281 Gd $190

SAUER SILVER CITY MARSHAL
Same as Western Marshal except has nickel plated frame, brass
grip frame, blued cylinder and barrel, pearlite grips. Imported
from 1973 to 1981.
.44 Magnum . . . . NiB $377 Ex $289 Gd $219
Combination .357 Magnum and 9mm Para.
.45 Colt and .45 Auto. . . . . . . NiB $362 Ex $270 Gd $180
Combination .44 Magnum
and .44-40 . . . . NiB $365 Ex $270 Gd $214

SAUER TEXAS MARSHAL
Same as Western Marshal except nickel plated, has pearlite
grips. Imported from 1973 to 1981.
.357 Magnum or .45 Colt . . . . . NiB $362 Ex $270 Gd $204
.44 Magnum . . . . NiB $365 Ex $303 Gd $214

Combination .357 Magnum and 9mm Para.,
.45 Colt and .45 Auto . . . . NiB $388 Ex $321 Gd $225
Combination .44 Magnum
and .44-40 . . . . NiB $395 Ex $332 Gd $239
.22 LR . . . . NiB $321 Ex $244 Gd $189
Combination .22 LR
and .22 WMR . . . . NiB $336 Ex $265 Gd $189

SAUER WESTERN MARSHAL SA REVOLVER
Calibers: .22 LR (disc.), .357 Magnum, .44 Magnum,
.45 Auto. Also in two-cylinder combinations: .22 WMR
(disc.), 9mm Para., .44-40, .45 Auto. Six-round cylinder,
bbl. lengths: 5.5-inch (disc.), 6-inch, 11.75 inches overall
(with 6-inch bbl.). Weight: 46 oz. Fixed sights. Blued finish.
Originally furnished w/simulated stag plastic grips. Recent
production has smooth rosewood grips. Made from 1968
by J. P. Sauer & Sohn, Eckernforde, Germany. Imported from
1973 to 1981.
.357 Magnum or .45 LC . . . . . . NiB $357 Ex $265 Gd $200
.44 Magnum . . . . NiB $377 Ex $290 Gd $219
Combination .357 Magnum and 9mm Para.,
.45 Colt and .45 Auto. . . . . . . NiB $385 Ex $270 Gd $214
Combination .44 Magnum
and .44-40 . . . . NiB $385 Ex $270 Gd $214
.22 LR . . . . NiB $281 Ex $198 Gd $160
Combination .22 LR
and .22 WMR . . . . NiB $281 Ex $198 Gd $160

HECKLER & KOCH — Oberndorf am Neckar, Germany, and Columbus, GA; Asburn, VA; and Newington, NH; formerly Chantilly, VA

MODEL HK4 DA AUTO PISTOL

Calibers: .380 Automatic (9mm Short), .22 LR, .25 Automatic (6.35mm), .32 Automatic (7.65mm) w/conversion kits. Seven-round magazine (.380 Auto), 8-round in other calibers, 3.4-inch bbl., 6.19 inches overall. Weight: 18 oz. Fixed sights. Blued finish. Plastic grip. Disc. 1984.

.22 LR or .380 units to kit. . . . . NiB $536 Ex $388 Gd $265
.25 ACP or .32 ACP units to kit. . . . NiB $536 Ex $377 Gd $255
.380 units to kit w/.22
   conversion unit. . . . . NiB $530 Ex $357 Gd $225
.380 units to kit w/.22, .25, .32
   conversion units . . . . NiB $530 Ex $357 Gd $225

Heckler & Koch
Model HK4

MODEL HK45 . . . . NiB $1025 EX $800 GD $550

Semi-automatic. DA/SA. Caliber: .45 ACP; 10-rnd. magazine. 4.53-in. bbl. w/O-ring. Frame: polymer. Sights: low-profile, 3-dot. Finish: black. Grip: textured polymer w/grip panels. Length: 8.3-in. Weight: 31.2 oz. Imported from 2008 to date.
HK45 Tactical (DA/SA or DAO, thread bbl.,
intro. 2013). . . . . NiB $1225 Ex $930 Gd $680
HK45 Compact
(3.9-in. bbl., intro. 2008) . . . . NiB $1025 Ex $800 Gd $550
HK45 Compact Tactical (3.9-in. threaded bbl.,
intro. 2011). . . . . NiB $1225 Ex $930 Gd $680

MARK 23 DA
AUTO PISTOL. . . . . NiB $2356 Ex $1831 Gd $1290

Short-recoil semiautomatic pistol w/polymer frame and steel slide. Caliber: .45 ACP. 10-round magazine, 5.87-inch bbl., 9.65 inches overall. Weight: 43 oz. Seven interchangeable rear sight adjustment units w/3-dot system. Developed primarily in response to specifications by the Special Operations Command (SOCOM) for a Special Operations Forces Offensive Handgun Weapon System. Imported from 1996 to date.

Heckler & Koch
Mark 23

MODEL P7 K3 DA AUTO PISTOL

Caliber: .380 ACP. Eight-round magazine, 3.8 inch-bbl., 6.3 inches overall. Weight: About 26 oz. Adj. rear sight. Imported 1988 to 1994.
.380 Cal. . . . . NiB $2200 Ex $1785 Gd $1250
.22 LR conversion kit add, ... $1500
.32 ACP conversion kitadd, ... $1000

Heckler & Koch
Model P7K3

MODEL P7 M8 . . . . NiB $2250 Ex $1750 Gd $1175

Squeeze-cock SA semiautomatic pistol. Caliber: 9mm Para. Eight-round magazine, 4.13-inch bbl., 6.73 inches overall. Weight: 29.9 oz. Matte black or nickel finish. Adjustable rear sight. Imported from 1985 to 2005.

MODEL P7 M10

Caliber: .40 S&W. Nine-round magazine, 4.2-inch bbl., 6.9 inches overall. Weight: 43 oz. Fixed front sight blade, adj. rear w/3-dot system. Imported from 1992 to 1994.
Blued finish. . . . . NiB $3200 Ex $2500 Gd $1880
Nickel finish add, ... 20%

MODEL P7 M13. . . . . NiB $3200 Ex $2500 Gd $1880

Caliber: 9mm. 13-round magazine, 4.13-inch bbl., 6.65 inches

Heckler & Koch
Model P7M13

**Heckler & Koch
Model P7 (PSP)**

**Heckler & Koch
Model P9S DA**

Heckler & Koch USP45

**Heckler & Koch
Model USP9 Compact (Stainless)**

overall. Weight: 34.42 oz. Matte black finish. Adj. rear sight. Imported 1985 to 1994.

MODEL P7 (PSP). . . . . NiB $1200 Ex $900 Gd $720
Caliber: 9mm Para. Eight-round magazine, 4.13-inch bbl., 6.54 inches overall. DA. Weight: About 33.5 oz. Blued finish. Imported 1983 to 1985 and 1990 with limited availability.
European model, add 15%

MODEL P9S DA AUTOMATIC PISTOL
Calibers: 9mm Para., .45 Automatic. Nine-round (9mm) or 7-round (.45 Auto) magazine. Four-inch bbl., 7.63 inches overall. Weight: 32 ounces. Fixed sights. Blued finish. Contoured plastic grips. This model disc. 1986.
9mm . . . . NiB $893 Ex $663 Gd $486
.45 Automatic . . . . NiB $918 Ex $713 Gd $500

MODEL P9S TARGET COMPETITION KIT
Same as Model P9S Target except comes w/Extra 5.5-inch bbl. and bbl. weights. Also available w/walnut competition grip.
w/standard grip . . . . NiB $3000 Ex $2300 Gd $1810
w/competition grip . . . . NiB $4000 Ex $3000 Gd $2000

MODEL P30. . . . . NiB $950 Ex $680 Gd $480
Semi-automatic. DA/SA. Caliber: 9mm or .40 S&W; 15 or 13-rnd. magazine. 3.85-in. bbl. Frame: polymer. Sights: low-profile, 3-dot. Finish: black. Grip: textured polymer w/grip panels. Length: 7.12-in. Weight: 26 oz. Imported from 2007 to date.
P30SK (3.27-in. bbl.) . . . . NiB $950 Ex $660 Gd $450
P30L (4.45-in. bbl.) . . . . NiB $950 Ex $660 Gd $450

MODEL P2000. . . . . NiB $850 Ex $660 Gd $450
Semi-automatic. DA/SA, DAO or LEM trigger. Caliber: 9mm, .357 SIG (2005-2012) or .40 S&W; 12 or 13-rnd. magazine. 3.66-in. bbl. Frame: polymer. Sights: low-profile, 3-dot. Finish: black. Grip: textured polymer w/ modular backstrap. Length: 6.85-in. Weight: 24.96 oz. Imported from 2004 to date.
**P2000 SK (3.26-in. bbl.,
2005 to date)** . . . . NiB $950 Ex $680 Gd $495

MODEL SP5K. . . . . NiB $2699 Ex $2600 Gd $2400
Semi-automatic commercial version of H&K MP5. SA. Caliber: 9mm; 10 or 30-rnd. magazine. 4.53-in. bbl. Frame: polymer. Sights: fixed front, adj. rear. Finish: black. Grip: textured polymer. Length: 13.9-in. Weight: 4.2 lbs. Imported from 2016 to date.

MODEL SP89 . . . . NiB $4960 Ex $4160 Gd $3740
Semiautomatic, recoil-operated, delayed roller-locked bolt system. Caliber: 9mm Para. 15-round magazine, 4.5-inch bbl., 13 inches overall. Weight: 68 oz. Hooded front sight, adj. rotary-aperture rear. Imported 1989 to 1993.

MODEL USP . . . . NiB $928 Ex $627 Gd $468
Polymer integral grip/frame design w/recoil reduction system. Calibers: 9mm Para., .40 S&W or .45 ACP. 15-round (9mm) or 13-round (.40 S&W and .45ACP) magazine, 4.13- or 4.25-inch bbl., 6.88 to 7.87 inches overall. Weight: 26.5-30.4 oz. Blade front sight, adj. rear w/3-dot system. Matte black finish. Stippled black polymer grip. Available in SA/DA or DAO. Imported 1993 to date.
Stainless finish. . . . . NiB $816 Ex $510 Gd 332
w/Tritium sights, add $100
w/ambidextrous decocking lever, add $30

MODEL USP9 COMPACT.......NiB $860 Ex $660 Gd $450
Caliber: 9mm. 10-round magazine, 4.25-inch bbl., 7.64 inches overall. Weight: 25.5 oz. Short recoil w/modified Browning action. 3-dot sighting system. Polymer frame w/integral grips, blued slide finish. Imported from 1993 to date.
Stainless slide finish ....NiB $740 Ex $500 Gd $375
w/ambidextrous decocking lever, add $75

MODEL USP40 COMPACT
Caliber: .40 S&W. 10-round magazine, 3.58- inch bbl., 6.81 inches overall. Weight: 27 oz. Short recoil w/modified Browning action. 3-dot sighting system. Polymer frame w/ integral grips, blued slide finish. Imported from 1993 to date.
Blued finish...............NiB $857 Ex $615 Gd $437
Stainless finish.............NiB $774 Ex $627 Gd $431
w/ambidextrous decocking lever, add $50

MODEL USP45 COMPACT ... NiB $918 Ex $615 Gd $410
Caliber: .45 ACP. Eight-round magazine, 3.8- inch bbl., 7.09 inches overall. Weight: 28 oz. Short recoil w/modified Browning action. 3-dot sighting system. Polymer frame w/integral grips. Imported from 1998 to date.
Stainless slide finish ....NiB $816 Ex $639 Gd $431
w/ambidextrous decocking lever, add $50
50th Anniversary
(1 of 1,000)............NiB $1199 Ex $947 Gd $709

MODEL USP EXPERT ......NiB $1301 Ex $1142 Gd $842
Caliber: .45 ACP. 10-round magazine, 6.2- inch bbl., 9.65 inches overall. Weight: 30 oz. Adjustable 3-dot target sights. Short recoil modified Browning action w/recoil reduction system. Reinforced polymer frame w/integral grips and match-grade slide. Imported from 1999 to 2009.

MODEL USP TACTICAL .....NiB $1178 Ex $933 Gd $638
SOCOM Enhanced version of the USP Standard Model, w/4.92-inch threaded bbl. Chambered for .45 ACP only. Imported from 1998 to date.

MODEL VP9.............NiB $719 EX $700 GD $680
Semi-automatic. Striker-fired. Caliber: 9mm; 10 or 15-rnd. magazine. 4.0-in. bbl. Frame: polymer. Sights: fixed, low-profile, 3-dot. Finish: black. Grip: textured polymer w/modular grip panels. Length: 7.3-in. Weight: 25.56 oz. Imported from 2014 to date.
VP40 (.40 S&W, intro. 2015) ..NiB $719 Ex $700 Gd $680

MODEL VP 70Z AUTO PISTOL NiB $791 Ex $536 Gd $377
Caliber: 9mm Para. 18-round magazine, 4.5-inch bbl., 8 inches overall. Weight: 32.5 oz. DA Fixed sights. Blued slide, polymer receiver and grip. Disc. 1986.

HELWAN
See listings under Interarms.

HENRY REPEATING ARMS — BAYONNE, NJ

MARE'S LEG RIMFIRE .... NiB $440 Ex $390 Gd $320
Lever-action pistol. SA. Caliber: .22 S/L/LR, 10-rnd. magazine. 12.8-in. bbl. Sights: adj rear. Finish: blue. Grip: smooth wood. Made from 2011 to date. Mare's Leg Pistol .22... NiB $440 Ex $390 Gd $320

MARE'S LEG PISTOL CENTERFIRE....NiB $975 Ex $870 Gd $620
Lever-action pistol. SA. Caliber: .357 Mag., .44 Mag., or .45 Long Colt, 5-rnd. magazine. 12.9-in. bbl. Sights: adj rear.

Heckler & Koch Model USP45
Compact 50th Anniversary

Heckler & Koch
Model USP Expert

Heckler & Koch
Model USP Tactical

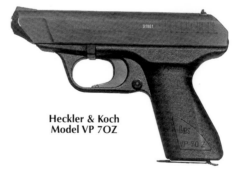

Heckler & Koch
Model VP 7OZ

Finish: blue or brass receiver, blue bbl. Made from 2011 to date.

HEIZER DEFENSE — PEVELY, MO

MODEL PS1 POCKET
SHOTGUN.............. NiB $449 Ex $410 Gd $340
Single-shot derringer, break action. DAO. Caliber: .45 ACP/410 gauge. 3.25-in. bbl. Frame: stainless steel. Sights: fixed. Finish:

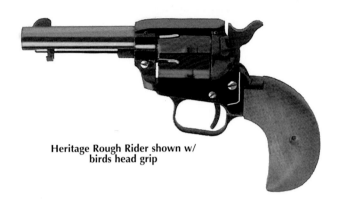

Heritage Rough Rider shown w/ birds head grip

Heritage Sentry

matte stainless. Grip: textured aluminum w/storage for 2 extra cartridges. Weight: 21 oz. Length: 4.6 in. Made from 2013 to date.
PAR1 (5.56 caliber)........**NiB $399 Ex $480 Gd $380**
PAK1 (7.62x39mm caliber)....**NiB $399 Ex $480 Gd $380**

HERITAGE MANUFACTURING — Opa Locka, FL

Acquired by Taurus Int'l. in 2012

MODEL H-25 AUTO PISTOL
Caliber: .25 ACP. Six-round magazine, 2.5-inch bbl., 4.63 inches overall. Weight: 12 oz. Fixed sights. Blued or chrome finish. Made 1995 to 1999.
Blued......................**NiB $136 Ex $95 Gd $75**
Nickel, add..................................**$20**

ROUGH RIDER SA REVOLVER
Calibers: .22 LR, .22 Mag. Six-round cylinder. bbl. lengths: 2.75, 3.75, 4.75, 6.5 or 9 inches. Weight: 31-38 oz. Blade front sight, fixed rear. High-polished blued finish w/gold accents. Smooth walnut grips. Made from 1993 to date.
.22 LR.....................**NiB $247 Ex $115 Gd $95**
.22 LR/.22 Mag. combo......**NiB $291 Ex $179 Gd $110**

SENTRY DA REVOLVER
Calibers: .22 LR, .22 Mag., .32 Mag., 9mm or .38 Special.

Six- or 8-round (rimfire) cylinder, 2- or 4-inch bbl., 6.25 inches overall (2-inch bbl.). Ramp front sight, fixed rear. Blued or nickel finish. Checkered polymer grips. Made from 1993 to 1997.
Blued.....................**NiB $131 Ex $95 Gd $75**
Nickel, add..................................**$15**

STEALTH DA AUTO PISTOL...**NiB $241 Ex $179 Gd $101**
Calibers: 9mm, .40 S&W. 10-round magazine, 3.9-inch bbl., weight: 20.2 oz. Gas-delayed blowback, double action only. AmbidExtrous trigger safety. Blade front sight, drift-adj. rear. Black chrome or stainless slide. Black polymer grip frame. Made from 1996 to 2000.

HI-POINT FIREARMS — Mansfield, OH

MODEL JS-9MM
AUTO PISTOL..............**NiB $158 Ex $101 Gd $75**
Caliber: 9mm Para. Eight-round magazine, 4.5-inch bbl., 7.75 inches overall. Weight: 39 oz. Fixed low-profile sights w/3-dot system. Matte blue, matte black or chrome finish. Checkered synthetic grips. Made from 1990 to 2000.

MODEL JS-9MM COMPETITION
PISTOL (STALLARD).........**NiB $151 Ex $90 Gd $69**
Similar to standard JS-9 except w/4-inch compensated bbl. w/ shortened slide and adj. sights. 10-round magazine, 7.25 inches overall. Weight: 30 oz. Made from 1998 to 2006.

MODEL JS-9MM/C-9MM COMPACT PISTOL
(BEEMILLER)................**NiB $148 Ex $90 Gd $75**
Similar to standard JS-9 except w/3.5-inch bbl. and shortened slide w/alloy or polymer frame. 6.72 inches overall. Weight: 29 oz. or 32 oz. Three-dot-style sights. Made from 1993 to date.

MODEL CF-.380
POLYMER...................**NiB $158 Ex $88 Gd $61**
Caliber: .380 ACP. Eight-round magazine, 3.5-inch bbl., 6.72 inches overall. Weight: 32 oz. Three-dot sights. Made from 1994 to date.

MODEL JS-.40/JC-.40 AUTO PISTOL
(IBERIA)...................**NiB $171 Ex $110 Gd $75**
Similar to Model JS-9mm except in caliber .40 S&W.

MODEL JS-.45/JH-.45 AUTO PISTOL
(HASKELL).................**NiB $150 Ex $101 Gd $70**
Similar to Model JS-9mm except in caliber .45 ACP w/7-round magazine and two-tone Polymer finish.

J. C. HIGGINS
See Sears, Roebuck & Company.

HIGH STANDARD SPORTING FIREARMS — East Hartford, CT
Formerly High Standard Mfg. Co., Hamden, ConnecticutA long-standing producer of sporting arms, High Standard disc. its operations in 1984. See new High Standard models under separate entry, HIGH STANDARD MFG. CO., INC.

NOTE: *For ease in finding a particular firearm, High Standard handguns are grouped into three sections: Automatic pistols,* *derringers and revolvers. For a complete listing, please refer to the Index.*

- AUTOMATIC PISTOLS -

MODEL A
HAMMERLESS. . . . . **NiB $847 Ex $748 Gd $497**
Caliber: .22 LR. 10-round magazine, bbl. lengths: 4.5-, 6.75-inch. 11.5 inches overall (6.75-inch bbl.). Weight: 36 oz. (in 6.75-inch bbl.). Adj. target sights. Blued finish. Checkered walnut grips. Made from 1938 to 1942.

MODEL B
AUTOMATIC PISTOL . . . . **NiB $668 Ex $444 Gd $367**
Original Standard pistol. Hammerless. Caliber: .22 LR. 10-round magazine, bbl. lengths: 4.5-, 6.75-inch, 10.75 inches overall (with 6.75-inch bbl.). Weight: 33 oz. (6.75-inch bbl.). Fixed sights. Blued finish. Hard rubber grips. Made from 1932 to 1942.

MODEL C
AUTOMATIC PISTOL . . . . **NiB $979 Ex $826 Gd $549**
Same as Model B except in .22 Short. Made 1935 to 1942.

MODEL D
AUTOMATIC PISTOL . . . . **NiB $1020 Ex $774 Gd $544**
Same general specifications as Model A but heavier bbl., weight: 40 oz. (6.75-inch bbl.). Made from 1937 to 1942.

DURA-MATIC
. . . . **NiB $362 Ex $301 Gd $204**
Takedown. Caliber: .22 LR. 10-round magazine, 4.5 or 6.5 inch interchangeable bbl., 10.88 inches overall (6.5-inch bbl.). Weight: 35 oz. (in 6.5-inch bbl.). Fixed sights. Blued finish. Checkered grips. Made from 1952 to 1970.

MODEL E
AUTOMATIC PISTOL . . . . . . **NiB $1275 Ex $1051 Gd $929**
Same general specifications as Model A but w/Extra heavy bbl. and thumbrest grips. Weight: 42 oz. (6.75-inch bbl.). Made 1937 to 1942.

FIELD-KING AUTOMATIC PISTOL FIRST MODEL
Same general specifications as Sport-King but w/heavier bbl. and target sights. Late model 6.75-inch bbls. have recoil stabilizer and lever take-down feature. Weight: 43 oz. (6.75-inch bbl.). Made from 1951 to 1958.
w/one bbl. . . . . **NiB $683 Ex $529 Gd $408**
w/both bbls., add **$204**

FIELD-KING AUTOMATIC PISTOL SECOND MODEL
Same general specifications as First Model Field-King but w/button take-down and marked FK 100 or FK 101.
w/one bbl. . . . . **NiB $852 Ex $588 Gd $324**
w/both bbls., add **$204**

FLITE-KING AUTOMATIC PISTOL — FIRST MODEL
Same general specifications as Sport-King except in .22 Short w/aluminum alloy frame and slide and marked FK 100 or FK 101. Weight: 26 oz. (6.5-inch bbl.). Made 1953-58.
w/one bbl. . . . . **NiB $668 Ex $469 Gd $342**
w/both bbls. . . . . **NiB $872 Ex $660 Gd $546**

High Standard
Model A

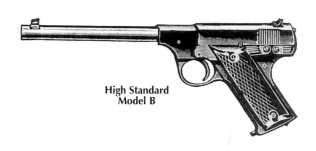

High Standard
Model B

High Standard
Model D

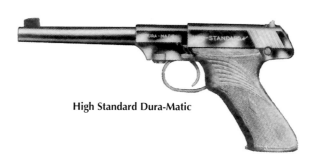

High Standard Dura-Matic

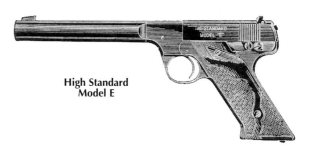

High Standard
Model E

**High Standard
G-380**

**High Standard
Model G-B**

**High Standard
Model G-E**

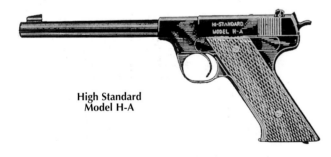

**High Standard
Model H-A**

**High Standard
Model H-B**

FLITE-KING AUTOMATIC PISTOL — SECOND MODEL
Same as Flite-King—First Model except w/steel frame and marked in the 102 or 103 series. Made from 1958 to 1966.
Model 102 . . . . NiB $556 Ex $398 Gd $265
Model 103 . . . . NiB $536 Ex $388 Gd $219

MODEL G-380
AUTOMATIC PISTOL . . . . NiB $668 Ex $571 Gd $408
Lever takedown. Visible hammer. Thumb safety. Caliber: .380 Automatic. Six-round magazine, 5-inch bbl., weight: 40 oz. Fixed sights. Blued finish. Checkered plastic grips. Made 1943 to 1950.

MODEL G-B AUTOMATIC PISTOL
Lever takedown. Hammerless. Interchangeable bbls. Caliber: .22 LR. 10-round magazine, bbl. lengths: 4.5, 6.75 inches, 10.75 inches overall (with 6.75-inch bbl.). Weight: 36 oz. (with 6.75-inch bbl.). Fixed sights. Blued finish. Checkered plastic grips. Made 1948 to 1951.
w/one bbl. . . . . NiB $689 Ex $500 Gd $365
w/both bbls. . . . . NiB $893 Ex $704 Gd $576

MODEL G-D AUTOMATIC PISTOL
Lever takedown. Hammerless. Interchangeable bbls. Caliber: .22 LR. 10-round magazine, bbl. lengths: 4.5, 6.75 inches. 11.5 inches overall (with 6.75-inch bbl.). Weight: 41 oz. (6,75-inch bbl.). Target sights. Blued finish. Checkered walnut grips. Made 1948 to 1951.
w/one bbl. . . . . NiB $1076 Ex $917 Gd $709
w/both bbls. . . . . NiB $1275 Ex $1048 Gd $898

MODEL G-E AUTOMATIC PISTOL
Same general specifications as Model G-D but w/Extra heavy bbl. and thumbrest grips. Weight: 44 oz. (with 6.75-inch bbl.). Made from 1949 to 1951.
w/one bbl. . . . . NiB $1488 Ex $1266 Gd $1015
w/both bbls. . . . . NiB $1692 Ex $1470 Gd $1200

MODEL H-A
AUTOMATIC PISTOL . . . . . . NiB $2230 Ex $1355 Gd $859
Same as Model A but w/visible hammer, no thumb safety. Made from 1939 to 1942.

MODEL H-B
AUTOMATIC PISTOL . . . . NiB $816 Ex $590 Gd $433
Same as Model B but w/visible hammer, no thumb safety. Made from 1940 to 1942.

MODEL H-D
AUTOMATIC PISTOL . . . . . . NiB $1282 Ex $1122 Gd $806
Same as Model D but w/visible hammer, no thumb safety. Made from 1939 to 1942.

MODEL H-DM
AUTOMATIC PISTOL . . . . NiB $663 Ex $524 Gd $429
Also called H-D Military. Same as Model H-D but w/thumb safety. Made from 1941 to 1951.

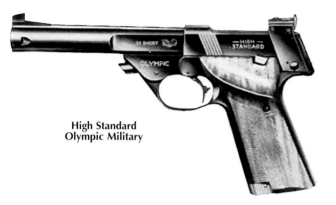

High Standard
Olympic Military

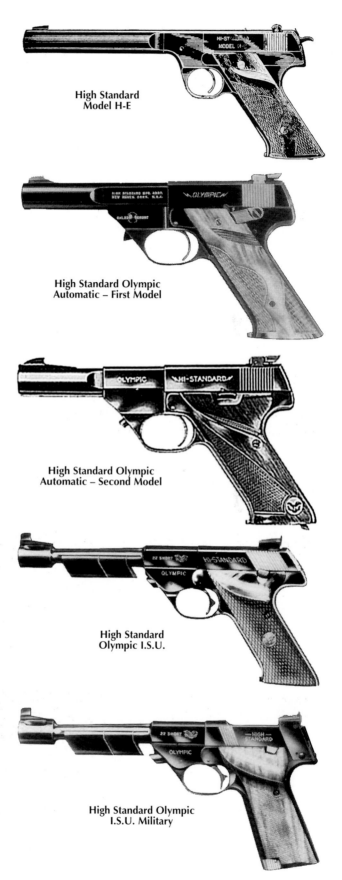

High Standard
Model H-E

High Standard Olympic
Automatic – First Model

High Standard Olympic
Automatic – Second Model

High Standard
Olympic I.S.U.

High Standard Olympic
I.S.U. Military

MODEL H-E
AUTOMATIC PISTOL . . . . . NiB $2275 Ex $2142 Gd $1197
Same as Model E but w/visible hammer, no thumb safety. Made from 1939 to 1942.

OLYMPIC AUTOMATIC PISTOL FIRST MODEL (G-O)
Same general specifications as Model G-E but in .22 Short w/ light alloy slide. Made from 1950 to 1951.
w/one bbl. . . . . NiB $1785 Ex $1153 Gd $629
w/both bbls, add. $408

OLYMPIC AUTOMATIC SECOND MODEL
Same general specifications as Supermatic but in .22 Short w/light alloy slide. Weight: 39 oz. (6.75-inch bbl.). Made 1951 to 1958.
w/one bbl. . . . . NiB $1325 Ex $1076 Gd $730
w/both bbls, add. $306

OLYMPIC AUTOMATIC PISTOL,
THIRD MODEL . . . . NiB $1213 Ex $984 Gd $734
Same as Supermatic Trophy w/bull bbl. except in .22 Short. Made from 1963 to 1966.

OLYMPIC COMMEMORATIVE
Limited edition of Supermatic Trophy Military issued to commemorate the only American-made rimfire target pistol ever to win an Olympic gold medal. Highly engraved w/Olympic rings inlaid in gold. Deluxe presentation case. Two versions issued: In 1972 (.22 LR) and 1980 (.22 Short).
1972 issue. . . . . NiB $6523 Ex $5416 Gd $3550
1980 issue. . . . . NiB $2243 Ex $1877 Gd $1215

OLYMPIC I.S.U. . . . . NiB $1316 Ex $1020 Gd $798
Same as Supermatic Citation except caliber .22 Short, 6.75- or 8-inch tapered bbl. w/stabilizer, detachable weights. Made from 1958 to 1977. Eight-inch bbl. disc. in 1966.

OLYMPIC I.S.U. MILITARY . . . NiB $1120 Ex $940 Gd $702
Same as Olympic I.S.U. except has military grip and bracket rear sight. Intro. in 1965. Disc.

OLYMPIC MILITARY . . . . NiB $1142 Ex $932 Gd $755
Same as Olympic — Third Model except has military grip and bracket rear sight. Made in 1965.

SHARPSHOOTER
AUTOMATIC PISTOL . . . . NiB $385 Ex $267 Gd $197
Takedown. Hammerless. Caliber: .22 LR. 10-round magazine, 5.5-inch bull bbl., 9 inches overall. Weight: 42 oz. Micrometer rear sight, blade front sight. Blued finish. Plastic grips. Made from 1971 to 1983.

High Standard Sport-King Automatic — First Model

High Standard Sport-King Automatic — Second Model

High Standard Sport-King Automatic — Third Model

High Standard Supermatic

SPORT-KING AUTOMATIC PISTOL FIRST MODEL

Takedown. Hammerless. Interchangeable barrels. Caliber: .22 LR. 10-round magazine, barrel lengths: 4.5-, 6.75-inches. 11.5 inches overall (with 6.75-inch barrel). Weight: 39 oz. (with 6.75-inch barrel). Fixed sights. Blued finish. Checkered plastic thumbrest grips. Made from 1951 to 1958. Note: 1951 to 1954 production has lever takedown as in "G" series. Later version (illustrated at left) has push-button takedown.

w/one bbl. . . . . NiB $388 Ex $306 Gd $220
w/both bbls. . . . . NiB $590 Ex $500 Gd $408

SPORT-KING AUTOMATIC PISTOL
SECOND MODEL . . . . NiB $357 Ex $279 Gd $204

Caliber: .22 LR. 10-round magazine, 4.5- or 6.75 inch interchangeable bbl. 11.25 inches overall (with 6.75-inch barrel). Weight: 42 oz. (with 6.75-inch barrel). Fixed sights. Blued finish. Checkered grips. Made from 1958 to 1970.

SPORT-KING AUTOMATIC PISTOL
THIRD MODEL . . . . NiB $305 Ex $204 Gd $135

Similar to Sport-King — Second Model with same general specifications for weight and length. Blued or nickel finish. Introduced in 1974. Disc.

SPORT-KING LIGHTWEIGHT

Same as standard Sport-King except lightweight has forged aluminum alloy frame. Weight: 30 oz. with 6.75-inch barrel Made from 1954 to 1965.

w/one bbl. . . . . NiB $590 Ex $380 Gd $255
w/both bbls. . . . . NiB $791 Ex $602 Gd $453

SUPERMATIC AUTOMATIC PISTOL

Takedown. Hammerless. Interchangeable bbls. Caliber: .22 LR. 10-round magazine, barrel lengths: 4.5-, 6.75-inches. Late model 6.75-inch barrel have recoil stabilizer feature. Weight: 43 oz. (with 6.75-inch barrel) 11.5 inches overall (with 6.75-inch barrel). Target sights. Elevated serrated rib between sights. Adjustable barrel weights add 2 or 3 oz. Blued finish. Checkered plastic thumbrest grips. Made from 1951 to 1958.

w/one bbl. . . . . NiB $872 Ex $683 Gd $509
w/both bbls. . . . . NiB $1070 Ex $893 Gd $714

SUPERMATIC CITATION

Same as Supermatic Tournament except 6.75-, 8- or 10-inch tapered bbl. with stabilizer and two removable weights. Also furnished with Tournament's 5.5-inch bull barrel, adjustable trigger pull, recoil-proof click-adjustable rear sight (barrel-mounted on 8- and 10-inch barrels), checkered walnut thumbrest grips on bull barrel model. Currently manufactured with only bull barrel. Made from 1958 to 1966.

High Standard Mfg. Co. 10-X Supermatic Citation (current mfg.)

**High Standard Victor
Solid Rib Barrel**

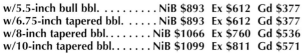

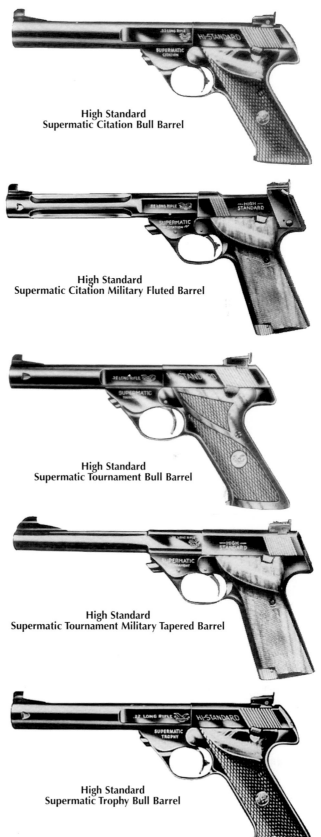

**High Standard
Supermatic Citation Bull Barrel**

**High Standard
Supermatic Citation Military Fluted Barrel**

**High Standard
Supermatic Tournament Bull Barrel**

**High Standard
Supermatic Tournament Military Tapered Barrel**

**High Standard
Supermatic Trophy Bull Barrel**

w/5.5-inch bull bbl. . . . . NiB $893 Ex $612 Gd $377
w/6.75-inch tapered bbl. . . . . NiB $893 Ex $612 Gd $377
w/8-inch tapered bbl. . . . . . . NiB $1066 Ex $760 Gd $536
w/10-inch tapered bbl. . . . . . NiB $1099 Ex $811 Gd $571

SUPERMATIC CITATION MILITARY
Same as Supermatic Citation except has military grip and bracket rear sight as in Supermatic Trophy. Made from 1965 to 1973.
w/bull bbl. . . . . NiB $897 Ex $581 Gd $499
w/fluted bbl. . . . . NiB $964 Ex $806 Gd $602

SUPERMATIC
TOURNAMENT. . . . . NiB $734 Ex $587 Gd $362
Takedown. Caliber: .22 LR. 10-round magazine, interchangeable 5.5-inch bull or 6.75-inch heavy tapered bbl., notched and drilled for stabilizer and weights. 10 inches overall (with 5.5-inch bbl.). Weight: 44 oz. (5.5-inch bbl.). Click adj. rear sight, undercut ramp front. Blued finish. Checkered grips. Made from 1958 to 1966.

SUPERMATIC TOURNAMENT
MILITARY . . . . NiB $1305 Ex $997 Gd $836
Same as Supermatic Tournament except has military grip. Made from 1965 to 1971.

SUPERMATIC TROPHY
Same as Supermatic Citation except with 5.5-inch bull bbl., or 7.25-inch fluted bbl., w/detachable stabilizer and weights, Extra magazine, High-luster blued finish, checkered walnut thumbrest grips. Made from 1963 to 1966.
w/bull bbl. . . . . NiB $1305 Ex $1090 Gd $638
w/fluted bbl. . . . . NiB $1305 Ex $1090 Gd $638

SUPERMATIC TROPHY MILITARY
Same as Supermatic Trophy except has military grip and bracket rear sight. Made from 1965 to 1984.
w/bull bbl. . . . . NiB $1357 Ex $1060 Gd $760
w/fluted bbl. . . . . NiB $1408 Ex $1120 Gd $813

THE VICTOR AUTOMATIC . . . NiB $3299 Ex $2798 Gd $2550
Takedown. Caliber: .22 LR. 10-round magazine, 4.5-inch solid or vent rib and 5.5-inch vent rib, interchangeable bbl., 9.75 inches overall (with 5.5-inch bbl.). Weight: 52 oz. (with 5.5-inch bbl.). Rib mounted target sights. Blued finish. Checkered walnut thumbrest grips. Standard or military grip configuration. Made from 1972 to 1984 (standard-grip model made from1974 to 1975).

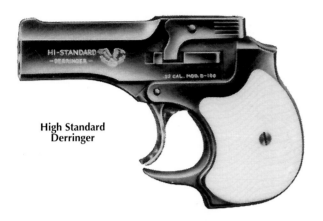

**High Standard
Derringer**

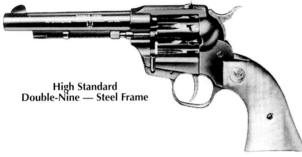

**High Standard
Double-Nine — Steel Frame**

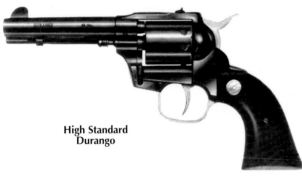

**High Standard
Durango**

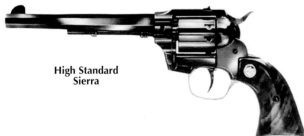

**High Standard
Sierra**

- DERRINGERS -

DERRINGER

Hammerless, double action, two-round, double bbl. (over/under). Calibers: .22 Short, Long, LR or .22 Magnum Rimfire, 3.5-inch bbls., 5 inches overall. Weight: 11 oz. Standard model has blued or nickel finish w/plastic grips. Presentation model is goldplated in walnut case. Standard model made from 1963 (.22 S-L-LR) and 1964 (.22 MRF) to 1984. Gold model, made from 1965 to 1983.

Standard model (blue) . . . . NiB $332 Ex $225 Gd $204
Standard model (nickel) . . . . . . NiB $332 Ex $225 Gd $204
Standard model
  (Electroless nickel). . . . . NiB $337 Ex $291 Gd $230
Gold Presentation
  One Derringer. . . . . NiB $541 Ex $362 Gd $286
Silver Presentation
  One Derringer. . . . . NiB $592 Ex $431 Gd $342
Presentation Set, Matched pair, consecutive
  numbers (1965 only) . . . . NiB $1392 Ex $1180 Gd $836

- REVOLVERS -

CAMP GUN . . . . NiB $270 Ex $220 Gd $189
Same as Sentinel Mark I/Mark IV except has 6-inch bbl., adj. rear sight, target-style checkered walnut grips. Caliber: .22 LR or .22 WMR. Made from 1976 to 1983.

DOUBLE-NINE DA REVOLVER —ALUMINUM FRAME
Western-style version of Sentinel. Blued or nickel finish w/ simulated ivory, ebony or stag grips, 5.5-inch bbl., 11 inches overall. Weight: 27.25 oz. Made from 1959 to 1971.
Blue model . . . . NiB $255 Ex $190 Gd $150

DOUBLE-NINE—STEEL FRAME
Similar to Double-Nine—Aluminum Frame, w/same general specifications except w/steel frame and has Extra cylinder for .22 WMR, walnut grips. Intro. in 1971. Disc.
Blue model . . . . NiB $291 Ex $225 Gd $179
Nickel model. . . . . NiB $306 Ex $225 Gd $190

DOUBLE-NINE DELUXE . . . . . . NiB $326 Ex $240 Gd $198
Same as Double-Nine Steel Frame except has adj. target rear sight. Intro. in 1971. Disc.

DURANGO
Similar to Double-Nine—Steel Frame except .22 LR only, available w/4.5- or 5.5-inch bbl. Made from 1971 to 1973.
Blue model . . . . NiB $275 Ex $189 Gd $150
Nickel model. . . . . NiB $301 Ex $219 Gd $170

HIGH SIERRA DA REVOLVER
Similar to Double-Nine—Steel Frame except has 7-inch octagon bbl., w/gold-plated grip frame, fixed or adj. sights. Made 1973 to 1983.
w/fixed sights . . . . NiB $352 Ex $286 Gd $214
w/adj. sights . . . . NiB $362 Ex $306 Gd $230

HOMBRE
Similar to Double-Nine—Steel Frame except .22 LR only, lacks single-action type ejector rod and tube, has 4.5-inch bbl. Made from 1971 to 1973.
Blue model . . . . NiB $281 Ex $204 Gd $143
Nickel model. . . . . NiB $306 Ex $220 Gd $165

KIT GUN DA REVOLVER . . . . . NiB $275 Ex $214 Gd $150
Solid frame, swing-out cylinder. Caliber: .22 LR. Nine-round cylinder, 4-inch bbl., 9 inches overall. Weight: 19 oz. Adj. rear sight, ramp front. Blued finish. Checkered walnut grips. Made from 1970 to 1973.

LONGHORN ALUMINUM FRAME
Similar to Double-Nine—Aluminum Frame except has Longhorn hammer spur, 4.5-, 5.5- or 9.5-inch bbl., Walnut, simulated pearl or simulated stag grips. Blued finish. Made from 1960 to 1971.
w/4.5- or 5.5-inch bbl. . . . . . . NiB $357 Ex $254 Gd $190
w/9.5-inch bbl . . . . NiB $357 Ex $254 Gd $190

High Standard Longhorn
Steel Frame

High Standard
Kit Gun

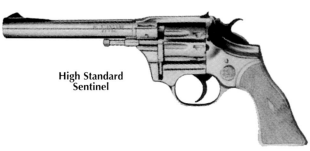

High Standard
Sentinel

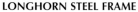

LONGHORN STEEL FRAME
Similar to Double-Nine — Steel Frame except has 9.5-inch bbl.
w/fixed or adj. sights. Made from 1971 to1983
w/fixed sights . . . . NiB $362 Ex $270 Gd $204
w/adj. sights . . . . NiB $377 Ex $316 Gd $229

NATCHEZ . . . . NiB $418 Ex $270 Gd $209
Similar to Double-Nine — Aluminum Frame except 4.5-inch
bbl., 10 inches overall, weight: 25.25 oz., blued finish, simulated ivory bird's-head grips. Made 1961-66.

POSSE . . . . NiB $281 Ex $180 Gd $148
Similar to Double-Nine — Aluminum Frame except 3.5-inch
bbl., 9 inches overall, weight: 23.25 oz. Blued finish, brass-
grip frame and trigger guard, walnut grips. Made from 1961
to 1966.

SENTINEL DA REVOLVER
Solid frame, swing-out cylinder. Caliber: .22 LR. Nine-round
cylinder, 3- 4- or 6-inch bbl. Nine inches overall (with 4-inch-
bbl.). Weight: 19 oz. (with 4-inch bbl.). Fixed sights. Aluminum
frame. Blued or nickel finish. Checkered grips. Made from
1955 to 1956.
Blue model . . . . NiB $302 Ex $156 Gd $120
Blue/green model . . . . NiB $577 Ex $439 Gd $319
Gold model. . . . . NiB $555 Ex $397 Gd $317
Nickel model. . . . . NiB $270 Ex $214 Gd $158
Pink model . . . . NiB $536 Ex $306 Gd $180

SENTINEL DELUXE
Same as Sentinel except w/4- or 6-inch bbl., wide trigger, drift-
adj. rear sight, two-piece square-butt grips. Made from 1957 to
1974. Note: Designated Sentinel after 1971.
Blue model . . . . NiB $270 Ex $170 Gd $128
Nickel model. . . . . NiB $296 Ex $189 Gd $160

SENTINEL IMPERIAL
Same as Sentinel except has onyx-black or nickel finish, two-
piece checkered walnut grips, ramp front sight. Made from
1962 to 1965.
Blue model . . . . NiB $270 Ex $179 Gd $130
Nickel model. . . . . NiB $281 Ex $189 Gd $143

High Standard
Longhorn Aluminum Frame

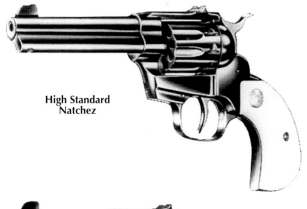

High Standard
Natchez

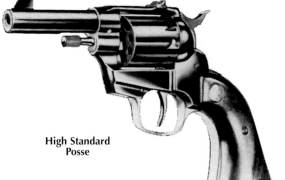

High Standard
Posse

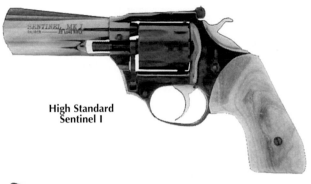

**High Standard
Sentinel I**

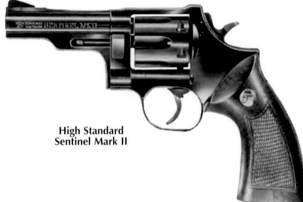

**High Standard
Sentinel Mark II**

**High Standard
Sentinel Mark III**

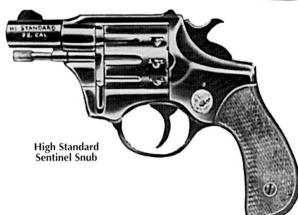

**High Standard
Sentinel Snub**

SENTINEL MARK 1 DA REVOLVER
Steel frame. Caliber: .22 LR. Nine-round cylinder, bbl. lengths: 2-, 3-, 4-inch, 6.88 inches overall (with 2-inch bbl.). Weight: 21.5 oz. (2-inch bbl.). Ramp front sight, fixed or adj. rear. Blued or nickel finish. Smooth walnut grips. Made from 1974 to 1983.

Blue model . . . . NiB $265 Ex $219 Gd $179
Nickel model. . . . . NiB $296 Ex $255 Gd $190
w/adj. sights . . . . NiB $337 Ex $270 Gd $225

SENTINEL MARK II
DA REVOLVER . . . . NiB $326 Ex $255 Gd $179
Caliber: .357 Magnum. Six-round cylinder, bbl. lengths: 2.5-, 4-, 6-inch, 9 inches overall w/4-inch bbl., weight: 38 oz. (with 4-inch bbl.). Fixed sights. Blued finish. Walnut service or combat-style grips. Made from 1974 to 1976.

SENTINEL MARK III . . . . NiB $326 Ex $255 Gd $175
Same as Sentinel Mark II except has ramp front and adj. rear sights. Weight: 40 oz. (with 4-inch bbl.). Blued finish. Made 1974 to 1976.

SENTINEL MARK IV
Same as Sentinel Mark I except in .22 WMR. Made 1974 to 1983.

Blue model . . . . NiB $301 Ex $230 Gd $175
Nickel model. . . . . NiB $326 Ex $265 Gd $198
w/adj. sights . . . . NiB $352 Ex $255 Gd $220

SENTINEL SNUB
Same as Sentinel Deluxe except w/2.75-inch bbl., (7.25 inches overall, weight: 15 oz.), checkered bird's head-type grips. Made 1957 to 1974.

Blued finish. . . . . NiB $255 Ex $190 Gd $148
Nickel finish . . . . NiB $274 Ex $160 Gd $109

HIGH STANDARD MFG. CO., INC. — Houston, TX
In 1993, High Standard acquired original assets and moved to Houston, Texas. The first Texas-manufactured firearms began shipping in March 1994 to date.

VICTOR 10X AUTO PISTOL . . . NiB $1120 Ex $840 Gd $540
Caliber: .22 LR. 10-round magazine, 5.5-inch bbl., 9.5 inches overall. Weight: 45 oz. Checkered walnut grips. Blued finish. Made from 1994 to date.

OLYMPIC I.S.U. AUTOMATIC PISTOL
Same specifications as the 1958 I.S.U. issue. See listing under previous High Standard Section.

Olympic I.S.U. model . . . . NiB $592 Ex $345 Gd $270
Olympic I.S.U. military model . . . NiB $816 Ex $577 Gd $336

SPORT KING AUTO PISTOL . . . NiB $694 Ex $434 Gd $305
Caliber: .22 LR. 10-round magazine, 4.5- or 6.75-inch bbl., 8.5 or 10.75 inches overall. Weight: 44 oz. (with 4.5-inch bbl.), 46 oz. (with 6.75-inch bbl.). Fixed sights, slide mounted. Checkered walnut grips. Parkerized finish. Manufactured in limited quantities.

SUPERMATIC CITATION
AUTO PISTOL. . . . . NiB $536 Ex $399 Gd $254
Caliber: .22 LR. 10-round magazine, 5.5- or 7.75-inch bbl., 9.5 or 11.75 inches overall. Weight: 44 oz. (with 5.5-inch bbl.), 46 oz. (with 7.75-inch bbl.). Frame-mounted, micro-adj. rear sight, undercut ramp front sight.

Blued or Parkerized finish. Made from 1994 to 2003.
.22 Short conversion. . . . . NiB $408 Ex $337 Gd $255

CITATION MS
AUTO PISTOL . . . . NiB $821 Ex $638 Gd $474
Similar to the Supermatic Citation except has 10-inch bbl., 14 inches overall. Weight: 49 oz. Made from 1994 to date.

SUPERMATIC TOURNAMENT . NiB $745 Ex $377 Gd $274
Caliber: .22 LR. 10-round magazine, bbl. lengths: 4.5, 5.5, or 6.75 inches, overall length: 8.5, 9.5 or 10.75 inches. Weight: 43, 44 or 45 oz. depending on bbl. length. Micro-adj. rear sight, undercut ramp front sight. Checkered walnut grips. Parkerized finish. Made from 1995 to 1997.

SUPERMATIC TROPHY. . . . . . NiB $719 Ex $356 Gd $220
Caliber: .22 LR. 10-round magazine, 5.5 or 7.25-inch bbl., 9.5 or 11.25 inches overall. Weight: 44 oz. (with 5.5-inch bbl.). Micro-adj. rear sight, undercut ramp front sight. Checkered walnut grips w/thumbrest. Blued or Parkerized finish. Made from 1994 to date.
.22 Short Conversion . . . . . . NiB $1301 Ex $890 Gd $779

VICTOR AUTOMATIC. . . . . . . NiB $723 Ex $475 Gd $270
Caliber: .22 LR.10-round magazine, 4.5- or 5.5-inch ribbed bbl., 8.5 or 9.5 inches overall. Weight: 45 oz. (with 4.5-inch bbl.), 46 oz. (with 5.5-inch bbl.). Micro-adj. rear sight, post front. Checkered walnut grips. Blued or Parkerized finish. Made from 1994 to date.
.22 Short conversion. . . . . . . NiB $1193 Ex $925 Gd $780

HOPKINS & ALLEN ARMS CO. — Norwich, CT
See listings of comparable Harrington & Richardson and Iver Johnson models for values.

INGRAM — Powder Springs, GA
See listings under M.A.C. (Military Armament Corp.)

Note: *Military Armament Corp. ceased production of the select-fire automatic, M10 (9mm & .45 ACP) and M11 (.380 ACP) in 1977. Commercial production resumed on semiautomatic versions under the M.A.C. banner until 1982.*

INLAND MANUFACTURING — Dayton, Ohio

MODEL 1911A1 . . . . NiB $749 Ex $700 Gd $680
Similar to US Military 1911A1 pistol. Semi-automatic. SA. Caliber: .45 ACP; 7-rnd. magazine. 5.0-in. bbl. Frame: steel. Sights: fixed. Finish: parkerized. Grip: checkered polymer. Length: 8.5 in. Weight: 39 oz. Made from 2014 to date.

MODEL M1 ADVISOR . . . . NiB $749 Ex $700 Gd $680
Similar to US Military M1 Carbine pistol. Semi-automatic. SA. Caliber: .30 Carbine; 15-rnd. magazine. 12 in. bbl. Receiver: steel. Sights: fixed front, adj. rear. Finish: parkerized. Grip: smooth wood. Length: 19.75 in. Weight: 4.4 lbs. Made from 2015 to date.

INTERARMS — Alexandria, VA
Also see Bersa.

Interarms/Helwan Brigadier

Interarms Virginian SA Revolver

HELWAN BRIGADIER
AUTO PISTOL. . . . . NiB $265 Ex $203 Gd $143
Caliber: 9mm Para. Eight-round magazine, 4.25-inch bbl., 8 inches overall. Weight: 32 oz. Blade front sight, dovetailed rear. Blued finish. Grooved plastic grips. Imported from 1987 to 1995.

VIRGINIAN DRAGOON SA REVOLVER
Calibers: .357 Magnum, .44 Magnum, .45 Colt. Six-round cylinder. Bbls.: 5- (not available in .44 Magnum), 6-, 7.5-, 8.38-inch (latter only in .44 Magnum w/adj. sights), 11.88 inches overall with (6-inch bbl.). Weight: 48 oz. (with 6-inch bbl.). Fixed sights or micrometer rear and ramp front sights. Blued finish w/color-casetreated frame. Smooth walnut grips. SWISSAFE base pin safety system. Mfg. by Interarms Industries Inc., Midland, VA. from 1977 to 1984.
Standard Dragoon. . . . . NiB $388 Ex $281 Gd $214
Engraved Dragoon . . . . NiB $785 Ex $530 Gd $362
Deputy model . . . . NiB $377 Ex $274 Gd $179
Stainless . . . . NiB $398 Ex $265 Gd $165

VIRGINIAN REVOLVER
SILHOUETTE MODEL. . . . . . . NiB $385 Ex $274 Gd $244
Same general specifications as regular model except designed in stainless steel w/untapered bull bbl., lengths of 7.5, 8.38 and 10.5 inches. Made from 1985 to 1986.

VIRGINIAN SA REVOLVER. . . . NiB $388 Ex $270 Gd $265
Similar to Colt Single Action Army except has base pin safety system. Imported from 1973-76. (See also listing under Hämmerli.)

INTRATEC U.S.A., INC. — Miami, FL

CATEGORY 9 DAO
SEMIAUTOMATIC. . . . . NiB $270 Ex $177 Gd $120
Blowback action w/polymer frame. Caliber: 9mm Par Eight-round magazine, 3-inch bbl., 7.7 inches overall. Weight: 18 oz. TExtured black polymer grips. Matte black finish. Made from 1993 to 2000.

**Japanese
Model 14 (1925)**

**Japanese
Model 26 DAO Revolver**

CATEGORY 40
DAO SEMIAUTOMATIC . . . . . NiB $270 Ex $177 Gd $120
Locking-breech action w/polymer frame. Caliber: .40 S&W. Seven-round magazine, 3.25-inch bbl., 8 inches overall. Weight: 21 oz. TExtured black polymer grips. Matte black finish. Made from 1994 to 2000.

CATEGORY 45
DAO SEMIAUTOMATIC . . . . . NiB $295 Ex $184 Gd $133
Locking-breech action w/polymer frame. Caliber: .45 ACP. Six-round magazine, 3.25-inch bbl., 8 inches overall. Weight: 21 oz. TExtured black polymer grips. Matte black finish. Made from 1994 to 2000.

MODEL PROTEC .25 ACP DA SEMIAUTOMATIC
Caliber: .25 ACP. 10-round magazine, 2.5-inch bbl., 5 inches overall. Weight: 14 oz. Wraparound composition grips. Black Teflon, satin grey or Tec-Kote finish. Disc. 2000.
ProTec .25 standard . . . . NiB $128 Ex $88 Gd $61
ProTec .25 w/satin or Tec-Kote . . . NiB $130 Ex $90 Gd $65

MODEL TEC-DC9 SEMIAUTOMATIC
Caliber: 9mm 20- or 36-round magazine, 5-inch bbl., weight: 50-51 oz. Open fixed front sight, adj. rear. Military nonglare blued or stainless finish.
Tec-9 w/blued finish . . . . NiB $510 Ex $332 Gd $270
Tec-9 w/Tec Kote finish . . . . . . NiB $546 Ex $342 Gd $301
Tec 9S w/stainless finish . . . . . NiB $576 Ex $398 Gd $301

MODEL TEC-DC9M SEMIAUTOMATIC
Same specifications as Model Tec-9 except has 3-inch bbl. without shroud and 20-round magazine, blued or stainless finish.
Tec-9M w/blued finish . . . . NiB $546 Ex $337 Gd $281
Tec-9MS w/stainless finish . . . . NiB $622 Ex $398 Gd $255

MODEL TEC-22T SEMIAUTOMATIC
Caliber: .22 LR. 10/.22-type 30-round magazine, 4-inch bbl., 11.19 inches overall. Weight: 30 oz. Protected post front sight, adj. rear sight. Matte black or Tec-Kote finish. Made from 1991 to 1994.
Tec-22T standard . . . . NiB $434 Ex $220 Gd $189
Tec-22TK Tec-Kote, add. $50

TEC-38 DERRINGER . . . . NiB $183 Ex $129 Gd $101
Calibers: .22 Mag., .32 H&R Mag., .357 Mag., .38 Special. Two-round capacity, 3-inch blued bbl., 4.63 inches overall. Weight: 13 oz. Fixed sights. Synth. black frame. Double-action. Made from 1986 to 1988.

ISRAEL ARMS — Kfar Sabs, Israel
Imported by Israel Arms International, Houston, TX.

BUL-M5 LOCKED BREECH (2000)
AUTO PISTOL. . . . . NiB $398 Ex $235 Gd $148
Similar to the M1911 U.S. Government model. Caliber: .45 ACP. Seven-round magazine, 5-inch bbl., 8.5 inches overall. Weight: 38 oz. Blade front and fixed, low-profile rear sights.

KAREEN MK II (1500) AUTO PISTOL
Single-action only. Caliber: 9mm Para. 10-round magazine, 4.75-inch bbl., 8 inches overall. Weight: 33.6 oz. Blade front sight, rear adjustable for windage. TExtured black composition or rubberized grips. Blued, two-tone, matte black finish. Imported from 1997 to 1998.
Blued or matte black finish . . . . NiB $386 Ex $301 Gd $219
Two-tone finish . . . . NiB $556 Ex $386 Gd $304
Meprolite sights, add $50

KAREEN MK II COMPACT
(1501) AUTO PISTOL . . . . NiB $386 Ex $290 Gd $204
Similar to standard Kareen MKII except w/3.85-inch bbl., 7.1 inches overall. Weight: 32 oz. Imported 1999 to 2000.

GOLAN MODEL (2500) AUTO PISTOL
Single or double action. Caliber: 9mm Para., .40 S&W. 10-round magazine, 3.85-inch bbl., 7.1 inches overall. Weight: 34 oz. Steel slide and alloy frame w/ambidExtrous safety and decocking lever. Matte black finish. Imported 1999.
9mm Para. . . . . NiB $954 Ex $755 Gd $536
.40 S&W . . . . NiB $954 Ex $755 Gd $536

GAL MODEL
(5000) AUTO PISTOL . . . . NiB $437 Ex $289 Gd $220
Caliber: .45 ACP. Eight-round magazine, 4.25-inch bbl., 7.25 inches overall. Weight: 42 oz. Low profile 3-dot sights. Combat-style black rubber grips. Imported from 1999 to 2001.

JAPANESE MILITARY PISTOLS — Tokyo, Japan
Manufactured by Government Plant.

MODEL 14 (1925)
AUTOMATIC PISTOL . . . . . . NiB $1423 Ex $1009 Gd $658
Modification of the Nambu Model 1914, changes chiefly intended to simplify mass production. Standard round trigger guard or oversized guard for use w/gloves. Caliber: 8mm Nambu. Eight-round magazine, 4.75-inch bbl., 9 inches overall. Weight: About 29 oz. Fixed sights. Blued finish. Grooved wood grips. Intro. 1925 and mfd. through WW II.

MODEL 26 DAO REVOLVER NiB $1586 Ex $1120 Gd $779
Top-break frame. Caliber: 9mm. Six-round cylinder w/ automatic Extractor/ejector, 4.7-inch bbl., adopted by the Japanese Army from 1893 to 1914, replaced by the Model 14 Automatic Pistol but remained in service through World War II.

MODEL 94 (1934)
AUTOMATIC PISTOL . . . . NiB $780 Ex $464 Gd $342
Poorly designed and constructed, this pistol is unsafe and can be fired merely by applying pressure on the sear, which is Exposed on the left side. Caliber: 8mm Nambu. Six-round magazine, 3.13-inch bbl., 7.13 inches overall. Weight: About 27 oz. Fixed sights. Blued finish. Hard rubber or wood grips. Intro. in 1934, principally for Export to Latin American countries, production continued thru WW II.

Japanese Model 94 (1934)

NAMBU MODEL
1914 AUTOMATIC PISTOL . . . NiB $1389 Ex $989 Gd $785
Original Japanese service pistol, resembles Luger in appearance and Glisenti in operation. Caliber: 8mm Nambu. Seven-round magazine, 4.5-inch bbl., 9 inches overall. Weight: About 30 oz. Fixed front sight, adj. rear sight. Blued finish. Checkered wood grips. Made from 1914 to 1925.

JENNINGS FIREARMS INC. — Irvine, CA
Currently Manufactured by Bryco Arms, Irvine, California. Previously by Calwestco, Inc. & B.L. Jennings. See additional listings under Bryco Arms.

Jennings Model J Auto Pistol

MODEL J-22 AUTO PISTOL
Calibers: .22 LR, .25 ACP. Six-round magazine, 2.5-inch bbl., about 5 inches overall. Weight: 13 oz. Fixed sights. Chrome, satin nickel or black Teflon finish. Walnut, grooved black Cycolac or resin-impregnated wood grips. Made from 1981-85 under Jennings and Calwestco logos; disc. 1985 by Bryco Arms.
Model J-22 . . . . NiB $81 Ex $50 Gd $40
Model J-25 . . . . NiB $91 Ex $61 Gd $50

IVER JOHNSON ARMS, INC. — Jacksonville, AR
Operation of this company dates back to 1871, when Iver Johnson and Martin Bye partnered to manufacture metallic cartridge revolvers. Johnson became the sole owner and changed the name to Iver Johnson's Arms & Cycle Works, which it was known as for almost 100 years. Modern management shortened the name, and after several owner changes the firm was moved from Massachusetts, its original base, to Jacksonville, Arkansas. In 1987, the American Military Arms Corporation (AMAC) acquired the operation, which subsequently ceased in 1993.

NOTE: *For ease in finding a particular firearm, Iver Johnson handguns are divided into two sections: Automatic Pistols (below) and Revolvers, which follow. For the complete handgun listing, please refer to the Index.*

- AUTOMATIC PISTOLS -

9MM DA AUTOMATIC . . . . NiB $474 Ex $357 Gd $265
Caliber: 9mm. Six-round magazine, 3-inch bbl., 6.5 inches overall. Weight: 26 oz. Blade front sight, adj. rear. Smooth hardwood grip. Blued or matte blued finish. Intro. 1986.

COMPACT .25 ACP . . . . NiB $273 Ex $190 Gd $148
Bernardelli V/P design. Caliber: .25 ACP. Five-round magazine,

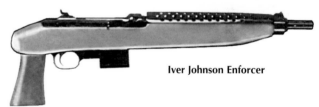

Iver Johnson Enforcer

2.13-inch bbl., 4.13 inches overall. Weight: 9.3 oz. Fixed sights. Checkered composition grips. Blued slide, matte blued frame and color-casehardened trigger. Made from 1991 to 1993.

ENFORCER . . . . NiB $893 Ex $643 Gd $431
Caliber: .30 U.S. Carbine. Five-, 15-, or 30-round magazine, 9.5-inch bbl., weight: 5.5 lbs. Adj. sights. Walnut stock. Made 1986.

I.J. SUPER ENFORCER . . . . NiB $893 Ex $643 Gd $431
Caliber: .30 U.S. Carbine. Fifteen- or 30-round magazine, 9.5-inch bbl., 17 inches overall. Weight: 4 pounds. Adj. peep rear sight, blade front. American walnut stock. Made from 1978 to 1993.

PONY AUTOMATIC PISTOL
Caliber: .380 Auto. Six-round magazine, 3.1-inch bbl., 6.1 inches overall. Blue, matte blue, nickel finish or stainless. Weight: 20 oz. Wooden grips. Smallest of the locked breech automatics. Made from 1982-88. Reintro. 1989-91.
Blue or matte blue finish . . . . . NiB $434 Ex $342 Gd $270
Nickel finish . . . . NiB $464 Ex $345 Gd $290
Deluxe finish . . . . NiB $464 Ex $377 Gd $281

Iver Johnson
Model TP

Iver Johnson
Model 55 Target

Iver Johnson
Model 55-S

Iver Johnson
Model 56 Blank Revolver

Iver Johnson
Model 57A Target

MODEL TP-22 DA
AUTOMATIC. . . . . NiB $316 Ex $219 Gd $160
Calibers: .22 LR, Seven-round magazine, 2.85-inch bbl., 5.39 inches overall. Blued finish. Weight: 14.46 oz. Made from 1982 to 1989.

MODEL TP25 DA
POCKET PISTOL . . . . NiB $271 Ex $190 Gd $143
Double-action automatic. Caliber: .25 ACP. Seven-round magazine, 3-inch bbl., 5.5 inches overall. Weight: 12 oz. Black plastic grips and blued finish. Made from 1981 to 1982.

TRAILSMAN AUTOMATIC PISTOL
Caliber: .22 LR. 10-round magazine, 4.5 or 6-inch bbl., 8.75 inches overall (with 4.5-inch bbl.). Weight: 46 oz. Fixed target-type sights. Checkered composition grips. Made 1985-91.
Standard model. . . . . NiB $306 Ex $220 Gd $160
Deluxe model . . . . NiB $321 Ex $230 Gd $170

- REVOLVERS -

MODEL 55
TARGET DA REVOLVER . . . . . . NiB $237 Ex $160 Gd $115
Solid frame. Caliber: .22 LR. Eight-round cylinder, bbl. lengths: 4.5-, 6-inches. 10.75 inches overall (with 6-inch bbl.). Weight: 30.5 oz. (with 6-inch bbl.). Fixed sights. Blued finish. Walnut grips. Note: Original model designation was 55; changed to 55A when loading gate was added in 1961. Made 1955-60.

MODEL 55-S REVOLVER. . . . . . NiB $265 Ex $165 Gd $110
Same general specifications as the Model 55 except for 2.5-inch bbl. and small, molded pocket-size grip.

MODEL 56
BLANK REVOLVER . . . . NiB $128 Ex $81 Gd $55
Solid frame. Caliber: .22 blanks only. Eight-round cylinder, 2.5-inch solid bbl., 6.75 inches overall. Weight: 10 oz.

MODEL 57A
TARGET DA REVOLVER . . . . . . NiB $255 Ex $143 Gd $101
Solid frame. Caliber: .22 LR. Eight-round cylinder, bbl. lengths: 4.5, and 6-inches. 10.75 inches overall. Weight: 30.5 oz. with 6-inch bbl. Adj. sights. Blued finish. Walnut grips. Note: Original model designation was 57, changed to 57A when loading gate was added in 1961. Made from 1961 to 1978.

MODEL 66 TRAILSMAN
DA REVOLVER . . . . NiB $306 Ex $209 Gd $160
Hinged frame. Rebounding hammer. Caliber: .22 LR. Eight-round cylinder, 6-inch bbl., 11 inches overall. Weight: 34 oz. Adj. sights. Blued finish. Walnut grips. Made 1985-91.

MODEL 67
VIKING DA REVOLVER . . . . . . **NiB $273 Ex $165 Gd $110**
Hinged frame. Caliber: .22 LR. Eight-round cylinder, bbl. lengths: 4.5- and 6-inches, 11 inches overall (with 6-inch bbl.). Weight: 34 oz. (with 6-inch bbl.). Adj. sights. Walnut grips w/ thumbrest. Made 1964 to 1978.

MODEL 67S VIKING
SNUB REVOLVER . . . . **NiB $286 Ex $189 Gd $179**
DA. Hinged frame. Calibers: .22 LR, .32 S&W Short and Long, .38 S&W. Eight-round cylinder in .22, 5-round in .32 and .38 calibers; 2.75-inch bbl. Weight: 25 oz. Adj. sights. Tenite grips. Made from 1964 to 1978.

MODEL 1900 DA REVOLVER . . . . NiB $158 Ex $90 Gd $65
Solid frame. Calibers: .22 LR, .32 S&W, .32 S&W Long, .38 S&W. Seven-round cylinder in .22 cal. , 6-round (.32 S&W), 5-round (.32 S&W Long, .38 S&W); bbl. lengths: 2.5-, 4.5- and 6-inches. Weight: 12 oz. (in .32 S&W w/2.5-inch bbl.). Fixed sights. Blued or nickel finish. Hard rubber grips. Made from 1900 to 1941.

MODEL 1900
TARGET DA REVOLVER . . . . . . **NiB $222 Ex $175 Gd $135**
Solid frame. Caliber: .22 LR. Seven-round cylinder, bbl. lengths: 6- and 9.5-inches. Fixed sights. Blued finish. Checkered walnut grips. (This earlier model does not have counterbored chambers as in the Target Sealed 8. Made from 1925 to 1942.)

AMERICAN BULLDOG DA REVOLVER
Solid frame. Calibers: .22 LR, .22 WMR, .38 Special. Six-round cylinder in .22, 5-round in .38. Bbl. lengths: 2.5-, 4-inch. 9 inches overall (with 4-inch bbl.). Weight: 30 oz. (with 4-inch bbl.). Adj. sights. Blued or nickel finish. Plastic grips. Made from 1974 to 1976.
.38 Special . . . . **NiB $464 Ex $286 Gd $204**
Other calibers . . . . **NiB $464 Ex $286 Gd $204**

ARMSWORTH MODEL 855 SA . . . NiB $464 Ex $290 Gd $198
Hinged frame. Caliber: .22 LR. Eight-round cylinder, 6-inch bbl., 10.75 inches overall. Weight: 30 oz. Adj. sights. Blued finish. Checkered walnut one-piece grip. Adj. finger rest. Made from 1955 to 1957.

CADET DA REVOLVER . . . . NiB $255 Ex $165 Gd $101
Solid frame. Calibers: .22 LR, .22 WMR, .32 S&W Long, .38 S&W, .38 Special. Six- or 8-round cylinder in .22, 5-round in other calibers, 2.5-inch bbl., 7 inches overall. Weight: 22 oz. Fixed sights. Blued finish or nickel finish. Plastic grips. Note: Loading gate added in 1961, .22 cylinder capacity changed from 8 to 6 rounds in 1975. Made 1955 to 1977.

CATTLEMAN SA REVOLVER . . . NiB $369 Ex $301 Gd $170
Patterned after the Colt Army SA revolver. Calibers: .357 Magnum, .44 Magnum, .45 Colt. Six-round cylinder. Bbl. lengths: 4.75-, 5.5- (not available in .44), 6- (.44 only), 7.25-inch. Weight: About 41 oz. Fixed sights. Blued bbl., and cylinder color-casehardened frame, brass grip frame. One-piece walnut grip. Made by Aldo Uberti, Brescia, Italy, from 1973 to 1978.
.44 Magnum, add **$50**

CATTLEMAN BUCKHORN SA REVOLVER
Same as standard Cattleman except has adj. rear and ramp front sights. Bbl. lengths: 4.75- (.44 only), 5.75- (not available

Iver Johnson
Model 66 Trailsman

Iver Johnson
Model 67 Viking

Iver Johnson
Model 67S Viking Snub

Iver Johnson
Model 1900 Target

Iver Johnson
Cadet

in .44), 6- (.44 only), 7.5- or 12-inches bbl., weight: About 44 oz. Made from 1973 to 1978.
.357 Magnum or .45
  Colt w/12-inch bbl. . . . . **NiB $439 Ex $326 Gd $219**
.357 Magnum or .45

Iver Johnson
Cattleman

Iver Johnson
Champion .22 Target

Iver Johnson
Protector Sealed 8

Iver Johnson
Rookie

Iver Johnson
Safety Hammer

Colt w/5.75- or 7.5-inch bbl. NiB $342 Ex $255 Gd $158
.44 Magnum, w/12-inch bbl. . . NiB $459 Ex $367 Gd $279
.44 Magnum, other bbls.. . . . . . NiB $439 Ex $326 Gd $219

CATTLEMAN BUNTLINE SA REVOLVER
Same as Cattleman Buckhorn except has 18-inch bbl., walnut shoulder stock w/brass fittings. Weight: About 56 oz. Made from 1973 to 1978.

.44 Magnum . . . . NiB $443 Ex $332 Gd $225
Other calibers. . . . . NiB $443 Ex $332 Gd $225

CATTLEMAN
TRAIL BLAZER . . . . NiB $377 Ex $274 Gd $189
Similar to Cattleman Buckhorn except .22 caliber has interchangeable .22 LR and .22 WMR cylinders, 5.5- or 6.5-inch bbl., weight: About 40 oz. Made from 1973 to 1978.

CHAMPION 822
.22 TARGET SA . . . . NiB $499 Ex $326 Gd $175
Hinged frame. Caliber: .22 LR. Eight-round cylinder. Single action. Counterbored chambers as in Sealed 8 model, 6-inch bbl., 10.75 inches overall. Weight: 28 oz. Adj. target sights. Blued finish. Checkered walnut grips, adj. finger rest. Made from 1938 to 1948.

DELUXE TARGET. . . . . NiB $305 Ex $225 Gd $175
Same as Sportsman except has adj. sights. Made 1975-76.

PROTECTOR SEALED 8
DA REVOLVER . . . . NiB $453 Ex $337 Gd $204
Hinged frame. Caliber: .22 LR. Eight-round cylinder, 2.5-inch bbl., 7.25 inches overall. Weight: 20 oz. Fixed sights. Blued finish. Checkered walnut grips. Made from 1933 to 1949.

ROOKIE DA REVOLVER . . . . NiB $270 Ex $204 Gd $90
Solid frame. Caliber: .38 Special. Five-round cylinder, 4-inch bbl., 9-inches overall. Weight: 30 oz. Fixed sights. Blued or nickel finish. Plastic grips. Made from 1975 to 1977.

SAFETY HAMMER
DA REVOLVER . . . . NiB $342 Ex $170 Gd $105
Hinged frame. Calibers: .22 LR, .32 S&W, .32 S&W Long, .38 S&W. Seven-round cylinder in .22 cal.,or 6-round (.32 S&W Long), 5-round (.32 S&W, .38 S&W). bbl. lengths: 2, 3, 3.25, 4, 5 or 6 inches. Weight w/4-inch bbl.: 15 oz. (.22, .32 S&W), 19.5 oz. (.32 S&W Long) or 19 oz. (.38 S&W). Fixed sights. Blued or nickel finish. Hard rubber, round butt grips or square butt, rubber or walnut grips available. Note: .32 S&W Long and .38 S&W models built on heavy frame. Made 1892-1950.

SAFETY HAMMERLESS
DA REVOLVER . . . . NiB $337 Ex $219 Gd $129
Similar to the Safety Hammer Model except w/shrouded hammerless frame. Made from 1895 to 1950.

SIDEWINDER
DA REVOLVER. . . . . NiB $281 Ex $179 Gd $110
Solid frame. Caliber: .22 LR. Six- or 8-round cylinder, bbl. lengths: 4.75, 6 inches; 11.25 inches overall (with 6-inch bbl.). Weight: 31 oz. (with 6-inch bbl.). Fixed sights. Blued or nickel finish w/plastic staghorn grips or color-casehardened frame w/walnut grips. Note: Cylinder capacity changed from 8 to 6 rounds in 1975. Made from1961 to 1978

SIDEWINDER "S". . . . . NiB $281 Ex $179 Gd $110
Same as Sidewinder except has interchangeable cylinders in .22 LR and .22 WMR, adj. sights. Intro. 1974. Disc.

SPORTSMAN
DA REVOLVER . . . . NiB $222 Ex $165 Gd $109
Solid frame. Caliber: .22 LR. Six-round cylinder. Bbl. lengths: 4.75-, 6-inches, 10.75 inches overall (with 6-inch bbl.). Weight: 30.5 oz. (with 6-inch bbl.). Fixed sights. Blued finish. Plastic grips. Made 1974 to 1976.

**Iver Johnson
Sidewinder**

**Iver Johnson
Supershot Sealed 8**

Iver Johnson Target Sealed 8

SUPERSHOT .22 DA
REVOLVER . . . . NiB $273 Ex $175 Gd $119
Hinged frame. Caliber: .22 LR. Seven-round cylinder, 6-inch bbl. Fixed sights. Blued finish. Checkered walnut grips. This earlier model does not have counterbored chambers as in the Supershot Sealed 8. Made from 1929 to 1949.

SUPERSHOT 9
DA REVOLVER . . . . NiB $273 Ex $175 Gd $119
Same as Supershot Sealed 8 except has nine non-counterbored chambers. Made from 1929 to 1949.

SUPERSHOT
MODEL 844 DA . . . . NiB $336 Ex $204 Gd $129
Hinged frame. Caliber: .22 LR. Eight-round cylinder, bbl. lengths: 4.5- or 6-inch, 9.25 inches overall (with 4.5-inch bbl.). Weight: 27 oz. (4.5-inch bbl.). Adj. sights. Blued finish. Checkered walnut one-piece grip. Made 1955-56.

SUPERSHOT SEALED
8 DA REVOLVER . . . . NiB $316 Ex $180 Gd $140
Hinged frame. Caliber: .22 LR. Eight-round cylinder, 6-inch bbl., 10.75 inches overall. Weight: 24 oz. Adj. target sights. Blued finish. Checkered walnut grips. Postwar model does not have adj. finger rest as earlier version. Made 1931-57.

SWING-OUT DA REVOLVER
Calibers: .22 LR, .22 WMR, .32 S&W Long, .38 Special. Six-round cylinder in .22, 5-round in .32 and .38. Two, 3-, 4-inch plain bbl., or 4- 6-inch vent rib bbl., 8.75 inches overall (with 4-inch bbl.). Fixed or adj. sights. Blue or nickel finish. Walnut grips. Made in 1977.
w/plain barrel, fixed sights . . . . NiB $220 Ex $158 Gd $115
w/vent rib, adj. sights . . . . NiB $204 Ex $148 Gd $110

TARGET 9 DA REVOLVER . . . . . NiB $265 Ex $180 Gd $135
Same as Target Sealed 8 except has nine non-counterbored chambers. Made from 1929 to 1946.

TARGET SEALED
8 DA REVOLVER . . . . NiB $273 Ex $166 Gd $135
Solid frame. Caliber: .22 LR. Eight-round cylinder, bbl. lengths: 6- and 10-inches. 10.75 inches overall (with 6-inch bbl.).

Weight: 24 oz. (with 6-inch bbl.). Fixed sights. Blued finish. Checkered walnut grips. Made from 1931 to 1957.

TRIGGER-COCKING
SA TARGET . . . . NiB $321 Ex $239 Gd $187
Hinged frame. First pull on trigger cocks hammer, second pull releases hammer. Caliber: .22 LR. Eight-round cylinder, counterbored chambers, 6-inch bbl., 10.75 inches overall. Weight: 24 oz. Adj. target sights. Blued finish. Checkered walnut grips. Made 1940 to 1947.

KAHR ARMS — Worcester, MA
Formerly Pearl River, New York.

MODEL K9 DAO AUTO PISTOL
Caliber: 9mm Para. Seven-round magazine, 3.5-inch bbl., 6 inches overall. Weight: 24 oz. Fixed sights. Matte black, electroless nickel, Birdsong Black-T or matte stainless finish. Wraparound textured polymer or hardwood grips. Made from 1994 to 2003.
Duo-Tone finish . . . . NiB $587 Ex $464 Gd $321
Electroless nickel finish . . . . . . NiB $657 Ex $577 Gd $395
Black-T finish . . . . NiB $740 Ex $602 Gd $464
Matte stainless finish . . . . NiB $785 Ex $631 Gd $453
Kahr Lady K9 model . . . . NiB $530 Ex $345 Gd $270
Elite model . . . . NiB $836 Ex $610 Gd $399
Tritium Night Sights, add $100

MODEL K40 DAO AUTO PISTOL
Similar to Model K9 except chambered .40 S&W w/5- or 6-round magazine, Weight: 26 oz. Made from 1997 to 2003.
Matte black finish . . . . NiB $590 Ex $433 Gd $321
Electroless nickel finish . . . . . . NiB $668 Ex $595 Gd $395
Black-T finish . . . . NiB $740 Ex $562 Gd $362
Matte black stainless finish . . . . NiB $653 Ex $485 Gd $345
**Covert model
(shorter grip-frame)** . . . . NiB $536 Ex $395 Gd $306
Elite model . . . . NiB $826 Ex $602 Gd $437
Tritium Night Sights, add $100

MODEL MK9 DAO AUTO PISTOL
Similar to Model K9 except w/Micro-Compact frame. Six- or 7- round magazine, 3- inch bbl., 5.5 inches overall. Weight: 22 oz. Stainless or Duo-Tone finish. Made from 1993 to 2003.
Duo-Tone finish . . . . NiB $665 Ex $530 Gd $398
**Matte stainless
finish** . . . . NiB $437 Ex $347 Gd $301
Elite model . . . . NiB $830 Ex $544 Gd $429
Tritium Night Sights, add $100

Kahr Model K9

Kel-Tec Model P-11

CW SERIES DAO AUTO PISTOL NiB $425 Ex $325 Gd $250
Caliber: 9mm Para., .40 S&W, .45 ACP. Seven-round magazine (9mm Para), 3.6-inch bbl., 6 inches overall. Weight: 15.8 oz. Fixed sights. Textured black polymer frame, matte stainless steel slide. Made from 2005 (9mm para), 2008 (.40 S&W, .45 ACP).

CM SERIES DAO AUTO PISTOL NiB $450 Ex $350 Gd $250
Caliber: 9mm Para., .40 S&W, .45 ACP. Six-round magazine (9mm Para), 3-inch bbl., 6 inches overall. Weight: 15.8 oz. Fixed sights. Textured black polymer frame, matte stainless steel slide. Made from 2011 (9mm para), 2012 (.40 S&W), 2013 (.45 ACP).

E9 DAO AUTO PISTOL . . . . . . NiB $425 Ex $340 Gd $250
Caliber: 9mm Para. Seven-round magazine, 3.5-inch bbl., 6 inches overall. Weight: 15.8 oz. Fixed sights. Textured black polymer frame. Made from 1997, reintro. 2003.

MK MICRO SERIES
DAO AUTO PISTOL . . . . NiB $450 Ex $350 Gd $250
Caliber: 9mm Para., .40 S&W. Six-round magazine (9mm para), 3-inch bbl., 5.5 inches overall. Weight: 15.8 oz. Fixed sights., Matte stainless steel slide and frame. Made from 1998-99 (9mm para), intro. 1999 (.40 S&W).

T SERIES DAO AUTO PISTOL . . NiB $600 Ex $450 Gd $290
Caliber: 9mm Para., .40 S&W. 8-round magazine (9mm para), 4-inch bbl., 6.5 inches overall. Weight: 26 oz. Fixed sights., Matte stainless steel slide and frame, wood grips. Made from 2002 (9mm para), 2004 (.40 S&W).

TP SERIES DAO AUTO PISTOL . . . NiB $500 Ex $430 Gd $285
Similar to T series except polymer frame and matte stainless steel slide. Made from 2004.

KBI, INC — Harrisburg, PA

MODEL PSP-.25 AUTO PISTOL . . . NiB $308 Ex $244 Gd $157
Caliber: .25 ACP. Six-round magazine, 2.13-inch bbl., 4.13 inches overall. Weight: 9.5 oz. All-steel construction w/dual safety system. Made 1994.

KEL-TEC CNC INDUSTRIES, INC. — Cocoa, FL

P-11 DAO PISTOL
Caliber: 9mm Parabellum or .40 S&W. 10-round magazine, 3.1- inch bbl., 5.6 inches overall. Weight: 14 oz. Blade front sight, drift adjustable rear. Aluminum frame w/steel slide. Checkered black, gray, or green polymer grips. Matte blue, nickel, stainless steel or Parkerized finish. Made from 1995 to date.
9mm . . . . NiB $305 Ex $214 Gd $156
.40 S&W . . . . NiB $590 Ex $399 Gd $243
Parkerized finish, add $75
Nickel finish (disc. 1995) add $75
Stainless finish, (1996 to date) add $75
Tritium Night Sights, add $90
.40 S&W conversion kit, add $204

P-32 . . . . NiB $291 Ex $170 Gd $90
Semi-auto, double-action. Cal.: .32 ACP. Internal block safety. 7-round mag. Bbl.: 2.68 inches; Parkerized, blue, or chrome finish. Choice of ivory or colored grips. Weight: 6.6 oz.

P-3AT . . . . NiB $301 Ex $180 Gd $95
Similar to P-32. Cal.: .380 ACP. Bbl.: 2.76 inches. 6-round mag. Black composite frame with Parkerized steel slide. Weight: 8.3 oz.

P-40 . . . . NiB $290 Ex $175 Gd $88
Semi-auto, double-action. 9- or 10-round mag. Composite frame with steel slide. Bbl.: 3.3 inches. Parkerized, blue, or chrome finish. Made from 1999 to 2001.
Parkerized finish, add $50
Hard chrome finish, add. $70

PLR-16 . . . . NiB $638 Ex $495 Gd $281
M-16-type gas operated. Cal.: .223 Rem., 10-round mag. Bbl.: 9.2 inches. Upper w/Picatinny accessory rail. Black composite frame. Weight: 3.2 lbs.

PLR-22 . . . . NiB $357 Ex $265 Gd $170
Similar to PLR-16 except in .22 LR; 26-round mag. Weight: 2.8 lbs.

PF-9. . . . . NiB $306 Ex $198 Gd $143
Similar to P-11, cal.: 9 mm Para. Bbl.: 3.1 inches. 7-round mag., lower accessory rail. Black finish. Weight: 12.7 oz. Limited production in 2006, reintro. 2008.
Parkerized finish, add $50
Hard chrome finish, add. $65

Kimber Model Classic .45

PMR-30. . . . . NiB $408 Ex $301 Gd $189
Cal.: .22 Mag. Bbl.: 4.3 inches. 30-round mag, blowback action, manual safety. Picatinny accessory rail. Steel slide and bbl., fiber optic sights. Weight: 19.5 oz. Made 2010 to date.

KIMBER MANUFACTURING, INC. — Yonkers, NY
Formerly Kimber of America, Inc.

MODEL CLASSIC .45
Similar to Government 1911 built on steel, polymer or alloy full-size or compact frame. Caliber: .45 ACP. Seven-, 8-, 10- or 14-round magazine, 4- or 5-inch bbl., 7.7 or 8.75 inches overall. Weight: 28 oz. (Compact LW), 34 oz. (Compact or Polymer) or .38 oz. (Custom FS). McCormick low-profile combat or Kimber adj. target sights. Blued, matte black oxide or stainless finish. Checkered custom wood or black synthetic grips. Made from 1994 to date.
Custom (matte black) . . . . NiB $882 Ex $599 Gd $431
Custom Royal (polished blue) . . . . NiB $774 Ex $612 Gd $443
Custom stainless (satin stainless) . . . NiB $737 Ex $577 Gd $439
Custom Target (matte black) . . . NiB $755 Ex $581 Gd $453
Target Gold Match
    (polished blue) . . . . NiB $1020 Ex $755 Gd $587
Target stainless Match
    (polished stainless) . . . . NiB $852 Ex $669 Gd $474
Polymer (matte black) . . . . NiB $852 Ex $669 Gd $474
Polymer Stainless
    (satin stainless slide) . . . . NiB $967 Ex $784 Gd $577
Polymer Target
    (matte black slide) . . . . NiB $918 Ex $744 Gd $536
Compact (matte black) . . . . NiB $644 Ex $541 Gd $377
Compact stainless
    (satin stainless) . . . . NiB $714 Ex $559 Gd $437
Compact LW (matte
black w/alloy frame) . . . . NiB $733 Ex $577 Gd $408

SERIES II MODELS
Similar to Classic 1911 models except includes firing pin block safety and denoted with "II" following all model names. Size configurations vary per model and include from smallest to largest: Micro (2.75-in. bbl., micro frame), Ultra (3-in. bbl., short frame), Ultra+ (3-in. bbl., full size frame), Compact (4-in. bbl., short frame), Pro (4-in. bbl., full size frame), Custom (5-in. bbl., full size frame). Made from 2001 to date.
Aegis II (intro. 2006) . . . . . . NiB $1200 Ex $1140 Gd $840
CDP II (intro. 2000) . . . . NiB $1150 Ex $1095 Gd $805
Compact II . . . . NiB $960 Ex $912 Gd $500
Covert II (intro. 2007) . . . . . NiB $1450 Ex $1100 Gd $650
Crimson Cary II (laser grip) . . NiB $1050 Ex $900 Gd $735
Custom II . . . . NiB $730 Ex $525 Gd $330
Custom II Stainless . . . . NiB $855 Ex $655 Gd $365
Custom Royal II . . . . NiB $1900 Ex $1000 Gd $580
Eclipse II (intro. 2002) . . . . $1100 Ex $1045 Gd $570
Gold Match II . . . . NiB $1300 Ex $1000 Gd $580
Master Carry II (intro. 2013). . . . NiB $1330 Ex $1265 Gd $931
Micro Carry
    (intro. 2013, .380 ACP) . . . . NiB $580 Ex $475 Gd $375
Raptor II (intro. 2004) . . . . . NiB $1300 Ex $1235 Gd $910
Super Carry II (intro. 2010). . . NiB $1350 Ex $1285 Gd $945
Tactical II (intro. 2003). . . . . NiB $1130 Ex $1075 Gd $795
Ultra Carry II (intro. 1999). . . . NiB $800 Ex $760 Gd $560
Custom Royal II . . . . NiB $1900 Ex $1000 Gd $580

MODEL MICRO SERIES
Scaled down 1911-style. Semi-automatic. SA. Caliber: .380 ACP, 7-rnd magazine. 2.75-in. bbl. Frame: aluminum. Sights: steel fixed. Finish: numerous. Grip: numerous. Weight: 13 oz. Length: 5.6 in. Made from 2012 to date.
Laser grip, add $200
Bel Air (turquoise frame/stainless slide,
    ivory micarta grip) . . . . NiB $802 Ex $790 Gd $690
Carry Advocate
    (two-tone finish, brown or purple grip) . NiB $714 Ex $700
    Gd $680
Crimson Carry (two-tone finish,
    laser grip) . . . . NiB $839 Ex $800 Gd $710
CDP (two-tone, rosewood grip) NiB $869 Ex $800 Gd $610
DC (matte black, rosewood grip) . . . NiB $877 Ex $810 Gd $710
Diamond (matte stainless frame/engraved slide,
    ivory micarta grip) . . . . NiB $1013 Ex $1000 Gd $980
Raptor (matte black,
    zebrawood grip) . . . . NiB $815 Ex $800 Gd $780
Raptor Stainless
    (stainless finish) . . . . NiB $842 Ex $810 Gd $790
RCP (matte black,
    rosewood grip) . . . . NiB $775 Ex $710 Gd $680
Sapphire (stainless frame/blue engraved slide,
    blue G10 grip) . . . . NiB $1013 Ex $1000 Gd $980
Stainless (stainless finish, rosewood
    grip) . . . . NiB $597 Ex $560 Gd $500
Two-Tone (rosewood grip) . . . . NiB $597 Ex $580 Gd $500

MODEL MICRO 9 SERIES
Similar to Micro except in 9mm, 6-rnd. magazine. Made from 2015 to date.
Crimson Carry (two-tone finish,
    laser grip) . . . . NiB $894 Ex $870 Gd $720
Stainless (stainless finish,
    rosewood grip) . . . . NiB $654 Ex $610 Gd $570
Two-Tone finish
    (rosewood grip) . . . . NiB $654 Ex $610 Gd $570

MODEL SOLO SERIES
Hammerless design. Semi-automatic. DAO striker firer. Caliber: .380 ACP, 7-rnd magazine. 2.7-in. bbl. Frame: aluminum. Sights: steel fixed, 3-dot. Finish: numerous. Grip: numerous. Weight: 17 oz. Length: 5.6 in. Made from 2012 to date.
Laser grip, add $200
Carry (black frame/stainless slide,
    black checkered synthetic) . . . NiB $815 Ex $800 Gd $770
CDP LG (two-tone, laser grip) . . . NiB $1223 Ex $1100 Gd $920
Crimson Carry (two-tone finish,
    laser grip) . . . . NiB $1073 Ex $1000 Gd $960

DC (matte black, black checkered
  micarta) . . . . NiB $904 Ex $890 Gd $800
Sapphire (stainless frame/blue engraved slide,
  blue G10 grip) . . . . NiB $1291 Ex $1200 Gd $990
Stainless (stainless finish, black
  checkered synthetic) . . . . . . NiB $815 Ex $800 Gd $770

Lahti Automatic Pistol

KORTH — Lollar, Germany

Previously Ratzeburg, Germany. Currently imported by Korth USA (Earl's Repair Service, Tewkberry, MA). Previously by Keng's Firearms Specialty, Inc., Beeman Precision Arms; Osborn Beeman Precision Arms; Osborne's and Mandall Shooting Supply.

REVOLVERS COMBAT, SPORT, TARGET
Calibers: .357 Mag. and .22 LR w/interchangeable combination cylinders of .357 Mag./9mm Para. or .22 LR/.22 WMR also .22 Jet, .32 S&W and .32 H&R Mag. Bbls: 2.5-, 3-, 4-inch (combat) and 5.25- or 6-inch (target). Weight: 33 to 42 oz. Blued, stainless, matte silver or polished silver finish. Checkered walnut grips. Imported 1967 to date.
Standard rimfire model. . . . NiB $4590 Ex $2735 Gd $1895
Standard centerfire model . NiB $6899 Ex $5100 Gd $4029
ISU Match Target model . . . NiB $7429 Ex $5433 Gd $3329
Custom stainless finish, add $485
Matte silver finish, add $689
Polished silver finish, add $950

SEMI-AUTOMATIC PISTOL
Calibers: 30 Luger, 9mm Para., .357 SIG, .40 S&W, 9x21mm. 10- or 14-round magazine, 4- or 5-inch bbl., all-steel construction, recoil-operated. Ramp front sight, adj. rear. Blued, stainless, matte silver or polished silver finish. Checkered walnut grips. Limited import from 1988 .
Standard model . . . . NiB $6495 Ex $5040 Gd $3934
Matte silver finish, add $332
Polished silver finish, add $791

KRISS USA — Chesapeake, VA

North American extension of the Switzerland based KRISS Group.

MODEL VECTOR SPD . . . . NiB $1349 Ex $1300 Gd $1200
Semi-automatic. Multi-caliber platform. Closed bolt delayed blow-beck system design for minimal recoil. Caliber: 9mm or .45 ACP, 17- or 15-rnd 9mm, 13- or 25-rnd .45 ACP, uses Glock magazine. 5.5-in. bbl., threaded muzzle. Frame: polymer. Sights: flip-up adj. Finish: matte black. Grip: textured polymer. Weight: 5.9 lbs. Length: 16.75 in. Imported from 2011 to date.
Alpine, FDE, or ODG finish, add $70

LAHTI — Sweden & Finland
Mfd. by Husqvarna Vapenfabriks A. B. Huskvarna, Sweden, and Valtion Kivaar Tedhas ("VKT") Jyväskyla, Finland.

AUTOMATIC PISTOL
Caliber: 9mm Para. Eight-round magazine, 4.75-inch bbl., weight: About 46 oz. Fixed sights. Blued finish. Plastic grips. Specifications given are those of the Swedish Model 40 but also apply in general to the Finnish Model L-35, which differs only slightly. A considerable number of Swedish Lahti pistols were imported and sold in the U.S. The Finnish

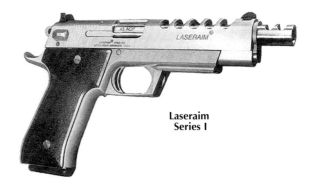

Laseraim
Series I

model, somewhat better made, is rare. Finnish Model L-35 adopted 1935. Swedish Model 40 adopted 1940, mfd. through 1944.
Finnish L-35 model
  (1st Variation). . . . . NiB $4120 Ex $3020 Gd $2455
Swedish 40 model. . . . . NiB $648 Ex $449 Gd $332

L.A.R. MANUFACTURING, INC. — West Jordan, UT

MARK I GRIZZLY WIN. MAG. AUTOMATIC PISTOL
Calibers: .357 Mag., .45 ACP, .45 Win. Mag. Seven-round magazine, 6.5-inch bbl., 10.5 inches overall. Weight: 48 oz. Fully adj. sights. Checkered rubber combat-style grips. Blued finish. Made from 1983 to date. 8- or 10-inch bbl., Made from 1987 to 1999.
.357 Mag. (6.5 inch barrel). . . . NiB $918 Ex $643 Gd $434
.45 Win. Mag.(6.5 inch barrel) NiB $918 Ex $740 Gd $444
8-inch barrel. . . . . NiB $1237 Ex $1040 Gd $943
10-inch barrel. . . . . NiB $1320 Ex $1118 Gd $1029

MARK 4 GRIZZLY
AUTOMATIC PISTOL . . . . NiB $918 Ex $740 Gd $629
Same general specifications as the L.A.R. Mark I except chambered for .44 Magnum, has 5.5- or 6.5-inch bbl., beavertail grip safety, matte blued finish. Made from 1991 to 1999.

MARK 5 AUTO PISTOL. . . . . . NiB $918 Ex $734 Gd $631
Similar to the Mark I except chambered in 50 Action Express. Six-round magazine, 5.4- or 6.5-inch bbl., 10.6 inches overall (with 5.4-inch bbl.). Weight: 56 oz. Checkered walnut grips. Made 1993 to 1999.

L.A.R. Mark I Grizzly

**Laseraim
Series II**

**Laseraim Series III
w/LA93 Illusion III scope**

**Llama Model IIIA
Deluxe Chrome Engraved First Issue**

LASERAIM TECHNOLOGIES, INC. — Little Rock, AR

Series I SA Auto Pistol Calibers: .40 S&W, .45 ACP, 10mm. Seven or 8- round magazine, 3.875- or 5.5-inch dual-port compensated bbl., 8.75 or 10.5 inches overall. Weight: 46 or 52 oz. Fixed sights w/Laseraim or adjustable Millet sights. TExtured black composition grips. Extended slide release, ambidExtrous safety and beveled magazine well. Stainless or matte black Teflon finish. Made from 1993 to 1999.

Series I w/adjustable sights.... NiB $362 Ex $255 Gd $188
Series I w/fixed sights .... NiB $362 Ex $255 Gd $188
Series I w/fixed sights (HotDot).. NiB $479 Ex $270 Gd $203
Series I Dream Team (RedDot).. NiB $479 Ex $ 270 Gd $203
Series I Illusion (Laseraim) .... NiB $479 Ex $270 Gd $203

SERIES II SA AUTO PISTOL
Similar to Series I except w/stainless finish and no bbl., compensator. Made from 1993 to 1996.
Series II w/adjustable sights ... NiB $530 Ex $365 Gd $265
Series II w/fixed sights ...... NiB $530 Ex $365 Gd $265
Series II Dream Team .... NiB $602 Ex $437 Gd $279
Series II Illusion .... NiB $540 Ex $439 Gd $321

SERIES III SA AUTO PISTOL
Similar to Series II except w/serrated slide and 5-inch compensated bbl., only. Made 1994. Disc.
Series III w/adjustable sights .. NiB $632 Ex $536 Gd $398
Series III w/fixed sights....... NiB $632 Ex $599 Gd $362

VELOCITY SERIES SA AUTO PISTOL
Similar to Series I except chambered for .357 Sig. or .400 Cor-Bon, 3.875-inch unported bbl., (compact) or 5.5-inch dual-port compensated bbl. Made from 1993 to 1999. See illustration previous page.
Compact model (unported).... NiB $362 Ex $290 Gd $204
Government model (ported)... NiB $362 Ex $290 Gd $204
w/wireless laser (HotDot), add.................... $175

LIGNOSE — Suhl, Germany
Aktien-Gesellschaft "Lignose" Abteilung
The following Lignose pistols were manufactured from 1920 to the mid-1930s. They were also marketed under the Bergmann name.

EINHAND MODEL 2A
POCKET AUTO PISTOL ...... NiB $434 Ex $305 Gd $209
As the name implies, this pistol is designed for one-hand operation, pressure on a "trigger" at the front of the guard retracts the slide. Caliber: .25 Auto. (6.35 mm). Six-round magazine, 2-inch bbl., 4.75 inches overall. Weight: About 14 oz. Blued finish. Hard rubber grips.

MODEL 2 POCKET
AUTO PISTOL.............. NiB $362 Ex $237 Gd $175
Conventional Browning type. Same general specifications as Einhand Model 2A but lacks the one-hand operation.

EINHAND MODEL
3A POCKET AUTO PISTOL.... NiB $479 Ex $369 Gd $270
Same as the Model 2A except has longer grip, 9-round magazine, weight: About 16 oz.

LLAMA — Vitoria, Spain
Manufactured by Gabilondo y Cia, Vitoria, Spain, imported by S.G.S., Wanamassa, New Jersey.

**Llama Model IIIA
Deluxe Blue Engraved Second Issue**

Llama Model XA First Issue

NOTE: *For ease in finding a particular Llama handgun, the listings are divided into two groupings: Automatic Pistols (below) and Revolvers, which follow. For a complete listing of Llama handguns, please refer to the index.*

-AUTOMATIC PISTOLS -

MODEL IIIA
AUTOMATIC PISTOL . . . . NiB $337 Ex $170 Gd $109
Caliber: .380 Auto. Seven-round magazine, 3.69-inch bbl., 6.5 inches overall. Weight: 23 oz. Adj. target sights. Blued finish. Plastic grips. Intro. 1951. Disc.

MODELS IIIA, XA, XV DELUXE
Same as standard Model IIIA, XA and XV except engraved w/ blued or chrome finish and simulated pearl grips.
Chrome-engraved finish . . . . . . NiB $365 Ex $306 Gd $219
Blue-engraved finish . . . . NiB $356 Ex $290 Gd $204

Llama Model CE-IIIA

MODEL VIII
AUTOMATIC PISTOL . . . . NiB $377 Ex $306 Gd $255
Caliber: .38 Super. Nine-round magazine, 5-inch bbl., 8.5 inches overall. Weight: 40 oz. Fixed sights. Blued finish. Wood grips. Intro. in 1952. Disc.

MODELS VIII, IXA, XI DELUXE
Same as standard Models VIII, IXA and XI except finish (chrome engraved or blued engraved) and simulated pearl grips. Disc. 1984.
Chrome-engraved finish . . . . . . NiB $377 Ex $290 Gd $190
Blue-engraved finish . . . . NiB $377 Ex $290 Gd $190

MODEL IXA
AUTOMATIC PISTOL . . . . NiB $377 Ex $290 Gd $190
Same as model VIII except .45 Auto, 7-round magazine,

MODEL XA
AUTOMATIC PISTOL . . . . NiB $377 Ex $290 Gd $190
Same as model IIIA except .32 Auto, 8-round magazine,

MODEL XI
AUTOMATIC PISTOL . . . . NiB $377 Ex $290 Gd $190
Same as model VIII except 9mm Para.

MODEL XV

Llama Model Compact

AUTOMATIC PISTOL . . . . NiB $321 Ex $255 Gd $170
Same as model XA except .22 LR.

MODELS BE-IIIA,
BE-XA, BE-XV . . . . NiB $530 Ex $332 Gd $235
Same as models IIIA, XA and XV except w/blued-engraved fin-

Llama Model C-XI

Llama M-82
DA Auto

ish. Made from 1977-84.

MODELS BE-VIII,
BE-IXA, BE-XI DELUXE . . . . NiB $530 Ex $398 Gd $281
Same as models VIII, IXA and XI except w/blued-engraved finish. Made from 1977 to 1984.

MODELS C-IIIA, C-XA, C-XV . . NiB $408 Ex $365 Gd $259
Same as models IIIA, XA and XV except in satin chrome.

MODELS C-VIII, C-IXA, C-XI . . NiB $475 Ex $357 Gd $244
Same as models VIII, IXA and XI except in satin chrome.

MODELS CE-IIIA,
CE-XA, CE-XV . . . . NiB $398 Ex $347 Gd $230
Same as models IIIA, XA and XV except w/chrome engraved finish. Made from 1977 to 1984.

MODELS CE-VIII,
CE-IXA, CE-XI . . . . NiB $475 Ex $357 Gd $244
Same as models VIII, IXA and XI, w/except chrome engraved finish. Made from 1977 to 1984.

COMPACT FRAME
AUTO PISTOL. . . . . NiB $345 Ex $270 Gd $204
Calibers: 9mm Para., .38 Super, .45 Auto. Seven-, 8- or 9-round magazine, 5-inch bbl., 7.88 inches overall. Weight: 34 oz. Blued, satin-chrome or Duo-Tone finishes. Made from 1986 to 1997. Duo-Tone disc. 1993.

DUO-TONE LARGE
FRAME AUTO PISTOL . . . . NiB $449 Ex $368 Gd $305
Caliber: .45 ACP. Seven-round magazine, 5-inch bbl., 8.5 inches overall. Weight: 36 oz. Adj. rear sight. Blued finished

w/satin chrome. Polymer black grips. Made from 1991 to 1993.

DUO-TONE SMALL
FRAME AUTO PISTOL . . . . NiB $306 Ex $209 Gd $150
Calibers: .22 LR, .32 and .380 Auto. Seven- or 8-round magazine, 3.69 inch bbl., 6.5 inches overall. Weight: 23 oz. Square-notch rear sight, Partridge-type front. Blued finish w/chrome. Made from 1990 to 1993.

MODEL G-IIIA DELUXE . . . NiB $2520 Ex $1944 Gd $1659
Same as Model IIIA except gold damascened w/simulated pearl grips. Disc. 1982.

LARGE-FRAME AUTOMATIC PISTOL (IXA)
Caliber: .45 Auto. 7-rnd. magazine, 5-in. bbl., weight: 2 lbs., 8 oz. Adj. rear sight, Partridge-type front. Walnut grips or teakwood on satin chrome model. Later models w/polymer grips.
Blued finish. . . . . NiB $369 Ex $258 Gd $198
Satin chrome finish. . . . . NiB $538 Ex $444 Gd $290

M-82 DA
AUTOMATIC PISTOL . . . . NiB $587 Ex $398 Gd $270
Caliber: 9mm Para. 15-round magazine, 4.25-inch bbl., 8 inches overall. Weight: 39 oz. Drift-adj. rear sight. Matte blued finish. Matte black polymer grips. Made from 1988 to 1993.

M-87 COMPETITION
PISTOL . . . . NiB $1029 Ex $816 Gd $634
Caliber: 9mm Para. 15-round magazine, 5.5-inch bbl., 9.5 inches overall. Weight: 40 oz. Low-profile combat sights. Satin nickel finish. Matte black grip panels. Built-in ported compensator to minimize recoil and muzzle rise. Made 1989-93.

MICRO-MAX SA AUTOMATIC PISTOL
Caliber: .380 ACP. Seven-round magazine, 3.125-inch bbl., weight: 23 oz. Blade front sight, drift adjustable rear w/3-dot system. Matte blue or satin chrome finish. Checkered polymer grips. Imported from 1997 to 2005.
Matte blue finish. . . . . NiB $281 Ex $204 Gd $165
Satin chrome finish. . . . . NiB $288 Ex $230 Gd $219

MINI-MAX SA AUTOMATIC PISTOL
Calibers: 9mm, .40 S&W or .45 ACP. Six- or 8-round magazine, 3.5-inch bbl., 8.3 inches overall. Weight: 35 oz. Blade front sight, drift adjustable rear w/3-dot system. Matte blue, Duo-Tone or satin chrome finish. Checkered polymer grips. Imported 1996 to 2005. Reintroduced 2016 to date.
Duo-Tone finish . . . . NiB $290 Ex $204 Gd $158
Matte blue finish. . . . . NiB $306 Ex $220 Gd $170
Satin chrome finish. . . . . NiB $326 Ex $240 Gd $190
Stainless (disc.) . . . . NiB $359 Ex $301 Gd $235

MINI-MAX II SA AUTOMATIC PISTOL
Cal: .45 ACP only. 10-round mag., 3.625 inch bbl., 7.375 inch overall. Wt: 37 oz. Blade front sight, drift adj. rear w/3-dot system. Shortened barrel and grip. Matte and Satin Chrome finish. Imp. 2005.
Matte blue finish. . . . . NiB $290 Ex $225 Gd $170
Satin chrome finish. . . . . NiB $316 Ex $255 Gd $189

MAX-I SA AUTOMATIC PISTOL
Calibers: 9mm or .45 ACP. 7- or 9-round magazine, 4.25- to 5.125-inch bbl., weight: 34 or 36 oz. Blade front sight, drift adj.

Llama MINI-MAX II

Llama MAX-I

Llama Comanche I

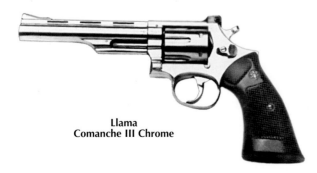

Llama Comanche III Chrome

rear w/3-dot system. Matte blue, Duo-Tone or satin chrome finish. Checkered black rubber grips. Imported from 1995 to 1999. Reintroduced 2016 to date.

Duo-Tone finish . . . . NiB $306 Ex $265 Gd $198
Matte blue finish. . . . . NiB $301 Ex $240 Gd $189
Satin chrome finish . . . . NiB $316 Ex $270 Gd $219

MAX-II SA AUTOMATIC PISTOL
Same as the MAX-I with 4.25 bbl. except w/10-round mag. Weight 40 oz., made 2005.
Matte blue finish. . . . . NiB $306 Ex $265 Gd $198
Satin chrome finish . . . . NiB $332 Ex $270 Gd $219

OMNI 45 DOUBLE-ACTION
AUTOMATIC PISTOL . . . . NiB $437 Ex $291 Gd $220
Caliber: .45 Auto. Seven-round magazine, 4.25-inch bbl., 7.75 inches overall. Weight: 40 oz. Adj. rear sight, ramp front. Highly polished deep blued finish. Made from 1984-86.

OMNI 9MM DOUBLE-ACTION
AUTOMATIC. . . . . NiB $469 Ex $347 Gd $290
Same general specifications as .45 Omni except chambered for 9mm w/13-round magazine. Made from 1983-86.

SINGLE-ACTION
AUTOMATIC PISTOL . . . . NiB $485 Ex $386 Gd $270
Calibers: .38 Super, 9mm, .45 Auto. Nine-round magazine (7-round for .45 Auto), 5-inch bbl., 8.5 inches overall. Weight: 2 lbs., 8 oz. Intro. in 1981.

SMALL-FRAME AUTOMATIC PISTOL
Calibers: .380 Auto (7-round magazine), .22 RF (8-round magazine), 3.69-inch bbl., weight: 23 oz. Partridge-blade front sight, adj. rear. Blued or satin-chrome finish. Disc. 1997.
Blued finish. . . . . NiB $255 Ex $204 Gd $165
Satin-chrome finish . . . . NiB $270 Ex $220 Gd $175

- REVOLVERS -

MARTIAL DOUBLE-
ACTION REVOLVER . . . . NiB $255 Ex $170 Gd $120
Calibers: .22 LR, .38 Special. Six-round cylinder, bbl. lengths: 4-inch (.38 Special only) or 6-inch; 11.25 inches overall (w/6-inch bbl.). Weight: About 36 oz. w/6-inch bbl. Target sights. Blued finish. Checkered walnut grips. Made from 1969 to 1976.

MARTIAL DOUBLE-ACTION DELUXE
Same as standard Martial except w/satin chrome, chrome-engraved, blued engraved or gold damascened finish. Simulated pearl grips. Made from 1969 to 1976.
Satin-chrome finish . . . . NiB $306 Ex $225 Gd $165
Chrome-engraved finish . . . . . . NiB $581 Ex $431 Gd $286
Blue-engraved finish . . . . NiB $638 Ex $453 Gd $332
Gold-damascened finish . . . NiB $2810 Ex $2647 Gd $2299

COMANCHE I . . . . NiB $270 Ex $204 Gd $160
Same general specifications as Martial .22. Made 1977 to 1982.

COMANCHE II . . . . NiB $265 Ex $189 Gd $150
Same general specifications as Martial .38. Made 1977-82.

COMANCHE III . . . . NiB $306 Ex $219 Gd $144
Caliber: .357 Magnum. Six-round cylinder, 4-inch bbl., 9.25 inches overall. Weight: 36 oz. Adj. rear sight, ramp front. Blued finish. Checkered walnut grips. Made from 1975 to 1995. Note: Prior to 1977, this model was designated

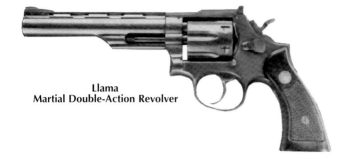

Llama
Martial Double-Action Revolver

Luger 1900
American Eagle

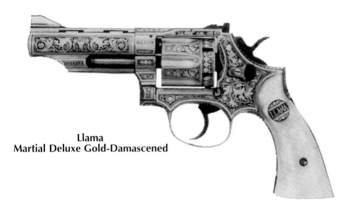

Llama
Martial Deluxe Gold-Damascened

LORCIN ENGINEERING CO., INC. — Mira Loma, CA

MODEL L-22
SEMIAUTOMATIC PISTOL . . . . . . NiB $120 Ex $90 Gd $70
Caliber: 22 LR. Nine-round magazine, 2.5-inch bbl., 5.25 inches overall. Weight: 16 oz. Blade front sight, fixed notch rear w/3-dot system. Black Teflon or chrome finish. Black, pink or pearl composition grips. Made from 1990 to 1998.

MODEL L-25, LT-.25 SEMIAUTOMATIC PISTOL
Caliber: 25 ACP. Seven-round magazine, 2.4-inch bbl., 4.8 inches overall. Weight: 12 oz. (LT-25) or 14.5 oz. (L-25). Blade front sight, fixed rear. Black Teflon or chrome finish. Black, pink or pearl composition grips. Made from 1989-98.
Model L-25 . . . . NiB $89 Ex $61 Gd $40
Model LT-25 . . . . NiB $79 Ex $50 Gd $35
Model Lady Lorcin . . . . NiB $81 Ex $55 Gd $35

MODEL L-32
SEMIAUTOMATIC PISTOL . . . . NiB $90 Ex $65 Gd $50
Caliber: 32 ACP. Seven-round magazine, 3.5-inch bbl., 6.6 inches overall. Weight: 27 oz. Blade front sight, fixed notch rear. Black Teflon or chrome finish. Black composition grips. Made from 1992 to 1998.

MODEL L-380 SEMIAUTOMATIC PISTOL
Caliber: .380 ACP. Seven- or 10-round magazine, 3.5-inch bbl., 6.6 inches overall. Weight: 23 oz. Blade front sight, fixed notch rear. Matte Black finish. Grooved black composition grips. Made 1994 to 1998.
Model L-380 (10-round) . . . . NiB $158 Ex $95 Gd $65
Model L-380 (13-round) . . . . NiB $128 Ex $90 Gd $61

MODEL L9MM SEMIAUTOMATIC PISTOL
Caliber: 9mm Parabellum. 10- or 13-round magazine, 4.5-inch bbl., 7.5 inches overall. Weight: 31 oz. Blade front sight, fixed notch rear w/3-dot system. Black Teflon or chrome finish. Black composition grips. Made from 1992 to 1998.
Model L-9mm (7-round) . . . . NiB $158 Ex $95 Gd $65
Model L-9mm (10-round) . . . . NiB $158 Ex $95 Gd $65

O/U DERRINGER . . . . NiB $198 Ex $105 Gd $70
Caliber: .38 Special/.357 Mag., .45LC. Two-round derringer. 3.5-inch bbls. 6.5 inches overall. Weight: 12 oz. Blade front sight, fixed notch rear. Stainless finish. Black composition grips. Made from 1996-98.

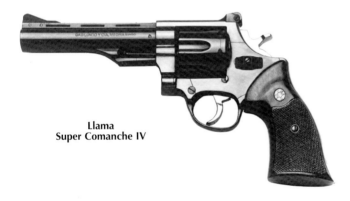

Llama
Super Comanche IV

"Comanche."

COMANCHE III CHROME . . . . NiB $362 Ex $270 Gd $204
Same gen. specifications as Comanche III except has satin chrome finish, 4- or 6-inch bbl. Made from 1975 to 1995.

SUPER COMANCHE IV . . . . . . NiB $388 Ex $301 Gd $204
Caliber: .44 Magnum. Six-round cylinder, 6-inch bbl., 11.75 inches overall. Weight: 50 oz. Adj. rear sight, ramp front. Polished deep blued finish. Checkered walnut grips. Disc. 1998.

SUPER COMANCHE V . . . . NiB $362 Ex $270 Gd $214
Caliber: .357 Mag. Six-round cylinder, 4-, 6- or 8.5-inch bbl., weight: 48 ozs. Ramped front blade sight, click-adj. Rear. Made from 1980 to 1988.

LUGER — Manufactured by Deutsche Waffen und Munitionsfabriken (DWM), Berlin, Germany

1900 AMERICAN EAGLE . . **NiB $6900 Ex $6555 Gd $4830**
Caliber: 7.65 mm. Eight-round magazine; thin, 4.75-inch; tapered bbl.; 9.5 inches overall. Weight: 32 oz. Fixed rear sight, dovetailed front sight. Grip safety. Checkered walnut grips. Early-style toggle, narrow trigger, wide guard, no stock lug. American Eagle over chamber. Estimated 8,000 production.

1900 COMMERCIAL. . . . . **NiB $6910 Ex $6565 Gd $4837**
Same specifications as Luger 1900 American Eagle except DWM on early-style toggle, no chamber markings. Estimated 8000 production.

1900 SWISS . . . . **NiB $6700 Ex $6365 Gd $4700**
Same specifications as Luger 1900 American Eagle except Swiss cross in sunburst over chamber. Estimated 9,000 production.

1902 AMERICAN EAGLE. . . **NiB $16,650 Ex $14,000 Gd $12,990**
Caliber: 9mm Para. Eight-round magazine, 4-inch heavy tapered bbl., 8.75 inches overall. Weight: 30 oz. Fixed rear sight, dovetailed front sight. Grip safety. Checkered walnut grips. American Eagle over chamber, DWM on early-style toggle, narrow trigger, wide guard, no stock lug. Estimated 700 production.

1902 CARBINE
Caliber: 7.65mm. Eight-round magazine, 11.75-inch tapered bbl., 16.5 inches overall. Weight: 46 oz. Adj. 4-position rear sight, long ramp front sight. Grip safety. Checkered walnut grips and forearm. DWM on early-style toggle, narrow trigger, wide guard, no chamber markings, stock lug. Estimated 3,200 production.
Model 1902 carbine
   (gun only) . . . . **NiB $12,245 Ex $11,353 Gd $7015**
Model 1902 carbine
   (gun only, American Eagle), add **45%**
w/issued stock and matching numbers, add **20%**
w/original stock and non-matching numbers, deduct. . . **20%**

1902 CARTRIDGE
COUNTER. . . . . **NiB $45,200 Ex $38,990 Gd $29,900**
Caliber: 9mm Para. Eight-round magazine, Heavy, tapered 4-inch bbl., 8.75 inches overall. Weight: 30 oz. Fixed rear sight, dovetailed front sight. Grip safety. Checkered walnut grips. DWM on dished toggle w/lock, American Eagle over chamber when marked. No stock lug. Estimated production unknown.

1902 COMMERCIAL . . . **NiB $13,600 Ex $10,895 Gd $5,500**
Same basic specifications as Luger 1902 Cartridge Counter except DWM on early-style toggle, narrow trigger, wide guard, no chamber markings, no stock lug. Estimated 400 production.

1902 AMERICAN EAGLE . . . **NiB $16,600 Ex $13,995 Gd $7,900**
Same basic specifications as Luger 1902 Commercial except American Eagle over chamber, DWM on early-style toggle, narrow trigger, wide guard, no stock lug. Estimated 700 production.

1902 AMERICAN EAGLE CARTRIDGE
COUNTER. . . . . **NiB $45,200 Ex $38,650 Gd $15,088**
Same basic specifications as Luger 1902 Cartridge Counter except American Eagle over chamber, DWM on early-style toggle, narrow trigger, wide guard, no stock lug. Estimated 700 production.

1904 GL "BABY" . . **NiB $197,500 Ex $166,000 Gd $110,000**
Caliber: 9mm Para. Seven-round magazine, 3.25-inch bbl., 7.75 inches overall. Weight: Approx. 20 oz. Serial number

10077B. "GL" marked on rear of toggle. Georg Luger's personal sidearm. Only one made in 1904.

1904 NAVAL
(REWORKED) . . . . **NiB $14,000 Ex $11,000 Gd $8,250**
Caliber: 9mm Para. Eight-round magazine, bbl., length altered to 4 inches., 8.75 inches overall. Weight: 30 oz. Adj. two-position rear sight, dovetailed front sight. Thumb lever safety. Checkered walnut grips. Heavy tapered bbl., DWM on new-style toggle w/lock, 1902 over chamber. w/or without grip safety and stock lug. Estimated 800 production. Untouched original (rare) worth $50,000.

1906 (11.35MM). . . **NiB $119,000 Ex $95,900 Gd $66,500**
Caliber: .45 ACP. Six-round magazine, 5-inch bbl., 9.75 inches overall. Weight: 36 oz. Fixed rear sight, dovetailed front sight. Grip safety. Checkered walnut grips. GL monogram on rear toggle link, larger frame w/altered trigger guard and trigger, no proofs, no markings over chamber. No stock lug. Only two were known to be made. Note: This version of the Luger pistol is the most valuable nExt to the "GL" Baby Luger.

1906 AMERICAN EAGLE
(7.65MM) . . . . **NiB $4235 Ex $3300 Gd $2200**
Caliber: 7.65mm. Eight-round magazine, thin 4.75-inch tapered bbl., 9.5 inches overall. Weight: 32 oz. Fixed rear sight, dovetailed front sight. Grip safety. Checkered walnut grips. DWM on new-style toggle, American Eagle over chamber. No stock lug. Estimated 8,000 production.

1906 AMERICAN EAGLE (9MM). . . **NiB $4600 Ex $4370 Gd $2000**
Same basic specifications as the 7.65mm 1906 except in 9mm Para. w/4-inch barrel, 8.75 inches overall, weight: 30 oz. Estimated 3,500 production.

1906 BERN (7.65MM). . . . . **NiB $4430 Ex $2520 Gd $1996**
Same basic specifications as the 7.65mm 1906 American Eagle except checkered walnut grips w/.38-inch borders, Swiss Cross on new-style toggle, Swiss proofs, no markings over chamber, no stock lug. Estimated 17,874 production.

1906 BRAZILIAN (7.65MM) . . . . **NiB $3550 Ex $3375 Gd $1910**
Same general specifications as the 7.65mm 1906 American Eagle except w/Brazilian proofs, no markings over chamber, no stock lug. Estimated 4,500 produced.

1906 BRAZILIAN (9MM) . . **NiB $1691 Ex $1390 Gd $1039**
Same basic specifications as the 9mm 1906 American Eagle except w/Brazilian proofs, no markings over chamber, no stock lug. Production fewer than 4,000 estimated.

1906 COMMERCIAL. . . . . . **NiB $4000 Ex $3400 Gd $1500**
Calibers: 7.65mm or 9mm. Same specifications as the 1906 American Eagle versions (above) except no chamber markings and no stock lug. Estimated production: 6,000 (7.65mm) and 3,500 (9mm).

1906 DUTCH . . . . **NiB $4200 Ex $3699 Gd $2809**
Caliber: 9mm Para. Same specifications as the 9mm 1906 American Eagle except tapered bbl., w/proofs, no markings over chamber, no stock lug. Arsenal rework. Estimated 3,000 production.
Original finish, add **100%**
1906 LOEWE
AND COMPANY. . . . . **NiB $4823 Ex $3899 Gd $2744**
Caliber: 7.65mm. Eight-round magazine, 6-inch tapered bbl.,

10.75 inches overall. Weight: 35 oz. Adj. two-position rear sight, dovetailed front sight. Grip safety. Checkered walnut grips. Loewe & Company over chamber, Naval proofs, DWM on new-style toggle, no stock lug. Estimated production unknown.

1906 NAVY
Caliber: 9mm Para. Eight-round magazine, 6-inch tapered bbl., 10.75 inches overall. Weight: 35 oz. Adj. two-position rear sight, dovetailed front sight. Grip safety and thumb safety w/lower marking (1st issue), higher marking (2nd issue). Checkered walnut grips. No chamber markings, DWM on new-style toggle w/o lock, but w/stock lug. Est. production: 9,000 (lst issue); 2,000 (2nd issue).
First issue . . . . NiB $7020 Ex $5630 Gd $4490

1906 NAVY COMMERCIAL. . NiB $5600 Ex $5320 Gd $2350
Same as the 1906 Navy except lower marking on thumb safety, no chamber markings. DWM on new-style toggle, w/stock lug and commercial proofs. Estimated 3,000 production.

1906 PORTUGUESE ARMY. . NiB $3400 Ex $3230 Gd $1720
Same specifications as the 7.65mm 1906 American Eagle except w/Portuguese proofs, crown and crest over chamber. No stock lug. Estimated 3,500 production.

1906 PORTUGUESE NAVAL . . . . NiB $11,560 Ex $9260 Gd $7300
Same as the 9mm 1906 American Eagle except w/Portuguese proofs, crown and anchor over chamber, no stock lug.

1906 RUSSIAN . . . . . NiB $18,650 Ex $15,767 Gd $12,890
Same general specifications as the 9mm 1906 American Eagle except thumb safety has markings concealed in up position, DWM on new-style toggle, DWM bbl., proofs, crossed rifles over chamber. Estimated production unknown.

1906 SWISS . . . . NiB $3900 Ex $2709 Gd $2100
Same general specifications as the 7.65mm 1906 American Eagle Luger except Swiss Cross in sunburst over chamber, no stock lug. Estimated 10,300 production.

1906 SWISS (REWORK) . . . NiB $3750 Ex $3250 Gd $2000
Same basic specifications as the 7.65mm 1906 Swiss except in bbl. lengths of 3.63, 4 and 4.75 inches, overall length 8.38 inches (with 4-inch bbl.). Weight 32 oz. (with 4-inch bbl.). DWM on new-style toggle, bbl., w/serial number and proof marks, Swiss Cross in sunburst or shield over chamber, no stock lug. Estimated production unknown.

1906 SWISS POLICE. . . . . . NiB $3189 Ex $2910 Gd $2397
Same general specifications as the 7.65mm 1906 Swiss except DWM on new-style toggle, Swiss Cross in matted field over chamber, no stock lug. Estimated 10,300 production.

1908 BULGARIAN . . . . NiB $3860 Ex $2450 Gd $2600
Caliber: 9mm Para. Eight-round magazine, 4-inch tapered bbl., 8.75 inches overall. Weight: 30 oz. Fixed rear sight dovetailed front sight. Thumb safety w/lower marking concealed. Checkered walnut grips. DWM chamber marking, no proofs, crown over shield on new-style toggle lanyard loop, no stock lug. Estimated production unknown.

1908 COMMERCIAL. . . . . . NiB $2560 Ex $2010 Gd $1713
Same basic specifications as the 1908 Bulgarian except higher marking on thumb safety. No chamber markings, commercial

proofs, DWM on new-style toggle, no stock lug. Estimated 4,000 production.

1908 ERFURT MILITARY. . . NiB $2555 Ex $2055 Gd $1824
Caliber: 9mm Para. Eight-round magazine, 4-inch tapered bbl., 8.75 inches overall. Weight: 30 oz. Fixed rear sight dovetailed front sight. Thumb safety w/higher marking concealed. Checkered walnut grips. Serial number and proof marks on barrel, crown and Erfurt on new-style toggle, dated chamber, but no stock lug. Estimated production unknown.

1908 MILITARY
Same general specifications as the 9mm 1908 Erfurt Military Luger except first and second issue have thumb safety w/higher marking concealed, serial number on bbl., no chamber markings, proofs on frame, DWM on new-style toggle but no stock lug. Estimated production: 10,000 (first issue) and 5000 (second issue). Third issue has serial number and proof marks on barrel, dates over chamber, DWM on new-style toggle but no stock lug. Estimated 3,000 production.
First issue . . . . NiB $2460 Ex $2160 Gd $1645
Second issue . . . . NiB $2010 Ex $1605 Gd $1320
Third issue. . . . . NiB $2299 Ex $1897 Gd $1645

1908 NAVY. . . . . NiB $8405 Ex $79849 Gd $3475
Same basic specifications as the 9mm 1908 military Lugers except w/6-inch bbl, adj. two-position rear sight, no chamber markings, DWM on new-style toggle, w/stock lug. Estimated 26,000 production.

1908 NAVY (COMMERCIAL) . . . NiB $6600 Ex $6270 Gd $4620
Same specifications as the 1908 Naval Luger except no chamber markings or date. Commercial proofs, DWM on new-style toggle, w/stock lug. Estimated 1,900 produced.

1914 ERFURT ARTILLERY. . . NiB $4670 Ex $4435 Gd $3040
Caliber: 9mm Para. Eight-shot magazine, 8-inch tapered bbl., 12.75 inches overall. Weight: 40 oz. Artillery rear sight, Dovetailed front sight. Thumb safety w/higher marking concealed. Checkered walnut grips. Serial number and proof marks on barrel, crown and Erfurt on new-style toggle, dated chamber, w/stock lug. Estimated production unknown.

1914 ERFURT MILITARY. . . NiB $2170 Ex $2061 Gd $1190
Same specifications as the 1914 Erfurt Artillery except w/4-inch bbl., and corresponding length, weight, etc.; fixed rear sight. Estimated 3,000 production.

1914 NAVY. . . . . NiB $6000 Ex $5700 Gd $3000
Same specifications as 9mm 1914 Lugers except has 6-inch bbl. w/corresponding length and weight, adj. two-position rear sight. Dated chamber, DWM on new-style toggle, w/stock lug. Estimated 40,000 produced.

1914–1918 DWM ARTILLERY . . . NiB $3600 Ex $3090 Gd $1997
Caliber: 9mm Para. Eight-shot magazine, 8-inch tapered bbl., 12.75 inches overall. Weight: 40 oz. Artillery rear sight, dovetailed front sight. Thumb safety w/higher marking concealed. Checkered walnut grips. Serial number and proof marks on barrel, DWM on new-style toggle, dated chamber, w/stock lug. Estimated 3,000 production.

1914–1918 DWM MILITARY. . . . NiB $2200 Ex $1899 Gd $1100
Same specifications as the 9mm 1914-1918 DWM Artillery except w/4-inch tapered bbl., and corresponding length, weight, etc., and fixed rear sight. Production unknown.

1920 CARBINE
Caliber: 7.65mm. Eight-round magazine, 11.75-inch tapered bbl., 15.75 inches overall. Weight: 44 oz. Four-position rear sight, long ramp front sight. Grip (or thumb) safety. Checkered walnut grips and forearm. Serial numbers and proof marks on barrel, no chamber markings, various proofs, DWM on new-style toggle, w/stock lug. Estimated production unknown.

gun only . . . . NiB $7430 Ex $7058 Gd $3000
w/shoulder stock, add. **35%**

1920 NAVY CARBINE . . . . . NiB $4800 Ex $4560 Gd $3360
Caliber: 7.65mm. Eight-round magazine, 11.75-inch tapered bbl., 15.75 inches overall. Two-position sliding rear sight. Naval military proofs and no forearm. Production unknown.

1920 COMMERCIAL . . . . . . NiB $1450 Ex $1250 Gd $1018
Calibers: 7.65mm, 9mm Para. Eight-round magazine, 3.63-, 3.75-, 4-, 4.75-, 6-, 8-, 10-, 12-, 16-, 18- or 20-inch tapered bbl., overall length: 8.375 to 24.75 inches. Weight: 30 oz. (with 3.63-inch bbl.). Varying rear sight configurations, dovetailed front sight. Thumb safety. Checkered walnut grips. Serial numbers and proof marks on barrel, no chamber markings, various proofs, DWM or crown over Erfurt on new-style toggle, w/stock lug. Production not documented.

1920 POLICE . . . . NiB $1410 Ex $1200 Gd $931
Same specifications as 9mm 1920 DWM w/some dated chambers, various proofs, DWM or crown over Erfurt on new-style toggle, identifying marks on grip frame, w/stock lug. Estimated 3,000 production.

1923 COMMERICAL . . . . . NiB $1600 Ex $1520 Gd $1120
Calibers: 7.65mm and 9mm Para. Eight-round magazine, 3.63, 3.75, 4, 6, 8, 12 or 16-inch tapered bbl., overall length: 8.38 inches (with 3.63-inch bbl.). Weight: 30 oz. (with 3.63-inch bbl.). Various rear sight configurations, dovetailed front sight. Thumb lever safety. Checkered walnut grips. DWM on new-style toggle, serial number and proofs on barrel, no chamber markings, w/stock lug. Estimated 15,000 production.

1923 DUTCH COMMERICAL . . . NiB $2320 Ex $2088 Gd $1872
Same basic specifications as 1923 Commercial Luger w/ same caliber offerings, but only 3.63 or 4-inch bbl. Fixed rear sight, thumb lever safety w/arrow markings. Production unknown.

1923 KRIEGHOFF
COMMERCIAL . . . . NiB $2340 Ex $2223 Gd $1638
Same specifications as 1923 Commercial Luger, w/same caliber offerings but bbl., lengths of 3.63, 4, 6, and 8 inches. "K" marked on new-style toggle. Serial number, proofs and Germany on barrel. No chamber markings, but w/ stock lug. Production unknown.

1923 SAFE AND LOADED . . . NiB $2460 Ex $2337 Gd $1722
Same caliber offerings, bbl., lengths and specifications as the 1923 Commercial except thumb lever safety, "safe" and "loaded" markings, w/stock lug. Estimated 10,000 production.

1923 STOEGER
Same general specifications as the 1923 Commercial Luger with the same caliber offerings and bbl., lengths of 3.75, 4, 6,

Luger 1923 Stoeger

8 and up to 24 inches. Thumb lever safety. DWM on new-style toggle, serial number and/or proof marks on barrel. American Eagle over chamber but no stock lug. Estimated production less than 1000 (also see Stoeger listings). Note: Qualified appraisals should be obtained on all Stoeger Lugers with bbl. lengths over 8 inches to ensure accurate values.

3.75-, 4-, or 6-inch bbl. . . . NiB $5660 Ex $5377 Gd $2730
8-inch bbl. . . . . NiB $6350 Ex $6035 Gd $2255

1926 "BABY"
PROTOTYPE . . . . . . NiB $112,750 Ex $90,295 Gd $62,355
Calibers: 7.65mm Browning and 9mm Browning (short). Five-round magazine, 2.31-inch bbl., about 6.25 inches overall. Small-sizedframe and toggle assembly. Prototype for a Luger "pocket pistol," but never manufactured commercially. Checkered walnut grips, slotted for safety. Only four known to exist, but as many as a dozen could have been made.

1929 SWISS . . . . NiB $2017 Ex $1486 Gd $989
Caliber: 7.65mm. Eight-round magazine, 4.75-inch tapered bbl., 9.5 inches overall. Weight: 32 oz. Fixed rear sight, dovetailed front sight. Long grip safety and thumb lever w/S markings. Stepped receiver and straight grip frame. Checkered plastic grips. Swiss Cross in shield on new-style toggle. Serial numbers and proofs on barrel, no markings over chamber and no stock lug. Estimated 1,900 production.

1934 KRIEGHOFF COMMERCIAL
(SIDE FRAME) . . . . NiB $ 7100 Ex $6350 Gd $2895
Caliber: 7.65mm or 9mm Para. Eight-round magazine, bbl. lengths: 4, 6, and 8 inches, overall length: 8.75 (with 4-inch bbl.). Weight: 30 oz. (with 4-inch bbl.). Various rear sight configurations w/dovetailed front sight. Thumb lever safety. Checkered brown plastic grips. Anchor w/H K Krieghoff Suhl on new-style toggle, but no chamber markings. Tapered bbl., w/serial number and proofs; w/stock lug. Estimated 1,700 production.

1934 KRIEGHOFF S CODE MODELS
Caliber: 9mm Para. Eight-round magazine, 4-inch tapered bbl., 8.75 inches overall. Weight: 30 oz. Fixed rear sight, dovetailed front sight. Thumb lever safety. Anchor w/H K Krieghoff Suhl on new-style toggle, S dated chamber, bbl., proofs and stock lug. Early model: Checkered walnut or plastic grips. Estimated 2,500 production. Late model: Checkered brown plastic grips. Estimated 1,200 production.
Early model. . . . . NiB $4660 Ex $4077 Gd $2976

Late model . . . . NiB $4460 Ex $3900 Gd $1464

1934 BYF . . . . NiB $2170 Ex $1950 Gd $1000
Caliber: 9mm Para. Eight-round magazine, 4-inch tapered bbl., 8.75 inches overall. Weight: 30 oz. Fixed rear sight, dovetailed front sight. Thumb lever safety. Checkered walnut or plastic grips. "byf" on new-style toggle, serial number and proofs on bbl., 41-42 dated chamber and w/stock lug. Estimated 3,000 productlon.

1934 MAUSER S/42 K. . . . . . NiB $7950 Ex $6800 Gd $3500
Caliber: 9mm Para. Eight-round magazine, 4-inch tapered bbl., 8.75 inches overall. Weight: 30 oz. Fixed rear sight dovetailed front sight. Thumb lever safety. Checkered walnut or plastic grips. "42" on new-style toggle, serial number and proofs on barrel, 1939-40 dated chamber markings and w/stock lug. Estimated 10,000 production.

**1934 MAUSER S/42
(DATED)** . . . . NiB $2244 Ex $2117 Gd $1599
Same specifications as Luger 1934 Mauser 42 except 41 dated chamber markings and w/stock lug. Production unknown.

**1934 MAUSER BANNER
(MILITARY)** . . . . NiB $4190 Ex $3455 Gd $3097
Same specifications as Luger 1934 Mauser 42 except Mauser in banner on new-style toggle, tapered bbl., w/serial number and proofs usually, dated chamber markings and w/stock lug. Production unknown.

**1934 MAUSER BANNER
COMMERCIAL** . . . . NiB $4400 Ex $3760 Gd $3156
Same specifications as Luger 1934 Mauser 42 except checkered walnut grips. Mauser in banner on new-style toggle, tapered bbl., usually w/serial number and proofs, no chamber markings, but w/ stock lug. Production unknown.

**1934 MAUSER
BANNER DUTCH** . . . . NiB $3787 Ex $3375 Gd $3099
Same specifications as Luger 1934 Mauser 42 except checkered walnut grips. Mauser in banner on new-style toggle, tapered bbl., w/caliber, 1940 dated chamber markings and w/stock lug. Production unknown.

1934 MAUSER LATVIAN. . . NiB $3260 Ex $2355 Gd $1989
Caliber: 7.65mm. Eight-round magazine, 4-inch tapered bbl., 8.75 inches overall. Weight: 30 oz. Fixed square-notched rear sight, dovetailed Partridge front sight. Thumb lever safety. Checkered walnut stocks. Mauser in banner on new-style toggle, 1937 dated chamber markings and w/stock lug. Production unknown.

**1934 MAUSER
(OBERNDORF)** . . . . NiB $3155 Ex $2535 Gd $1733
Same as 1934 Mauser 42 except checkered walnut grips. Oberndorf 1934 on new-style toggle, tapered bbl., w/proofs and caliber, Mauser banner over chamber and w/stock lug (also see Mauser).

1934 SIMSON-S TOGGLE . . . NiB $4459 Ex $4188 Gd $3799
Same as 1934 Mauser 42 except checkered walnut grips, "S" on new-style toggle, tapered bbl., w/proofs and S/N, no chamber markings; w/stock lug. Estimated 10,000 production.

**42 MAUSER
BANNER (BYF)** . . . . NiB $3877 Ex $3078 Gd $2689
Same specifications as Luger 1934 Mauser 42 except weight:

**Luger S42 (shown with toggle
locked back)**

32 oz. Mauser in banner on new-style toggle, tapered bbl., w/serial number and proofs usually, dated chamber markings and w/stock lug. Estimated 3,500 production.

**ABERCROMBIE AND
FITCH** . . . . NiB $5465 Ex $4876 Gd $2879
Calibers: 7.65mm and 9mm Para. Eight-round magazine, 4.75-inch tapered bbl., 9.5 inches overall. Weight: 32 oz. Fixed rear sight, dovetailed front sight. Grip safety. Checkered walnut grips. DWM on new-style toggle Abercrombie & Fitch markings on barrel, Swiss Cross in sunburst over chamber, no stock lug. Est. 100 production.

**DUTCH ROYAL
AIR FORCE** . . . . NiB $3324 Ex $2190 Gd $998
Caliber: 9mm Para. Eight-round magazine, 4-inch tapered bbl., 8.75 inches overall. Weight: 30 oz. Fixed rear sight dovetailed front sight. Grip safety and thumb safety w/markings and arrow. Checkered walnut grips. DWM on new-style toggle, bbl., dated w/serial number and proofs, no markings over chamber, no stock lug. Estimated 4,000 production.

DWM (G DATE) . . . . NiB $2189 Ex $1953 Gd $1645
Caliber: 9mm Para. Eight-round magazine, 4-inch tapered bbl., 8.75 inches overall. Weight: 30 oz. Fixed rear sight, dovetailed front sight. Thumb lever safety. Checkered walnut grips. DWM on new-style toggle, serial number and proofs on barrel, G (1935 date) over chamber and w/stock lug. Production unknown.

DWM AND ERFURT . . . . . . NiB $1357 Ex $1134 Gd $876
Caliber: 9mm Para. Eight-round magazine, 4- or 6-inch tapered bbl., overall length: 8.75 or 10.75 inches. Weight: 30 or 38 oz. Fixed rear sight, dovetailed front sight. Thumb safety. Checkered walnut grips. Serial numbers and proof marks on barrel, double dated chamber, various proofs, DWM or crown over Erfurt on new-style toggle and w/stock lug. Production unknown.

KRIEGHOFF 36. . . . . NiB $4550 Ex $3799 Gd $1899
Caliber: 9mm Para. Eight-round magazine, 4-inch tapered bbl., 8.75 inches overall. Weight: 30 oz. Fixed rear sight, dovetailed front sight. Thumb lever safety. Checkered brown plastic grips. Anchor w/H K Krieghoff Suhl on new-style toggle, 36 dated chamber, serial number and proofs on barrel and w/stock lug. Estimated 700 production.

KRIEGHOFF DATED (1936 - 1945)
Same specifications as Luger Krieghoff 36 except 1936-45 dated chamber, bbl. proofs. Est. 8,600 production.

1936, 1937 and 1940 . . . . . NiB $5500 Ex $4779 Gd $2735
1938 and 1941 . . . . NiB $6500 Ex $5779 Gd $2735
1942 thru 1943, add 60%
1945, add 110%

KRIEGHOFF (GRIP SAFETY)... NiB $4977 Ex $3965 Gd $2790
Same specifications as Luger Krieghoff 36 except grip safety and thumb lever safety. No chamber markings, tapered bbl., w/serial number, proofs and caliber, no stock lug. Production unknown.

MAUSER BANNER
(GRIP SAFETY) . . . . NiB $2874 Ex $2050 Gd $1465
Caliber: 7.65mm. Eight-round magazine, 4.75-inch tapered bbl., 9.5 inches overall. Weight: 30 oz. Fixed rear sight, dovetailed front sight. Grip safety and thumb lever safety. Checkered walnut grips. Mauser in banner on new-style toggle, serial number and proofs on barrel, 1939 dated chamber markings, but no stock lug. Production unknown.

MAUSER BANNER 42
(DATED) . . . . NiB 2170 Ex $1196 Gd $100
Caliber: 9mm Para. Eight-round magazine, 4-inch tapered bbl., 8.75 inches overall. Weight: 30 oz. Fixed rear sight, dovetailed front sight. Thumb lever safety. Checkered walnut or plastic grips. Mauser in banner on new-style toggle serial number and proofs on bbl., (usually) 1942 dated chamber markings and stock lug. Production unknown.

MAUSER BANNER
(SWISS PROOF) . . . . NiB $3460 Ex $2830 Gd $1540
Same specifications as Luger Mauser Banner 42 except checkered walnut grips and 1939 dated chamber.

MAUSER FREISE . . . . NiB $4960 Ex $4090 Gd $2866
Same specifications as Mauser Banner 42 except checkered walnut grips, tapered bbl. w/proofs on sight block and Freise above chamber. Production unknown.

S/42
Caliber: 9mm Para. Eight-round magazine, 4-inch tapered barrel. 8.75 inches overall. Weight: 30 oz. Fixed rear sight, dovetailed front sight. Thumb lever safety. Checkered walnut grips. S/42 on new-style toggle, serial number and proofs on barrel and w/stock lug. Dated Model: Has dated chamber; estimated 3000 production. G Date: Has G (1935 date) over chamber; estimated 3000 production. K Date: Has K (1934 date) over chamber; production unknown.

Dated model . . . . NiB $6780 Ex $5977 Gd $4538
G date model . . . . NiB $2669 Ex $2380 Gd $2010
K date model . . . . NiB $6876 Ex $5986 Gd $4610

RUSSIAN COMMERCIAL . . . NiB $3146 Ex $2548 Gd $1713
Caliber: 7.65mm. Eight-round magazine, 3.63-inch tapered bbl., 8.38 inches overall. Weight: 30 oz. Fixed rear sight, dovetailed front sight. Thumb lever safety. Checkered walnut grips. DWM on new-style toggle, Russian proofs on barrel, no chamber markings but w/stock lug. Production unknown.

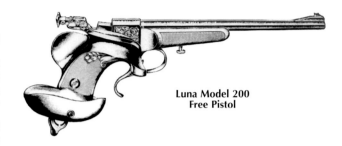

Luna Model 200
Free Pistol

SIMSON AND COMPANY
Calibers: 7.65mm and 9mm Para. Eight-round magazine, Weight: 32 oz. Fixed rear sight, dovetailed front sight. Thumb lever safety. Checkered walnut grips. Simson & Company Suhl on new-style toggle, serial number and proofs on barrel, date over chamber and w/stock lug. Estimated 10,000 production.

Simson and Company
(9mm w/1925 date) . . . . . . NiB $6300 Ex $5300 Gd $300
Simson and Company
(undated) . . . . NiB $4300 Ex $3650 Gd $200
Simson and Company
(S code) . . . . NiB $5600 Ex $4800 Gd $2389

VICKERS-DUTCH . . . . NiB $4375 Ex $3968 Gd $3316
Caliber: 9mm Para. Eight-round magazine, 4-inch tapered bbl., 8.75 inches overall. Weight: 30 oz. Fixed rear sight, dovetailed front sight. Grip safety and thumb lever w/arrow markings. Checkered walnut grips (coarse). Vickers LTD on new-style toggle, no chamber markings, dated barrel but no stock lug. Estimated 10,000 production.

LUNA FREE PISTOL — Zella-Mehlis, Germany
Originally mfd. by Ernst Friedr. Buchel and later by Udo Anschutz.

MODEL 200 FREE PISTOL . . NiB $1198 Ex $1027 Gd $784
Single-shot. System Aydt action. Set trigger. Caliber: .22 LR. Eleven-inch bbl., weight: 40 oz. Target sights. Blued finish. Checkered and carved walnut grip and forearm; improved design w/adj. hand base on later models of Udo Anschutz manufacture. Made prior to WWII.

M.A.C. (Military Armament Corp.) — Ducktown, TN

INGRAM MODEL 10 AUTO PISTOL
Select fire (NFA-Title II-Class III) SMG based on Ingram M10 blowback system using an open bolt design with or without telescoping stock. Calibers: 9mm or .45 ACP. Cyclic rate: 750 RPM (9mm) or 900 RPM (.45 ACP). 32- or 30-round magazine, 5.75-inch threaded bbl. (to accept muzzle brake) bbl. Extension or suppressor, 10.5 inches overall w/o stock or 10.6 (w/telescoped stock) and 21.5 (w/Extended stock). Weight: 6.25 pounds. Front protected post sight, fixed aperture rear sight.

9mm model . . . . NiB $1113 Ex $920 Gd $669
ACP model . . . . NiB $998 Ex $877 Gd $668
w/bbl. extension, add $255
w/suppressor, add $587

INGRAM MODEL 10A1S SEMIAUTOMATIC
Similar to the Model 10 except (Class I) semiautomatic w/ closed bolt design to implement an interchangable component system to easily convert to fire 9mm and .45 ACP.

9mm model . . . . NiB $408 Ex $332 Gd $225
.45 ACP model . . . . NiB $431 Ex $342 Gd $235
w/bbl. extension, add $204
w/fake suppressor, add $225

INGRAM MODEL 11 SEMIAUTOMATIC
Similar to the Model 10A1 except (Class I) semiautomatic chambered .380 ACP.

.380 ACP model . . . . NiB $862 Ex $714 Gd $536
w/bbl. extension, add $204
w/fake suppressor, add $225

MAC — Philippines

Manufactured in Philippines and imported by Eagle Imports, Wanamassa, New Jersey. Series-70 style.

1911 BOBCUT SERIES . . . . NiB $978 Ex $910 Gd $870
Similar 1911 Classic except w/4.35-in. bbl. and bobcat frame.

1911 CLASSIC SERIES . . . . NiB $609 Ex $570 Gd $500
1911 platform. Semi-automatic. SA. Caliber: .45 ACP; 8-rnd. magazine. 5 in. bbl. Frame: steel. Sights: adj. rear, fiber optic front. Finish: blue, black chrome, hard chrome. Grip: textured hardwood. Length: 8.88 in. Weight: 40.56 oz. Beavertail, magwell. Imported from 2011 to date.
hard chrome or black chrome finish, add...$70

1911 BULLSEYE SERIES . . . . NiB $1219 Ex $1180 Gd $1000
Similar 1911 Classic except w/6-in. bbl.
hard chrome finish, add $70

3011 SSD SERIES . . . . NiB $1215 Ex $570 Gd $500
1911 platform. Semi-automatic. SA. Caliber: .40 S&W or .45 ACP; 14-rnd. magazine. 5-in. bbl. Frame: steel. Sights: adj. rear, fiber optic front. Finish: deep blue, hard chrome. Grip: checkered aluminum. Length: 8.91 in. Weight: 46.54 oz. Beavertail, magwell funnel.
3011 SSD Tactical (accessory rail), add $90

MAGNUM RESEARCH, INC. (MRI) —
Minneapolis, MN
Originally mfd. by IMI (Isreal Military Industries). MRI purchased by Kahr Arms in 2010.

BABY EAGLE
SEMI-AUTOMATIC . . . . NiB $577 Ex $479 Gd $365
DA. Calibers: 9mm, .40 S&W, .41 AE. 15-shot magazine (9mm), 9-round magazine (.40 S&W), 10-round magazine (.41 AE), 4.75-inch bbl., 8.15 inches overall. Weight: 35.4 oz. Combat sights. Matte blued finish. Imported from 1991-96 and 1999 to 2007.

BABY EAGLE II
SEMI-AUTOMATIC . . . . NiB $656 Ex $430 Gd $335
Similar to Baby Eagle except w/accessory rail. Imported from 2008 to date.

BFR LONG CYLINDER
REVOVER . . . . NiB $1050 Ex $780 Gd $550
SA. Calibers: .30-30 Win., .444 Marlin, .45 LC/.410, .450 Marlin, .45-70 Gov't., .460 S&W Mag., and .50 S&W Mag. 5-round cylinder, bbl. lengths: 7.5- or 10-in. Stainless finish. Weight: 4-4.4 lbs.Rubber grips. Made from 1999 to date.

BFR SHORT
CYLINDER REVOVER . . . . . . NiB $1050 Ex $780 Gd $550
SA. Calibers: .44 Mag., .454 Casull, .475 Linebaugh, and .480 Ruger, 5-round cylinder, bbl. lengths: 5-, or 7.5-in. Stainless finish. Rubber grips. Weight: 3.2-4.4 lbs. Made 1999 to date.

DESERT EAGLE MK VII SEMIAUTOMATIC
Gas-operated. Calibers: .357 Mag., .41 Mag., .44 Mag., .50 Action Express (AE). Eight- or 9-round magazine, 6-inch w/ standard bbl., or 10- and 14-inch w/polygonal bbl., 10.6 inches overall (with 6-inch bbl.). Weight: 52 oz. (w/alum. alloy frame) to 67 oz. (w/steel frame). Fixed or adj. combat sights. Combat-type trigger guard. finish: Military black oxide, nickel, chrome, stainless or blued. Wraparound rubber grips. Made from 1983 to 1995 and 1998 to 2001.

.357 standard (steel)
  or alloy (6-inch bbl.) . . . . NiB $903 Ex $658 Gd $562
.357 stainless steel (6-inch bbl.) . . . . NiB $940 Ex $704 Gd $536
.41 Mag. standard (steel) or alloy
  (6-inch bbl.) . . . . NiB $1099 Ex $831 Gd $638
.41 Mag. stainless steel
  (6-inch bbl.) . . . . NiB $1145 Ex $984 Gd $780
.44 Mag. standard (steel) or alloy
  (6-inch bbl.) . . . . NiB $1015 Ex $798 Gd $567
.44 Mag. stainless steel
  (6-inch bbl.) . . . . NiB $991 Ex $806 Gd $559
.50 AE Magnum standard . . . . NiB $1135 Ex $968 Gd $689
For 10-inch bbl., add . . . . NiB $204 Ex $148 Gd $110
For 14-inch bbl., add . . . . NiB $225 Ex $175 Gd $128

DESERT EAGLE MARK XIX SEMI-AUTOMATIC PISTOL
Interchangeable component system based on .50-caliber frame. Calibers: .357 Mag., .44 Mag., .50 AE. Nine-, 8-, 7-round magazine, 6- or 10-inch bbl. w/dovetail design and cross slots to accept scope rings. Weight: 70.5 oz. (6-inch bbl.) or 79 oz. 10.75 or 14.75 inches overall. Sights: Post front and adjustable rear. Blue, chrome or nickel finish; available brushed, matte or polished. Hogue soft rubber grips. Made from 1995 to 1998.

.357 Mag. and .44 Mag.
  (w/6-inch bbl.) . . . . NiB $1400 Ex $1150 Gd $900
.50 AE (w/6-inch bbl.) . . . . NiB $1435 Ex $1164 Gd $989
w/10-inch bbl., add $100
Two caliber conversion (bbl., bolt & mag.), add $444
XIX Platform System (three-caliber conversion kit
  w/six bbls.) . . . . NiB $4335 Ex $3799 Gd $3260
XIX6 System (two-caliber conversion kit
  w/two 6-inch bbls.) . . . . . NiB $2675 Ex $2254 Gd $1969
XIX10 System (two-caliber conversion
  kit w/two 10-inch bbls.) . . . NiB $2150 Ex $1720 Gd $1196
Custom shop finish, add $20%
24K gold finish, add $40%

MICRO DESERT EAGLE. . . . . . NiB $647 Ex $380 Gd $265
DAO. Calibers: .380 ACP. 6-shot magazine, 2-2-inch bbl. Weight: 14 oz. Imported from 2009 to 2013.

(ASAI) MODEL ONE PRO .45 PISTOL
Calibers: .45 ACP or .400 COR-BON, 3.75- inch bbl., 7.04 or 7.83 (IPSC Model) inches overall. Weight: 23.5 (alloy frame)

Magnum Research Model Desert Eagle Mark XIX shown w/optional Leupold scope

Magnum Research Model One Pro .45

Magnum Research SSP-91 Lone Eagle Pistol shown w/Optional Leupold Scope

or 31.1 oz. 10-round magazine. Short recoil action. SA or DA mode w/de-cocking lever. Steel or alloy grip-frame. Textured black polymer grips. Imported from 1998.

Model 1P45 . . . . NiB $740 Ex $567 Gd $399
Model 1C45/400 (compensator kit), add $204
Model 1C400NC (400 conversion kit), add $150

MOUNTAIN EAGLE SEMIAUTOMATIC

Caliber: .22 LR. 15-round polycarbonate resin magazine, 6.5-inch injection-molded polymer and steel bbl., 10.6 inches overall. Weight: 21 oz. Ramp blade front sight, adj. rear. Injection-molded, checkered and textured grip. Matte black finish. Made 1992 to 1996.

Standard, w/6-inch bb . . . . NiB $214 Ex $160 Gd $143
Compact, w/4.5-inch bbl . . . . . . NiB $190 Ex $143 Gd $110
Target, w/8-inch bbl . . . . NiB $240 Ex $150 Gd $120

SSP-91 LONE EAGLE PISTOL

Single-shot action w/interchangeable rotating breech bbl., assembly. Calibers: .22 LR, .22 Mag., .22 Hornet, .22-250, .223 Rem., .243 Win., 6mm BR, 7mm-08, 7mm BR, .30-06, .30-30, .308 Win., .35 Rem., .357 Mag., .44 Mag., .444 Marlin. 14-inch interchangeable bbl. assembly, 15 inches overall. Weight: 4.5 lbs. Black or chrome finish. Made from 1991 to 2001.

Black finish . . . . NiB $434 Ex $321 Gd $165
Chrome finish . . . . NiB $464 Ex $342 Gd $186
Extra 14-inch bbl., black finish $150
Extra 14-inch bbl., chrome finish, ... $175
Ambidextrous stock assembly (only) $220
w/muzzle brake, add $408
w/open sights, add $45

MAUSER — Oberndorf, Germany, Waffenfabrik Mauser of Mauser-Werke A.G.

MODEL 80-SA AUTOMATIC . . . NiB $577 Ex $395 Gd $255
Caliber: 9mm Para. 13-round magazine, 4.66-inch bbl., 8 inches overall. Weight: 31.5 oz. Blued finish. Hardwood grips. Made 1992 to 1996.

MODEL 90 DA AUTOMATIC . . NiB $530 Ex $354 Gd $234
Caliber: 9mm Para. 14-round magazine, 4.66-inch bbl., 8 inches overall. Weight: 35 oz. Blued finish. Hardwood grips. Made 1992 to 1996.

MODEL 90 DAC COMPACT . . . NiB $571 Ex $405 Gd $270
Caliber: 9mm Para. 14-round magazine, 4.13-inch bbl., 7.4 inches overall. Weight: 33.25 oz. Blued finish. Hardwood grips. Made 1992 to 1996.

MODEL 1898 (1896) "BROOMHANDLE" MILITARY AUTO PISTOL

Caliber: 7.63mm Mauser, but also chambered for 9mm Mauser and 9mm Para. w/the latter being identified by a large red "9" in the grips. 10-round box magazine, 5.25-inch bbl., 12 inches overall. Weight: 45 oz. Adj. rear sight. Blued finish. Walnut grips. Made from 1897 to 1939. Note: Specialist collectors recognize a number of variations at significantly higher values. Price here is for more common commercial and military types with original finish.

Commercial model (pre-war) . . . NiB $3520 Ex $2735 Gd $1096
Commercial model
 (wartime) . . . . NiB $3015 Ex $2512 Gd $1040
Red 9 Commercial model
 (fixed sight) . . . . NiB $3265 Ex $2979 Gd $1049
Red 9 WWI Contract
 (tangent sight) . . . . NiB $3300 Ex $2670 Gd $1300
w/stock sssembly (matching S/N), add $1300

MODEL HSC DA AUTO PISTOL

Calibers: .32 Auto (7.65mm), .380 Auto (9mm Short). Eight-round (.32) or 7-round (.380) magazine, 3.4-inch bbl., 6.4 inches overall. Weight: 23.6 oz. Fixed sights. Blued or nickel finish. Checkered walnut grips. Made from 1938 to 1945 and from 1968 to 1996.

Military model
 (low grip screw) . . . . NiB $6200 Ex $5110 Gd $2820
Commercial model (wartime) . . . NiB $536 Ex $398 Gd $249
Nazi military model (pre-war) . . . NiB $1148 Ex $974 Gd $632
Nazi military model (wartime) . . . . NiB $600 Ex $499 Gd $270
French production (postwar) . . . . NiB $474 Ex $398 Gd $239

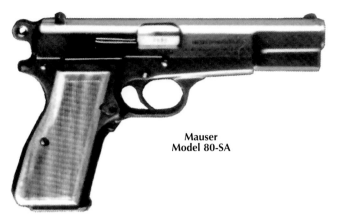

**Mauser
Model 80-SA**

**Mauser
Model 90-DA**

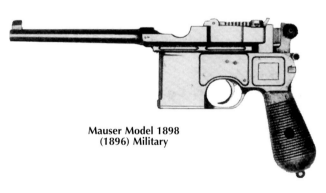

**Mauser Model 1898
(1896) Military**

**Mauser Parabellum Luger
shown w/6-in. barrel**

Mauser production (postwar) . . . NiB $497 Ex $377 Gd $235
**Recent importation
    (Armes De Chasse)** . . . . NiB $478 Ex $398 Gd $270
**Recent importation
    (Interarms)** . . . . NiB $388 Ex $289 Gd $230
**Recent importation
    (European Amer. Arms)** . . . . . NiB $328 Ex $196 Gd $115
**Recent importation
    (Gamba, USA)** . . . . NiB $431 Ex $316 Gd $194
**American Eagle model
    (1 of 5000)** . . . . NiB $562 Ex $433 Gd $319

LUGER LANGE PISTOL 08
Caliber: 9mm Para. Eight-inch bbl., Checkered grips. Blued finish. Accessorized w/walnut shoulder stock, front sight tool, spare magazine, leather case. Currently in production. Commemorative version made in limited quantities w/ivory grips and 14-carat gold monogram plate.
**Commemorative model
    (100 produced)** . . . . NiB $2855 Ex $2330 Gd $1875
**Commemorative matched
    pair** . . . . NiB $5423 Ex $4412 Gd $3099
Cartridge counter model . . . NiB $4010 Ex $2907 Gd $2017
**Carbine model (w/matching
    buttstock)** . . . . NiB $8025 Ex $6309 Gd $3718

PARABELLUM LUGER AUTO PISTOL
Current commercial model. Swiss pattern with grip safety. Calibers: 7.65mm Luger, 9mm Para. Eight-round magazine, bbl. lengths: 4-, 6-inch, 8.75 inches overall (with 4-inch bbl.). Weight: 30 oz. (with 4-inch bbl.). Fixed sights. Blued finish. Checkered walnut grips. Made from 1970 to date. Note: Pistols of this model sold in the U.S. have the American Eagle stamped on the receiver.
Standard model (blue) . . . . . NiB $1603 Ex $1230 Gd $704

POCKET MODEL 1910 AUTO PISTOL
Caliber: .25 Auto (6.35mm). Nine-round magazine, 3.1-inch bbl., 5.4 inches overall. Weight: 15 oz. Fixed sights. Blued finish. Checkered walnut or hard rubber grips. Made 1910-34.
Model 1910 (standard) . . . . NiB $691 Ex $461 Gd $306
Model 1910 (w/side latch) . . . . NiB $546 Ex $431 Gd $309

POCKET MODEL 1914 . . . . . . NiB $691 Ex $485 Gd $314
Similar to Pocket Model 1910. Caliber: .32 Auto (7.65mm). Eight-round magazine, 3.4-inch bbl., 6 inches overall. Weight: 21 oz. Fixed sights. Blued finish. Checkered walnut or hard rubber grips. Made 1914 to 1934

POCKET MODEL 1934 . . . . NiB $816 Ex $595 Gd $410
Similar to Pocket Models 1910 and 1914 in the respective calibers. Chief difference is in the more streamlined, one-piece grips. Made from 1934 to 1939.

WTP MODEL I AUTO PISTOL . NiB $779 Ex $610 Gd $413
"Westentaschen-Pistole" (Vest Pocket Pistol). Caliber: .25 Automatic (6.35mm). Six-round magazine, 2.5-inch bbl., 4 inches overall. Weight: 11.5 oz. Blued finish. Hard rubber grips. Made from 1922 to 1937.

**WTP MODEL II
AUTO PISTOL** . . . . NiB $1398 Ex $1137 Gd $895
Similar to Model I but smaller and lighter. Caliber: .25 Automatic (6.35mm). Six-round magazine, 2-inch bbl., 4 inches overall. Weight: 9.5 oz. Blued finish. Hard rubber grips. Made from 1938 to 1940.

GRADING: **NiB** = New in Box   **Ex** = Excellent or NRA 95%   **Gd** = Good or NRA 68%

MERWIN HULBERT & CO. — New York, NY

FIRST MODEL
FRONTIER ARMY . . . . NiB $9679 Ex $8023 Gd $6029
SA .44 caliber, 7.5-inch bbl. Square butt, open top, scoop flutes on cylinder, two screws above trigger guard.

SECOND MODEL
FRONTIER ARMY . . . . NiB $8617 Ex $7608 Gd $6138
Similar to First Model except one screw above trigger guard.

SECOND MODEL
POCKET ARMY . . . . NiB $7740 Ex $ 6487 Gd $5009
Similar to Second Model except has bird's-head butt instead of square butt, 3.5- or 7-in. (scarce) bbl. Some models may be marked "Pocket Army."

THIRD MODEL
FRONTIER ARMY . . . . NiB $6995 Ex $3429 Gd $2152
Caliber: .44, 7-inch round bbl. with no rib, single action. Square butt, top strap, usually has conventional fluting on cylinder but some have scoop flutes.

THIRD MODEL DA
FRONTIER ARMY . . . . NiB $6775 Ex $5254 Gd $4890
Similar to Third Model Frontier Army SA except is double action.

THIRD MODEL
POCKET ARMY . . . . NiB $7610 Ex $5366 Gd $4997
Caliber: .44, 3.5- or 7.5-inch bbl. with no rib. Single action, bird's-head butt, top strap.

THIRD MODEL
POCKET ARMY DA . . . . NiB $6648 Ex $5096 Gd $3930
Similar to Third Model Pocket Army SA except DA.

FOURTH MODEL
FRONTIER ARMY . . . . NiB $9010 Ex $8188 Gd $4992
Caliber: .44, 3.5- 5- or 7-inch unique ribbed bbl. Single action, square butt, top strap, conventional flutes on cylinder.

FOURTH MODEL FRONTIER
ARMY DA . . . . NiB $8189 Ex $5883 Gd $5409
Similar to Fourth Model Frontier Army SA DA.

NOTE: *The following handguns are foreign copies of Merwin Hulbert Co. guns and may be marked as such, or as "Sistema Merwin Hulbert," but rarely with the original Hopkins & Allen markings. These guns will usually bring half or less of a comparable genuine Merwin Hulbert product.*

FIRST POCKET MODEL . . . NiB $2270 Ex $1996 Gd $1416
Caliber: .38 Special, 5-round cylinder (w/cylinder pin Exposed at front of frame), single action. Spur trigger; round loading hole in recoil shield, no loading gate.

SECOND POCKET MODEL . . . NiB $1815 Ex $1595 Gd $1416
Similar to First Pocket Model except has sliding loading gate.

THIRD POCKET MODEL . . . . NiB $1633 Ex $1270 Gd $1111
Similar to First Pocket Model except has enclosed cylinder pin.

THIRD POCKET MODEL W/TRIGGER
GUARD . . . . NiB $1517 Ex $1319 Gd $1133
Similar to First Pocket Model except w/conventional trigger guard.

SMALL FRAME

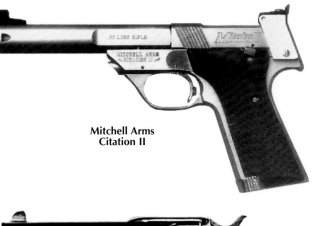

Mitchell Arms
Citation II

Mitchell Arms SA
Army Revolver

POCKET MODEL . . . . NiB $1360 Ex $1120 Gd $601
Caliber: .38 Spec., 5-rnd. cylinder, DA, may have hammer spur.

SMALL FRAME
POCKET MODEL 32 . . . . NiB $1377 Ex $1190 Gd $979
Similar to Medium Frame Pocket Model except .32 caliber, 7-round cylinder, double action.

TIP-UP MODEL 22 . . . . NiB $1579 Ex $1367 Gd $1056
Similar to S&W Model One except .22 caliber, 7-round cylinder, spur trigger. Scarce.

MITCHELL ARMS, INC. — Santa Ana, CA

MODEL 1911 GOLD SIGNATURE
Caliber: .45 ACP. Eight-round mag, 5-inch bbl., 8.75 inches overall. Weight: 39 oz. Interchangeable blade front sight, drift-adj. combat or fully adj. rear. Smooth or checkered walnut grips. Made 1994 to 1996.
Blued model w/fixed sights. . . . NiB $512 Ex $393 Gd $301
Blued model w/adj. sights. . . . . NiB $554 Ex $456 Gd $412
Stainless model w/fixed sights . . . NiB $709 Ex $549 Gd $464
Stainless model w/adj. sights . . . . NiB $755 Ex $601 Gd $530

ALPHA MODEL AUTO PISTOL
Dual action w/interchangeable trigger modules. Caliber: .45 ACP. Eight-round magazine, 5-inch bbl., 8.75 inches overall. Weight: 39 oz. Interchangeable blade front sight, drift-adj. rear. Smooth or checkered walnut grips. Blued or stainless finish. Made in 1994. Advertised in 1995 but not manufactured.

AMERICAN EAGLE
LUGER PISTOL . . . . NiB $900 Ex $678 Gd $369

**Mitchell Arms
Sharpshooter II**

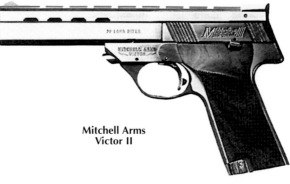

**Mitchell Arms
Victor II**

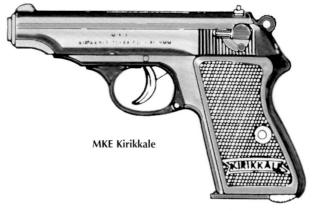

MKE Kirikkale

**MOA Maximum
Carbine Pistol**

**Mossberg Brownie
"Pepperbox" Pistol**

Stainless-steel re-creation of the American Eagle Parabellum auto pistol. Caliber: 9mm Para. Seven-round magazine, 4-inch bbl., 9.6 inches overall. Weight: 26.6 oz. Blade front sight, fixed rear. Stainless finish. Checkered walnut grips. Made from 1993 to 1994.

CITATION II AUTO PISTOL . . . NiB $433 Ex $309 Gd $228
Re-creation of the High Standard Supermatic Citation Military. Caliber: .22 LR. 10-round magazine, 5.5-inch bull bbl. or 7.25 fluted bbl., 9.75 inches overall (5.5-inch bbl.). Weight: 44.5 oz. Ramp front sight, slide-mounted micro-adj. rear. Satin blued or stainless finish. Checkered walnut grips w/thumbrest. Made 1992 to 1996.

OLYMPIC I.S.U.
AUTO PISTOL. . . . . NiB $659 Ex $556 Gd $434
Similar to the Citation II model except chambered in .22 Short, 6.75-inch round tapered bbl. w/stabilizer and removable counterweights. Made from 1992 to 1996.

SHARPSHOOTER I
AUTO PISTOL. . . . . NiB $362 Ex $288 Gd $212
Re-creation of the High Standard Sharpshooter. Caliber: .22 LR. 10-round magazine, 5-inch bull bbl., 10.25 inches overall. Weight: 42 oz. Ramp front sight, slide-mounted micro-adj. rear. Satin blued or stainless finish. Checkered walnut grips w/ thumbrest. Made 1992 to 1996.

SA SPORT KING II . . . . NiB $304 Ex $226 Gd $170
Caliber: .22 LR. 10-round magazine, 4.5- or 6.75-inch bbl., 9 or 11.25 inches overall. Weight: 39 or 42 oz. Checkered walnut or black plastic grips. Blade front sight and drift adjustable rear. Made 1993 to 1994.

SA ARMY REVOLVER
Calibers: .357 Mag., .44 Mag., .45 Colt/.45 ACP. Six-round cylinder. bbl., lengths: 4.75, 5.5, 7.5 inches, weight: 40-43 oz. Blade front sight, grooved top strap or adj. rear. Blued or nickel finish w/color-casehardened frame. Brass or steel backstrap/ trigger guard. Smooth one-piece walnut grips. Imported from 1987-94 and 1997. Disc.
Standard model w/blued finish . . NiB $431 Ex $319 Gd $235
Standard model w/nickel finish. . . . NiB $464 Ex $398 Gd $303
Standard model w/steel
  backstrap . . . . NiB $541 Ex $422 Gd $317
.45 Combo w/blued finish . . . . NiB $544 Ex $429 Gd $346
.45 Combo w/nickel finish . . . . NiB $601 Ex $562 Gd $433

TROPHY II
AUTO PISTOL. . . . . NiB $464 Ex $337 Gd $270

Similar to the Citation II model except w/gold-plated trigger and gold-filled markings. Made from 1992 to 1996.

VICTOR II AUTO PISTOL . . . . . NiB $544 Ex $419 Gd $342
Re-creation of the High Standard Victor w/full-length vent rib. Caliber: .22 LR. 10-round magazine, 4.5- or 5.5-inch bbl., 9.75 inches overall (with 5.5-inch bbl.). Weight: 52 oz. (with 5.5-inch bbl.). Rib-mounted target sights. Satin blued or stain-

---

GRADING: **NiB** = New in Box   **Ex** = Excellent or NRA 95%   **Gd** = Good or NRA 68%   **255**

less finish. Checkered walnut grips w/thumbrest. Made from 1992 to 1996.

GUARDIAN ANGEL
DERRINGER . . . . NiB $158 Ex $120 Gd $101
Hammerless, double-action O/U derringer w/interchangeable drop-in breech block. Calibers: .22 LR, .22 WRM. Two-round capacity. Two-inch bbl., 5 inches overall. Weight: 12 oz. Blue, nickel or gold finish. Blade front and fixed rear sights. Checkered black grips. Made from 1996 to 1997.

GUARDIAN II. . . . . NiB $327 Ex $235 Gd $169
Caliber: .38 Special, Six-round cylinder, 2-, 4- or 6-inch bbl., 8.5 inches overall (with 4-inch bbl.). Weight: 32 oz (with 4-inch bbl.). Blade ramp front and fixed rear sights. Checkered combat or target grips. Blued finish. Made in 1995.

GUARDIAN III . . . . NiB $369 Ex $272 Gd $181
Same specifications as Guardian II model except w/adjustable rear sights. Made in 1995.

TITAN II DA . . . . NiB $295 Ex $259 Gd $175
Caliber: .357 Mag. Six-round cylinder. 2-, 4- or 6-inch bbl., 7.75 inches overall (with 4-inch bbl.). Weight: 38 oz (with 4-inch bbl.). Blade front and fixed rear sights. Crane mounted cylinder release. Blued or stainless finish. Made in 1995.

TITAN III DA. . . . . NiB $345 Ex $204 Gd $119
Same specification as the Titan II except w/adjustable rear sight. Made in 1995.

MKE — Ankara, Turkey
Manufactured by Makina ve Kimya Endüstrisi Kurumu.

KIRIKKALE DA
AUTOMATIC PISTOL . . . . NiB $399 Ex $283 Gd $212
Similar to Walther PP. Calibers: .32 Auto (7.65mm), .380 Auto (9mm Short). Seven-round magazine, 3.9-inch bbl., 6.7 inches overall. Weight: 24 oz. Fixed sights. Blued finish. Checkered plastic grips. Made from 1948 to 1988. Note: This is a Turkish Army standard service pistol.

MOA CORPORATION — Dayton, OH

MAXIMUM SINGLE-SHOT PISTOL
Calibers: .22 Hornet to .454 Casull Mag. Armoloy, Chromoloy or stainless falling block action fitted w/blued or stainless 8.75-, 10- or 14-inch Douglas bbl., weight: 60-68 oz. Smooth walnut grips. Made from 1986.
Chromoloy receiver
   (blued bbl.) . . . . NiB $806 Ex $588 Gd $475
Armoloy receiver (blued bbl.) . . . NiB $933 Ex $836 Gd $497
Stainless receiver (blued bbl.) . . NiB $1028 Ex $916 Gd $689
w/stainless bbl., add $306
w/Extra bbl., add $388

MAXIMUM CARBINE PISTOL
Similar to Maximum Pistol except w/18-inch bbl. Made intermittently from 1986-88 and from 1994 to date.
MOA Maximum (blued bbl.) . . . NiB $984 Ex $780 Gd $601
**MOA Maximum
   (stainless bbl.).** . . . . NiB $1100 Ex $890 Gd $597

O.F. MOSSBERG & SONS, INC. — North Haven, CT

BROWNIE "PEPPERBOX" PISTOL NiB $816 Ex $562 Gd $375
Hammerless, top-break, double-action, four bbls. w/revolving firing pin. Caliber: .22 LR, 2.5-inch bbls., weight: 14 oz. Blued finish. Serrated grips. Approximately 37,000 made from 1919-32.

MODEL 715P PISTOL . . . . NiB $308 Ex $270 Gd $260
Semi-automatic. Uses a Model 702 Plinkster barreled action. Caliber: .22 LR, 10- or 20-rnd. magazine. 6-inch bbl. Weight: 48 oz. Blued finish. Polymer grips. Made from 2014 to present.
w/red dot optic, add. $45
Duck Commander, add. $100

NAMBU
See Listings under Japanese Military Pistols.

NAVY ARMS COMPANY — Martinsburg, WV

MODEL 1873 SA REVOLVER
Calibers: .44-40, .45 Colt. Six-round cylinder, bbl. lengths: 3, 4.75, 5.5, 7.5 inches, 10.75 inches overall (with 5.5-inch bbl.). Weight: 36 oz. Blade front sight, grooved topstrap rear. Blued w/color-casehardened frame or nickel finish. Smooth walnut grips. Made from 1991 to 2009.
**Blued finish w/brass
   backstrap** . . . . NiB $468 Ex $357 Gd $235
**U.S. Artillery model w/5-inch
   bbl.** . . . . NiB $544 Ex $386 Gd $270
**U.S. Cavalry model w/7-inch
   bbl** . . . . NiB $544 Ex $386 Gd $270
Bisley model . . . . NiB $536 Ex $359 Gd $225
Sheriff's model (disc. 1998). . . . NiB $434 Ex $356 Gd $220

MODEL 1875 SCHOFIELD REVOLVER
Replica of S&W Model 3, top-break single-action w/auto ejector. Calibers: .44-40 or .45 LC. Six-round cylinder, 5- or 7-inch bbl., 10.75 or 12.75 inches overall. Weight: 39 oz. Blade front sight, square-notched rear. Polished blued finish. Smooth walnut grips. Made from 1999 to 2009.
Cavalry model (7-inch bbl.) . . . NiB $668 Ex $544 Gd $336
**Deluxe Cavalry model
   (engraved)** . . . . NiB $1720 Ex $1398 Gd $1176
Wells Fargo model (5-inch bbl.). . NiB $840 Ex $636 Gd $447
**Deluxe Wells Fargo
   model (engraved)** . . . . NiB $1479 Ex $1266 Gd $1122
**Hideout model
   (3.5-inch bbl.)** . . . . NiB $748 Ex $590 Gd $398

1875 REMINGTON
SA REVOLVER . . . . NiB $398 Ex $283 Gd $194
Replica of Remington Model 1875. Calibers: .357 Magnum, .44-40, .45 Colt. Six-round cylinder, 7.5-inch bbl., 13.5 inches overall. Weight: About 48 oz. Fixed sights. Blued or nickel finish. Smooth walnut grips. Made in Italy c.1955-1980 and 1994 to 2000. Originally marketed in the U.S. as Replica Arms Model 1875 (that firm was acquired by Navy Arms Co).

FRONTIER SA REVOLVER . . . . . NiB $397 Ex $290 Gd $224
Calibers: .22 LR, .22 WMR, .357 Mag., .45 Colt. Six-round cylinder, bbl. lengths: 4.5-, 5.5-, 7.5-inches, 10.25 inches overall (with 4.5-inch bbl.). Weight: About 36 oz. (with 4.5-inch bbl.).

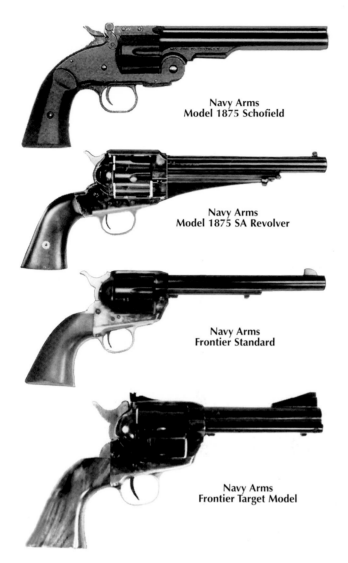

Navy Arms
Model 1875 Schofield

Navy Arms
Model 1875 SA Revolver

Navy Arms
Frontier Standard

Navy Arms
Frontier Target Model

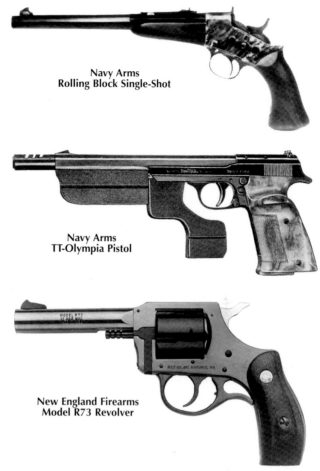

Navy Arms
Rolling Block Single-Shot

Navy Arms
TT-Olympia Pistol

New England Firearms
Model R73 Revolver

Fixed sights. Blued bbl., and cylinder, color-casehardened frame, brass grip frame. One-piece smooth walnut grip. Imported from 1975 to 1979.

FRONTIER TARGET MODEL . . . NiB $416 Ex $312 Gd $225
Same as standard Frontier except has adj. rear sight and ramp front sight. Imported from 1975 to 1979.

BUNTLINE FRONTIER . . . . NiB $569 Ex $467 Gd $342
Same as Target Frontier except has detachable shoulder stock and 16.5-inch bbl. Calibers: .357 Magnum and .45 Colt only. Made from 1975 to 1979.

LUGER AUTOMATIC . . . . NiB $166 Ex $112 Gd $88
Caliber: .22 LR, standard or high velocity. 10-round magazine, bbl. length: 4.5 inches, 8.9 inches overall. Weight: 1 lb., 13.5 oz. Square blade front sight w/square notch, stationary rear sight. Walnut checkered grips. Non-reflecting black finish. Made 1986 to 1988.

**ROLLING BLOCK
SINGLE-SHOT PISTOL . . . . NiB $418 Ex $345 Gd $231**

Calibers: .22 LR, .22 Hornet, .357 Magnum. Eight-inch bbl., 12 inches overall. Weight: About 40 oz. Adjustable sights. Blued bbl., color-casehardened frame, brass trigger guard. Smooth walnut grip and forearm. Imported from 1965 to 1980.

TT-OLYMPIA PISTOL . . . . NiB $283 Ex $214 Gd $170
Reproduction of the Walther Olympia Target Pistol. Caliber: .22 LR. Eight inches overall 4.6-inch bbl., weight: 28 oz. Blade front sight, adj. rear. Blued finish. Checkered hardwood grips. Imported 1992 to 1994.

NEW ENGLAND FIREARMS — Gardner, MA

In 1987, New England Firearms was established as an independent company producing select H&R models under the NEF logo. In 1991, H&R 1871, Inc. was formed from the residual of the parent company and took over the New England Firearms facility. H&R 1871 produced firearms under both their logo and the NEF brand name until 1999, when the Marlin Firearms Company acquired the assets of H&R 1871. Purchased by Freedom Group in 2008.

MODEL R73 REVOLVER . . . . NiB $158 Ex $98 Gd $67
Caliber: .32 H&R Mag. Five-round cylinder, 2.5- or 4-inch bbl., 8.5 inches overall (with 4-inch bbl.). Weight: 26 oz. (with 4 inch bbl.). Fixed or adjustable sights. Blued or nickel finish.

Walnut-finish hardwood grips. Made from 1988 to 1999.

MODEL R92 REVOLVER . . . . **NiB $137 Ex $90 Gd $64**
Same general specifications as Model R73 except chambered for .22 LR. Nine-round cylinder. Weight: 28 oz. w/4 inch bbl., Made 1988 to 1999.

MODEL 832 STARTER PISTOL . . **NiB $148 Ex $101 Gd $75**
Calibers: .22 Blank, .32 Blank. Nine- and 5-round cylinders, respectively. Push-pin swing-out cylinder. Solid wood grips w/ NEF medallion insert.

ULTRA REVOLVER . . . . **NiB $170 Ex $109 Gd $70**
Calibers: .22 LR, .22 Mag. Nine-round cylinder in .22 LR, 6-round cylinder in .22 Mag., 4- or 6-inch ribbed bull bbl., 10.75 inches overall (with 6-inch bbl.). Weight: 36 oz. (with 6-inch bbl.). Blade front sight, adj. square-notched rear. Blued or nickel finish. Walnut-finish hardwood grips. Made from 1989 to 1999.

LADY ULTRA REVOLVER . . . . . **NiB $169 Ex $144 Gd $106**
Same basic specifications as the Ultra except in .32 H&R Mag. w/5-round cylinder and 3-inch ribbed bull bbl., 7.5 inches overall. Weight: 31 oz. Made from 1992 to 1999.

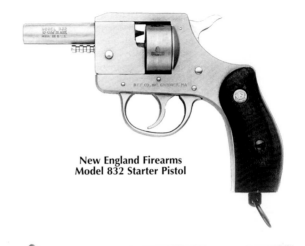

New England Firearms
Model 832 Starter Pistol

NORTH AMERICAN ARMS — Provo, UT

MODEL .22LR. . . . . **NiB $175 Ex $149 Gd $70**
Same as Model 22S except chambered for .22 LR., is 3.88-inches overall, weight: 4.5 oz. Made from 1975 to date.

MODEL 22S MINI REVOLVER . . **NiB $170 Ex $150 Gd $70**
Single-Action. Caliber: .22 Short. Five-round cylinder, 1.13-inch bbl., 3.5-inches overall. Weight: 4 oz. Fixed sights. Stainless steel. Plastic grips. Made from 1975 to date.

MODEL 450 MAGNUM EXPRESS
Single-Action. Calibers: .450 Magnum Express, .45 Win. Mag. Five-round cylinder, 7.5- or 10.5-inch bbl., matte or polished stainless steel finish. Walnut grips. Presentation case. Disc. 1984.
Matte stainless model . . . . . **NiB $1259 Ex $1066 Gd $808**
Polished stainless model . . . . **NiB $1528 Ex $1234 Gd $856**
w/10-inch bbl., add $281
w/combo cylinder, add. $255

BLACK WIDOW REVOLVER
SA. Calibers: .22 LR., .22 WMR. Five-round cylinder, 2-inch heavy vent bbl., 5.88-inches overall. Weight: 8.8 oz. Fixed or adj. sights. Full-size black rubber grips. Stainless steel brush finish. Made from 1990 to date.
Adj. sight model . . . . **NiB $257 Ex $188 Gd $135**
Adj. sight combo model, add $45
Fixed sight model . . . . **NiB $257 Ex $188 Gd $135**
Fixed sight combo model, add $40

GUARDIAN DAO PISTOL . . . . **NiB $377 Ex $286 Gd $198**
Caliber: .25 ACP, .32 ACP or .380. Six-round magazine (.32 ACP), 2-inch bbl., 4.4 inches overall. Weight: 13.5 oz. Fixed sights. Black synthetic grips. Stainless steel. Made from 1997 to date.

MINI-MASTER TARGET REVOLVER
SA. Calibers: .22 LR., .22 WMR. Five-round cylinder, 4-inch heavy vent rib bbl., 7.75-inches overall. Weight: 10.75 oz. Fixed or adj. sights. Black rubber grips. Stainless steel brush finish. Made from 1990 to date.

Ortgies
Pocket Automatic Pistol

Adj. sight model . . . . **NiB $270 Ex $214 Gd $165**
Adj. sight combo model, add $35
Fixed sight model . . . . **NiB $270 Ex $214 Gd $165**
Fixed sight combo model, add $35

NORWEGIAN MILITARY PISTOLS — Manufactured by Kongsberg Vaapenfabrikk, Government Arsenal at Kongsberg, Norway

MODEL 1912 . . . . **NiB $2885 Ex $2289 Gd $1588**
Same as the model 1914 except has conventional slide stop. Only 500 were made.

MODEL 1914
AUTOMATIC PISTOL . . . . **NiB $511 Ex $378 Gd $283**
Similar to Colt Model 1911 .45 Automatic w/same general specifications except has lengthened slide stop. Made 1919-46.

OLYMPIC ARMS, INC. — Olympia, WA

OA-93 AR SEMIAUTOMATIC PISTOL
AR-15 style receiver with no buffer tube or charging handle. Caliber: .223 Rem. or 7.62x39mm. Five-, 20- or 30-round detachable magazine, 6-, 9- or 14-inch stainless steel bbl., 15.75 inches overall w/6-inch bbl., weight: 4 lbs., 3 oz. Flattop

upper with no open sights. VortEx flash suppressor. A2 stow-away pistol grip and forward pistol grip. Made 1993-94. Note: All post-ban versions of OA-93 style weapons are classified by BATF as "Any Other Weapon" and must be transferred by a Class III dealer. Values listed here are for limited-production, pre-ban guns.

(.223 Rem.) . . . . NiB $1134 Ex $871 Gd $687
(7.62x39mm) . . . . NiB $2234 Ex $1669 Gd $1378

OA-96 AR SEMI-AUTOMATIC
PISTOL . . . . NiB $904 Ex $804 Gd $637
Similar to Model OA-93 AR except w/6.5-inch bbl. only chambered for .223 Rem. Additional compliance modifications include a fixed (nonremovable) well-style magazine and no forward pistol grip. Made from 1996 to 2000.

WHITNEY WOLVERINE . . . . . . NiB $294 Ex $265 Gd $235
Similar to original Whitney Wolverine from 1950s except w/ polymer frame and ventalated rib. .22 LR, 10-rnd. magazine. Finish: black, pink, desert tan, coyote brown. Weight: 19.2 oz. Made from 2010 to date.

ORTGIES PISTOLS — Erfurt, Germany
Manufactured by Deutsche Werke A.G.

POCKET
AUTOMATIC PISTOL . . . . NiB $399 Ex $305 Gd $225
Calibers: .32 Auto (7.65mm), .380 Auto (9mm). Seven-round magazine (.380 cal.), 8-round (.32 cal.), 3.25-inch bbl., 6.5-inches overall. Weight: 22 oz. Fixed sights. Blued finish. Plain walnut grips. Made in 1920's.

VEST POCKET
AUTOMATIC PISTOL . . . . NiB $365 Ex $289 Gd $203
Caliber: .25 Auto (6.35mm). Six-round magazine, 2.75-inch bbl., 5.19 inches overall. Weight: 13.5 oz. Fixed sights. Blued finish. Plain walnut grips. Made in 1920's.

PARA USA, INC. — Pineville, NC
Purchased by Freedom Group in 2012.

LIMITED EDITION SERIES
Custom-tuned and fully accessorized "Limited Edition" versions of standard "P" Models. Enhanced-grip frame and serrated slide fitted w/match-grade bbl., and full-length recoil spring guide system. Beavertail grip safety and skeletonized hammer. Ambidextrous safety and trigger-stop adjustment. Fully adjustable or contoured low-mount sights. For pricing see individual models.

P-10 SA AUTO PISTOL
Super compact. Calibers: .40 S&W, .45 ACP. 10-round magazine, 3-inch bbl., weight: 24 oz. (alloy frame) or 31 oz. (steel frame). Ramp front sight and drift adjustable rear w/3-dot system. Steel or alloy frame. Matte black, Duo-Tone or stainless finish. Made from 1997 to 2002.
Alloy model . . . . NiB $637 Ex $540 Gd $413
Duo-Tone model . . . . NiB $688 Ex $581 Gd $464
Stainless steel model . . . . NiB $693 Ex $577 Gd $447
Steel model . . . . NiB $648 Ex $536 Gd $410
Limited model (tuned & accessorized), add $150

P-12 COMPACT AUTO PISTOL

Calibers: .45 ACP. 11-round magazine, 3.5-inch bbl., 7-inches overall. Weight: 24 oz. (alloy frame). Blade front sight, adj. rear w/3-dot system. Textured composition grips. Matte black alloy or steel finish. Made from 1990 to 2003.
Model P1245 (alloy) . . . . NiB $779 Ex $606 Gd $530
Model P1245C (steel) . . . . NiB $857 Ex $686 Gd $541
Limited model (tuned & accessorized), add $150

P-13 AUTO PISTOL
Same general specifications as Model P-12 except w/12-round magazine, 4.5-inch bbl., 8-inches overall. Weight: 25 oz. (alloy frame). Blade front sight, adj. rear w/3-dot system. TExtured composition grips. Matte black alloy or steel finish. Made from 1993 to 2003.
Model P1345 (alloy) . . . . NiB $779 Ex $606 Gd $530
Model P1345C (steel) . . . . NiB $772 Ex $586 Gd $337
Limited model
(tuned & accessorized), add $150

P-14 AUTO PISTOL
Caliber: .45 ACP. 13-round magazine, 5-inch bbl., 8.5 inches overall. Weight: 28 oz. Alloy frame. Blade front sight, adj. rear w/3-dot system. TExtured composition grips. Matte black alloy or steel finish. Made from 1990 to 2003.
Model P1445 (alloy) . . . . NiB $685 Ex $474 Gd $332
Model P1445C (stainless) . . . . . NiB $755 Ex $546 Gd $395
Limited model (tuned & accessorized), add $128

P-15 AUTO PISTOL
Caliber: .40 S&W. 10-round magazine, 4.25-inch bbl., 7.75 inches overall. Weight: 28 to 36 oz. Steel, alloy or stainless receiver. Matte black, Duotone or stainless finish. Made 1996 to 1999.
Model P1540 (alloy) . . . . NiB $740 Ex $495 Gd $362
Model P1540C (steel) . . . . NiB $665 Ex $544 Gd $468
Duotone stainless model . . . . . . NiB $740 Ex $495 Gd $362
Stainless model . . . . NiB $700 Ex $602 Gd $536

P-16 SA AUTO PISTOL
Caliber: .40 S&W. 10- or 16-round magazine, 5-inch bbl., 8.5 inches overall. Weight: 40 oz. Ramp front sight and drift adjustable rear w/3-dot system. Carbon steel or stainless frame. Matte black, Duotone or stainless finish. Made from 1995 to 2002.
Blue steel model . . . . NiB $683 Ex $536 Gd $437
Duotone model . . . . NiB $709 Ex $572 Gd $362
Stainless model . . . . NiB $740 Ex $576 Gd $485
Limited model (tuned & accessorized), add $175

P-18 SA AUTO PISTOL
Caliber: 9mm Parabellum. 10- or 18-round magazine, 5-inch bbl., 8.5 inches overall. Weight: 40 oz. Dovetailed front sight and fully adjustable rear. Bright stainless finish. Made from 1998 to 2003.
Stainless model . . . . NiB $816 Ex $652 Gd $523
Limited model (tuned & accessorized), add $150

PXT SINGLE STACK SERIES AUTO PISTOL
Caliber: 9mm Para. , .38 Super or .45 ACP. Eight- or 9-round (9mm Para) magazine, 3-, 3.5-, 4.25-, 5- or 6-inch bbl., 8.5 inches overall (5-in. bbl.). Weight: 30 oz. (5-in. bbl.). Steel or stainless frame. Blade front sight, adj. rear w/3-dot system. Textured composition grips. Matte black alloy or steel finish. Made from 2004 to date.
1911 OPS (disc. 2008) . . . . NiB $980 Ex $931 Gd $450
1911 LTC (intro. 2009) . . . . NiB $780 Ex $741 Gd $330
1911 Wild Bunch (intro. 2011) . . . NiB $660 Ex $550 Gd $340
GI Expert (intro. 2009) . . . . NiB $580 Ex $440 Gd $355

Olympic Arms OA-93

**Para-Ordnance
P-12 Compact**

**Para-Ordnance
P-14 Auto Pistol**

Slim Hawg (.45 ACP, 3-in. bbl.)...NiB $860 Ex $670 Gd $400

PXT HIGH CAPACITY SERIES AUTO PISTOL
Similar to PXT Single Stack series except 10-, 14-, or 18-round magazine. Made from 2004 to date.
P14.45 (.45 ACP, 14-rnd.
  magazine)................NiB $880 Ex $650 Gd $410

P18.9 (9mm Para, 18-rnd.
  magazine)..............NiB $1030 Ex $840 Gd $470
Warthog (.45 ACP, 10-rnd.
  magazine)...............NiB $900 Ex $700 Gd $400

PHOENIX ARMS — Ontario, CA

MODEL HP22/HP25 SA
AUTO PISTOLS............. NiB $170 Ex $95 Gd $66
Caliber: .22 LR, .25 ACP. 10-round magazine, 3-inch bbl., 5.5 inches overall. Weight: 20 oz. Checkered synthetic grips. Blade front sight, adj. rear. Blue, chrome or nickel finish. Made from 1994 to date.

MODEL HP RANGE-MASTER TARGET SA
AUTO PISTOL............... NiB $170 Ex $95 Gd $66
Similar to Model HP .22 except w/5.5-inch target bbl. and Extended magazine, Ramp front sight, adj. notch rear on vent rib. Checkered synthetic grips. Blue or satin nickel finish. Made from 1998 to date.

MODEL HP RANGE-MASTER DELUXE TARGET
SA AUTO PISTOL........... NiB $204 Ex $165 Gd $110
Similar to Model HP Rangemaster Target model except w/dual-2000 laser sight and custom wood grips. Made from 1998 to date.

RAVEN SA AUTO PISTOL........ NiB $88 Ex $61 Gd $45
Caliber: .25 ACP. Six-round magazine, 2.5 inch bbl., 4.75 inches overall. Weight: 15 oz. Ivory, pink pearl, or black slotted stocks. Fixed sights. Blue, chrome or nickel finish. Made from 1993 to 1998.

PLAINFIELD MACHINE COMPANY — Dunellen, NJ
This firm disc. operation about 1982.

MODEL 71 AUTOMATIC PISTOL
Calibers: .22 LR, .25 Automatic w/conversion kit available. 10-round magazine (.22 LR) or 8-round (.25 Auto), 2.5-inch bbl., 5.13 inches overall. Weight: 25 oz. Fixed sights. Stainless steel frame/slide. Checkered walnut grips. Made from 1970-82.
.22 LR or .25 Auto ....NiB $200 Ex $177 Gd $128
w/conversion kit............NiB $222 Ex $188 Gd $119

MODEL 72 AUTOMATIC PISTOL
Same as Model 71 except has aluminum slide, 3.5-inch bbl., 6 inches overall. Made from 1970 to 1982
.22 LR or .25 Auto only ......NiB $220 Ex $177 Gd $101
w/conversion kit............NiB $235 Ex $166 Gd $128

POLISH MILITARY PISTOLS — Radom, Poland
Manufactured at Lucznik Arms Factory.

MODEL P-64............... NiB n/a Ex $250 Gd $125
SA/DA. Similar to Walther PPK. Caliber: 9x18mm Makarov. 3.3-in. bbl., 22 ozs. Military surplus. Made 1965 to date.

MODEL P-83 WANAD .... NiB n/a Ex $350 Gd $220
SA/DA. Caliber: 9x18mm Makarov. 8-round magazine. 3.5-in. bbl., 26 ozs. Military surplus. Made 1983 to date.

Plainfield Model 71

Plainfield Model 72

Radom P-35

PROFESSIONAL ORDNANCE, INC. — Lake Havasu City, AZ

MODEL CARBON-15 TYPE 20
SEMIAUTOMATIC PISTOL . . . . NiB $944 Ex $819 Gd $581
Similar to Carbon-15 Type 97 except w/unfluted barrel.
Weight: 40 oz. Matte black finish. Made from 1999 to 2000.

MODEL CARBON-15 TYPE 97
SEMIAUTOMATIC PISTOL . . . NiB $1030 Ex $927 Gd $588
AR-15 operating system w/recoil reduction system. Caliber:
.223 Rem. 10-round magazine, 7.25-inch fluted bbl., 20
inches overall. Weight: 46 oz. Ghost ring sights. Carbon-fiber
upper and lower receivers w/Chromoly bolt carrier. Matte
black finish. Checkered composition grip. Made from 1996
to 2003.

RADOM — Radom, Poland
Manufactured by the Polish Arsenal.

P-35 AUTOMATIC PISTOL
Variation of the Colt Government Model .45 Auto. Caliber:
9mm Para. Eight-round magazine, 4.75-inch bbl., 7.75 inches
overall. Weight: 29 oz. Fixed sights. Blued finish. Plastic grips.
Made from 1935 thru WWII.
Commercial model
  (Polish Eagle) . . . . NiB $4599 Ex $4370 Gd $2555
Nazi military model
  (w/slotted backstrap) . . . . . NiB $1629 Ex $1199 Gd $877
Nazi military model
  (w/takedown lever) . . . . . . NiB $1300 Ex $1000 Gd $431
Nazi military model
  (No takedown lever or slot) . . NiB $459 Ex $356 Gd $232
Nazi military model (Parkerized), add $357

RANDALL FIREARMS COMPANY — Sun Valley, CA
*The short-lived Randall firearms Company (1982 to 1984)
was a leader in the production of stainless steel semi-autimatic
handguns, particularly in left-handed configurations. Prices
shown are for production models. Add 50% for prototype
models (t-prefix on serial numbers) and $125 for guns with
serial numbers below 2000. Scare models (C311, C332, etc.,
made in lots of four pieces or less) valued substantially higher
to avid collectors.*

MODEL A111 . . . . NiB $791 Ex $479 Gd $316
Caliber: .45 Auto. Barrel: 5 inches. Round-slide top; right-hand
model. Sights: Fixed. Total production: 3,431 pieces.

MODEL A112 . . . . NiB $920 Ex $689 Gd $581
Calibers: 9mm. Barrel: 5 inches. Round-slide top; right-hand
model. Sights: Fixed.

MODEL A121 . . . . NiB $734 Ex $643 Gd $377
Caliber: .45 Auto. Barrel: 5 inches. Flat-slide top; right-hand
model. Sights: Fixed.

MODEL A211 . . . . NiB $785 Ex $571 Gd $479
Caliber: .45 Auto. Barrel: 4.25 inches. Round-slide top; right-
hand model. Sights: Fixed.

P-83 Wanad

MODEL A232 . . . . NiB $1560 Ex $1357 Gd $1100
Caliber: 9mm. Barrel: 4.25 inches. Flat-slide top; right-hand model. Sights: Fixed.

MODEL A331 . . . . NiB $1808 Ex $1566 Gd $1234
Caliber: .45 Auto. Barrel: 4.25 inches. Flat-slide top; right-hand model. Sights: Fixed.

MODEL B111 . . . . NiB $1270 Ex $1124 Gd $890
Caliber: .45 Auto. Barrel: 5 inches. Round-slide top; left-hand model. Sights: Fixed. Toatal production: 297 pieces

MODEL B131 . . . . NiB $1470 Ex $1326 Gd $1152
Caliber: .45 Auto. Barrel: 5 inches. Flat-slide top; left-hand model. Sights: Millet. Total production: 225 pieces.

MODEL B311 . . . . NiB $1632 Ex $1418 Gd $1206
Caliber: .45 Auto. Barrel: 4.25 inches. Round-slide top; left-hand model. Sights: Fixed. Total production: 52 pieces.

MODEL B312 LEMAY . . . . . NiB $5170 Ex $1669 Gd $3090
Caliber: 9mm. Barrel: 4.25 inches. Round-slide top; left-hand model. Sights: Fixed. Total production: 9 pieces.

MODEL B331 . . . . NiB $1800 Ex $1589 Gd $1356
Caliber: .45 Auto. Barrel: 4.25 inches. Flat-slide top; left-hand model. Sights: Millet. Total production: 45 pieces.

RECORD-MATCH PISTOLS — Zella-Mehlis, Germany. Manufactured by Udo Anschütz

MODEL 200 FREE PISTOL . . . NiB $1039 Ex $760 Gd $616
Basically the same as Model 210 except w/different stock design and conventional set trigger, spur trigger guard. Made prior to WW II.

MODEL 210 FREE PISTOL . . NiB $1355 Ex $1206 Gd $919
System Martini action, set trigger w/button release. Caliber: .22 LR. Single-shot, 11-inch bbl., weight: 46 oz. Target sights micrometer rear. Blued finish. Carved and checkered walnut forearm and stock w/adj. hand base. Also made w/ dual action (Model 210A); weight 35 oz. Made prior to WWII.

REISING ARMS CO. — Hartford, CT

TARGET AUTOMATIC PISTOL . . .NiB $1132 Ex $862 Gd $587
Hinged frame. Outside hammer. Caliber: .22 LR. 12-round magazine, 6.5-inch bbl., fixed sights. Blued finish. Hard rubber grips. Made 1921 to 1924.

REMINGTON ARMS COMPANY — Madison, NC
Manufacturing in Ilion, New York; Lonoke, AR; and Mayfield, KY. Owned by the Freedom Group.

MODEL 51 AUTOMATIC PISTOL
Calibers: .32 Auto, .380 Auto. Seven-round magazine, 3.5-inch bbl., 6.63 inches overall. Weight: 21 oz. Fixed sights. Blued finish. Hard rubber grips. Made from 1918 to 1926.
.32 ACP . . . . NiB $887 Ex $780 Gd $453
.380 ACP . . . . NiB $899 Ex $790 Gd $495

MODEL 95 DOUBLE DERRINGER
SA. Caliber: 41 Short Rimfire. Three-inch double bbls. (superposed), 4.88 inches overall. Early models have long hammer spur and two-armed Extractor, but later guns have short hammer spur and sliding Extractor (a few have no Extractor). Fixed blade front sight and grooved rear. finish: Blued, blued w/nickel-plated frame or fully nickel-plated; also w/factory engraving. Grips: Walnut, checkered hard rubber, pearl, ivory. Weight: 11 oz. Made 1866-1935. Approximately 150,000 were manufactured. Note: Duringthe 70 years of its production, serial numbering of this model was repeated two or three times. Therefore, aside from hammer and Extractor differences between the earlier and later models, the best clue to the age of a Double Derringer is the stamping of the company's name on the top of the bbl., or side rib. Prior to 1888, derringers were stamped "E. Remington & Sons, Ilion, N.Y." on one side rib and "Elliot's Patent Dec. 12, 1865" on the other (Type I-early & mid-production) and on the top rib (Type I-late production). In 1888-1911, "Remington Arms Co., Ilion, N.Y." and patent date were stamped on the top rib (Type II) and from 1912-35 "Remington Arms - U.M.C. Co., Ilion, N.Y." and patent date were stamped on the top rib.
Model 95 (Early Type I,
    w/o Extractor) . . . . NiB $6600 Ex $5000 Gd $3800
Model 95 (Mid Type I,
    w/Extractor) . . . . NiB $11,000 Ex $8000 Gd $4000
Model 95 (Late Type I,
    w/Extractor) . . . . NiB $5000 Ex $4219 Gd $1000
M95 (TYPE II
    produced 1888-1911) . . . . NiB $3700 Ex $2588 Gd $909
Model 95 (Type III,
    produced 1912-35) . . . . . NiB $3600 Ex $3000 Gd $1099
Factory-engraved model w/ivory
    or pearl grips, add 40%

NEW MODEL SINGLE-SHOT TARGET PISTOL
Also called Model 1901 Target. Rolling-block action. Calibers: .22 Short & Long, .25 Stevens, .32 S&W, .44 S&W Russian. 10-inch half-octagon bbl., 14 inches overall. Weight: 45 oz. (.22 cal.). Target sights. Blued finish. Checkered walnut grips and forearm. Made from 1901 to 1909.
Model 1901 (.22 caliber) . . NiB $3750 Ex $2550 Gd $1203
Model 1901
    (.25 Stevens, .32 S&W) . . .NiB $3449 Ex $2988 Gd $1380
Model 1901 (.44 Russian) . . NiB $3969 Ex $2709 Gd $1190

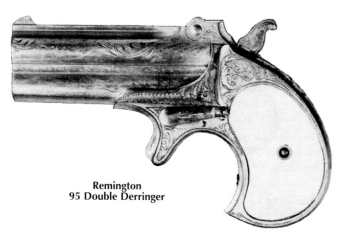

**Remington
95 Double Derringer**

**Record-Match
Model 200 Free Pistol**

MODEL XP-100
SINGLE-SHOT PISTOL. . . . . . NiB $984 Ex $622 Gd $464
Bolt action. Caliber: 221 Rem. Fireball. 10.5-inch vent rib bbl., 16.75 inches overall. Weight: 3.75 lbs. Adj. rear sight, blade front, receiver drilled and tapped for scope mounts. Blued finish. One-piece brown nylon stock. Made from 1963 to 1988.

MODEL XP-100
CUSTOM PISTOL. . . . . NiB $1096 Ex $755 Gd $596
Bolt-action, single-shot, long-range pistol. Calibers: .223 Rem., 7mm-08 or .35 Rem. 14.5-inch bbl., standard contour or heavy. Weight: About 4.25 lbs. Currently in production.

MODEL XP-100 SILHOUETTE . NiB $984 Ex $622 Gd $464
Same general specifications as Model XP-100 except chambered for 7mm BR Rem. and 35 Rem. 14.75-inch bbl., weight: 4.13 lbs. Made from 1987 to 1992.

MODEL XP-100
VARMINT SPECIAL. . . . . NiB $984 Ex $622 Gd $464
Bolt-action, single-shot, long-range pistol. Calibers: .223 Rem., 7mm BR. 14.5-inch bbl., 21.25 inches overall. Weight: About 4.25 lbs. One-piece Du Pont nylon stock w/universal grips. Made from 1986 to 1992.

MODEL XP-100R
CUSTOM REPEATER
Same general specifications as Model XP-100 Custom except 4- or 5- round repeater chambered for .22-250, .223 Rem.,

.250 Savage, 7mm-08 Rem., .308 Win., .35 Rem. and .350 Rem. Mag. Kevlar-reinforced synthetic or fiberglass stock w/ blind magazine and sling swivel studs. Made from 1992-94 and from 1998 to 1999.
**Model XP-100R (fiberglass
  stock) . . . . NiB $984 Ex $622 Gd $464**
**Model XP-100R KS (kevlar
  stock) . . . . NiB $984 Ex $622 Gd $464**

NOTE: *The following Remington derringers were produced from the mid-1860s through the mid-1930s. The Zig-Zag model is reputed to be the first cartridge handgun ever produced at the Remington plant. Few if any Remington derringers Exiswt in "new" or "in box" condition, therefore, guns in 90-percent condition command top price.*

ZIG-ZAG DERRINGER . . . . NiB $6155 Ex $5875 Gd $4145
Caliber: .22S, L, LR. Six shot, six-barrel (rotating) cluster. 3-inch bbl., blued, ring trigger. Two-piece rubber grips. Fewer than 1,000 pieces produced from 1861 to 1863.

ELIOT'S FIVE-SHOT
DERRINGER. . . . . NiB $1897 Ex $1268 Gd $1091
Caliber: .22S, L, LR. Five shot, five-barrel fixed cluster. 3-inch bbl., ring trigger, blue and/or nickel finish. Two-piece rubber, walnut, ivory or pearl grips.

ELIOT'S FOUR-SHOT
DERRINGER. . . . . NiB $5000 Ex $4275 $3795
Caliber: .32. Four shot, four-barrel fixed cluster. 3-3/8 inch bbl., ring trigger, blue and/or nickel finish. Two-piece rubber, walnut, ivory or pearl grips. Approx. 25,000 pieces (.22 and .32) produced.

VEST POCKET
DERRINGER. . . . . NiB $3255 Ex $2920 Gd $2635
Caliber: .22, .30, .32, .41 rimfire . Two shot, various bbl. lengths, blue or nickel finish. Two-piece walnut grips. Spur trigger. Made from 1865 to 1888.

OVER AND UNDER
DERRINGER. . . . . NiB $6270 Ex $4720 Gd $3955
Caliber: .41 rimfire. Two shot, 3-inch super imposed bbl., spur trigger, blue and/or nickel finish. Two-piece rubber, walnut, ivory or pearl grips. Oscillating firing pin. Produced 1866-1934. Also known as Double Derringer or Model 95. Type 1 and variatitons bear maker's name, patent data stamped between the barrels, with or without Extractor. Types Two and Three marked "Remington Arms Company, Ilion, NY. Type Four marked on top of barrel, "Remington Arms-U.M.C. Co. Ilion, NY."

MODEL 1866
ROLLING BLOCK PISTOL. . .NiB $6210 Ex $4329 Gd $3144
Caliber: .50 rimfire. Single-shot, 8-1/2 inch round, blue finish. Walnut grip and forearm. Spur trigger. Made from 1866-67. Mistakenly designated as Model 1865 Navy. Top values are for military-marked, pristine pieces. Very few of these guns remain in original condition.

MODEL 1870 NAVY
ROLLING BLOCK PISTOL. . .NiB $4225 Ex $3199 Gd $1905
Caliber: .50 centerfire. Single shot, 7-inch round bbl. Standard trigger with trigger guard, walnut grip and forearm. Approx. 6,400 pieces made from 1870-75. Modified for the

Navy from Model 1866. Higher values are for 8--inch commercial version without proof marks.

RIDER'S
MAGAZINE PISTOL . . . . NiB $3577 Ex $2885 Gd $2389
Caliber: .32. Five shot, 3-inch octagon bbl. blued (add 50 percent for case-hardened receiver). Walnut, rosewood, ivory or pearl grips. Spur trigger. Made from 1871 to 1888.

ELIOT'S VEST POCKET SINGLE-SHOT
DERRINGER . . . . NiB $3387 Ex $1109 Gd $879
Caliber: .41 rimfire. Single-shot, 2-1/2-inch round bbl., blue and/or nickel finish. Also known as "Mississippi Derringer." Two-piece walnut grips. Spur trigger. Approx. 10,000 made from 1867 to 1888.

MODEL 1890 SINGLE-ACTION
REVOLVER . . . . . . NiB $15,210 Ex $14,070 Gd $7680
Caliber: .41 centerfire . Six shot, 5-3/4 or 7-1/2-inch round bbl., blue or nickel finish. Standard trigger with trigger guard. Two-piece ivory or pearl grips with Remington monogram. nickel finish valued about 15 percent less.

MODEL 1911
REMINGTON UMC. . . . . NiB $7000 Ex $5550 Gd $1650
Caliber: .45 ACP. WWII military contract production. Blued finish. Made from 1918 to 1919, with serial numbers 1 to 21,676.

MODEL 1911A1
REMINGTON RAND. . . . NiB $2500 Ex $2079 Gd $1086
Caliber: .45 ACP. Parkerized finish. Two-piece walnut grips. Made from 1943-45 by Remington Rand Co., not Remington Arms Co.

Model 1911 R1. . . . . NiB $774 Ex $660 Gd $510
1911 platform. Semi-automatic. SA. Caliber: .45 ACP; 7-rnd. magazine. 5.0-in. bbl. Frame: steel. Sights: fixed. Finish: high polish blue. Grip: checkered double diamond walnut. Length: 8.5 in. Weight: 38.5 oz. Made from 2014 to date.
Carry model (extended beavertail, ambi.
  safety) . . . . .NiB $1067 Ex $1000 Gd $880
Carry Commander model (4.25-in. bbl., extended beavertail, ambi. safety) . . . . .NiB $1067 Ex $1000 Gd $880
Carry Commander CT model (4.25-in. bbl., laser grip) NiB $1350 Ex $1100 Gd $880
Commander model (4.25-in. bbl.) . . NiB $774 Ex $660 Gd $510
Enhanced model (extended beavertail, ambi.
  safety). . . . . NiB $837 Ex $790 Gd $700
Enhanced stainless model (extended beavertail, ambi. safety, stainless). . . . . NiB $990 Ex $880 Gd $750
Enhanced threaded bbl. model (extended beavertail, ambi. safety, thread bbl.) . . . . NiB $959 Ex $960 Gd $850
Stainless model (stainless) . . . NiB $837 Ex $790 Gd $700

MODEL R51 . . . . NiB $448 EX $390 GD $340
Semi-automatic. Caliber: 9mm; 7-rnd. magazine. 3.4-in. bbl. Frame: aluminum. Sights: fixed. Finish: matte black. Grip: checkered polymer. Length: 6.6 in. Weight: 22 oz. Made 2014; rereleased 2016 to date.

MODEL RM380 . . . . NiB $436 EX $400 GD $380
Semi-automatic. DAO. Caliber: .380 ACP; 6-rnd. magazine. 2.9-in. bbl. Frame: aluminum. Sights: fixed. Finish: matte

black. Grip: checkered polymer. Length: 5.27 in. Made 2016 to date.

RG (Röhm Gesellschaft)—Germany
Imported by R.G. Industries, Miami, FL., then manufactured until 1986.

MODEL 23 . . . . NiB $115 Ex $88 Gd $70
SA/DA. 6-round magazine, swing-out cylinder. Caliber: .22 LR. 1.75- or 3.38-inch bbl., Overall length: 5.13 and 7.5 inches. Weight: 16-17 oz. Fixed sights. Blued or nickel finish. Disc. 986.

MODEL 38S
SA/DA. Caliber: .38 Special. Six-round magazine, swing-out cylinder. Three- or 4-inch bbl., overall length: 8.25 and 9.25 inches. Weight: 32-34 oz. Windage-adj. rear sight. Blued finish. Disc. 1986.
w/plastic grips. . . . . NiB $177 Ex $140 Gd $101
w/wood grips. . . . . NiB $212 Ex $130 Gd $95

ROHRBAUGH FIREARMS — Long Island, NY
Purchased by Remington inJanuary 2014.

MODEL R9 . . . . NiB $1349 Ex $1300 Gd $1200
Semi-automatic. DAO. Caliber: .380 ACP or 9mm, 6-rnd. magazine. 2.9-in. bbl. Frame: aluminum. Sights: fixed. Finish: matte black or two-tone. Grip: smooth polymer. Weight: 13.5 oz. Length: 5.2 in. Made from 2002 to 2014.

ROSSI — São Leopoldo, Brazil
Manufactured by Amadeo Rossi S.A., imported by BrazTech, Int'l., in Miami, Florida; previously by Interarms, Alexandria, VA.

MODEL 31 DA REVOLVER. . . . NiB $144 Ex $78 Gd $62
Caliber: .38 Special. Five-round cylinder, 4-inch bbl., weight: 20 oz. Blued or nickel finish. Disc. 1985.

MODEL 51 DA REVOLVER. . . . NiB $147 Ex $82 Gd $61
Caliber: .22 LR. Six-round cylinder, 6-inch bbl., weight: 28 oz. Blued finish. Disc. 1985.

MODEL 68 . . . . NiB $177 Ex $147 Gd $101
Caliber: .38 Special. Five-round magazine, 2- or 3-inch bbl., overall length: 6.5 and 7.5 inches. Weight: 21-23 oz. Blued finish. Nickel finish available w/3-inch bbl. Disc. 1998.

MODEL 84 DA REVOLVER. . NiB $209 Ex $160 Gd $110
Caliber: .38 Special. 6-rnd. cylinder, 3-in. bbl., 8-in. overall. Weight: 27.5 oz. Stainless steel finish. Imported 1984 to 1986.

MODEL 85 DA REVOLVER. . NiB $209 Ex $160 Gd $110
Same as Model 84 except has vent rib. Imported 1985-86.

MODEL 88 DA REVOLVER
Caliber: .38 Special. Five-round cylinder, 2- or 3-inch bbl., weight: 21 oz. Stainless steel finish. Imported from 1988 to 98.
Model 88 (disc.) . . . . NiB $219 Ex $180 Gd $148
Model 88 Lady Rossi

(round butt) . . . . **NiB $225 Ex $189 Gd $152**

MODEL 88/2 DA REVOLVER NiB $219 Ex $180 Gd $140
Caliber: .38 Special. Five-round cylinder, 2- or 3-inch bbl., 6.5 inches overall. Weight: 21 oz. Stainless steel finish. Imported 1985 to 1987.

MODEL 89 DA REVOLVER. . . NiB $184 Ex $110 Gd $75
Caliber: .32 S&W. Six-round cylinder, 3-inch bbl., 7.5 inches overall. Weight: 17 oz. Stainless steel finish. Imported 1989 to 1990.

MODEL 94 DA REVOLVER . . . NiB $175 Ex $109 Gd $88
Caliber: .38 Special. Six-round cylinder, 3-inch bbl., 8 inches overall. Weight: 29 oz. Imported from 1985 to 1988.

MODEL 95 (951) REVOLVER NiB $219 Ex $175 Gd $141
Caliber: .38 Special. 6-rnd. cylinder, 3-in. bbl., 8-in. overall. Weight: 27.5 oz. Vent rib. Blued finish. Imported 1985 to 1990.

MODEL 351/352 REVOLVERS
Caliber: .38 Special. Five-round cylinder, 2-inch bbl., 6.87 inches overall. Weight: 22 oz. Ramp front and rear adjustable sights. Stainless or matte blued finish. Imported 1999 to date.
Model 351 (matte blue finish)NiB $362 Ex $255 Gd $186
Model 352 (stainless finish) . NiB $437 Ex $326 Gd $265

MODEL 461/462 REVOLVERS
Caliber: .357 Magnum. Six-round cylinder, 2-inch heavy bbl., 6.87 inches overall. Weight: 26 oz. Rubber grips w/ serrated ramp front sight. Stainless or matte blued finish. Imported 1999 to date.
Model 461 (matte blue finish)NiB $365 Ex $265 Gd $188
Model 462 (stainless finish) . NiB $439 Ex $290 Gd $219

MODEL 511 DA REVOLVER. . NiB $195 Ex $170 Gd $75
Similar to the Model 51 except in stainless steel. Imported 1986 to 1990.

MODEL 515 DA REVOLVER. . NiB $214 Ex $105 Gd $70
Calibers: .22 LR, .22 Mag. Six-round cylinder, 4-inch bbl., 9 inches overall. Weight: 30 oz. Red ramp front sight, adj. square-notched rear. Stainless finish. Checkered hardwood grips. Imported from 1994 to 1998.

MODEL 518 DA REVOLVER. . NiB $214 Ex $105 Gd $70
Similar to the Model 515 except in caliber .22 LR. Imported from 1993 to 1998.

MODEL 677 DA REVOLVER. NiB $225 Ex $180 Gd $128
Caliber: .357 Mag. Six-round cylinder, 2-inch bbl., 6.87 inches overall. Weight: 26 oz. Serrated front ramp sight, channel rear. Matte blue finish. Contoured rubber grips. Imported 1997-98.

MODEL 720 DA REVOLVER. NiB $235 Ex $170 Gd $141
Caliber: .44 Special. Five-round cylinder, 3-inch bbl., 8 inches overall. Weight: 27.5 oz. Red ramp front sight, adj. square-notched rear. Stainless finish. Checkered Neoprene combat-style grips. Imported from 1992 to 1998.

MODEL 841 DA REVOLVER. NiB $319 Ex $225 Gd $160
Same general specifications as Model 84 except has 4-inch bbl., (9 inches overall), weight: 30 oz. Imported 1985-86.

MODEL 851 DA REVOLVER. NiB $336 Ex $259 Gd $158
Same general specifications as Model 85 except w/3-or 4-inch bbl., 8 inches overall (with 3-inch bbl.). Weight: 27.5 oz. (with 3-inch bbl.). Red ramp front sight, adj. square-notched rear. Stainless finish. Checkered hardwood grips. Imported from 2001 to 2009 to date.

MODEL 877 DA REVOLVER . . . NiB $230 Ex $160 Gd $110
Same general specifications as Model 677 except stainless steel. Made from 1996 to date.

MODEL 941 DA REVOLVER . . . . NiB $214 Ex $109 Gd $82
Caliber: .38 Special. Six-round cylinder, 4-inch bbl., 9 inches overall. Weight: 30 oz. Blued finish. Imported from 1985-86.

MODEL 951 DA REVOLVER . . . . NiB $214 Ex $109 Gd $82
Previous designation M95 w/same general specifications.

MODEL 971 DA REVOLVER
Caliber: .357 Magnum. Six-round cylinder, 2.5-, 4- or 6-inch bbl., 9 inches overall (with 4-inch bbl.). Weight: 36 oz. (with 4-inch bbl.). Blade front sight, adj. square-notched rear. Blued or stainless finish. Checkered hardwood grips. Imported from 1988 to 1998.
Blued finish. . . . . .NiB $219 Ex $166 Gd $129
Stainless finish. . . . . .NiB $240 Ex $175 Gd $101
w/compensated bbl., add $25

MODEL 971 VRC
DA REVOLVER . . . . .NiB $321 Ex $270 Gd $175
Same general specifications as Model 971 stainless except w/ ventilated rib and compensated bbl. Made 1988 to 1998.

MODEL 972 . . . . NiB $380 Ex $330 Gd $260
Similar to Model 971 except stainless steel, 6-in. bbl. Imported from 2001 to date.

CYCLOPS DA REVOLVER . . . . . NiB $425 Ex $362 Gd $274
Caliber: .357 Mag. Six-round cylinder, 6- or 8-inch compensated slab-sided bbl., 11.75 or 13.75 inches overall. Weight: 44 oz. or 51 oz. Undercut blade front sight, fully adjustable rear. B-Square scope mount and rings. Stainless steel finish. Checkered rubber grips. Made from 1997 to 1998.

DA REVOLVER . . . . .NiB $220 Ex $170 Gd $124
Calibers: .22 LR, .32 S&W Long, .38 Special. 5-rnd. (.38) or 6-rnd. cylinder (other calibers), bbl. lengths: 3-, 6-inches. Weight: 22 oz. (3-inch bbl.). Adj. Rear sight, ramp front. Blued or nickel finish. Wood or plastic grips. Imported from 1965-91.

MATCHED PAIR . . . . NiB $380 Ex $330 Gd $260
Single-shot, break action w/interchangeable bbls. SA. Caliber: .22 LR or .45 Long Colt/410 gauge. 11-in. bbl. Frame: steel. Sights: fixed front, adj. rear. Finish: blue. Grip: textured rubber. Made from 2012 to date.

RANCH HAND . . . . NiB $597 Ex $500 Gd $380
Lever-action Mare's Leg style pistol. SA. Caliber: .357 Mag., .44 Mag., or .45 Long Colt, 6-rnd. magazine. 12-in. bbl. Sights: adj rear. Finish: blue. Made from 2010 to 2016.

SPORTSMAN'S .22 . . . . NiB $279 Ex $219 Gd $170
Caliber: .22 LR. Six-round magazine, 4-inch bbl., 9 inches overall. Weight: 30 oz. Stainless steel finish. Disc. 1991.

**Ruger Mark I Target w/5.5-inch
Untapered Bull Barrel**

Ruger Mark II

**Ruger Mark II
22/45**

RUBY — Manufactured by Gabilondo y Urresti, Eibar, Spain, and others

7.65MM
AUTOMATIC PISTOL . . . . NiB $342 Ex $255 Gd $129
Secondary standard service pistol of the French Army in world wars I and II. Essentially the same as the Alkartasuna (see separate listing). Other manufacturers: Armenia Elgoibarresa y Cia., Eceolaza y Vicinai y Cia., Hijos de Angel Echeverria y Cia., Bruno Salaverria y Cia., Zulaika y Cia., all of Eibar, Spain-Gabilondo y Cia., Elgoibar Spain; Ruby Arms Company, Guernica, Spain. Made from 1914 to 1922.

RUGER — Southport, CT
Manufactured by Sturm, Ruger & Co. Rugers made in 1976 are designated "Liberty" in honor of the U.S. Bicentennial and bring a premium of approximately 25% in value over regular models.

NOTE: *For ease in finding a particular Ruger handgun, the listings are divided into two groups: Automatic/Single-Shot Pistols (below) and Revolvers, which follow. For a complete listing, please refer to the index.*

- AUTOMATIC/SINGLE-SHOT PISTOLS -

22 CHARGER AUTOMATIC . . . NiB $330 Ex $230 Gd $180
Uses Ruger 10/22 action. Caliber: .22 LR, 10-in. bbl., black/grey laminated pistol grip and forend, bipod, matte black finish. Made from 2008 to 2012.

AMERICAN . . . . NiB $579 Ex $500 Gd $480
Semi-automatic. Striker fired. Caliber: 9mm or .45 ACP, 10 or 17-rnd magazine. 4.2- or 4.5-in. bbl. Frame: polymer. Sights: fixed. Finish: matte black. Grip: modular polymer inserts. Weight: 30-31.5 oz. Length: 7.5-8 in. Made from 2016 to date.

HAWKEYE SINGLE-SHOT
PISTOL . . . . NiB $2555 Ex $2427 Gd $1000
Built on a SA revolver frame w/cylinder replaced by a swing-out breechblock and fitted w/a bbl., w/integral chamber. Caliber: .256 Magnum. 8.5-inch bbl., 14.5 inches overall. Weight: 45 oz. Blued finish. Ramp front sight, click adj. rear. Smooth walnut grips. Made from 1963 to 1965 (3,300 produced).

MARK I TARGET MODEL AUTOMATIC PISTOL
Caliber: .22 LR. 10-round magazine, 5.25- and 6.88-inch heavy tapered or 5.5-inch untapered bull bbl., 10.88 inches overall (with 6.88-inch bbl.). Weight: 42 oz. (in 5.5- or 6.88-inch bbl.). Undercut target front sight, adj. rear. Blued finish. Hard rubber grips or checkered walnut thumbrest grips. Made from 1952 to 1982.
Standard model . . . . NiB $877 Ex $791 Gd $612
w/red medallion . . . . NiB $975 Ex $859 Gd $712
Walnut grips, add $434

MARK II AUTOMATIC PISTOL
Caliber: .22 LR, standard or high velocity 10-round magazine, 4.75- or 6-inch tapered bbl., 8.31 inches overall (with 4.75-inch bbl.). Weight: 36 oz. Fixed front sight, square notch rear. Blued or stainless finish. Made from 1982 to 2004.
Blued . . . . NiB $265 Ex $305 Gd $158
Stainless . . . . NiB $321 Ex $265 Gd $204
Bright stainless (ltd. prod.
   5,000 in 1982) . . . . NiB $590 Ex $479 Gd $346

MARK II 22/45 AUTOMATIC PISTOL
Same general specifications as Ruger Mark II .22 LR except w/blued or stainless receiver and bbl., in four lengths: 4-inch tapered w/adj. sights (P4), 4.75-inch tapered w/fixed sights (KP4), 5.25-inch tapered w/adj. sights (KP 514) and 5.5-inch bull (KP 512). Fitted w/Zytel grip frame of the same design as the Model 1911 45 ACP. Made from 1993 to 2004.
Model KP4 (4.75-inch bbl.) . . . . NiB $255 Ex $177 Gd $140
Model KP512, KP514
   (w/5.5- or 5.25-inch bbl.) . . . . NiB $365 Ex $229 Gd $126
Model P4, P512
   (Blued w/4- or 5.5-inch bbl.) NiB $270 Ex $216 Gd $160

MARK II BULL BARREL MODEL
Same as standard Mark II except for bull bbl. (5.5- or 10-inch).

Ruger P-89

Ruger P-90

Weight: About 2.75 lbs.
Blued finish . . . . NiB $319 Ex $237 Gd $175
Stainless finish (intro. 1985) . . . NiB $430 Ex $379 Gd $128

MARK II GOVERNMENT MODEL AUTO PISTOL
Civilian version of the Mark II used by U.S. Armed Forces. Caliber: .22LR. 10-round magazine, 6.88-inch bull bbl., 11.13 inches overall. Weight: 44 oz. Blued or stainless finish. Made from 1986 to 1999.
Blued model (MK687G
  commercial) . . . . NiB $388 Ex $286 Gd $198
Stainless steel model
  (KMK678G commercial) . . . . NiB $444 Ex $337 Gd $270
w/U.S. markings (military model) . . . NiB $1148 Ex $910 Gd $629

MARK II TARGET MODEL
Caliber: .22 LR. 10-round magazine, 4-, 5.5- and 10-inch bull bbl. or 5.25- and 6.88-inch heavy tappered bbl., weight: 38 oz. to 52 oz. 11.13 inches overall (with 6.88-inch bbl.). Made 1982 to 2004.
Blued. . . . . NiB $375 Ex $303 Gd $128
Stainless steel . . . . NiB $444 Ex $377 Gd $290

MARK III AUTOMATIC PISTOL
Similar to Mark II pistol except w/magazine button on left side grip, tapered bolt ears, and improved ejection port. Made from 2005 to date.
Blued. . . . . NiB $389 Ex $190 Gd $120

MARK III TARGET AUTOMATIC PISTOL
Same as Mark III pistol except w/tapered barrel, adj. rear sight, laminated grips. Made from 2005 to date.
Blued. . . . . NiB $460 Ex $240 Gd $180
Stainless steel . . . . NiB $569 Ex $290 Gd $190
Government Competition . . . . . NiB $659 Ex $350 Gd $250

MARK III 22/45 AUTOMATIC PISTOL
Similar to Mark II 22/45 pistol except w/Mark III improvements. Made from 2005 to 2012.
Blued. . . . . NiB $265 Ex $180 Gd $140
Stainless steel . . . . NiB $335 Ex $200 Gd $150
Hunter (fluted bbl.). . . . . NiB $435 Ex $250 Gd $170
Lite (2012 to date) . . . . NiB $499 Ex $330 Gd $270
Target (4- or 5.5-in. bull bbl.) . . NiB $359 Ex $255 Gd $175
Threaded Barrel (2011 to date) NiB $449 Ex $230 Gd $175

MODEL LCP AUTOMATIC PISTOL NiB $379 Ex $230 Gd $150
DOA. Caliber: .380 ACP, 6- or 7-round magazine, 2.75 in. bbl. Weight: 9.4 oz. Fixed sights. Made from 2008 to date.
w/Crimsontrace sight, add $150
w/LaserMax sight, add $75
Stainless steel slide finish . . . . . NiB $429 Ex $225 Gd $175

MODEL LC9 PISTOL . . . . NiB $379 Ex $230 Gd $150
DAO. Caliber: 9mm. 7- or 9-round magazine, 3.12 inch bbl. Weight: 17.1 oz. Fixed 3-dot sights. Blued finish. Made from 2011 to date.
w/Crimsontrace sight, add $150
w/LaserMax sight, add $75

MODEL LC380 PISTOL . . . . . . NiB $379 Ex $230 Gd $150
Similar to LC9 pistol except chambered in .380 ACP. Blued finish. Made from 2013 to date.
w/Crimsontrace sight, add $150
w/LaserMax sight, add $75

MODEL P-85 AUTOMATIC PISTOL
Caliber: 9mm. DA, recoil-operated. 15-round capacity, 4.5 inch bbl., 7.84 inches overall. Weight: 32 oz. Fixed rear sight, square-post front. Available w/decocking levers, ambidExtrous safety or in DA only. Blued or stainless finish. Made from 1987 to 1992.
Blued finish. . . . . NiB $332 Ex $214 Gd $110
Stainless steel finish . . . . NiB $439 Ex $365 Gd $291

MODEL P-89 AUTOMATIC PISTOL
Caliber: 9mm. DA w/slide-mounted safety levers. 15-round magazine, 4.5-inch bbl., 7.84 inches overall. Weight: 32 oz. Square-post front sight, adj. rear w/3-dot system. Blued or stainless steel finish. Grooved black Xenoy grips. Made from 1992 to 2007.
P-89 blued . . . . NiB $434 Ex $321 Gd $225
P-89 stainless . . . . NiB $546 Ex $453 Gd $388

MODEL P-89 DAC/DAO AUTO PISTOLS
Similar to the standard Model P-89 except the P-89 DAC has ambidExtrous decocking levers. The P-89 DAO operates in double-action-only mode. Made from 1991 to 2009.
P-89 DAC blued . . . . NiB $431 Ex $316 Gd $225
P-89 DAC/DAO stainless . . . . . NiB $530 Ex $431 Gd $316

MODEL P-90, KP90 DA AUTOMATIC PISTOL
Caliber: .45 ACP. Seven-round magazine, 4.5-inch bbl., 7.88 inches overall. Weight: 33.5 oz. Square-post front

**Ruger P-93
Compact**

sight adj. square-notched rear w/3-dot system. Grooved black Xenoy composition grips. Blued or stainless finish. DAC model has ambidExtrous decocking levers. Made from 1991 to 2010.

Model P-90 blued . . . . NiB $530 Ex $342 Gd $240
Model P-90 DAC (decocker). . . NiB $530 Ex $342 Gd $240
Model KP-90 DAC stainless. . . . NiB $536 Ex $367 Gd $270
Model KP-90 DAC (decocker). . NiB $536 Ex $367 Gd $270

MODEL P-91 DA AUTOMATIC PISTOL
Same general specifications as the Model P-90 except chambered for .40 S&W w/12-round double-column magazine, Made 1992 to 1994.

Model P-91 DAC (decockers) . . NiB $444 Ex $289 Gd $225
Model P-91 DAO (DA only) . . . NiB $444 Ex $289 Gd $225

MODEL P-93D AUTO PISTOL
Similar to the standard Model P-89 except w/3.9-inch bbl., (7.3 inches overall). Weight: 31 oz. Stainless steel finish. Made from 1993 to 2004.

Model P-93 DAC (decocker)
   (disc. 1994). . . . . NiB $444 Ex $289 Gd $225
Model P-93 Stainless. . . . . NiB $485 Ex $357 Gd $283

MODEL P-94 AUTOMATIC PISTOL
Similar to the Model P-91 except w/4.25-inch bbl., Calibers: 9mm or .40 S&W. Blued or stainless steel finish. Made 1994 to 2004.

Model KP-94 DAC
   (S/S decocker) . . . . NiB $444 Ex $289 Gd $225
Model KP-94 DAO
   (S/S dble. action only) . . . . . NiB $444 Ex $289 Gd $225
Model P-94 DAC
   (Blued decocker) . . . . NiB $444 Ex $289 Gd $225
Model P-94 DAO
   (blued dble. action only) . . . NiB $395 Ex $290 Gd $198

MODEL P-95PR AUTO PISTOL
Caliber: 9mm Parabellum. 10-round magazine, 3.9-inch bbl., 7.3 inches overall. Weight: 27 oz. Square-post front sight, drift adjustable rear w/3-dot system. Molded polymer grip-frame fitted w/stainless or chrome-moly slide. AmbidExtrous decocking levers (P-95D) or double action only (DAO). Matte black or stainless finish. Made 1997 to date.

P-95 blued . . . . NiB $444 Ex $289 Gd $225
KP-95PR stainless . . . . NiB $398 Ex $270 Gd $190

MODEL P-97D AUTOMATIC PISTOL
Caliber: .45 ACP. Eight-round magazine, 4.5- inch bbl., 7.25 inches overall. Weight: 30.5 oz. Square-post front sight adj. square-notched rear w/3-dot system. Grooved black Xenoy composition grips. Blued or stainless finish. DAC model has ambidExtrous decocking levers. Made from 2002 to 2004.

Model KP-97 DAO stainless . . . NiB $444 Ex $289 Gd $225
Model P-97D DAC (decockers) . . NiB $377 Ex $306 Gd $219

MODEL P-345 AUTOMATIC PISTOL
SA/DA. Caliber: .45 ACP. 8-round magazine, 4.25-in. bbl. Black polymer frame w/rail, blued steel slide. Weight: 29 oz. Fixed sights. Ambidextrous safety or decocking levers. Made from 2005 to 2012.

P345 . . . . NiB $490 Ex $340 Gd $225
KP345 (decocker) . . . . NiB $520 Ex $350 Gd $230

MODEL P-944 . . . . NiB $450 Ex $300 Gd $220
Similar to Model P-94 except in .40 S&W, ambidextrous safety and blued finish. Many variations of safety type, decocker or DAO. Made from 1999 to 2010.

Stainless finish, add. $50

MODEL SR22. . . . . NiB $399 Ex $265 Gd $230
SA/DA. Caliber: .22 LR. 10-round magazine, 3.25-in. bbl. Polymer frame, steel slide w/front/rear serrations. Weight: 17.5 oz. 3-dot adj. sights. Blued finish. Two backstrap inserts. Made 2012 to date.

Threaded barrel, add. $50
Two-tone finish, add $30

MODEL SR9. . . . . NiB $399 Ex $265 Gd $230
Striker fired system. Caliber: 9mm. 10- or 17-round magazine, 4.1-in. bbl. Polymer frame w/reversible backstrap. Weight: 26.5 oz. 3-dot low profile sights. Black stainless, brushed stainless, or OD green finish. Made 2007 to date.

Black stainless finish . . . . NiB $529 Ex $400 Gd $280
Matte stainless finish. . . . . NiB $529 Ex $400 Gd $280
OD green finish (2009-10) . . . . NiB $529 Ex $400 Gd $280

MODEL SR9C . . . . NiB $529 Ex $360 Gd $280
Similar to SR9 except compcat version w/3.5-in. bbl. Made 2010 to date.

MODEL SR40. . . . . NiB $529 Ex $360 Gd $280
Similar to SR9 except chambered in .40 S&W. Made 2011 to date.

MODEL SR40C . . . . NiB $529 Ex $360 Gd $280
Similar to SR40 except compcat version w/3.5-in. bbl. Made 2011 to date.

MODEL SR45. . . . . NiB $529 Ex $360 Gd $280
Similar to SR9 except chambered in .45 ACP. Made 2013 to date.

MODEL SR1911. . . . . NiB $829 Ex $470 Gd $330
1911 platform. Caliber: .45 ACP. 5-in. bbl., 7- and 8-round magazine. Stainless steel, checkered cocobola grips. Navak 3-dot sights. Made 2011 to date.

Commander model (4.25-in. bbl.). . . NiB $829 Ex $470 Gd $330

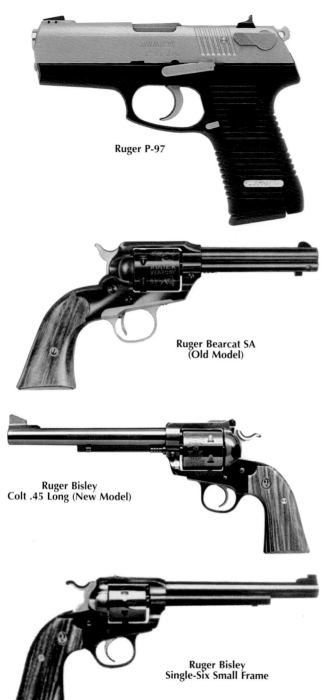

Ruger P-97

**Ruger Bearcat SA
(Old Model)**

**Ruger Bisley
Colt .45 Long (New Model)**

**Ruger Bisley
Single-Six Small Frame**

STANDARD MODEL AUTOMATIC PISTOL
Caliber: .22 LR. Nine-round magazine, 4.75- or 6-in. bbl., 8.75 inches overall (with 4.75-inch bbl.). Weight: 36 oz. (with 4.75 inch bbl.). Fixed sights. Blued finish. Hard rubber or checkered walnut grips. Made from 1949 to 1952. Known as the "Red Eagle Automatic," this early type is now a collector's item. Note: After the death of Alexander Sturm in 1951, the color of the eagle on the grip medallion was changed from red to black

Ruger Blackhawk

as a memorial. Made from 1952 to 1981.
w/red eagle medallion . . . . NiB $689 Ex $536 Gd $431
w/black eagle medallion. . . . . . NiB $430 Ex $379 Gd $170
Walnut grips, add $40

- REVOLVERS -

BEARCAT, SUPER
(OLD MODEL) . . . . NiB $602 Ex $365 Gd $291
Same general specifications as Bearcat except has steel frame. Weight: 25 oz. Made from 1971 to 1974.

NEW MODEL BEARCAT REVOLVER
Same general specifications as Super Bearcat except all steel frame and trigger guard. Interlocked mechanism and transfer bar. Calibers: .22 LR and .22WMR. Interchangeable 6-round cylinders (disc. 1996). Smooth walnut stocks w/Ruger medallion. Made from 1994 to date.
Convertible model (disc.
1996 after factory recall) . . . . . NiB $469 Ex $362 Gd $291
Standard model (.22 LR only). . . NiB $485 Ex $326 Gd $225

BISLEY SA REVOLVER, LARGE FRAME
Calibers: .357 Mag., .41 Mag. .44 Mag., .45 Long Colt. 7.5-inch bbl., 13 inches overall. Weight: 48 oz. Non-fluted or fluted cylinder, no engraving. Ramp front sight, adj. rear. Satin blued or stainless. Made from 1986 to date.
Blued finish. . . . . NiB $485 Ex $365 Gd $270
Vaquero/Bisley (blued w/case
    colored fr.) . . . . NiB $612 Ex $474 Gd $398
Vaquero/Bisley (stainless
    steel) . . . . NiB $587 Ex $434 Gd $357
w/ivory grips, add. $50

BISLEY SINGLE-SIX REVOLVER, SMALL FRAME
Calibers: .22 LR and .32 Mag. Six-round cylinder, 6.5-inch bbl., 11.5 inches overall. Weight: 41 oz. Fixed rear sight, blade front. Blue finish. Goncalo Alves grips. Made 1986 to date.
.22 caliber. . . . . NiB $485 Ex $365 Gd $270
.32 H&R Mag. . . . . NiB $693 Ex $601 Gd $479

BLACKHAWK SA CONVERTIBLE (OLD MODEL)
Same as Blackhawk except has Extra cylinder. Caliber combinations: .357 Magnum and 9mm Para., .45 Colt and .45 Automatic. Made 1967 to 1972.
.357/9mm combo (early w/o
    prefix S/N) . . . . .NiB $556 Ex $437 Gd $290
.357/9mm combo (late
    w/prefix S/N) . . . . NiB $556 Ex $437 Gd $290
.45 LC/.45 ACP combo
(1967-85 & 1999 to date). . . . . NiB $556 Ex $437 Gd $290

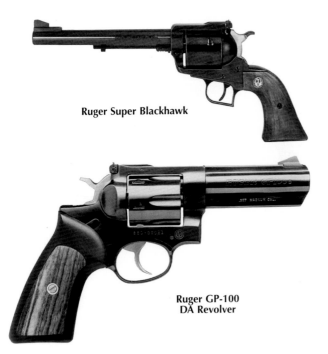

Ruger Super Blackhawk

**Ruger GP-100
DA Revolver**

Ruger New Model Blackhawk Convertible

.30 Carbine, .357 Mag. . . . . NiB $510 Ex $432 Gd $325
.41 Mag. . . . . NiB $760 Ex $660 Gd $265
.45 Colt. . . . . NiB $875 Ex $532 Gd $255

BLACKHAWK SA "FLAT-TOP" REVOLVER (OLD MODEL)
Similar to standard Blackhawk except w/"Flat Top" cylinder strap. Calibers: .357 Mag. or .44 Mag. Six-round fluted cylinder, 4.625-, 6.5-, 7.5- or 10-inch bbl., adj. rear sight, ramp front. Blued finish. Black rubber or smooth walnut grips. Made from 1955 to 1962.
.357 Mag. (w/4.625-inch
   bbl.) . . . . NiB $1235 Ex $1148 Gd $975
.357 Mag. (w/6.5-inch bbl.) . . . NiB $479 Ex $342 Gd $198
.357 Mag. (w/10-inch bbl.) . . NiB $2540 Ex $1650 Gd $1030
.44 Mag. (w/fluted cylinder/4.625-inch
   bbl.) . . . . NiB $1336 Ex $1270 Gd $1030
.44 Mag. (w/fluted cylinder/ 6.5-inch
   bbl.) . . . . NiB $1020 Ex $666 Gd $408
.44 Mag. (w/fluted cylinder/ 10-inch
   bbl.) . . . . NiB $2540 Ex $1945 Gd $1779

GP-100 DA REVOLVER
Caliber: .357 Magnum. Three- to 4-inch heavy bbl., or 6-inch standard or heavy bbl., Overall length: 9.38 or 11.38 inches. Cushioned grip panels. Made from 1986 to date.
Blued finish. . . . . NiB $590 Ex $434 Gd $274
Stainless steel finish . . . . NiB $570 Ex $410 Gd $290

GP-100 MATCH CHAMPION . . . NiB $899 Ex $580 Gd $430
Similar to GP-100 except yuned for competiotion w/slab side, half under lug 4.25-in. bbl. Matte stainless finish. Hogue stippled hardwood grip. Made from 2014 to date.

LCR DAO REVOLVER. . . . . NiB $545 Ex $670 Gd $300
DAO. Caliber: .22 LR, .22 WMR, .38 Spl.+P, or .357 Mag. Hammless design, polymer fire control housing, monolithic aluminum frame, stainless cylinder, 1.87-in. bbl., fixed sights, Hogue rubber grip. Made from 2010 to date.
.357 Mag., add. $80
Crimson Trace laser grips, add. $280
LCRX model (external hammer), add. $50
LCRX model (3-in. bbl.), add $20

NEW MODEL BLACKHAWK SA REVOLVER
Safety transfer bar mechanism. SA. Calibers: .30 Carbine, .357 Magnum, .357 Maximum, .41 Magnum, .44 Magnum, .44 Special, .45 Colt. Six-round cylinder, bbl. lengths: 4.63-inch (.357, .41, .45 Colt); 5.5 inch (.44 Mag., .44 Spec.); 6.5-inch (.357, .41, .45 Long Colt); 7.5-inch (.30, .45, .44 Special, .44 Mag.); 10.5-inch in .44 Mag; 10.38 inches overall (.357 Mag. w/4.63-inch bbl.). Weight: 40 oz. (.357 w/4.63-inch bbl.). Adj. rear sight, ramp front. Blued finish or stainless steel; latter only in .357 or .45 LC. Smooth walnut grips. Made from 1973 to date.
Blued finish. . . . . NiB $464 Ex $326 Gd $203
High-gloss stainless (.357 Mag.,
   .45 LC) . . . . NiB $459 Ex $316 Gd $190
Satin stainless (.357 Mag.,
   .45 LC) . . . . NiB $418 Ex $332 Gd $265
.357 Maximum SRM (1984-85). . . NiB $452 Ex $357 Gd $226

NEW MODEL BLACKHAWK BISLEY
Similar to New Model Blackhawk except w/Bisley shaped grip and hammer, fluted or unfluted cylinder. Made 1986 to date.
Blued finish. . . . . NiB $799 Ex $430 Gd $320
Unfluted cylinder, add $120

**Ruger Blackhawk High-Gloss Stainless
(New Model) .357 Magnum**

BLACKHAWK SA REVOLVER (OLD MODEL)
Calibers: .30 Carbine, .357 Mag., .41 Mag., .45 Colt. Six-round cylinder, bbl. lengths: 4.63-inch (.357, .41, .45 caliber), 6.5-inch (.357, .41 caliber), 7.5-inch (.30, .45 caliber). 10.13 inches overall (.357 Mag. w/4.63-inch bbl.). Weight: 38 oz. (.357 w/4.63-inch bbl.). Ramp front sight, adj. rear. Blued finish. Checkered hard rubber or smooth walnut grips. Made from 1955 to 1962.

**Ruger Single-Six SSM
(New Model)**

**Ruger Super Blackhawk
(New Model)**

**Ruger Super Single-Six
Convertible (New Model)**

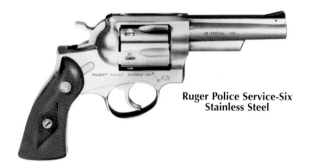

**Ruger Police Service-Six
Stainless Steel**

Same general specifications as standard Single-Six except chambered for .32 H&R Magnum cartridge. Bbl. lengths: 4.63, 5.5, 6.5 or 9.5 inches.

NEW MODEL SUPER BLACKHAWK SA REVOLVER
Safety transfer bar mechanism. SA. Caliber: .44 Magnum. Six-round cylinder, 5.5-inch, 7.5-inch and 10.5-inch bull bbl. 13.38 inches overall. Weight: 48 oz. Adj. rear sight, ramp front. Blued and stainless steel finish. Smooth walnut grips. Made 1973 to date, 5.5-inch bbl. made from 1973 to date.
Blued finish. . . . . NiB $570 Ex $477 Gd $281
High-gloss stainless
   (1994-96) . . . . NiB $580 Ex $486 Gd $290
Satin stainless steel . . . . NiB $570 Ex $480 Gd $295
Stainless steel Hunter
   (intro. 2002) . . . . NiB $780 Ex $490 Gd $295

NEW MODEL SUPER BLACKHAWK BISLEY
Similar to New Model Super Blackhawk except w/Bisley shaped grip and hammer, fluted or unfluted cylinder. Made from 1986 to date.
Blued finish. . . . . NiB $729 Ex $330 Gd $260
Stainless Hunter model. . . . . . . NiB $859 Ex $480 Gd $340

NEW MODEL SUPER SINGLE-SIX CONVERTIBLE REVOLVER
Safety transfer bar mechanism. SA. Calibers: .22 LR and .22 WMR. Interchangeable 6-round cylinders. Bbl. lengths: 4.63, 5.5, 6.5, 9.5 inches. 10.81 inches overall (with 4.63 inch bbl.). Weight: 33 oz. (with 4.63-inch bbl.). Adj. rear sight, ramp front. Blued finish or stainless steel; latter only w/5.5- or 6.5-inch bbl., smooth walnut grips. Made from 1994 to 2004.
Blued finish. . . . . NiB $500 Ex $306 Gd $190
Stainless steel . . . . NiB $530 Ex $316 Gd $219
Stainless steel Hunter
   (intro. 2002) . . . . NiB $660 Ex $560 Gd $295
Stainless steel Hunter 17 HMR/.17
   Mach 2 (2005-06) . . . . NiB $760 Ex $560 Gd $295

NEW MODEL VAQUERO. . . . . NiB $590 Ex $431 Gd $316
Similar to Vaquero except w/smaller pre-1962 XR-3 style grip frame, reverse indexing cylinder, recontoured hammer, beveled cylinder, cresent shaped ejector rod. Blued w/case-color or bright stainless finish. Checkered rubber or smooth rosewood grips. Made 2005 to date.

NEW MODEL VAQUERO BISLEY . . . NiB $810 Ex $440 Gd $315
Similar to New Model Vaquero except w/Bisley shaped grip and hammer, fluted cylinder. Made from 2009 to date.

POLICE SERVICE-SIX
Same general specifications as Speed-Six except has square butt. Stainless steel models and 9mm Para. caliber available w/ only 4-inch bbl., Made from 1971 to 1988.
.38 Special, blued finish. . . . . . NiB $434 Ex $306 Gd $230
.38 Special, stainless steel . . . . NiB $345 Ex $290 Gd $270
.357 Magnum or 9mm Para.,
   blued finish . . . . NiB $444 Ex $309 Gd $235
.357 Magnum, stainless steel . . NiB $439 Ex $306 Gd $225

REDHAWK DA REVOLVER
Calibers: .357 Mag., .41 Mag., .45 LC, .44 Mag. Six-round cylinder, 5.5-and 7.5-inch bbl., 11 and 13 inches overall, respectively. Weight: About 52 oz. Adj. rear sight, interchange-

NEW MODEL BLACKHAWK CONVERTIBLE
Same as New Model Blackhawk except has Extra cylinder. Blued finish only. Caliber combinations: .357 Magnum/9mm Para., .44 Magnum/.44-40, .45 Colt/.45 ACP. (Limited Edition Buckeye Special .32-20/.32 H&R Mag. or .38-40/10mm). Made from 1973 to 1985. Reintro. 1999.
.32-20/.32 H&R Mag. (1989-90) . . . NiB $556 Ex $386 Gd $259
.38-40/10mm (1990-91) . . . . . NiB $556 Ex $386 Gd $259
.357/9mm combo . . . . NiB $556 Ex $386 Gd $259
.44/.44-40 combo (disc.1982) . NiB $834 Ex $579 Gd $389
.45 LC/.45 ACP combo (disc. 1985) . . NiB $556 Ex $386 Gd $259

NEW MODEL SUPER SINGLE-SIX SSM
SA REVOLVER. . . . . NiB $555 Ex $480 Gd $209

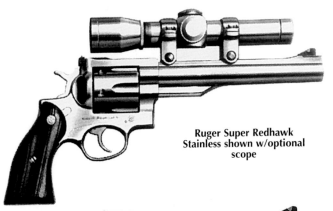

Ruger Super Redhawk Stainless shown w/optional scope

Ruger Redhawk

Ruger Super Redhawk Stainless

Ruger Single-Six

able front sights. Stainless finish. Made from 1979 to 2009; .357 Mag. disc. 1986. Alloy steel model w/blued finish intro. in 1986 in .41 Mag. and .44 Mag. calibers.

Blued finish	NiB $620	Ex $450	Gd $270
Stainless steel	NiB $789	Ex $499	Gd $300

SUPER REDHAWK DA REVOLVER
Calibers: .44 Mag., .454 Casull and .480 Ruger. Six-round cylinder, 7.5- to 9.5- inch bbl., 13 to 15 inches overall. Weight: 53 to 58 oz. Integral scope mounting system w/stainless rings. Adjustable rear sight. Cushioned grip panels. Made from 1987 to date.

Model .44 Mag. 7.5- inch bbl., stainless	NiB $795	Ex $546	Gd $434
Model .44 Mag. 9.5- inch bbl., stainless	NiB $830	Ex $577	Gd $444
Model .454 Casull & .480 Ruger Stainless/target gray stainless	NiB $862	Ex $590	Gd $474
Alaskan (intro. 2005)	NiB $880	Ex $590	Gd $480

SECURITY-SIX DA REVOLVER
Caliber: .357 Magnum, handles .38 Special. Six-round cylinder, bbl. lengths: 2.25-, 4-, 6-inch, 9.25 inches overall (with 4-inch bbl.). Weight: 33.5 oz. (with 4-inch bbl.). Adj. rear sight, ramp front. Blued finish or stainless steel. Square butt. Checkered walnut grips. Made 1971 to 1985.

Blued finish	NiB $410	Ex $280	Gd $214
Stainless steel	NiB $420	Ex $300	Gd $265

SINGLE-SIX REVOLVER (OLD MODEL)
Calibers: .22 LR, .22 WMR. Six-round cylinder. bbl., lengths: 4.63, 5.5, 6.5, 9.5 inches, 10.88 inches overall (with 5.5-inch bbl.). Weight: About 35 oz. Fixed sights. Blued finish. Checkered hard rubber or smooth walnut grips. Made 1953-73. Note: Pre-1956 model w/flat loading gate is worth about twice as much as later version.

Standard	NiB $879	Ex $602	Gd $439
Convertible (w/two cylinders, .22 LR/.22 WMR)	NiB $561	Ex $398	Gd $272

SINGLE-SIX - LIGHTWEIGHT NiB $1086 Ex $816 Gd $530
Same general specifications as Single-Six except has 4.75-inch bbl., lightweight alloy cylinder and frame, 10 inches overall length, weight: 23 oz. Made in 1956.

SINGLE-NINE . . . . NiB $639 Ex $380 Gd $280
Same general specifications as New Model Single-Six except chambered in .22 WMR, 9-round cylinder, 6.5-in. bbl. Stainless steel. Made in 2013 to date.

SINGLE-TEN . . . . NiB $639 Ex $370 Gd $270
Same general specifications as New Model Single-Six except w/10-round cylinder, 5.5-in. bbl. Stainless steel. Made in 2012 to date.

SP101 DA REVOLVER
Calibers: .22 LR, .32 Mag., 9mm, .38 Special+P, .357 Mag. Five- or 6-round cylinder, 2.25-, 3.06- or 4-inch bbl., weight: 25-34 oz. Stainless steel finish. Cushioned grips. Made from 1989 to date.

Standard model	NiB $530	Ex $321	Gd $204
DAO model (DA only, spurless hammer)	NiB $530	Ex $321	Gd $204

SPEED-SIX DA REVOLVER
Calibers: .38 Special, .357 Magnum, 9mm Para. Six-round cylinder, 2.75-, 4-inch bbl., (9mm available only w/2.75-inch bbl.). 7.75 inches overall (2.75-inch bbl.). Weight: 31 oz. (with 2.75-inch bbl.). Fixed sights. Blued or stainless steel finish; latter available in .38 Special (with 2.75 inch bbl.), .357 Magnum and 9mm w/either bbl., Round butt. Checkered walnut grips. Made from 1973 to 1987.

blued finish	NiB $439	Ex $272	Gd $190
stainless steel	NiB $449	Ex $303	Gd $214
9mm Para., blued finish	NiB $689	Ex $522	Gd $440
9mm Para., stainless steel	NiB $690	Ex $540	Gd $442

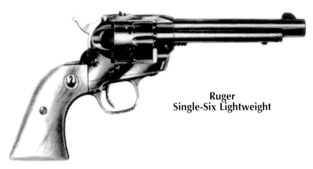

Ruger
Single-Six Lightweight

Ruger
Super Single-Six Convertible

Ruger Single-Six Fixed Sight

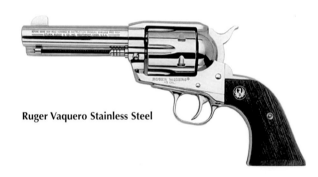

Ruger Vaquero Stainless Steel

Ruger Vaquero Blued

Ruger Speed-Six Stainless Steel

SUPER BLACKHAWK (OLD MODEL)

SA w/heavy frame and unfluted cylinder. Caliber: .44 Magnum. Six-round cylinder. 6.5- or 7.5-inch bbl., Adj. rear sight, ramp front. Steel or brass grip frame w/square-back trigger guard. Smooth walnut grips. Blued finish. Made from 1956 to 1973.

w/6.5-inch bbl., ... NiB $1316 Ex $1148 Gd $918
w/7.5-inch bbl., ... NiB $806 Ex $385 Gd $281
w/brass gripframe . . . . NiB $1599 Ex $1316 Gd $1153

VAQUERO . . . . NiB $590 Ex $431 Gd $316

SA. Calibers: .357 Mag., .44-40, .44 Magnum, .45 Colt. Six-round cylinder. Bbl. lengths: 4.625, 5.5, 7.5 inches, 13.63 inches overall (with 7.5-inch bbl.). Weight: 41 oz. (with 7.5-inch bbl.). Blade front sight, grooved topstrap rear. Blued w/color casehardened frame or polished stainless finish. Smooth rosewood grips w/Ruger medallion. Made from 1993 to 2004.

VAQUERO BISLEY . . . . NiB $575 Ex $460 Gd $230

Similar to Vaquero except w/Bisley shaped grip and hammer, fluted cylinder. Blued or bright stainless finish. Made from 1999 to 2004.

RUSSIAN SERVICE PISTOLS — Manufactured by Government plants at Tula and elsewhere

Note: *Tokarev-type pistols have also been made in Hungary, Poland, Yugoslavia, People's Republic of China, N. Korea.*

MODEL TT30 TOKAREV SERVICE AUTOMATIC

Modified Colt-Browning type. Caliber: 7.62mm Russian Auto (also uses 7.63mm Mauser Auto cartridge). Eight-round magazine, 4.5-inch bbl., 7.75 inches overall. Weight: About 29 oz. Fixed sights. Made from 1930 to mid-1950s. Note: A slightly modified version w/improved locking system and different disconnector was adopted in 1933.

Standard Service Model
  TT30 . . . . NiB $1239 Ex $1127 Gd $918
Standard Service Model
  TT33 . . . . NiB $2490 Ex $2285 Gd $1879
Recent imports (distinguished by importer
  marks) . . . . NiB $209 Ex $158 Gd $109

MODEL PM

MAKAROV PISTOL . . . . NiB $3000 Ex $2445 Gd $2000
Double-action, blowback design. Semi-automatic. Caliber: 9x18mm Makarov. Eight-round magazine, 3.8-inch bbl., 6.4 inches overall. Weight: 26 oz. Blade front sight, square-notched

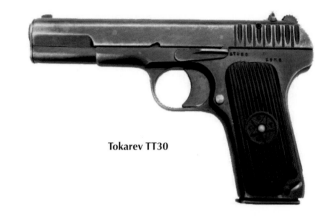

Tokarev TT30

Sako Model .22-.32 Olympic

Sauer 1930 Pocket

rear. Checkered composition grips. Numerous examples exist from former Eastern Bloc countries such as Bulgaria and East Germany as well as China.

Standard Service Model PM
(Pistole Makarov) . . . . NiB $3595 Ex $3125 Gd $2890
Recent non-Russian imports (distinguished
  by importer marks) . . . . NiB $434 Ex $306 Gd $170

SAKO — Riihimaki, Finland
Manufactured by Oy Sako Ab.

.22-.32 OLYMPIC PISTOL (TRIACE)

Calibers: .22 LR, .22 Short, .32 S&W Long. Five-round magazine, 6- or 8.85- (.22 Short) inch bbl., weight: About 46 oz. (.22 LR); 44 oz. (.22 Short); 48 oz. (.32). Steel frame. ABS plastic, anatomically designed grip. Non-reflecting matte black upper surface and chromium-plated slide. Equipped w/carrying case and tool set. Limited importation from 1983 to 1989.
Sako .22 or .32
  Single pistol . . . . NiB $1355 Ex $1240 Gd $1090
Sako Triace, triple-barrel set
  w/wooden grip . . . . NiB $2647 Ex $2279 Gd $2045

SAUER — Germany
Manufactured through WW II by J. P. Sauer & Sohn, Suhl, Germany. Now manufactured by J. P. Sauer & Sohn, GmbH, Ecmernförde, West Germany. Also see listings under Sig Sauer for automatic pistols, Hawes for single action revolvers.

MODEL 1913 POCKET PISTOL . . NiB $342 Ex $240 Gd $179
Semi-automatic pistol. Caliber: .32 ACP (7.65mm). Seven-round magazine, 3-inch bbl., 5.88 inches overall. Weight: 22 oz. Fixed sights. Blued finish. Black hard rubber grips. Made from 1913 to 1930.

MODEL 1930 POCKET AUTOMATIC PISTOL
Authority Model (Behorden Model). Successor to Model 1913, has improved grip and safety. Caliber: .32 Auto (7.65mm). Seven-round magazine, 3-inch bbl., 5.75 inches overall. Weight: 22 oz. Fixed sights. Blued finish. Black hard rubber grips. Made from 1930-38. Note: Some pistols made w/indicator pin showing when cocked. Also mfd. w/dual slide and receiver; this type weight: about 7 oz. less than the standard model.
Steel model . . . . NiB $405 Ex $290 Gd $203
Dural (alloy) model . . . . NiB $1454 Ex $1367 Gd $1209

MODEL 38H DA AUTOMATIC PISTOL
Calibers: .25 Auto (6.35mm), .32 Auto (7.65mm), .380 Auto (9mm). Specifications shown are for .32 Auto model. Seven-round magazine, 3.25-inch bbl., 6.25 inches overall. Weight: 20 oz. Fixed sights. Blued finish. Black plastic grips. Also made in dual model weighing about 6 oz. less. Made 1938-1945. Note: This pistol, designated Model .38, was mfd. during WW II for military use. Wartime models are inferior in design to earlier production, as some lack safety lever.
.22 caliber . . . . NiB $5625 Ex $3410 Gd $2200
.32 ACP . . . . NiB $643 Ex $410 Gd $281
.32 ACP (w/Nazi proofs) . . . . . NiB $709 Ex $453 Gd $326
.380 ACP . . . . NiB $4500 Ex $4255 Gd $3975

POCKET .25 (1913) . . . . NiB $398 Ex $286 Gd $214
Smaller version of Model 1913, issued about same time as .32 caliber model. Caliber: .25 Auto (6.35mm). Seven-round magazine, 2.5-inch bbl., 4.25 inches overall. Weight: 14.5 oz. Fixed sights. Blued finish. Black hard rubber grips. Made 1913 to 1930.

SAVAGE ARMS — Utica, NY

MODEL 101 SA SINGLE-SHOT
PISTOL . . . . NiB $255 Ex $170 Gd $105
Barrel integral w/swing-out cylinder. Calibers: .22 Short, Long, LR. 5.5-inch bbl. Weight: 20 oz. Blade front sight, slotted rear, adj. for windage. Blued finish. Grips of compressed, impregnated wood. Made 1960 to 1968.

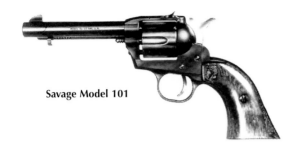

Savage Model 101

Savage Model 1907

Sears/J.C. Higgins
Model 88 DA Revolver

MODEL 501/502F "STRIKER" SERIES PISTOLS
Calibers: .22 LR., and .22 WMR. 5- or 10- round magazine, 10-inch bbl., 19 inches overall. Weight: 4 lbs. Drilled and tapped sights for scope mount (installed). AmbidExtrous rear grip. Made from 2000 to 2005.
Model 501F, .22 LR. . . . . NiB $359 Ex $206 Gd $165
Model 502F, .22 WMR . . . . NiB $301 Ex $190 Gd $158

MODEL 510/516 "STRIKER" SERIES PISTOLS
Calibers: .223 Rem., .22-250 Rem., .243 Win., 7mm-08 Rem., .260 Rem., and .308 Win. Three-round magazine, 14-inch bbl., 22.5 inches overall. Drilled and tapped for scope mounts. Left hand bolt with right hand ejection. Stainless steel finish. Made from 1998 to 2005.
Model 510F. . . . . NiB $495 Ex $395 Gd $235
Model 516FSAK . . . . NiB $546 Ex $474 Gd $230
Model 516FSS. . . . . NiB $546 Ex $474 Gd $230
Model 516FSAK . . . . NiB $704 Ex $468 Gd $408
Model 516BSS. . . . . NiB $755 Ex $500 Gd $437

MODEL 1907 AUTOMATIC PISTOL
Caliber: .32 ACP, 10-round magazine, 3.25-inch bbl., 6.5 inches overall. Weight: 19 oz. Checkered hard rubber or steel grips marked "Savage Quality," circling an Indian-head logo. Optional pearl grips. Blue, nickel, silver or gold finish. Made from 1910 to 1917.
Blued model (.32 ACP) . . . . . . NiB $610 Ex $430 Gd $175
Blued model (.380 ACP) . . . . . . NiB $709 Ex $495 Gd $326

MODEL 1915 AUTOMATIC PISTOL
Same general specifications as the Savage Model 1907 except the Model 1915 is hammerless and has a grip safety. It is also chambered for both the .32 and .380 ACP. Made froim 1915 to 1917.
.32 ACP. . . . . NiB $930 Ex $729 Gd $500
.380 ACP. . . . . NiB $1400 Ex $857 Gd $643

U.S. ARMY TEST MODEL . . . . NiB $12,650 Ex $8990 Gd $653
Caliber: .45 ACP, Seven-round magazine w/Exposed hammer. An enlarged version of the Model 1910 manufactured for military trials between 1907 and 1911. Note: Most "Trial Pistols" were refurbished and resold as commercial models. Values are for original Government Test Issue models.

MODEL 1917 AUTOMATIC PISTOL
Same specifications as 1910 Model except has spur-type hammer and redesigned, heavier grip. Made from 1917 to 1928.
.32 ACP. . . . . NiB $564 Ex $445 Gd $279
.380 ACP. . . . . NiB $646 Ex $486 Gd $336

SCCY INDUSTRIES — Daytona Beach, FL

CPX-1 . . . . NiB $334 Ex $290 Gd $220
Semi-automatic. DAO. Caliber: 9mm, 10-rnd magazine. 3.1-in. bbl. Frame: polymer with thumb safety. Sights: fixed. Finish: matte black, pink, purple, FDE, and many other colors. Grip: textured polymer. Weight: 15 oz. Length: 5.7 in. Made from 2013 to date.

CPX-2 . . . . NiB $314 Ex $280 Gd $210
Similar to CPX-1 except w/o thumb safety. Made from 2011 to date.

SEARS, ROEBUCK & COMPANY — Chicago, IL

J.C. HIGGINS MODEL 80
AUTO PISTOL. . . . . NiB $281 Ex $165 Gd $109
Caliber: .22 LR. 10-round magazine, 4.5- or 6.5-inch interchangeable bbl., 10.88 inches overall (with 6.5-inch bbl.). Weight: 41 oz. (with 6.5-inch bbl.). Fixed Partridge sights. Blued finish. Checkered grips w/thumbrest.

J.C. HIGGINS MODEL 88
DA REVOLVER . . . . NiB $209 Ex $105 Gd $75
Caliber: .22 LR. Nine-round cylinder, 4- or 6-inch bbl., 9.5 inches (with 4-inch bbl.). Weight: 23 oz. (with 4-inch bbl.). Fixed sights. Blued or nickel finish. Checkered plastic grips.

J.C. HIGGINS RANGER
DA REVOLVER . . . . NiB $219 Ex $137 Gd $88
Caliber: .22 LR. Nine-round cylinder, 5.5-inch bbl., 10.75 inches overall. Weight: 28 oz. Fixed sights. Blued or chrome finish. Checkered plastic grips.

SECURITY INDUSTRIES OF AMERICA — Little Ferry, NJ

MODEL PM 357
DA REVOLVER . . . . NiB $255 Ex $198 Gd $160
Caliber: .357 Magnum. Five-round cylinder, 2.5-inch bbl., 7.5 inches overall. Weight: 21 oz. Fixed sights. Stainless steel. Walnut grips. Made 1975. Disc.

Security Industries of America Model PM 357

Security Industries of America Model PPM 357

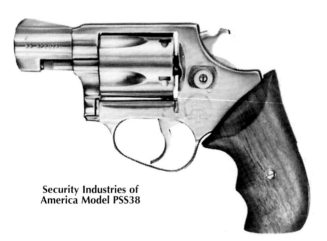

Security Industries of America Model PSS38

MODEL PPM357

DA REVOLVER . . . . NiB $255 Ex $198 Gd $160
Caliber: .357 Magnum. Five-round cylinder, 2-inch bbl., 6.13 inches overall. Weight: 18 oz. Fixed sights. Stainless steel. Walnut grips. Made in 1975. Note: Spurless hammer (illustrated) was disc. in 1975; this model has the same conventional hammer as other Security revolvers.

MODEL PSS 38 DA REVOLVER . . . NiB $197 Ex $112 Gd $90
Caliber: .38 Special. Five-round cylinder, 2-inch bbl., 6.5 inch-

es overall. Weight: 18 oz. Fixed sights. Stainless steel. Walnut grips. Intro. 1973. disc.

R. F. SEDGLEY, INC, — Philadelphia, PA

BABY HAMMERLESS
EJECTOR REVOLVER . . . . NiB $704 Ex $556 Gd $290
DA. Solid frame. Folding trigger. Caliber: .22 Long. Six-round cylinder, 4 inches overall. Weight: 6 oz. Fixed sights. Blued or nickel finish. Rubber grips. Made 1930 to 1939.

L. W. SEECAMP, INC. — Milford, CT

LWS .25 DAO PISTOL . . . . NiB $439 Ex $398 Gd $281
Caliber: .25 ACP. Seven-round magazine, 2-inch bbl., 4.125 inches overall. Weight: 12 oz. Checkered black polycarbonate grips. Matte stainless finish. No sights. Made from 1981 to 1985.

LWS .32 DAO PISTOL
Caliber: .32 ACP. Six-round magazine, 2-inch bbl., 4.25 inches overall. Weight: 12.9 oz. Ribbed sighting plane with no sights. Checkered black LExon grips. Stainless steel. Made from 1985 to date. Limited production results in inflated resale values.
Matte stainless finish. . . . . NiB $464 Ex $398 Gd $272
Polished stainless finish, add. $128

LWS .380
DAO PISTOL. . . . . NiB $795 Ex $650 Gd $470
Similar to LWS 32 except chambered in .380 ACP. Made from 2000 to date.

SHERIDAN PRODUCTS, INC. — Racine, WI

KNOCKABOUT
SINGLE-SHOT PISTOL . . . . NiB $305 Ex $189 Gd $108
Tip-up type. Caliber: .22 LR, Long, Short; 5-inch bbl., 6.75 inches overall. Weight: 24 oz. Fixed sights. Checkered plastic grips. Blued finish. Made from 1953 to 1960.

SIG — Neuhausen am Rheinfall, Switzerland

See also listings under SIG-Sauer.
MODEL P210-1 PISTOL . . . NiB $2878 Ex $2662 Gd $2288
Semi-automatic. Calibers: .22 LR, 7.65mm Luger, 9mm Para. Eight-round magazine, 4.75-inch bbl., 8.5 inches overall. Weight: 33 oz. (.22 cal.) or 35 oz. (7.65mm, 9mm). Fixed sights. Polished blued finish. Checkered wood grips. Made from 1949 to 1986.

MODEL P210-2. . . . . NiB $1835 Ex $1590 Gd $1409
Same as Model P210-1 except has sandblasted finish, plastic grips. Not avail. in .22 LR. Disc. 2002.

MODEL P210-5
TARGET PISTOL . . . . NiB $2330 Ex $2190 Gd $1902
Same as Model P210-2 except has 6-inch bbl., micrometer adj. rear sight, target front sight, adj. trigger stop, 9.7 inches overall. Weight: About 38.3 oz. Disc. 2007.

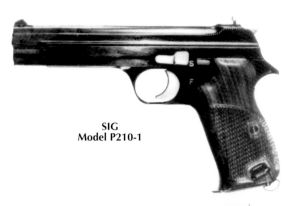

**SIG
Model P210-1**

**SIG
Model P210-6 Target Pistol**

**SIG Sauer
P220**

**SIG Sauer
P225**

MODEL P210-6
TARGET PISTOL . . . . NiB $1910 Ex $1720 Gd $1525
Same as Model P210-2 except has micrometer adj. rear sight, target front sight, adj. trigger stop. Weight: About 37 oz. Disc. 1987.

P210 .22 CONVERSION UNIT, add $1525
Converts P210 pistol to .22 LR. Consists of bbl., w/recoil spring, slide and magazine,

---

SIG SAUER — Neuhausen, Switzerland and Exeter, NH
Manufactured by J. P. Sauer & Sohn of Germany, SIG of Switzerland, and other manufacturers.

MODEL MOSQUITO . . . . NiB $408 Ex $350 Gd $270
Similar to P226 except chambered in .22 LR. Finish: numerous finish options. Weight: 24.6 oz. Made from 2005 to date.
Sporter model (long slide, disc. 2012), add $80
Pink, FDE, or OD green finish, add $20
Threaded bbl., add $30

MODEL P220 DA/DAO AUTOMATIC PISTOL
Calibers: 22LR, 7.65mm, 9mm Para., .38 Super, .45 ACP. Seven-round in .45 ACP, 9-round in other calibers, 4.4-inch bbl., 8 inches overall. Weight: 26.5 oz. (9mm). Fixed sights. Blue, electroless nickel, K-Kote, Duo/nickel or Ilaflon finish. Alloy frame. Checkered plastic grips. Imported from 1976 to date. Note: Also sold in U.S. as Browning BDA.
Blue finish . . . . NiB $918 Ex $734 Gd $499
Duo/nickel finish . . . . NiB $1030 Ex $712 Gd $523
Nickel finish . . . . NiB $988 Ex $784 Gd $546
K-Kote finish . . . . NiB $974 Ex $693 Gd $474
Ilaflon finish . . . . NiB $969 Ex $689 Gd $507
.22 LR conversion kit, add $434
w/Siglite sights, add $100

MODEL P220 CARRY . . . . . . NiB $1108 Ex $930 Gd $730
Compact version of the P220 full size w/3.9-in. bbl. Made from 2007 to date.
**Model P220 Carry Elite (Siglite sights,
 Stainless finish), add** $200
**Model P220 Carry Elite (Siglite sights, Nitron finish, 2009-
 2012), add** $300
**Model P220 Carry Equinox (two-tone slide, Siglite sights,
 blackwood grip), add** $100
Model P220 Carry SAS (SIG Anti-Snag treatment), add . . . $50

MODEL P220 COMPACT
NITRON . . . . NiB $1170 Ex $950 Gd $710
Subcompact version of the P220 full size w/3.9-in. bbl., shorter frame, DA/SA or SAO trigger. Made from 2007 to 2015.
Model P220 Compact (two-tone finish), add $80
Model P220 Compact SAS (SIG Anti-Snag treatment) . . . NiB
 $1170 Ex $950 Gd $710

MODEL P220 SPORT
AUTOMATIC . . . . NiB $1415 Ex $1119 Gd $1016
Similar to Model P220 except .45 ACP only w/4.5-inch compensated bbl., 10-round magazine, adj. target sights. Weight: 46.1 oz. Stainless finish. Made from 1999 to date.

MODEL P224 NITRON . . . . . . NiB $1108 EX $890 GD $630
Compact version of the P229. Caliber: 9mm, .40 S&W or .357 SIG; 10-, 12-, or 15-rnd. magazine depending on caliber. Finish: Nitron. Grip: E2 style textured polymer. Weight: 29.0 oz. Length: 6.7 in. DA/SA or DAK trigger. Made from 2012 to 2015.

SIG Sauer P230

Model P224 Equinox (night sights, G10 grip), add $100
Model P224 Extreme (black and grey Hogue Piranha grip,
Siglite sights, short reset trigger), add $80
Model P224 Nickel (nickel slide, black frame finish),
add $20

MODEL P225 DA AUTOMATIC
Caliber: 9mm Para. Eight-round magazine, 3.85-inch bbl., 7 inches overall. Weight: 26.1 oz. Blue, nickel, K-Kote, Duo/nickel or Ilaflon finish.
Blued finish . . . . NiB $628 Ex $556 Gd $431
Duo/nickel finish . . . . NiB $669 Ex $588 Gd $500
Nickel finish . . . . NiB $700 Ex $612 Gd $478
K-Kote finish . . . . NiB $700 Ex $612 Gd $478
w/Siglite sights, add $128

MODEL P225-A1 . . . . NiB $1122 EX $990 GD $890
Reintroduction of the P225 with ergonomic enhancements. Finish: Nitron. Grip: checkered G10. Weight: 30.5 oz. Length: 6.9 in. Made from 2015 to date.
Model P225-A1 Classic (blued finish, checkered American
hardwood grip) . . . . NiB $1079 Ex $900 Gd $880

MODEL P226 DA/DAO AUTOMATIC
Caliber: .357 SIG, 9mm Para., .40 S&W, 10- or 15-round magazine, 4.4-inch bbl., 7.75 inches overall. Weight: 29.5 oz. Alloy frame. Blue, electroless nickel, K-Kote, Duo/nickel or Nitron finish. Imported from 1983 to date.
Blued finish . . . . NiB $882 Ex $724 Gd $444
Duo/nickel finish . . . . NiB $898 Ex $809 Gd $496
Nickel finish . . . . NiB $804 Ex $659 Gd $478
K-Kote finish . . . . NiB $804 Ex $639 Gd $485
Nitron finish
(blackened stainless) . . . . NiB $826 Ex $658 Gd $479
w/Siglite sights, add $100

MODEL P226 X SERIES
Design evolution of the P226 X-Five series. Made from 2014 to date.
P226 X All Around
(DA/SA trigger) . . . . NiB $2250 Ex $1960 Gd $1600
P226 X Classic (SAO trigger,
wood grip) . . . . NiB $2680 Ex $2400 Gd $1860
P226 X Entry (SAO trigger,
polymer grip, fixed sights) . NiB $1760 Ex $1560 Gd $1210
P226 X Match (SAO trigger,
laminated grips, adj. sights) NiB $1730 Ex $1510 Gd $1110
P226 X Open (SAO trigger, G10 grips, 5-in.
compensated bbl.) . . . . NiB $4850 Ex $4460 Gd $3560
P226 X Super Match (5- or 6-in. bbl.,
adj. sights) . . . . NiB $3040 Ex $2710 Gd $2260

P226 X Tactical (SAO trigger,
Nitron finish) . . . . NiB $1680 Ex $1500 Gd $1130

MODEL P226 X-FIVE SERIES
Similar to P226 except customized by SIG Mastershop. Calibers: 9mm or .40 S&W. 5-in. bbl. Sights: adj. Trigger: adj. SA. Grips: checkered wood or polymer. Weight: 47.2 oz. Made from 2005 to 2012.
P226 X-Five (wood grips) . . . NiB $2750 Ex $2400 Gd $1700
P226 X-Five All Around (ergonomic grip frame, mfg. 2007 to
2012) . . . . NiB $1700 Ex $1430 Gd $980
P226 X-Five Competition (polymer grips, mfg. 2007 to 2012)
. . . . NiB $1980 Ex $1730 Gd $1250
P226 X-Five Tactical (ergonomic grip frame, Nitron finish,
mfg. 2007 to 2012) . . . . NiB $1700 Ex $1430 Gd $980

MODEL P227 . . . . NiB $1108 Ex $800 Gd $700
Semi-automatic. DA/SA. Caliber: .45 ACP; 10-rnd. magazine. 4.4-in. bbl. Frame: alloy w/picatinny rail. Sights: contrast or Siglite. Finish: matte black. Grip: textured polymer. Weight: 32 oz. Length: 7.7 in. Made from 2013 to date.
Model P227 Carry (3.9-in. bbl.) NiB $1108 Ex $800 Gd $700
Model P227 Carry SAS (3.9-in. bbl., Gen 2) . . . NiB $1150 Ex
$995 Gd $750
Model P227 Equinox
(two-tone finish) . . . . NiB $1250 Ex $1050 Gd $950
Model P227R (threaded bbl.) . . . NiB $1230 Ex $1050 Gd $950

MODEL P228 DA AUTOMATIC
Same general specifications as Model P226 except w/3.86-inch bbl., 7.13 inches overall. 10- or 13-round magazine, Imported 1990 to 1997.
Blued finish . . . . NiB $831 Ex $709 Gd $455
Duo/nickel finish . . . . NiB $860 Ex $755 Gd $499
Electroless nickel finish . . . . . . NiB $895 Ex $780 Gd $530
K-Kote finish . . . . NiB $882 Ex $743 Gd $541
w/Siglite night sights, add $130

MODEL M11-A1 (P228) . . . . . . NiB $1149 EX $900 GD $800
Semi-automatic. DA/SA. Caliber: 9mm; 15-rnd. magazine. 3.9-in. bbl. Frame: alloy w/o picatinny rail. Sights: Siglite. Finish: matte black. Grip: textured polymer. Weight: 32 oz. Length: 7.1 in. Commercial version of M11 Issued to US Naval Aviation. Made from 2013 to date.
Model M11-A1 Desert (FDE finish), add $100
Model M11-A1 threadedbbl., add $120

MODEL P229 DA/DAO AUTOMATIC
Same general specifications as Model P228 except w/3.86-inch bbl., 10- or 12-round magazine, weight: 32.5 oz. Nitron or Satin Nickel finish. Imported from 1991 to date.
Nitron finish
(Blackened stainless) . . . . . . NiB $860 Ex $755 Gd $464
Satin nickel finish . . . . NiB $890 Ex $791 Gd $500
For Siglite nite sights, add $128

MODEL P229
SPORT AUTOMATIC . . . . . . NiB $1292 Ex $1035 Gd $871
Similar to Model P229 except .357 SIG only w/4.5-inch compensated bbl., adj. target sights. Weight: 43.6 oz. Stainless finish. Made from 1998 to 2003. Reintroduced 2003 to 2005.

MODEL P230 DA AUTOMATIC PISTOL
Calibers: .22 LR, .32 Auto (7.65mm), .380 Auto (9mm Short), 9mm Ultra. 10-round magazine in .22, 8-round in .32, 7-round in 9mm; 3.6-inch bbl., 6.6 inches overall. Weight: 18.2 oz. or 22.4 oz. (steel frame). Fixed sights. Blued or stainless finish.

Plastic grips. Imported 1976 to 1996.
Blued finish..............NiB $530 Ex $408 Gd $308
Stainless finish (P230SL)......NiB $602 Ex $500 Gd $367

MODEL P232 DA/DAO AUTOMATIC PISTOL
Caliber: .380 ACP. Seven-round magazine, 3.6-inch bbl., 6.6 inches overall. Weight: 16.2 oz. or 22.4 oz. (steel frame). Double/single action or double action only. Blade front and notch rear drift adjustable sights. Alloy or steel frame. Automatic firing pin lock and heelmounted magazine release. Blue, Duo or stainless finish. Stippled black composite stocks. Imported 1997 to date.
Blued finish..............NiB $576 Ex $467 Gd $316
Duo finish................NiB $601 Ex $498 Gd $321
Stainless finish............NiB $588 Ex $523 Gd $433
w/Siglite night sights, add........................$65

MODEL P238 NITRON ....NiB $680 Ex $550 Gd $480
Semi-automatic. SA. Caliber: .380 ACP; 6-rnd. magazine. 2.7-in. bbl. Frame: alloy. Sights: Siglite. Finish: matte black. Grip: textured grooved polymer. Weight: 15.2 oz. Length: 5.5 in. Numerous finishes available. Made from 2009 to date.
Model P238 Blackwood (two-tone finish), add.......$100
Model P238 Rosewood (checkered rosewood grip), add.....$100
Model P238 Extreme (7+1 capacity), add............$90

MODEL P245................NiB $845 Ex $700 Gd $690
Semi-automatic. DA/SA. Caliber: .45 ACP; 6 and 8-rnd. magazine. 3.9-in. bbl. Frame: alloy. Sights: contrast. Finish: blue, two-tone. Grip: textured polymer. Weight: 30 oz. Made from 1999 to 2006.

MODEL P239 DA/DAO AUTOMATIC PISTOL
Caliber: .357 SIG, 9mm Parabellum or .40 S&W. Seven- or 8-round magazine, 3.6-inch bbl., 6.6 inches overall. Weight: 28.2 oz. Double/single action or double action only. Blade front and notch rear adjustable sights. Alloy frame w/stainless slide. AmbidExtrous frame- mounted magazine release. Matte black or Duo finish. Stippled black composite stocks. Made from 1996 to date.
Matte black finish..........NiB $590 Ex $524 Gd $301
DAO finish ....NiB $638 Ex $530 Gd $365
w/Siglite night sights, add $128

MODEL P250 FULL SIZE......NiB $466 Ex $415 Gd $370
Semi-automatic. Striker fire. Caliber: 9mm, .357 SIG, .40 S&W, .45ACP; 17-, 14- or 10-rnd. magazine depending on caliber. 4.7-in. bbl. Frame: polymer, modular grip frames allows trigger group to be swapped from frame sizes. Sights: contrast or Siglite. Finish: matte black. Grip: textured polymer. Weight: 29.4 oz. Made from 2008 to 2013.
Model P250 Compact, add......................$90
Model P250 Compact Diamond, add.............$80
Model P250 Subcompact, add $110
Model P250 TacPac (compact frame, holster), add.....$100

MODEL P290RS.............NiB $570 Ex $495 Gd $450
Semi-automatic. DAO. Caliber: 9mm; 6- or 8-rnd. magazine. 2.9-in. bbl. Frame: polymer. Sights: contrast or Siglite. Finish: matte black also numerous finishes available. Grip: textured polymer. Weight: 29.4 oz. Made from 2011 to date.

MODEL P320 NITRON ....NiB $713 Ex $630 Gd $520
Semi-automatic. SFO or DAO. Caliber: 9mm or .40 S&W; 17- or 14-rnd. magazine depending on caliber. 4.7-in. bbl. Frame: polymer w/modular grip panels. Sights: contrast or Siglite. Finish: matte black. Grip: textured polymer. Weight: 29.4 oz. Made from 2014 to date.

Model P320 Carry Nitron
(3.9-in. bbl.) ....NiB $713 Ex $630 Gd $520

MODEL P938 ROSEWOOD.....NiB $805 Ex $690 Gd $560
Similar to P238 except chambered in 9mm. Numerous finished and grip styles. Made from 2012 to date.
Model P938 Blackwood (two-tone finish), add........$20
Model P938 BRG (black rubber finger groove grip), add...$30

MODEL P400..............NiB $1414 Ex $1120 Gd $990
AR15 style gas system. Semi-automatic. Caliber: 5.56; 30-rnd. magazine. 9.0-in. bbl. Frame: forged aluminum. Sights: flip-up, adj. Finish: matte black. Grip: textured polymer. Weight: 6.5 lbs. Includes SB15 stabilizing brace. Made from 2014 to date.
Model P400 Elite (SBX brace)... NiB $1656 Ex $1500 Gd $1375

MODEL P516.............NiB $1754 Ex $1480 Gd $1275
AR15 style except short stroke piston system. Semi-automatic. Caliber: 5.56; 10-rnd. magazine. 5.7- or 10.0-in. bbl. Frame: forged aluminum. Sights: flip-up, adj. Finish: matte black. Grip: textured polymer. Weight: 6.5 lbs. Includes SB15 stabilizing brace. Made from 2010 to date.

MODEL P522................NiB $467 Ex $420 Gd $380
Blow-back system. Semi-automatic. Caliber: .22 LR; 10- or 25-rnd. magazine. 10.6-in. bbl. Frame: polymer. Sights: adj. Finish: matte black. Grip: textured polymer. Weight: 6.5 lbs. Made 2010 only, reintro. 2014 to date.

MODEL P556XI...........NiB $1470 Ex $1350 Gd $1170
3-position gas system. Semi-automatic. Caliber: 5.56 or 7.62x39mm; 30-rnd. magazine. 10.0-in. bbl. Frame: forged aluminum. Sights: flip-up, adj. Finish: matte black. Grip: textured polymer. Weight: 6.8 lbs. Includes SB15 stabilizing brace. Made from 2014 to date.

MODEL P716.............NiB $2252 Ex $2000 Gd $1890
AR15 style except short stroke piston system. Semi-automatic. Caliber: 7.62x51mm NATO; 10-rnd. magazine. 12.5-in. bbl. Frame: forged aluminum. Sights: flip-up, adj. Finish: matte black. Grip: textured polymer. Weight: 8.6 lbs. Includes SB15 stabilizing brace. Made from 2015 to date.

MODEL SP2022.............NiB $640 Ex $550 Gd $480
Semi-automatic. DA/SA. Caliber: 9mm or .40 S&W; 10-, 12-, or 15-rnd. magazine depending on caliber. 3.9-in. bbl. Frame: polymer. Sights: contrast or Siglite. Finish: matte black. Grip: textured polymer. Weight: 29.0 oz. Made from 2011 to date.
Model SP2022 Two-tone, add.....................$90
Model SP2022 Nitron TB (threaded bbl.), add........$100
Model SP2022 FDE (FDE finish), add.................$60
Model SP2022 TacPac (holster), add.................$100

MODEL 1911 GSR CARRY SERIES
Similar to 1911 GSR except w/4-in. bbl. Made from 2007 to date.
**Model 1911 GSR Carry (Nitron or two-tone
finish, 2007-2012)** ....NiB $1130 Ex $980 Gd $730
**Model 1911 GSR Carry Fastback (fastback frame,
mfg. 2012 only)** ....NiB $1170 Ex $1130 Gd $730
**Model 1911 GSR Carry Nightmare (black finish w/
stainless controls)**.........NiB $1240 Ex $1180 Gd $860
**Model 1911 GSR Carry Scorpion
(FDE finish)**..............NiB $1210 Ex $1170 Gd $850
**Model 1911 GSR Carry Spartan "Molon Labe"
(bronze finish), add** $300

Model 1911 GSR CarryTacops (accessory rail, ambi.
   safety, Ergo TX grip, mfg. 2012 only), deduct. $90
Threaded bbl., add $60

MODEL 1911 GSR COMPACT SERIES

Similar to 1911 GSR Carry except w/4-in. bbl. and short frame.
Made from 2007 to date.
Model 1911 GSR Compact (Nitron or two-tone finish,
   2007-2009). . . . . NiB $1170 Ex $980 Gd $730
Model 1911 GSR Compact C3
   (two-tone finish). . . . . NiB $1040 Ex $930 Gd $730
Model 1911 GSR Compact RCS
   (dehorned treatment), add. $50

MODEL 1911 GSR. . . . . NiB $1140 Ex $990 Gd $880

1911 style platform w/SIG styling on slide. Semi-automatic.
SA. Caliber:.40 S&W or .45 ACP; 8-rnd. magazine. 5-in. match
grade bbl. Sights: Novak or low-profile. Finish: numerous.
Grip: numerous material and textures. Weight: 41.0 oz. Made
from 2004 to date.
Model 1911 GSR Desert (desert tan finish), deduct $10
Model 1911 GSR Extreme (G-10 grips, mfg.
   2012 only), deduct. $80
Model 1911 GSR Fastback (bobtail frame, mfg.
   2012 only), deduct. $80
Model 1911 GSR Max (competition ready), add $500
Model 1911 GSR Nightmare (bobtail frame), add $200
Model 1911 GSR POW-MIA
   (engraved, mfg. 2012 only), add $300
Model 1911 GSR Railed Tacpac
   (accessory rail, holster, mag. pouch), add $100
Model 1911 GSR STX (two-tone finish), add $100
Model 1911 GSR Scorpion (FED finish), add $200
Model 1911 GSR Spartan "Molon Labe"
   (bronze finish), add $400
Model 1911 GSR Stainless
   (.45 ACP only, disc. 2013), add $90
Model 1911 GSR TTT
   (.45 ACP only, two-tone finish, disc. 2012), add $90
Model 1911 GSR Tacops
   (accessory rail, ambi. safety, Ergo TX grip), add. $100
Model 1911 GSR Target
   (Nitron or stainless finish, 2011-2012), add. $90
Model 1911 GSR XO
   (.45 ACP only, Nitron or stainless finish), deduct. $50
Threaded bbl., add $50

MODEL 1911 MATCH ELITE. . . . NiB $1140 Ex $990 Gd $860

Similar to 1911 Traditional except chambered in 9mm, .40
S&W or .45 ACP; 8-rnd. magazine. 5-in. bbl. Sights: adj. target.
Finish: stainless or two-tone. Grip: Hogue wood. Made from
2011 to 2012.

MODEL 1911 TRADITIONAL STAINLESS SERIES

Similar to 1911 Traditional except stainless steel construction
and chambered in 9mm, .38 Super, .40 S&W or .45 ACP. Made
from 2014 to date.
Model 1911 Traditional Stainless
   Match Elite. . . . . NiB $1170 Ex $1030 Gd $780
Model 1911 Traditional Stainless Nightmare
   (fastback frame) . . . . NiB $1240 Ex $1090 Gd $830
Model 1911 Traditional Stainless Scorpion
   (FED finish). . . . . NiB $1210 Ex $1080 Gd $830

MODEL 1911 TRADITIONAL . . . NIB $1140 Ex $990 Gd $860

1911 full size style platform w/traditional slide styling. Semi-
automatic. SA. Caliber: .40 S&W or .45 ACP; 8-rnd. magazine.
5-in. bbl. Sights: low-profile Siglite. Finish: reverse two-tone.
Grip: Hogue wood. Weight: 41.0 oz. Made from 2011 to 2012.
Model 1911 Traditional Compact
   (3.9-in. bbl., 2011-2012) . . . NiB $1140 Ex $990 Gd $860
Model 1911 Traditional Tacops NiB $1220 Ex $930 Gd $760

MODEL 1911-22 . . . . NIB $460 EX $400 Gd $320

Similar to a full size 1911platform except chambered in .22
LR. Semi-automatic. SA. Caliber: .40 S&W or .45 ACP; 8-rnd.
magazine. 5-in. bbl. Sights: low-profile Siglite. Finish: black,
camo, FDE or OD green. Grip: Hogue rosewood. Weight: 34
oz. Made from 2011 to date.

SMITH & WESSON — Springfield, MA

NOTE: *For ease in locating a particular S&W handgun, the
listings are divided into two groupings: Automatic/Single-Shot
Pistols (below) and Revolvers (page 156). For a complete
handgun listing, please refer to the index.*

*In 1957 S&W started to use a number system for each
model. Models with a dash followed by a one, two or three
digit number indicate a model that has had a design and/or
production change, i.e.: Model 29-2 indicates this Model 29
was produced during the second design and/or production
change. To determine the model number of a revolver, swing
out the cylinder and where the yoke meets the frame the model
name is stamped.*

*Since 1990 S&W's Performance Center has been building
or modfiying existing guns. Many handguns have come out
of the shop and it is difficult to keep an accurate account-
ing of all models and variants. Note that guns from the
Performance Center in the past decade are marked with the
Performance Center logo on the frame. Champion and Pros
Series handguns are designed in collaboration with professional competition shooters. Since 2007, S&W began the
Classics Series reissuing revolvers with aestetics of classic
revolver models.*

- AUTOMATIC/SINGLE-SHOT PISTOLS -

MODEL 35 (1913)
AUTOMATIC PISTOL . . . . NiB $979 Ex $780 Gd $469
Caliber: 35 S&W Auto. Seven-round magazine, 3.5-inch bbl.,
(hinged to frame). 6.5 inches overall. Weight: 25 oz. Fixed sights.
Blued or nickel finish. Plain walnut grips. Made from 1913 to 1921.

MODEL 32
AUTOMATIC PISTOL . . . . . NiB $3097 Ex $2315 Gd $1699
Caliber: .32 Automatic. Same general specifications as .35
caliber model, but barrel is fastened to the receiver instead of
hinged. Made from 1924 to 1937.

MODEL 22A SPORT SERIES
Caliber: .22 LR. 10-round magazine, 4-, 5.5- or 7-inch standard
(A-series) or bull bbl., (S-series). Single action. Eight, 9.5 or 11
inches overall. Weight: 28 oz. to 33 oz. Partridge front sight,
fully adjustable rear. Alloy frame w/stainless slide. Blued finish.
Black polymer or Dymondwood grips. Made 1997-2014.
Model 22A (w/4-inch bbl.) . . . . NiB $255 Ex $190 Gd $105

**Smith & Wesson
Model 22A Sport Series**

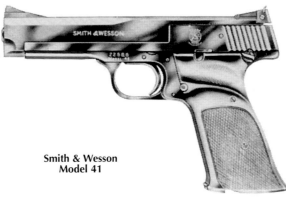

**Smith & Wesson
Model 41**

**Smith & Wesson
Model 22S Sport Series
w/Dymondwood Grips**

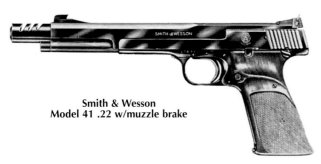

**Smith & Wesson
Model 41 .22 w/muzzle brake**

Model 22A (w/5.5-inch bbl.) . . NiB $265 Ex $204 Gd $120
Model 22A (w/7-inch bbl.) . . . . NiB $265 Ex $204 Gd $120
Model 22S (w/5.5-inch bbl.) . . . NiB $362 Ex $290 Gd $214
Model 22S (w/7-inch bbl.) . . . . NiB $395 Ex $337 Gd $265
w/bull bbl., add $65
w/Dymondwood grips, add $100

MODEL 39 9MM DA AUTO PISTOL
Calibers: 9mm Para. Eight-round magazine, 4-inch barrel. Overall length: 7.44-inches. Steel or alloy frames. Weight: 26.5 oz. (w/alloy frame). Click adjustable rear sight, ramp front. Blued or nickel finish. Checkered walnut grips. Made 1954-82. Note: Between 1954 and 1966, 927 pistols were

produced w/steel instead of alloy. In 1970, Model 39-1 w/alloy frame and steel slide. In 1971, Model 39-2 was introduced as an improved version of the original Model 39 w/modified Extractor. Model 39 (early production) 1954-70.
First series (S/N 1000-2600) . . . NiB $1566 Ex $1418 Gd $1299
9mm blue (w/steel frame & slide,
   produced 1966) . . . . NiB $1866 Ex $1618 Gd $1299
9mm blue (w/alloy frame) . . . . NiB $622 Ex $437 Gd $225
Nickel finish, add $45
Models 39-1, 39-2 (late production, 1970-82),
   9mm blue (w/alloy frame) . . . NiB $534 Ex $331 Gd $220
Nickel finish, add $50

MODEL 41 .22 AUTOMATIC PISTOL
Caliber: .22 LR, .22 Short (not interchangeably). 10-round magazine, bbl. lengths: 5-, 5.5-, 7.75-inches; latter has detachable muzzle brake, 12 inches overall (with 7.75-inch bbl.). Weight: 43.5 oz. (with 7.75-inch bbl.). Click adj. rear sight, undercut Partridge front. Blued finish. Checkered walnut grips w/thumbrest. 1957 to date.
.22 LR model. . . . . NiB $1200 Ex $870 Gd $529
.22 Short model (w/counter-
   weights & muzzle brake) . . . NiB $2700 Ex $1299 Gd $1120
w/Extended sight, add. $128
w/muzzle brake, add $50

MODEL 46 .22
AUTO PISTOL. . . . . NiB $1225 Ex $765 Gd $448
Caliber: .22 LR. 10-round magazine, bbl. lengths: 5-, 5.5-, 7-inches. 10.56 inches overall (with 7-inch bbl.). Weight: 42 oz. (with 7-inch bbl.). Click adj. rear sight, undercut Partridge front. Blued finish. Molded nylon grips w/thumbrest. Only 4,000 produced. Made from 1957 to 1966.

MODEL 52 .38 MASTER AUTO
Caliber: .38 Special (midrange wadcutter only). Five-round magazine, 5-inch bbl., overall length: 8.63 inches. Weight: 41 oz. Micrometer click rear sight, Partridge front on ramp base. Blued finish. Checkered walnut grips. Made from 1961 to 1963.
Model 52 (1961-63) . . . . NiB $1109 Ex $915 Gd $546
Model 52-1 (1963-71). . . . . . . NiB $1029 Ex $915 Gd $546
Model 52-2 (1971-93). . . . . . . NiB $1029 Ex $915 Gd $546
Model 52-A USA Marksman (fewer
   than 100 mfg.) . . . . NiB $3820 Ex $3470 Gd $3139

**Smith & Wesson
Model 52**

**Smith & Wesson
Model 59**

**Smith & Wesson
Model 422**

**Smith & Wesson
Model 439**

MODEL 59 9MM DA AUTO
Similar specifications as Model 39 except has 14-round staggered column magazine, checkered nylon grips. Made 1971 to 1981.

Model 59, blue . . . . NiB $549 Ex $431 Gd $290
Model 59, nickel. . . . . NiB $600 Ex $444 Gd $326
Model 59 (early production
   w/smooth grip frame). . . . NiB $1647 Ex $1508 Gd $1015

MODEL 61 ESCORT POCKET AUTOMATIC PISTOL
Caliber: .22 LR. Five-round magazine, 2.13-inch bbl., 4.69 inches overall. Weight: 14 oz. Fixed sights. Blued or nickel finish. Checkered plastic grips. Made from 1970 to 1974.

Model 61, blue . . . . NiB $380 Ex $270 Gd $165
Model 61, nickel. . . . . NiB $431 Ex $316 Gd $220

MODEL 410 AUTO PISTOL . . . NiB $561 Ex $444 Gd $244
Caliber: .40 S&W. Double action. 10-round magazine, 4-inch bbl., 7.5 inches overall. Weight: 28.5 oz. Alloy frame w/steel slide. Post front sight, fixed rear w/3-dot system. Matte blue finish. Checkered synthetic grips w/straight backstrap. Made from 1996 to 2007.

MODEL 411 AUTO PISTOL . . . NiB $530 Ex $433 Gd $386
Similar to S&W Model 915 except in caliber .40 S&W. 11-round magazine, made from 1994 to 1996.

MODEL 422 SA AUTO PISTOL
Caliber: .22 LR. 10-round magazine, 4.5- or 6-inch bbl., 7.5 inches overall (with 4.5-inch bbl.). Weight: 22-23.5 oz. Fixed or adjustable sights. Checkered plastic or walnut grips. Blued finish. Made from 1987 to 1996.

Standard model. . . . . NiB $220 Ex $175 Gd $150
Target model. . . . . NiB $274 Ex $198 Gd $170

MODEL 439 9MM AUTOMATIC
DA. Caliber: 9mm Para. Two 8-round magazines, 4-inch bbl., 7.44 inches overall. Alloy frame. Weight: 30 oz. Serrated ramp square front sight, square notch rear. Checkered walnut grips. Blued or nickel finish. Made from 1979 to 1988.

Model 439, blue . . . . NiB $530 Ex $368 Gd $306
Model 439, nickel. . . . . NiB $529 Ex $386 Gd $316
w/adjustable sights, add $40

MODEL 457
COMPACT AUTO PISTOL. . . . . NiB $571 Ex $434 Gd $265
Caliber: .45 ACP. Double action. Seven-round magazine, 3.75-inch bbl., 7.25 inches overall. Weight: 29 oz. Alloy frame w/steel slide. Post front sight, fixed rear w/3-dot system. Bobbed hammer. Matte blue finish. Wraparound synthetic grip w/straight backstrap. Made from 1996 to 2006.

MODEL 459 DA AUTOMATIC
Caliber: 9mm Para. Two 14-round magazines, 4-inch bbl., 7.44 inches overall. Alloy frame. Weight: 28 oz. Blued or nickel finish. Made from 1979 to 1987.

Model 459, blue . . . . NiB $485 Ex $431 Gd $319
Model 459, nickel. . . . . NiB $527 Ex $475 Gd $377
FBI Model (brushed finish) . . . . NiB $733 Ex $599 Gd $437

MODEL 469
(MINI) AUTOMATIC. . . . . NiB $485 Ex $388 Gd $270
DA. Caliber: 9mm Para. Two 12-round magazines, 3.5-inch bbl., 6.88 inches overall. Weight: 26 oz. Yellow ramp front

Smith & Wesson
Model 459

Smith & Wesson
Model 645

Smith & Wesson
Model 469

Smith & Wesson
Model 639

sight, dovetail mounted square-notch rear. Sandblasted blued finish. Optional ambidExtrous safety. Made from 1982 to 1988.

MODEL 539 DA AUTOMATIC
Similar to Model 439 except w/steel frame. Caliber: 9mm Para. Two 8-round magazines, 4-inch bbl., 7.44 inches overall. Weight: 36 oz. Blued or nickel finish. Made 1980-83.
Model 539, blue . . . . NiB $590 Ex $486 Gd $368
Model 539, nickel . . . . NiB $601 Ex $530 Gd $408
w/adjustable sights, add $50

MODEL 559 DA AUTOMATIC
Similar to Model 459 except w/steel frame. Caliber: 9mm Para. Two 14-round magazines, 4-inch bbl., 7.44 inches overall. Weight: 39.5 oz. Blued or nickel finish. (3750 produced) Made 1980 to 1983.
Model 559, blue . . . . NiB $612 Ex $536 Gd $408
Model 559, nickel . . . . NiB $648 Ex $561 Gd $444
w/adjustable sights, add $50

MODEL 622 SA AUTO PISTOL
Same general specifications as Model 422 except w/stainless finish. Made from 1989 to 1996.
Standard model . . . . NiB $265 Ex $197 Gd $120
Target model . . . . NiB $309 Ex $212 Gd $146

MODEL 639 AUTOMATIC . . . . NiB $530 Ex $377 Gd $304
Caliber: 9mm Para. Stainless. Two 12-round magazines, 3.5-inch bbl., 6.9 inches overall. Weight: 36 oz. Made 1986-88.

MODEL 645 DA AUTOMATIC
Caliber: .45 ACP. Eight-round. 5-inch bbl., overall length: 8.5 inches. Weight: Approx. 38 oz. Red ramp front, fixed rear sights. Stainless. Made from 1986-88.
Model 645 (w/fixed sights) . . . . NiB $601 Ex $433 Gd $346
Model 645 (w/adjustable sights) NiB $638 Ex $464 Gd $366

MODEL 659 9MM AUTOMATIC
DA. Similar to S&W Model 459 except weight: 39.5 oz. and finish is satin stainless steel finish. Made from 1983-88.
Model 659 (w/fixed sights) . . . . NiB $517 Ex $419 Gd $326
Model 659 (w/adjustable sights) . . . NiB $528 Ex $444 Gd $356

MODEL 669 AUTOMATIC . . . . NiB $559 Ex $345 Gd $274
Caliber: 9mm. 12-round magazine, 3.5 inch bbl., 6.9 inches overall. Weight: 26 oz. Serrated ramp front sight w/red bar, fixed rear. Non-glare stainless steel finish. Made from 1986-88.

MODEL 745 AUTOMATIC PISTOL
Caliber: .45 ACP. Eight-round magazine, 5-inch bbl., 8.63 inches overall. Weight: 38.75 oz. Fixed sights. Blued slide,

Smith & Wesson
Model 659

Smith & Wesson
Model 745

Smith & Wesson
Model 1026

stainless frame. Checkered walnut grips. Similar to the model 645, but w/o DA capability. Made from 1987-90.

w/standard competition
features . . . . NiB $760 Ex $549 Gd $433
IPSC Commemorative
(first 5,000). . . . . NiB $798 Ex $638 Gd $429

MODEL 908/910 AUTO PISTOLS
Caliber: 9mm Parabellum. Double action. Eight-round (Model 908), 9-round (Model 909) or 10-round (Model 910) magazine; 3.5- or 4-inch bbl.; 6.83 or 7.38 inches overall. Weight: 26 oz. to 28.5 oz. Post front sight, fixed rear w/3-dot system. Matte blue steel slide w/alloy frame. Delrin synthetic wrap-around grip w/straight backstrap. Made from 1994 to date.
Model 908 . . . . NiB $541 Ex $397 Gd $272
Model 909 (disc 1996) . . . . NiB $479 Ex $347 Gd $239
Model 910 . . . . NiB $497 Ex $348 Gd $255

MODEL 915 AUTO PISTOL . . . NiB $434 Ex $306 Gd $220
DA. Caliber: 9mm Para. 15-round magazine, 4-inch bbl., 7.5 inches overall. Weight: 28.5 oz. Post front sight, fixed square-notched rear w/3-dot system. Xenoy wraparound grip. Blued steel slide and alloy frame. Made from 1992-94.

MODEL 1000 SERIES DA AUTO
Caliber: 10mm. Nine-round magazine, 4.25- or 5-inch bbl., 7.88 or 8.63 inches overall. Weight: About 38 oz. Post front sight, adj. or fixed square-notched rear w/3-dot system. One-piece Xenoy wraparound grips. Stainless slide and frame. Made from 1990-94.
Model 1006 (fixed sights,
5-inch bbl.) . . . . NiB $724 Ex $530 Gd $433
Model 1006 (adj. sights,
5-inch bbl.). . . . . NiB $740 Ex $544 Gd $479
Model 1026 (fixed sights, 5-inch
bbl., decocking lever) . . . . . . NiB $724 Ex $530 Gd $433
Model 1066 (fixed
sights, 4.25 inch bbl.) . . . . . . NiB $678 Ex $530 Gd $362
Model 1076 (fixed sights, 4.25 inch bbl., frame-mounted
decocking lever, ... NiB $730 Ex $536 Gd $439
Model 1076 (same as above
w/Tritium night sight) . . . . . . NiB $730 Ex $536 Gd $439
Model 1086 (same as model
1076 in DA only) . . . . NiB $760 Ex $544 Gd $429

MODEL 2206 SA AUTOMATIC PISTOL
Similar to Model 422 except w/stainless-steel slide and frame, weight: 35-39 oz. Partridge front sight on adj. sight model; post w/white dot on fixed sight model. Plastic grips. Made from 1990-96.
Standard model. . . . . NiB $342 Ex $227 Gd $130
Target model . . . . NiB $377 Ex $239 Gd $178

MODEL 2213
SPORTSMAN AUTO . . . . NiB $279 Ex $180 Gd $119
Caliber: .22 LR. Eight-round magazine, 3-inch bbl., 6.13 inches overall. Weight: 18 oz. Partridge front sight, fixed square-notched rear w/3-dot system. Black synthetic molded grips. Stainless steel slide w/alloy frame. Made from 1992-99.

MODEL 2214
SPORTSMAN AUTO . . . . NiB $362 Ex $190 Gd $126
Same general specifications as Model 2214 except w/blued slide and matte black alloy frame. Made from 1990-99.

MODEL 3904/3906 DA AUTO PISTOL
Caliber: 9mm. Eight-round magazine, 4-inch bbl., 7.5 inches overall. Weight: 25.5 oz. (Model 3904) or 34 oz. (Model 3906).

Smith & Wesson
Model 3906

Smith & Wesson
Model 3953

Fixed or adj. sights. Delrin one-piece wraparound checkered grips. Alloy frame w/blued carbon steel slide (Model 3904) or satin stainless (Model 3906). Made from 1989 to 1991.

Model 3904 w/adj. sights . . . . . NiB $536 Ex $362 Gd $287
Model 3904 w/fixed sights . . . . NiB $497 Ex $328 Gd $249
Model 3904 w/Novak LC sight . . . NiB $536 Ex $362 Gd $287
Model 3906 w/adj. sights   . . . . . NiB $576 Ex $497 Gd 431
Model 3906 w/Novak LC
  sight . . . . NiB $546 Ex $499 Gd $366

MODEL 3913/3914 DA AUTOMATIC
Caliber: 9mm Parabellum (Luger). Eight-round magazine, 3.5-inch bbl., 6.88 inches overall. Weight: 25 oz. Post front sight, fixed or adj. square-notched rear. One-piece Xenoy wraparound grips w/straight backstrap. Alloy frame w/stainless or blued slide. Made from 1990 to 1999.

Model 3913 stainless . . . . NiB $577 Ex $449 Gd $346
Model 3913LS Lady Smith stainless
  w/contoured trigger guard . . . NiB $755 Ex $588 Gd $479
Model 3913TSW (intro. 1998) . . . NiB $739 Ex $596 Gd $479
Model 3914 blued compact
  (disc 1995) . . . . NiB $559 Ex $467 Gd $386

MODEL 3953/3954 DA AUTO PISTOL
Same general specifications as Model 3913/3914 except double action only. Made from 1990 to 2002.

Model 3953 stainless,
  double action only . . . . NiB $590 Ex $444 Gd $396
Model 3954 blued, double
  action only (disc. 1992) . . . . . NiB $530 Ex $431 Gd $340

MODEL 4000 SERIES DA AUTO
Caliber: .40 S&W. 11-round magazine, 4-inch bbl., 7.88 inches overall. Weight: 28-30 oz. w/alloy frame or 36 oz. w/ stainless frame. Post front sight, adj. or fixed square-notched rear w/2 white dots. Straight backstrap. One-piece Xenoy wraparound grips. Blued or stainless finish. Made between 1991 to 1993.

Model 4003 stainless w/alloy
  frame . . . . NiB $658 Ex $498 Gd $388
Model 4003 TSW w/
S&W Tactical options . . . . NiB $870 Ex $779 Gd $608
Model 4004 blued w/alloy
  frame . . . . NiB $601 Ex $449 Gd $397
Model 4006 stainless
  frame, fixed sights. . . . . NiB $711 Ex $562 Gd $431
Model 4006 stainless
  frame, Adj. sights . . . . NiB $744 Ex $634 Gd $498
Model 4006 TSW w/
S&W Tactical options . . . . . . NiB $855 Ex $760 Gd $475
Model 4013 stainless frame,
  fixed sights . . . . NiB $622 Ex $419 Gd $377
Model 4013 TSW w/
S&W Tactical options . . . . . . NiB $855 Ex $760 Gd $475
Model 4014 blued, fixed sights
  (disc. 1993) . . . . NiB $581 Ex $419 Gd $398
Model 4026 w/decocking
  Lever (disc. 1994) . . . . NiB $659 Ex $562 Gd $449
Model 4043 DA only, stainless
  w/alloy frame . . . . NiB $693 Ex $580 Gd $497
Model 4044 DA only,
  blued w/alloy frame . . . . NiB $569 Ex $448 Gd $346
Model 4046 DA only, stainless
  frame, fixed sights. . . . . NiB $739 Ex $668 Gd $499
Model 4046 TSW w/
S&W Tactical options . . . . . . NiB $700 Ex $632 Gd $485
Model 4046 DA only, stainless
  frame, Tritium night sight . . . NiB $724 Ex $634 Gd $475

MODEL 4013/4014 DA AUTOMATIC
Caliber: .40 S&W. Eight-round capacity, 3.5-inch bbl., 7 inches overall. Weight: 26 oz. Post front sight, fixed Novak LC rear w/3-dot system. One-piece Xenoy wraparound grips. Stainless or blued slide w/alloy frame. Made from 1991 to 1996.

Model 4013 w/stainless slide
  (disc. 1996) . . . . NiB $643 Ex $536 Gd $327
Model 4013 Tactical w/stainless
  slide . . . . NiB $860 Ex $693 Gd $588
Model 4014 w/blued slide
  (disc. 1993) . . . . NiB $587 Ex $464 Gd $328

MODEL 4053/4054 DA AUTO PISTOL
Same general specifications as Model 4013/4014 except double action only. Alloy frame fitted w/blued steel slide. Made from 1991 to 1997.

Model 4053 DA only w/stainless
  slide . . . . NiB $668 Ex $530 Gd $458
Model 4053 TSW w/ S&W
  Tactical options. . . . . NiB $760 Ex $648 Gd $541
Model 4054 DA only w/blued slide
  (disc. 1992) . . . . NiB $709 Ex $464 Gd $378

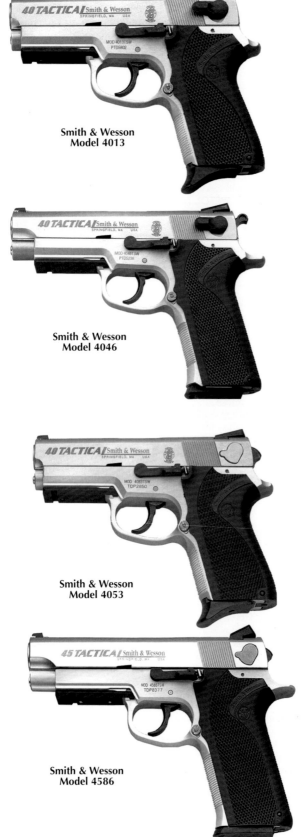

Smith & Wesson
Model 4013

Smith & Wesson
Model 4046

Smith & Wesson
Model 4053

Smith & Wesson
Model 4586

MODEL 4500 SERIES DA AUTOMATIC

Caliber: .45 ACP. Six-, 7- or 8-round magazine, bbl. lengths: 3.75, 4.25 or 5 inches; 7.13 to 8.63 inches overall. Weight: 34.5 to 38.5 oz. Post front sight, fixed Novak LC rear w/3-dot system or adj. One-piece Xenoy wraparound grips. Satin stainless finish. Made from 1991 to 1997.

Model 4505 w/fixed sights,
   5-inch bbl. . . . . NiB $693 Ex $597 Gd $386
Model 4505 w/Novak LC sight,
   5-inch bbl. . . . . NiB $653 Ex $578 Gd $431
Model 4506 w/fixed sights,
   5-inch bbl. . . . . NiB $744 Ex $581 Gd $523
Model 4506 w/Novak LC sight,
   5-inch bbl. . . . . NiB $755 Ex $590 Gd $500
Model 4513T (TSW) w/3.75-inch
   bbl.Tactical Combat . . . . NiB $781 Ex $633 Gd $499
Model 4516 w/3.75-inch bbl . . .NiB $724 Ex $622 Gd $479
Model 4526 w/5-inch bbl., alloy frame,
   decocking lever, fixed sights . . .NiB $734 Ex $590 Gd $500
Model 4536, decocking lever . . . NiB $734 Ex $590 Gd $500
Model 4546, w/3.75-inch bbl.,
   DA only . . . . NiB $734 Ex $590 Gd $500
Model 4553T (TSW) w/3.75-inch
   bbl. Tactical Combat. . . . . . . NiB $780 Ex $665 Gd $459
Model 4556, w/3.75-inch bbl.,
   DA only . . . . NiB $700 Ex $601 Gd $397
Model 4563 TSW w/4.25-inch bbl.
   Tactical Combat . . . . NiB $779 Ex $658 Gd $499
Model 4566 w/4.25-inch bbl., ambidextrous
   safety, fixed sights. . . . . NiB $693 Ex $536 Gd $453
Model 4566 TSW w/4.25-inch
   bbl. Tactical Combat. . . . . . . NiB $693 Ex $536 Gd $453
Model 4576 w/4.25-inch bbl.,
   decocking lever. . . . . NiB $691 Ex $607 Gd $449
Model 4583T TSW w/4.25-inch bbl.
   Tactical Combat . . . . NiB $780 Ex $665 Gd $459
Model 4586 w/4.25-inch bbl.,
   DA only . . . . NiB $780 Ex $610 Gd $500
Model 4586 TSW w/4.25-inch bbl.
   Tactical Combat . . . . NiB $734 Ex $590 Gd $500

MODEL 5900 SERIES DA AUTOMATIC

Caliber: 9mm. 15-round magazine, 4-inch bbl., 7.5 inches overall. Weight: 26-38 oz. Fixed or adj. sights. One-piece Xenoy wraparound grips. Alloy frame w/stainless-steel slide (Model 5903) or blued slide (Model 5904) stainless-steel frame and slide (Model 5906). Made from 1990 to 1997.

Model 5903 w/adjustable
   sights . . . . NiB $693 Ex $556 Gd $386
Model 5903 w/Novak LC rear
   sight . . . . NiB $780 Ex $691 Gd $386
Model 5903 TSW w/4-inch bbl.,
   Tactical Combat . . . . NiB $767 Ex $658 Gd $497
Model 5904 w/adjustable
   sights . . . . NiB $581 Ex $468 Gd $376
Model 5904 w/Novak LC rear
   sight . . . . NiB $599 Ex $474 Gd $398
Model 5905 L/C Adjustable
   Sights . . . . NiB $693 Ex $549 Gd $398
Model 5905 w/Novak LC rear
   sight . . . . NiB $733 Ex $634 Gd $464

Smith & Wesson Model 5904 w/ Adjustable Sights

Model 5906 w/adjustable
   sights . . . . NiB $658 Ex $544 Gd $439
Model 5906 w/Novak LC rear
   sight . . . . NiB $658 Ex $544 Gd $439
Model 5906 w/Tritium night
   sight . . . . NiB $755 Ex $650 Gd $562
Model 5906 TSW w/4-inch bbl.,
   Tactical Combat . . . . NiB $862 Ex $733 Gd $544
Model 5924 w/anodized frame,
   blued slide . . . . NiB $659 Ex $508 Gd $337
Model 5926 w/stainless frame,
   decocking lever. . . . . NiB $644 Ex $543 Gd $444
Model 5943 w/alloy frame/
   stainless slide, DA only . . . . . NiB $601 Ex $444 Gd $351
Model 5943 TSW w/4-inch bbl.,
   DA only . . . . NiB $650 Ex $546 Gd $429
Model 5944 w/alloy frame/
   blued slide, DA only . . . . NiB $689 Ex $556 Gd $456
Model 5946 w/stainless frame/slide,
   DA only . . . . NiB $658 Ex $534 Gd $376
Model 5946 TSW w/4-inch bbl.,
   DA only . . . . NiB $774 Ex $632 Gd $337

MODEL 6900 COMPACT SERIES
Double action. Caliber: 9mm. 12-round magazine, 3.5-inch bbl., 6.88 inches overall. Weight: 26.5 oz. AmbidExtrous safety. Post front sight, fixed Novak LC rear w/3-dot system. Alloy frame w/blued carbon steel slide (Model 6904) or stainless steel slide (Model 6906). Made 1989 to 1997.
Model 6904 . . . . NiB $601 Ex $499 Gd $377
Model 6906 w/fixed sights . . . . NiB $621 Ex $546 Gd $499
Model 6906 w/Tritium night
   sight . . . . NiB $843 Ex $621 Gd $500
Model 6926 w/decocking lever . . NiB $691 Ex $587 Gd $374
Model 6944 in DA only . . . . NiB $612 Ex $546 Gd $342
Model 6946
   in DA only ,fixed sights. . . . . NiB $709 Ex $577 Gd $395
Model 6946 w/Tritium night
   sight . . . . NiB $709 Ex $544 Gd $433

M&P9 AUTOMATIC PISTOL . . . NiB $569 Ex $320 Gd $270
Striker fired action. Caliber: 9mm. 10- or 17-round magazine, 4.25-in. bbl., polymer frame w/three interchangeable grip inserts and accessory rail, low profile fixed sights, w/ or w/o thumb safety. Weight: 24 oz. Black Melonite finish. Made from 2006 to date.
M&P9L (5-in. bbl.,
   discont. 2010) . . . . NiB $575 Ex $400 Gd $330
M&P9 Compact (3.5-in. bbl.) . . NiB $569 Ex $320 Gd $270
M&P9 JG (Julie Goloski-Golob design collaboration,
   discont. 2012). . . . . NiB $465 Ex $330 Gd $280
M&P9 VTAC (Viking Tactics design collaboration, 4.5-in. bbl.
   w/full size frame, FDE finish) . . . NiB $799 Ex $430 Gd $330

M&P9 C.O.R.E.
AUTOMATIC PISTOL . . . . NiB $729 Ex $480 Gd $350
Similar to M&P9 or M&P40 except set up for competition w/ optic mount, fixed 3-dot sights. Made from 2013 to date.

M&P9 PRO SERIES
AUTOMATIC PISTOL . . . . NiB $699 Ex $410 Gd $310
Similar to M&P9 except w/5-in. bbl., fiber optic Novak sights, optic ready. Made from 2012 to date.

M&P40 AUTOMATIC PISTOL . . . NiB $569 Ex $320 Gd $270
Similar to M&P9 except in .40 S&W w/10- or 15-round magazine. Made from 2006 to date.
M&P40 Compact (3.5-in. bbl.) . . . NiB $569 Ex $320 Gd $270
M&P40 VTAC (Viking Tactics design collaboration, 4.5-in.
   bbl. w/full size frame, FDE finish) . . NiB $799 Ex $430 Gd $330

M&P40 PRO SERIES
AUTOMATIC PISTOL . . . . NiB $699 Ex $410 Gd $310
Similar to M&P40 except w/5-in. bbl., fiber optic Novak sights, optic ready. Made from 2012 to date.

M&P45 AUTOMATIC PISTOL . . . NiB $599 Ex $330 Gd $270
Similar to M&P9 except in .45 ACP w/10-round magazine. Made from 2006 to date.
M&P45 Compact (4-in. bbl.) . . . NiB $599 Ex $330 Gd $270

M&P357 AUTOMATIC PISTOL . . . NiB $585 Ex $380 Gd $280
Similar to M&P9 except in .357 SIG w/10- or 15-round magazine. Made from 2006 to 2010.
M&P357 Compact (3.5-in. bbl.) . . . NiB $585 Ex $380 Gd $280

M&P BODYGUARD
AUTOMATIC PISTOL . . . . NiB $380 Ex $240 Gd $185
DAO. Caliber: .380 ACP. 6-nd. magazine, 2.75-in. bbl., polymer frame. Weight: 11.9 oz. Black Melonite finish. Made 2014 to date.

SIGMA SW380
AUTOMATIC PISTOL . . . . NiB $536 Ex $357 Gd $290
Caliber: .380 ACP. Double-action only. Six-round magazine, 3-inch bbl., weight: 14 oz. Black integral polymer gripframe w/checkered back and front straps. Fixed channel sights. Polymer frame w/hammerless steel slide. Made from 1994 to 1996.

SIGMA SW9 SERIES AUTOMATIC PISTOL
Caliber: 9mm Parabellum. Double action only. 10-round magazine, 3.25-, 4- or 4.5-inch bbl., weight: 17.9 oz. to 24.7 oz. Polymer frame w/hammerless steel slide. Post front sight and drift adjustable rear w/3-dot system. Gray or black integral polymer gripframe w/checkered back and front straps. Made from 1994 to 1996.
Model SW9C (compact w/3.25-inch
   bbl.) . . . . NiB $500 Ex $425 Gd $326

Smith & Wesson
Model 1

Model SW9F (blue slide w/4.5-inch
  bbl.) . . . . NiB $500 Ex $425 Gd $326
Model SW9M (compact w/3.25-inch
  bbl.) . . . . NiB $342 Ex $255 Gd $165
Model SW9V (stainless slide w/4-inch
  bbl.) . . . . NiB $408 Ex $304 Gd $229
Tritium night sight, add. $25

M&P SHIELD
AUTOMATIC PISTOL . . . . NiB $449 Ex $280 Gd $210
Similar to M&P9 and M&P40 except sub-compact variant
w/3.1-in. bbl., 6-, 7- or 8-round magazine. Weight: 19 oz.
Black Melonite finish. Made from 2012 to date.

MODEL SW22 VICTORY. . . . . . NiB $409 EX $380 Gd $310
Semi-automatic. SA. Caliber:.22 LR; 10-rnd. magazine. 5.5-in.
bbl. Sights: fiber optic front, adj. rear. Finish: stainless. Grip:
textured polymer. Weight: 36.0 oz. Made from 2016 to date.
Threaded bbl., add $20
Camo finish, add. $10

SW40 SERIES AUTOMATIC PISTOL
Same general specifications as SW9 series except chambered
for .40 S&W w/4- or 4.5-inch bbl., weight: 24.4 to 26 oz. Made
1994 to 1998.
Model SW40C (compact w/4-inch
  bbl.) . . . . NiB $497 Ex $346 Gd $249
Model SW40F (blue slide w/4.5-inch
  bbl.) . . . . NiB $497 Ex $346 Gd $249
Model SW40V (stainless slide
  w/4-inch bbl.) . . . . NiB $497 Ex $346 Gd $249
w/Tritium night sight, add. $25

MODEL 1891 SINGLE-SHOT TARGET PISTOL,
FIRST MODEL
Hinged frame. Calibers: .22 LR, .32 S&W, .38 S&W. Bbl.
lengths: 6-, 8- and 10-inches, approx. 13.5 inches overall (with
10-inch bbl.). Weight: About 25 oz. Target sights, barrel catch
rear adj. for windage and elevation. Blued finish. Square butt,
hard rubber grips. Made 1893-1905. Note: This model was
available also as a combination arm w/accessory .38 revolver
bbl. and cylinder enabling conversion to a pocket revolver.
It has the frame of the .38 SA revolver Model 1891 w/side
flanges, hand and cylinder stop slots.
Single-shot pistol, .22 LR . . NiB $2890 Ex $2643 Gd $2425
Single-shot pistol, .32 S&W
  or .38 S&W. . . . . NiB $2320 Ex $1996 Gd $1748
Combination set, revolver
and single-shot barrel . . . . . NiB $3635 Ex $3145 Gd $2869

MODEL 1891 SINGLE-SHOT TARGET PISTOL,
SECOND MODEL . . . . NiB $2797 Ex $2466 Gd $1580
Similar to the First Model except side flanges, hand and stop
slots eliminated, cannot be converted to revolver, redesigned
rear sight. Caliber: .22 LR only, 10-inch bbl. only. Made from
1905 to 1909.

PERFECTED SINGLE-SHOT TARGET PISTOL
Similar to Second Model except has double-action lockwork.
Caliber: .22 LR only, 10-inch bbl. Checkered walnut grips,
Extended square-butt target type. Made 1909-23. Note: In
1920 and thereafter, this model was made w/barrels having
bore diameter of .223 instead of .226 and tight, short chamber-
ing. The first group of these pistols was produced for the U.S.
Olympic Team of 1920, thus the designation Olympic Model.
Pre-1920 type . . . . NiB $2314 Ex $1945 Gd $1566
Olympic model . . . . NiB $2665 Ex $2380 Gd $2235

STRAIGHT LINE SINGLE-SHOT
TARGET PISTOL . . . . NiB $3345 Ex $3267 Gd $3095
Frame shaped like that of an automatic pistol, barrel swings
to the left on pivot for Extracting and loading, straight-line
trigger and hammer movement. Caliber: .22 LR. 10-inch bbl.,
11.25 inches overall. Weight: 34 oz. Target sights. Blued finish.
Smooth walnut grips. Supplied in metal case w/screwdriver
and cleaning rod. Made from 1925 to 1936.

- REVOLVERS -

MODEL 1 HAND EJECTOR
DA REVOLVER . . . . NiB $2670 Ex $2000 Gd $1289
First Model. Forerunner of the .32 Hand Ejector and
Regulation Police models, this was the first S&W revolver
of the solid-frame, swing-out cylinder type. Top strap of this
model is longer than those of later models, and it lacks the
usual S&W cylinder latch. Caliber: .22 Long. Bbl., lengths:
3.25-, 4.25-, and 6-inches. Fixed sights. Blued or nickel
finish. Round butt, hard rubber stocks. Made from 1896 to
1903.

NO. 3 SA FRONTIER . . . . . NiB $5170 Ex $4350 Gd $3095
Caliber: .44-40 WCF. Bbl., lengths: 4-, 5- and 6.5-inch. Fixed
or target sights. Blued or nickel finish. Round, hard rubber or
checkered walnut grips. Made from 1885 to 1908.

NO. 3 SA (NEW MODEL) . . NiB $7245 Ex $6095 Gd $4270
Hinged frame. Six-round cylinder. Caliber: .44 S&W Russian.
Bbl., lengths: 4-, 5-, 6-, 6.5-, 7.5- and 8-inches. Fixed or target
sights. Blued or nickel finish. Round, hard rubber or checkered
walnut grips. Made from 1878 to 1908. Note: Value shown is
for standard model. Specialist collectors recognize numerous
variations w/a range of higher values.
Performance Center Schofield Model of 2000
  (modern repro) . . . . NiB $1800

NO. 3 SA TARGET. . . . . . . NiB $6996 Ex $3890 Gd $3175
Hinged frame. Six-round cylinder. Calibers: .32/.44 S&W,
.38/.44 S&W Gallery & Target. 6.5-inch bbl. only. Fixed or
target sights. Blued or nickel finish. Round, hard rubber or
checkered walnut grips. Made from 1887 to 1910.

MODEL 10 .38 MILITARY & POLICE DA
Also called Hand Ejector Model of 1902, Hand Ejector
Model of 1905, Model K. Manufactured substantially in its
present form since 1902, this model has undergone numerous changes, most of them minor. Round- or square-butt

**Smith & Wesson
Model 10 (Two-inch Barrel)**

**Smith & Wesson
Model 12 (Two-inch Barrel)**

**Smith & Wesson Model 13
(Heavy Barrel)**

**Smith & Wesson
Model 14**

models, the latter intro. in 1904. Caliber: .38 Special. Six-round cylinder, bbl. lengths: 2-(intro. 1933), 4-, 5-, 6- and 6.5-inch (latter disc. 1915) also 4-inch heavy bbl., (intro. 1957); 11.13 inches overall (square-butt model w/6-inch bbl.). Round-butt model is 1/4-inch shorter, weight: About 1/2 oz. less. Fixed sights. Blued or nickel finish. Checkered walnut grips, hard rubber available in round-butt style. Current Model 10 has short action. Made 1902 to date. Note: S&W Victory Model, wartime version of the M & P .38, was produced for the U.S. Government from 1940 to the end of the war. A similar revolver, designated .38/200 British Service Revolver, was produced for the British Government during the same period. These arms have either brush-polish or sandblast blued finish, and most of them have plain, smooth walnut grips, lanyard swivels.

Model of 1902 (1902-05) . . . . . NiB $639 Ex $536 Gd $362
Model of 1905 (1905-40) . . . . NiB $1165 Ex $910 Gd $602
.38/200 British Service
   (1940-45) . . . . NiB $1165 Ex $910 Gd $602
Victory Model (1942-45) . . . . . NiB $643 Ex $529 Gd $425
Model of 1944 (1945-48) . . . . NiB $785 Ex $431 Gd $319
Model 10 (1948-date) . . . . NiB $530 Ex $437 Gd $319

**MODEL 10 .38 MILITARY
& POLICE HEAVY BARREL** . . . . NiB $632 Ex $499 Gd $337
Same as standard Model 10 except has heavy 4-inch bbl., weight: 34 oz. Made from 1957 to 1986.

MODEL 10 CLASSICS SERIES . . NiB $632 Ex $499 Gd $337
Recent manufacture of Model 10 except chambered in .38 Spl.+P and w/heavy 4-in. bbl., fixed sights, blued finish, checkered wood grips. Made from 2010 to date.

**MODEL 12 .38 M&P
AIRWEIGHT** . . . . NiB $544 Ex $388 Gd $290
Same as standard Military & Police except has light alloy frame, f8rnished w/2- or 4-inch bbl. only, weight: 18 oz. (w/2-inch bbl.). Made from 1952 to 1986.

**MODEL 12/13 (AIR FORCE MODEL)
DA REVOLVER** . . . . NiB $536 Ex $439 Gd $265
Special "Air Force" Model designed with alloy cylinder and frame to be used as a "Survival Weapon" for air crews. Athough this weapon was actually a first-series Model 12, the Air Force stamped "M13" on the top strap. Issued 1953 but recalled for function problems in 1954.

**MODEL 13 .357
MILITARY/POLICE** . . . . NiB $487 Ex $318 Gd $204
Same as Model 10 .38 Military & Police Heavy Barrel except chambered for .357 Magnum and .38 Special w/3- or 4-inch bbl. Round or square butt configuration. Made 1974-98.

**MODELS 14 (K-38) AND 16 (K-32) MASTERPIECE
REVOLVERS**
Calibers: .22 LR, .22 Magnum Rimfire, .32 S&W Long, .38 Special. Six-round cylinder. DA/SA. Bbl. lengths: 4- (.22 WMR only), 6-, 8.38-inch (latter not available in K32), 11.13 inches overall (with 6-inch bbl.). Weight: 38.5 oz. (with 6-inch bbl.). Click adj. rear sight, Partridge front. Blued finish. Checkered walnut grips. Made from 1947 to date. (Model 16 disc. 1974; 3,630 produced; reissued 1990 to 1993.)
Model 14 (K-38 DA) . . . . NiB $577 Ex $318 Gd $209
Model 14 (K-38 SA, 6-in. bbl.) . . . NiB $693 Ex $366 Gd $220
Model 14 (K-38 SA, 8.38-in. bbl.) . . . . . NiB $474 Ex $351 Gd $259
Model 16 (K-32 DA) 1st Issue . . NiB $3500 Ex $3316 Gd $889
Model 16 (K-32 DA) . . . . NiB $2579 Ex $1138 Gd $974

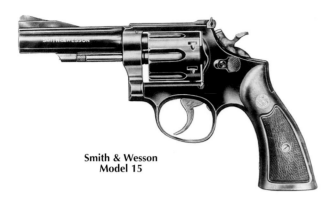

**Smith & Wesson
Model 15**

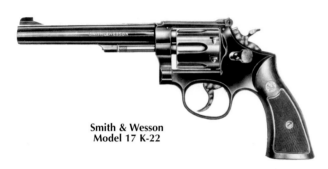

**Smith & Wesson
Model 17 K-22**

**Smith & Wesson
Model 18 (See Model 15 for description)**

**Smith & Wesson
Model 19 (Round Butt)**

MODEL 14 CLASSICS SERIES . . . .NiB $695 Ex $375 Gd $340
Recent manufacture of Model 14 except chambered in .38 Spl.+P and 6-in. bbl., adj. sights, blued or nickel finish, checkered wood grips. Made from 2009 to 2011.

MODELS 15 (.38) AND 18 (.22) COMBAT MASTERPIECE DA REVOLVERS
Same as K-22 and K-38 Masterpiece but w/2- (.38) or 4-inch bbl., and Baughman quick-draw front sight. 9.13 inches overall w/4-inch bbl., Weight: 34 oz. (.38 cal.). Made 1950-99.
Model 15 . . . . .NiB $805 Ex $602 Gd $456
Model 18 (disc. 1985) . . . . .NiB $691 Ex $523 Gd $487
w/target options TH & TT, add $50

MODEL 15 CLASSICS SERIES . . . .NiB $780 Ex $300 Gd $270
Recent manufacture of Model 15 except chambered in .38 Spl.+P and 4-in. bbl., adj. sights, blued finish, checkered wood grips. Made from 2010 to 2011.

MODEL 17 K-22 MASTERPIECE DA REVOLVER
Caliber: 22 LR. Six-round cylinder, Bbl lengths: 4, 6 or 8.38 inches. 11.13 inches overall (with 6-inch bbl.). Weight: 38 oz. (with 6-inch bbl.). Partridge-type front sight, S&W micrometer click rear. Checkered walnut Service grips with S&W momogram. S&W blued finish. Made from 1947-93 and from 1996-98.
Model 17 (4-inch bbl.) . . . . NiB $632 Ex $453 Gd $347
Model 17 (6-inch bbl.) . . . . . . .NiB $632 Ex $453 Gd $347
Model 17 (8.38-inch bbl.) . . . . .NiB $823 Ex $546 Gd $479
w/target options TH & TT, add $50

MODEL 17 CLASSICS SERIES. . . . NiB $989 Ex $480 Gd $430
Recent manufacture of Model 17 except w/6-in. bbl., adj. sights, blued finish, checkered wood grips. Made from 2009 to date.

MODEL 18 . . . . .NiB $750 Ex $480 Gd $420
Similar to Model 17 except w/4-in. bbl., adj. sights, blued finish, checkered wood grips. Made from 1949 to 1986.

MODEL 18 CLASSICS SERIES . . . .NiB $695 Ex $400 Gd $360
Recent manufacture of Model 18. Made from 2009 to 2011.

MODEL 19 .357 COMBAT MAGNUM DA REVOLVER
Caliber: .357 Magnum. Six-round cylinder, bbl. lengths: 2.5 (round butt), 4, or 6 inches, 9.5 inches overall (with 4-inch bbl.). Weight: 35 oz. (with 4-inch bbl.). Click adj. rear sight, ramp front. Blued or nickel finish. Target grips of checkered Goncalo Alves. Made from 1956 to date (2.5- and 6-inch bbls. were disc. in 1991).
Model 19 (2.5-inch bbl.) . . . . . .NiB $601 Ex $431 Gd $319
Model 19 (4-inch bbl.) . . . . . . .NiB $601 Ex $431 Gd $319
Model 19 (6-inch bbl.) . . . . . . .NiB $601 Ex $431 Gd $319
Model 19 (8.38-inch bbl.) . . . . .NiB $601 Ex $431 Gd $319
w/target options TH & TT, add $75

MODEL 20 .38/44 HEAVY DUTY DA
Caliber: .38 Special. Six-round cylinder, bbl. lengths: 4, 5 and 6.5 inches;10.38 inches overall (with 5-inch bbl.). Weight: 40 oz. (with 5-inch bbl.). Fixed sights. Blued or nickel finish. Checkered walnut grips. Short action after 1948. Made from 1930-56 and from 1957 to 67.
Pre-World War II . . . . .NiB $1970 Ex $1770 Gd $525
Post-war . . . . .NiB $2270 Ex $1620 Gd $910

Smith & Wesson
Model 19 (Square Butt)

Smith & Wesson
Model 22/32 Target Revolver

Smith & Wesson
Model 20

Smith & Wesson
Model 22

Smith & Wesson
Model 22/32 Kit Gun

MODEL 21 .44 MILITARY DA REVOLVER
Postwar version of the 1926 Model 44 Military. Caliber: .44 Special, 6-round cylinder. Bbl. lengths: 4-, 5- and 6.5-inches. 11.75 inches overall (w/6.5-inch bbl.) Weight: 39.5 oz. (w/6.5-inch bbl.). Fixed front sight w/square-notch rear sight; target model has micrometer click rear sight adj. for windage and elevation. Checkered walnut grips w/S&W monogram. Blued or nickel finish. Made 1950 to 1967.
Model 21 (4- or 5-inch bbl.) . . . NiB $2979 Ex $2035 Gd $809
Model 21 (6.5-inch bbl.), add. 50%

MODEL 22 1950 ARMY DA . . . NiB $2025 Ex $1735 Gd $816
Postwar version of the 1917 Army w/same general specifications except redesigned hammer. Made from 1950 to 1967.

MODEL 22 CLASSICS SERIES. . . NiB $850 Ex $470 Gd $420
Recent manufacture of Model 22 except in .45 ACP, 4- or 5.5-in. bbl., blued finish, Altamont wood grip. Made 2007-10.

MODEL 22 CLASSICS SERIES
MODEL OF 1917 . . . . NiB $999 Ex $470 Gd $420
Recent manufacture of Model 1917 except in .45 ACP, 5.5-in. bbl., N-Frame, lanyard loop, blued finish, Altamont wood grip. Made from 2008 to 2012.

.22/.32 TARGET DA REVOLVER
Also known as the "Bekeart Model." Design based upon ".32 Hand Ejector." Caliber: .22 LR (recessed head cylinder for high-speed cartridges intro. 1935). Six-round cylinder, 6-inch bbl., 10.5 inches overall. Weight: 23 oz. Adj. target sights. Blued finish. Checkered walnut grips. Made from 1911-53. Note: In 1911, San Francisco gun dealer Phil Bekeart, who suggested this model, received 292 pieces. These are the true "Bekeart Model" revolvers and are marked with separate identification numbers on the base of the wooden grip.
.22/.32 Standard Model . . . . . NiB $1160 Ex $760 Gd $498
.22/.32 (early prod. 1-3000), add 20%
.22/.32 Bekeart model . . . . . NiB $1565 Ex $1329 Gd $752

.22/.32 KIT GUN . . . . NiB $850 Ex $580 Gd $319
Same as .22/.32 Target except has 2- or 4-inch bbl., round grips, 6 or 8 inches overall, weight: 19-21oz. Made 1935-53.

Smith & Wesson
Model 23

Smith & Wesson
Model 24 Target

Smith & Wesson
Model 25 Target

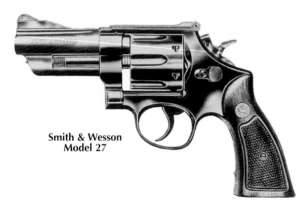

Smith & Wesson
Model 27

MODEL 23 .38-44 OUTDOORSMAN DA REVOLVER

Target version of the .38/44 Heavy Duty. 6.5- or 8.75-inch bbl., weight: 41.75 oz. Target sights, micrometer-click rear on postwar models. Blued or nickel finish. 1950 transition model has ribbed barrel, redesigned hammer. Made from 1930 to 1967.

Pre-war model (plain bbl.) . . . NiB $2555 Ex $1958 Gd $1278
Post-war (ribbed bbl.) . . . . . . NiB $1724 Ex $1398 Gd $780

MODEL 24 1950 .44 TARGET DA REVOLVER

Postwar version of the 1921 Model .44 Hand Ejector. .44 Special with 4-, 5- or 6.5-inch ribbed bbl., redesigned hammer, micrometer click rear sight. Matte or polished blue finish. Made from 1950-67. Model 24 reintroduced in 1983 only.

**Model 24 (1950 w/6.5-inch
    bbl.** . . . . NiB $2770 Ex $1696 Gd $897
Model 24 (1950) w/4-inch bbl., add. 20%
Model 24 (1950) w/5-inch bbl., add. 100%
**Model 24 (1950) w/polished
    blue finish, add** 25%
**Model 24 (1950)
    w/nickel finish, add** 65%
**Model 24 .44 Target reintroduced (7,500 produced
    in 1983-84) (w/4-inch bbl.)** . . . . NiB $760 Ex $560 Gd $402
Model 24 (w/6.5-inch bbl.) . . . . NiB $730 Ex $553 Gd $365
**Model 24-3 .44
Lew Horton Special
w/3-inch bbl. (prod. in 1983)** . . NiB $860 Ex $654 Gd $380
**Classics w/6.5-inch bbl.
    (2008-2012)** . . . . NiB $770 Ex $554 Gd $370
Classics w/ nickel finish, add 8%

MODEL 24-6
CLASSICS SERIES . . . . NiB $770 Ex $470 Gd $420

Recent manufacture of Model 24 except in .45 ACP, 3- or 6.5-in. bbl., blued or nickel finish, square butt wood grip. Made from 2006 to 2012.

MODEL 25 1955 .45 TARGET DA REVOLVER

Same as 1950 Model .44 Target, but chambered for .45 ACP, .45 Auto Rim or .45 LC w/4-, 6- or 6.5-inch bbl. Made from 1955 to 1991 in several variations. Note: In 1961, the .45 ACP was designated Model 25-2, and in 1978 the .45 LC was designated Model 25-5.

**Model 25 1955 .45 Target
.45 ACP w/4- or 6-inch bbl.** . . . . NiB $780 Ex $587 Gd $434
.45 ACP w/6.5-inch pinned bbl . . . NiB $767 Ex $660 Gd $449
.45 LC early production . . . NiB $4245 Ex $4040 Gd $3779
**Model 25-2 .45 ACP
Lew Horton Special w/3-inch
    bbl** . . . . NiB $541 Ex $453 Gd $346
Model 25-2 (w/4-inch bbl.). . . . . NiB $601 Ex $485 Gd $402
Model 25-3 (w/6.5-inch bbl.) . . NiB $734 Ex $544 Gd $429
**Model 25-5 .45 LC w/4-inch
    bbl.** . . . . NiB $601 Ex $484 Gd $377
Model 25-3 (w/6.5-inch bbl.) . . NiB $648 Ex $530 Gd $362
**Model 25 Classics
    (reintro. 2008)** . . . . NiB $980 Ex $530 Gd $362

MODEL 25 CLASSICS SERIES . . . . NiB $1010 Ex $470 Gd $420

Recent manufacture of Model 25 except w/3- or 6.5-in. bbl., blued or nickel finish, square butt, wood grip. Made from 2007 to date.

MODEL 26 1950 .45 LIGHT TARGET DA REVOLVER

Similar to 1950 Model Target except w/lighter bbl. Note: Lighter profile was not well received. (Only 2,768 produced)

**Model 26 (.45 ACP or .45 Auto Rim
    w/6.5-inch bbl.)** . . . . NiB $4590 Ex $4295 Gd $3988
**Model 26 .45 LC, (200
    produced)** . . . . NiB $4590 Ex $4295 Gd $3988
w/4- or 5-inch bbl., ... $50

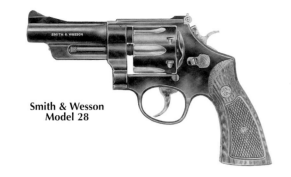

**Smith & Wesson
Model 28**

**Smith & Wesson
Model 29**

**Smith & Wesson
Model 31**

MODEL 27 .357 MAGNUM DA

Caliber: .357 Magnum. Six-round cylinder, bbl. lengths: 3.5-, 4-, 5-, 6-, 6.5-and 8.38-inches, 11.38 inches overall (with 6-inch bbl.). Weight: 44 oz. (with 6-inch bbl.). Adj. target sights, Baughman quick-draw ramp front sight on 3.5-inch bbl., Blued or nickel finish. Checkered walnut grips. Made from 1935-94. Note: Until 1938, the .357 Magnum was custom made in any barrel length from 3.5-inch to 8.75-inch. Each of these revolvers was accompanied by a registration certificate and has its registration number stamped on the inside of the yoke. Postwar magnums have a redesigned hammer w/shortened fall and the new S&W micrometer click rear sight.
Pre-war model
(Reg number on yoke). . . . . NiB $893 Ex $730 Gd $615
Pre-war model w/out reg
number . . . . NiB $862 Ex $653 Gd $612
Early model w/pinned bbl.,
recessed cyl. . . . . NiB $895 Ex $755 Gd $624
Late model w/8. 38-inch bbl. . . NiB $895 Ex $755 Gd $624
Late model w/3.5 to 5-inch bbl . . NiB $895 Ex $755 Gd $624
Late model, other bbl. lengths . . NiB $915 Ex $785 Gd $612

MODEL 27 CLASSICS SERIES . . NiB $1020 Ex $470 Gd $420
Recent manufacture of Model 25 except w/4- or 6.5-in. bbl., blued or nickel finish, wood grip. Made from 2008 to date.

MODEL 28 HIGHWAY PATROLMAN
Caliber: .357 Magnum. Six-round cylinder, bbl. lengths: 4- or 6-inches, 11.25 inches overall (with 6-inch bbl.). Weight: 44 oz. (with 6-inch bbl.). Adj. rear sight, ramp front. Blued finish. Checkered walnut grips, Magna or target type. Made from 1954 to 1986.
Pre-war registered model
(reg number on yoke) . . . . . . .NiB $893 Ex $780 Gd $610
Pre-war model without registration
number . . . . .NiB $1190 Ex $975 Gd $700
Early model w/pinned bbl.,
recessed cylinder, 5-screws . NiB $895 Ex $734 Gd $632
Late model, all bbl. lengths. . . . NiB $536 Ex $362 Gd $255

MODEL 29 .44 MAGNUM DA REVOLVER
Caliber: .44 Magnum. Six-round cylinder. bbl., lengths: 4-, 5-, 6.5-, 8.38-inches. 11.88 inches overall (with 6.5-inch bbl.). Weight: 47 oz. (with 6.5-inch bbl.). Click adj. rear sight, ramp front. Blued or nickel finish. Checkered Goncalo Alves target grips. Made from 1956 to 1998. Early Production Standard Series (disc. 1983)
3-Screw model (1962-83) . . . . .NiB $970 Ex $843 Gd $686
4-Screw model (1957-61) . . .NiB $2200 Ex $1693 Gd $880
5-Screw model (1956-57) . .NiB $3497 Ex $2895 Gd $2630
w/5-inch bbl., 3- or 4-screw models, add 100%Late
Production standard series (disc. 1998)
Model 29 (w/4- or 6.5-inch
bbl.) . . . . .NiB $870 Ex $669 Gd $432
Model 29 (w/3-inch bbl.,
Lew Horton Special) . . . . .NiB $920 Ex $689 Gd $432
Model 29 (w/8.38-inch bbl.). . .NiB $895 Ex $679 Gd $432
Model 29 Classic (w/5- or 6.5-inch
bbl.) . . . . .NiB $610 Ex $539 Gd $332
Model 29 Classic (w/8.38-inch
bbl.) . . . . .NiB $630 Ex $540 Gd $345
Model 29 Classic DX (w/6.5-in. and
8.38-in. bbl.) . . . . .NiB $1260 Ex $648 Gd $556
Model 29 Classic DX (w/5-inch
bbl.) . . . . .NiB $1410 Ex $798 Gd $656
Model 29 Magna Classic (w/7.5-inch
ported bbl.).**. . . . . .NiB $1170 Ex $859 Gd $537
Model 29 Silhouette (w/10.63-inch
bbl.) . . . . .NiB $860 Ex $656 Gd $437

MODEL 29 CLASSICS SERIES . . NiB $999 Ex $480 Gd $420
Recent manufacture of Model 29 except w/3-, 4- or 6.5-in. bbl., blued or nickel finish, wood grip. Made from 2008 to date.

MODEL 30 .32 HAND EJECTOR
DA REVOLVER . . . . .NiB $554 Ex $469 Gd $356
Caliber: .32 S&W Long. Six-round cylinder, bbl. lengths: 2- (intro. 1949), 3-, 4- and 6-inches, 8 inches overall (with 4-inch bbl.). Weight: 18 oz. (with 4-inch bbl.). Fixed sights. Blued or nickel finish. Round, checkered walnut or hard rubber grips. Made from 1903-76.

MODELS 31 & 33 REGULATION POLICE DA REVOLVER
Same basic type as .32 Hand Ejector except has square butt-grips. Calibers: .32 S&W Long (Model 31) .38 S&W (Model 33). Six-round cylinder in .32 cal., 5-round in .38 caliber. Bbl., lengths: 2- (intro. 1949), 3-, 4- and 6-inches in .32 cal., 4-inch only in .38 cal., 8.5 inches overall (with 4-inch bbl.). Weight:

**Smith & Wesson
Model 32**

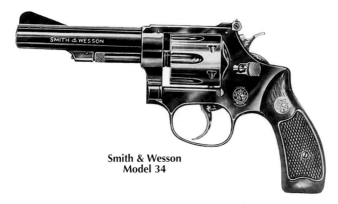

**Smith & Wesson
Model 34**

**Smith & Wesson
Model 36**

**Smith & Wesson
Model 37**

18 oz. (.38 cal. w/4-inch bbl.), 18.75 oz. (.32 cal. w/4-inch bbl.). Fixed sights. Blued or nickel finish. Checkered walnut grips. Made from 1917. Model 33 disc. in 1974; Model 31 disc. in 1992.

Model 31 . . . . NiB $546 Ex $306 Gd $255
Model 33 . . . . NiB $448 Ex $283 Gd $198

MODEL 32 DA REVOLVER . . . NiB $546 Ex $467 Gd $219
Hinged frame. Caliber: .32 S&W. Five-round cylinder, bbl. lengths: 3-, 3.5- and 6-inches. Fixed sights. Blued or nickel finish. Hard rubber grips. Made from 1880-1919. Note: Value shown applies generally to the several varieties. exception is the rare first issue of 1880 (identified by squared sideplate and serial no. 1 to 30) valued up to $2,500.

MODEL 32 TERRIER DA . . . . . . NiB $479 Ex $342 Gd $255
Caliber: .38 S&W. Five-round cylinder, 2-inch bbl., 6.25 inches overall. Weight: 17 oz. Fixed sights. Blued or nickel finish. Checkered walnut or hard rubber grips. Built on .32 Hand Ejector frame. Made from 1936-74.

**MODEL 33 .32-20 MILITARY & POLICE
DA REVOLVER** . . . . NiB $2845 Ex $2719 Gd $2530
Same as M&P 38 except chambered for .32-20 Winchester cartridge. First intro. in the 1899 model, M&P revolvers were produced in this caliber until about 1940. Values same as M&P .38 models.

MODEL 34 DA REVOLVER . . . . NiB $756 Ex $408 Gd $305
Caliber: .22 LR. Six-shot cylinder, 2-inch or 4-inch bbl. and round or square grips, blued or nickel finish. Made from 1936-91.

**MODEL 35 1953
.22/.32 TARGET** . . . . NiB $772 Ex $590 Gd $362
Same general specifications as previous model .22/.32 Target except has micrometer-click rear sight. Magna type target grips. Weight: 25 oz. Made from 1953-74.

MODEL 36 CHIEFS SPECIAL DA
Based on .32 Hand Ejector w/frame lengthened to permit longer cylinder for .38 Special cartridge. Caliber: .38 Special. Five-round cylinder, bbl. lengths: 2- or 3-inches, 6.5 inches overall (with 2-inch bbl.). Weight: 19 oz. Fixed sights. Blued or nickel finish. Checkered walnut grips, round or square butt. Made from 1952 to date.

Blued model . . . . NiB $638 Ex $425 Gd $255
Nickel model. . . . . NiB $648 Ex $437 Gd $265
Early model (5-screw, small trigger
  guard, S/N 1-2500). . . . . NiB $668 Ex $541 Gd $386
Model 36 Ladysmith
  (1990-2008) . . . . NiB $480 Ex $290 Gd $186

**MODEL 37 AIRWEIGHT
CHIEFS SPECIAL** . . . . NiB $500 Ex $366 Gd $225
Same general specifications as standard Chiefs Special except has light alloy frame, weight: 12.5 oz. w/2-inch bbl., blued finish only. Made from 1954 to 1995

MODEL 38 BODYGUARD AIRWEIGHT DA REVOLVER
Shrouded hammer. Light alloy frame. Caliber: .38 Special. Five-round cylinder, 2- or 3-inch bbl., 6.38 inches overall (w/2-inch bbl). Weight: 14.5 oz. Fixed sights. Blued or nickel finish. Checkered walnut grips. Made from 1955 to 1998.

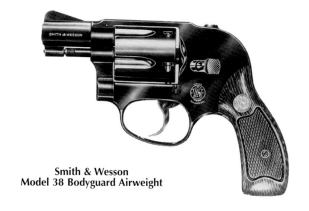

**Smith & Wesson
Model 38 Bodyguard Airweight**

Blued model . . . . NiB $479 Ex $347 Gd $235
Nickel model. . . . . NiB $500 Ex $362 Gd $274
**Early model (pinned bbl. &
    recessed cyl., pre-1981)** . . . . NiB $485 Ex $342 Gd $243

MODEL .38 DA REVOLVER. . . . NiB $945 Ex $734 Gd $544
Hinged frame. Caliber: .38 S&W. Five-round cylinder, bbl. lengths: 4-, 4.25-, 5-, 6-, 8- and 10-inch. Fixed sights. Blued or nickel finish. Hard rubber grips. Made from 1880-1911. Note: Value shown applies generally to the several varieties. exceptions are the first issue of 1880 (identified by squared sideplate and serial no. 1 to 4,000) and the 8- and 10-inch bbl. models of the third issue (1884 to 1995).

MODEL .38 HAND EJECTOR DA
Military & Police — First Model. Resembles Colt New Navy in general appearance, lacks bbl., lug and locking bolt common to all later S&W hand ejector models. Caliber: .38 Long Colt. Six-round cylinder, bbl. lengths: 4-, 5-, 6- and 6.5-inch, 11.5 inches overall (with 6.5-inch bbl.). Fixed sights. Blued or nickel finish. Round, checkered walnut or hard rubber grips. Made from 1899 to 1902.
**Standard model
(civilian issue)** . . . . NiB $1870 Ex $1322 Gd $1132
Army Model (marked U.S.
Army Model, 1000 issued) . NiB $3725 Ex $3397 Gd $2935
Navy Model (marked USN,
    1000 issued) . . . . NiB $4495 Ex $3800 Gd $3412

**.38 MILITARY & POLICE
TARGET DA.** . . . . NiB $3725 Ex $3397 Gd $2740
Target version of the Military & Police w/standard features of that model. Caliber: .38 Special, six-inch bbl. Weight: 32.25 oz. Adj. target sights. Blued finish. Checkered walnut grips. Made from 1899 to1940. For values, add $175 for corresponding M&P 38 models.

**MODEL .38
PERFECTED DA.** . . . . NiB $1465 Ex $1336 Gd $1145
Hinged frame. Similar to earlier .38 DA Model but heavier frame, side latch as in solid-frame models, improved lockwork. Caliber: .38 S&W. Five-round cylinder, bbl. lengths: 3.25, 4, 5 and 6 inches. Fixed sights. Blued or nickel finish. Hard rubber grips. Made 1909 to 1920.

MODEL 40 CENTENNIAL DA HAMMERLESS REVOLVER
Similar to Chiefs Special but has Safety Hammerless-type mechanism w/grip safety. Two-inch bbl. Weight: 19 oz. Made from 1953 to 1974.
Blued model . . . . NiB $633 Ex $437 Gd $398
Nickel model. . . . . NiB $1319 Ex $1109 Gd $895

MODEL 42 CENTENNIAL AIRWEIGHT
Same as standard Centennial model except has light alloy frame, weight: 13 oz. Made from 1954 to 1974.
Blued model . . . . NiB $648 Ex $429 Gd $351
Nickel model. . . . . NiB $1250 Ex $1062 Gd $884

MODEL 42 CLASSICS SERIES . . NiB $999 Ex $480 Gd $420
Recent manufacture of Model 42 except in .38 Spl.+P w/1.87-in. bbl., aluminum frame, grip safety, blued finish, checkered wood grip. Made from 2009 to 2010.

**MODEL 43 1955 .22/.32
KIT GUN AIRWEIGHT** . . . . NiB $760 Ex $543 Gd $274
Same as Model 34 Kit Gun except has light alloy frame, square grip. Furnished w/3.5-inch bbl., weight: 14.25 oz. Made 1954 to 1974.

MODEL 44 1926 MILITARY DA REVOLVER
Same as the early New Century model with Extractor rod casing but lacking the "Triple Lock" feature. Caliber: .44 S&W Special. Six-round cylinder, bbl. lengths: 4, 5 and 6.5 inches, 11.75 inches overall (with 6.5-inch bbl.). Weight: 39.5 oz. (with 6.5-inch bbl.). Fixed sights. Blued or nickel finish. Checkered walnut grips. Made 1926 to 1941.
Standard model. . . . . NiB $3715 Ex $3409 Gd $3135
**Target model w/6.5-inch bbl.,
    target sights, blued** . . . . . NiB $3715 Ex $3409 Gd $3095

.38 AND .44 DA REVOLVERS
Also called Wesson Favorite (lightweight model), Frontier (caliber .44-40). Hinged frame. Six-round cylinder. Calibers: .44 S&W Russian, .38-40, .44-40. Bbl. lengths: 4-, 5-, 6- and 6.5-inch. Weight: 37.5 oz. (with 6.5-inch bbl.). Fixed sights. Blued or nickel finish. Hard rubber grips. Made from 1881 to 1913, Frontier disc. 1910.
Standard model, .44
    Russian . . . . NiB $10,930 Ex $9795 Gd $6579
Standard model, .38-40 . . . NiB $6030 Ex $5095 Gd $1479
Frontier model . . . . NiB $5089 Ex $3240 Gd $1939
Favorite model . . . . NiB $10,600 Ex $8499 Gd $2977

.44 HAND EJECTOR MODEL DA REVOLVER
First Model, New Century, also called "Triple Lock" because of its third cylinder lock at the crane. Six-round cylinder. Calibers: .44 S&W Special, .450 Eley, .455 Mark II. Bbl. lengths: 4-, 5-, 6.5- and 7.5-inch. Weight: 39 oz. (with 6.5-inch bbl.). Fixed sights. Blued or nickel finish. Checkered walnut grips. Made 1907 to 1966. Second Model is basically the same as New Century except crane lock ("Triple Lock" feature) and Extractor rod casing eliminated. Calibers: .44 S&W Special .44-40 Win. .45 Colt. Bbl. lengths: 4-, 5-, 6.5- and 7.5-inch; 11.75 inches overall (with 6.5-inch bbl.). Weight: 38 oz. (with 6.5-inch bbl.). Fixed sights. Blued or nickel finish. Checkered walnut grips. Made from 1915 to 1937.
**First Model w/triple lock (1907-15)
Standard model,
    .44 S&W Special.** . . . . . . NiB $4735 Ex $4380 Gd $4335
**Standard model
    other calibers** . . . . NiB $2865 Ex $2555 Gd $2339
**British .455
    Target model** . . . . NiB $3520 Ex $3299 Gd $1135
**Second Model
    w/o triple lock (1915-37)** . . NiB $3520 Ex $3266 Gd $1117
.44 S&W Special . . . . NiB $2420 Ex $2119 Gd $1972
**Second model,
    other calibers** . . . . NiB $5200 Ex $4190 Gd $3977

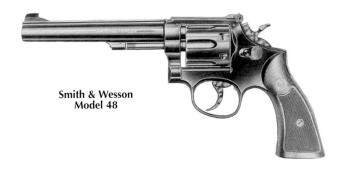

Smith & Wesson
Model 48

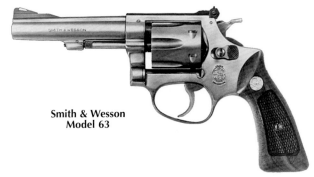

Smith & Wesson
Model 63

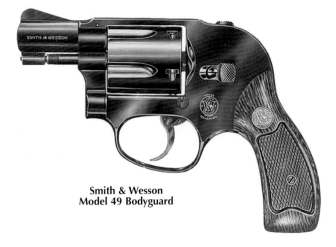

Smith & Wesson
Model 49 Bodyguard

Smith & Wesson
Model 64

Smith & Wesson
Model 57

Smith & Wesson
Model 60

.44 HAND EJECTOR, SECOND MODEL
DA REVOLVER . . . . **NiB $2425 Ex $2174 Gd $1981**
Basically the same as New Century except crane lock ("Triple Lock" feature) and Extractor rod casing eliminated. Calibers: .44 S&W Special .44-40 Win. .45 Colt. Bbl. lengths: 4-, 5-, 6.5- and 7.5-inches, 11.75 inches overall (with 6.5-inch bbl.). Weight: .38 oz. (with 6.5-inch bbl.). Fixed sights. Blued or nickel finish. Checkered walnut grips. Made from 1915 to 1937.

MODEL 48 (K-22) MASTERPIECE M.R.F. DA REVOLVER
Caliber: .22 Mag. and .22 LR. Six-round cylinder, bbl. lengths: 4, 6 and 8.38 inches, 11.13 inches overall (w/ 6-inch bbl.). Weight: 39 oz. Adj. rear sight, ramp front. Made from 1959 to 1986.
Model 48 (4- or 6-inch bbl.) . . . **NiB $862 Ex $668 Gd $495**
Model 48 (8.38-inch bbl.) . . . . . **NiB $826 Ex $612 Gd $439**
w/target options TH & TT, add $75

MODEL 48 CLASSICS SERIES . . **NiB $999 Ex $480 Gd $420**
Recent manufacture of Model 48 except w/4- or 6-in. bbl., blued finish, checkered wood grip. Made from 2010 to date.

MODEL 49 BODYGUARD
Same as Model 38 Bodyguard Airweight except has steel frame, weight: 20.5 oz. Made from 1959 to 1996.
Blued model . . . . **NiB $478 Ex $337 Gd $244**
Nickel model. . . . . **NiB $530 Ex $377 Gd $270**

MODEL 51 1960 .22/.32
KIT GUN. . . . . **NiB $755 Ex $549 Gd $319**
Same as Model 34 Kit Gun except chambered for .22 WMR 3.5-inch bbl., weight: 24 oz. Made from 1960 to 1974.

**Smith & Wesson
Model 66 Combat Magnum**

**Smith & Wesson
Model 67 Combat Masterpiece**

MODEL 53 .22 REM. JET DA
Caliber: .22 Rem. Jet C.F. Magnum. Six-round cylinder (inserts permit use of .22 Short, Long, or LR cartridges). Bbl. lengths: 4, 6, 8.38 inches, 11.25 inches overall (with 6-inch bbl.). Weight: 40 oz. (with 6-inch bbl.). Micrometer-click rear sight ramp front. Checkered walnut grips. Made from 1960 to 1974.
Model 53 (4- or 6-inch bbl.) . . . NiB $933 Ex $749 Gd $633
Model 53 (8.38-inch bbl.) . . . . NiB $1040 Ex $844 Gd $704
w/target options TH & TT, add $75

MODEL 57 .41 MAGNUM DA REVOLVER
Caliber: 41 Magnum. Six-round cylinder, bbl. lengths: 4-, 6-, 8.38-inch. Weight: 40 oz. (with 6-inch bbl.). Micrometer click rear sight, ramp front. Target grips of checkered Goncalo Alves. Made from 1964 to 1993.
Model 57 (w/4- or 6-inch bbl.) NiB $812 Ex $627 Gd $429
Model 57 (w/8.63-inch bbl.) . . . NiB $852 Ex $677 Gd $449
Model 57 (w/pinned bbl., recessed cylinder), add 10%

MODEL 57 CLASSICS SERIES NiB $1010 Ex $470 Gd $420
Recent manufacture of Model 57 except w/4- or 6-in. bbl., blued finish, checkered wood grip. Made from 2009 to date.

MODEL 58 .41 MILITARY& POLICE
DA REVOLVER . . . . NiB $855 Ex $709 Gd $576
Caliber: 41 Magnum. Six-round cylinder, 4-inch bbl. 9.25 inches overall. Weight: 41 oz. Fixed sights. Checkered walnut grips. Made from 1964 to 1982.

MODEL 58 CLASSICS SERIES . . NiB $780 Ex $470 Gd $420
Recent manufacture of Model 58 except w/blued or nickel finish, checkered wood grip. Made from 2009 to 2011.

MODEL 60 STAINLESS DA
Caliber: .38 Special or .357 Magnum. Five-round cylinder, bbl. lengths: 2, 2.1 or 3 inches, 6.5 or 7.5 inches overall. Weight: 19 to 23 oz. Square-notch rear sight, ramp front. Satin finish stainless steel. Made from 1965-96 (.38 Special) and from 1996 to date (.357/.38).
.38 Special (disc. 1996) . . . . . . NiB $474 Ex $346 Gd $270
.357 Mag. . . . . NiB $498 Ex $366 Gd $283
Lady Smith (w/smaller grip) . . . NiB $544 Ex $377 Gd $280

MODEL 63 (1977)
KIT GUN DA. . . . . NiB $474 Ex $319 Gd $265
Caliber: .22 LR. Six-round cylinder, 2- or 4-inch bbl., 6.5 or 8.5 inches overall. Weight: 19 to 24.5 oz. Adj. rear sight, ramp front. Stainless steel. Checkered walnut or synthetic grips.

MODEL 64 .38 M&P
STAINLESS . . . . NiB $498 Ex $362 Gd $287
Same as standard Model 10 except satin-finished stainless steel, square butt w/4-inch heavy bbl., or round butt w/2-inch bbl. Made from 1970 to date.

MODEL 65 .357 MILITARY/
POLICE STAINLESS . . . . NiB $499 Ex $357 Gd $290
Same as Model 13 except satin-finished stainless steel. Made 1974 to 2004.
Lady Smith (w/smaller grip) . . . NiB $540 Ex $377 Gd $302

MODEL 66 .357 COMBAT MAGNUM STAINLESS
Same as Model 19 except satin-finished stainless steel. Made from 1971 to date.
Model 66 (2.5-inch bbl.) . . . . . . NiB $536 Ex $439 Gd $328
Model 66 (3-inch bbl.) . . . . NiB $536 Ex $431 Gd $303
Model 66 (4-inch bbl.) . . . . NiB $536 Ex $431 Gd $303
Model 66 (6-inch bbl.) . . . . NiB $562 Ex $456 Gd $346
w/target options TH & TT, add $65

MODEL 67 .38 COMBAT
MASTERPIECE STAINLESS. . . . . NiB $597 Ex $440 Gd $337
Same as Model 15 except satin-finished stainless steel available only w/4-inch bbl. Made from 1972-1988 and from 1991-1998.

MODEL 68 .38 COMBAT
MASTERPIECE STAINLESS. . . . . NiB $831 Ex $668 Gd $601
Same as Model 66 except w/4- or 6-inch bbl., chambered for .38 Special. Made to accommodate CA Highway Patrol because they were not authorized to carry .357 magnums. Made from 1976 yo 1983. (7,500 produced)

125th Anniversary Commemorative
Issued to celebrate the 125th anniversary of the 1852 partnership of Horace Smith and Daniel Baird Wesson. Standard Edition is a Model 25 revolver in .45 Colt w/6.5-inch bbl., bright blued finish, gold-filled bbl., roll mark "Smith & Wesson 125th Anniversary," sideplate marked w/gold-filled Anniversary seal, smooth Goncalo Alves grips, in presentation case w/ nickel silver Anniversary medallion and book, "125 Years w/ Smith & Wesson," by Roy Jinks. Deluxe Edition is same except revolver is Class A engraved w/gold-filled seal on sideplate, ivory grips, Anniversary medallion is sterling silver and book is leather bound. Limited to 50 units. Total issue is 10,000 units, of which 50 are Deluxe Edition and two are a Custom Deluxe Edition and not for sale. Made in 1977.
Standard edition . . . . NiB $648 Ex $377 Gd $305
Deluxe edition . . . . NiB $2579 Ex $2365 Gd $2094

MODEL 242 AIRLITE TI
CENTENNIAL . . . . **NiB $500 Ex $300 Gd $220**
DAO. Caliber: .38 Spl.+P. 7-round titanium cylinder, 2.5-in. bbl., alloy L-frame. Uncle Mike's boot grip. Made 1990 only.

MODEL 296 AIRLITE TI
CENTENNIAL . . . . **NiB $650 Ex $400 Gd $260**
DAO. Caliber: .44 Spl. 5-round titanium cylinder, 2.5-in. bbl., alloy L-frame. Uncle Mike's boot grip. Made 1990 only.

MODEL 310 NIGHTGUARD . . **NiB $895 Ex $540 Gd $360**
SA/DA. Caliber: .40 S&W or 10mm. 6-round stainless cylinder, 2.5-in. bbl., scandium alloy N-frame. Fixed sights. Pachmayr grip. Made 2009 to 2010.

MODEL 315 NIGHTGUARD . . . **NiB $895 Ex $540 Gd $360**
SA/DA. Caliber: .40 S&W or 10mm. 6-round stainless cylinder, 2.5-in. bbl., scandium alloy N-frame. Fixed sights. Pachmayr grip. Made 2009 to 2010.

MODEL 317 AIRLITE DA REVOLVER
Caliber: .22 LR. Eight-round cylinder, 1.88- or 3-in. bbl., 6.3 or 7.2 inches overall. Weight: 9.9 oz. or 11 oz. Ramp front sight, notched frame rear. Aluminum, carbon fiber, stainless and titanium construction. Brushed aluminum finish. Synthetic or Dymondwood grips. Made from 1997 to date.
w/1.88-in. bbl. . . . . **NiB $590 Ex $380 Gd $306**
w/3-in. bbl. . . . . **NiB $683 Ex $453 Gd $356**
w/Dymondwood grips, add **$100**

MODEL 325 NIGHTGUARD . . . **NiB $830 Ex $430 Gd $350**
SA/DA. Caliber: .45 ACP. 6-round stainless cylinder, 2.5-in. bbl., alloy N-frame. Fixed sights. Weight: 26.5 oz. Pachmayr rubber grip. Made 2008 to 2012.

MODEL 325 PD-AIRLITE SC. . . . **NiB $800 Ex $490 Gd $340**
SA/DA. Caliber: .45 ACP. 6-round titanium cylinder, 2.5- or 4-in. bbl., scandium alloy N-frame. Weight: 21.5-25 oz. Hogue rubber grip. Made 2004 to 2007.

MODEL 327 NIGHTGUARD . . . **NiB $830 Ex $430 Gd $350**
SA/DA. Caliber: .357 Mag. 8-round stainless cylinder, 2.5-in. bbl., alloy N-frame. Fixed sights. Weight: 28 oz. Pachmayr rubber grip. Made 2008 to 2012.

MODEL 327 PD-AIRLITE SC. . . . **NiB $960 Ex $460 Gd $320**
SA/DA. Caliber: .357 Mag. 8-round titanium cylinder, 4-in. bbl., scandium alloy N-frame. Fixed sights. Weight: 28 oz. Wood grip. Made 2008 to 2009.

MODEL 329
NIGHTGUARD . . . . **NiB $830 Ex $430 Gd $350**
SA/DA. Caliber: .44 Mag. 6-round stainless cylinder, 2.5-in. bbl., alloy N-frame. Fixed sights. Weight: 28 oz. Pachmayr rubber grip. Made 2008 to 2012.

MODEL 329
PD-AIRLITE SC. . . . . **NiB $1160 Ex $530 Gd $350**
SA/DA. Caliber: .44 Mag. 6-round titanium cylinder, 4-in. bbl., scandium alloy N-frame. Fixed sights. Weight: 28 oz. Wood grip. Made 2003 to date.

MODEL 331 AIRLITE TI
CHIEFS SPECIAL . . . . **NiB $675 Ex $465 Gd $310**
SA/DA. Caliber: .32 H&R Mag. 6-round titanium cylinder, 1.87-in. bbl., alloy J-frame. Fixed sights. Weight: 28 oz. Wood or Uncle Mike's grip. Made 1999 to 2003.

MODEL 332 AIRLITE TI
CENTENNIAL . . . . **NiB $575 Ex $455 Gd $310**
DAO. Caliber: .32 H&R Mag. 6-round titanium cylinder, 1.87-in. bbl., alloy J-frame. Fixed sights. Weight: 28 oz. Uncle Mike's grip. Made 1999 to 2003.

MODEL 337 AIRLITE TI
CHIEFS SPECIAL . . . . **NiB $675 Ex $465 Gd $310**
SA/DA. Caliber: .38 Spl.+P. 5-round titanium cylinder, 1.87-in. bbl., alloy J-frame. Fixed sights. Weight: 12 oz. Made 1999 to 2003.

MODEL 337 AIRLITE TI
KIT GUN . . . . **NiB $600 Ex $350 Gd $290**
SA/DA. Caliber: .38 Spl.+P. 5-round cylinder, 3.12-in. bbl., J-frame. Fixed sights. Weight: 12 oz. Made 2000 to 2003.

MODEL 337 PD AIRLITE TI . . . **NiB $585 Ex $345 Gd $315**
SA/DA. Caliber: .38 Spl.+P. 5-round titanium cylinder, 1.87-in. bbl., alloy J-frame. Fixed sights. Weight: 10.7 oz. Made 2000 to 2003.

MODEL 340 AIRLITE SC
CENTENNIAL . . . . **NiB $775 Ex $410 Gd $350**
DAO. Caliber: .357 Mag. 5-round titanium cylinder, 1.87-in. bbl., alloy J-frame. Fixed sights. Weight: 10.7 oz. Made 2001 to 2008.

MODEL 340 PD-AIRLITE SC
CENTENNIAL . . . . **NiB $775 Ex $410 Gd $350**
DAO. Caliber: .357 Mag. 5-round titanium cylinder, 1.87-in. bbl., alloy J-frame. HiViz fixed sights. Weight: 10.7 oz. Made 2000 to date.

MODEL 340 M&P
CENTENNIAL . . . . **NiB $869 Ex $500 Gd $280**
DAO. Caliber: .357 Mag. 5-round stainless cylinder, 1.87-in. bbl., alloy J-frame. HiViz fixed sights. Weight: 10.7 oz. Made 2007 to date.

MODEL 342 AIRLITE TI
CENTINNIAL . . . . **NiB $575 Ex $355 Gd $310**
DAO. Caliber: .38 Spl.+P. 5-round titanium cylinder, 1.87-in. bbl., alloy J-frame. Fixed sights. Weight: 12 oz. Made 1999 to 2003.

MODEL 342 PD AIRLITE TI
CENTINNIAL . . . . **NiB $575 Ex $355 Gd $310**
DAO. Caliber: .38 Spl.+P. 5-round titanium cylinder, 1.87-in. bbl., alloy J-frame. Fixed sights. Weight: 10.8 oz. Made 1999 to 2003.

MODEL 351 PD AIRLITE SC
CHEIFS SPECIAL . . . . **NiB $759 Ex $400 Gd $310**
SA/DA. Caliber: .22 WMR. 7-round cylinder, 1.87-in. bbl., alloy J-frame. Fixed sights. Weight: 10.6 oz. Made 2004 to date.

MODEL 351 PD AIRLITE
CENTINNIAL . . . . **NiB $689 Ex $375 Gd $300**
DAO. Caliber: .22 WMR. 7-round cylinder, 1.87-in. bbl., alloy J-frame. Fixed sights. Weight: 11 oz. Made 2010 to date.

MODEL 357 PD . . . . **NiB $815 Ex $405 Gd $345**
SA/DA. Caliber: .41 Mag. 6-round titanium cylinder, 4-in. bbl., scandium alloy N-frame. HiViz front, adj. rear sights. Weight: 27.5 oz. Ahrends wood grip. Made 2005 to 2007.

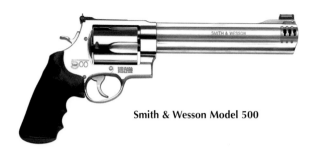

Smith & Wesson Model 500

MODEL 357 NIGHTGUARD . . NiB $895 Ex $430 Gd $355
SA/DA. Caliber: .41 Mag. 6-round stainless cylinder, 2.5-in. bbl., alloy N-frame. Fixed sights. Weight: 29.7 oz. Rubber grip. Made 2010 only.

**MODEL 360 AIRLITE SC
CHEIFS SPECIAL . . . .** NiB $780 Ex $410 Gd $345
SA/DA. Caliber: .357 Mag. 5-round titanium cylinder, 1.87-in. bbl., alloy J-frame. Fixed sights. Weight: 12 oz. Hogue rubber grip. Made 2001 to 2007.
Kit Gun model (3.1-in. bbl.). . . . NiB $775 Ex $440 Gd $330

**MODEL 360 PD AIRLITE SC
CHEIFS SPECIAL . . . .** NiB $1020 Ex $400 Gd $345
SA/DA. Caliber: .357 Mag. 5-round titanium cylinder, 1.87-in. bbl., alloy J-frame. Fixed sights. Weight: 12 oz. Hogue rubber grip. Matte grey finish. Made 2002 to date.

**MODEL 360 M&P
CHEIFS SPECIAL . . . .** NiB $1020 Ex $400 Gd $345
SA/DA. Caliber: .357 Mag. 5-round stainless cylinder, 1.87-in. bbl., scandium alloy J-frame. Fixed sights. Weight: 13.3 oz. Rubber grip. Matte black finish. Made 2007 to 2010.

**MODEL 386 AIRLITE SC
MOUNTAIN LITE . . . .** NiB $660 Ex $3700 Gd $325
SA/DA. Caliber: .357 Mag. 7-round titanium cylinder, 2.5- or 3.1-in. bbl., scandium alloy L-frame. HiViz front, adj. rear sights. Weight: 18.5 oz. Rubber grip. Matte black finish. Made 2001 to 2007.

MODEL 386 PD-AIRLITE SC . . . NiB $1020 Ex $400 Gd $345
SA/DA. Caliber: .357 Mag. 7-round titanium cylinder, 2.5-in. bbl., scandium alloy L-frame. Adj. sights. Weight: 17.5 oz. Hogue rubber grip. Matte grey finish. Made 2001 to 2005.

MODEL 386 SC/S . . . . NiB $780 Ex $390 Gd $340
SA/DA. Caliber: .357 Mag. 7-round stainless cylinder, 2.5-in. bbl., scandium alloy L-frame. Adj. sights. Weight: 21.2 oz. Made 2007 to 2008.

MODEL 386 NIGHTGUARD . . NiB $750 Ex $460 Gd $410
SA/DA. Caliber: .357 Mag. 7-round stainless cylinder, 2.5-in. bbl., alloy L-frame. Fixed sights. Weight: 24.5 oz. Made 2008 to 2012.

**MODEL 386 XL HUNTER
AIRLITE SC. . . . .** NiB $795 Ex $430 Gd $380
SA/DA. Caliber: .357 Mag. 7-round stainless cylinder, 6-in. bbl., alloy L-frame. Fixed sights. Weight: 30 oz. Matte black finish. Made 2010 to 2012.

**MODEL 396 AIRLITE TI
MOUNTAIN LITE. . . . .** NiB $625 Ex $360 Gd $320
SA/DA. Caliber: .44 Spl. 5-round titanium cylinder, 3.1-in. bbl., alloy L-frame. Adj. sights. Weight: 18 oz. Matte grey finish. Made 2001 to 2004.

MODEL 396 NIGHTGUARD. . . NiB $825 Ex $480 Gd $430
SA/DA. Caliber: .44 Spl. 5-round stainless cylinder, 2.5-in. bbl., alloy L-frame. Fixed sights. Weight: 24.2 oz. Made 2008 to 2009.

MODEL 431 AIRWEIGHT . . . . NiB $525 Ex $355 Gd $300
SA/DA. Caliber: .32 H&R Mag. 6-round cylinder, 2-in. bbl., J-frame. Fixed sights. Blued finish. Made 2004 to 2005.

**MODEL 431 CENTENNIAL
AIRWEIGHT. . . . .** NiB $5505 Ex $380 Gd $310
DAO. Caliber: .32 H&R Mag. 6-round cylinder, 2-in. bbl., J-frame. Fixed sights. Blued finish. Made 2004 to 2005.

MODEL 438 AIRWEIGHT . . . . NiB $525 Ex $355 Gd $300
SA/DA. Caliber: .38 Spl.+P. 5-round cylinder, 1.87-in. bbl., J-frame. Fixed sights. Weight: 15 oz. Matte black finish. Made 2004 to 2005.

**MODEL 442 AIRWEIGHT
CENTINNIAL . . . .** NiB $470 Ex $220 Gd $180
DAO. Caliber: .38 Spl.+P. 5-round cylinder, 1.87-in. bbl., J-frame. Fixed sights. Weight: 15 oz. Matte black, blued, or nickel finish. Made 1993 to date.
442 Pro Series (moon clips). . . . NiB $499 Ex $230 Gd $190

MODEL 469 V/XVR . . . . NiB $1370 Ex $700 Gd $600
SA/DA. Caliber: .460 S&W Mag. 5-round cylinder, 5- or 8.5-in. bbl., X-frame. HiViz adj. sights. Matte stainless finish. Made 2005 to date.

MODEL 500
Caliber: .500 S&W Magnum. Uses S&W's largest revolver frame: X-frame. 5-round cylinder, bbl. lengths: 4, 6.5 and 8.38 inches, ported barrel, overall length: 15 inches (8.38-inch bbl.). Weight: 71.9 oz. (8.38-inch bbl.). Interchangeable front sight, micrometer-click adj. rear. Synthetic grip. Satin stainless finish. Made from 2003 to date.
w/6- or 8.38-inch bbl.. . . . . . . NiB $1299 Ex $740 Gd $459
**w/4-inch bbl. , add $70
w/ factory HI-VIZ sights (8.38-in. bbl.), add $70**

**MODEL 520
DA REVOLVER . . . .** NiB $556 Ex $410 Gd $321
Caliber: .357 Mag. Six-round cylinder. N-Frame w/4-inch bbl. Weight: 40 oz. Fixed sights. In 1980, 3000 pieces were made for the N.Y. State Police but that agency did not purchase those firearms, so they were sold commercially.

**MODEL 547
DA REVOLVER . . . .** NiB $816 Ex $709 Gd $499
Caliber: 9mm. Six-round cylinder, bbl. length: 3 or 4 inches, 7.31 inches overall. Weight: 32 oz. Square-notch rear sight, ramp front. Disc. 1986.

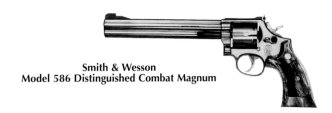

Smith & Wesson
Model 586 Distinguished Combat Magnum

Smith & Wesson
Model 625

Smith & Wesson
Model 629 Classic

Smith & Wesson
Model 629

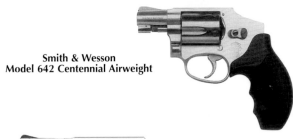

Smith & Wesson
Model 642 Centennial Airweight

Smith & Wesson
Model 640

MODEL 581 DISTINGUISHED
SERVICE MAGNUM . . . . NiB $7˘50 Ex $520 Gd $420
SA/DA. Caliber: .357 Mag. 6-round cylinder, 4-in. full lug bbl., L-frame, fixed sights, blued or nickel finish. Made from 1981 to 1992.
Nickel finish, add $25

MODEL 586 DISTINGUISHED COMBAT MAGNUM
Caliber: .357 Magnum. Six-round cylinder, bbl. lengths: 4, 6 and 8.38 inches, overall length: 9.75 inches (with 4-inch bbl.). Weight: 42, 46, 53 oz., respectively. Red ramp front sight, micrometer-click adj. rear. Checkered grip. Blued or nickel finish. Made 1980 to 1999.
Model 586 (w/4- or 6-inch bbl.) NiB $691 Ex $479 Gd $345
Model 586 (w/8.63-inch bbl.) . . NiB $709 Ex $499 Gd $359
Model 586 (w/adjustable front sight), add $50
Model 586 (w/nickel finish), add $65

MODEL 610 DA REVOLVER . . . NiB $755 Ex $612 Gd $500
Similar to Model 625 except in caliber .40 S&W/10mm. Magna classic grips. Made from 1990 to 1991 and from 1998 to 2004.

MODEL 610 CLASSIC . . . . NiB $860 Ex $580 Gd $480
SA/DA. Caliber: .40 S&W/10mm. 6-round fluted or unfluted cylinder. 4-, 5- or 6.5-in. full lug bbl. N-frame, Adj. sights, stainless finish. Made from 1990; 1998 to 2005; 2009.
10-round cylinder, add $80

MODEL 617 K-22
MASTERPIECE . . . . NiB $830 Ex $480 Gd $360
SA/DA. Caliber: .22 LR. 6- or 10-round cylinder. 4-, 6- or 8.37-in. full lug bbl. K-frame, Adj. sights, matte stainless finish, Hogue rubber grips. Made from 1990 to date.
Semi-target model w/4- or 6-inch
 bbl. . . . . NiB $648 Ex $530 Gd $362
Target model w/6-inch bbl. . . . . NiB $648 Ex $530 Gd $362
Target model w/8.38-inch bbl. . NiB $615 Ex $485 Gd $332
w/10-round cylinder, add $128

MODEL 619 . . . . NiB $450 Ex $230 Gd $190
SA/DA. Caliber: .357 Mag. 7-round cylinder. 5-in. bbl. L-frame, fixed sights, matte stainless finish, rubber grips. Made from 2005 to 2006.

MODEL 620 . . . . NiB $450 Ex $230 Gd $190
SA/DA. Caliber: .357 Mag. 7-round cylinder. 4-in. bbl., L-frame, adj. sights, matte stainless finish, rubber grips. Made from 2005 to 2009.

MODEL 624 . . . . NiB $750 Ex $530 Gd $460
SA/DA. Caliber: .44 Spl. 6-round cylinder. 4- or 6.5-in. bbl., N-frame, adj. sights, matte stainless finish. Made from 1986 to 1987.

MODEL 625 DA REVOLVER . . . NiB $866 Ex $733 Gd $569
Same general specifications as Model 25 except 3-, 4- or 5-inch bbl., round-butt Pachmayr grips and satin stainless steel finish. Made 1989 to 2007.

MODEL 625 JM . . . . NiB $979 Ex $480 Gd $430
SA/DA. Caliber: .45 ACP. 6-round cylinder. 3-, 4- or 5-in. full lug bbl., N-frame, adj. sights, matte stainless finish, made in colaboration with competitive shooter Jerry Miculek. Made from 1988 to date.

MODEL 627 DA REVOLVER . . . NiB $730 Ex $427 Gd $337
SA/DA. Caliber: .357 Mag. unfluted cylinder, 5.5-in. full lug bbl., N-frame, adj. sights, satin stainless steel finish. Made from 1989 to 2008.

MODEL 627 . . . . NiB $730 Ex $427 Gd $337
SA/DA. Caliber: .357 Mag. 8-round cylinder. 4-in. bbl., N-frame, adj. sights, satin stainless steel finish. Made from 2008 to 2009.

MODEL 629 DA REVOLVER
Same as Model 29 in .44 Magnum except in stainless steel. Classic made from 1990 to date.

w/ 3-inch bbl.(Backpacker model) . . . . NiB $774	Ex $567	Gd $408
w/4- or 6-inch bbls. . . . . NiB $774	Ex $567	Gd $408
w/8.38-inch bbl. . . . . NiB $774	Ex $567	Gd $408
Classic model (w/5- or 6.5-inch bbl.) . . . . NiB $829	Ex $581	Gd $444
Classic model (w/8.38-inch bbl.) . . . . NiB $685	Ex $576	Gd $469
Classix DX model (w/6.5-inch bbl.) . . . . NiB $685	Ex $576	Gd $469
Classic DX model (w/8.38-inch bbl.) . . . . NiB $685	Ex $576	Gd $469
Magna Classic model . . . . NiB $979	Ex $680	Gd $530

MODEL 631 DA REVOLVER
Similar to Model 31 except chambered for .32 H&R Mag. Goncalo Alves combat grips. Made in 1991 to 1992.

Fixed sights, 2-inch bbl. . . . . . . NiB $800	Ex $659	Gd $246
Adjustable sights, 4-inch bbl., add		10%
Lady Smith, 2-inch bbl. . . . . NiB $410	Ex $329	Gd $246
Lady Smith, 2-inch bbl. (black stainless). . . . . NiB $420	Ex $329	Gd $246

MODEL 632 CENTENNIAL DA REVOLVER
Same general specifications as Model 640 except chambered for .32 H&R Mag. 2- or 3-inch bbl., weight: 15.5 oz. Stainless slide w/alloy frame. Fixed sights. Santoprene combat grips. Made 1991 to 1992.

w/2-inch bbl. . . . . NiB $693	Ex $408	Gd $321
w/3-inch bbl. . . . . NiB $789	Ex $485	Gd $930

MODEL 637 CHIEFS SPECIAL AIRWEIGHT
DA REVOLVER . . . . NiB $485 Ex $357 Gd $289
Same general specifications as Model 37 except w/clear anodized fuse alloy frame and stainless cylinder. 560 made in 1991 and reintroduced in 1996.

MODEL 638 BODYGUARD
AIRWEIGHT DA . . . . NiB $468 Ex $367 Gd $326
Same general specifications as Model .38 except w/clear anodized fuse alloy frame and stainless cylinder. 1,200 made in 1990 and reintroduced in 1998.

MODEL 640 CENTENNIAL DA . . NiB $648 Ex $398 Gd $326
Caliber: .38 Special. Five-round cylinder, 2, 2.1 or 3-inch bbl., 6.31 inches overall. Weight: 20-22 oz. Fixed sights. Stainless finish. Smooth hardwood service grips. Made 1990 to date.

MODEL 642 CENTENNIAL AIRWEIGHT
DA Revolver . . . . NiB $479 Ex $365 Gd $290
Same general specifications as Model 640 except w/stainless steel/aluminum alloy frame and finish. Weight 15.8 oz.

Santoprene combat grips. Made from 1990-93 and reintroduced 1996.

Lady Smith model
(w/smaller grip) . . . . NiB $648	Ex $478	Gd $377
2.125-in. bbl. w/ PowerPort (2009-2010), add.		$150
Pro Series w/ full moon clips (intro. 2010), add.		$30

MODEL 648
DA REVOLVER . . . . NiB $695 Ex $506 Gd $450
Same general specifications as Models 17/617 except in stainless and chambered for .22 Mag. Made from 1990 to 1993.
Model 648-2 (2003-2005). . . . . NiB $660 Ex $500 Gd $390

MODEL 649 BODYGUARD
DA REVOLVER . . . . NiB $644 Ex $369 Gd $290
Caliber: .38 Special. Five-round cylinder, bbl. length: 2 inches, 6.25 inches overall. Weight: 20 oz. Square-notch rear sight ramp front. Stainless frame and finish. Made from 1986 to date.

MODEL 650 . . . . NiB $856 Ex $680 Gd $525
Caliber: .22 Mag. Six-round cylinder, 3-inch bbl., 7 inches overall. Weight: 23.5 oz. Serrated ramp front sight, fixed square-notch rear. Round butt, checkered walnut monogrammed grips. Stainless steel finish. Made 1983 to 1986.

MODEL 651 STAINLESS DA
Caliber: .22 Mag. Rimfire. Six-round cylinder, bbl. length: 3 and 4 inches, 7 and 8.63 inches, respectively, overall. Weight: 24.5 oz. Adj. rear sight, ramp front. Made from 1983 to 1987 and from 1990 to 1998. Note: .22 LR cylinder available during early production.

w/3- or 4-inch bbl. . . . . NiB $561	Ex $366	Gd $345
w/extra cylinder . . . . NiB $862	Ex $386	Gd $365

MODEL 657 REVOLVER
Caliber: 41 Mag. Six-round cylinder. Bbl. lengths: 4, 6 or 8.4 inches; 9.6, 11.4, and 13.9 inches overall. Weight: 44.2, 48 and 52.5 oz. Serrated black ramp front sight on ramp base click rear, adj. for windage and elevation. Satin finished stainless steel. Made from 1986 to 2008.

w/4- or 6-inch bbl. . . . . NiB $601	Ex $433	Gd $398
w/8.4-inch bbl. . . . . NiB $882	Ex $464	Gd $377

MODEL 681 DSM. . . . . NiB $464 Ex $329 Gd $255
Same as S&W Model 581 except in stainless finish only. Made 1991 to 1993.

MODEL 686
Same as S&W Model 586 Distinguished Combat Magnum except in stainless finish w/additional 2.5-inch bbl. Made from 1991 to date.

w/2.5-inch bbl. . . . . NiB $639	Ex $434	Gd $332
w/4- or 6-inch bbl. . . . . NiB $639	Ex $434	Gd $332
w/8.63-inch bbl. . . . . NiB $639	Ex $434	Gd $332
Model 686 (w/adjustable front sight), add		$50

MODEL 686 PLUS
Same as standard Model 686 Magnum except w/7-round cylinder and 2.5-, 4- or 6-inch bbl. Made from 1996 to date.

w/2.5-inch bbl. . . . . NiB $689	Ex $617	Gd $499
w/4-inch bbl. . . . . NiB $704	Ex $595	Gd $408
w/6-inch bbl. . . . . NiB $700	Ex $631	Gd $429

MODEL 696 . . . . NiB $546 Ex $386 Gd $337
Caliber: .44 S&W Special. L-Frame w/five-round cylinder, 3-inch shrouded bbl., 8.38 inches overall. Weight: 48 oz. Red ramp front sight, micrometer-click adj. rear. Checkered synthetic grip. Satin stainless steel. Made from 1997 to 2002.

MODEL 940 CENTENNIAL DA . . NiB $479 Ex $367 Gd $290
Same general specifications as Model 640 except chambered for 9mm. Two- or 3-inch bbl., Weight: 23-25 oz. Santoprene combat grips. Made from 1991 to 1998.

MODEL 1891
SA REVOLVER . . . . NiB $2779 Ex $2465 Gd $2190
Hinged frame. Caliber: .38 S&W. Five-round cylinder, bbl. lengths: 3.25, 4, 5 and 6-inches. Fixed sights. Blued or nickel finish. Hard rubber grips. Made 1891-1911. Note: Until 1906, an accessory single-shot target bbl. (see Model 1891 Single-Shot Target Pistol) was available for this revolver.
w/extra .22 single-shot bbl. . . NiB $5300 Ex $4220 Gd $3690

MODEL 1917 ARMY DA REVOLVER
Caliber: .45 Automatic, using 3-cartridge half-moon clip or .45 Auto Rim, without clip. Six-round cylinder, 5.5-inch bbl., 10.75 inches overall. Weight: 36.25 oz. Fixed sights. Blued finish (blue-black finish on commercial model, brush polish on military). Checkered walnut grips (commercial model, smooth on military). Made under U.S. Government contract 1917-19 and produced commercially 1919-1941. Note: About 175,000 of these revolvers were produced during WW I. The DCM sold these to NRA members during the 1930s at $16.15 each.
Commercial model . . . . NiB $2500 Ex $2168 Gd $1870
Military model . . . . NiB $1860 Ex $1640 Gd $1389

K-22 MASTERPIECE DA . . . NiB $5100 Ex $4390 Gd $2724
Improved version of K-22 Outdoorsman w/same specifications but w/micrometer-click rear sight, short action and antibacklash trigger. Fewer than 1,100 manufactured in 1940.

K-22 OUTDOORSMAN DA NiB $2552 Ex $1906 Gd $1392
Design based on the .38 Military & Police Target. Caliber: .22 LR. Six-round cylinder, 11.13 inches overall. Weight: 35 oz. Adj. target sights. Blued finish. Checkered walnut grip. Made 1931 to 1940.

K-32 AND K-38 HEAVY MASTERPIECES
Same as K32 and K38 Masterpiece but w/heavy bbl. Weight: 38.5 oz. Made 1950-53. Note: All K32 and K38 revolvers made after September 1953 have heavy bbls. and the "Heavy Masterpiece" designation was disc. Values for Heavy Masterpiece models are the same as shown for Models 14 and 16. (See separate listing).

K-32 TARGET
DA REVOLVER . . . . NiB $18,600 Ex $15,400 Gd $9900
Same as .38 Military & Police Target except chambered for .32 S&W Long cartridge, slightly heavier bbl., weight: 34 oz. Only 98 produced. Made from 1938 to 1940.

LADY SMITH (MODEL M HAND EJECTOR) DA REVOLVER
Caliber: .22 LR. Seven-round cylinder, bbl. length: 2.25-, 3-, 3.5- and 6-inch (Third Model only), approximately 7 inches overall w/3.5-inch bbl., weight: About 9.5 oz. Fixed sights, adj. target sights available on Third Model. Blued or nickel finish. Round butt, hard rubber grips on First and Second models; checkered walnut or hard rubber square buttgrips on Third Model. First Model —1902-06: Cylinder locking bolt operated

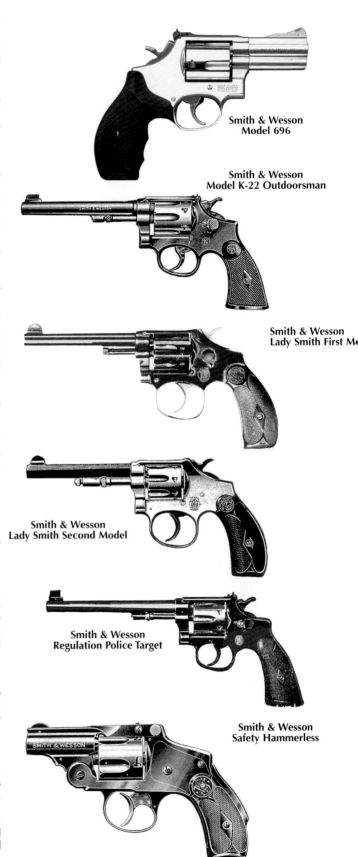

Smith & Wesson
Model 696

Smith & Wesson
Model K-22 Outdoorsman

Smith & Wesson
Lady Smith First M‹

Smith & Wesson
Lady Smith Second Model

Smith & Wesson
Regulation Police Target

Smith & Wesson
Safety Hammerless

by button on left side of frame, no bbl., lug and front locking bolt. Second Model —1906-11: Rear cylinder latch eliminated, has bbl. lug, forward cylinder lock w/draw-bolt fastening. Third Model —1911-21: Same as Second Model except has square grips, target sights and 6-inch bbl. available. Note: Legend has it that a straight-laced D.B. Wesson ordered discontinuance of the Lady Smith when he learned of the little revolver's reputed popularity w/ladies of the evening. The story, which undoubtedly has enhanced the appeal of this model to collectors, is not true: The Lady Smith was disc. because of difficulty of manufacture and high frequency of repairs.

First model . . . . NiB $3140 Ex $2130 Gd $1696
Second model . . . . NiB $2315 Ex $1779 Gd $1015
Third model, w/fixed sights,
    2.25- or 3.5-inch bbl. . . NiB $2315 Ex $1779 Gd $1015
Third model, w/fixed sights,
    6-inch bbl. . . . . NiB $2315 Ex $1779 Gd $1015
Third model, w/adj. sights,
    6-inch bbl. . . . . NiB $2215 Ex $1888 Gd $934

REGULATION POLICE
DA (I Frame) . . . . NiB $811 Ex $602 Gd $434
Calibers: .32 S&W (6-round) or .38 S&W (5-round) built on .32 Hand Ejector frames. Two-, 3-, 3.25-, 4-, 4.25- or 6-inch bbl., weight: 20-24 oz. Fixed sights. Blue or nickel finish. Checkered walnut grips. Made 1917-57. Note: After 1957 "J" Frames replaced the older "I" Frames and designations changed to Model 31 and 33 respectively.
Regulation Police, .32 S&W . . NiB $1097 Ex $920 Gd $599
Regulation Police, .38 S&W . . NiB $1097 Ex $920 Gd $599

REGULATION POLICE TARGET DA
Target version of the Regulation Police w/standard features of that model. Calibers: .32 S&W Long or .38 S&W. 6-inch bbl., 10.25 inches overall. Weight: 20 oz. Adjustable target sights. Blue or nickel finish. Checkered walnut grips. Made from about 1917 to 1957.
Regulation Police Target,
    .32 S&W . . . . NiB $2600 Ex $2470 Gd $780
Regulation Police Target,
    .38 S&W (pre-war) . . . . . . NiB $3000 Ex $2855 Gd $900

SAFETY HAMMERLESS . . . . NiB $1396 Ex $1178 Gd $1024
Also called New Departure Double Action. Hinged frame. Calibers: .32 S&W, .38 S&W. Five-round cylinder, bbl. lengths: 2, 3- and 3.5-inch (.32 cal.) or 2-, 3.25-, 4-, 5- and 6-inch (.38 cal.); 6.75 inches overall (.32 cal. w/3-inch bbl.) or 7.5 inches (.38 cal. w/3.25-inch bbl.). Weight: 14.25 oz. (.32 cal. w/3-inch bbl.) or 18.25 oz. (.38 cal. 2.5-inch bbl.). Fixed sights. Blued or nickel finish. Hard rubber grips. Made from 1888 to 1937 (.32 cal.); 1887 to 1941 (.38 cal. w/various minor changes.)

TEXAS RANGER
COMMEMORATIVE . . . . NiB $658 Ex $359 Gd $270
Issued to honor the 150th anniversary of the TExas Rangers. Model 19 .357 Combat Magnum w/4-inch bbl., sideplate stamped w/TExas Ranger Commemorative Seal, smooth Goncalo Alves grips. Special Bowie knife in presentation case. 8,000 sets made in 1973. Top value is for set in new condition.

SPHINX ENGINEERING S.A. — Matten b. Interlaken, Switzerland
North American extension of the Switzerland based KRISS Group based in Chesapeake, VA.

MODEL AT-380 DA PISTOL
Caliber: .380 ACP. 10-round magazine, 3.27- inch bbl., 6.03

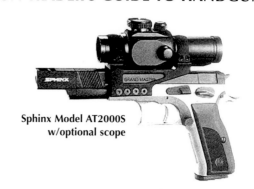

Sphinx Model AT2000S
w/optional scope

inches overall. Weight: 25 oz. Stainless steel frame w/blued slide or Palladium finish. Slide latch w/ambidExtrous magazine release. Imported from 1993 to 1996.
Two-tone (w/blued slide) . . . . . NiB $474 Ex $336 Gd $240
w/Palladium finish . . . . NiB $561 Ex $431 Gd $336

NOTE: *The AT-88 pistol series was previously manufactured by ITM in Switzerland and imported by Action Arms before Sphinx-Muller resumed production of these firearms, now designated as the AT-2000 series.*

MODEL 2000S DA AUTOMATIC PISTOL
Calibers: 9mm Parabellum, .40 S&W. 15- or 11-round magazine respectively, 4.53-inch bbl., (S-standard), 3.66-inch bbl., (P-compact), 3.34-inch bbl., (H-subcompact), 8.25 inches overall. Weight: 36.5 oz. Fixed sights w/3-dot system. Stainless frame w/blued slide or Palladium finish. AmbidExtrous safety. Checkered walnut or neoprene grips. Imported 1993 to 1996.
Standard model . . . . NiB $990 Ex $903 Gd $581
Compact model . . . . NiB $890 Ex $755 Gd $536
Sub-compact model . . . . NiB $890 Ex $755 Gd $536
.40 S&W, add $50
Palladium finish, add $100

MODEL AT2000C/2000CS COMPETITOR
Similar to the Model AT2000S except also chambered for 9x21mm. 10-round magazine, 5.31-inch compensated bbl., 9.84 inches overall. Weight: 40.56 oz. Fully adjustable BoMar or ProPoint sights. Made 1993 to 1996.
w/Bomar sight . . . . NiB $1844 Ex $1599 Gd $1418
w/ProPoint sight . . . . NiB $2254 Ex $1923 Gd $1690

MODEL AT2000GM/GMS GRAND MASTER
Similar to the AT2000C except single action only w/square trigger guard and Extended beavertail grip. Imported 1993-96.
w/BoMar sight . . . . NiB $1872 Ex $1624 Gd $1375
w/ProPoint sight . . . . NiB $2179 Ex $1919 Gd $1699

SPD STANDARD . . . . NiB $1295 EX $1100 GD $830
Semi-automatic. DA/SA. Caliber: 9mm; 10- or 17-rnd. magazine. 4.5-in. bbl. Sights: fiber optic front, adj. rear or fixed white dot. Finish: matte black. Grip: textured polymer w/ modular grip inserts. Length: 8.3-in. Weight: 31.6 oz. Made from 2012 to date.
SPD Compact (3.7-in. bbl.) . . . . . NiB $999 Ex $980 Gd $900
SPD Subcompact (3.1-in. bbl.) . . . NiB $949 Ex $900 Gd $880

SPRINGFIELD ARMORY — Geneseo, IL
Formerly U.S. Government run Springfield Armory in Springfield, Massachusetts. Springfield Armory name purchased in 1974 for commercial/civilian manufacturing.

MODEL M1911 SERIES AUTO PISTOL
Springfield builds the "PDP" (Personal Defense Pistol) Series based on the self-loading M 1911-A1 pistol (military specifi-

**Springfield Armory
1911-A1 Post '90 Series Trophy Model**

**Springfield Armory
1911-A1 PDP Series Defender**

**Springfield Armory
1911-A1 Champion**

**Springfield Armory
1911-A1 Compact**

**Springfield Armory
M1911-A1 Ultra
Compact Parkerized**

**Springfield
Armory
M1911-A1 Ultra
Compact Bi-Tone**

cations model) as adopted for a standard service weapon by the U.S. Army. With enhancements and modifications they produce a full line of firearms including Ultra-Compacts, Lightweights, Match Grade and Competition Models. For values see specific models.

MODEL 1911-A1 GOVERNMENT

Calibers: 9mm Para., .38 Super, .40 S&W, 10mm or .45 ACP., 7-, 8-, 9- or 10-round magazine, 4- or 5-inch bbl., 8.5 inches overall. Weight: 36 oz. Fixed combat sights. Blued, Parkerized or Duo-Tone finish. Checkered walnut grips. Note: This is an Exact duplicate of the Colt M1911-A1 that was used by the U.S. Armed Forces as a service weapon.

Blued finish . . . . NiB $453 Ex $347 Gd $265
Parkerized finish . . . . NiB $453 Ex $347 Gd $265

MODEL 1911-A1 (PRE '90 SERIES)

Calibers: 9mm Parabellum, .38 Super, 10mm, .45 ACP. Seven-, 8-, 9- or 10-round magazine, bbl. length: 3.63, 4, 4.25 or 5 inches, 8.5 inches overall. Weight: 36 oz. Fixed combat sights. Blued, Duo-Tone or Parkerized finish. Checkered walnut stocks. Made 1985 to 1990.

Government model (blued) . . . . NiB $453 Ex $347 Gd $265
**Government model
  (Parkerized)** . . . . NiB $621 Ex $436 Gd $362
Bullseye model (wadcutter) . NiB $1474 Ex $1345 Gd $866
**Combat Commander model
  (blued)** . . . . NiB $474 Ex $386 Gd $321
**Combat Commander model
  (Parkerized)** . . . . NiB $650 Ex $475 Gd $353
Commander model (blued) . . . . NiB $479 Ex $306 Gd $219
Commander model (Duo-Tone) NiB $567 Ex $473 Gd $397
Commander model (Parkerized) NiB $650 Ex $536 Gd $386
Compact model (blued) . . . . . NiB $ 470 Ex $347 Gd $265
Compact model (Duo-Tone) . . . NiB $559 Ex $500 Gd $434
Compact model (Parkerized) . . . NiB $668 Ex $500 Gd $342
Defender model (blued) . . . . . . NiB $546 Ex $434 Gd $290
Defender model (Parkerized) . . NiB $704 Ex $556 Gd $377
**Defender model
  (Custom Carry)** . . . . NiB $540 Ex $429 Gd $326
**National Match model
  (Hardball)** . . . . NiB $829 Ex $709 Gd $546
Trophy Master (Competition) NiB $1355 Ex $1265 Gd $918
**Trophy Master
  (Distinguished)** . . . . NiB $2152 Ex $2030 Gd $1234
Trophy Master (Expert) . . . . NiB $1723 Ex $1528 Gd $1322

MODEL 1911-A1 (CUSTOM LOADED SERIES)

1911 style operating system w/steel or alloy frame. Calibers: 9mm Parabellum, .38 Super, .40 S&W, 10mm, .45 ACP. Seven-, 8-, 9- or 10-round magazine, bbl. length: 3.63, 4, 4.25 or 5 inches; 8.5 inches overall. Weight: 28 oz. to 36 oz. Fixed combat sights. Blued, Duo-Tone, Parkerized or stainless finish. Checkered composition or walnut stocks. Made 1990 to 1998.

Mil-Spec model (blued) . . . . . . NiB $595 Ex $419 Gd $340
Mil-Spec model (Parkerized) . . . NiB $809 Ex $644 Gd $444
Standard model (blued) . . . . . . NiB $879 Ex $689 Gd $499
Standard model (Parkerized) . . NiB $1068 Ex $998 Gd $826
Standard model (stainless) . . . . NiB $806 Ex $699 Gd $497
Trophy model (blued) . . . . . . NiB $1440 Ex $1240 Gd $989
Trophy model (Hi-Tone) . . . NiB $1437 Ex $1245 Gd $1029
Trophy model (stainless) . . . . . . NiB $709 Ex $577 Gd $429

MODEL 1911-A1 PDP SERIES

PDP Series (Personal Defense Pistol). Calibers: .38 Super, .40 S&W, .45 ACP. Seven-, 8-, 9-, 10-, 13- or 17-round magazine, bbl. length: 4, 5, 5.5 or 5.63 inches, 9 to 11 inches overall w/ compensated bbl. Weight: 34.5 oz. to 42.8 oz. Post front sight, adjustable rear w/3-dot system. Blued, Duo-Tone, Parkerized or stainless finish. Checkered composition or walnut stocks. Made from 1991 to 1998.

Defender model (blued) . . . . . . NiB $910 Ex $780 Gd $586

Defender model (Duo-Tone)... NiB $910 Ex $780 Gd $586
Defender model (Parkerized) .. NiB $910 Ex $780 Gd $586
.45 ACP Champion Comp
  (blued) .... NiB $780 Ex $562 Gd $431
.45 ACP Compact Comp HC
  (blued) .... NiB $602 Ex $453 Gd $398
.380 Sup Factory Comp (blued) NiB $740 Ex $546 Gd $431
.45 ACP Factory Comp (blued) NiB $866 Ex $780 Gd $544
.380 Sup Factory Comp HC
  (blued) .... NiB $740 Ex $546 Gd $398
.45 ACP Factory Comp HC
  (blued) .... NiB $733 Ex $789 Gd $556

MODEL M1911-A1 CHAMPION
Calibers: .380 ACP, 9mm Para., .45 ACP. Six- or 7-round magazine, 4-inch bbl. Weight: 26.5 to 33.4 oz. Low profile post front sight and drift adjustable rear w/3-dot sighting system. Commander-style hammer and slide. Checkered walnut grips. Blue, Bi-Tone, Parkerized or stainless finish. Made from 1992 to 2002.
.380 ACP standard
  (disc. 1995) .... NiB $850 Ex $807 Gd $479
.45 ACP (parkerized or blued) NiB $700 Ex $665 Gd $480
.45 ACP (Bi-Tone) (B/H Model) NiB $912 Ex $790 Gd $386
.45 ACP (stainless) .... NiB $742 Ex $707 Gd $522
.45 ACP Super Tuned (1997-1999) NiB $850 Ex $807 Gd $479

MODEL M1911-A1 COMPACT
Similar to the standard M1911 w/champion length slide on a steel or alloy frame w/a shortened grip. Caliber: .45 ACP. Six- or 7-round magazine (10+ law enforcement only), 4-inch bbl. weight: 26.5 to 32 oz. Low profile sights w/3-dot system. Checkered walnut grips. Matte blue, Duo-Tone or Parkerized finish. Made 1991 to 1996.
Compact (Parkerized) .... NiB $464 Ex $380 Gd $290
Compact (blued) .... NiB $464 Ex $380 Gd $290
Compact (Duo-Tone) .... NiB $577 Ex $500 Gd $434
Compact (stainless)......... NiB $556 Ex $376 Gd $270
Compact Comp (ported)..... NiB $882 Ex $792 Gd $587
High capacity (blued)....... NiB $595 Ex $369 Gd $321
High capacity (stainless)..... NiB $831 Ex $638 Gd $499

MODEL M1911-A1 ULTRA COMPACT
Similar to M1911 Compact except chambered for .380 ACP or .45 ACP. 6- or 7-round magazine, 3.5-inch bbl., weight: 22 oz. to 30 oz. Matte Blue, Bi-Tone, Parkerized (military specs) or stainless finish. Made from 1995 to 2003.
.380 ACP Ultra (disc. 1996) ... NiB $740 Ex $585 Gd $388
.45 ACP Ultra (Parkerized
  or blued)............... NiB $740 Ex $585 Gd $388
.45 ACP Ultra (Bi-Tone) ...... NiB $844 Ex $709 Gd $500
.45 ACP (stainless) .... NiB $740 Ex $585 Gd $388
.45 ACP ultra high capacity
  (Parkerized) .... NiB $740 Ex $585 Gd $388
.45 ACP ultra high capacity
  (blued) .... NiB $780 Ex $615 Gd $499
.45 ACP ultra high capacity
  (stainless) .... NiB $780 Ex $615 Gd $499
.45 ACP V10 ultra comp
  (Parkerized) .... NiB $979 Ex $806 Gd $495
.45 ACP V10 ultra comp
  (blued) .... NiB $979 Ex $806 Gd $495
.45 ACP V10 ultra comp
  (stainless) .... NiB $979 Ex $806 Gd $495
.45 ACP V10 ultra (super
  tuned) .... NiB $1090 Ex $974 Gd $577

MODEL 1911-A1 TRP (TACITCAL RESPONSE PISTOL) OPERATOR
SA AUTO PISTOL .... NiB $1620 Ex $1460 Gd $780
1911 style operating system w/steel frame. Caliber: .45 ACP. Seven-round magazine, bbl. length: 5 inches; 8.5 inches over-all. Weight: 36 oz. Fixed combat sights. Black Armory Kote or stainless finish. Checkered front strap, composition stocks. Made from 2008 to date.

MODEL 1911-A1 LONG SLIDE CUSTOM LOADED
SA AUTO PISTOL .... NiB $1100 Ex $960 Gd $480
1911 style operating system w/steel frame. Caliber: .45 ACP or .45 Super. Seven-round magazine, bbl. length: 6 inches; 8.5 inches overall. Weight: 36 oz. Fixed combat sights. Black Armory Kote or stainless finish. Checkered wood stocks. Made from 2001 to 2012.

MODEL EMP (ENHANCED
MICRO PISTOL)........... NiB $1175 EX $800 GD $600
Similar to 1911-style semi-automatic except in 9mm Parabellum or .40 S&W, and 3-in. bull bbl.

FIRECAT AUTOMATIC PISTOL
Calibers: 9mm, .40 S&W. Eight-round magazine (9mm) or 7-round magazine (.40 S&W), 3.5-inch bbl., 6.5 inches overall. Weight: 25.75 oz. Fixed sights w/3-dot system. Checkered walnut grip. Matte blued finish. Made from 1991 to 1993.
9mm .... NiB $556 Ex $408 Gd $289
.40 S&W .... NiB $556 Ex $408 Gd $289

PANTHER AUTO PISTOL ..... NiB $606 Ex $453 Gd $346
Calibers: 9mm, .40 S&W. 15-round magazine (9mm) or 11-round magazine (.40 S&W), 3.8-inch bbl., 7.5 inches overall. Weight: 28.95 oz. Blade front sight, rear adj. for windage w/3-dot system. Checkered walnut grip. Matte blued finish. Made from 1991 to 1993.

MODEL P9 DA COMBAT SERIES
Calibers: 9mm, .40 S&W, .45 ACP. Magazine capacity: 15-round (9mm), 11-round (.40 S&W) or 10-round (.45 ACP), 3.66-inch bbl., (Compact and Sub-Compact), or 4.75-inch bbl., (Standard), 7.25 or 8.1 inches overall. Weight: 32 to 35 oz. Fixed sights w/3-dot system. Checkered walnut grip. Matte blued, Parkerized, stainless or Duo-Tone finish. Made from 1990 to 1994.
Compact model (9mm,
  Parkerized) .... NiB $464 Ex $342 Gd $279
Sub-Compact model (9mm,
  Parkerized) .... NiB $433 Ex $309 Gd $235
Standard model (9mm,
  Parkerized) .... NiB $498 Ex $377 Gd $304
w/blued finish, add........... $50
w/Duo-Tone finish, add......... $100
w/stainless finish, add......... $128
.40 S&W, add $35
.45 ACP add $50

MODEL P9 COMPETITION SERIES
Same general specifications as Model P9 except in target configuration w/5-inch bbl., (LSP Ultra) or 5.25-inch bbl. Factory Comp model w/dual port compensator system, Extended safety and magazine release.
Factory Comp model
  (9mm Bi-Tone) .... NiB $648 Ex $444 Gd $337
Factory Comp model
  (9mm stainless) .... NiB $733 Ex $431 Gd $281
IPSC Ultra model
  (9mm Bi-Tone) .... NiB $689 Ex $431 Gd $270
LSP Ultra model
  (9mm stainless).......... NiB $785 Ex $580 Gd $425
.40 S&W, .45 ACP: add........ $128

MODEL RANGE OFFICER..... NiB $800 Ex $680 Gd $460
Similar to 1911-style semi-automatic except in 9mm Parabellum or .45 ACP only, 5-in. match bbl., adj. sights. Finish: blued or stainless finish.
stainless, add................. $100

Springfield Armory
P9 Combat

Springfield Armory Panther

MODEL XD-S . . . . NiB $599 Ex $470 Gd $355
Similar to XD and XD(M) series except with single stack magazine, 3.3- or 4-in. bbl., fiber optic sights. Finish: blued or two-tone. Made from 2013 to date.
two-tone, add $100
laser sight, add $100

MODEL XD MOD.2 . . . . NiB $500 Ex $450 Gd $345
Similar to XD and XD(M) series except with modified grip and Grip Zone with 3 grip texture types, fiber optic sights. Sub-Compact (3- or 3.3-in bbl.), Service (4-in. bbl.), and Tactical (5-in. bbl.). Made from 2015 to date.

XD SERIES
Based on HS 2000 pistol manufactured in Croatia. Striker fired. Calibers: 9mm, .357 SIG, .40 S&W, .45 ACP or .45 G.A.P. Polymer frame. 9-, 10-, 12- or 15-rnd. magazine depending on caliber. Matte black or bi-tone finish. Imported 2002 to date.
5-in. bbl. NiB $599 Ex $400 Gd $270
4-in. bbl. NiB $580 Ex $370 Gd $240
3-in. bbl. NiB $550 Ex $370 Gd $240

XD(M) SERIES . . . . NiB $697 Ex $470 Gd $320
Similar to XD series except w/modular backstraps, diagonal slide serrations. Striker fired. Calibers: 9mm, .40 S&W, or .45 ACP. Bbl. lengths: 3.8- or 4.5-in. Made 2008 to date.
Compact . . . . NiB $700 Ex $470 Gd $320
Competition . . . . NiB $780 Ex $550 Gd $350

S.P.S. — Spain

Manufactured in Spain and imported by Eagle Imports, Wanamassa, New Jersey. Series-70 style.

SPS PANTERA SERIES . . . . . . NiB $1895 Ex $1320 Gd $1200
1911 platform. Semi-automatic. SA. Caliber: 9mm, .40 S&W, or .45 ACP; 12, 16-, or 21-rnd. magazine depending on cali-

ber. 5-in. bbl. Frame: steel. Sights: adj. rear, fiber optic front. Finish: blue, black chrome, hard chrome. Grip: glass filled nylon. Length: 8.71 in. Weight: 36.68 oz. Beavertail, magwell. Competition ready. Imported from 2011 to date.

SPS VISTA LONG . . . . NiB $1907 Ex $1880 Gd $1730
Similar to Pantera except chambered in .38 Super, 5.5-in. bbl. w/compensator, optic mount. Designed for IPSC, USPSA, and IDPA competition.
SPS Vista Short (5-in. bbl.) . . NiB $1907 Ex $1880 Gd $1730

STALLARD ARMS — Mansfield, OH
See listings under Hi-Point.

STAR — Eibar, Spain
Manufactured by Star, Bonifacio Echeverria, S.A.

MODEL 30M DA AUTO PISTOL NiB $431 Ex $288 Gd $189
Caliber: 9mm Para. 15-round magazine, 4.38-inch bbl., 8 inches overall. Weight: 40 oz. Steel frame w/combat features. Adj. sights. Checkered composition grips. Blued finish. Made from 1984 to 1991.

MODEL 30PK DA AUTO PISTOL NiB $431 Ex $288 Gd $189
Same gen. specifications as Star Model 30M except 3.8-inch bbl., weight: 30 oz. Alloy frame. Made from 1984 to 1989.

MODEL 31P DA AUTO PISTOL
Same general specifications as Model 30M except removable backstrap houses complete firing mechanism. Weight: 39.4 oz. Made from 1990 to 1994.
Blued finish. . . . . NiB $431 Ex $288 Gd $189
Starvel finish, add $50

MODEL 31 PK DA AUTO PISTOL . . . NiB $431 Ex $288 Gd $189
Same general specifications as Model 31P except w/alloy frame. Weight: 30 oz. Made from 1990 to 1997.

MODEL A AUTOMATIC PISTOL . . NiB $365 Ex $259 Gd $169
Modification of the Colt Government Model .45 Auto, which it closely resembles, but lacks grip safety. Caliber: .38 Super. Eight-round magazine, 5-inch bbl., 8 inches overall. Weight: 35 oz. Fixed sights. Blued finish. Checkered grips. Made from 1934-97. (No longer imported.)

MODELS AS, BS, PS . . . . NiB $500 Ex $380 Gd $279
Same as Models A, B and P except have magazine safety. Made in 1975.

MODEL B . . . . NiB $498 Ex $365 Gd $259
Same as Model A except in 9mm Para. Made 1934 to 1975.

MODEL BKM . . . . NiB $398 Ex $306 Gd $225
Similar to Model BM except has aluminum frame weight: 25.6 oz. Made from 1976 to 1992.

**MODEL BKS STARLIGHT
AUTOMATIC PISTOL . . . . NiB $431 Ex $279 Gd $209**
Light alloy frame. Caliber: 9mm Para. Eight-round magazine, 4.25-inch bbl., 7 inches overall. Weight: 25 oz. Fixed sights. Blued or chrome finish. Plastic grips. Made from 1970 to 1981.

MODEL BM AUTOMATIC PISTOL
Caliber: 9mm. Eight-round magazine, 3.9-inch bbl., 6.95 inches overall. Weight: 34.5 oz. Fixed sights. Checkered walnut grips. Blued or Starvel finish. Made from 1976 to 1992.
Blued finish. . . . . NiB $367 Ex $279 Gd $220
Starvel finish . . . . NiB $380 Ex $304 Gd $240

MODEL CO POCKET
AUTOMATIC PISTOL . . . . NiB $316 Ex $217 Gd $126
Caliber: .25 Automatic (6.35mm), 2.75-inch bbl., 4.5 inches overall. Weight: 13 oz. Fixed sights. Blued finish. Plastic grips. Made from 1941 to 197.

MODEL CU STARLET
POCKET PISTOL . . . . NiB $291 Ex $198 Gd $124
Light alloy frame. Caliber: .25 Auto (6.35mm). Eight-round magazine, 2.38-inch bbl., 4.75 inches overall. Weight: 10.5 oz. Fixed sights. Blued or chrome-plated slide w/frame anodized in black, blue, green, gray or gold. Plastic grips. Made from 1957 to 1997. (U.S. importation disc. 1968.)

MODEL F
AUTOMATIC PISTOL . . . . NiB $362 Ex $268 Gd $130
Caliber: .22 LR. 10-round magazine, 4.5-inch bbl., 7.5 inches overall. Weight: 25 oz. Fixed sights. Blued finish. Plastic grips. Made from 1942 to 1967.

MODEL F
OLYMPIC RAPID-FIRE . . . . NiB $556 Ex $408 Gd $230
Caliber: .22 Short. Nine-round magazine, 7-inch bbl., 11.06 inches overall. Weight: 52 oz. w/weights. Adj. target sight. Adj. 3-piece bbl. weight. Aluminum alloy slide. Muzzle brake. Plastic grips. Made from 1942 to 1967.

MODEL FM
. . . . NiB $362 Ex $279 Gd $171
Similar to Model FR except has heavier frame w/web in front of trigger guard, 4.25-inch heavy bbl., Weight: 32 oz. Made from 1972 to 1991.

MODEL FR
. . . . NiB $362 Ex $279 Gd $171
Similar to Model F w/same general specifications but restyled, has slide stop and adj. rear sight. Made from 1967 to 1972.

MODEL FR SPORT
. . . . NiB $398 Ex $306 Gd $229
Same as Model FR except has 6-inch bbl., weight: 28 oz. Also avail. in chrome finish. Made from 1967 to 1991.

MODEL FS
. . . . NiB $362 Ex $309 Gd $165
Same as regular Model F but w/6-inch bbl. and adj. sights. Weight: 27 oz. Made from 1942 to 1967.

MODEL HK LANCER
AUTOMATIC PISTOL . . . . NiB $319 Ex $225 Gd $249
Similar to Starfire w/same general specifications except .22 LR. Made from 1955 to 1968.

MODEL HN
AUTOMATIC PISTOL . . . . NiB $431 Ex $279 Gd $220
Caliber: .380 Auto (9mm Short). Six-round magazine, 2.75-inch bbl., 5.56 inches overall. Weight: 20 oz. Fixed sights. Blued finish. Plastic grips. Made from 1934 to 1941.

MODEL H
. . . . NiB $357 Ex $281 Gd $165
Same as Model HN except .32 Auto (7.65mm), 7-round magazine, weight: 20 oz. Made from 1934 to 1941.

MODEL I
AUTOMATIC PISTOL . . . . NiB $398 Ex $302 Gd $177
Caliber: .32 Auto (7.65mm). Nine-round magazine, 4.81-inch bbl., 7.5 inches overall. Weight: 24 oz. Fixed sights. Blued finish. Plastic grips. Made from 1934 to 1936.

MODEL IN
. . . . NiB $434 Ex $290 Gd $175
Same as Model I except caliber .380 Auto (9mm Short), 8-round magazine, weight: 24.5 oz. Made from 1934-36.

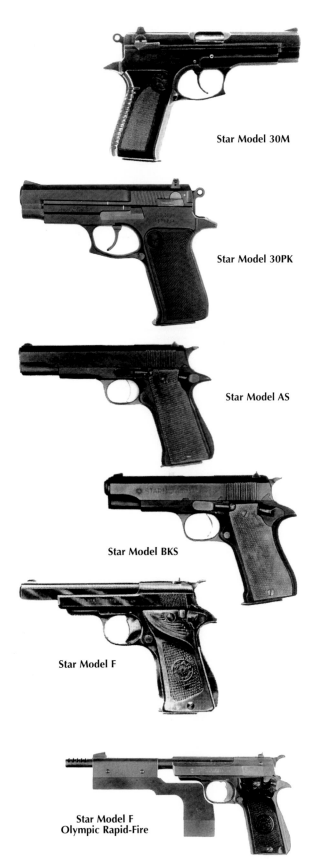

Star Model 30M

Star Model 30PK

Star Model AS

Star Model BKS

Star Model F

Star Model F
Olympic Rapid-Fire

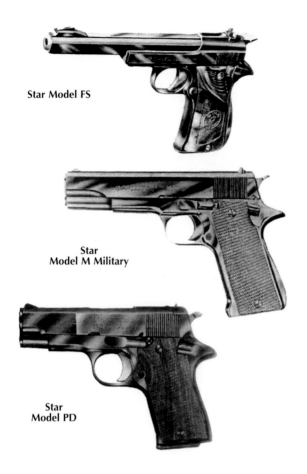

Star Model FS

Star
Model M Military

Star
Model PD

MODEL M MILITARY
AUTOMATIC PISTOL . . . . NiB $398 Ex $337 Gd $219
Modification of the Model M without grip safety. Calibers: 9mm Bergmann (Largo), .45 ACP, 9mm Para. Eight-round magazine except 7-shot in .45 caliber, 5-inch bbl., 8.5 inches overall. Weight: 36 oz. Fixed sights. Blued finish. Checkered grips. Made from 1934 to 1939.

MODELS M40, M43, M45 FIRESTAR AUTO PISTOLS
Calibers: 9mm, .40 S&W, .45 ACP. Seven-round magazine (9mm) or 6-round (other calibers). 3.4-inch bbl., 6.5 inches overall. Weight: 30.35 oz. Blade front sight, adj. rear w/3-dot system. Checkered rubber grips. Blued or Starvel finish. Made 1990 to 1997.
M40 blued (.40 S&W) . . . . NiB $367 Ex $289 Gd $232
M40 Starvel (.40 S&W) . . . . NiB $398 Ex $304 Gd $239
M43 blued (9mm) . . . . NiB $365 Ex $294 Gd $237
M43 Starvel (9mm) . . . . NiB $398 Ex $304 Gd $239
M45 blued (.45 ACP) . . . . NiB $357 Ex $270 Gd $120
M45 Starvel (.45 ACP) . . . . NiB $377 Ex $290 Gd $143

MEGASTAR AUTOMATIC PISTOL
Calibers: 10mm, .45 ACP. 12-round magazine, 4.6-inch bbl., 8.44 inches overall. Weight: 47.6 oz. Blade front sight, adj. rear. Checkered composition grip. finishes: Blued or Starvel. Made from 1992 to 1997.
Blued finish, 10mm or .45 ACP . . . NiB $500 Ex $397 Gd $274
Starvel finish, 10mm or .45 ACP . . . NiB $544 Ex $416 Gd $305

MODEL P . . . . NiB $464 Ex $345 Gd $283
Same as Model A except caliber .45 Auto, has 7-round magazine. Made from 1934 to 1975.

MODEL PD AUTOMATIC PISTOL
Caliber: .45 Auto. Six-round magazine, 3.75-inch bbl., 7 inches overall. Weight: 25 oz. Adj. rear sight, ramp front. Blued or Starvel finish. Checkered walnut grips. Made from 1975 to 1992.
Blued finish . . . . NiB $398 Ex $304 Gd $224
Starvel finish . . . . NiB $422 Ex $342 Gd $270

MODEL S . . . . NiB $319 Ex $220 Gd $159
Same as Model SI except caliber .380 Auto (9mm), 7-round magazine, weight: 19 oz. Made from 1941 to 1965.

MODEL SI
AUTOMATIC PISTOL . . . . NiB $316 Ex $225 Gd $130
Reduced-size modification of the Colt Government Model .45 Auto, lacks grip safety. Caliber: .32 Auto (7.65mm). Eight-round magazine, 4-inch bbl., 6.5 inches overall. Weight: 20 oz. Fixed sights. Blued finish. Plastic grips. Made from 1941 to 1965.

STARFIRE DK
AUTOMATIC PISTOL . . . . NiB $453 Ex $337 Gd $255
Light alloy frame. Caliber: .380 Automatic (9mm Short). Seven-round magazine, 3.13-inch bbl. 5.5 inches overall. Weight: 14.5 oz. Fixed sights. Blued or chrome-plated slide w/frame anodized in black, blue, green, gray or gold. Plastic grips. Made 1957-97. U.S. importation disc. 1968.

MODEL SUPER A
AUTOMATIC PISTOL . . . . NiB $499 Ex $431 Gd $220
Caliber: .38 Super. Improved version of Model A but has disarming bolt permitting easier takedown, cartridge indicator, magazine safety, take-down magazine, improved sights w/luminous spots for aiming in darkness. This is the standard service pistol of the Spanish Armed Forces, adopted 1946.

MODEL SUPER B AUTOMATIC PISTOL
Caliber: 9mm Para. Similar to Model B except w/improvements described under Model Super A. Made 1946 to 1990.
Super blued finish . . . . NiB $453 Ex $342 Gd $225
Starvel finish . . . . NiB $456 Ex $366 Gd $249

MODELS SUPER M, SUPER P . . NiB $852 Ex $685 Gd $478
Calibers: .45 ACP, 9mm Parabellum or 9mm Largo, (Super M) and 9mm Parabellum (Super P). Improved versions of the Models M & P w/same general specifications, but has disarming bolt permitting easier takedown, cartridge indicator, magazine safety, take-down magazine, improved sights w/luminous spots for aiming in darkness.

MODELS SUPER SI, SUPER S . . NiB $332 Ex $239 Gd $274
Same general specifications as the regular Model SI and S except w/improvements described under Super Star. Made 1946 to 1972.

MODEL SUPER SM . . . . NiB $398 Ex $386 Gd $204
Similar to Model Super S except has adj. rear sight, wood grips. Made from 1973 to 1981.

SUPER TARGET MODEL . . . NiB $1595 Ex $1396 Gd $1309
Same as Super Star model except w/adj. target sight. (Disc.)

ULTRASTAR DA
AUTOMATIC PISTOL . . . . NiB $365 Ex $290 Gd $200
Calibers: 9mm Parabellum or .40 S&W. Nine-round magazine, 3.57-inch bbl., 7 inches overall. Weight: 26 oz. Blade front, adjustable rear w/3-dot system. Polymer frame. Blue metal finish. Checkered black polymer grips. Imported from 1994 to 1997.

STENDA-WERKE — Suhl, Germany

POCKET AUTOMATIC PISTOL . NiB $337 Ex $279 Gd $160
Essentially the same as the Beholla (see listing of that pistol for specifications). Made circa 1920-.25. Note: This pistol may be marked "Beholla" along w/the Stenda name and address.

STERLING ARMS CORPORATION — Gasport, NY

MODEL 283 TARGET 300
AUTO PISTOL . . . . NiB $189 Ex $109 Gd $90
Caliber: .22 LR. 10-round magazine, bbl. lengths: 4.5-, 6- 8-inch. 9 inches overall w/4.5-inch bbl., Weight: 36 oz. w/4.52-inch bbl. Adj. sights. Blued finish. Plastic grips. Made from 1970 to 1971.

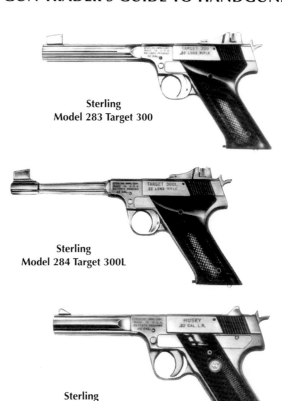

Sterling
Model 283 Target 300

MODEL 284 TARGET 300L . . . . . NiB $179 Ex $115 Gd $90
Same as Model 283 except has 4.5- or 6-inch Luger-type bbl. Made from 1970 to 1971.

MODEL 285 HUSKY . . . . NiB $179 Ex $115 Gd $90
Same as Model 283 except has fixed sights, 4.5-inch bbl only. Made from 1970 to 1971.

Sterling
Model 284 Target 300L

MODEL 286 TRAPPER . . . . NiB $129 Ex $115 Gd $90
Same as Model 284 except w/fixed sights. Made 1970-71.

MODEL 287 PPL-.380
AUTOMATIC PISTOL . . . . NiB $179 Ex $115 Gd $90
Caliber: .380 Auto. Six-round magazine, 1-inch bbl., 5.38 inches overall. Weight: 22.5 oz. Fixed sights. Blued finish. Plastic grips. Made from 1971 to 1972.

Sterling
Model 285 Husky

MODEL 300
AUTOMATIC PISTOL . . . . NiB $150 Ex $90 Gd $75
Caliber: .25 Auto. Six-round magazine, 2.33-inch bbl., 4.5 inches overall. Weight: 13 oz. Fixed sights. Blued or nickel finish. Plastic grips. Made from 1972 to 1983.

MODEL 300S . . . . NiB $179 Ex $115 Gd $90
Same as Model 300 except in stainless steel. Made 1976-83.

MODEL 302 . . . . NiB $179 Ex $115 Gd $90
Same as Model 300 except in .22 LR. Made 1973 to 1983.

Sterling
Model 286 Trapper

MODEL 302S . . . . NiB $179 Ex $115 Gd $90
Same as Model 302 except in stainless steel. Made 1976-83.

MODEL 400 DA
AUTOMATIC PISTOL . . . . NiB $309 Ex $214 Gd $129
Caliber: .380 Auto. Seven-round magazine, 3.5-inch bbl., 6.5 inches overall. Weight: 24 oz. Adj. rear sight. Blued or nickel finish. Checkered walnut grips. Made from 1975 to 1983.

Sterling
Model 300

MODEL 400S . . . . NiB $309 Ex $214 Gd $129
Same as Model 400 except stainless steel. Made1977-83.

MODEL 450 DA AUTO PISTOL . . NiB $309 Ex $214 Gd $129
Caliber: .45 Auto. Eight-round magazine, 4-inch bbl., 7.5 inches overall. Weight: 36 oz. Adj. rear sight. Blued finish. Smooth walnut grips. Made from 1977 to 1983.

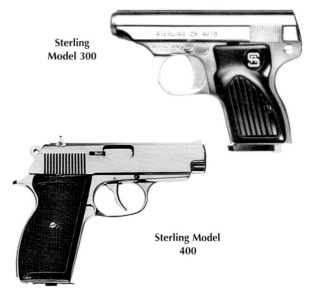

MODEL PPL-22
AUTOMATIC PISTOL . . . . NiB $309 Ex $214 Gd $129
Caliber: .22 LR. 10-round magazine, 1-inch bbl., 5.5 inches overall. Weight: About 24 oz. Fixed sights. Blued finish. Wood grips. Only 382 made in 1970 to 1971.

Sterling Model
400

J. STEVENS ARMS & TOOL CO. — Chicopee Falls, MA

This firm was established in Civil War era by Joshua Stevens, for whom the company was named. In 1999 Savage Arms began manufacture of Stevens designs.

NO. 10 SINGLE-SHOT
TARGET PISTOL . . . . NiB $249 Ex $207 Gd $160
Caliber: .22 LR. 8-inch bbl., 11.5 inches overall. Weight: 37 oz. Target sights. Blued finish. Hard rubber grips. In External appearance this arm resembles an automatic pistol but it has a tip-up action. Made from 1919 to 1939.

NO. 35 OFFHAND MODEL SINGLE-SHOT
TARGET PISTOL . . . . NiB $377 Ex $301 Gd $255
Tip-up action. Caliber: .22 LR. Bbl. lengths: 6, 8, 10, 12.25 inches. Weight: 24 oz. w/6-inch bbl. Target sights. Blued finish. Walnut grips. Note: This pistol is similar to the earlier "Gould" model. Made from 1907 to 1939.

NO. 35 OFFHAND SINGLE-SHOT
PISTOL/SHOTGUN . . . . NiB $377 Ex $301 Gd $255
Same general specifications as the standard No. 35 pistol except chambered for the .410 shotshell. Six-, 8-, 10-, or 12-inch half-ocatagonal bbl., iron frame either blued, nickel plated, or casehardened. BATF Class 3 license required to purchase. Made from 1923 to 1942.

NO. 36 SINGLE-SHOT PISTOL . . NiB $842 Ex $577 Gd $439
Tip-up action. Calibers: .22 Short and LR, .22 WRF, .25 Stevens, .32 Short Colt, .38 Long Colt, .44 Russian. 10- or 12-inch half-octagonal bbl., iron or brass frame w/nickel plated finish. Blued bbl. Checkered walnut grips. Made from 1880 to 1911.

NO. 37 SINGLE-SHOT PISTOL. . NiB $1020 Ex $836 Gd $544
Similar specifications to the No. 38 except the finger spur on the trigger guard has been omitted. Made from 1889 to 1919.

NO. 38 SINGLE-SHOT PISTOL NiB $536 Ex $437 Gd $247
Tip-up action. Calibers: .22 Short and LR, .22 WRF, .25 Stevens, .32 Stevens, .32 Short Colt. Iron or brass frame. Checkered grips. Made from 1884 to 1903.

NO. 41 TIP-UP
SINGLE-SHOT PISTOL . . . . NiB $342 Ex $281 Gd $204
Tip-up action. Caliber: .22 Short, 3.5-inch half-octagonal bbl. Blued metal parts w/optional nickel frame. Made from 1896 to1915.

STEYR — Steyr, Austria

GB SEMIAUTOMATIC PISTOL
Caliber: 9mm Para. 18-round magazine, 5.4-inch bbl., 8.9 inches overall. Weight: 2.9 lbs. Post front sight, fixed, notched rear. Double, gas-delayed, blow-back action. Made from 1981 to 1988.
Commercial model . . . . NiB $680 Ex $530 Gd $337
Military model
   (Less than 1000 imported) . . NiB $800 Ex $652 Gd $377

STEYR-HAHN (M12) AUTOMATIC PISTOL
Caliber: 9mm Steyr. Eight-round fixed magazine, charger loaded; 5.1-inch bbl., 8.5 inches overall. Weight: 35 oz. Fixed sights. Blued finish. Checkered wood grips. Made from 1911-19. Adopted by the Austro-Hungarian Army in 1912. Note: Confiscated by the Germans in 1938, an estimated 250,000 of these pistols were converted to 9mm Para. and stamped w/an identifying "08" on the left side of the slide. Mfd. by Osterreichische Waffenfabrik-Gesellschaft.
Commercial model (9mm Steyr) . . NiB $544 Ex $468 Gd $377
Military model (9mm Steyr-Austro
   -Hungarian Army) . . . . NiB $568 Ex $479 Gd $229
Military model (9mm Parabellum
   Conversion marked "08") . . NiB $1033 Ex $879 Gd $498

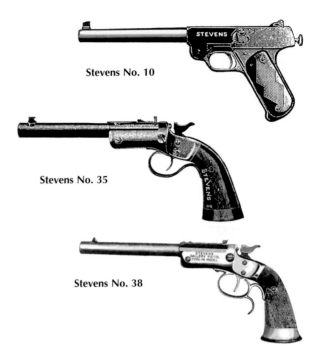

Stevens No. 10

Stevens No. 35

Stevens No. 38

C-A1 SERIES . . . . NiB $560 Ex $500 Gd $400
Similar to M-A1 series pistol but with smaller frame and 12 or 17-rnd. magazine.

L-A1 SERIES . . . . NiB $560 Ex $500 Gd $400
Similar to M-A1 series pistol but with full size frame, 4.5-in. bbl., 12 or 17-rnd. magazine.

M SERIES . . . . NiB $610 Ex $510 Gd $410
Semi-automatic. DAO. Caliber: 9mm, .40 S&W or .357 SIG; 10-rnd. magazine. Sights: trapezoidal. Weight: 28 oz. Polymer frame. Finish: matte black. One of the first pistols to use an integrate safety lock. Made from 1999 to 2002.

M-A1 SERIES . . . . NiB $560 Ex $500 Gd $400
Updated Model M series. Semi-automatic. Striker firer. Caliber: 9mm, .40 S&W or .357 SIG; 10-, 12-, or 15-rnd. magazine depending on caliber. 3.5- or 4-in. bbl. Sights: trapezoidal. Weight: 27 oz. Polymer frame. Finish: matte black. One of the first pistols to use an integrate safety lock. Made from 2004 to 2099, reintro. 2010.

S-A1 SERIES . . . . NiB $560 Ex $500 Gd $400
Similar to M-A1 series pistol but with smaller frame and 10-rnd. magazine.

MODEL SPP . . . . NiB $895 Ex $810 Gd $610
Semi-automatic. SA. Caliber: 9mm; 15- or 30-rnd. magazine. 5.9-in. bbl. Weight: 44 oz. Polymer construction. Made from 1992 to 1993.

STI INTERNATIONAL — Georgetown, TX

Note: STI uses a numerical code with model names to designate bbl. length, i.e. Lawman 5.0 features a 5-inch bbl. STI produces two platform types: 1911 single stack metal frame and 2011 double stack wide body polymer/steel frame. Magazine capacity as follows: 1911 style pistols have a 6- or 7-rnd. (.45 ACP); 7- or 8-rnd. (.40 S&W/10mm Auto); 8-, 9- or 10-rnd. (9mm) magazine. 2011 platform pistols have a 10-, 12-, or 14-rnd. (.45 ACP); 12-, 14-, 17-, or 22-rnd. (.40 S&W/10mm Auto); and 15-, 17-, 20-, or 26-rnd. (9mm/.38 Super) magazine.

—2011 SERIES—

MODEL APERIO . . . . **NiB $2199 Ex $1630 Gd $1030**
Semi-automatic. SA. 2011 style platform. Caliber: 9mm, .40
S&W, or .45 ACP. 5-in. island bbl. Weight: 38 oz. Polymer/
steel wide body frame. Sights: fiber optic front, adj. Bomar rear.
Finish: blue. Made from 2010 to date.

MODEL DVC 3-GUN . . . . . **NiB $2999 Ex $2150 Gd $1550**
Semi-automatic. SA. 2011 style platform. Caliber: 9mm. 5.4-in.
bushing bbl. Polymer/steel wide body frame. Sights: adj. rear,
fiber optic front. Finish: black. Made from 2015 to date.

MODEL DVC CLASSIC . . . **NiB $2799 Ex $2150 Gd $1550**
Semi-automatic. SA. Colt 1911 style platform. Caliber: 9mm,
.40 S&W or .45 ACP. 5.4-in. bushing bbl. Steel frame. Sights:
adj. rear, fiber optic front. Grips: VZ Operator II. Finish: hard
chrome. Made from 2015 to date.

MODEL DVC LIMITED . . . **NiB $2999 Ex $2150 Gd $1550**
Semi-automatic. SA. 2011 style platform. Caliber: 9mm or
.40 S&W. 5-in. bull bbl. Weight: 41 oz. Polymer/steel wide
body frame. Sights: adj. Bomar rear, ramped front. Finish: hard
chrome. Slide and dust cover cuts. Made from 2015 to date.

MODEL DVC OPEN . . . . . **NiB $3999 Ex $32150 Gd $2550**
Semi-automatic. SA. 2011 style platform. Caliber: 9mm or .38
Super. 5-in. trubor bbl. Weight: 48 oz. Polymer/steel wide body
frame. Sights: C-More red dot. Finish: hard chrome. Made from
2015 to date.

—1911 SERIES—

MODEL DUTY ONE . . . . . . **NiB $1380 Ex $1030 Gd $655**
Semi-automatic. SA. 1911 style platform. Caliber: 9mm, .40
S&W, or .45 ACP. 3-, 4-, 5-in. bushing bbl. Steel frame. Sights:
tritium. Finish: matte blue. Grip: textured G10. Made from
2013 to date.

MODEL DUTY CT . . . . **NiB $1288 Ex $955 Gd $610**
Semi-automatic. SA. 1911 style platform. Caliber: 9mm, .40
S&W, or .45 ACP. 5-in. bull bbl. Steel frame w/ rail. Sights:
fixed. Finish: matte blue. Made from 2006 to 2008.

MODEL EAGLE . . . . **NiB $1899 Ex $1590 Gd $1000**
Semi-automatic. SA. 2011 style platform. Caliber: 9mm or .40
S&W. 5- or 6-in. bushing bbl. Polymer/steel wide body frame.
Sights: ramped front, ledge rear. Finish: matte blue. Made from
1998 to date.

MODEL EDGE . . . . **NiB $2199 Ex $1630 Gd $1030**
Semi-automatic. SA. 2011 style platform. Caliber: 9mm, .38
Super, .40 S&W, or .45 ACP. 5-in. bull bbl. Polymer/steel wide
body frame. Sights: fiber optic front, adj. Bomar rear. Finish:
blue. Made from 1998 to date.

MODEL ELECTRA . . . . **NiB $1399 Ex $1090 Gd $700**
Semi-automatic. SA. 1911 style platform. Caliber: 9mm or
.45 ACP. 3-in. bull bbl. Aluminum frame. Sights: tritium front/
rear. Grips: textured G10. Finish: two-tone. Made from 2010
to date.

MODEL ESCORT . . . . **NiB $1299 Ex $930 Gd $580**
Semi-automatic. SA. 1911 style platform. Caliber: 9mm or .45
ACP. 3.24-in. bull bbl. Aluminum frame. Sights: fixed white
dot. Grips: ultra thin cocobolo. Finish: two-tone. Made from
2009 to date.

MODEL EXECUTIVE . . . . . **NiB $2699 Ex $1980 Gd $1245**
Semi-automatic. SA. 2011 style platform. Caliber: 9mm, .40
S&W, or .45 ACP. 5-in. bull bbl. Polymer/steel wide body
frame. Sights: fiber optic front, adj. Bomar rear. Finish: hard
chrome. Made from 2001 to date.

MODEL G.I. . . . . **NiB $874 Ex $660 Gd $420**
Semi-automatic. SA. 1911 style platform. Caliber: .45 ACP.
5-in. bushing bbl. Steel frame. Sights: G.I. style fixed. Grips:
smooth wood. Finish: matte blue. Made from 2010 to 2015.

MODEL GP6 . . . . **NiB $660 Ex $555 Gd $405**
Semi-automatic. DA/SA. Mfg. by Grand Power. Caliber: 9mm.
4.25-in. bbl. Steel frame. Sights: adj. Weight: 26.1 oz. Finish:
blued. Made from 2009 to 2012.

MODEL GM . . . . **NiB $3680 Ex $3740 Gd $1730**
Semi-automatic. SA. 2011 style platform. Caliber: 9mm or .38
Super. 5.5-in. Trubor bbl. w/ compensator. Weight: 44.6 oz.
Polymer/steel wide body frame. Sights: C-More red dot. Finish:
blue/hard chrome. Made from 2012 to date.

MODEL GUARDIAN . . . . **NiB $1299 Ex $880 Gd $550**
Semi-automatic. SA. 1911 style platform. Caliber: 9mm or .45
ACP. 3.9-in. bull bbl. Steel frame. Sights: fixed white dot. Grips:
ultra thin cocobolo. Finish: two-tone.

MODEL GUARDIAN 2011 . **NiB $1899 Ex $1480 Gd $890**
Semi-automatic. SA. 2011 style platform. Caliber: 9mm. 3.9-in.
bull bbl. Polymer/steel wide body frame. Sights: fixed white
dot. Finish: two-tone. Made from 2016 to date.

MODEL HAWK . . . . **NiB $1899 Ex $1480 Gd $890**
Semi-automatic. SA. 1911 style platform. Caliber: various. 4.3-
in. bbl. Aluminum or steel frame. Made from 1993 to 1999.

MODEL HEX TACTICAL SS
Semi-automatic. SA. Caliber: 9mm or .45 ACP. 4- or 5-in. bushing bbl. Steel frame. Sights: ledge rear, fiber optic front. Grips:
VZ Alien (1911) or black (2011). Finish: black cerakote. Made
from 2016 to date.
1911 platform . . . . **NiB $2099 Ex $1950 Gd $1350**
2011 platform . . . . **NiB $2599 Ex $1950 Gd $1350**

MODEL LAWMAN . . . . **NiB $1299 Ex $930 Gd $580**
Semi-automatic. SA. 1911 style platform. Caliber: 9mm or .45
ACP. 3-, 4.15-, or 5-in. bull (3-in.) or bushing bbl. Steel frame.
Sights: ramped front, TAS rear. Grips: textured G10. Finish:
black cerakote. Made from 2005 to date.

MODEL LEGEND . . . . **NiB $1299 Ex $930 Gd $580**
Semi-automatic. SA. 1911 style platform. Caliber: 9mm, .38
Super, .40 S&W, or .45 ACP. 5-in. bull bbl. Steel frame. Sights:
competition. Finish: blued or hard chrome. Made from 2007
to 2015.

MODEL MARAUDER . . . . . . **NiB $2399 Ex $1580 Gd $990**
Semi-automatic. SA. 2011 style platform. Caliber: 9mm. 5-in.
bushing bbl. Polymer/steel wide body frame. Sights: fiber optic
front, TAS rear. Finish: black cerakote. Made from 2014 to date.

MODEL MATCH MASTER . **NiB $2999 Ex $2370 Gd $1500**
Semi-automatic. SA. 2011 style platform. Caliber: 9mm or .38
Super. 4.26-in. trubor bbl. Polymer/steel wide body frame.
Sights: C-More red dot. Finish: blue. Made from 2009 to date.

MODEL NEMESIS . . . . **NiB $870 Ex $730 Gd $455**
Semi-automatic. SA. 1911 style platform. Caliber: 7x23mm.
2.5-in. bbl. Steel frame. Made from 2010 to 2011.

MODEL NIGHT HAWK . . . . **NiB $2136 Ex $1400 Gd $860**
Semi-automatic. SA. 2011 style platform. Caliber: .45 ACP. 4.3-
in. bbl. Polymer/steel wide body frame. Finish: blued. Made
from 1997 to 1999.

MODEL NITRO 10 . . . . **NiB $1599 Ex $1130 Gd $710**
Semi-automatic. SA. 1911 style platform. Caliber: 10mm Auto.
5-in. bull or bushing bbl. Steel frame. Sights: ramped front,
ledge rear. Grips: textured G10. Finish: blued.

MODEL OFF DUTY . . . . **NiB $1599 Ex $1130 Gd $710**
Semi-automatic. SA. 1911 style platform. Caliber: 9mm or .45
ACP. 3-in. bbl. Steel frame. Sights: ramped front, ledge rear.
Grips: cocobolo. Finish: blued or hard chrome. Made from
2009 to 2013.

MODEL PERFECT 10 . . . . . NiB $2699 Ex $1955 Gd $1230
Semi-automatic. SA. 2011 style platform. Caliber: 10mm Auto. 6-in. bull bbl. Polymer/steel wide body frame. Sights: competition front, adj. Bomar rear. Finish: blue. Made from 2009 to date.

MODEL RANGE MASTER . . NiB $1599 Ex $1210 Gd $755
Semi-automatic. SA. 1911 style platform. Caliber: 9mm or .45 ACP. 5-in. bull bbl. Steel frame. Sights: competition front, LPA rear. Grips: textured cocobolo. Finish: matte blue. Made from 2005 to date.

MODEL RANGER II . . . . NiB $1181 Ex $880 Gd $555
Semi-automatic. SA. 1911 style platform. Caliber: 9mm, .40 S&W, or .45 ACP. 3.9- or 4.15-in. bull bbl. Steel frame. Sights: fixed. Weight: 29- oz. Grips: checkered double diamond mahogany. Finish: blued or hard chrome. Made from 2001 to 2015.

MODEL ROGUE . . . . NiB $1025 Ex $830 Gd $580
Semi-automatic. SA. 1911 style platform. Caliber: 9mm. 3-in. bull bbl. Aluminum frame. Sights: integral sights. Weight: 21 oz. Finish: two-tone. Made from 2009 to 2015.

MODEL SENTINEL . . . . NiB $2099 Ex $1780 Gd $1130
Semi-automatic. SA. 1911 style platform. Caliber: 9mm and .45 ACP. 5-in. bushing bbl. Sights: ramped tritium front, TAS tritium rear. Grips: textured G10. Finish: hard chrome. Made from 2007 to 2008.

MODEL SENTINEL PREMIER . . . . . NiB $2099 Ex $1780 Gd $1130
Semi-automatic. SA. 1911 style platform. Caliber: 9mm or .45 ACP. 5-in. bushing bbl. Steel frame. Sights: tritium. Finish: hard chrome. Made from 2009 to date.

MODEL SENTRY . . . . NiB $1755 Ex $1310 Gd $830
Semi-automatic. SA. 1911 style platform. Caliber: 9mm, .40 S&W or .45 ACP. 5-in. bushing bbl. Steel frame. Sights: adj. Weight: 35.3 oz. Grips: checkered cocobolo. Finish: blued or hard chrome. Made from 2009 to 2015.

MODEL SHADOW . . . . NiB $1475 Ex $1100 Gd $700
Semi-automatic. SA. 1911 style platform. Caliber: 9mm, .40 S&W or .45 ACP. 3-in. bull bbl. Aluminum frame. Sights: tritium. Weight: 23.4 oz. Grips: ultra thin G10. Finish: matte black. Made from 2010 to 2015.

MODEL SPARTAN . . . . NiB $745 Ex $580 Gd $635
Semi-automatic. SA. 1911 style platform. Caliber: 9mm or .45 ACP. 3-, 4-, or 5-in. bull bbl. Commander size steel frame. Sights: fixed. Weight: 32.7 oz. Grips: checkered double diamond mahogany. Finish: parkerized. Made from 2012 to date.

MODEL STEEL MASTER . . . NiB $2999 Ex $2370 Gd $1500
Semi-automatic. SA. 2011 style platform. Caliber: 9mm. 4.26-in. trubor bbl. Polymer/steel wide body frame. Sights: C-More red dot. Finish: blue. Made from 2009 to date.

MODEL TACTICAL . . . . NiB $2099 Ex $1580 Gd $990
Semi-automatic. SA. 2011 style platform. Caliber: 9mm, .40 S&W, or .45 ACP. 4-, 4.15-, or 5-in. bull bbl. Polymer/steel wide body frame. Sights: ramped front, ledge rear. Finish: black cerakote. Made from 2014 to date.

MODEL TACTICAL SS . . . . . NiB $1899 Ex $1460 Gd $950
Semi-automatic. SA. 1911 style platform. Caliber: 9mm or .45 ACP. 3.75-, 4.15-, or 5-in. thrd. bull bbl. Steel frame. Sights: ramped front, ledge rear. Grips: textured G10. Finish: black cerakote. Made from 2013 to date.

MODEL TARGET MASTER . . NiB $1799 Ex $1360 Gd $860
Semi-automatic. SA. 1911 style platform. Caliber: 9mm or .45 ACP. 6-in. bull bbl. Steel frame. Sights: aristocrat front, trisetrear. Grips: textured cocobolo. Finish: blue.

MODEL TEXICAN . . . . NiB $1344 Ex $1010 Gd $610
Revolver. SA. Colt SAA style platform. Caliber: .45 LC, 6-shot cylinder. 5.5-in. bbl. Steel frame. Sights: fixed. Grips: textured hard rubber. Weight: 36 oz. Finish: case hardened frame; blue bbl., cylinder, backstrap and trigger guard. Made from 2007 to 2010.

MODEL TROJAN . . . . NiB $1299 Ex $910 Gd $580
Semi-automatic. SA. 1911 style platform. Caliber: 9mm, .38 Super, .40 S&W, or .45 ACP. 5-in. bushing bbl. Steel frame. Sights: fixed rear, fiber optic front. Grips: cocobolo. Finish: blued. Made from 1999 to date.
Model Trojan Lite (aluminum frame), add $100

MODEL TRUBOR . . . . NiB $2899 Ex $2370 Gd $1500
Semi-automatic. SA. 2011 style platform. Caliber: 9mm or .38 Super. 5-in. trubor bbl. Polymer/steel wide body frame. Sights: C-More red dot. Finish: blue. Made from 1999 to date.

MODEL TRUSIGHT . . . . . . NiB $1985 Ex $1530 Gd $910
Semi-automatic. SA. 2011 style platform. Caliber: 9mm, .40 S&W, or .45 ACP. 5-in. bull bbl. w/ expansion chamber. Polymer/steel wide body frame. Sights: adj. competition. Finish: blued, polished slide. Made from 2006 to 2009.

MODEL USPSA DOUBLE STACK . . NiB $2425 Ex $2010 Gd $1210
Semi-automatic. SA. 2011 style platform. Caliber: 9mm, .40 S&W or .45 ACP. 5-in. bushing bbl. Polymer/steel wide body frame. Sights: adj. competition. Weight: 38.3 oz. Finish: blued. Made from 2009 to 2012.

MODEL USPSA SINGLE STACK . . . NiB $1976 Ex $1500 Gd $930
Semi-automatic. SA. 1911 style platform. Caliber: 9mm, .38 Super, .40 S&W or .45 ACP. 5-in. bushing bbl. Steel frame. Sights: adj. competition. Weight: 38.3 oz. Finish: blued. Made from 2009 to 2015.
[add these with STI]_____
Swiss Service Pistols
Note: Produced by SIG, Neuhausen, Switzerland; also see SIG and SIG Sauer.

MODEL P 210 . . . . NiB $3000 Ex $2500 Gd $1500
Semi-automatic. SA. 9mm Parabellum; 8-rnd magazine. 4.75-in. bbl. Frame-mounted manual safety. Finish: blued. Adopted 1949, in service thru 1975. Note: The Model P 210 was all adopted by the Danish Military as the Model M49.

STOEGER LUGERS — South Hackensack, NJ
Formerly manufactured by Stoeger Industries, So. Hackensack, New Jersey; later by Classic Arms, Union City, New Jersey.

AMERICAN EAGLE LUGER
Caliber: 9mm Para. 7-rnd. magazine, 4- or 6-in. bbl., 8.25 inches overall (with 4-inch bbl.). or 10.25 inches (with 6-inch bbl.). Weight: 30 or 32 oz. Checkered walnut grips. Stainless steel w/brushed or matte black finish. Intro. 1994. Disc.
Model P-08 stainless (4-inch bbl.) . . . . NiB $774 Ex $499 Gd $366
Navy model (6-inch bbl.) . . . . . NiB $854 Ex $811 Gd $400
w/matte black finish, add $85

STANDARD LUGER . . . . NiB $299 Ex $137 Gd $101
Caliber: .22 LR. 10-round magazine, 4.5- or 5.5-inch bbl., 8.88 inches overall (with 4.5-inch bbl.). Weight: 29.5 oz. (with 4.5-inch bbl.). Fixed sights. Black finish. Smooth wood grips. Made 1969 to 1986.

STEEL FRAME LUGER . . . . NiB $290 Ex $133 Gd $95
Caliber: .22 LR. 10-round magazine, 4.5-inch bbl., 8.88 inches overall. Blued finish. Checkered wood grips. Features one piece forged and machined steel frame. Made 1980 to 1986.

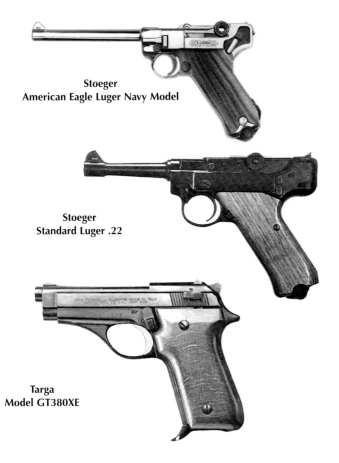

**Stoeger
American Eagle Luger Navy Model**

**Stoeger
Standard Luger .22**

**Targa
Model GT380XE**

TARGET LUGER
.22 AUTO PISTOL . . . . NiB $227 Ex $160 Gd $110
Same as Standard Luger .22 except has target sights 9.38 inches overall w/4.5-inch bbl., Checkered wood grips. Made from 1975 to 1986.

SWISS SERVICE PISTOLS — Switzerland

NOTE: *Produced by SIG, Neuhausen, Switzerland; also see SIG and SIG Sauer.*

MODEL P 210 . . . . NiB $3000 Ex $2500 Gd $1500
Semi-automatic. SA. 9mm Parabellum; 8-rnd magazine. 4.75-in. bbl. Frame-mounted manual safety. Finish: blued. Adopted 1949, in service thru 1975. Note: The Model P 210 was adopted by the Danish Military as the Model M49.

TARGA PISTOLS — Italy
Manufactured by Armi Tanfoglio Guiseppe.
MODEL GT26S
AUTO PISTOL . . . . NiB $166 Ex $98 Gd $79
Caliber: .25 ACP. Six-round magazine, 2.5-inch bbl., 4.63 inches overall. Weight: 15 oz. fixed sights. Checkered composition grips. Blued or chrome finish. Disc. 1990.

MODEL GT32 AUTO PISTOL
Caliber: .32 ACP. Six-round magazine, 4.88-inch bbl., 7.38 inches overall. Weight: 26 oz. fixed sights. Checkered composition or walnut grips. Blued or chrome finish.

Blued finished . . . . NiB $166 Ex $109 Gd $88
Chrome finish . . . . NiB $179 Ex $118 Gd $89

MODEL GT380 AUTOMATIC PISTOL
Same as the Targa GT32 except chambered for .380 ACP.
Blued finish. . . . . NiB $179 Ex $118 Gd $89
Chrome finish . . . . NiB $197 Ex $137 Gd $101

MODEL GT380XE
AUTOMATIC PISTOL . . . . NiB $220 Ex $165 Gd $101
Caliber: .380 ACP. 11-round magazine, 3.75-inch bbl., 7.38 inches overall. Weight: 28 oz. Fixed sights. Blued or satin nickel finish. Smooth wooden grips. Made from 1980 to 1990.

TAURUS INT'L. MFG. — Porto Alegre, Brazil
Manufactured by FORJAS TAURUS S.A. Porto Alegre, Brazil; imported Miami, FL.

NOTE: *For ease in locating a particular Taurus handgun, the listings are divided into two groupings: Automatic Pistols (page 192) and Revolvers (below). For a complete handgun listing, please refer to the index.*

- REVOLVERS -

MODEL GAUCHO. . . . . NiB $425 Ex $285 Gd $245
SA. Colt SAA reproduction. Caliber: .357 Mag., .44-40, or .45 LC. Six-round cylinder, 4.75-, 5.5-, 7.5- or 12-in. bbl. Blued, case color, matte or bright stainless finish. Made from 2005 to 2007.

MODEL 17C . . . . NiB $300 Ex $190 Gd $170
SA/DA. Caliber: .17 HMR or .17 Mach 2. 8-round cylinder, 2-, 4-, 5-in. bbl. Adj. sights, rubber grips. Blued finish. Made from 2003 to 2007.
Ultra-Lite (2-in. bbl.). . . . . NiB $340 Ex $200 Gd $180
Polished stainless finish. . . . . . . NiB $330 Ex $195 Gd $175

MODEL 17IB . . . . NiB $295 Ex $185 Gd $170
SA/DA. Caliber: .17 HMR or .17 Mach 2. 8- or 9-round cylinder, 1.75-in. bbl. Adj. sights, rubber grips. Blued finish. Made from 2005 to 2007.
Matte stainless finish. . . . . NiB $330 Ex $195 Gd $175

MODEL 17 TRACKER. . . . . NiB $481 Ex $265 Gd $225
SA/DA. Caliber: .17 HMR. 7-round cylinder, 4-, 6.5-, 8.6-in. vent rib bbl. Adj. sights, rubber grips. Made from 2003 to date.
Matte stainless, add $50
Two-tone finish, add $50
**Silhoutte model (12-in. bbl., optic mount,
     discont. 2004).** . . . . NiB $320 Ex $205 Gd $185

MODEL 21T TRACKER. . . . . . . NiB $330 Ex $205 Gd $185
SA/DA. Caliber: .218 Bee. 7-round cylinder, 6.5-in. vent rib bbl. Adj. sights, rubber grips. Made from 2003 to 2005.

MODEL 22H
RAGING HORNET. . . . . NiB $800 Ex $530 Gd $455
SA/DA. Caliber: .22 Hornet. 8-round cylinder, 10-in. vent rib bbl. Adj. sights, optic mount, rubber grips. Made from 1999 to 2004.

MODEL 30C RAGING THIRTY
HUNTER . . . . NiB $800 Ex $530 Gd $455
SA/DA. Caliber: .30 Carbine. 8-round cylinder, 12-in. vent rib full lug bbl. Adj. sights, optic mount, adj. trigger, rubber grips. Made from 2003 to 2004.
**Silhoutte model (12-in. half lug bbl., optic mount,
     discont. 2004).** . . . . NiB $795 Ex $525 Gd $450

MODEL 44 DA REVOLVER
Caliber: .44 Mag. Six-round cylinder, 4-, 6.5-, or 8.38-inch bbl. Weight: 44.75 oz., 52.5 or 57.25 oz. Brazilian hardwood grips. Blued or stainless steel finish. Made from 1994 to 2004.
Blued finish. . . . . NiB $433 Ex $327 Gd $220

Taurus Model .44

Taurus Model 66

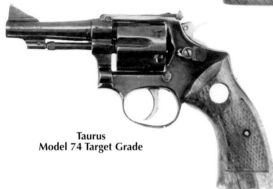

Taurus
Model 74 Target Grade

Taurus Model 80

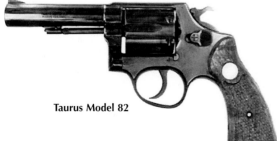

Taurus Model 82

Model 44SS Stainless finish
(intro. 1994) . . . . NiB $600 Ex $487 Gd $274

MODEL 44C TRACKER. . . . . . . NiB $646 Ex $430 Gd $380
SA/DA. Caliber: .44 Mag. 5-round cylinder, 4-in. ported bbl.
Blued or matte stainless finish. Made from 2005 to date.

MODEL 45-410 "THE JUDGE". . . . NiB $610 Ex $355 Gd $300
SA/DA. Caliber: .45 LC/.410 3-in. chamber. 5-round cylinder,
2.5-, 3-, 6.5-in. bbl. Blued or matte stainless finish. Made from
2006 to date.
Ultra-Lite . . . . NiB $580 Ex $400 Gd $355

MODEL 45-410 "THE JUDGE"
PUBLIC DEFENDER . . . . NiB $610 Ex $355 Gd $300
SA/DA. Caliber: .45 LC/.410 2.5-in. chamber. 5-round stainless
or titanium cylinder, 2-in. bbl. smaller hammer. Blued or matte
stainless finish. Made from 2009 to date.
Ultra-Lite . . . . NiB $580 Ex $400 Gd $355
Polymer frame. . . . . NiB $550 Ex $400 Gd $355

MODEL 65 DA REVOLVER
Caliber: .357 Magnum. 6-round cylinder, 3- or 4-inch bbl.,
weight: 32 oz. Front ramp sight, square notch rear. Checkered
walnut target grip. Royal blued or satin nickel finish. Imported
1992 to 1997 and from 1999 to date.
Blue finish. . . . . NiB $398 Ex $289 Gd $171
Stainless finish. . . . . NiB $427 Ex $351 Gd $212

MODEL 66 DA REVOLVER
Calibers: .357 Magnum, .38 Special. Six-round cylinder, 3-, 4-
and 6-inch bbl., weight: 35 oz. Serrated ramp front sight, rear
click adj. Checkered walnut grips. Royal blued or nickel finish.
Imported 1992-1997 and from 1999 to date.
Blue finish. . . . . NiB $500 Ex $351 Gd $212
Model 66SS Stainless finish. . . . . NiB $550 Ex $398 Gd $229

MODEL 73 DA REVOLVER . . . . NiB $211 Ex $121 Gd $101
Caliber: .32 Long. Six-round cylinder, 3-inch heavy bbl., weight:
20 oz. Checkered grips. Blued or satin nickel finish. Disc. 1993.

MODEL 76 TARGET . . . . NiB $244 Ex $279 Gd $118
Caliber: .32 S&W Long. Six-round cylinder, 3-inch bbl., 8.25
inches overall. Weight: 20 oz. Adj. rear sight, ramp front. Blued or
nickel finish. Checkered walnut grips. Made from 1971 to 1990.

MODEL 80 DA REVOLVER
Caliber: .38 Special. Six-round cylinder, bbl. lengths: 3, 4 inches, 9.25 inches overall (with 4-inch bbl.). Weight: 30 oz. (with
4-inch bbl.) Fixed sights. Blued or nickel finish. Checkered
walnut grips. Made 1996 to 1997.
Blued finish. . . . . NiB $214 Ex $140 Gd $98
Model 80SS Stainless finish. . . . . NiB $431 Ex $337 Gd $258

MODEL 82 HEAVY BARREL
Same as Model 80 except has heavy bbl., weight: 33 oz. w/4-
inch bbl., Made from 1971 to date.
Blued finish. . . . . NiB $366 Ex $290 Gd $212
Model 82SS Stainless finish
(intro. 1993) . . . . NiB $437 Ex $327 Gd $259

MODEL 83 HEAVY BARREL TARGET GRADE
Same as Model 84 except has heavy bbl., weight: 34.5 oz.
Made from 1977 to date.
Blued finish. . . . . NiB $255 Ex $160 Gd $105
Model 83SS Stainless finish. . . . . NiB $281 Ex $198 Gd $128

MODEL 84 TARGET
GRADE REVOLVER . . . . NiB $312 Ex $235 Gd $170
Caliber: .38 Special. Six-round cylinder, 4-inch bbl., 9.25
inches overall. Weight: 31 oz. Adj. rear sight, ramp front. Blued
or nickel finish. Checkered walnut grips. from 1971 to 1989.

MODEL 85 DA REVOLVER
Caliber: .38 Special. Five-round cylinder, 2- or 3-inch. bbl.,
weight: 21 oz. Fixed sights. Checkered walnut grips. Blued,

Taurus Model 83

Taurus Model 84

Taurus
Model 85 Concealed Hammer

Taurus Model 86

Taurus
Model 85 w/Spur Hammer

satin nickel or stainless-steel finish. Model 85CH is the same as the standard version except for concealed hammer. Made from 1997 to 2012.

Blued or satin nickel finish . . . . NiB $377 Ex $302 Gd $143
Stainless steel finish . . . . NiB $437 Ex $362 Gd $189
Titanium Ultra-Lightweight . . . . NiB $540 Ex $370 Gd $320

MODEL 85PLYB2
"PROTECTOR PLY" . . . . NiB $355 Ex $230 Gd $210
SA/DA. Caliber: .38 Spl.+P. Five-round blued or matte stainless cylinder, 1.25- or 1.75-in. vent rib bbl., polymer frame. Weight: 16.5 oz. Fixed fiber optic sights. Made from 2011 to 2012.

MODEL VIEW (85VTA) . . . . NiB $599 Ex $500 Gd $420
Revolver. DAO. Caliber: .38 Spl., 5-shot cylinder. 1.41-in. bbl. Weight: 8 oz. Unique clear Lexan side plate, stainless frame, bobbed hammer, small checkered polymer grip. Sights: fixed. Finish: matte stainless, gold color hammer. Made 2014 only.

MODEL 86 CUSTOM TARGET
DA REVOLVER . . . . NiB $301 Ex $208 Gd $110
Caliber: .38 Special. Six-round cylinder, 6-inch bbl., 11.25 inches overall. Weight: 34 oz. Adj. rear sight, Partridge-type front. Blued finish. Checkered walnut grips. Made 1971-94.

MODEL 94 DA REVOLVER
Same as Model 74 except .22 LR. w/9-round cylinder, 3- or 4-inch bbl., weight: 25 oz. Blued or stainless finish. Made from 1971 to date.

Blued finish . . . . NiB $362 Ex $306 Gd $219
Model 94SS Stainless finish . . . . NiB $386 Ex $348 Gd $255

MODEL 96 TARGET SCOUT . . . NiB $301 Ex $209 Gd $112
Same as Model 86 except in .22 LR. Made from 1971 to 1998.

MODEL 380 IB . . . . NiB $433 Ex $310 Gd $205
Revolver. DAO. Caliber: .380 ACP, 5-shot cylinder. 1.75-in. bbl. Weight: 15.5 oz. Bobbed hammer. Sights: fixed. Finish: blued. Made from 2012 to date.

MODEL 431 DA REVOLVER
Caliber: .44 Spec. Five-round cylinder, 3- or 4-inch solid-rib bbl. w/ejector shroud. Weight: 35 oz. w/4-inch bbl., Serrated ramp front sight, notched topstrap rear. Blued or stainless finish. Made 1992 to 1997.

Blued finish . . . . NiB $239 Ex $198 Gd $144
Stainless finish . . . . NiB $434 Ex $306 Gd $265

MODEL 441 DA REVOLVER
Similar to the Model 431 except w/6-inch bbl. and fully adj. target sights. Weight: 40 oz. Made from 1991 to 1997.

Blued finish . . . . NiB $306 Ex $237 Gd $144
Stainless finish . . . . NiB $434 Ex $306 Gd $225

MODEL 445 DA REVOLVER
Caliber: .44 Special. Five-round cylinder, 2-inch bbl., 6.75 inches overall. Weight: 28.25 oz. Serrated ramp front sight, notched frame rear. Standard or concealed hammer. Santoprene I grips. Blue or stainless finish. Imported from 1997 to 2003.

Blued finish . . . . NiB $306 Ex $239 Gd $190
Stainless finish . . . . NiB $342 Ex $265 Gd $204

MODEL 454 DA RAGING BULL REVOLVER
Caliber: .454 Casull. Five-round cylinder, ported 6.5- or 8.4-inch vent rib bbl., 12 inches overall (w/6.5-inch bbl.). Weight: 53 or 63 oz. Partridge front sight, micrometer adj. rear. Santoprene I or walnut grips. Blue or stainless finish. Imported 1997 to date.

Blued finish . . . . NiB $862 Ex $730 Gd $587
Stainless finish . . . . NiB $877 Ex $791 Gd $648

MODEL 605 POLYMER
PROTECTOR PLY . . . . NiB $371 Ex $320 Gd $235
Revolver. DA/SA. Caliber: .357 Mag., 5-shot cylinder. 2-in. bbl. Weight: 19.75 oz. Polymer frame, blued or stainless steel cylinder. Sights: fixed. Finish: matte stainless/blued or blued. Made from 2011 to date.

stainless cylinder, add $20

MODEL 669/669VR DA REVOLVER

Caliber: .357 Mag. Six-round cylinder, 4- or 6-inch solid-rib bbl. w/ejector shroud Model 669VR has vent rib bbl., weight: 37 oz. w/4-inch bbl., Serrated ramp front sight, micro-adj. rear. Royal blued or stainless finish. Checkered Brazilian hardwood grips. Made from 1989 to 1998.

Blued finish. . . . . NiB $283 Ex $214 Gd $165
Stainless finish. . . . . NiB $362 Ex $286 Gd $240
Model 669VR, blued finish . . . . NiB $301 Ex $225 Gd $175
Model 669VR, stainless finish . . NiB $362 Ex $286 Gd $255

MODEL 741/761 DA REVOLVER

Caliber: .32 H&R Mag. Six-round cylinder, 3- or 4-inch solid-rib bbl. w/ejector shroud. Weight: 20 oz. w/3-inch bbl., Serrated ramp front sight, micro-adj. rear. Blued or stainless finish. Checkered Brazilian hardwood grips. Made 1991-97.

Blued finish. . . . . NiB $225 Ex $129 Gd $90
Stainless finish . . . . NiB $291 Ex $204 Gd $150
MODEL 761(6-inch bbl.,
    34 oz., blued finish) . . . . NiB $281 Ex $204 Gd $143

MODEL 941 TARGET REVOLVER

Caliber: .22 Magnum. Eight-round cylinder. Solid-rib bbl. w/ ejector shroud. Micro-adj. rear sight. Brazilian hardwood grips. Blued or stainless finish.

Blued finish. . . . . NiB $357 Ex $306 Gd $204
Stainless finish. . . . . NiB $408 Ex $365 Gd $274

- AUTOMATIC PISTOLS -

CURVE . . . . NiB $392 Ex $300 Gd $250
Semi-automatic. DAO. Caliber: .380 ACP, 6-rnd. magazine. 2.5-in. bbl. Weight: 10.2 oz. Unique polymer frame curved to fit body when carry. Finish: blued. Carry clip. Integrated laser and light. Made from 2015 to date.

MODEL 22 PLY . . . . NiB $285 Ex $177 Gd $101
DAO. Caliber: .22 LR. 8-round magazine, tip-up 2.3-in. bbl., polymer frame. Weight: 10.8 oz. Fixed sights. Made from 2012 to date.

MODEL 25 PLY . . . . NiB $285 Ex $177 Gd $101
Similar to Model 22 PLY model except chambered in .25 ACP. Made from 2012 to date.

MODEL PT-22 . . . . NiB $285 Ex $177 Gd $101
SA/DA. Caliber: .22 LR. Nine-round magazine, 2.75-inch bbl., weight: 12.3 oz. Fixed open sights. Brazilian hardwood grips. Blued finish. Made from 1991 to date.

MODEL PT-24/7 . . . . NiB $455 Ex $300 Gd $260
DAO. Caliber: 9mm, .40 S&W or .45 ACP. 10-, 12-, 15, or 17-round magazine, 4-in. bbl. Polymer frame w/blued or stainless slide. 3-dot sights. Accessory rail. Made from 2004 to 2005.

MODEL PT-24/7

PRO FULL SIZE . . . . NiB $420 Ex $290 Gd $240
SA with DA second strike trigger. Caliber: 9mm, .40 S&W or .45 ACP. 10-, 12-, 15, or17-round magazine, 4-in. bbl. Polymer frame w/blued or stainless slide. 3-dot sights. Acessory rail. Made from 2006 to 2010.
Pro Compact (3.1-in. bbl.) . . . . NiB $420 Ex $280 Gd $250
Pro Long Slide (5.2-in. bbl.) . . . NiB $450 Ex $295 Gd $255

MODEL PT-24/7 G2 . . . . NiB $530 Ex $300 Gd $260
SA with DA second strike trigger. Caliber: 9mm, .40 S&W or .45 ACP. 10-, 12-, 15, or17-round magazine, 4-in. bbl. Polymer frame w/interchangeable backstraps, ambidextrous controls, blued or stainless slide. 3-dot sights. Acessory rail. Made from 2011 to date.
Compact (3.1-in. bbl.) . . . . NiB $530 Ex $300 Gd $260

MODEL PT-24/7 OSS . . . . NiB $480 Ex $330 Gd $290
Similar to PT-24/7 Pro Full Size except w/5.25-in. bbl. and tan or black polymer frame. Made from 2007 to 2010.

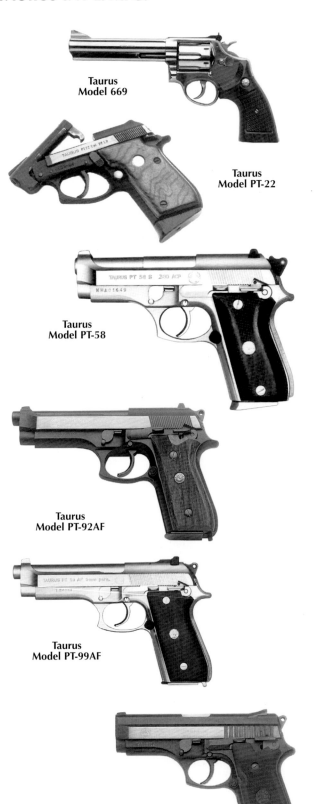

Taurus
Model 669

Taurus
Model PT-22

Taurus
Model PT-58

Taurus
Model PT-92AF

Taurus
Model PT-99AF

Taurus
Model PT-908

MODEL PT-25 . . . . NiB $285 Ex $170 Gd $92
Same general specifications as Model PT 22 except in .25 ACP w/eight-round magazine. Made from 1992 to date.

MODEL PT-58 . . . . NiB $408 Ex $332 Gd $240
Caliber: .380 ACP. Twelve-round magazine, 4-inch bbl., 7.2 inches overall. Weight: 30 oz. Blade front sight, rear adj. for windage w/3-dot sighting system. Blued, satin nickel or stainless finish. Made from 1988 to 1996.

MODEL PT-92AF
SA/DA. Similar to Beretta M92 SB-F. Caliber: 9mm Para. 15-round magazine, 5-inch bbl., 8.5 inches overall. Weight: 24 oz. Blade front sight, notched bar rear. Smooth Brazilian walnut grips. Blued, satin nickel or stainless finish. Made from 1991 to date.
Blued finish. . . . . NiB $670 Ex $377 Gd $286
Satin nickel finish . . . . NiB $720 Ex $418 Gd $319
Stainless finish. . . . . NiB $679 Ex $398 Gd $306
Deluxe (blue/gold or
   stainless/gold). . . . . NiB $520 Ex $390 Gd $300

MODEL PT-92AFC COMPACT PISTOL
Same general specs as Model PT-92AF except w/13-round magazine, 4.25-inch bbl., 7.5 inches overall. Weight: 31 oz. Made 1991 to 1996
Blued finish. . . . . NiB $362 Ex $283 Gd $214
Satin nickel finish . . . . NiB $408 Ex $328 Gd $266
Stainless finish. . . . . NiB $434 Ex $346 Gd $220

MODEL PT-99AF
SEMI-AUTOMATIC PISTOL. . . . NiB $530 Ex $437 Gd $301
Same general specifications as Model PT-92AF except rear sight is adj. for elevation and windage, and finish is blued or satin nickel.

MODEL PT-100 DA AUTOMATIC PISTOL
Caliber: .40 S&W. Eleven-round magazine, 5-inch bbl., weight: 34 oz. Fixed front sight, adj. rear w/3-dot system. Smooth hardwood grip. Blued, satin nickel or stainless finish. Made from 1991 to 1997.
Blued finish. . . . . NiB $500 Ex $444 Gd $362
Satin finish . . . . NiB $546 Ex $469 Gd $377
Stainless finish. . . . . NiB $536 Ex $444 Gd $367

MODEL PT-101 DA AUTOMATIC PISTOL
Same general specifications as Model 100 except w/micrometer click adj. sights. Made from 1992 to 1996.
Blued finish. . . . . NiB $536 Ex $444 Gd $367
Satin nickel finish . . . . NiB $576 Ex $453 Gd $367
Stainless finish. . . . . NiB $536 Ex $444 Gd $367

MODEL PT-111 MILLENNIUM DAO PISTOL
Caliber: 9mm Parabellum. 10-round magazine, 3.12-inch bbl., 6 inches overall. Weight: 19.1 oz. Fixed low-profile sights w/3-dot system. Black polymer grip/frame. Blue or stainless slide. Imported from 1998 to 2004.
Blue finish. . . . . NiB $362 Ex $265 Gd $130
Stainless finish. . . . . NiB $380 Ex $286 Gd $185

MODEL PT-132 . . . . NiB $355 Ex $265 Gd $210
Semi-automatic. DAO. Caliber: .32 ACP, 10-rnd. magazine. 4-in. bbl. Weight: 16 oz. Polymer frame. Finish: blued or stainless steel. Made from 2001 to 2004.

MODEL PT-132 MILLENNIUM PRO . NiB $375 Ex $300 Gd $225
Similar to PT-132 expect DA/SA trigger, Heinie sights. Made from 2005 to 2011.

MODEL PT-138 . . . . NiB $350 Ex $255 Gd $180
Similar to PT-132 except .380 ACP. Made from 1998 to 2004.
PT-140 (.40 S&W, 1999-2004) . NiB $350 Ex $255 Gd $180
PT-145 (.45 ACP, 2000-2003) . . NiB $400 Ex $315 Gd $245

MODEL PT-138 MILLENNIUM PRO . . . NiB $395 Ex $300 Gd $230
Similar to PT-132 Millennium Pro except .380 ACP. Made from 2005 to 2011.
PT-140 Millennium Pro (.40 S&W, 2003-2012) . NiB $395 Ex $290 Gd $215
PT-145 Millennium Pro (.45 ACP, 2003-2012) . . NiB $395 Ex $290 Gd $215

MODEL PT-609 . . . . NIB $535 Ex $435 Gd $330
Semi-automatic. DA/SA. Caliber: 9mm, 13-rnd. magazine. 3.25-in. bbl. Weight: 19.7 oz. Polymer frame. Made from 2007 to 2010.

MODEL PT-709 SLIM . . . . NIB $316 Ex $300 Gd $200
Semi-automatic. DA/SA w/ Strike Two capability. Caliber: 9mm, 7-rnd. magazine. 3-in. bbl. Weight: 19 oz. Polymer frame. Sights: fixed. Finish: black or stainless. Made from 2008 to 2012, reintro. 2014 to date.

MODEL PT-732 TCP . . . . NIB $295 Ex $300 Gd $200
Semi-automatic. DAO. Caliber: .32 ACP, 6-rnd. magazine. 3.3-in. bbl. Weight: 10.2 oz. Polymer frame. Sights: fixed. Finish: black or pink. Made from 2011 to 2012.
Model PT-7328 TCP (.380 ACP) NiB $356 Ex $260 Gd $175

MODEL PT-740 SLIM . . . . NIB $316 Ex $300 Gd $200
Similar to PT-709 SLIM except in .40 S&W, 6-rnd. magazine. Made from 2011 to date.

MODEL PT-809 . . . . NIB $486 Ex $350 Gd $225
Semi-automatic. DA/SA w/ Strike Two capability. Caliber: 9mm, 17-rnd. magazine. 4-in. bbl. Weight: 30.2 oz. Polymer frame w/ accessory rail. Ambidextrous 3-position safety. External hammer. Sights: Novak fixed. Finish: black tennifer. Made from 2007 to date.
Model PT-809 Compact (3.5-in. bbl.) . NiB $486 Ex $350 Gd $225
Model PT-840 (.40 S&W) . . . . . NiB $486 Ex $350 Gd $225
Model PT-840 Compact (3.5-in. bbl.) . NiB $486 Ex $350 Gd $225
Model PT-845 (.45 ACP) . . . . . . NiB $486 Ex $350 Gd $225

MODEL PT-908 SEMIAUTOMATIC PISTOL
Caliber: 9mm Para. Eight-round magazine, 3.8-inch bbl., 7 inches overall. Weight: 30 oz. Post front sight, drift-adj. combat rear w/3-dot system. Blued, satin nickel or stainless finish. Made 1993 to 1997.
Blued finish. . . . . NiB $357 Ex $286 Gd $204
Satin nickel finish . . . . NiB $388 Ex $316 Gd $205
Stainless finish. . . . . NiB $431 Ex $321 Gd $265

MODEL PT-911 COMPACT SEMIAUTOMATIC PISTOL
Caliber: 9mm Parabellum. 10-round magazine, 3.75-inch bbl., 7.05 inches overall. Weight: 28.2 oz. Fixed low-profile sights w/3-dot system. Santoprene II grips. Blue or stainless finish. Imported from 1997 to date.
Blued finish. . . . . NiB $546 Ex $408 Gd $270
Stainless finish. . . . . NiB $546 Ex $408 Gd $270

MODEL PT-938 COMPACT SEMIAUTOMATIC PISTOL
Caliber: 380 ACP. 10-round magazine, 3.72-inch bbl., 6.75 inches overall. Weight: 27 oz. Fixed low-profile sights w/3-dot system. Santoprene II grips. Blue or stainless finish. Imported 1997 to 2005.
Blue finish. . . . . NiB $499 Ex $357 Gd $265
Stainless finish. . . . . NiB $469 Ex $377 Gd $286

MODEL PT-940 COMPACT SEMIAUTOMATIC PISTOL
Caliber: .40 S&W. 10-round magazine, 3.75-inch bbl., 7.05 inches overall. Weight: 28.2 oz. Fixed low-profile sights w/3-dot system. Santoprene II grips. Blue or stainless finish. Imported from 1997 to date.
Blue finish. . . . . NiB $546 Ex $437 Gd $290
Stainless finish. . . . . NiB $571 Ex $499 Gd $316

MODEL PT-945 COMPACT SEMIAUTOMATIC PISTOL
Caliber: .45 ACP. Eight-round magazine, 4.25-inch bbl., 7.48 inches overall. Weight: 29.5 oz. Fixed low-profile sights

w/3-dot system. Santoprene II grips. Blue or stainless finish. Imported from 1995 to date.

Blue finish. . . . . .NiB $601 Ex $530 Gd $377
Stainless finish. . . . . .NiB $587 Ex $437 Gd $316

MODEL PT-957 . . . . NiB $523 Ex $365 Gd $240
Similar to PT-945 except in .357 SIG. Made from 1999 to 2003.

MODEL PT-1911 . . . . NiB $729 Ex $555 Gd $370
Semi-automatic. SA. Colt 1911 style platform. Caliber: .38 Super, 9mm, .40 S&W or .45 ACP; 8- (.40 S&W, .45 ACP) or 9- (.38 Super, 9mm) rnd. magazine. 5-in. bbl. Weight: 32 oz. Steel or aluminum frame, steel slide w/ front/rear serrations. Sights: Heinie fixed. Grips: wood. Finish: blued or two-tone. Made from 2005 to date.

MODEL PT-1911 COMPACT (4.25-IN. BBL.). . . NiB $490 Ex $360 Gd $275
stainless finish, add $180
PT-1911FS (fixed sights, .45 ACP only)NiB $685 Ex $460 Gd $355

MODEL PT-1911B-1. . . . . NiB $834 Ex $750 Gd $600
Similar to PT-1911 except with accessory rail. Made from 2009 to 2011.

MODEL PT-2011 DT INTEGRAL NiB $570 Ex $420 Gd $290
Semi-automatic. DA/SA w/ trigger safety. Caliber: .380 ACP or 9mm; 11- (.380 ACP) or 13/15- (9mm) rnd. magazine. 3.2-in. bbl. Weight: 21-24 oz. Aluminum frame, steel slide. Sights: adj. rear. Grips: black polymer. Finish: matte black or stainless. Made 2012 only.

MODEL PT-2011 DT HYBRID . NiB $585 Ex $430 Gd $290
Similar to Model PT-2011 DT Integral except 9mm or .40 S&W. Made from 2012 to 2013.

MODEL PT-2045 . . . . NiB $570 Ex $420 Gd $290
Semi-automatic. DA/SA. Caliber: .45 ACP; 12-rnd. magazine. 4.2-in. bbl. Weight: 32 oz. Combined features of 800 series, 24/7 series and 24/7 OSS series. Made in 2009 only.

TEXAS ARMS — Waco, TX

DEFENDER DERRINGER. . . . . .NiB $306 Ex $218 Gd $120
Calibers: 9mm, .357 Mag., .44 Mag., .45 ACP, .45 Colt/.410. Three-inch bbl., 5 inches overall. Weight: 21 oz. Blade front sight, fixed rear. Matte gun-metal gray finish. Smooth grips. Made from 1993 to 1999.

TEXAS LONGHORN ARMS — Richmond, TX

"THE JEZEBEL" PISTOL. . . . . .NiB $337 Ex $265 Gd $200
Top-break, single-shot. Caliber: .22 Short, Long or LR. Six-inch half-round bbl., 8 inches overall. Weight: 15 oz. Bead front sight, adj. rear. One-piece walnut grip. Stainless finish. Intro. in 1987.

SA REVOLVER CASED SET
Set contains one each of the Texas Longhorn Single Actions. Each chambered in the same caliber and w/the same serial number. Intro. in 1984.
Standard set . . . . .NiB $1620 Ex $1400 Gd $1000
Engraved set . . . . .NiB $1820 Ex $1615 Gd $1219

**SOUTH TEXAS ARMY LIMITED
EDITION SA REVOLVER**. . . NiB $1840 Ex $1418 Gd $1120
Calibers: All popular centerfire pistol calibers. Six-round cylinder, 4.75-inch bbl.,10.25 inches overall. Weight: 40 oz. Fixed sights. Color casehardened frame. One-piece deluxe walnut grips. Blued bbl., Intro. in 1984.

**SESQUICENTENNIAL
SA REVOLVER**. . . . . .NiB $2613 Ex $2114 Gd $1489

Thompson/Center
Vent Rib Barrel

TThompson/Center
Contender Bull Barrel

Same as South Texas Army Limited Edition except engraved and nickel-plated w/one-piece ivory grip. Intro. in 1986.

**TEXAS BORDER SPECIAL
SA REVOLVER**. . . . . .NiB $1744 Ex $1316 Gd $954
Same as South Texas Army Limited Edition except w/3.5-inch bbl. and bird's-head grips. Intro. in 1984.

**WEST TEXAS FLAT TOP
TARGET SA REVOLVER**. . . . .NiB $1633 Ex $1316 Gd $896
Same as South TExas Army Limited Edition except w/choice of bbl. lengths from 7 .5 to 15 inches. Same special features w/ flat-top style frame and adj. rear sight. Intro. in 1984.

THOMPSON — West Hurley, NY
Manufactured by Auto-Ordnance Corporation; owned by Kahr Arms. Also see Auto-Ordnance handgun section.

MODEL 1927A-5 . . . . .NiB $1071 Ex $855 Gd $668
Similar to Thompson Model 1928A submachine gun except has no provision for automatic firing, does not have detachable buttstock. Caliber: .45 Auto, 20-round detachable box magazine (5-, 15- and 30-round box magazines, 39-round drum also available), 13-inch finned bbl., overall length: 26 inches. Weight: About 6.75 lbs. Adj. rear sight, blade front. Blued finish. Walnut grips. Intro. in 1977.

THOMPSON/CENTER ARMS — Rochester, NH
Acquired by Smith & Wesson in 2006.

CONTENDER SINGLE-SHOT PISTOL
Break frame, underlever action. Calibers: (rimfire) .22 LR. .22 WMR, 5mm RRM; (standard centerfire), .218 Bee, .22 Hornet, .22 Rem. Jet, .221 Fireball, .222 Rem., .25-35, .256 Win. Mag., .30 M1 Carbine, .30-30, .38 Auto, .38 Special .357 Mag./ Hot Shot, 9mm Para., .45 Auto, .45 Colt, .44 Magnum/Hot Shot; (wildcat centerfire) .17 Ackley Bee, .17 Bumblebee, .17 Hornet, .17 K Hornet, .17 Mach IV, .17-.222, .17-.223, .22 K Hornet, .30 Herrett, .357 Herrett, .357-4 B&D. Interchangeable bbls.: 8.75- or 10-inch standard octagon (.357 Mag., .44 Mag.

and .45 Colt available w/detachable choke for use w/Hot Shot cartridges); 10-inch w/vent rib and detachable internal choke tube for Hot Shots, .357 and .44 Magnum only; 10-inch bull bbl., .30 or .357 Herrett only. 13.5 inches overall w/10-inch bbl., Weight: 43 oz. (w/standard 10-inch bbl.). Adj. rear sight, ramp front; vent rib model has folding rear sight, adj. front; bull bbl., available w/or w/o sights. Lobo 1.5/ scope and mount (add $40 to value). Blued finish. Receiver photoengraved. Checkered walnut thumbrest grip and forearm (pre-1972 model has different grip w/silver grip cap). Made from 1967 to date, w/the following revisions and variations.

Standard model.	NiB $419	Ex $321	Gd $204
Vent rib model	NiB $439	Ex $342	Gd $230
Bull bbl. model, w/sights	NiB $434	Ex $326	Gd $214
Bull bbl. model, without sights	NiB $431	Ex $316	Gd $204
Extra standard bbl, add			$255
Extra vent rib or bull bbl, add			$306

CONTENDER BULL BARREL . . . NiB $408 Ex $321 Gd $204
Caliber offerings of the bull bbl. version Expanded in 1973 and 1978, making it the Contender model w/the widest range of caliber options: .22 LR, .22 Win. Mag., .22 Hornet, .223 Rem., 7mm T.C.U., 7x30 Waters, .30 M1 Carbine, .30-30 Win., .32 H&R Mag., .32-20 Win., .357 Rem. Max., .357 Mag., 10mm Auto, .44 Magnum, .445 Super Magnum. 10-inch heavy bbl., Partridge-style iron sights. Contoured Competitor grip. Blued finish.

CONTENDER INTERNAL
CHOKE MODEL . . . . NiB $434 Ex $347 Gd $225
Originally made in 1968-69 w/octagonal bbl., this Internal Choke version in .45 Colt/.410 caliber only was reintroduced in 1986 w/10-inch bull bbl. Vent rib also available. Fixed iron rear sight, bead front. Detachable choke screws into muzzle. Blued finish. Contoured American black walnut Competitor grip, also since 1986, has nonslip rubber insert permanently bonded to back of grip.
w/bull bbl, add $50
w/vent rib, add $61

CONTENDER OCTAGON
BARREL . . . . NiB $388 Ex $290 Gd $204
The original Contender design, this octagonal bbl., version began to see the discontinuance of caliber offerings in 1980. Now it is available in .22 LR only, 10-inch octagonal bbl., Partridge-style iron sights. Contoured Competitor grip. Blued finish.

CONTENDER STAINLESS
Similar to the standard Contender models except stainless steel w/blued sights. Black Rynite forearm and ambidExtrous finger-groove grip. Made from 2006 to date.
Standard SS model (10-inch bbl.)	NiB $469	Ex $386	Gd $306
SS Super 14	NiB $377	Ex $291	Gd $143
SS Super 16	NiB $377	Ex $291	Gd $143

CONTENDER SUPER (14 IN./16 IN.)
Calibers: .22 LR, .222 Rem., .223 Rem., 6mm T.C.U., 6.5mm T.C.U., 7mm T.C.U., 7x30 Waters, .30 Herrett, .30-30 Win., .357 Herrett, .357 Rem. Max., .35 Rem., 10mm Auto, .44 Mag., .445 Super Mag. 14- or 16.25-inch bull bbl., 18 or 20.25 inches overall. Weight: 43-65 oz. Partridge-style ramp front sight, adj. target rear. Blued finish. Made from 1978 to 1997.
Super 14	NiB $380	Ex $306	Gd $204
Super 16	NiB $380	Ex $306	Gd $204

CONTENDER TC ALLOY II
Calibers: .22 LR, .223 Rem., .357 Magnum, .357 Rem. Max., .44 Magnum, 7mm T.C.U., .30-30 Win., .45 Colt/.410 (w/ internal choke), .35 Rem. and 7-30 Waters (14-inch bbl.). 10- or 14-inch bull bbl. or 10-inch vent rib bbl. (w/internal choke). All metal parts permanently electroplated w/T/C Alloy II, which is harder than stainless steel, ensuring smoother action, 30 percent longer bbl. life. Other design specifications the same as late model Contenders. Made from 1986 to 1989.
w/10-inch bull bbl.	NiB $377	Ex $306	Gd $214
w/vent rib bbl. and choke	NiB $464	Ex $377	Gd $286
Super 14	NiB $388	Ex $306	Gd $219

ENCORE SINGLE-SHOT PISTOL
Similar to the standard Contender models except w/10-, 12- or 15-inch bbl., Calibers: .22-250 Rem., .223 Rem., .243 Win., .260 Rem., .270 Win., 7mm BR Rem., 7mm-08 Rem., 7.62x39mm, .308 Win., .30-06 Spfd., .44 Rem. Mag., .444 Marlin, .45-70 Govt., .45 LC/410. Blue or stainless finish. Walnut or composition, ambidExtrous finger-groove grip. Hunter Model w/2.5-7x pistol scope. Note: Encore bbls. are not interchangeable with Contender models. Made from 1998 to date.
w/10-inch bbl. (blue, disc.)	NiB $561	Ex $499	Gd $270
w/12-inch bbl., blued	NiB $561	Ex $499	Gd $270
w/15-inch bbl., blued	NiB $576	Ex $464	Gd $286
Hunter model w/2,5-7x scope	NiB $755	Ex $546	Gd $365
Encore model (stainless finish), add			$25

G2 CONTENDER SINGLE-SHOT PISTOL
Similar to the Contender model except w/12- or 14-in. bbl., various rimfire and centerfire calibers. Walnut grip. Note: older Contender bbls. are compatiable with G2 Contenter models. Made from 2002 to 2012.
Blued finish.	NiB $650	Ex $400	Gd $350
Stainless finish.	NiB $695	Ex $425	Gd $370

PRO-HUNTER SINGLE-SHOT
PISTOL . . . . NiB $655 Ex $430 Gd $360
Similar to the Contender model except w/15-in. fluted stainless steel bbl., various calibers. Walnut or composite grip. Made from 2006 to 2012.

TISAS — Trabzon, Turkey
Est. 1993. Mfg. of pistols currently imported by Zenith Firearms, Afton, VA.

TISAS ZIG M 45 . . . . NiB $500 Ex $480 Gd $450
1911 style platform. Semi-automatic. SA. Caliber: .45 ACP, 8-rnd. magazine. 4-in. bbl. Frame: alloy. Sights: fixed. Finish: matte black. Grip: checkered wood. Ambidextrous thumb safety. Imported from 2016 to date.
Zig PC 1911 (5-in. brrl., rail)	NiB $550	Ex $510	Gd $490
Zig PCS 1911 (matte stainless, rail)	NiB $550	Ex $510	Gd $490
Zig PCS 9 (matte stainless, rail, 9mm)	NiB $550	Ex $510	Gd $490

TISAS ZIGNA FC . . . . NiB $550 EX $510 Gd $490
Semi-automatic. DA/SA. Caliber: 9mm, 15-rnd. magazine. 4.6-in. bbl. Frame: alloy. Sights: fixed. Finish: matte stainless. Grip: textured polymer. Ambidextrous thumb safety. Imported from 2016 to date.
Tisas Zigna KC (4.1-in. brrl.) . . . . NiB $550 Ex $510 Gd $490

TISAS FATIH 13 . . . . NiB $400 EX $380 GD $300
Beretta style open slide. Semi-automatic. DA/SA. Caliber: .380 ACP, 13-rnd. magazine. 3.9-in. bbl. Frame: alloy. Sights: fixed. Finish: matte black. Grip: textured polymer. Ambidextrous thumb safety. Imported from 2016 to date.

UBERTI — Ponte Zanano, Italy

Manufactured by Aldo Uberti, imported by Uberti USA, Inc. Manufactures many reproduction revolvers for a variety of companies including EMF, Taylor's & Co., and Cimarron Firearms.

1851 NAVY CONVERSION . . NiB $569 Ex $470 Gd $260
Revolver. SA. Replica of Colt 1851 Navy Conversion. Caliber: .38 Spl., 6-shot cylinder. 4.75-, 5.5-, or 7.5-in. bbl. Finish: case-hardened frame; blued bbl., cylinder; and brass trigger guard and backstrap. Octagon bbl., ejector rod. Grips: 1-piece smooth walnut. Sights: fixed. Made from 2007 to date.

1860 ARMY CONVERSION . . NiB $589 Ex $480 Gd $265
Revolver. SA. Replica of Colt 1860 Army Conversion. Caliber: .38 Spl. or .45 LC, 6-shot cylinder. 4.75-, 5.5-, or 8-in. bbl. Overall length: 13.8-in. Weight: 41.6 oz. Finish: case-hardened frame; blued bbl., cylinder, backstrap and trigger guard. Round bbl. Grips: 1-piece smooth walnut. Sights: fixed. Made from 2007 to date.

1871 NAVY OPEN-TOP . . . . . NiB $539 Ex $470 Gd $260
Revolver. SA. Replica of Colt 1871 Navy Open-Top. Caliber: .38 Spl. or .45 LC, 6-shot cylinder. 4.75-, 5.5-, or 7.5-in. bbl. Finish: case-hardened frame; blued bbl., cylinder; and brass backstrap trigger guard. Round bbl., ejector rod. Grips: 1-piece smooth walnut. Sights: fixed. Made from 2002 to date.

1871 ROLLING BLOCK
TARGET PISTOL . . . . NiB $418 Ex $321 Gd $230
Single shot. Calibers: .22 LR, .22 Magnum, .22 Hornet and .357 Magnum; 9.5-inch bbl., 14 inches overall. Weight: 44 oz. Ramp front sight, fully adjustable rear. Smooth walnut grip and forearm. Color casehardened frame w/brass trigger guard. Blued half-octagon or full round barrel. Made 2002 to 2006.

1872 ARMY OPEN-TOP . . . . . . NiB $569 Ex $475 Gd $265
Revolver. SA. Replica of Colt 1872 Army Open-Top. Caliber: .38 Spl. or .45 LC, 6-shot cylinder. 7.5-in. bbl. Finish: case-hardened frame; blued bbl., cylinder, backstrap and trigger guard. Round bbl. Grips: 1-piece smooth walnut. Sights: fixed. Made from 2002 to date.

1873 CATTLEMAN SA REVOLVER
Calibers: .357 Magnum, .38-40, .44-40, .44 Special, .45 Long Colt, .45 ACP. Six-round cylinder, Bbl length: 3.5, 4.5, 4.75, 5.5, 7.5 or 18 inches; 10.75 inches overall (5.5-inch bbl.). Weight: 38 oz. (5.5-inch bbl.). Color casehardened steel frame w/steel or brass back strap and trigger guard. Nickel-plated or blued barrel and cylinder. First issue imported from 1997 to 2004; new models from 2002 to date.

First issue	NiB $459	Ex $386	Gd $235
Bisley	NiB $459	Ex $386	Gd $235
Bisley (flattop)	NiB $459	Ex $386	Gd $235
Buntline (reintroduced 1992) .	NiB $500	Ex $395	Gd $244
Quick Draw	NiB $459	Ex $386	Gd $235
Sabre (bird head)	NiB $459	Ex $386	Gd $235
Sheriff's model	NiB $459	Ex $386	Gd $235
Convertible cylinder, add $75			
Stainless steel, add $150			
Steel backstrap and trigger guard, add $75			
Target sights, add $75			

1873 HORSEMAN . . . . NiB $549 Ex $400 Gd $255
Revolver. SA. Replica of Colt 1873 SAA. Caliber: .22 LR, .38 Spl., .44 Mag. or .45 LC, 6-shot cylinder. 4.75, 5.5-, or 7.5-in. bbl. Finish: case-hardened frame; blued bbl., cylinder, back-

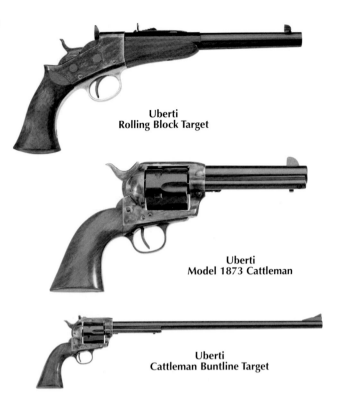

Uberti
Rolling Block Target

Uberti
Model 1873 Cattleman

Uberti
Cattleman Buntline Target

strap and trigger guard. Grips: 1-piece smooth walnut. Sights: fixed. Coil main spring, wide trigger, transfer bar safety system. Made from 2013 to date.

1875 NO. 3 TOP BREAK . . . . . NiB $1079 Ex $800 Gd $500
Revolver. SA. Replica of S&W No. 3. Caliber: .38 Spl., .44-40 or .45 LC, 6-shot cylinder. 3.5-, 5, or 7-in. bbl. Finish: case-hardened, blued or nickel. Grips: 2-piece smooth walnut or pearl. Sights: fixed. Made from 2005 to date.
nickel finish, add $300

1875 REMINGTON OUTLAW
Replica of Model 1875 Remington. Calibers: .357 Mag., .44-40, .45 ACP, .45 Long Colt. Six-round cylinder, 5.5- to 7.5-inch bbl., 11.75 to13.75 inches overall. Weight: 44 oz. (with 7.5 inch bbl). Color casehardened steel frame w/steel or brass back strap and trigger guard. Blue or nickel finish.
Blue finish . . . . NiB $479 Ex $366 Gd $219
Nickel finish (disc. 1995) . . . . . NiB $541 Ex $473 Gd $321
Convertible cylinder
(.45 LC/.45 ACP), add $50

1890 REMINGTON POLICE
Similar to Model 1875 Remington except without the web under the ejector housing.
Blue Model . . . . NiB $464 Ex $346 Gd $198
Nickel finish (disc. 1995) . . . NiB $862 Ex $704 Gd $345
Convertible Cylinder (.45 LC/.45 ACP), add $50

NO. 3 RUSSIAN TOP BREAK . NiB $1079 Ex $800 Gd $500
Similar to 1875 No. 3 Top Break except .44 Russian or .45 LC only. 6.5-in. bbl. Finish: case-hardened/blued or nickel. Grips: 2-piece smooth walnut. Sights: fixed. Trigger spur. Made from 2005 to date.
nickel finish, add $300

BIRD'S HEAD . . . . NiB $569 Ex $420 Gd $265
Similar to new model Cattleman except bird's head grip. Caliber: .357 Mag. or .45 LC, 6-shot cylinder. 3.5-, 4.75, or 5.5-in. bbl. Finish: case-hardened frame; blued bbl., cylinder, backstrap and trigger guard. Grips: 1-piece smooth walnut. Sights: fixed. Made from 1997 to date.

BISLEY . . . . NiB $609 Ex $445 Gd $280
Similar to new model Cattleman except Replica of Colt Bisley. Caliber: .357 Mag. or .45 LC, 6-shot cylinder. 4.75, 5.5-, or 7.5-in. bbl. Finish: case-hardened frame; blued bbl., cylinder, backstrap and trigger guard. Grips: 1-piece smooth walnut. Sights: fixed. Made from 1997 to date.

REMINGTON 1858
NEW ARMY CONVERSION . . . NiB $589 Ex $480 Gd $265
Revolver. SA. Replica of Remington 1858 New Army Conversion. Caliber: .45 LC, 6-shot cylinder. 8-in. bbl. Overall length: 13.8-in. Weight: 41.6 oz. Finish: blued. Octagon bbl. Grips: 2-piece smooth walnut. Sights: fixed. Made from 2007 to date.

STALLION . . . . NiB $449 Ex $350 Gd $220
Revolver. SA. Replica of Colt SAA. Caliber: .22 LR or .38 Spl., 6-shot cylinder. 4.75 or 5.5-in. bbl. Finish: case-hardened frame; blued bbl. and cylinder; brass backstrap and trigger guard. Round bbl. Grips: 1-piece smooth walnut. Sights: fixed. Made from 1999 to date.
conversion model (.22 LR/.22 Mag.), add. $70
steel backstrap and trigger guard, add $50
Stallion Target (adj. sights), add $70

STALLION 10-SHOT . . . . NiB $499 Ex $325 Gd $210
Similar to Stallion except .22 LR only, 10-shot cylinder. Made from 2010 to date.
Stallion Target 10-Shot (adj. sights), add. $70

ULTRA LIGHT ARMS, INC — Granville, WV
MODEL 20 SERIES PISTOLS
Calibers: .22-250 thru .308 Win. Five-round magazine, 14-inch bbl., weight: 4 lbs. Composite Kevlar, graphite reinforced stock. Benchrest grade action available in right- or left-hand models. Timney adjustable trigger w/three function safety. Bright or matte finish. Made 1987 to 1999.
Model 20 Hunter's Pistol
  (disc. 1989). . . . . NiB $1295 Ex $1057 Gd $974
Model 20 Reb Pistol
  (disc. 1999). . . . . NiB $1508 Ex $1345 Gd $1199

UNIQUE — Hendaye, France
Manufactured by Manufacture d'Armes des Pyrénées. Currently imported by Nygord Precision Products, previously by Beeman Precision Arms.

MODEL B/CF
AUTOMATIC PISTOL . . . . NiB $220 Ex $115 Gd $70
Calibers: .32 ACP, .380 ACP. 9-rnd. (.32) or 8-rnd. (.38) magazine, 4-inch bbl., 6.6 inches overall. Weight: 24.3 oz. Blued finish. Plain or thumbrest plastic grips. Intro. in 1954. Disc.

MODEL D2 . . . . NiB $326 Ex $219 Gd $177
Same as Model D6 except has 4.5-inch bbl., 7.5 inches overall, weight: 24.5 oz. Made from 1954. Disc.

MODEL D6
AUTOMATIC PISTOL . . . . NiB $332 Ex $239 Gd $118
Caliber: .22 LR. 10-round magazine, 6-inch bbl., 9.25 inches overall. Weight: About 26 oz. Adj. sights. Blued finish. Plain or thumbrest plastic grips. Intro. in 1954. Disc.

MODEL DES/32U RAPID FIRE PISTOL
Caliber: .32 S&W Long (wadcutter). Five- or 6-round magazine, 5.9-inch bbl., weight: .40.2 oz. Blade front sight, micro-

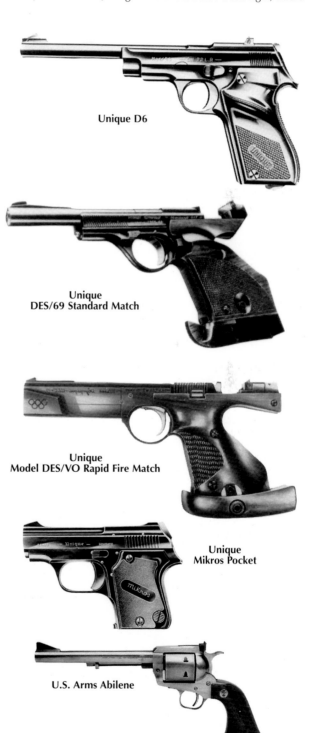

Unique D6

Unique
DES/69 Standard Match

Unique
Model DES/VO Rapid Fire Match

Unique
Mikros Pocket

U.S. Arms Abilene

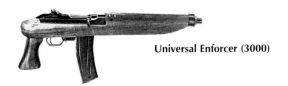

Universal Enforcer (3000)

Uzi
Semi-automatic Pistol

adj. rear. Trigger adj. for weight and position. Blued finish. Stippled handrest grips. Imported from 1990 to date.

Right-hand model . . . . NiB $1418 Ex $1316 Gd $1155
Left-hand model . . . . NiB $1486 Ex $1366 Gd $1220

MODEL DES/69-U STANDARD MATCH PISTOL
Caliber: .22 LR. Five-round magazine, 5.9-inch bbl., w/250 gm counterweight. 10.6 inches overall. Trigger adjusts for position and pull. Weight: 35.3 oz. Blade front sight, micro-adj. rear. Checkered walnut thumbrest grips w/adj. handrest. Blued finish. Imported from 1969 to 1999.

Right-hand model . . . . NiB $1234 Ex $1138 Gd $909
Left-hand model . . . . NiB $1240 Ex $1144 Gd $941

MODEL DES 823U RAPID FIRE
MATCH AUTOMATIC PISTOL NiB $1122 Ex $950 Gd $836
Caliber: .22 Short. Five-round magazine, 5.9-inch bbl., 10.4 inches overall. Weight: 43 oz. Click adj. rear sight blade front. Checkered walnut thumbrest grips w/adj. handrest. Trigger adj. for length of pull. Made from 1974 to 1998.

KRIEGSMODELL L
AUTOMATIC PISTOL . . . . NiB $362 Ex $255 Gd $180
Caliber: .32 Auto (7.65mm). Nine-round magazine, 3.2-inch bbl., 5.8 inches overall. Weight: 26.5 oz. Fixed sights. Blued finish. Plastic grips. Mfd. during German occupation of France 1940 to 194545. Note: Bears the German military acceptance marks and may have grips marked "7.65m/m 9 SCHUSS."

MODEL L
AUTOMATIC PISTOL . . . . NiB $283 Ex $204 Gd $149
Calibers: .22 LR, .32 Auto (7.65mm), .380 Auto (9mm Short). 10-round magazine in .22, 7 in .32, 6 in .380; 3.3-inch bbl.; 5.8 inches overall. Weight: 16.5 oz. (.380 Auto w/light alloy frame), 23 oz. (w/steel frame). Fixed sights. Blued finish. Plastic grips. Intro. in 1955. Disc.

MODEL MIKROS POCKET
Automatic Pistol . . . . NiB $225 Ex $150 Gd $97
Calibers: .22 Short, .25 Auto (6.35mm). Six-round magazine, 2.25-inch bbl., 4.44 inches overall. Weight: 9.5 oz. (light alloy frame), 12.5 oz. (steel frame.). Fixed sights. Blued finish. Plastic grips. Intro. in 1957. Disc.

MODEL RR
AUTOMATIC PISTOL . . . . NiB $218 Ex $109 Gd $68
Postwar commercial version of WWII Kriegsmodell w/same general specifications. Intro. in 1951. Disc.

MODEL 2000-U MATCH PISTOL
Caliber: .22 Short. Designed for U.I.T. rapid fire competition. Five-round top-inserted magazine, 5.5-inch bbl., w/five vents

for recoil reduction. 11.4 inches overall. Weight: 43.4 oz. Special light alloy frame, solid steel slide and shock absorber. Stippled French walnut w/adj. handrest. Imported from 1990 to 1996.

Right-hand model . . . . NiB $1367 Ex $1199 Gd $1122
Left-hand model . . . . NiB $1398 Ex $1250 Gd $1196

UNITED STATES ARMS CORPORATION — Riverhead, NY

ABILENE SA REVOLVER
Safety Bar action. Calibers: .357 Mag., .41 Mag., .44 Mag., .45 Colt and .357/9mm convertible model w/two cylinders. Six-round cylinder, bbl. lengths: 4.63-, 5.5-, 6.5-inch, 7.5- and 8.5-inches in .44 Mag. only. Weight: About 48 oz. Adj. rear sight, ramp front. Blued finish or stainless steel. Smooth walnut grips. Made 1976 to 1983.

.44 Magnum, blued finish . . . . . NiB $365 Ex $306 Gd $225
Magnum, stainless steel . . . . . . NiB $437 Ex $336 Gd $265
Other calibers, blued finish . . . NiB $327 Ex $209 Gd $200
.357 Magnum, stainless steel . . NiB $433 Ex $342 Gd $266
Convertible, .357 Mag./9mm
  Para., blued finish . . . . NiB $362 Ex $224 Gd $207

UNITED STATES FIRE ARMS MFG CO., INC. — Hartford, CT

Manufacturer of high quality reproduction Colt SAA revolver and Colt 1911 pistols from 1995 to 2012. The facility was once located in the old Colt factory building.

1910 COMMERCIAL MODEL
AUTOMATIC PISTOL . . . . . . NiB $1650 Ex $1300 Gd $800
Full size 1911-style pistol. Caliber: .45 ACP, 7-round magazine, 5-inch bbl., 8.3 inches overall. High polish Armory Blue finish, checkered walnut grips. Made from 2006 to 2009.
1911 Military Model (similar
  Colt 1911 rollmarks) . . . . NiB $1650 Ex $1300 Gd $800
1911 Super 38 (.38 Super) . NiB $1650 Ex $1300 Gd $800

SINGLE ACTION ARMY REVOLVER
PREMIUM GRADE . . . . NiB $910 Ex $660 Gd $400
Calibers: .22 LR, .22 WMR, .32-20, .357 Mag., .38 Special, .38-40, .41 Colt, .44-40, .44 Special, .45 Long Colt, .45 ACP. Six-round cylinder, Bbl length: 3, 4, 4.75, 5.5, 7.5 or 10 inches. Dome Blue, Old Armory, Bone Case or nickel finish.
Flat Top (adj. sights) . . . . NiB $1509 Ex $1186 Gd $710
U.S. Pre-War . . . . NiB $1400 Ex $1000 Gd $610
New Buntline Special (16-in. bbl.,
  skeleton stock) . . . . NiB $1900 Ex $1550 Gd $990
Bisley . . . . NiB $1560 Ex $1210 Gd $710
Sheriff's Model . . . . NiB $1060 Ex $900 Gd $500
Rodeo (matte finish) . . . . NiB $700 Ex $500 Gd $350
Cowboy (Dome Blue finish,
  brown rubber grips) . . . . . . NiB $775 Ex $600 Gd $400
Omni-Potent (Bisley grip) . . . NiB $1500 Ex $1060 Gd $675

MODEL ZIP . . . . NiB $269 Ex $200 Gd $190
Semi-automatic. SA. Caliber: .22 LR, comparable w/ Ruger 10/22 magazine. 5.25-in. bbl. Length: 7.75 in. Weight: 15.2 oz. Unique polymer frame/grip. Sights: none, rail. Finish: black or gray. Made from 2013 to date.

UNIVERSAL FIREARMS CORPORATION — Hialeah, FL

This company was purchased by Iver Johnson Arms in the mid-1980s, when the Enforcer listed below was disc. An improved version was issued under the Iver Johnson name (see separate listing).

ENFORCER (3000)
SEMIAUTOMATIC PISTOL . . . . NiB $479 Ex $337 Gd $265
M-1 Carbine-type action. Caliber: 30 Carbine. Five-, 15- or 30-round clip magazine, 10.25-inch bbl., 17.75 inches overall. Weight: 4.5 lbs. (with 30-round magazine). Adj. rear sight, blade front. Blued finish. Walnut stock w/pistol grip and handguard. Made from 1964 to 1983.

UZI — Israel

Manufactured by Israel Military Industries, Israel currently imported by UZI America.

SEMIAUTOMATIC PISTOL . . . NiB $1044 Ex $855 Gd $658
Caliber: 9mm Para. 20-round magazine, 4.5-inch bbl., about 9.5 inches overall. Weight: 3.8 lbs. Front post-type sight, rear open-type, both adj. Disc. in 1993.

"EAGLE" SERIES SEMIAUTOMATIC DA PISTOL
Caliber: 9mm Parabellum, .40 S&W, .45 ACP (Short Slide). 10-round magazine, 3.5-, 3.7- and 4.4-inch bbl., weight: 32 oz. to 35 oz. Blade front sight, drift adjustable tritium rear. Matte blue finish. Black synthetic grips. Imported from 1997 to 1998.
Compact model (DA or DAO) . . . NiB $540 Ex $406 Gd $317
Polymer compact model . . . . . NiB $540 Ex $496 Gd $317
Full-size model . . . . NiB $540 Ex $496 Gd $317
Short slide model . . . . NiB $540 Ex $496 Gd $317

WALTHER — Manufactured by German, French, Swiss and U.S. firms

The following Walther pistols were made before and during World War II by Waffenfabrik Walther, Zella-Mehlis (Thür.), Germany.

MODEL 1
AUTOMATIC PISTOL . . . . NiB $900 Ex $581 Gd $316
Caliber: .25 Auto (6.35mm). Six-round. 2.1-inch bbl., 4.4 inches overall. Weight: 12.8 oz. Fixed sights. Blued finish. Checkered hard rubber grips. Intro. in 1908.

MODEL 2 AUTOMATIC PISTOL
Caliber: .25 Auto (6.35mm). Six-round magazine, 2.1-inch bbl., 4.2 inches overall. Weight: 9.8 oz. Fixed sights. Blued finish. Checkered hard rubber grips. Intro. in 1909.
Standard model. . . . . NiB $663 Ex $468 Gd $227
Pop-up sight model . . . . NiB $1950 Ex $1345 Gd $1188

MODEL 3
AUTOMATIC PISTOL . . . . . NiB $4010 Ex $3286 Gd $1005
Caliber: .32 Auto (7.65mm). Six-round magazine, 2.6-inch bbl., 5 inches overall. Weight: 16.6 oz. Fixed sights. Blued finish. Checkered hard rubber grips. Intro. in 1910.

MODEL 4
AUTOMATIC PISTOL . . . . NiB $556 Ex $425 Gd $235
Caliber: .32 Auto (7.65mm). Eight-round magazine, 3.5-inch bbl., 5.9 inches overall. Weight: 18.6 oz. Fixed sights. Blued finish. Checkered hard rubber grips. Made from 1910 to 1918.

Walther Model 5

Walther Model 8

Walther Model 9

Walther PP
(Prewar)

MODEL 5
AUTOMATIC PISTOL . . . . NiB $660 Ex $541 Gd $204
Improved version of Model 2 w/same general specifications, distinguished chiefly by better workmanship and appearance. Intro. in 1913.

MODEL 6
AUTOMATIC PISTOL . . . . . NiB $9570 Ex $7933 Gd $5420
Caliber: 9mm Para. Eight-round magazine, 4.75-inch bbl., 8.25 inches overall. Weight: 34 oz. Fixed sights. Blued finish. Checkered hard rubber grips. Made from 1915-17. Note: The 9mm Para. cartridge is too powerful for the simple blow-back system of this pistol, so firing is not recommended.

MODEL 7

AUTOMATIC PISTOL . . . . NiB $759 Ex $553 Gd $301
Caliber: .25 Auto. (6.35mm). Eight-round magazine, 3-inch bbl., 5.3 inches overall. Weight: 11.8 oz. Fixed sights. Blued finish. Checkered hard rubber grips. Made from 1917 to 1918.

MODEL 8

AUTOMATIC PISTOL . . . . NiB $770 Ex $639 Gd $240
Caliber: .25 Auto. (6.35mm). Eight-round magazine, 2.88-inch bbl., 5.13 inches overall. Weight: 12.38 oz. Fixed sights. Blued finish. Checkered plastic grips. Made from 1920 to 1945.

MODEL 8 LIGHTWEIGHT

AUTOMATIC PISTOL . . . . NiB $733 Ex $530 Gd $422
Same as standard Model Eight except about 25 percent lighter due to use of aluminum alloys.

MODEL 9 VEST POCKET

AUTOMATIC PISTOL . . . . NiB $779 Ex $577 Gd $396
Caliber: .25 Auto (6.35mm). Six-round magazine, 2-inch bbl., 3.94 inches overall. Weight: 9 oz. Fixed sights. Blued finish. Checkered plastic grips. Made from 1921 to 1945.

MODEL HP DOUBLE-ACTION AUTOMATIC

Prewar commercial version of the P38 marked with an "N" proof over an "Eagle" or "Crown." The "HP" is an abbreviation of "Heeres Pistole" (Army Pistol). Caliber: 9mm Para. 8-round magazine, 5-inch bbl., 8.38 inches overall. Weight: About 34.5 oz. Fixed sights. Blued finish. Checkered wood or plastic grips. The Model HP is distinguished by its notably fine material and workmanship. Made from 1937 to 1944. (S/N range 1000-25900)
First production (Swedish Trials
model H1000-H2000) . . . . . NiB $3595 Ex $2765 Gd $2064
Standard commercial production
(2000-24,000) . . . . NiB $2152 Ex $1825 Gd $1743
War production - marked "P38"
(24,000-26,000) . . . . NiB $1722 Ex $1550 Gd $1289
w/Nazi proof "Eagle/359," add $270

OLYMPIA FUNFKAMPF

MODEL AUTOMATIC . . . . . NiB $3266 Ex $2430 Gd $2220
Caliber: .22 LR. 10-round magazine, 9.6-inch bbl., 13 inches overall. Weight: 33 oz., less weight. Set of 4 detachable weights. Adj. target sights. Blued finish. Checkered grips. Intro. in 1936.

OLYMPIA HUNTING

MODEL AUTOMATIC . . . . . NiB $2762 Ex $2430 Gd $2220
Same general specifications as Olympia Sport Model but w/4-inch bbl., Weight: 28.5 oz.

OLYMPIA RAPID

FIRE AUTO. . . . . NiB $2550 Ex $1620 Gd $1244
Caliber: .22 Short. Six-round magazine, 7.4-inch bbl., 10.7 inches overall. Weight: (without 12.38 oz. detachable muzzle weight,) 27.5 oz. Adj. target sights. Blued finish. Checkered grips. Made 1936 to 1940.

OLYMPIA SPORT

MODEL AUTOMATIC . . . . . NiB $2090 Ex $1398 Gd $1269
Caliber: .22 LR. 10-round magazine, 7.4-inch bbl., 10.7 inches overall. Weight: 30.5 oz., less weight. Adj. target sights. Blued finish. Checkered grips. Set of four detachable weights was supplied at Extra cost. Made about 1936 to 1940.

P38 MILITARY DA AUTOMATIC

Modification of the Model HP adopted as an official German Service arm in 1938 and produced throughout WW II by Walther (code "ac"), Mauser (code "byf") and a few other manufacturers. General specifications and appearance same as Model HP, but w/a vast difference in quality, the P38 being a mass-produced military pistol. Some of the late wartime models were very roughly finished and tolerances were quite loose.

War Production w/Walther banner (1940)
Zero S/N 1st issue
  (S/N01-01,000) . . . . NiB $8130 Ex $6160 Gd $2445
Zero S/N. 2nd issue
  (S/N 01,000-03,500) . . . . NiB $6515 Ex $5125 Gd $2309
Zero S/N. 3rd issue
  (S/N 03,500-013,000) . . . NiB $3130 Ex $2112 Gd $1021

WALTHER CONTRACT PISTOLS (LATE 1940-44)
"480" code Series
  (S/N 1-7,600) . . . . NiB $5745 Ex $3937 Gd $1590
"ac" code Ser. w/no date
  (S/N 7,350-9,700) . . . . . . NiB $6079 Ex $4390 Gd $2244
"ac" code Ser. w/.40 below
  code (S/N 9,700-9,900A) NiB $4435 Ex $3866 Gd $1879
"ac40" code inline Ser.
  (S/N 1-9,900B) . . . . NiB $2360 Ex $1966 Gd $909
"ac" code Ser. w/41 below code
  (S/N 1-4,5001) . . . . NiB $1897 Ex $1633 Gd $974
"ac" code Ser. w/42 below code
  (S/N 4,5001-9,300K) . . . . NiB $1610 Ex $1364 Gd $869
"ac" code Ser. w/43 date
  (inline or below) . . . . NiB $831 Ex $633 Gd $478
"ac" code Ser. w/45
  (inline or below) . . . . NiB $780 Ex $599 Gd $439

MAUSER CONTRACT PISTOLS (LATE 1942-44)
"byf" code Ser. w/42 date
  (19,000 prod.) . . . . NiB $1418 Ex $1023 Gd $816
"bcf" code Ser. w/43, 44 or 45 date
  (inline or below) . . . . NiB $984 Ex $744 Gd $612
"svw" code Ser. (French prod. w/Nazi
  proofs) . . . . NiB $1316 Ex $1066 Gd $693
"svw" code Ser. (French prod.
  w/star proof) . . . . NiB $576 Ex $500 Gd $376

SPREEWERKE CONTRACT PISTOLS (LATE 1942-45)
"cyq" code 1st Ser. w/Eagle over
  359 (500 prod.) . . . . NiB $1866 Ex $1598 Gd $1135
"cyq" code Standard Ser.
  (300,000 prod.) . . . . NiB $989 Ex $590 Gd $478
"cyq" code "0" Ser.
  (5,000 prod.) . . . . NiB $1132 Ex $741 Gd $562

MODEL PP DA AUTOMATIC PISTOL

Polizeipistole (Police Pistol). Calibers: .22 LR (5.6mm), .25 Auto (6.35mm), .32 Auto (7.65mm), .380 Auto (9mm). Eight-round magazine, (7-round in .380), 3.88-inch bbl., 6.94 inches overall. Weight: 23 oz. Fixed sights. Blued finish. Checkered plastic grips. 1929-45. Post-War production and importation 1963 to 2000.

NOTE: *Wartime models are inferior in quality to prewar commercial pistols.*

COMMERICAL MODEL WITH CROWN "N" PROOF

.22 cal. . . . . NiB $1599 Ex $1033 Gd $713
.25 cal. . . . . NiB $8554 Ex $3390 Gd $1729
.32 cal. . . . . NiB $890 Ex $568 Gd $376
.32 cal. (w/Dural alloy frame) NiB $1025 Ex $979 Gd $377
.32 cal. (w/Verchromt Fin.,
  pre-war) . . . . NiB $3560 Ex $2533 Gd $907

.32 cal. (A.F.Stoeger Contract,
pre-war) . . . . NiB $2550 Ex $1656 Gd $691
.32 cal. (Allemagne French
contract, pre-war). . . . . . . NiB $1489 Ex $1189 Gd $712
.380 cal. (w/Comm. Crown
"N" proof) . . . . NiB $1578 Ex $1266 Gd $831
.380 cal. (w/Verchromt Fin.,
pre-war) . . . . NiB $2779 Ex $2465 Gd $1109

WARTIME MODEL WITH EAGLE "N" PROOF
.32 cal. (w/Waffenampt
proofs) . . . . NiB $980 Ex $544 Gd $475
.32 cal. (w/Eagle "C" Nazi Police
markings) . . . . NiB $1056 Ex $744 Gd $496
.32 cal. (w/Eagle "F" Nazi Police
markings) . . . . NiB $1060 Ex $748 Gd $500
.32 cal. (w/NSKK
markings) . . . . NiB $3277 Ex $3417 Gd $1100
.32 cal. (w/NSDAP Gruppe
markings) . . . . NiB $2660 Ex $2245 Gd $1033
.380 cal. (w/Waffenampt
proofs) . . . . NiB $1440 Ex $1187 Gd $899

COMMERCIAL MODEL (POST-WAR)
.22 cal. (German manufacture) . NiB $1203 Ex $1032 Gd $601
.32 cal. (German
manufacture) . . . . NiB $1044 Ex $806 Gd $577
.380 cal. (German
manufacture) . . . . NiB $1181 Ex $1099 Gd $444
.22 cal. (French manufacture). . NiB $601 Ex $498 Gd $290
.32 cal. (French manufacture). . NiB $601 Ex $498 Gd $290
.380 cal. (French manufacture) NiB $610 Ex $567 Gd $289
.22, .32 or .380 Cal.
(other foreign manuf.) . . . . NiB $449 Ex $346 Gd $240

MODEL PP SPORT DA AUTOMATIC PISTOL
Target version of the Model PP. Caliber: .22 LR. Eight-round magazine, 5.75- to 7.75 inch bbl. w/adjustable sights. Blue or nickel finish. Checkered plastic grips w/thumbrest. Made from 1953 to 1970.
Walther manufacture . . . . . . NiB $1233 Ex $730 Gd $464
Manurhin manufacture. . . . . . NiB $990 Ex $834 Gd $561
C Model (comp./SA). . . . . . . NiB $1294 Ex $920 Gd $668
w/nickel finish, add $204
w/matched bbl., weights, add $100

MODEL PP DELUXE ENGRAVED
These elaborately engraved models are available in blued finish, silver- or gold-plated.
Blued finish . . . . NiB $ 1667 Ex $1462 Gd $1230
Silver-plated . . . . NiB $1922 Ex $1530 Gd $1306
Gold-plated. . . . . NiB $2130 Ex $1830 Gd $1488
w/ivory grips, add. $281
w/presentation case, add $4750
.22 caliber, add. $75
.380 caliber, add. 100%

MODEL PP LIGHTWEIGHT
Same as standard Model PP except about 25 percent lighter due to use of aluminum alloys (Dural). Values 40 percent higher. (See individual listings).

MODEL PP SUPER
DA PISTOL . . . . NiB $1066 Ex $831 Gd $623
Caliber: 9x18mm. Seven-round magazine, 3.6-inch bbl., 6.9 inches overall. Weight: 30 oz. Fixed sights. Blued finish. Checkered plastic grips. Made from 1973 to 1979.

MODEL PP 7.65MM
PRESENTATION . . . . NiB $2100 Ex $1596 Gd $1214
Made of soft aluminum alloy in green-gold color, these pistols were not intended to be fired.

MODEL PPK DOUBLE-ACTION AUTOMATIC PISTOL
Polizeipistole Kriminal (Detective Pistol). Calibers: .22 LR (5.6mm), .25 Auto (6.35mm), .32 Auto (7.65mm), .380 Auto (9mm). Seven-round magazine, (6-round in .380), 3.25-inch bbl., 5.88 inches overall. Weight: 19 oz. Fixed sights. Blued finish. Checkered plastic grips.

Note: *Wartime models are inferior in workmanship to prewar commercial pistols. Made 1931 to 1945.*

NOTE: *After both World Wars, the Walther manufacturing facility was required to cease the production of "restricted" firearms as part of the armistice agreements. Following WW II, Walther moved its manufacturing facility from the original location in Zella/Mehilis, Germany to Ulm/Donau. In 1950, the firm Manufacture de Machines du Haut Rhine at Mulhouse, France was licensed by Walther and started production of PP and PPK models at the Manurhin facility in 1952. The MK II Walthers as produced at Manurhin were imported in the U.S. until 1968 when CGA importation requirements restricted the PPK firearm configuration from further importation. As a result, Walther developed the PPK/S to conform to the new regulations and licensed Interarms to produce the firearm in the U.S. from 1986-99. From 1984-86, Manurhin imported PP and PPK/S type firearms under the Manurhin logo. Additional manufacturing facilities (both licensed & unlicensed) that produced PP and PPK type firearms were established after WW II in various locations and other countries including: China, France, Hungary, Korea, Romania and Turkey. In 1996, Walther was sold to UmarEx Sportwaffen GmbH and manufacturing facilities were relocated in Arnsberg, Germany. In 1999, Walther formed a partnership with Smith and Wesson and selected Walther firearms were licensed for production in the U.S.*

COMMERCIAL MODEL W/EAGLE PROOF (PREWAR)
.22 cal. . . . . NiB $2560 Ex $1735 Gd $1509
.25 cal. . . . . NiB $10,620 Ex $6387 Gd $4960
.32 cal. . . . . NiB $1533 Ex $831 Gd $567
.380 cal. . . . . NiB $4530 Ex $3789 Gd $3320

WARTIME MODEL W/EAGLE "N" PROOF
.22 cal. . . . . NiB $2522 Ex $1733 Gd $1458
.22 cal. (w/Dural frame). . . NiB $1920 Ex $1779 Gd $1357
.32 cal. . . . . NiB $1599 Ex $1022 Gd $879
.32 cal. (w/Dural frame). . . NiB $1199 Ex $ 1022 Gd $879
.32 cal. (w/Verchromt Fin.,
Pre-War). . . . . NiB $1199 Ex $1022 Gd $879
.380 cal. . . . . NiB $3885 Ex $2345 Gd $2097
.380 cal. (w/Dural frame). . NiB $3885 Ex $2345 Gd $2097
.380 cal. (w/Verchromt Fin.,
Pre-War). . . . . NiB $3885 Ex $2345 Gd $2097
.32 cal. (w/Waffenampt
proofs) . . . . NiB $2132 Ex $882 Gd $453
.32 cal. (w/Eagle "C" Nazi
Police markings) . . . . NiB $2132 Ex $882 Gd $453
.32 cal. (w/Eagle "F" Nazi
Police markings) . . . . NiB $2566 Ex $1145 Gd $650
.32 cal. (w/NSKK markings). . NiB $2366 Ex $1918 Gd $1333
.32 cal. (w/NSDAP
Gruppe markings). . . . . . NiB $8560 Ex $5788 Gd $1225
.380 cal. (w/Waffenampt
proofs) . . . . NiB $1474 Ex $1198 Gd $1029

COMMERCIAL MODEL (POST-WAR)
.22 cal. (German manufacture) . . . NiB $1076 Ex $945 Gd $411
.32 cal. (German manufacture) . . . NiB $850 Ex $601 Gd $383
.380 cal. (German manufacture) . . . NiB $1091 Ex $591 Gd $498
.22 cal. (French manufacture) . . NiB $2212 Ex $924 Gd $538
.32 cal. (French manufacture) . . NiB $857 Ex $651 Gd $437
.380 cal. (French manufacture) . . NiB $1173 Ex $839 Gd $452
.22, .32 or .380 cal. (other foreign
    manuf.) . . . . NiB $332 Ex $281 Gd $201

COMMERCIAL MODEL (U.S. PRODUCTION 1986-2001)
.380 cal. (w/blue finish) . . . . . . NiB $658 Ex $499 Gd $403
.380 cal. (w/nickel finish) . . . . . NiB $658 Ex $499 Gd $403
.32 or .380 Cal. (stainless steel) . . NiB $658 Ex $499 Gd $403

MODEL PPK DELUXE ENGRAVED
These elaborately engraved models are available in blued finish, chrome-, silver- or gold-plated.
Blued finish . . . . NiB $1932 Ex $1543 Gd $1199
Chrome-plated . . . . NiB $3087 Ex $2156 Gd $1779
Silver-plated . . . . NiB $2234 Ex $1789 Gd $1418
Gold-plated. . . . . NiB $2567 Ex $1979 Gd $1598
w/ivory grips, add. $306
w/Presentation case, add $791
.22 cal, add. $75
.25 cal, add. $128
.380 cal, add. $110

MODEL PPK LIGHTWEIGHT
Same as standard Model PPK except about 25 percent lighter due to aluminum alloys. Values 50 percent higher.

MODEL PPK 7.65MM
PRESENTATION . . . . NiB $1856 Ex $1418 Gd $966
Made of soft aluminum alloy in green-gold color, these pistols were not intended to be fired.

MODEL PPK/S DA AUTOMATIC PISTOL
Designed to meet the requirements of the U.S. Gun Control

Walther PPK (WW II)

Walther PPK Silver-Plated

Act of 1968, this model has the frame of the PP and the shorter slide and bbl., of the PPK. Overall length: 6.1 inches. Weight: 23 oz. Other specifications are the same as those of standard PPK except steel frame only. German, French and U.S. production 1971 to date. U.S. version made by Interarms 1978-1999, Smith & Wesson production from 2002-2009.
.22 cal. (German manufacture) . . NiB $1336 Ex $1016 Gd $660
.32 cal. (German manufacture) . . NiB $997 Ex $789 Gd $497
.380 cal. (German
    manufacture) . . . . NiB $1321 Ex $997 Gd $577
.22 cal. (French manufacture) . . NiB $968 Ex $760 Gd $561
.32 cal. (French manufacture) . . NiB $973 Ex $781 Gd $577
.380 cal. (French
    manufacture) . . . . NiB $944 Ex $632 Gd $500
.22, .32 or .380 cal., blue
    (U.S. manufacture) . . . . NiB $638 Ex $508 Gd $398
.22, .32 or .380 cal.,
    stainless (U.S. manufacture) NiB $638 Ex $508 Gd $398

NOTE: *Interarms (Interarmco) acquired a license from Walther in 1978 to manufacturer PP and PPK models at the Ranger Manufacturing Co., Inc. in Gadsden, Alabama. In 1988 the Ranger facility was licensed as EMCO and continued to produce Walther firearms for Interarms until 1996. From 1996-99, Black Creek in Gadsden, Alabama, produced Walther pistols for Interarms. In 1999, Smith & Wesson acquired manufacturing rights for Walther firearms at the Black Creek facility.*

MODELS PPK/S DELUXE ENGRAVED
These elaborately engraved models are available in blued finish, chrome-, silver- or gold-plated.
Blued finish. . . . . NiB $1634 Ex $1216 Gd $1094
Chrome-plated . . . . NiB $1552 Ex $1268 Gd $976
Silver-plated . . . . NiB $1755 Ex $1296 Gd $966
Gold-plated. . . . . NiB $1889 Ex $1566 Gd $1034

NOTE: *The following Walther pistols are now manufactured by Carl Walther, Waffenfabrik, Ulm/Donau, Germany.*

SELF-LOADING
SPORT PISTOL . . . . NiB $866 Ex $856 Gd $546
Caliber: .22 LR. 10-rnd. magazine, bbl. lengths: 6- and 9-in. 9.88 inches overall w/6-inch bbl. Target sights. Blued finish. One-piece, wood or plastic grips, checkered. Intro. in 1932.

MODEL FREE PISTOL . . . . . NiB $1533 Ex $1367 Gd $1159
Single-Shot. Caliber: .22 LR. 11.7-inch heavy bbl., Weight: 48 oz. Adj. grips and target sights w/electronic trigger. Importation disc. 1991.

MODEL GSP TARGET AUTOMATIC PISTOL
Calibers: .22 LR, .32 S&W Long Wadcutter. Five-round magazine, 4.5-inch bbl., 11.8 inches overall. Weights: 44.8 oz. (.22 cal.) or 49.4 oz. (.32 cal.). Adj. target sights. Black finish. Walnut thumbrest grips w/adj. handrest. Made 1969 to 1994.
.22 LR . . . . NiB $1598 Ex $1432 Gd $889
.32 S&W Long Wadcutter . . NiB $2773 Ex $2513 Gd $2122
Conversion unit. .22 Short or .22 LR, add $1071

MODEL OSP RAPID
FIRE TARGET PISTOL . . . . . NiB $1744 Ex $1509 Gd $1345
Caliber: .22 Short. Five-round magazine, 4.5-inch bbl., 11.8 inches overall. Weight: 42.3 oz. Adj. target sights. Black finish. Walnut thumbrest grips w/adj. handrest. .22 LR conversion unit available (add $281.) Made from 1968 to 1994.

Walther
Free Pistol

Walther GSP

Walther P5

MODEL P4 (P38-LV)
DA PISTOL. . . . . NiB $844 Ex $712 Gd $448
Similar to P38 except has an uncocking device instead of a manual safety. Caliber: 9mm Para. 4.3-inch bbl., 7.9 inches overall. Other general specifications same as for current model P38. Made from 1974 to 1982.

MODEL P5 DA PISTOL. . . . . . NiB $1654 Ex $804 Gd $543
Alloy frame w/frame-mounted decocking levers. Caliber: 9mm Para. Eight-round magazine, 3.5-inch bbl., 7 inches overall. Weight: 28 oz. blued finish. Checkered walnut or synthetic grips. Made from 1997 to date.

MODEL P5 COMPACT
DA PISTOL . . . . NiB $1693 Ex $988 Gd $497
Similar to model P5 except w/3.1-inch bbl. and weight: 26 oz. Imported from 1987.

MODEL P1 DA AUTOMATIC
Postwar commercial version of the P38, has light alloy frame. Calibers: .22 LR, 7.65mm Luger, 9mm Para. Eight-round magazine, bbl., lengths: 5.1-inch in .22 caliber, 4.9- inch in 7.65mm and 9mm, 8.5 inches overall. Weight: 28.2 oz. Fixed sights. Nonreflective black finish. Checkered plastic grips. Made from 1957 to 1989. Note: The "P1" was W. German Armed Forces official pistol.
.22 LR . . . . NiB $805 Ex $644 Gd $433
Other calibers. . . . . NiB $806 Ex $610 Gd $398

MODEL P38 DELUXE ENGRAVED PISTOL
Elaborately engraved, available in blued or chrome-, silver- or gold-plated finish.
Blued finish. . . . . NiB $2077 Ex $1566 Gd $1028
Chrome-plated . . . . NiB $1776 Ex $1432 Gd $998
Silver-plated . . . . NiB $1712 Ex $1429 Gd $1043
Gold-plated. . . . . NiB $1987 Ex $1603 Gd $1163

MODEL P38K . . . . NiB $886 Ex $781 Gd $468
Short-barreled version of current P38, the "K" standing for "kurz" (meaning short). Same general specifications as standard model except 2.8-inch bbl., 6.3 inches overall, weight: 27.2 oz. Front sight is slide mounted. Caliber: 9mm Para. Made from 1974 to 1980.

MODEL P88 DA AUTOMATIC
PISTOL . . . . NiB $1132 Ex $988 Gd $774
Caliber: 9mm Para. 15-round magazine, 4-inch bbl., 7.38 inches overall. Weight: 31.5 oz. Blade front sight, adj. rear. Checkered black synthetic grips. External hammer w/ambidExtrous decocking levers. Alloy frame w/matte blued steel slide. Made 1987 to 1993.

MODEL P88 DA COMPACT
Similar to the standard P88 Model except w/10- or 13-round magazine, 3.8-inch bbl., 7.1 inches overall. Weight: 29 oz. Imported from 1993 to 2003.
Model P88
(early importation). . . . . . . NiB $1088 Ex $975 Gd $648
Model P88
(post 1994 importation) . . . . NiB $1088 Ex $975 Gd $648

MODEL P99 DA
AUTOMATIC PISTOL . . . . NiB $756 Ex $576 Gd $486
Calibers: 9mm Para., .40 S&W or 9x21mm. 10-round magazine, 4-inch bbl., 7.2 inches overall. Weight: 22-25 oz. AmbidExtrous magazine release, decocking lever and 3-function safety. Interchangeable front post sight, micro-adj. rear. Polymer gripframe w/blued slide. Imported from 1995 to date.

MODEL TPH DA POCKET PISTOL
Light alloy frame. Calibers: .22 LR, .25 ACP (6.35mm). Six-round magazine, 2.25-inch bbl., 5.38 inches overall. Weight: 14 oz. Fixed sights. Blued finish. Checkered plastic grips. Made 1968 to date. Note: Few Walther-made models reached the U.S. because of import restrictions. A U.S.-made version was mfd. by Interarms from 1986 to 1999.
German model . . . . NiB $1100 Ex $756 Gd $602
U.S. model . . . . NiB $900 Ex $743 Gd $436

NOTE: *The Walther Olympia Model pistols were manufactured 1952-1963 by Hämmerli AG Jagd-und Sportwaffenfabrik, Lenzburg, Switzerland, and marketed as "Hämmerli-Walther." See Hämmerli listings for specific data.*

OLYMPIA MODEL 200 AUTO PISTOL,
1952 TYPE. . . . . NiB $729 Ex $612 Gd $453
Similar to 1936 Walther Olympia Funfkampf Model.
Note: For Hammerli-Walther Models—200, 201, 202, 203, 204, and 205—see listings under Hammerli Section.

- CURRENT MFG. -

MODEL CCP. . . . . NiB $450 Ex $240 Gd $190
Semi-automatic. Striker-fire. Caliber: 9mm Parabellum, 8-rnd. magazine. 3.54-in. bbl. Weight: 22.3 oz. Steel slide, polymer frame w/ ergonomic Walther grip, accessory rail. Sights: low

profile adj. Finish: black or stainless. Features SOFTCOIL gas-delay blowback system. Made from 2014 to date.

MODEL P22 . . . . **NiB $380 Ex $280 Gd $180**
Semi-automatic. DA/SA. Caliber: .22 LR, 10-rnd. magazine. 3.4- or 5-in. bbl. Weight: 17 or 20 oz. Polymer frame, steel slide. Sights: adj. rear. Finish: matte black slide/green frame, black slide/black frame, or nickel slide/black frame. Made from 2002 to date.
laser sight, add **$30**
nickel finish, add. **$65**
Military model (black slide/tan frame). . . **NiB $380 Ex $280 Gd $180**
Tactical model (3.25-in. thrd. bbl.). . **NiB $450 Ex $350 Gd $255**
Target model (5-in. bbl.) . . . . . . **NiB $480 Ex $380 Gd $230**

MODEL PK380 . . . . **NiB $399 Ex $355 Gd $230**
Semi-automatic. DA/SA. Caliber: .380 ACP, 8-rnd. magazine. 43.6-in. bbl. Weight: 21 oz. Steel slide, polymer frame. Ambidextrous slide safety. Sights: fixed 3-dot. Finish: black or nickel slide, black frame. Accessory rail. Made from 2009 to date.
nickel finish, add. **$50**
laser sight, add **$50**

MODEL PPK . . . . **NiB $699 Ex $670 Gd $400**
Similar to PPK but manufactured in USA. Extended beavertail.

MODEL PPK/S . . . . **NiB $699 Ex $670 Gd $400**
Similar to PPK/S but manufactured in USA. Extended beavertail.

MODEL PPQ. . . . . **NiB $600 Ex $530 Gd $385**
Semi-automatic. Striker-fire. Caliber: 9mm Parabellum or .40 S&W, 15/12 (9mm) or 17/14 (.40) round magazine. 4-in. bbl. Weight: 24.5 oz. Steel slide, polymer frame with interchangeable backstraps. Ambidextrous slide and magazine release. Sights: adjustable. Finish: black. Loaded-chamber indicator, accessory rail, Quick Defense Trigger (Glock style). Made from 2011 to 2012.

MODEL PPQ M2. . . . . **NiB $650 Ex $560 Gd $330**
Similar to PPQ except with 4-, 4.1- (.40 S&W only), 4.6- (thread bbl., 9mm only), or 5-in. bbl. Ambidextrous magazine release button. Sights: low-profile combat. Finish: black. Made from 2013 to date.
5-in. bbl. model, add **$105**
PPQ M2 Navy (4.6-in. thrd. bbl.), add **$55**
PPQ M2 .22 LR . . . . **NiB $430 Ex $340 Gd $260**
PPQ M2 SD Tactical .22 LR . . . **NiB $450 Ex $350 Gd $260**

MODEL PPS CLASSIC . . . . **NiB $630 Ex $550 Gd $330**
Semi-automatic. Striker-fire. Caliber: 9mm Parabellum or .40 S&W, 6/7/8 (9mm) or 5/6/7 (.40) round magazine. 3.2-in. bbl. Weight: 21 oz. Steel slide, polymer frame with interchangeable backstraps. Ambidextrous magazine release. Sights: fixed. Finish: black. Cocking indicator, accessory rail, Glock style trigger, 3 magazine sizes. Made from 2008 to 2016.

MODEL PPS M2 . . . . **NiB $649 Ex $600 Gd $575**
Similar to PPS except push-button magazine release, ergonomic Walther grip, no accessory rail. Made from 2016 to date.

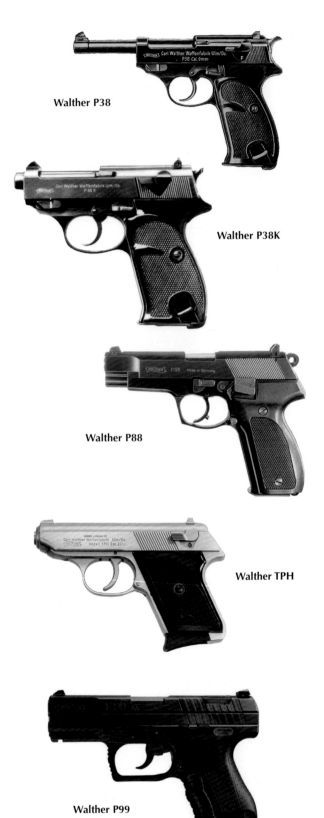

Walther P38

Walther P38K

Walther P88

Walther TPH

Walther P99

MODEL PPX . . . . **NiB $450 Ex $400 Gd $265**
Semi-automatic. DAO, hammer fired. Caliber: 9mm Parabellum
or .40 S&W, 16- (9mm) or 14- (.40) rnd. magazine. 4- or 4.6-in.
bbl. Weight: 21 oz. Steel slide, polymer frame. Ambidextrous
magazine release, slide stop. Sights: low profile 3-dot fixed
polymer. Finish: black. Accessory rail. Made from 2013 to date.

MODEL SP22-M1 . . . . **NiB $400 Ex $330 Gd $155**
Semi-automatic. SA. Caliber: .22 LR, 10-rnd. magazine. 4-in.
bbl. Weight: 27 oz. Steel slide, polymer frame. Sights: adj.
target. Made from 2008 to 2010.

MODEL SP22-M2 . . . . **NiB $400 Ex $330 Gd $155**
Similar to SP22-M1 except w/ 6-in. bbl. Made from 2008 to
2010.

MODEL SP22-M3 . . . . **NiB $480 Ex $405 Gd $205**
Similar to SP22-M2 except w/ top and bottom accessory rails.
Made from 2008 to 2010.

MODEL SP22-M4 . . . . **NiB $750 Ex $680 Gd $405**
Semi-automatic. SA. Caliber: .22 LR, 10-rnd. magazine. 6-in.
match grade bbl. Weight: 32.2 oz. Steel slide, wood target grip.
Sights: adj. target. Match trigger. Made from 2008 to 2010.

**Webley 9MM
Military Police Automatic**

**Webley Mark III
38 Military & Police Revolver**

**Webley-Fosbery Automatic
Revolver**

WARNER — Norwich, CT
Warner Arms Corp. or Davis-Warner Arms Co.

INFALLIBLE POCKET
AUTOMATIC PISTOL . . . . **NiB $507 Ex $356 Gd $253**
Caliber: .32 Auto. Seven-round magazine, 3-inch bbl., 6.5
inches overall. Weight: About 24 oz. Fixed sights. Blued finish.
Hard rubber grips. Made from 1917 to 1919.

WEBLEY & SCOTT LTD. — London and Birmingham, England

MODEL 1909 9MM MILITARY
& POLICE AUTOMATIC . . . **NiB $2090 Ex $1465 Gd $1288**
Caliber: 9mm Browning Long. Eight-round magazine, 8 inches
overall. Weight: 32 oz. Fixed sights. Blued finish. Checkered
Vulcanite grips. Made from 1909 to 1930.

MODEL 1907 HAMMER
AUTOMATIC . . . . **NiB $1006 Ex $866 Gd $207**
Caliber: .25 Automatic. Six-round magazine, overall length:
4.75 inches. Weight: 11.75 oz. No sights. Blued finish.
Checkered Vulcanite grips. Made from 1906 to 1940.

MODEL 1912 HAMMERLESS
AUTOMATIC. . . . . **NiB $1500 Ex $1306 Gd $1233**
Caliber: .25 Automatic. Six-round magazine, overall length:
4.25 inches, weight: 9.75 oz. Fixed sights. Blued finish.
Checkered Vulcanite grips. Made from 1909 to 1940.

MARK I 455
AUTOMATIC PISTOL . . . . . **NiB $2505 Ex $1988 Gd $1600**
Caliber: .455 Webley Auto. Seven-round magazine, 5-inch bbl.,
8.5 inches overall. Weight: About 39 oz. Fixed sights. Blued
finish. Checkered Vulcanite grips. Made 1913-31. Reissued
during WWII. Total production about 9,300. Note: Mark I No.
2 is same pistol w/adj. rear sight and modified manual safety.

MARK III 38 MILITARY & POLICE
DA REVOLVER . . . . **NiB $974 Ex $789 Gd $633**
Hinged frame. DA. Caliber: .38 S&W. Six-round cylinder, bbl.
lengths: 3- and 4-inches. 9.5 inches overall (with 4-inch bbl.).
Weight: 21 oz. (with 4-inch bbl.). Fixed sights. Blued finish.
Checkered walnut or Vulcanite grips. Made from 1897 to 1945.

MARK IV 22 CALIBER
TARGET REVOLVER . . . . **NiB $806 Ex $691 Gd $386**
Same frame and general appearance as Mark IV .38. Caliber: .22
LR. Six-round cylinder, 6-inch bbl., 10.13 inches overall. Weight:
34 oz. Target sights. Blued finish. Checkered grips. Disc. in 1945.

MARK IV 38 MILITARY & POLICE
DA REVOLVER . . . . **NiB $806 Ex $691 Gd $386**
Identical in appearance to the double-action Mark IV .22 w/
hinged frame except chambered for .38 S&W. Six-round cylinder, bbl. length: 3-, 4- and 5-inches; 9.13 inches overall (with
5-inch bbl.). Weight: 27 oz. (with 5-inch bbl.). Fixed sights.
Blued finish. Checkered grips. Made from 1929 to 1957.

MARK VI NO. 1 BRITISH SERVICE
DA REVOLVER . . . . **NiB $691 Ex $567 Gd $478**
Hinged frame. Caliber: 455 Webley. Six-round cylinder, bbl.
lengths: 4-, 6- and 7.5-inches; 11.25 inches overall (with 6-inch
bbl.). Weight: 38 oz. (with 6-inch bbl.). Fixed sights. Blued finish.
Checkered walnut or Vulcanite grips. Made from 1915 to 1947.

MARK VI 22
TARGET REVOLVER . . . . **NiB $1266 Ex $1096 Gd $909**
Same frame and general appearance as the Mark VI 455. Caliber: .22 LR. Six-round cylinder, 6-inch bbl., 11.25 inches overall. Weight: 40 oz. Target sights. Blued finish. Checkered walnut or Vulcanite grips. Disc. in 1945.

METROPOLITAN POLICE
AUTOMATIC PISTOL . . . . . **NiB $1629 Ex $1528 Gd $1266**
Calibers: .32 Auto, .380 Auto. Eight-round (.32) or 7-round (.380) magazine, 3.5-inch bbl., 6.25 inches overall. weight: 20 oz. Fixed sights. Blued finish. Checkered Vulcanite grips. Made from 1906-40 (.32) and 1908 to 1920 (.380).

R.I.C. MODELS DA REVOLVER NiB $950 Ex $700 Gd $500
Royal Irish Constabulary or Bulldog Model. Solid frame. Caliber: .455 Webley. Five-round cylinder, 2.25-inch bbl., weight: 21 oz. Fixed sights. Blued finish. Checkered walnut or vulcanite grips. Made from 1897-1939.

SEMIAUTOMATIC
SINGLE-SHOT PISTOL . . . . . **NiB $1090 Ex $ 916 Gd $617**
Similar in appearance to the Webley Metropolitan Police Automatic, this pistol is "semiautomatic" in the sense that the fired case is Extracted and ejected and the hammer cocked as in a blow-back automatic pistol; it is loaded singly and the slide manually operated in loading. Caliber: .22 Long, 4.5- or 9-inch bbl., 10.75 inches overall (with 9-inch bbl.). Weight: 24 oz. (with 9-inch bbl.). Adj. sights. Blued finish. Checkered Vulcanite grips. Made from 1911 to 1927.

SINGLE-SHOT
TARGET PISTOL . . . . **NiB $1588 Ex $1469 Gd $1190**
Hinge frame. Caliber: .22 LR. 10-inch bbl., 15 inches overall. Weight: 37 oz. Fixed sights on earlier models, current production has adj. rear sight. Blued finish. Checkered walnut or Vulcanite grips. Made from 1909.

WEBLEY-FOSBERY AUTOMATIC REVOLVER
Hinged frame. Recoil action revolves cylinder and cocks hammer. Caliber: 455 Webley. Six-round cylinder, 6-inch bbl., 12 inches overall. Weight: 42 oz. Fixed or adjustable sights. Blued finish. Checkered walnut grips. Made 1901-1939. Note: A few were produced in caliber .38 Colt Auto w/an 8-shot cylinder (very rare).
1901 model. . . . . **NiB $12,600 Ex $8600 Gd $5500**
1902 model .38 Colt (8-round), add, add. **300%**
1903 model. . . . . **NiB $10,000 Ex $7600 Gd $4600**
Target model w/adjustable sights, add **20%**

WESSON FIREARMS CO., INC. — Palmer, MA
Renamed Dan Wesson Firearms, Inc. Acquired by CZ-USA in 2005 and renamed Dan Wesson. Also see Dan Wesson for current production.

Note: *Models with a three digit model number that begins with a "7" are starinless steel models.*

MODEL 8 SERVICE
Same general specifications as Model 14 except caliber .38 Special. Made from 1971 to 1975. Values same as for Model 14.

MODEL 8-2 SERVICE
Similar as Model 14-2 except caliber .38 Special. Made from 1975 to date. Values same as for Model 14-2.

MODEL 9 TARGET
Same as Model 15 except caliber .38 Special. Made from 1971 to 1975. Values same as for Model 15.

MODEL 9-2 TARGET
Same as Model 15-2 except caliber .38 Special. Made from 1975 to date. Values same as for Model 15-2.

MODEL 9-2H HEAVY BARREL
Same general specifications as Model 15-2H except caliber .38 Special. Made from 1975 to date. Values same as for Model 15-2H. Disc. 1983.

MODEL 9-2HV VENT RIB HEAVY BARREL
Same as Model 15-2HV except caliber .38 Special. Made from 1975 to date. Values same as for Model 15-2HV.

MODEL 9-2V VENT RIB
Same as Model 15-2V except caliber .38 Special. Made from 1975 to date. Values same as for Model 15-2H.

MODEL 11 SERVICE DA REVOLVER
Caliber: .357 Magnum. Six-round cylinder. bbl. lengths: 2.5-, 4-, 6-inches interchangeable bbl. assemblies, 9 inches overall (with 4-inch bbl.). Weight: 38 oz. (with 4-inch bbl.). Fixed sights. Blued finish. Interchangeable grips. Made from 1970-71. Note: The Model 11 has an External bbl. nut.
w/one bbl. assembly and grip . . **NiB $274 Ex $180 Gd $101**
Extra bbl. assembly, add **$75**
Extra grip, add **$50**

MODEL 12 TARGET
Same general specifications as Model 11 except has adj. sights. Made from 1970-71.
w/one-bbl. assembly and grip . . **NiB $290 Ex $204 Gd $135**
Extra bbl. assembly, add **$75**
Extra grip, add **$50**

MODEL 14 SERVICE DA REVOLVER
Caliber: .357 Magnum. Six-round cylinder, bbl. length: 2.25-, 3.75, 5.75-inches; interchangeable bbl. assemblies, 9 inches overall (with 3.75-inch bbl.). Weight: 36 oz. (with 3.75-inch bbl.). Fixed sights. Blued or nickel finish. Interchangeable grips. Made 1971-75. Note: Model 14 has recessed bbl. nut.
w/one-bbl. assembly and grip . . **NiB $225 Ex $158 Gd $101**

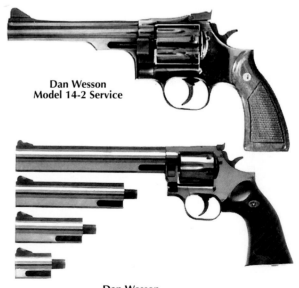

Dan Wesson
Model 14-2 Service

Dan Wesson
Model 15-2H Interchangeable Heavy Barrels

Extra bbl. assembly, add $61
Extra grip, add $25

MODEL 14-2 SERVICE DA REVOLVER
Caliber: .357 Magnum. Six-round cylinder, bbl. lengths: 2.5-, 4-, 6-, 8-inch; interchangeable bbl. assemblies, 9.25 inches overall (with 4-inch bbl.) Weight: 34 oz. (with 4-inch bbl.). Fixed sights. Blued finish. Interchangeable grips. Made from 1975 to 1995. Note: Model 14-2 has recessed bbl. nut.
w/one bbl. assembly
   (8 inch) and grip . . . . NiB $270 Ex $204 Gd $158
w/one bbl. assembly
   (other lengths) and grip . . . . NiB $270 Ex $204 Gd $158
Extra bbl. assembly, 8 inch, add $75
Extra bbl. assembly,
   other lengths, add $75
Extra grip, add $50

MODEL 15 TARGET
Same general specifications as Model 14 except has adj. sights. Made from 1971 to 1975.
w/one bbl. assembly and grip . . NiB $306 Ex $230 Gd $190
Extra bbl. assembly, add $75
Extra grip, add $50

MODEL 15-2 TARGET
Same general specifications as Model 14-2 except has adj. rear sight and interchangeable blade front; also avail. w/10-, 12- or 15-inch bbl., Made from 1975 to 1995.
w/one bbl. assembly (8 inch) and grip . . NiB $362 Ex $289 Gd $187
w/one bbl. assembly (10 inch)
   and grip . . . . NiB $362 Ex $289 Gd $187
w/one bbl. assembly
   (12 inch)/grip. Disc. . . . . NiB $362 Ex $289 Gd $187
w/one bbl. assembly
   (15 inch)/grip. Disc. . . . . NiB $362 Ex $289 Gd $187
w/one-bbl. assembly
   (other lengths)/grip. . . . . NiB $244 Ex $159 Gd $133
Extra bbl. assembly, add $75
Extra grip, add $50

MODEL 15-2H HEAVY BARREL
Same as Model 15-2 except has heavy bbl., assembly weight: with 4-inch bbl., 38 oz. Made from 1975 to 1983.
w/one bbl. assembly . . . . NiB $500 Ex $345 Gd $235
Extra bbl. assembly, add $75
Extra grip, add $50

MODEL 15-2HV VENT RIB HEAVY BARREL
Same as Model 15-2 except has vent rib heavy bbl. assembly; weight: (w/4-inch bbl.) 37 oz. Made from 1975 to 1995.
w/one bbl. assembly
   (8 inch) and grip . . . . NiB $303 Ex $240 Gd $162
w/one bbl. assembly
   (10 inch) and grip . . . . NiB $303 Ex $240 Gd $162
w/one bbl. assembly
   (12 inch) and grip . . . . NiB $303 Ex $240 Gd $162
w/one bbl. assembly
   (15 inch) and grip . . . . NiB $321 Ex $273 Gd $192
w/one bbl. assembly
   (other lengths) and grip . . . . NiB $198 Ex $241 Gd $163
Extra bbl. assembly (8 inch), add $75
Extra bbl. assembly (10 inch), add $75
Extra bbl. assembly (12 inch), add $75
Extra bbl. assembly (15 inch), add $75
Extra bbl. assembly (other lengths), add $75
Extra grip, add $50

MODEL 15-2V VENT RIB
Same as Model 15-2 except has vent rib bbl. assembly, weight: 35 oz. (with 4-inch bbl.). Made from 1975 to date. Values same as for 15-2H.

HUNTER PACS
Dan Wesson Hunter Pacs are offered in all Magnum calibers and include heavy vent rib 8-inch shrouded bbl., Burris scope mounts, bbl. changing tool in a case.

Model	NiB	Ex	Gd
HP22M-V	$893	$660	$473
HP22M-2	$733	$612	$447
HP722M-V	$843	$632	$439
HP722M-2	$806	$612	$408
HP32-V	$785	$571	$395
HP32-2	$691	$530	$425
HP732-V	$816	$597	$434
HP732-2	$755	$608	$449
HP15-V	$755	$608	$449
HP15-2	$780	$601	$437
HP715-V	$831	$654	$479
HP715-2	$755	$657	$478
HP41-V	$688	$556	$425
HP741-V	$841	$689	$495
HP741-2	$739	$607	$439
HP44-V	$884	$700	$536
HP44-2	$739	$607	$439
HP744-V	$933	$781	$576
HP744-2	$897	$738	$546
HP40-V	$616	$497	$366
HP40-2	$827	$691	$496
HP740-V	$988	$816	$590
HP740-2	$918	$729	$526
HP375-V	$595	$500	$356
HP375-2	$944	$786	$590
HP45-V	$734	$626	$439

WHITNEY FIREARMS COMPANY —
Hartford, CT
NOTE: *Since 2004 the Whitney Wolverine design is currently manufactured by Olympic Arms, Olympia, WA. Also see Olympic Arms.*

WOLVERINE AUTOMATIC PISTOL
Dural frame/shell contains all operating components. Caliber: .22 LR. 10-round magazine, 4.63-inch bbl., 9 inches overall. Weight: 23 oz. Partridge-type sights. Blued or nickel finish. Plastic grips. Made from 1955 to 1962.
Blue finish. . . . . NiB $680 Ex $575 Gd $383
Nickel finish . . . . NiB $1330 Ex $1080 Gd $610

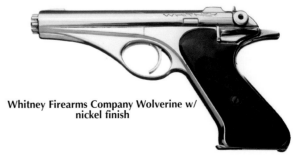

Whitney Firearms Company Wolverine w/ nickel finish

WICHITA ARMS — Wichita, Kansas

CLASSIC PISTOL
Caliber: Chambered to order. Bolt-action, single-shot. 11.25-inch octagonal bbl., 18 inches overall. Weight: 78 oz. Open micro sights. Custom-grade checkered walnut stock. Blued finish. Made from 1980 to 1997.
Standard . . . . **NiB $3310 Ex $2546 Gd $2245**
**Presentation grade
  (engraved)** . . . . **NiB $5379 Ex $3916 Gd $2166**

HUNTER PISTOL . . . . **NiB $1433 Ex $1096 Gd $872**
Bolt-action, single-shot. Calibers: .22 LR, .22 WRF, 7mm Super Mag., 7-30 Waters, .30-30 Win., .32 H&R Mag., .357 Mag., .357 Super Mag. 10.5-inch bbl., 16.5 inches overall, weight: 60 oz. No sights (scope mount only). Stainless steel finish. Walnut stock. Made from 1983 to 1994.

INTERNATIONAL PISTOL . . . . . **NiB $733 Ex $567 Gd $453**
Top-break, single-shot. SA. Calibers: 7-30 Waters, 7mm Super Mag., 7R (.30-30 Win. necked to 7mm), .30-30 Win. .357 Mag., .357 Super Mag., .32 H&R Mag., .22 Mag., .22 LR. 10- and 14-inch bbl. (10.5 inch for centerfire calibers). Weight: 50-71 oz. Partridge front sight, adj. rear. Walnut forend and grips.

MK-40 SILHOUETTE . . . . . . **NiB $1613 Ex $1407 Gd $1206**
Calibers: .22-250, 7mm IHMSA, .308 Win. Bolt-action, single-shot. 13-inch bbl., 19.5 inches overall. Weight: 72 oz. Wichita Multi-Range sight system. Aluminum receiver w/blued bbl., gray Fiberthane glass stock. Made from 1981 to 1994.

SILHOUETTE PISTOL . . . **NiB $1587 Ex. $1453 Gd $1356**
Calibers: .22-250, 7mm IHMSA 308 Win. Bolt-action, single-shot. 14.94-inch bbl., 21.38 inches overall. Weight: 72 oz. Wichita Multi-Range sight system. Blued finish. Walnut or gray Fiberthane glass stock. Walnut center or rear grip. Made from 1979 to 1994.

WILKINSON ARMS — Parma, ID

LINDA . . . . **NiB $680 Ex $557 Gd $360**
Semi-automatic. Caliber: 9mm Para. 31-rnd. magazine, 8.25-in. bbl., 12.25 inches overall. Weight: 77 oz. Rear peep sight w/blade front. Blued finish. Checkered composition grips. Made from 2000 to 2005.

SHERRY . . . . **NiB $274 Ex $188 Gd $126**
Semi-automatic. Caliber: .22 LR. 8-rnd. magazine, 2.13-in. bbl., 4.38 inches overall. Weight: 9.25 oz. Crossbolt safety. Fixed sights. Blued or blue-gold finish. Checkered composition grips. Made from 2000 to 2005.

DIANE . . . . **NiB $160 Ex $97 Gd $55**
Semi-automatic. Caliber: .25 ACP, 6-rnd. magazine, 2.125-in. bbl. Weight: 77 oz. Rear peep sight w/blade front. Blued finish. Checkered composition grips. Made from 2000 to 2005.

ZASTAVA ARMS — Serbia

NOTE: *Established in 1853, Zastava firearms have been imported into the U.S. by Century Arms International, EAA, Remington and others.*

CZ999 . . . . **NiB $475 Ex $420 Gd $265**
Semi-automatic. DA/SA. Caliber: 9mm, 10- or 15-rnd. maga-

Wilkinson Arms Linda

Zastava M88A

Zastava CZ999

zine, 4.25-in. bbl., 7.8 inches overall. Weight: 33.5 oz. Fixed sight. Finish: matte black. Checkered polymer grips. Made from 2013 to date.
CZ999 Compact (3.5-in. bbl.) . . **NiB $475 Ex $420 Gd $265**

M57 . . . . **NiB $310 Ex $300 Gd $180**
Similar to Soviet TT. Semi-automatic. SA. Caliber: 7.62x25mm Tokarev, 9-rnd. magazine, 4.5-in. bbl., 7.9 inches overall. Weight: 31 oz. Fixed sight. Finish: blued. Polymer grips. Manual safety. Made from 2013 to date.

M70A . . . . **NiB $310 Ex $300 Gd $180**
Similar to Soviet TT. Semi-automatic. SA. Caliber: 9mm, 9-rnd. magazine, 4.5-in. bbl., 7.9 inches overall. Weight: 31 oz. Fixed sight. Finish: blued. Polymer grips. Manual safety. Made from 2013 to date.

M88 . . . . **NiB $310 Ex $300 Gd $180**
Semi-automatic. SA. Caliber: 9mm, 9-rnd. magazine, 3.8-in. bbl., 6.9 inches overall. Weight: 29.9 oz. Fixed sight. Finish: blued. Polymer grips. Manual safety. Made from 2013 to date.

ZENITH FIREARMS — Afton, VA

Importer of H&K-licensed mfg. pistols, TISAS pistols and Girsan pistols all mfg. in Turkey.
Model MKE Z-5RS . . . . **NiB $1800 Ex $1700 Gd $1650**
Licensed version of H&K MP5 except semi-automatic. SA. Caliber: 9mm; 10 or 30-rnd. magazine. 8.9-in. bbl. Frame: polymer. Sights: fixed front, adj. rear. Finish: black. Grip: textured polymer. Length: 19.9-in. Weight: 5.5 lbs. Imported from 2016 to date.
w/SB Tactical Stabilizing Brace, add...$200
MKE Z-5P (5.8-in. bbl.) . . . . **NiB $1800 Ex $1700 Gd $1650**
MKE Z-5K (4.6-in. bbl.) . . . . **NiB $1750 Ex $1650 Gd $1600**

Appendix A: Online Auctions

Technology has opened up gun trading to be available 24/7/365. Online auctions enable sellers and buyers to connect as never before. If you have a gun to sell, all you need to do is create an account, type in a description, take a few digital pictures of the gun, and list it on an auction site. It's really that simple and that easy.

All the same federal, state, and local gun laws apply to selling and purchasing a gun online as when purchasing or selling one at a brick-and-mortar retailer. Know your local and state laws before working online to effect firearms purchases or sales. Also, perform your due diligence by contacting the seller prior to making a bid and obtaining as much information as you can about the item. Remember, if you bid on it and win, you own it.

There are four types of online auctions:

1. **Basic**—In a basic auction, the seller's staring price is the amount at which the seller is willing to sell the item.
2. **Dutch**—In a Dutch auction, a seller auctions two or more identical items and a buyer bids on the per-item cost for a total of however many items the seller is auctioning. For example if the bid is for $1.00 and there are ten items, the total price is $10.00.
3. **Reserve**—In a reserve auction, a seller has a minimum reserve price set for the item, i.e., the lowest price at which he agrees to sell the item. This amount is often hidden from bidders.
4. **Absolute or Penny**—Absolute or penny auctions start out at $.01 and have no reserve. The item is sold to the last bidder when the auction closes.

Online Auction Glossary

TEN- OR FIFTEEN-MINUTE RULE

After the last bid activity and/or an auction is ready to close, there is a time interval of ten to fifteen minutes, depending on the online auction's policy, that must pass to allow any last bids to be entered. Think of it as the "Going, going, gone!" statement made by a live auctioneer. If a bid is entered during the last ten or fifteen minutes, the ten- or fifteen-minute interval then resets. Only when the entire ten or fifteen minutes has passed is the auction considered closed.

AUTO BID OR PROXY BID

A buyer bids the maximum amount they are willing to pay for an item and the auto-bid function automatically enters the least amount to win and continues to automatically bid to the specified maximum. For example, Buyer 1 sets up an auto bid for $500, yet the current bid on the item is $450. Buyer 2 bids $475, so Buyer 1's auto bid places bids according to the bid increment of the auction until the maximum amount specified Buyer 1 is reached.

AUCTION TERMINOLOGY

Bid—The amount a buyer is willing to pay for an item.

Bid history—Shows the bids of buyers and time and date of bid. During a live auction, the bid amounts are hidden. After the auction closes, bid amounts per shown.

Bid increment—Amount the bid is increased by as specified by the seller.

Buy now—A displayed price the seller is willing to accept to end the auction.

FFL—Federal Firearms License. FFL holders are required to transfer a firearm from a seller to a buyer.

Feedback—Buyers and sellers can leave feedback on the auction transaction for public viewing. Typically, both sellers and buyers are rated on how well the transaction went between the buyer and seller.

Fixed price—An item that sells at a set price with no bidding.

Inspection period—Some auction websites require the seller to give the buyer a set time limit, usually three days, to inspect the item. If the buyer declines the item, the buyer is entitled to a full refund on the auction price. Return shipping of the item to the seller is paid for by the buyer.

Minimum bid—Total amount of the current high bid plus the bid increment.

Reserve price—Lowest price the seller is willing to accept. Typically, the reserve price is hidden.

Reserve Price Not Met/Reserve Price Met: In a reserve auction, "Reserve Price Not Met" or "Reserve Price Met" can be indicated.

Starting bid—The least amount a bidder is allowed to bid. This is set by the seller.

Watch list—A buyer can use a Watch List to track items they are interested in, and bid or not on the item. Items stay in a user's Watch List until deleted by a user, even if the item's auction has closed.

Appendix B: Gun Shows

GUN TRADING BASICS

As is the case when selling any collectible item, there is no substitute for research. The first step in shrewd gun trading is to know your firearm, its condition, and its value in your market. When it comes to "horse trading" there are no rules, but the conflict is always the same: Each party wants to come out a winner. Learn how to dicker.

Here are four tips for the new gun trader:

1. **Don't say too much.** Present the gun to the buyer and let them make comments and ask questions.
2. **Decide on a price.** A poker player's panache helps. Set a price too low and a buyer pounces on it. Set it too high and they might walk away. The right price will keep a buyer interested, which is why knowing your gun and its value is important.
3. **Don't lie or embellish.** Gun collectors know their guns. If your gun is not in original condition, has been refurbished, or is not what it appears to be, be honest and say so. If you don't know the answer to a question, say so.
4. **Know when to quit.** Trust your instincts. If a buyer or seller seems overeager, says the value is less than you know it is worth, or tells you the gun is illegal, a fake, or otherwise not what you say it is, back off and do more research.

GUN SHOWS

If you spend time buying and selling guns, you are going to make some great trades. Unfortunately, you are also going to be beaten in price by others who have more experience. Both gun shows and online gun auctions are excellent venues for buying and selling firearms, but attending gun shows is a chance to see a wide variety of firearms, their condition, and their value at the local level. This is the place to learn about guns and how their values are determined. Most dealers will gladly explain the nuances of gun's condition, why perfectly refurbished guns are worth so much less than a rusted, beat-up original, and what makes one gun worth so much while another seemingly similar model.

Unless otherwise noted, all gun shows in the US are open to the public. There are security requirements that must be followed, but, generally, anyone attending a gun show may bring with them unloaded guns for appraisal, sale, or trade. Laws vary from state to state, so be sure to check with the gun show promoters or local law enforcement before bringing a gun with you.

Typically, you will not get top dollar for your gun at a show. While huge crowds at gun shows can be a hindrance, you can use the crowd to your advantage by carrying your locked and tagged "For Sale" gun with you as you move around the booths. There will be buyers and dealers in the crowd who may stop you to discuss your firearm. Even if you do not make a sale, you can make valuable contacts for future transactions.

For a complete schedule of gun shows near you and around the country, go to gunshows-usa.com.

Appendix C: Curios & Relics

Curios and Relics (C&R) represent a segment of gun trading and collecting. Firearms designated as C&Rs have slightly different classification than newly manufactured firearms. Collectors often apply for a C&R license, which allows them to more easily collect firearms meeting this criteria.

The ATF website (atf.gov) has a complete list of firearms that are classified as C&R firearms. According to the ATF website:

Firearm curios or relics include firearms which have special value to collectors because they possess some qualities not ordinarily associated with firearms intended for sporting use or as offensive or defensive weapons. To be recognized as curios or relics, firearms must fall within one of the following categories:

1. *Have been manufactured at least 50 years prior to the current date, but not including replicas thereof; or*
2. *Be certified by the curator of a municipal, State, or Federal museum which exhibits firearms to be curios or relics of museum interest; or*
3. *Derive a substantial part of their monetary value from the fact that they are novel, rare, bizarre, or from the fact of their association with some historical figure, period, or event.*

The definition for C&R firearms found in ATF regulations 27 CFR § 478.11 does not specifically state that a firearm must be in its original condition to be classified as a C&R firearm. However, ATF Ruling 85-10, which discusses the importation of military C&R firearms, notes that they must be in original configuration and adds that a receiver is not a C&R item. Combining this ruling and the definition of C&R firearms, the Firearms Technology Branch (FTB) has concluded that a firearm must be in its original condition to be considered a C&R. It is also the opinion of the FTB, however, that a minor change such as the addition of scope mounts, non-original sights, or sling swivels would not remove a firearm from its original condition. Moreover, we have determined that replacing particular firearms parts with new parts that are made to the original design would also be acceptable, for example, replacing a cracked M1 Grand stock with a new wooden stock of the same design, but replacing the original firearm stock with a plastic stock would change its classification as a C&R item.

www.skyhorsepublishing.com

Appendix D: Handgun Collectors Organizations

Browning Collectors Association: browningcollectors.com

The Colt Collectors Association: coltcollectors.com

Glock Collectors Association: facebook.com/glockcollectorsassociation

The Remington Society of America: remingtonsociety.com

Ruger Collectors Association: rugercollectorsassociation.com

Smith & Wesson Collectors Association: theswca.org

References

Davis, Aarron. (2006). Standard Catalog of Luger. Iola, WI: Gun Digest Books.

Gibson, Randall. (1980). The Krieghoff Parabellum.

Goertz, J. and Bryans, D. (1997). German Small Arms Markings From Authentic Sources. Marceline, MO: Walsworth Publishing Co.

Hallock, Don and van de Kant , Joop. (2010) The Mauser Parabellum 1930-1946, Analysis of a Million Luger Pistols. HaKa Arms Publications Co.

Kuhnhausen, Jerry. (2001). The Colt Double Action Revolvers, Vol. I. McCall, ID: Heritage Gun Books

Kuhnhausen, Jerry. (2001). The Colt Single Action Revolvers. McCall, ID: Heritage Gun Books

Lee, Jerry. (2014). Standard Catalog of Ruger Firearms. Iola, WI: Gun Digest Books.

McHenry, Roy C. and Roper, Walter F. (2013) Smith & Wesson Hand Guns. New York: Skyhorse Publishing.

Nahas, Richard and Supica, Jim. (2007). Standard Catalog of Smith & Wesson, 3rd Edition. Iola, WI: Gun Digest Books.

Nonte, George C. (1975). Walther P-38 Pistol Manual. Desert Publications.

Rayburn, Bob. (1985). Colt Woodsman Pocket Guide 8th Edition. Self published.

Wilson, R.L. (1985). Colt: An American Legend. New York City: Abbeville Press.

Index

FEG (FEGYVERGYAN) (Continued)
Mark II APK-380 DA Automatic Pistol, 195
Model GKK-9 (92C) Auto Pistol, 195
Model GKK-45 Auto Pistol, 195
Model MBK-9HP Auto Pistol, 195
Model PA-63 Auto Pistol, 196
Model PJK-9HP Auto Pistol, 196
Model PSP-25 Auto Pistol, 196
Model SMC-22 Auto Pistol, 196
Model SMC-380 Auto Pistol, 196
Model SMC-918 Auto Pistol, 196

FIALA OUTFITTERS
Repeating Pistol, 196

F.I.E. CORPORATION
Arminius DA Standard Revolver, 196
Buffalo Scout SA Revolver, 196
Hombre SA Revolver, 196
Little Ranger SA Revolver, 196
Model A27BW "The Best" Semiauto, 196
Model TZ75 DA Semiautomatic, 197
Super Titan II, 197
Texas Ranger Single-Action Revolver, 197
Titan II Semiautomatic, 197
Titan Tiger Double-Action Revolver, 197
Yellow Rose SA Revolver, 197

FIREARMS INTERNATIONAL
Model D Automatic Pistol, 198
Regent DA Revolver, 198

FN BROWNING PISTOLS
6.35mm Pocket Auto Pistol, 198
Baby Auto Pistol, 199
Model 1900 Pocket Auto Pistol, 198
Model 1903 Military Auto Pistol, 198
Model 1910 Pocket Auto Pistol, 198
Model 1922 (10/22) Police/Military Auto, 198
Model 1935 Military Hi-Power Pistols, 198

FNH USA
Five-Seven, 199
FNP-9, 199
FNS-9, 199
FNX-9, 199
FNX-45 Series, 200

FOREHAND & WADSWORTH—See listings of comparable Harrington & Richardson and Iver Johnson Revolvers for values.

FORJAS TAURUS S.A.—See Taurus

FORT WORTH FIREARMS
Citation, 200
Match Master series, 200

Olympic, 200
Sharpshooter, 200
Sport King, 200
Trophy, 200
Victor, 200

FRANCAIS Le PISTOLS
Army Model Automatic Pistol, 200
Policeman Model Automatic Pistol, 200
Staff Officer Model Automatic Pistol, 200

FREEDOM ARMS
Model 97 Premier Grade SA Revolver, 200
Model 83 SA Revolver series and grades, 200
Model U.S. Deputy Marshal SA Revolver, 201
Model FA-L-22LR Mini-Revolver, 201
Model FA-S-22LR Mini-Revolver, 201
Model FA-S-22M Mini-Revolver, 201

FRENCH MILITARY PISTOLS
Model 1935A Automatic Pistol, 201
Model 1935S Automatic Pistol, 201
Model 1950 Automatic Pistol, 201
Model MAB F1 Automatic Pistol, 201
Model MAB P-15 Automatic Pistol, 201
Model MAB P-8 Automatic Pistol, 201

FROMMER PISTOLS
Baby Pocket Automatic Pistol, 202
Lilliput Pocket Automatic Pistol, 201
Stop Pocket Automatic Pistol, 201

Galena Handguns
Acceleratror, 202
AMT Backup, 202
Automag II, 202
Automag III, 202
Automag IV, 202
Automag 440, 202
Commando, 202
Hardballer, 202
Longslide, 202

GALESI PISTOLS
Automatic Pistol, 203
Model 6 Pocket Automatic Pistol, 202
Model 9 Pocket Automatic Pistol, 202

GIRSAN
MC 14, 203
MC 28 series, 203
MC 39 series, 203
MC 1911 series, 203

GLISENTI PISTOL
Brixia Model, 203
Model 1910 Italian Service Automatic, 203
Sosso Model, 203